Comedy, CHAOS, & Calamity

Comedy, CHAOS, & Calamity

A Weekly Commentary on
Donald Trump's Last
White House Residency
(Lest We Forget)

Kelly Paige

Disclaimer: Some of the content of this book is presented as a work of parody and should be viewed as such. These entries are intended for entertainment purposes only and are not associated with the original creators or any entities affiliated with the original works. By no means should they be considered a substitute for the original works, nor do they represent the views or opinions of the original artists, creators, or any affiliated parties.

The author of these parodies does not claim any rights to the original work and acknowledges the intellectual property rights of the original creators. These parodies are not endorsed by, directly affiliated with, maintained, authorized, or sponsored by the original creators or any of their affiliates.

This disclaimer is intended to clarify the purpose of these parodies and to respect and acknowledge the rights of the original creators. The aim is not to diminish or impugn the original works, but rather to offer a humorous or critical interpretation for entertainment purposes only.

Copyright © 2024 Kelly Paige. All rights reserved.

All rights reserved. No part of this publication may be reproduced, distributed, or transmitted in any form or by any means, including photocopying, recording, or other electronic or mechanical methods, without the prior written permission of the publisher, except in the case of brief quotations embodied in critical reviews and certain other noncommercial uses permitted by copyright law.

ISBN: 978-1-954049-03-1 - Paperback

ISBN: 978-1-954049-02-4 - eBook

HOW THIS BOOK IS ORGANIZED

First Readers' Feedback 7

Introduction 11

Weekly Email from the White House 15

Volume One – 2017 – Weekly Screeds & Resources 17
Volume Two– 2018 – Weekly Screeds & Resources 125
Volume Three – 2019 – Weekly Screeds & Resources 243
Volume Four – 2020 – Weekly Screeds & Resources 363

Fast Forward 500

Acknowledgements 502

Bibliography 505
    Section 1: (Mostly) Books………………………507
    Section 2: From the Good Book…………………516
    Section 3: Songs and Poems……………………..517

Index 521
    Section 1: All Things Trump……………………523
    Section 2: People…………………………………535
    Section 3: Places…………………………………562
    Section 4: Everything Else………………………576

This compilation is dedicated to YOU, my First Readers. I started this project for myself but stayed with it for all y'all. Here's a small sampling of the feedback that kept me going. **KP**

- WELL DONE on the song lyrics - bounces right along!!! How 'bout sending it to a prominent rabble-rousing singer??? Would love to see The Orange Ass's response. **PM**
- Oh, Kelly, This is just priceless!! **CG**
- Oh AMEN!!! to the weekly screed this week my friend! Really loved your use of "communication skills #1 tell people what you want/need ,using neutral language so much more effective than pummeling the obvious negatives DT spews every day. You ARE REALLY GOOD at what you do, every week!! **RM**
- Dear, Dear Kelly, I swear to God, I do NOT know how you could EVER top THIS! And I also know that you WILL! (I think you're superhuman or maybe an alien.) **LBB**
- You always manage to make me laugh (despite all the horror)! Well done! **MBD**
- I did not realize just how popular you are with the Trump group. So, I do want to thank you for getting all those awful emails so the rest of us don't have to. **SF**
- Excellent Kelly! I couldn't agree with you more!!!
  What WILL you do once he's gone???? :)   **SM**
- Kelly, Thanks for sharing these with me. You helped keep me sane through these past dark days. **LG**
- Keep 'em coming. I am assured that the Donald is reading them, and it has already made a difference. Your screed is the reason Mueller still has a job for instance. Really! **KR**
- The most hilarious yet; I'll be laughing for days! **KSH**
- Fantastic Kelly!! How informed and articulate you are. **SC**
- You are a stronger woman than I. I would vomit if texts like these arrived at my phone. **BC**
- Just wanted to comment that you had some really good links in this particular screed. You really know how to do your homework...Thanks for doing so! **BP**
- Well done Kelly… your song put a smile on my face. **NF**
- [When a Weekly Screed was sent out late]: Whew! A relief. Thought maybe it had gotten so bad you were throwing in the towel. Thank goodness you are not. **SF**

- Thanks again for starting my day off with another appreciation of your screed. I so admire your commitment to keeping your readers informed. I wonder how long Kelly will last? **EW**
- Thank you so much, Kelly - you are providing a real service. **KSH**
- Hi Kelly, I would like to take a moment to thank you specifically for spending your time/energy each and every week to inform us, coach us and guide us with your important brand of insight. Thank you Kelly, for the "shot in the arm" I need each week so I don't lose sight of the light at the end of the tunnel. **RMD**
- Love the Voltaire quote! And thank you for your screeds; I have enjoyed them so much! **PT**
- Love the rap song! You should send it to Ari Melber MSNBC. The rant was needed, not sure how much more of the dung we can take! Peace, love, and persistence! **WT**
- So happy you are home and recovering after your re-hospitalization. You have been so much on my mind.... Loving your weekly screed. Be safe and heal well cozy at home. **JA**
- Genius <3 Thank you for another fantastic Screed! \(^_^)/ **MV**
- Geez, I forgot you studied Russian. You are such a multiverse. **JPS**
- Thanks as usual, Kelly! It's all a bit easier to bear knowing that you will comment on it! **CM**
- Hi Kelly, I hope you are doing well! I just wanted to pop in and say thank you for these. It just makes my heart warm and fuzzy to see how diligently you write on! I hope that you are still considering eventually publishing this. **HS**
- Can I add a friend to your email list? He hates T and loves weed. **SJ**
- Another good report, how do you keep up with it? I really enjoy all of your writing. **GB**
- I really enjoyed the screed and links this week. Keep up the great work. And please consider turning this into a book once DT is out of office. It will make a great read. **JM**
- Hi Kelly, here's another friend of mine who would like to receive your weekly screed. I had sent her your Bad Santa. **SB**
- Nailed it again, sweetie!! Thanks for doing this, although I'm wondering if anyone "official" reads these. I take it you haven't heard anything from the West Wing. **MW**
- Kelly, this is just fantastic! HUGE thank you for letting me in on these little gems. I have read the October 8th and 15th Screed and will be looking forward to them every week now! You MUST publish these! **HS**

- Hey Darlin Girl :) Another fabulous Screed!!! Keep bringing them!! They buoy my spirits. **CC**
- Thanks for keeping me in the loop of your continuing dialogue with the Donald…surely he has to notice now that "screed" is gaining currency. **RH**
- Even though I don't agree with all your conclusions, you really should syndicate this. It's better than most anything out there ☺ **SSJ**
- Another good one Kelly. Is it a blessing or a bane to have Trump as your muse? **ML**
- Loyal FAN says " Kudos to you, my star pupil!" from your "seasoned" communications instructor, circa Boston, 1980's **RW**
- Another Awesome screed! I laughed and laughed! It was wonderful to talk, and I love you, my brilliant, clever, Forever Friend! **LW**
- Another great one, Kelly…I think you should submit these for some sort of publication. Really. **SM**
- Thank you, Kelly, for sharing these and for your creativity and hard work to keep us informed. So thankful those dark days are behind us. Take care! **PS**
- Dear Kelly, I think I speak for all when I say thank you for all of your hard work and dedication in getting the Weekly Screed out for all of these weeks. I don't know how you did it but thank you for hanging in there and keeping our attention focused on what was going on in the Nation's Capital. Our long nightmare is over and we can breathe again!! **MW**
- Your critical eye and wit will be missed, Kelly. Thank you for sharing your insights over the past years. And thank you for your service (-:), to apply an overused phrase. We'll miss your sharp analysis. **DF**
- Thanks for 4 years of dedication to humorously enlighten your readers with a weekly summary of The Impostor's idiotic blurts and antics. No doubt I'm not the only one who will miss your insightful Screeds! Thanks for the weekly morale boost and the giggles! **CC**
- Kelly, I just love this so much. You are fantastic. So looking forward to tomorrow, particularly seeing KAMALA get sworn in. YAH!!!! **CG**
- Thank you for 4 years of hard labor. **CH**
- There is a bitter sweetness in this final screed. I have loved your weekly screeds and looked forward to them and so I will miss them but at the same time thank goodness this mad man is out of office finally. Thanks for making the last four years more bearable. **JM**

INTRODUCTION

Introductions are in order. You don't know me, or of me. I'm not a journalist or a blogger or a political operative or an academic or an influencer. I've never had any desire to run for office, but I do vote in every single election, a) because it's my civic duty, and b) because I'm prone to complaint when the results are not to my liking and I figure I'd better have cast a ballot to earn that disaffection.

What I *am* is a retired bureaucrat and (for the last few years) a substitute teacher. I grew up in small-town Texas and a big suburb of Denver. I attended a public liberal arts college in western Colorado for my BA in History and French. Then I went to Indiana University for my MA in Russian History.

What followed was an extremely eclectic working life (which I hesitate to call a *career*) in corporate operations in Boston and New York and many foreign lands; non-profit management (overseas and in Alaska), and Oregon State government. I was in the Peace Corps (Kisangani, Zaire, now the Democratic Republic of Congo) and what I dubbed the War Corps (i.e., working as a civilian with the military in Korea, Guam, and Okinawa, Japan).

In the early '80s I went back to school for two more graduate degrees: a Certificate of Administration and Management from Harvard and an MBA in International Management form the Thunderbird School of Global Management in Arizona. In short, over-educated, unfocused, and underpaid.

Fast forward to my reasons for writing this book. When Donald Trump ascended to the Oval Office thanks to the Electoral College (see the US Constitution, Article II, Section 1, Clause 3) I was mightily annoyed and alarmed. What I was *not* was surprised, since Michael Moore had warned us in July of 2016 that Hillary Clinton was not going to be able to pull off the win. *

Most of my friends declared their intention to abandon the news. They were shocked and depressed. I got it. But I didn't feel I had that luxury, because my very own job depended on Trump's declared intention to Repeal and Replace Obamacare.

---

*Michael Moore's Once-Shocking Prediction of a Trump Presidency Now Feels Very Prescient (hollywoodreporter.com)

Since the fall of 2013, I had been working at the State of Oregon Health Authority on a team tasked with implementing the Patient Protection and Affordable Care Act throughout the state. My assigned region was the "Frontier": a bunch of huge counties in Eastern Oregon that comprised almost half the landmass and about 3% of the population of the entire state.

My job involved working with community partners (health care workers, non-profit organizations, insurance agents, schools, tribes, county governments, hospitals, prisons, etc.) whose missions included helping their clients obtain health care coverage. I drove about 3,000 miles per month, led a lot of meetings, and conducted hours and hours of training on the ever-changing systems required to enroll applicants for expanded Medicaid or a Marketplace plan. Every November, at Open Enrollment time, we all participated in a live conference call with President Obama, thanking us for our efforts on behalf of the ACA. I really loved my job, and I had to pay attention.

Watching Trump's Inauguration ceremony and aftermath, I figured I would be in a state of sustained outrage for the next four years. At the same time, I found many of his antics so hilarious that they served to mitigate the horror. Acting on my operating principle of "Everyone's Entitled to My Opinion," I made a New Year's Resolution to share my perspective on every week's events first with Trump, and then my nearest and dearest.

Step One: Write it up. Call it *The Weekly Screed*.

Step Two: Go to Contact Us | The White House, and select "Share Your Thoughts With the President." Fill in the form. Yes, *all* of your contact information is required.

Step Three: Copy and paste *The Weekly Screed* into the text box labeled "What Would You Like to Say?" where you are informed that "2000 characters allowed. These messages are being captured and archived in compliance with the Presidential Records Act or the Federal Records Act." Got it.

Step Four: Hit "Send" and wait for the formulaic email to acknowledge receipt of your message. Week after week, that's all I got back, no matter how vituperous my comments.

Step Five: Copy in an email to selected List of Contacts, along with links to "resources."

I soon added my book club members and work colleagues. Recipients grew to include my hair stylist, neighbors, old boyfriends, and a nurse who took care of me in the recovery room after my first knee replacement surgery.

Others I never met in person but were sent *The Weekly Screed* by *their* friends or family, and then signed up. Almost all of these people were like-minded progressives but several were conservatives who love me anyway and were on my holiday newsletter list. By the end, I was foisting this project on 250+ souls every single week.

I took pains not to say anything that could be construed as threatening. I didn't want the Secret Service circling my cul-de-sac. But I was not polite. I also did a great deal of research to back up my findings. The links to those resources were sent to my email list, along with anecdotes of a more personal nature. Not every Issue was a rant. Sometimes I was seized by the doggerel gene (thanks, Dad) and felt compelled to wax poetic, or send my message via haiku or fractured song lyrics.

So all of this is duplicated here: the two hundred and ten Screeds, the emails, the research, the updates. I never missed a week in four years. I sent out the first missive on the Sunday following the American Carnage inauguration spectacle (January 22, 2017) and the last on the day following the Biden-Harris inauguration (January 21, 2021). Some were penned while I was on vacation or recovering from (three) surgeries. One was composed in a hospital. I was working full time for the first three years. The fourth was the Year of the Plague.

By the end, I was so thoroughly sick of The Donald that I threw all of my work product into a huge orange bin and shoved it into the nether region of my attic. I toyed with the idea of putting this out sooner but figured everyone else was OVER him as well. But, as we have seen, he hasn't "moved on" or allowed us to either. So I decided to dedicate my summer vacation to publishing this weighty tome. If I change even one person's mind, or vote, it will be my contribution to Saving the World.

How do I characterize this book? It's certainly not a comprehensive history of the Trump White House years (I've resisted calling it a "presidency") but it *is* a week-by-week recounting of selected events. I attempted to cover the full spectrum of his misdeeds: the repugnant cabinet and judicial appointments; the constant mendacity and malapropisms; the casual misogyny and racism; the overwhelming lack of empathy or intelligence which gave rise to his horrific domestic and foreign policies.

Whenever I could, I tried to make it funny, but it's not all political satire. I almost always wrote directly to The Donald, but it's not a record of our correspondence, as I never received back any communication (except for the aforementioned weekly email from the Office of White House Correspondence.) Sometimes I wrote about myself, but it's definitely not a memoir.

So you, the reader, get to decide what any or all of this means to you! My last Screed and my subtitle include the admonition "Lest We Forget" which is, ultimately, my reason for publishing this book. While the Trump Celebrity President reality show was (thankfully) not renewed for a second season in 2020, it's star is desperate for a comeback in 2024. I don't *ever* want to write another book about Trump, but I hope you are in some measure informed and entertained by this one.

Kelly Paige.

Lake Oswego, Oregon.

September 2024

Week after week, I poured out my heart, soul, and brain to The Donald.

Week after week, this is all I ever got back……

THE WHITE HOUSE
WASHINGTON

Dear Ms. Paige,

Thank you for contacting the White House. We are carefully reviewing your message.

President Donald J. Trump believes the strength of our country lies in the spirit of the American people and their willingness to stay informed and get involved. President Trump appreciates your taking the time to reach out.

For more information about the steps President Trump is taking to keep the American people safe, strengthen our Nation, and preserve liberty and prosperity, please click here.

Sincerely,

The Office of Presidential Correspondence

Table of Contents - Volume One – 2017

Issue	Topic	Date	Days Left in Office	Page
1	Trumped Up	Jan 22	1459	22
2	Alternative Facts	Jan 29	1452	24
3	Already a Total Disaster	Feb 5	1445	26
4	Reprehensible	Feb 12	1438	28
5	A Fine-Tuned Machine	Feb 19	1431	30
6	CPAC 2017	Feb 26	1424	32
7	Drug Addled	Mar 5	1417	34
8	Trumpcare	Mar 12	1410	36
9	Budget Anti-Christ	Mar 19	1403	38
10	Don't Believe Everything You Think	Mar 26	1396	40
11	Counting the Days	Apr 2	1389	42
12	Flipper in Chief	Apr 9	1382	44
13	Sustained Outrage	Apr 16	1375	46
14	POTUS Ignoramus	Apr 23	1368	48
15	100 Days of Despair and Duplicity	Apr 30	1361	50
16	Freedom From Health Care	May 7	1354	52
17	An Explanation to the Nation	May 14	1347	54
18	Nut Jobs & Witch Hunts	May 21	1340	56
19	International Embarrassment in Chief	May 28	1333	58
20	Hater in Chief	Jun 4	1326	60
21	Prevaricator in Chief	Jun 11	1319	62
22	Birthday Boy	Jun 18	1312	64
23	The Grinch Who Stole Health Care	Jun 25	1305	66
24	O Canada	Jul 2	1298	68
25	From Putin, With Love	Jul 9	1291	70
26	DJTJ at Trump Tower	Jul 16	1284	72
27	Smelling Something Rotten	Jul 23	1277	74
28	Little Skirmisher	Jul 30	1270	76
29	Working Vacay	Aug 6	1263	78
30	Fire and Fury	Aug 13	1256	80
31	Losing Our Culture	Aug 20	1249	82

32	Rabble Rouser	Aug 27	1242	86
33	What Exactly is a Screed?	Sep 3	1235	88
34	Blowhard	Sep 10	1228	90
35	Mowing in America	Sep 17	1221	92
36	Madman Across the Water	Sep 24	1214	94
37	God Bless Trump's USA	Oct 1	1207	96
38	Moron in Chief	Oct 8	1200	98
39	President of the Virgin Islands	Oct 15	1193	100
40	Commander in Grief	Oct 22	1186	102
41	One of the World's Greatest Memories	Oct 29	1179	104
42	A Papadopoulos for Christmas	Nov 5	1172	106
43	Too Soon	Nov 12	1165	108
44	Creep in Chief	Nov 19	1158	110
45	#45	Nov 26	1151	112
46	Then and Now	Dec 3	1144	114
47	The Last Good Republican	Dec 10	1137	116
48	Idiot in Chief	Dec 17	1130	118
49	Bad Santa	Dec 24	1123	120
50	Special Impeachment Issue #1	Dec 31	1116	122

Dear Readers, I present to You:

Trump's First Year as Acting President of the United States (POTUS)

Much **Comedy**, Plenty of **CHAOS**, Episodic **Calamity**

.....And So It Begins.....

The Weekly Screed: January 22, 2017 (Volume I, Issue 1)

TO: The Donald – Trumped Up

FROM: Kelly - First of Many, I'm Afraid

Donald, I didn't vote for you. I occasionally watched *The Apprentice* when I needed a laugh. You were so pretentious and pompous. Your Trump Tower dwelling was hilariously garish. I never understood why anyone would consider working for you for a year to be a prize worth winning. As of last Wednesday, we're all stuck with you as "President," may heaven help us. But you'll never be My President. Here's why, *this* week:

- I spent hours watching the hurried confirmation hearings of your nominees for DOE, HHS, Treasury, and Attorney General. To a person, I found them to be unctuous, unqualified, and unethical.

- I watched your inauguration speech. It would have been risible were it not so repulsive. American Carnage doesn't yet exist in Oregon, where I live, but I expect to see it soon, with hundreds of thousands losing their health care (and their lives) under your tenure.

- I saw both you and your press secretary LIE about the size of your crowds and the D.C. Metro ridership statistics, and the media.

- You had the appallingly bad taste to actually LIE *to the faces* of CIA personnel (whom you had only recently compared to Nazis) in front of the Memorial Wall.

- You signed an Executive Order directing all federal agencies to "relieve" Americans of the "burdens" placed on them by the Affordable Care Act. You are an idiot.

- I got out my thesaurus to look up all the synonyms for the word LIE, since I know I will grow weary of using just the one word to describe the utterances of you, your staff, your Cabinet, and your party in the months to come. The most wonderful match for the verb "to lie" was "To Trump Up." Until you resign, or are impeached, I'm sure I will find many occasions to use that phrase.
- P.S. I know that you have a short attention span, and "like bullets or I like as little as possible" so I will endeavor to keep this to one page a week, in your preferred format.

Resources - Volume I – Issue 1

I'm starting a new tradition: sending an email to The Donald every week (via the official White House website) with a list of reasons why he is Not My President. Should be easy !! I figure if I don't issue any actual threats, I should be okay. Just want to let them know that someone besides the press is paying attention! The first offering is attached...............Kelly

"The Inaugural Address," *Whitehouse.gov*, January 20, 2017
The Inaugural Address – The White House (archives.gov)

Rich Schapiro and Denis Slattery, "Trump Press Secretary Sean Spicer Claims Inauguration Drew 'Largest Audience Ever' in a Conference Light on Facts", *New York Daily News*, January 22, 2017 Trump press secretary Sean Spicer claims inauguration drew 'largest audience ever' in a conference light on facts – New York Daily News (nydailynews.com)

Jon Sharman, "Donald Trump 'Should be Ashamed' of Inauguration Crowd Remarks at CIA Headquarters, Ex-Director Says," *Independent*, January 22, 2017. Donald Trump 'should be ashamed' of inauguration crowd remarks at CIA headquarters, ex-director says | The Independent | The Independent

Steve Benen, "In Intelligence Briefings, Trump Prefers 'As Little as Possible'", *Rachael Maddow Show – MSNBC,* January 18, 2017. In intelligence briefings, Trump prefers 'as little as possible' (msnbc.com)

The Weekly Screed: January 29, 2017 (Volume I, Issue 2)

TO:	The Donald – POTUS of Alternative Facts

FROM:	Kelly – Already Gob Smacked

Wow. So many awful acts to pick from but am honoring my pledge to keep it to one page of bulleted items….so here's why you are Not My President *this* week:

- The establishment of edicts and exigencies based on "alternative facts." Of all the ludicrous utterances of Kellyanne Conway, this took the prize.

- Your continued obsession with the size of your………audience.
  While all this may seem like a new reality show to ***you*** ("Celebrity President!"), the rest of us can actually *look* at the crowd-size photos and draw the conclusion that more people showed up for Obama's 2009 inauguration than for yours. Get over it. This isn't the Nielsen ratings.

- Your trumped-up fantasy about the 3-5 million "illegals" who voted for Hillary. More voters disliked YOU than disliked her. You lost the popular vote big-time and are only occupying the White House due to the anachronistic Electoral College and Russian hijinks.

- Your executive order reinstating the "Global Gag Rule" against organizations supporting all methods of family planning. Women will die.

- Your executive order directing the construction of your Preposterous Wall (which WE will have to pay for, because Mexico never, ever will). I have two words for you: Ladders. Tunnels.

- Twitter diplomacy and advocacy of torture. Are you high???
  I have an MBA in International Business and have lived and worked all over the world. You are a clear and present danger to all nations AND our troops. Get off your phone and let the remaining grown-ups at State and Defense try to keep you from destroying the world.

- Your half-baked ban on Syrian refugees and other nationals from Muslim countries <u>where you do not do business</u>. Unconstitutional and heartless.
  A recruiting tool for ISIS and Al Qaeda. People will die.

Resources - Volume I – Issue 2

Dear Recipients of The Weekly Screed:
If you are afraid of being sent to Guantanamo or being hacked due to your email appearing on the receiving end of this, please let me know and I can remove you (or send to an alternate email). If it makes you feel any better, I'm using a different email (AOL) to send this out from the one I'm using to communicate with The Donald (GMAIL).

Will he ever read these? Probably not. But at least one of his minions will have to read it to delete it..........It's my own little protest. My left knee doesn't let me march in the streets for hours, but I don't have carpal tunnel syndrome yet, so as long as I can type I can voice my dismay. I have no fear of running out of outrages.........Kelly

Kellyanne Conway: Press Secretary Sean Spicer Gave 'Alternative Facts' | Meet The Press | NBC News. Bing video, January 22, 2017. Kellyanne Conway: Press Secretary Sean Spicer Gave 'Alternative Facts' | Meet The Press | NBC News - Bing video

Emery, David. "Donald Trump Claims 3 to 5 Million People Voted Illegally." Snopes, January 25, 2017. Trump Claims Without Evidence that 3 to 5 Million Voted Illegally, Vows Investigation | Snopes.com

Redden, Molly. "'Global gag rule' reinstated by Trump, curbing NGO abortion services abroad." The Guardian. January 23, 2017. . 'Global gag rule' reinstated by Trump, curbing NGO abortion services abroad | 'Global gag rule' | The Guardian

"Full text of Trump's executive order on 7-nation ban, refugee suspension." CNN. January 28, 2017. Full text of Donald Trump's executive order on 7-nation ban, refugee suspension.

The Weekly Screed: February 5, 2017 (Volume I, Issue 3)

TO: **The Donald. I told my friends who voted for you that you would be a <u>Total Disaster</u>. Sometimes, I just <u>hate</u> it when I'm right.**

FROM: **Kelly. Having a hard time keeping the list of outrages to one page.**

Gosh. We are only two weeks into this catastrophe, but it seems like much longer. So let's get right to it: Here are the reasons you are Not My President this week:

- Your harebrained Executive Order mandating that for every new regulation signed, two have to go away. Good government doesn't operate on the same principles as downsizing your closet.

- The Monday Night Massacre relieving Sally Yates of her position as Acting Attorney General………. This was a shrewd move on her part. Now that you've made her a martyr to defending the Constitution, offers from the private sector will be pouring in. Your press release categorizing her as "weak on borders and very weak on illegal immigration" only showcases your own colossal ignorance of how to keep America safe.

- Your tongue-tied announcement of your pick for SCOTUS, informing us that Gorsuch was being nominated "….of the Supreme Court to be of the Supreme Court." Huh? Pleeeze, Louise……….

- Trotting out your out-of-control National Security Advisor Michael Flynn to "put Iran on notice." Yeah, tough guy. Iran responds: you talkin' to me? I had figured it might take at least 6 months before we went to war with Persia, but I believe I need to re-think my timeline.

- Your embarrassing appearance at the National Prayer Breakfast (itself an exercise in total futility and hypocrisy), where you asked everyone to pray for Arnold Schwarzenegger's ratings on the re-booted "Apprentice."

- Bragging to the Australian Prime Minister about the size of your Electoral College win (unremarkable) but ending the call by whining that "this was the worst call by far" that you'd had with any other world leaders. What happened, Donny? Did he decline to tell you how fantastic you are?

Resources - Volume I – Issue 3

The White House. (n.d.). [Trump Archive] Presidential Executive Order on Reducing Regulation and Controlling Regulatory Costs – The White House (archives.gov)

Borger, Julian. "Iran Put 'on Notice' by Trump Administration After Missile Test." *The Guardian*, 1 Feb. 2017. Trump administration 'officially putting Iran on notice', says Michael Flynn | Iran | The Guardian

Horsley, Scott. "Trump Touts 'Apprentice' Ratings, Tells Prayer Breakfast to 'Pray for Arnold'." *NPR*, 2 Feb. 2017. Trump Touts Apprentice Ratings, Tells Prayer Breakfast: 'Pray For Arnold' Schwarzenegger : NPR

Rucker, Philip, and Karen DeYoung. "No 'G'Day, Mate': On Call with Australian PM, Trump Badgers and Brags." *The Washington Post*, 1 Feb. 2017. 'This was the worst call by far': Trump badgered, bragged, and abruptly ended phone call with Australian leader - The Washington Post

The Weekly Screed: February 12, 2017 (Volume I, Issue 4)

TO: The Donald: Reprehensible

FROM: Kelly: Persisting in Portland.

Dear Donald,

This week, for Valentine's Day, I adapted a beautiful love song just for you!

Reprehensible (Apologies to composer Irving Gordon)

Reprehensible, that's what you are:

Unendurable, hateful, bizarre.

Like a nightmare from which I can't wake,

You're a constant specter I can't shake.

Tweeting nonsense… fake facts you dispense….

Ignorant and vile in every way,

And till you're impeached, that's how you'll stay.

That's why, Donald, it's so crystal clear

You're the POTUS, thanks to Vladimir,

But Obama's still My President too.

Resources - Volume I – Issue 4

Unforgettable, as sung by Natalie & Nat King Cole

#nowwatching Natalie Cole LIVE - Unforgettable (youtube.com)

Unforgettable, about the song

"Unforgettable (Nat King Cole Song)." *Wikipedia*.

Unforgettable (Nat King Cole song) - Wikipedia

Unforgettable, the lyrics

Nat "King" Cole – Unforgettable Lyrics | Genius Lyrics

The Weekly Screed: February 19, 2017 (Volume I, Issue 5)

TO: The Donald: Driver of the "Fine-Tuned Machine"

FROM: Kelly: Proud of the press for exposing High-Level Lying

Let's Review: According to your jaw-dropping press conference last week, you characterize your administration as "a fine-tuned machine."

- However, as I watch the parade of mendacious rascals you call your cabinet enter (and, already! exit) the Clown Car of the celebrity circus you call a "presidency," I have another metaphor in mind.

- My current job is facilitating enrollment in Obamacare in rural eastern Oregon. I'm in seven big beautiful far-flung counties (in what we refer to as the "Oregon Outback") every month. I, too, am fortunate to drive *excellent* rented vehicles on these travels. Nevertheless, no matter how fine-tuned or well-oiled the SUV, other factors are always at play:

    1. Particularly this time of year, <u>Weather Hazards</u> (blizzards, freezing rain, black ice, etc.). Or, in your case, unexpected occurrences such as spontaneous protests against just about everything you've tried to do in the past 30 days. We don't like your policies or your people.

    2. Road hazards such as <u>Falling Rocks</u> or <u>Downed Trees.</u> I'm thinking Mike Flynn and Andrew Puzder and Monica Crowley and Vincent Viola. So sad that we won't have these fine folks as public servants.

    3. All too often, due to <u>Accidents or Road Work</u>, I see a big ole flashing neon sign proclaiming a message like "Highway Closed at Pendleton." I compare these blockages/detours to the number that various courts have done on your heartless Muslim Travel Ban.

    4. Impediments to my progress such as <u>Speed Limits</u>. I know it's annoying to have your super-powers limited by that pesky Constitution, but you simply must accept that you are *no longer* The Boss of Everything. And No Tweeting While Driving! Eyes on the road, for cryin' out loud!! You're gonna get us all killed!!

Resources - Volume I – Issue 5

Jacobs, Ben, Gambino, Lauren, and Siddiqui, Sabrina. "Trump Administration a Fine-Tuned Machine' – Press Conference Live." *The Guardian*, 16 Feb. 2017. Trump: I'm running a 'fine-tuned machine' | US news | The Guardian

Waldman, Paul. "Trump Says He Runs a 'Fine-Tuned Machine.' Here Are All the Ways That's Not True." *The Washington Post*, 17 Feb. 2017. Opinion | Trump says he runs a 'fine-tuned machine.' Here are the ways that's not true. - The Washington Post

"Trump Defends Agenda in News Conference." *The New York Times*, 16 Feb. 2017. 'A Fine-Tuned Machine' - The New York Times (nytimes.com)

The Weekly Screed: February 26, 2017 (Volume I, Issue 6)

TO: The Donald: Criminal in Chief at CPAC

FROM: Kelly: In a Constant State of Consternation

So much awful stuff happened at the **C**orrupt **P**erfidious **A**ssembly of **C**riminals (aka the Conservative Political Action Conference) that I feel obliged to dedicate this entire issue to that particular gathering:

- Steve Bannon, Ogre in Chief, was astonishingly candid in his outline of your "agenda":
    1. National Security consists of building your ridiculous and exorbitant "Great Wall," plus keeping out Syrian women and children who have been vetted for 2+ years.
    2. "Economic Nationalism," which punishes nations for trading with us, and will only exert taxes on American consumers.
    3. "Deconstruction of the Administrative State"….in other words, selecting cabinet secretaries guaranteed to destroy the agencies they head (EPA, Education, Justice, HHS, HUD).
- Then YOU took to the podium and , in a rambling stream of semi-conscious babble, regaled us with attacks on:
    1. Sweden (repeating the Fake News from FOX)
    2. Paris, which your friend "Jim "says has disappeared, but which I visited 14 months ago and found enchanting, as always….
    3. "Bad Dudes" which are being rounded up and deported (including those vicious single moms of American citizens who have lived here for decades)
    4. The Phony News: "Let there be no more sources." Huh???
- Obamacare ("A disaster," except for those whom it covers)
- You then opined that "We are all equal in the eyes of Almighty God," which may be true, if there is One, but (as George Orwell so famously noted), some animals [i.e., Rich White Guys] are "more equal than others."
- Hilariously, "no one loves it [the First Amendment] more than me" Donald, Puhleeeeez. And, most chillingly, your statement that "The Future Belongs to Us," which prompted me to revisit "Tomorrow Belongs to Me" from my favorite musical, *Cabaret*. Check it out. See if it gives you goose bumps too, although we might have gotten them for different reasons.

Resources - Volume I – Issue 6

Diamond, Jeremy. "Reince Priebus and Steve Bannon Emphasize Unity at CPAC." *CNN*, 23 Feb. 2017. CPAC 2017: Bannon offers up Trump agenda in rare public speaking appearance | CNN Politics

"Donald Trump Speaks at CPAC 2017." 23 Feb. 2017 **Guardian News**. (1893) The most bizarre moments from Donald Trump's CPAC speech - YouTube

"Tomorrow Belongs to Me." *Wikipedia*.

Tomorrow Belongs to Me - Wikipedia

"Tomorrow Belongs to Me" **Cabaret**

Tomorrow belongs to me - Cabaret (youtube.com)

The Weekly Screed: March 5, 2017 (Volume I, Issue 7)

TO: The Donald: Drug-Addled in D.C.

FROM: Kelly: Feeling Low in L.O.

I may not have mentioned this yet (as we are still really in the "getting to know you" phase of our relationship, aren't we?), but I live in the most well-educated, affluent, and least diverse community in all of Oregon: Lake Oswego

- While you might be tempted to consider us **_your_** kind of people, I hasten to inform you that this small city voted 67% for Hillary. [We also went for Bill twice and Obama in both 2008 and 2012).
- Yesterday, some of your supporters (or, as you referred to them: "I love the poorly educated!") tried to hold a march in the downtown area. They were outnumbered by your opponent's 3 to 1. SAD !

So, while I'm encouraged by the smarts and goodwill of my town, I am increasingly alarmed by your erratic behavior, as evidenced by the activities of the past week:

- First, we were all astounded that you were able to read your Fake State of the Union Speech that Steve Bannon wrote for you from the teleprompter, for an hour, without even once throwing a temper tantrum.
- Sadly, though, your shameless exploitation of the widow of the Navy Seal you so casually sent to his death was, even for you, a low point.
- But then you followed up in the wee small hours of Saturday morning with your LOL twitter rant accusing Barack Obama of wire-tapping Trump Tower. Silly Donald............don't you know that it was the Russians??

But I think I get it now. I read a few things this week that lead me to believe that Your Hair is Making You Crazy:

- Here are some of the <u>known</u> side effects of Propecia (finasteride) which your wack-a-doodle doctor says you have been ingesting for some time in order to maintain that *extraordinary* comb-over: sexual dysfunction (= Melania staying in NYC); mood swings (we see how those manifest); swelling of hands (haven't noticed that one); confusion (on constant display); and runny nose (that annoying sniffling during debates and speeches).
- I beg of you: just shave your head so 1) YOU won't have to take that drug anymore and 2) WE don't have to worry so much about nuclear war.

Resources - Volume I – Issue 7

"Remarks by President Trump in Joint Address to Congress." *The White House*. 28 February 2017. Remarks by President Trump in Joint Address to Congress – The White House (archives.gov)

Mayo Clinic. "Finasteride (Oral Route) Side Effects." *Mayo Clinic*. Finasteride (Oral Route) Side Effects - Mayo Clinic

The Weekly Screed: March 12, 2017 (Volume I, Issue 8)

TO: The Donald: Promising "a beautiful picture"

FROM: Kelly: Offering artistic inspiration

- Though I harbor *many* doubts that you will, or even can, fulfill the multiple assurances you offered your devotees whilst out on the hustings, please remember these:
1. You pledged to replace the Affordable Care Act with something "terrific," that is "so much better, so much better, so much better."
2. You declared that you would save Medicare and Medicaid without cutting benefits.
3. You swore that you "do cherish women, and I will take care of women."

- Then, in November, you professed to Leslie Stahl that Obamacare repeal would result in "great health care for much less money."
- And, in January, you attested that you were near completion of a health-care law that would deliver "insurance for everybody" with "lower numbers, much lower deductibles….in a much-simplified form. Much less expensive and much better." "It'll be another plan. But they'll be beautifully covered."
- You made us practically giddy with anticipation that this plan was "very much formulated down to the final strokes. We haven't put it in quite yet, but we're going to be doing it soon" [Oh…. give it to me, Big Guy….]
- You reassured us that "There was a philosophy in some circles that if you can't pay for it, you don't get it. That's not going to happen with us."

[Now I'm positively swooning….]

I soooo want to believe in you Donald, when you say that "What I do want is to be able to take care of people." REALLY?? Do you honestly mean it?? Then here's how you can astonish us all and fulfill this fervent desire: Go directly to the website of Physicians for a National Health Program. Here these canny caregivers have devised and explained a "Proposal for Single-Payer Health Care Reform."

- They've already done Everything!! They are Smart American Doctors, and they have come up with the Big Plan. They have outlined coverage, explicit capital funding, cost containment, and payments to hospitals and health care professionals. There's even a 23-page FAQ. You don't have to lift a finger.

- So, come hither, Donald. Give us the only thing that will work. Be a hero. It will be like Nixon going to China. Remember: You Alone Can Do It.

Resources - Volume I – Issue 8

"Interview on the Patient Protection and Affordable Care Act With Ezra Klein and Sarah Kliff of Vox." *The American Presidency Project*. Interview on the Patient Protection and Affordable Care Act With Ezra Klein and Sarah Kliff of Vox | The American Presidency Project (ucsb.edu)

"President-elect Trump Speaks to a Divided Country." *CBS News*. Lesley Stahl. November 13, 2016 President-elect Trump speaks to a divided country - CBS News

Physicians for a National Health Program. (n.d.). Physicians for a National Health Program - PNHP

The Weekly Screed: March 19, 2017 (Volume I, Issue 9)

TO: The Donald: The Budget Anti-Christ

FROM: Kelly: A dues-paying Unitarian

1. For this week's rumination, let's just *pretend* that you have actually read *any* of The Bible. We know you are fond of **"Two" Corinthians, 3:17**….which you referred to as "the whole ballgame."

2. But then you said that your *favorite* Bible verse was that "an eye for an eye" sentiment from **Exodus, 21:24**. BTW, that particular chapter is chock full of advice on how to treat slaves. Just sayin.'

3. Anyhoo, Jesus begs to differ with you…. when HE goes on at length in **Matthew 5:38-39**: "You have heard that it was said "an eye for an eye, and a tooth for a tooth.' But I say to you, do not resist one who is evil….and if anyone would sue you and take your coat, let him have your cloak as well." [But isn't it YOU who usually does the suing?]

4. Donald, by sheer coincidence, this passage is located in the *exact same* chapter as the Sermon on the Mount. Which I'm sure you memorized in Sunday school. [I know I did.] This brings me, somewhat circuitously, to my main topic today: your villainous and unsound "America First" budget proposal of March 15. (Beware the Ides of Trump?)

5. Because, really, what kind of spending plan do you think Jesus would put forth to Congress?
    - **More war (+ 52 Billion)?** Doubtful, as JC preached: "Blessed are the peacemakers, for they shall be called sons of God." [**Matthew 5:9**]
    - **Your Huge Stoopid wall (+2.6 Billion "down-payment")?** Did you realize that JC's main man the Apostle Paul escaped a homicidal plot in Damascus when his disciples helped him escape by lowering him over the city's wall in a basket?? [**Acts 9:25**] (Note to self: buy stock in giant baskets, as well as long ladders and big-time tunneling equipment.)
    - **Cuts to WIC and Meals on Wheels?** Let's return to **Matthew, 25:41-43**: [JC: "Depart from me, you cursed, into the eternal fire prepared for the devil and his angels; for I was hungry and you gave me no food, I was thirsty

and you gave me no drink, I was a stranger and you did not welcome me...] Gee, sounds like he was also pro-refugee.

6. Now, I realize that those of your ilk think that Barack Obama was actually THE Anti-Christ, but you have to admit that Jesus might propose a few amendments to your "blueprint" for the nation. I could go on and on....but I know I've reached the limit of your reading capability and attention span.

Resources - Volume I – Issue 9

Diamond, Jeremy. "Donald Trump Quotes 'Two Corinthians' at Liberty University." *CNN*, 18 Jan. 2016. Donald Trump's Liberty University speech inspires laughs, cheers | CNN Politics

Vanden Heuvel, Katrina. "An America-Last Budget." *The Washington Post*, 21 Mar. 2017. Opinion | An 'America last' budget - The Washington Post

The Weekly Screed: March 26, 2017 (Volume I, Issue 10)

TO: The Donald: Having a Very Bad Week

FROM: Kelly: Having my Best Week in Quite Some Time

- Donald, I was in Enterprise, Oregon, this week……….meeting with my heroic Community Partners who are (still) working hard to help all of the residents of deep-red- and-rural Wallowa County secure health coverage via Obamacare.

- Outside the local Safeway, I spied an old truck with a great bumper sticker:

    Don't Believe Everything You Think

- Who, I asked myself, could *best* use this trenchant advice? My new pen-pal Donald!!
  Let's illustrate with a table:

Everything You Think:	Don't Believe It, Because:
You think the American people like you because crowds of delusional ignoramuses show up at your 2020 campaign rallies	You have the lowest approval rating of ANY new POTUS in history
You think Congress is afraid of you	Threats of "I'm coming after you" result in a collective shrug and mutterings of "Meh"
You think President Obama "wire-tapped" you …..and that Great Britain helped	This is tin-foil hat stuff. Take your meds.
You think that you are devastatingly attractive to women	That ship, if it EVER got underway, has long since sailed.
You think that you are a WINNER	Massive protests in the streets, travel ban declared unconstitutional, Michael Flynn fired, FBI investigation of you and your team, your budget sucks, etc. [weren't we going to get "so tired of winning" ?????]

You think you are a Great Negotiator	Trumpcare goes down in flames….. [But you did get to clamber into that Mack Truck, shake your tiny fists, and blow the horn like a Really Big Boy.]
You think the USA is the greatest country on earth.	If you actually analyze the "well-being" statistics of the majority of our citizens, we compare miserably to Europe (especially the Nordic countries), Canada, and Japan.

Resources - Volume I – Issue 10

I know, I usually send this on Sunday (my Sabbath Ritual), but I'm going to the beach this weekend. No internet !

"Trump Says Republicans Will Lose in 2018 if They Don't Support GOP Health Care Bill." *NPR*, 21 Mar. 2017. Trump Tells Freedom Caucus Chair 'I'm Coming After You' In Health Care Meeting : NPR

Johnson, Jenna, and Chris Cillizza. "25 Quotes Capturing Donald Trump's Final Pitch to South Carolina." *The Washington Post*, 19 Feb. 2016. 25 quotes capturing Donald Trump's final pitch to South Carolina - The Washington Post

Scully, Sean. "Trump is Mercilessly Mocked on Twitter for Pulling Animated Faces While Honking Horn of Big Rig Mack Truck." *Daily Mail*, 24 Mar. 2017. Trump mercilessly mocked on Twitter for Mack Truck faces | Daily Mail Online

The Weekly Screed: April 2, 2017 (Volume I, Issue 11)

TO: The Donald: Our national and on-going April Fool's Day Joke

FROM: Kelly: Nobody's Fool

- Good afternoon, Donald. Today, I would like to tell you about the wonderful 2017 calendar I bought my husband for Christmas: **The Out of Office Countdown** calendar.

- Starting on January 20, we are given a number in bright red: 1461…..Days left.

- On January 21, we *only* have 1460 days to put up with you. And so on. You get the idea.

- Each month tells us how many months to go; gives us a suitable-for-framing photo of you, usually looking smarmy, enraged, dazed, or confused……….and a notable quote.

- January reaches back to February of 2000, when you opined: *"One of the key problems today is that politics is such a disgrace, good people don't go into government."*
Too true. Except for Barack Obama, Bernie Sanders, Jeff Merkley, Kirsten Gillebrand, etc.

- In February, Ivanka is in the photo also, and the monthly quote is your March 2006 confession to the ladies of The View: *"I've said if Ivanka weren't my daughter, perhaps I'd be dating her."* Family values indeed.

- March (46 months to go!!) takes us to a March 2011, interview on ABC's Good Morning America, when you boasted that *"The beauty of me is that I am very rich."*

- Donald, I don't think your inherited wealth has made you beautiful. It has made you Bigly Ugly.

- On the same topic, I recently re-read the story and watched a couple of movies of my favorite fairy tale, ***"Beauty and the Beast."***
- The story is that of a spoiled brat princeling who is cruel and contemptuous toward a beggar woman and is then cursed to assume the form of a monstrous hirsute animal with bad teeth (but really big paws)

until he is redeemed by the love of an intelligent and open-minded woman.

- Along the way, we are given subtle lessons about tolerance for "The Other," the value of knowledge, the deleterious effects of greed, and the virtues of empathy and compassion. I know, none of these things matter to you, but they should. And were you ever to avail yourself of this fable (in any of its iterations), you would clearly see yourself in both the foppish and ruthless pre-Beast prince…..and in the crassly ignorant and bombastic human suitors who also want to control the heroine.

So, DT, due to the fact that we still have 1389 days remaining of your incompetent and chaotic occupation of 1600 Pennsylvania Avenue, I remain, yours truly, Persisting in Portland….KP

Resources - Volume I – Issue 11

"2017 Donald Trump Out of Office Countdown Wall Calendar." *Sourcebooks*. Best independent book publisher (sourcebooks.com)

[Update: Sadly, no longer in print, although I did purchase and consult the 2018, 2019, and 2020 versions as well.]

Beauty and the Beast (disambiguation) - Wikipedia

The Weekly Screed: April 9, 2017 (Volume I, Issue 12)

TO: The Donald: Flipper in Chief

FROM: Kelly: It's All Sounding Terribly Familiar

- Good evening, Donald. I'm sure you are looking forward to my take on the week's events in Syria. You need wait no longer. Everyone's entitled to my opinion.
- But let's start with YOUR take on the Syrian crisis……..in 2013 and 2014. At the time, you repeatedly chided President Obama for even *considering* a retaliation against Syria, and *especially* if he didn't get authorization from Congress first:

  -- *"Again, to our very foolish leader, do not attack Syria – If you do many very bad things will happen...."* [Sep 2013] and

  -- *"The president must get Congressional approval before attacking Syria – big mistake if he does not!"* [Aug 2013]   and (my personal favorite):

  -- *"If Syria was forced to use Obamacare they would self-destruct without a shot being fired."* [Sep 2013]. Donald, you crack me up !
- And then a funny thing happened: Obama DID try to get Congress to vote on military action in Syria, only to be told by people such as Marco Rubio: "I remain unconvinced that the use of force proposed here will work."
- Of course, as Bill Maher pointed out, that would be Bombing While Black, so Congress could never go along with enabling such a radical action.

- Fast-forward to NOW: Our new CEO of the State Department opines that: "I think the status and the longer-term status of President Assad will be decided by the Syrian people."
- Bashar Assad thinks, hmmm, okay, I have the Green Light to do whatever I want and proceeds to explode sarin gas all over the people of Idlib province…………..two days later.
- You then blame Obama for the attack, (but then, again, two days later) decide to lob a few missiles into Syria after all (without consulting Congress), decrying the fact that "beautiful babies were cruelly murdered." Because now you are such a humanitarian.
- And, ever ready to weigh in, Marco Rubio gravely notes that: …. he doesn't think it's a coincidence that a suspected chemical weapons attack in Syria occurred shortly after Secretary of State Rex Tillerson suggested Syrian President Bashar Al-Assad could remain in power. [CNN]

- This triggered **my** recall of a meeting way back in July of 1990, when US Ambassador April Glaspie made nice with Saddam Hussein and assured him that Daddy Bush [George H.W., # 41] wished for "better relations with Iraq" and held "no opinion on the Arab-Arab conflicts, like your border disagreement with Kuwait."
- Oopsidoodle. Gulf War I.
- Then Shock and Awe in 2003 as Baby Bush [W, #43] decided to finish the job and make Iraq safe for Halliburton. We all know how well THAT turned out.

Now, I realize that you are just dipping your toes into the slimy edge of *this* quagmire, but I urge you to recall your prescient advice last year on this topic: --"We should not be focusing on Syria. You're going to end up in World War III over Syria if we listen to Hillary Clinton."

Resources - Volume I – Issue 12

Syria, of course. Ironically, the night of the missile strike, I was at the World Affairs Council of Oregon's International Speakers Series, listening to a talk by Tawakkol Karman, a woman from Yemen who (at 32 in 2011) was awarded the Nobel Peace Prize. She doesn't like The Donald either.

Krieg, G. "Trump Tweet on Syria and Obama." *CNN*, 6 Apr. 2017. Trump repeatedly to Obama in 2013: Don't attack Syria | CNN Politics

Nelson, Louis. "Marco Rubio, the Hawk, Turned Dovish on Syria in 2013." *Politico*, 6 May 2015. Marco Rubio 2016: The hawk turned dovish on Syria in 2013 - POLITICO

Labott, Elise. "Tillerson and Haley Deliver Different Messages on Syria's Assad." *CNN*, 30 Mar. 2017. US signals openness to Assad staying put | CNN Politics

Osnos, Evan. "Donald Trump Says Syria Chemical Attack Is 'Consequence of Obama's Weakness.'" *The Independent*, 5 Apr. 2017. Donald Trump blames Barack Obama's 'weakness' for Syria chemical attack - despite tweeting against intervention | The Independent | The Independent

Walt, Stephen M. "WikiLeaks, April Glaspie, and Saddam Hussein." *Foreign Policy*, 9 Jan. 2011. WikiLeaks, April Glaspie, and Saddam Hussein – Foreign Policy

The Weekly Screed: April 16, 2017 (Volume I, Issue 13)

TO: The Donald: The Easter Egomaniac

FROM: Kelly: Really? You couldn't let it go for One Week??

- So, I see you were up bright and early on this lovely morning, contemplating the most sacred of Christian holidays. And then blurted out:

"I did what was an almost an impossible thing to do for a Republican-easily won the Electoral College! Now Tax Returns are brought up again?"

6:07 AM - 16 Apr 2017

- And, just a few minutes later:

"Someone should look into who paid for the small, organized rallies yesterday. The election is over!" 6:13 AM - 16 Apr 2017

- Indeed, Donald, the massive catastrophe of the 2016 election IS over. Everyone gets it. But YOU can't stop bringing it up, no matter what the occasion: press conferences, signing your ludicrous Executive Orders, bragging to other heads of state, and tweeting about it incessantly. As in, mere moments before you tell the rest of us to stop focusing on it.
- I know……it was your one moment of glory, and it's hard to resist basking in it indefinitely. But the majority of the country is actually moving on:
We want to see your **2016** taxes. The ones not yet "under audit."
- And besides the tax fraud, we have many other matters to be perturbed about. But we can't march about everything every day.
- Yesterday, my sister, in her sweet little pink Pussy Cap, with her hand-lettered sign [He's Hiding Russian Investments], marched around the streets of her hometown. Believe me when I tell you that no one offered her remuneration.
- I was listening to NPR yesterday, when a Pulitzer Prize-winning journalist from the *Charleston Gazette-Mail* (West Virginia) shared with us his late editor's philosophy towards investigative reporting: Sustained Outrage.
- Donald, many of my friends and relatives have found it relatively easy to maintain this level of indignation ever since you started your *run* for the White House. Let alone your so-called election. Well past your odious installation ceremony. And continuing on as we awake in horror every day to your corrupt and benighted POTUS reality show.

Resources - Volume I – Issue 13

NBC News. "Trump Calls for Investigation of Tax Day Protesters, Tweets Election Over." NBC News, 2017. Trump Calls for Investigation Into Tax Day Protesters, Tweets 'Election Is Over!' (nbcnews.com)

NPR. "A Pulitzer-Winning Journalist's Advice, And Why He Does A Monthly Night Shift." NPR, April 15, 2017. A Pulitzer-Winning Journalist's Advice And Why He Does A Monthly Night Shift : NPR

The Weekly Screed: April 23, 2017 (Volume I, Issue 14)

TO:	The Donald: POTUS Ignoramus

FROM:	Kelly: Citizen Bibliophilius

Donald, I want to tell you a few things this week:

- Yesterday, my Pussy Capped sister, with her new sign "**Make America Think Again**," was once again marching in the streets. I realize it's hard for you to keep track of all these protests, what with the weekly golf retreats to Mar-a-Lago, but this one was in support of SCIENCE.
- As you may at some point discover, science is complicated (as is, to your amazement, health care policy and the political situation in the Koreas).
- One of the main reasons why you are Not My President is that you have appointed the most spectacularly dense and science-averse cabinet EVER:

    --On April 7, the *LA Times* reported that "Led by EPA Administrator <u>Scott Pruitt</u>, the Trump team is moving quickly to "return national environmental policy to a pre-scientific age." Because he's against "regulatory overreach."

    --And then there's <u>Betsy DeVos</u>, Secretary of Education, who does not believe in evolution, and is an active member of the Christian Reformed Church in North America. One of this fine denomination's stated doctrines is that "all scientific theories be subject to Scripture." Holy Moly.

    --Even our throwback Attorney General, <u>Jefferson Beauregard Sessions</u> wants in on the War on Science: he has announced that the DOJ will not renew the National Commission on *Forensic* Science. Who needs evidence?
- We should also consider your abysmal budget, which slashes government funding for every avenue of scientific research from the NIH to the EPA to NASA to NOAA.
- However, the most alarming, and potentially catastrophic, of your factual deprivations manifests in your attitude toward climate change. As you opined last September: *"And I think it's very low on the list. So I am not a believer, and I will, unless somebody can prove something to me, I believe there's weather. I believe there's change, and I believe it goes up and it goes down, and it goes up again. And it changes depending on years and centuries, but I am not a believer, and we have much bigger problems."*
- Bigger problems than breathing? Or Mar-a-Lago becoming Bajo-el-Mar when Florida sinks? Or when Club Med opens a resort in the Yukon?

- Donald, you are the Knucklehead in Chief. Please learn something.

Resources - Volume I – Issue 14

Horsey, David. "Pruitt Undermines Environmental Protections." *Los Angeles Times* April 7, 2017. Scott Pruitt undermines the EPA with anti-scientific ignorance - Los Angeles Times (latimes.com)

McCray, Rebecca. Edelman, Eric. "Disbanding the NCFS Will Lead to Worse Outcomes." *Slate*, 6 June 2017. Disbanding the NCFS will lead to worse outcomes. (slate.com)

Borenstein, Seth. "Trump Mocks Global Warming." *HuffPost*, 23 Sept. 2015. Donald Trump On Climate Change: 'I Believe It Goes Up And It Goes Down' | HuffPost Entertainment

The Weekly Screed: April 30, 2017 (Volume I, Issue 15)

TO: The Donald: 100 Days of Duplicity

FROM: Kelly: 100 Days of Despair

- Let's kick off this review with <u>your</u> evaluation: *"It's a false standard, 100 days, but I have to tell you, I don't think anybody has done what we've been able to do in 100 days, so we're very happy."*
- We are in agreement, Donald. No other Occupant of the White House has accomplished so little of his agenda (which <u>does</u> make me happy, along with the FBI investigation of you and your minions) yet inflicted such a disproportional amount of damage (which makes me SAD).
- I just reviewed your Contract With [On] the American Voter, where you promise to "restore honesty and accountability" and lay out 18 measures to clean up corruption, protect American workers, and beef up "security and the constitutional rule of law." There follows an outline of ten (count 'em, 10!) legislative measures that you will "work with Congress to introduce…. within the first 100 days of my Administration." Hah!
- Let's start with the circus act you *repeatedly* pledged to ringmaster **"on Day One"**: Repeal and Replace Obamacare. Despite having voted 60 times during the past 6 years, at an estimated cost of $87 million, to do just that, Paul Ryan and his cohorts couldn't even bring to a vote *either* of the TWO versions they recently concocted.
- Keeping score: that's a vote to repeal/replace around every 40 days during the Obama presidency, but only 2 *failures to vote* during your first 100.
I suggest they pick up the pace if they wanna keep their record intact.
- And who's to blame for this? The Democrats, you whined on March 24: ***"We were very close; it was a very tight margin. We had no Democrat support, no votes from the Democrats."*** Shocking.
- But now it seems you've shifted the focus of your ire to the document you swore on two Bibles to defend: the US Constitution. In an interview with Fox News (who else?) you placed the blame squarely on those pesky "checks and balances": ***"It's a very rough system. It's an archaic system … It's really a bad thing for the country."***
- Anyway, I'm running out of room, so I'd like to congratulate you on what I consider your most extraordinary accomplishments thus far: uniting the progressive and compassionate voices in this country; reinvigorating protest movements of all stripes; and Making Late Night TV Hilarious Again.

Resources - Volume I – Issue 15

Greetings, survivors (of the First 100 Days). We aren't at war with North Korea yet !

Anderson, Steve. "10 ways Congress could have spent $87 million (if they hadn't blown it on 60 Obamacare repeal votes)" Health Insurance. Org. October 1, 2015. 10 ways Congress could have spent $87 million | healthinsurance.org

Robinson, Joanna. "'The President Show' Proves We're Far From Peak Trump Impression." *GQ*, April 27, 2017. 'The President Show' Brings You the Donald Trump Impression You Didn't Know You Needed | GQ

The Weekly Screed: May 7, 2017 (Volume I, Issue 16)

TO: The Donald = AHCA: Amoral Hazardous Con Artist

FROM: Kelly = ACA: All-inclusive Coverage Advocate

- Oh, Donald, why didn't you listen to me? I am trying to save the nation, but also trying to save you from yourself.
- Obviously, you neglected to read (or consider) my advice from March 12, Volume I, Issue 8, the one where I handed you an Absolutely Fabulous *solution* to Repeal-and-Replace.
- It is, of course, Medicare for ALL, or single-payer, or heck, you can even call it IvankaCare if you want. Trust me; all those low-information voters (aka your "base") would love it!
- Instead, you went out and shilled for the R-and-R version that was finally mean-spirited enough to satisfy the fiendish "Freedom Caucus."
- Then, after you twisted enough arms in the House to get on board this "Freedom **FROM** Health Care" train, you held your little frat boy victory celebration in the Rose Garden. [Too soon, DT, too soon.]
- This display of Caucasian Condescension and Cluelessness was followed almost immediately by an astonishingly candid (and remarkably fact-based) admission to Australia's Prime Minister Malcolm Turnbull. Speaking at a press conference you acknowledged that you probably shouldn't mention the "fantastic health care" you are foisting on your citizens because "you [Australia] have better health care than we do."
- Wow. And I was giving you the benefit of the doubt that you had no idea what the provisions of the American Health Care Act actually were. That you were just supporting it because it replaced "Affordable" with "American" and so that HAD to make it better, right?
- But there you were, on national TV, conceding that the AHCA is really just a flaming pile of dingo feces compared to the coverage enjoyed by the Down-Under denizens.
- So, I checked it out and, by golly, learned that by every single health outcome I could find (e.g., hospital beds per capita, % of live births, life expectancy, etc.) Australia outperforms the US AND does it cheaper!
- I would imagine that we might suffer fewer casualties via poisonous creatures and shark bite, but that could be one of the few bright spots.
- Don't worry too much, Donald. The Senate has the long knives out for this wretched bill. Both of us will still have our jobs for a while……. I think.

Resources - Volume I – Issue 16

Good evening.

I came across a couple of quizzes from The New York Times which will reveal how much attention YOU are paying to this national catastrophe.

Full disclosure, I missed one on each quiz. But one of my results was: "You know more than he does." Duh.

They don't take too long. And they are fun. Enjoy !

Trump 100 Day Quizzes:

Collins, Gail. "The Trump 100-Day Quiz". *The New York Times* April 21, 2017. Opinion | The Trump 100-Day Quiz - The New York Times (nytimes.com)

Collins, Gail. "The Trump 100-Day Quiz, Part 2" *The New York Times* April 28, 2017. Opinion | The Trump 100-Day Quiz, Part 2 - The New York Times (nytimes.com)

Hope you have health insurance ! Use it NOW...........

The Weekly Screed: May 14, 2017 (Volume I, Issue 17)

TO: The Donald [in full confession mode]

FROM: Kelly [channeling his stream of consciousness]

An Explanation to the Nation:

I did not like this Comey guy showboating at the FBI.
At first, I tried to make you see I fired him over Hillary
because of that old email stink. Amazingly, you did not think
that was the reason! So, I met with Lester Holt and tried to set
the record straight on NBC (because I'm AWESOME on TV).

And in that little White House chat, I let it slip, right off the bat,
that I, The Donald, made the call (while letting others take the fall)
for ousting Comey. HERE is why I said I fired him: "It's a LIE!"
RUSSIA! MADE UP! Move along!! I swear that I did *nothing* Wrong!"

I'd asked him for his loyalty. He only promised "honesty."
In Moscow, that would get him killed. But with God's mercy I am filled.
So. *This* is what I *really* hate: I'm 6 foot 2, and he's six eight.
I have to look UP when he stands (and have you seen his giant hands?)
By his grandstanding I'm appalled. I fired him cuz he's Just. Too. Tall.

Resources - Volume I – Issue 17

Howdy, y'all.

It had to be about Comey this week. I knew the exact minute I heard about it on Tuesday why it had happened. I kept waiting for one of the pundits or comedians to come to the same conclusion that I did, but.........

NBC News. Trump Interview with Lester Holt. May 11, 2017. Trump Interview With Lester Holt: President Asked Comey If He Was Under Investigation - May 11, 2017 (youtube.com)

Kurtz, Judy. "How Tall is Donald Trump? Driver's License Raises Questions." December 23, 2016. **The Hill.** How tall is Donald Trump? Driver's license raises questions (thehill.com)

The Weekly Screed: May 21, 2017 (Volume I, Issue 18)

TO: The Donald: Whining about Nut Jobs and Witch Hunts

FROM: Kelly: The Amazing Week in Review

On **Monday** we were apprised that you bragged, during your Oval Office meeting with top Russian spies (excuse me, *officials*) about getting "the best intel." You then proceeded to *share* this classified info for "humanitarian reasons"....and to fight terrorism.....and because it was your "absolute right" to do so....and, well, because Putin had asked you to. Who could say no to that? Oh yeah, and that you had fired your FBI Director because he was "crazy, a real nut job." [Actually we don't learn this last tidbit till Friday.....from a *Russian* transcript of the meeting.]

On **Tuesday** we were pleased to learn that Comey (crazy like a fox) had kept detailed memos outlining all his conversations with you and that you had told him (on the day after you "fired" Michael Flynn) that Flynn was "a good guy" and that "I hope you can let this [the FBI investigation into Flynn's Russia ties] go." Nice try, Donald! Your first foray into Obstruction of Justice!

On **Wednesday** Deputy AG Rod Rosenstein appointed former FBI Director Robert Mueller as special counsel....to investigate your campaign's ties to Russia. The *really* bad news for you: he's just as tall as James Comey.

On **Thursday**, channeling Nixon, you decried ("with surety") this investigation as "the single greatest witch hunt" in American history. At which point Barack Obama, both Clintons, and the ghosts of 20 men and women executed during the Salem Witch Trials fell on the floor laughing. [The Catholic Church in Europe *burned* around 50,000 suspected witches, so we're just amateurs in this activity.]

On **Friday** we are told that a White House official close to YOU is "under scrutiny" and "a person of interest" in the new investigation; and that Comey is planning to testify before the Senate Intelligence Committee.

In summary, just a little couplet for this week's poetic offering:

I'd never elevate you to the status of a "witch;" instead, you're just (as Bill Maher says) "a whiny little bitch."

And you have nimbly jumped yourself from frying pan to fire. The logs are set, the kindling lit, and Mueller tends the pyre.

Resources - Volume I – Issue 18

Greetings.

I tried to outdo last week's All Doggerel memo, but there was just too much information !

Here's a good piece from USA Today that includes his tweets on the Oval Office meeting with the Russians.

Johnson, Kevin. "Donald Trump Shares Classified Information with Russian Officials." USA Today, May 16, 2017. Donald Trump says he has 'absolute right' to share 'facts' with Russia (usatoday.com)

Next week: An examination of what I'm sure will be at least a few hilarious international incidents..........Kelly

The Weekly Screed: May 28, 2017 (Volume I, Issue 19)

TO: The Donald: aka The International Embarrassment in Chief

FROM: Kelly: Channeling your report on:

What I did on my Big Spring Break!

I tried to bring World Peace by seeing nations and giving speeches on my First Vacation.

To followers of Jesus, Allah, Yahweh….my wisdom *should* have made them see things MY way.

But things did not always go as I planned. Melania refused to hold my hand.

My oration under the chandeliers did <u>not</u> make all those A-rabs stand and cheer.

I thought I'd score in Israel at least, but who knew that it's in the Middle East??

And who expected *anyone* would look at what I wrote in some museum's book?

And then compare My Words (they were So Great) with what Obama wrote, back in Oh-Eight??

At least I think I made it crystal clear those Russkies in my office didn't hear

That I had *EVER* named **Israeli** spies as helping us to capture ISIS guys.

So on to Europe where I met the Pope but all he seemed to do was pout and mope.

My ladies dressed in black from toe to head, like at my future funeral, so SAD!

The worst part of the trip was still to come: I had to handshake-wrestle that Macron.

And smile at all those losers in the NATO, and shove aside that dude from Montenegro.

To top it off, that concert in Manchester, and all those Russia stories seemed to fester

And stole away my limelight, so I hear. I think I'll go to Disneyland next year.

Resources - Volume I – Issue 19

Bennett, Brian. "Trump's First Foreign Trip Highlights His Unconventional Diplomacy." Los Angeles Times, May 27, 2017. From the shove to the orb, no single Trump moment from trip abroad stands out. There are too many - Los Angeles Times (latimes.com)

Marsden, Rachel. "Trump's Speech in Saudi Arabia Was an Awkward Misstep." Townhall, May 23, 2017. Trump's speech in Saudi Arabia was an awkward misstep (townhall.com)

Larison, Daniel. "Trump to Israelis: We Just Got Back from the Middle East." Slate, May 22, 2017. Trump to Israelis: "We just got back from the Middle East." (slate.com)

Drum, Kevin. "Trump Confirms His Intel Blabbing Originated in Israel." Mother Jones, May 22, 2017. Trump Confirms His Intel Blabbing Originated With Israel – Mother Jones

Manchester Arena bombing - Wikipedia

The Weekly Screed: June 4, 2017 (Volume I, Issue 20)

TO: The Donald: Hater in Chief

FROM: Kelly: Heartbroken in Portland

- So I've tried to keep it lively and jocular recently….a diversion from the awfulness of your every act. But something happened here in Portland recently, and there's just no way I can put an amusing spin on it.
- I'm speaking, of course, of the stabbing of three men on a light-rail train on May 26. These courageous citizens were standing up to the harassment of two young black women, one wearing a hijab.
- Their attacker, one Jeremiah Joseph Christian [oh, the irony] was screaming at them to "Pay taxes!" and "Go home. We need Americans here!" [Um, if they "go home," presumably to some other country (not their own) where the majority of teenage girls cover their hair, it might make it impossible for them to pay taxes here.] But I digress.
- What followed was bloody mayhem as Micah Fletcher (a 21-year-old poet and pizzeria employee) got in a shoving match with Christian, and Taliesin Myrddin Namkai-Meche (23, a consultant) and Ricky John Best (53, a former Marine) stood to intervene. Christian slashed all three with a knife.
- Best died at the scene, as a homeless man stripped him of his wedding ring and backpack. [This piece-of-crap perpetrator is now in custody.]
- Namkai-Meche died at a nearby hospital. Fletcher survived.
- Christian was arrested and queried police, "Think I stab (expletive) in the neck for fun? Oh yeah, you're right I do. I'm a patriot." Later in court he summed up his actions thusly: "Free speech or die, Portland. You got no safe space. This is America; get out if you don't like free speech."
- Gee, Donald….who does this remind me of? Who has been screaming at rallies, tweeting in the middle of the night, and signing despicable "Executive Orders," all designed to denigrate every demographic except Rich White Guys? Who gave this racist monster permission to kill people in the name of America First? Who is the most contemptible person ever to occupy the Oval Office? It took you three whole days to respond to this.
- I've been waxing poetic the past few weeks….but this week, the Hero Bard of the Train gets the last words. After coming out of surgery, he wrote:
    > *I am alive. I spat in the eye of hate and lived.*
    > *This is what we must do for one another.*
    > *We must live for one another.*

Resources - Volume I – Issue 20

It's a Somber Screed this week, my friends. I had to address the events of May 26, right here in Portland.

McLaughlin, Eliott C. "Portland Train Stabbing: What Happened." CNN, May 31, 2017. Portland train suspect: 'I hope everyone I stabbed died' | CNN

Wasserstrom, Shuly. KOIN 6 News Staff. "MAX Stabbing Suspect Unrepentant at Arraignment." KOIN, May 30, 2017. MAX stabbing suspect unrepentant at arraignment (koin.com)

Nashrulla, Tasneem. "A Man Stole from a Portland Train Stabbing Victim as He Lay Dying." BuzzFeed News, May 31, 2017. A Man Stole The Wedding Ring And Backpack Of One Of The Portland Train Stabbing Attack Victims (buzzfeednews.com)

Owens, Caitlin. "Trump's Response to the Portland Stabbing Does Little to Combat Hatred." Bustle, May 28, 2017. Trump's Response To The Portland Stabbing Does Little To Combat Hatred (bustle.com)

Kristof, Nicholas. "On a Portland Train, the Battlefield of American Values." The New York Times, May 30, 2017. Opinion | On a Portland Train, the Battlefield of American Values - The New York Times (nytimes.com)

The Weekly Screed: June 11, 2017 (Volume I, Issue 21)

TO: The Donald: Prevaricator in Chief

FROM: Kelly: Pursuing the Truth

- Watching James Comey's testimony before the Senate Select Committee on Intelligence on Thursday gave me a flashback to another time someone whose integrity I respect stood up (under oath) to another bully and fibber.
- It was in 2007, and a disgruntled (and sociopathic) private investigator had sued me and my employee (a former cop who was in charge of compliance efforts for the Oregon Board of Investigators.) I was the Executive Director of this licensing agency.
- The charges against me were dismissed before the trial, but my employee was still in the hot seat. At one point in the proceedings, when presented with untrue statements by the plaintiff, he characterized his accuser as a "Liar, liar, pants on fire." The jury loved it, and the State of Oregon won the lawsuit. Lordy, I sure was glad we hadn't settled with that P.I. **and** that we had copious records of all sorts (including taped phone conversations) that backed up our case.
- This brings me back to Comey, and his repeated reference to his concern that YOU (as opposed to the other two Presidents he had worked for) would most likely *lie about* his conversations and meetings with you.
- Donald, this would be a shocking accusation, but for our collective experience. Following your installation as POTUS, here are the things You Lied about *just in January*: your inauguration crowd (to both the CIA and to ABC News); "voter fraud" at a Congressional reception; two murders being committed during Obama's recent speech in Chicago; the Mexican President; the murder rate in Philadelphia; being in Scotland the day before the Brexit vote; and that Delta Airlines and protesters were responsible for the "big problems at airports" after your first try at the Muslim Travel Ban.
- Phew. That's a lot of LIES for just your first ten days in office!!!
So when Comey labels you a Liar, most of us nod our heads and say: Yup.
- As is my wont these past weeks, I'd like to wrap this up with a bit of verse, keeping in mind the testimony of my dear former colleague:
    > ***Tracking your mendacity is now a full-time gig.***
    > ***It's hard to keep up with the trumped-up falsehoods,***
    > ***small and big.***
    > ***Each morning, we tune in to radios, TVs, and browsers***
    > ***To learn about the latest conflagration in your trousers.***

Resources - Volume I – Issue 21

This week's memo addresses Comey (of course) and recalls the time I was sued by a Trumpian private investigator.

Georgantopoulos, Mary Ann. "President Trump's Lie List." BuzzFeed News, 2017.

Here's A Running List Of President Trump's Lies And Other Bullshit (buzzfeednews.com)

Shafer, Jack. "Why Donald Trump's Lies Don't Faze His Supporters." Politico, January 18, 2017. Trump's Lies vs. Your Brain - POLITICO Magazine

Finally, on my trip to Costco this weekend, I picked up Al Franken's latest: <u>Al Franken Giant of the Senate</u>

Which led me back to his 2003 book: <u>LIES And the Lying Liars Who Tell Them: A Fair and Balanced Look at the Right</u>

The latter could have been written last week...............just change the names.

The Weekly Screed: June 18, 2017 (Volume I, Issue 22)

TO: The Donald: Birthday Boy

FROM: Kelly: Marking the Occasion

- Wow……What a Week! The Attorney General shows up to testify before the Senate Intelligence Committee but can't remember ANYTHING intelligent; we learn that you are, in fact, under investigation (for obstruction of justice); another gun nut (this time a Sanders supporter, for cryin' out loud) vents his frustration by trying to take out the Republican Baseball team; Melania finally moves to Washington; it's Father's Day; and Donny turns 71.
- But what really made this week So Special was your First Full Cabinet Meeting. If you are going to have a great Birthday Party, clowns are in order. And they did not disappoint. I watched the whole thing on YouTube, and was able to divine the subtext of the expressions of awe and reverence:
- <u>Veep Mike Pence</u> gushed that it's been the greatest privilege of his LIFE to have to lawyer up while he waits in the wings for your impeachment.
- <u>Tom Price, M.D. (Health & Human Services)</u> declared that it was an Incredible Honor to be able to dismantle the nation's health care system in exchange for big tax cuts for the top 1%.
- <u>Jefferson Beauregard Sessions (AG)</u> actually remembered something and declared that law enforcement officers around the country were finally "so thrilled" to be able to fight rising crime under your esteemed leadership.
- <u>Rick Perry (Energy) and Scott Pruitt (Environmental Protection)</u> were both "honored to be on the team" and so excited to be able to get back to propping up the great polluting fossil fuel industries until we all suffocate.

Or get Raptured. Whichever comes first.
- <u>Betsy DeVos (Education)</u> offered that it was an "incredible privilege" to dismember public schools so that ALL students would be able to try to afford the religious/alternative-facts pedantry God clearly wanted for them.
- And on and on around the table it went, each man or woman determined to destroy the very agencies they were chosen to run; each more obsequious than the one before in their genuflections to the Dear Leader.

> *So, Donald, on your Birthday Week, you prompted adulation*
> *From all the clowns that you've sent in to decimate the nation.*
> *The only sour note came from that Mad Dog Mattis: Oops!*
> *Instead of praising YOU he had the nerve to praise the troops.*

Resources - Volume I – Issue 22

1) The truly pathetic Attorney General under questioning by another Nasty Woman:

Sen. Kamala Harris Goes After Atty. Gen Jeff Sessions | Los Angeles Times, June 13, 2017(1898) Sen. Kamala Harris Goes After Atty. Gen Jeff Sessions | Los Angeles Times - YouTube

2) The Great and Glorious Cabinet Meeting

The Great and Glorious Cabinet Meeting. "Trump Invites His Employees to Praise Him During Cabinet Meeting." YouTube, June 12, 2017. Trump Invites His Employees To Praise Him During Cabinet Meeting (youtube.com)

4) "Melania" gives Stephen Colbert an interview as she moves into the White House

The Late Show with Stephen Colbert. "Melania Gives Stephen Colbert an Interview as She Moves into the White House." YouTube, June 14, 2017. Melania Trump Gets Emotional About Moving Into The White House (youtube.com)

The Weekly Screed: June 25, 2017 (Volume I, Issue 23)

TO: **The Donald: The Grinch Who Stole Health Care**

FROM: **Kelly: With Apologies to Dr. Seuss**

Every Who down in Whoville likes health care a LOT.
But the Grinches who toil in the Congress, DO NOT!
The Donald [the Grinch-in-Chief] hates health care too
No one quite knows the reason; we don't have a clue.
It could be his head isn't screwed on just right.
It could be his ties and his shoes are too tight.
But I think that the most likely reason of all:
His heart [like his hands] is two sizes too small.

Whatever the reason (heart, hands, ties, or shoes)
He truly and deeply despises the Whos.
He thinks they are LOSERS, pathetic and dumb
And that all of the Whos should live under his thumb.
He promised so much when he campaigned last year:
The Whos would be WINNING at all they held dear.
Huge Jobs and Great Health Care! A Fantastic Wall!
The miners would dig up enough coal for all!!

But the more the Grinch thought of this whole "health care" thing,
The more the Grinch thought, "I don't have *enough* bling!"
The White House is shabby and ugly and old.
I just need to re-decorate it in gold!
But first I need Money. Now where can I find it?
To line the deep pockets of all my like-minded?"
Then he slithered and slunk, with a smile like a smirk,
And he realized just how this new plan could work:

"Instead of attending to all the Whos' welfare
I'll substitute Tax Cuts for Rich Folk for health care!
That Medicaid nonsense has just got to GO
And Planned Parenthood doesn't help who *I* know
So, it can go under and why would I care?
It's just for those lowly Who-Females out there.
The Whos are too lazy; their duties they shirk.
The little Who Children can go out and work!

The Disabled Whos can just pray for their lives.
The Elderly Whos, and their husbands and wives,
Can die in the streets---THAT's the health plan I see
Will do most to help all the Rich People like ME.
Obamacare we shall Repeal and Replace
And I will Grinch on with that smirk on my face.
This Christmas, instead of the Health Care I stole
I PROMISE to fill the Who-stockings with coal."

Resources - Volume I – Issue 23

So, I know it's not a "done deal" quite yet but seeing the direction the Republican health care bills are going (Mean and Meaner, as Oregon's wonderful Senator Jeff Merkley says), we are all done for. Therefore, this week I'm channeling my inner doctor (Seuss) and offering up my own take...........Kelly

Stafford, Dylan. "Trump's Health Care Promises." CNN, June 24, 2017. Trump's previous promises on health care | CNN Politics

U.S. Congress. "H.R.1628 - American Health Care Act of 2017." Congress.gov, 115th Congress (2017-2018). H.R.1628 - 115th Congress (2017-2018): American Health Care Act of 2017 | Congress.gov | Library of Congress

McEvers, Kelly. "Who Wins, Who Loses with Senate Health Care Bill." NPR, June 22, 2017. 9 Things To Know About The Senate Health Care Bill : Shots - Health News : NPR

Poem Analysis. "How the Grinch Stole Christmas by Dr. Seuss." Poem Analysis. How the Grinch stole Christmas by Dr. Seuss - Poem Analysis

The Weekly Screed: July 2, 2017 (Volume I, Issue 24)

TO: The Donald: Not Nearly as Handsome (or Smart…or Sane…) as Justin Trudeau

FROM: Kelly: Canadian Wanna-Be

- In Honor of the 150th Birthday of the Great Nation of Canada (July 1, 2017), I offer my own song…. hand over heart……

O Canada (American Refugee Anthem)	O Canada (Official National Anthem)
O Canada	O Canada
Will you please take me in?	Our home and native land
I'm scared enough to migrate to Baffin	True patriot love in all our sons command
With sinking heart, I have seen Trump rise	With glowing hearts we see thee rise
And he's making us less free	The True North strong and free!
From the Travel Ban to his Russian pals	From far and wide, O Canada,
He's a plague on the country.	We stand on guard for thee.
I'd live anywhere: P.E.I. to B.C.	God keep our land glorious and free!
O Canada, you're where I long to be.	O Canada, we stand on guard for thee.
O Canada, open your arms to me!	O Canada, we stand on guard for thee!

- Seriously, Donald, ever since I dated a hunky hockey player from Halifax in the '70s, I've wanted to be a Canadian.
- I even sent away for the immigration forms in 2004, and could have squeaked in then (age, education, speak French…).
- But now I'm too old and not wealthy enough. So, I'm stuck in Oregon. [Which is a pretty great place compared to the rest of the nation.]
- Sadly, though, even The People's Republic of Portland is still at the mercy of YOU and your tweeting thumbs.
- Please resign and go build your new hotel in Turkmenistan or obstruct some more justice so we can end this national nightmare.

Resources - Volume I – Issue 24

O Canada ! Happy 150th Birthday...........I've written you a song !
For those of you who are out of practice, here's a link to the official anthem so you can sing along..........It's an unusual version, but I really like this one-man a cappella Barbershop "Quartet":

Oh Canada – Trudbol Barbershop Quartet – Julien Neel – July 4, 2013

O Canada (Canadian Anthem) - Trudbol Barbershop Quartet (youtube.com)

BuzzFeedVideo. "Can Americans Pass the Canadian Citizenship Test?" YouTube, May 8, 2016. Can Americans Pass The Canadian Citizenship Test? (youtube.com)

"O Canada, the Anthem and Its History." Wikipedia, 2017. O Canada - Wikipedia

The Star Editorial Board. "Gender-Neutral Anthem Would Have Been Fine Birthday Gift to Canada." The Toronto Star, June 28, 2017. Gender-neutral anthem would have been fine birthday gift to Canada: Editorial (thestar.com)

The Weekly Screed: July 9, 2017 (Volume I, Issue 25)

TO: The Donald: I Just Can't Quit You, Vlad

FROM: Kelly: I Just Can't Wait to See All the Stuff Putin Has on You.

In honor of the first official meeting of you two evil Bozos, I've fractured the lyrics to one of my James Bond themes.

From Putin, With Love

From Russia with love, I'll fly to Don.

The G-20 meeting will go on

In Hamburg despite the riots and fights

I'm coming from Russia with love.

I've met Sexy Rexy* and Mike Flynn too,

But you were the one I desired.

We're both Bad Guys with pride, so I can't let

You see my disdain; in case you'd say "nyet."

From Russia I played you so I'd see

What favors you would return to me.

You're POTUS because I put you there.

Your fealty I ask you to swear.

Donald, every person in every US Intelligence agency is convinced, beyond a shadow of a doubt, that Russia hacked Hillary to put YOU in the White House. But Vladimir gives you that winning smile and, hand to God (or Lenin), promises, as the former head of the KBG, that he would NEVER interfere in a US election. And you try to convince us that you "believe" him. And then propose a US/Russian cyber-security partnership. As a way to "move forward." To ensure that EVERY election pleases our Kremlin overlords. This is treason, pure and simple.

Resources - Volume I – Issue 25

*Tillerson, Rex (Secretary of State)

Theme song from the 1963 James Bond film of the same name. Sung by Matt Munro. MATT MONRO ~ From Russia With Love ~ (youtube.com)

Cassidy, John. "The Trump-Putin Bromance Is Back On." *The New Yorker*, July 9, 2017. The Trump-Putin Bromance Is Back On | The New Yorker

CNN Editorial Staff. "Donald Trump and Vladimir Putin: Timeline of Political Interactions." *CNN*, March 28, 2017 80 times Trump talked about Putin - CNN.com

Dowd, Maureen "Opinion | Vlad, The Trump Impaler." *The New York Times*, July 8, 2017. Opinion | Vlad, the Trump Impaler - The New York Times (nytimes.com)

Maybe Putin taught him a nice toast:

To our get-together! May we meet up more often!

Russian: Выпьем за то, что мы здесь собрались, и чтобы чаще собирались!

But I will leave you with the more traditional:

За твоё здоровье! [za tva-jó zda-ró-vye]

Nasdrovye, All Yall............келли

The Weekly Screed: July 16, 2017 (Volume I, Issue 26)

TO: The Donald: Clearly a "High Quality" Parental Unit

FROM: Kelly: I'm loving ALL of this

Dear DT, for the past 25 weeks I've been writing to YOU, but would you please pass this one along to your "Good Boy"?

- **Dear Donald Jr.,** first of all, I'd like to express my condolences. I've had my own Daddy issues, but nothing as horrific as dealing with the psychotic imbecile you are so unfortunately named after.
- By the way, have you ever noticed how many "juniors" turn out to be mentally disturbed? [I've read that a 1971 study says 3 times the general population] Or is this just a function of having an uber-narcissist for a father… think George Foreman Jr., George Foreman III, IV, V, VI, etc.
- But I digress. I must tell you that if I were named Donald Trump, Jr., and I had received that now infamous June 3, 2016, email from "Best, Rob", I would have jumped on it too. You've been trying to impress your toxic and abusive Daddy-O all your life, and here was your Big Chance.
- For me, the most telling thing about your response was NOT "**I love it**."
- It was the things you *didn't* respond with that's gonna take all y'all *down.*
- For example, "Say what? This is just *PART* **'of Russia and its government's support for Mr. Trump'**?? Golly gee, this is swell!! What are the other parts? When did this start? Does *Dad* know about this?"
- OR, "Rob, how are you so familiar with sending back-channel ultra-sensitive and incriminating '**info to your father via Rhona'**?? It's almost as hard to get my dad's secretary's contact info as it is his!"
- So yeah, all of this is appalling, and illegal, and you (and especially Jared) are in some extremely scalding water right now, which will only get more scorching once you have to testify about this whole incident under oath.
- But the person in the most trouble here is really Dear Old Dad. Are we seriously supposed to believe that you lame-ass Three Musketeers didn't clear this titillating little meeting with King Donald before you took it?
- In the meantime, I must quote Charlie Pierce, writing for Esquire, "This then, is Junior's official explanation: ***I thought we were colluding to ratf**k the Democratic candidate, and the presidential election in general, but then she started talking about getting the mobsters' money back. Bitch set me up.*** This is not an argument I would bring to court." Good luck, DJ.

Resources - Volume I – Issue 26

As a public service, I do this "opposition research" so you don't have to………

Why you shouldn't name your son after his father:

Davis, Veronica Wells. "Naming Your Son After His Dad: 14 Pros and Cons." *MadameNoire*, March 21, 2016 Naming Your Son After His Dad: 14 Pros And Cons (madamenoire.com)

The emails:

Yourish, Karen, et al. "Donald Trump Jr.'s Emails About Meeting With Russian Lawyer." *The New York Times*, July 11, 2017. Read the Emails on Donald Trump Jr.'s Russia Meeting - The New York Times (nytimes.com)

The tortured familial relationship

Parker, Nigel. "Inside Donald Trump Jr.'s Relationship with His Father." *People*, July 10, 2017. Donald Trump Jr.'s Relationship with His Father Through the Years (people.com)

This is really all about The Donald:

Abramson, Jill. "The Trump-Russia Drama Isn't Going Away. But We're Missing the Real Story." *The Guardian*, July 13, 2017. Donald Trump – not his son – is the real protagonist of the Russia drama | Jill Abramson | The Guardian

What do the Russians 'Have' on the Trump Family?

Weiss, Philip. "The Real Story Behind Donald Trump Jr.'s Russian Meeting." *Esquire*, July 12, 2017. What Do the Russians Have on the Trump Family? (esquire.com)

The Weekly Screed: July 23, 2017 (Volume I, Issue 27)

TO: The Donald: Outsourcer in Chief

FROM: Kelly: Smelling Something Rotten

Donald, I was inspired by your shameless and pandering "Made in America Week" to do some research into the provenance of your self-branded accouterment. While almost all of your shabby output has come from foreign lands, I found one category of Trumpola that *WAS* made in the Good Ole U S of A. This would be the line of <u>Trump Fragrances</u>. Let's have a look!

- Your first foray into celebrity odor bore the moniker: ***Donald Trump: The Fragrance Experience."*** I have to say, DT, this is really a hilarious name, but the "experience" must have been underwhelming cuz you dropped it.
- Then along came ***Success by Trump,*** purported to *"capture the spirit of the driven man. The scent is an inspiring blend of fresh juniper and iced red current, brushed with hints of coriander. As it evolves, the mix of frozen ginger, fresh bamboo leaves and geranium emerge taking center stage, while a masculine combination of rich vetiver, tonka beans, birch wood and musk create a powerful presence throughout wear."* Wow. I'm overcome.
- As you tweeted at the time: *My fragrance— "Success"—is flying off the shelves @macys. The perfect Christmas gift!* –November 13, 2012
- Last but not least was ***Empire by Trump,*** *"the perfect accessory for the confident man determined to make his mark with passion, perseverance, and drive. For those who aspire to create their own empire through personal achievement, this dynamic scent is both compelling and leaves a lasting impression. Bold notes of peppermint, spicy chai, and a hint of apple demand attention."* I'm sure all the scammed and swindled scholars at Trump University were reeking of the stuff.
- Sadly, these many fine aromas are past their shelf life and no longer available at Macy's (or anywhere else). So, I'm proposing the creation of a vigorous new *parfum* to commemorate the first six months of your reign:
- ***Hypocrisy by Trump***: a cunning admixture of essence of ignorance and ambergris interspersed with bouquet of braggadocio, bergamot, and bombast. Hints of peevishness, perversion, and pineapple mingle with compelling overtones of paranoia. Top notes of mendacity and intimidation command notice, distinguished by a soupçon of melancholy. Delusions of adequacy and entitlement combine with whiffs of vodka, urine of virgins, and stale borscht to complete the gut-punch of sensory overload. It will be HUGE.

Resources - Volume I – Issue 27

This week's communication focuses on Trump Fragrances, which actually were Made in America. Until they weren't.

Trump Toilet Water

- Wikipedia Contributors. "The Trump Organization." *Wikipedia, The Free Encyclopedia*. The Trump Organization - Wikipedia

- O'Malley, Katie. "Donald Trump Launches New Men's Fragrance: Empire by Trump." *The Independent*, March 24, 2015. Donald Trump launches new men's fragrance, Empire by Trump: 'Because every man has his own empire to build' | The Independent | The Independent

- AskMen Editorial Staff. "What's Really in Your Cologne?" *AskMen*. Surprising Ingredients Found In Cologne - AskMenReddit Contributors.

Why Nothing is Made in America anymore:

- Miller, Matt. "Donald Trump's Made in America Week." *GQ*, July 17, 2017. Trump's Made in America Week Shows Us Why Nothing Is Made in America Anymore | GQ

Made in each state:

- Chappell, Bill. "White House Highlights 'Made in America' Products From Each State." *NPR*, July 18, 2017 White House Highlights 'Made In America' Products From Each State : The Two-Way : NPR

Trump merch NOT "Made in the USA"

- Kessler, Glenn. "How Many Trump Products Were Made Overseas? Here's the Complete List." *The Washington Post*, August 26, 2016. https://www.washingtonpost.com/news/fact-checker/wp/2016/08/26/how-many-trump-products-were-made-overseas-heres-the-complete-list/

The Weekly Screed: July 30, 2017 (Volume I, Issue 28)

TO: **The Donald: Patron de Scaramouche**

FROM: **Kelly: Is this the real life? Is this just fantasy?**

- Donald, we've endured only one week of your new "Communications Director" Anthony Scaramucci (who isn't technically On the Job until next month. But has already hit the ground running his potty mouth at top speed.)
- Of course, I was compelled to do some research into "Bohemian Rhapsody" by Queen, as this lyric has become an annoying earworm since The Mooch's first press conference on July 21: " *I see a little silhouetto of a man, Scaramouche, Scaramouche, will you do the Fandango?*
Thunderbolt and lightning, Very, very frightening me."
- Here's what I found out: "***Scaramuccia*** *(literally "little skirmisher") is a stock clown character of the Italian commedia dell'arte…. he was often beaten by Harlequin for his boasting and cowardice."* [Thanks, Wikipedia!]
- Has there ever been a more perfect conflation of moniker and man? This profane buffoon comes straight from central casting to play the part of your personal *sicario*: "I'm a Wall Street guy. I'm more of a front-stabbing person," he reassured a grateful nation. Then he threatened to "fire everybody" at the White House who might divulge even publicly available information (such as his financial disclosure forms).
- As James Howard Kunstler blogged on July 28, "It's kind of like Paulie Walnuts of 'The Sopranos' wandered into the West Wing of 'Veep'. Somebody's gonna get whacked and it'll be a laugh-riot when it happens." I'm sure Sean Spicer and Reince Priebus are ROFL.
- Frankly, Mr. Mini-Me Bully Boy should fit right in with the general atmosphere of paranoia you work so hard to inspire. This week you've gone after your evil elf of an Attorney General (Jefferson Beauregard Sessions); the three Republican Senators who voted against the odious "Skinny Repeal" of the Affordable Care Act; and Dr. Tom Price (your repellent Secretary of Health and Human Services, who is concerned with neither).
- On Saturday, you taunted the entire health insurance industry by threatening the withdrawal of CSRs (cost-sharing reductions) so that Obamacare can descend into a death spiral and "implode."
- Whatever happened to "We're going to have insurance for everybody!"??
- Or is it as the song ends: *"Nothing really matters to me."* I believe this lyric sums up your real feelings toward all of us. True colors, Donald.

Resources - Volume I – Issue 28

Good morning, everyone! Since last Friday, Merriam-Webster reports an 8,185% increase in searches for "Scaramouch"......

- Wikipedia Contributors. "Scaramouche." *Wikipedia, The Free Encyclopedia*, July 10, 2024. Scaramouche - Wikipedia

- Queen. "Bohemian Rhapsody." YouTube, December 24, 2012. Queen - Bohemian Rhapsody (Official Lyric Video) (youtube.com)

- Kessler, Ted. "Queen: 20 Things You Probably Never Knew About 'Bohemian Rhapsody'." *NME*, July 12, 2016 Queen: 20 Things You Probably Never Knew About 'Bohemian Rhapsody' (nme.com)

- Collins Dictionary. "Hit Man." *Collins English-Italian Dictionary*. Italian Translation of "HIT MAN" | Collins English-Italian Dictionary (collinsdictionary.com)

- Kunstler, James Howard. "Words and Deeds." *Clusterfuck Nation*, July 9, 2017. Words and Deeds - Kunstler

- Ross, Casey. "Trump Warns Insurers and Congress on Health Care." *STAT News*, July 29, 2017. Trump threatens insurer payments — and health care enjoyed by Congress | STAT (statnews.com)

- Everett, Burgess. "Trump's Obamacare Promises." *Politico*, March 23, 2017. 6 promises Trump has made about health care - POLITICO

The Weekly Screed: August 6, 2017 (Volume I, Issue 29)

TO: The Donald: On a "Working" Vacation

FROM: Kelly: On the Job

- Donald, how are you doing? I mean, really? I know Change is Hard, and you've had some major personnel shake-ups in the past few days. Anyway, I completely get that you are in dire need of some R & R. [Pay no attention to that "Lazy Boy" <u>Newsweek</u> cover. MEAN.FAKE.NEWS.]
- But here's the thing, DT. For the past 29 weeks, you've generously supplied me with ample fodder for these little pen-pal memos. In fact, there has been many a Sunday when I have *struggled* to wade through the collective mayhem of the most recent seven days to find the one shining superlative Outrage of the Week.
- So that's why I'm genuinely concerned that you won't be able to hold up your end of the bargain, especially with your nasty new Chief of Staff (General Kelly) calling the shots at Boot Camp Bedminster.
- You *say* that there will be "calls and tweets," so I'm going to cross my fingers and take you at your word. For inspiration, I look to the August 3 airing of your "first impression" calls to Mexican President Enrique Peña Nieto (from Jan. 27) and Australian Prime Minister Malcolm Turnbull (made on Jan. 28). Here's my favorite stuff from each conversation:

<u>Thing One</u> – After threatening Mexican products with "tariffs at the border," blaming the "tough hombres" of Mexico for turning New Hampshire into a "drug-infested den" and acknowledging that "[Enrique] speaks better English than me [sic]," you actually commanded The Leader of Another Sovereign Nation to quit saying that Mexico would never pay for The Stoopid Wall. "I cannot negotiate under those circumstances" you whined. In other words, if he wouldn't lie for you, it would just be too darn hard to maintain *your* signature Big Lie. Unfair!

<u>Thing Two</u> – After congratulating Turnbull that "You are worse than I am" in his attitudes toward Middle Easterners, you still complain that even the *appearance* of vetting refugees "is going to kill me....I hate taking these people....They are not going to be wonderful people who go on to work for the local milk people." [Say what?] Finally, the self-inflicted coup de grâce: "...this is the most unpleasant call all day. Putin was a pleasant call. This is ridiculous....This is crazy." Click.

Donald, *please* phone more friends like these on your vacay, and I think we can all rest assured there will be Screed-worthy topics throughout August.

Resources - Volume I – Issue 29

Say it ain't so ! He's going on VACATION? Well, I'm not planning on one till September, so will still be hoping for fresh material to get us through the Dog Days of August.

- Estepa, Jessica. "Newsweek Calls President Trump 'Lazy Boy' on Its New Cover." *USA Today*, August 4, 2017. Newsweek calls President Trump a 'Lazy Boy' on its new cover (usatoday.com)

- Manchester, Julia. "Trump Claims New Jersey Getaway Is Not a Vacation." The Hill, August 4, 2017. Trump: New Jersey getaway is 'not a vacation' (thehill.com)

- Greg Miller, Julie Vitkovskaya, Reuben Fischer-Baum 'This deal will make me look terrible': Full transcripts of Trump's calls with Mexico and Australia. The Washington Post, August 3, 2017. Transcripts of Trump's calls with Mexico and Australia - Washington Post
Note that the leaders he is talking to always refer to him as 'Mr. President' while he always calls them by their first names. Such a boor.

Speaking of phone chats, Donald, I'm inspired to revisit another great tune and

(in the words of Blondie) invite you to take our relationship to a new level: ***Call Me!***

You call Fox and Friends, Dear Donald, and World Leaders too

But I won't need NO translation when I talk to you

Come down off your Game of Thrones; we both have some great cell phones—

Call me (call me) on the line, you can call me any anytime

Call me (call me), pick a fight, you can call me any day or night, Call ME!

The Weekly Screed: August 13, 2017 (Volume I, Issue 30)

TO: The Donald: Fire and Fury

FROM: Kelly: Remembering Korea and Guam

- Donald, as a good pen-pal, I've tried from time to time to reflect on some of my experiences that have relevance to the Outrage of the Week. Today, I'd like to tell you about a very interesting job I had in the mid '80s.
- While you were swaggering around Manhattan, cheating on Ivana with Marla, I was working at the Port of Incheon (Korea) and Apra Harbor (Guam) as an Executive Director for United Seamen's Service, aka USS.
- USS is a non-profit agency, sponsored by the US Navy, which supports the merchant marine. USS Centers purport to offer "a home away from home" (restaurants, bars, gift shops, and social services) to US military, port officials, and merchant seamen. It was the hardest work I ever did.
- Korea in 1985 was filled with student protests over the election of Chun Doo-hwan (it was the only time I got tear-gassed!) and saw the first exchange of visits between Seoul and Pyongyang. The economy was sputtering, and most Koreans were not allowed to get a passport or travel. I was the only Western female living in the city of Incheon, and the first woman to manage USS Incheon, which had a staff of 35 Korean employees.
- In 1986, I was transferred to USS Guam, where I arrived to manage a multi-national staff of 45, and found the agency being investigated by the US Department of Labor for failing to pay appropriate overtime pay; the center's restaurant failing its sanitation inspections (by the Navy); and a stalled dining room construction. On New Year's Eve, my gift shop manager Rose (a mother of two) was murdered in a drug deal gone bad.
- At the time, USS Headquarters was located in One World Trade Center, and my clueless bosses were always calling me in the middle of the night, saying "What time is it there now?" And I would always respond: "We're where America's day begins! It's now tomorrow at 3 am."
- I guess the whole point of this issue, Donald, is that (unlike you) I've been to the Demilitarized Zone between North and South Korea, and I've lived in (and still have friends in) these places that you so cavalierly dismiss:
"Let's see what he [Kim Jong-un] does with Guam."
- You are as crazy as Kim. I hope millions of Koreans and Americans who are in immediate harm's way survive your bellicose taunting.

Resources - Volume I – Issue 30

Were I still living on Guam, I would not be reassured by Trump's phone call to Governor Calvo:

Mr. Trump said: "I have to tell you; you have become extremely famous all over the world. They are talking about Guam; and they're talking about you." And when it comes to tourism, he added, "I can say this: You're going to go up, like, tenfold with the expenditure of no money." [New York Times]

So, this threat of nuclear annihilation thing is really just a Jobs Bill for the Mariana Islands. Got it. Anyway, this week's issue mostly deals with what I was doing in Korea and Guam in the '80s. Glad I was able to be there before they both become smoldering ash heaps. The agency I worked for no longer has a website, only a Wikipedia entry. Sadly, USS headquarters was destroyed on 9/11 [but had its offices on the 13th floor and everyone got out] and has now relocated to Jersey City. And the two centers I ran have both closed down.

Stephen Colbert: Where is Guam? War In Guam! Wait, Where Is That Again? (youtube.com)

Allen, Nick. "Guam: The Paradise Island That Hosts Nuclear Bombers and Is in North Korea's Crosshairs." *The Telegraph*, August 9, 2017. Where is Guam and why is North Korea threatening it with missiles? (telegraph.co.uk)

Rogers, Katie, and Peter Baker. "Trump's Threat of 'Fire and Fury' Raises Alarms in Asia." *The New York Times*, August 12, 2017. Trump Threats Are Wild Card in Showdown With North Korea - The New York Times (nytimes.com)

The Weekly Screed: August 20, 2017 (Volume I, Issue 31)

TO: The Donald: Bemoaning the Loss of Our "Culture"

FROM: Kelly: Remembering Bonham, "The Star of North Texas"

- Donald, first I'd like to talk to you about the events that recently occurred in Charlottesville, Virginia. The "Unite the Right" rally (whose most benign stated purpose was to protest the proposed removal of a Robert E. Lee statue) devolved into violent clashes between the Protesters (the National Socialist Movement, Identity Dixie, the KKK, etc.) and the Counter-Protesters (the National Council of Churches, Black Lives Matter, Refuse Fascism, etc.). This 2-day melee injured dozens and claimed the life of Heather Heyer after a car driven by a self-proclaimed white-supremacist Protester slammed his vehicle into a group of Counter-Protesters.
- You have sent quite a few mixed messages in response to this gathering of (let's face it) your "base" and the groups that disagree with you and them. At first you decried "the display of hatred, bigotry, and violence on many sides." Okay. Your standard false-equivalency assessment.
- Then you doubled down, claiming that there were "some very bad people in that group [the Protesters] but you also had people that were very fine people, on both sides." Hmmm. You hastened to exclude the "neo-Nazis and white nationalists" from the "fine people" contingent but could only come up with the "people protesting very quietly the taking down of the statue of Robert E. Lee" in the fine folk category. Because "they had a permit." Obtained, coincidentally I'm sure, by Jason Kessler, a Charlottesville native *and white supremacist.*
- According to you, the fine people at this little soiree were the ones who "felt very strongly about the monument to Robert E. Lee, a great general." You also alluded to people who were "changing history…and changing culture."
- Now, Donald, here's where you and I must agree to disagree. I would submit to you that the glorification of these Confederate monuments to the "Lost Cause" (aka The War of Northern Aggression) is perpetrated by the people *who want to change history*. The Civil War was fought to end slavery. The generals who fought it were traitors. This particular Robert E. Lee statue was erected in 1927, during the height of the Jim Crow era in the South, by racists *who wanted to reinstate the culture of slavery.* I have many kinfolk who still hold on to fantasies of "Southern heritage," and I know exactly what they are talking about when they voice those sentiments. I don't consider them "fine people" on this topic.
- So, while pondering your admiration of the "beautiful statues and monuments" littering the landscape of Dixie, I decided to check out the small Texas town I grew up in…. does it boast any tributes to the

glorious Confederacy? Thankfully, no.[Or I'd probably feel compelled to go down and protest.]
- Bonham is named for Col. James Butler Bonham, who died at the Alamo, and whose statue IS outside the courthouse in the town square. Other notable local landmarks include the Sam Rayburn Memorial Library (you probably never knew or cared that the longest serving Speaker of the House of Representatives was an actual Democrat from the Lone Star State) ….
- ….and a replica of Fort Inglish, built to protect early Texas settlers from the Native Americans who took exception to their usurpation of the territory. Coincidentally, the original fort was located on the grounds of the Veterans Medical Center, where my father worked when we resided in Bonham.
- Of course, when WE lived there (1954 – 60, when I was age 2-8) the town was segregated. As in "Colored" water fountains [I used to wonder just what color that water *was*] and "Niggrahs" confined to the balcony of the movie theatre and red-lined from the "nice" neighborhoods.
- I remember asking my mother (one Saturday while shopping at the JC Penney's located across from the courthouse and noticing patrons of a different complexion): "Why don't colored kids go to school or church?"
- "Now, honey, don't worry, they have their <u>own</u> school and church." Oh.
- Donald, just this March, in Ontario, Oregon, I met *another* person who lived in Bonham during those years. But he's black, and a few years older than I am. We had the same memories, but from dissimilar angles. So to speak.
- About a decade ago, I visited Bonham for the first time since we moved. Unlike many small towns in Texas, Bonham has grown since the 1950s. It has a Super Wal-Mart, and more eateries and shops and recreation. [Back in the day, my family belonged to the local "Country Club," which hosted the town's only golf course and swimming pool. No Negroes or Jews allowed.]
- My one overwhelming thought as I drove past my early haunts, was: Thank heavens my dad was transferred to Denver, Colorado. And I didn't have to <u>finish</u> growing up in Bonham and become thoroughly indoctrinated into the local "culture." It was such a lucky escape.
- Donald, I must apologize for going on here. I know that you are carefully crafting condolences to Heather's mother. When asked if you had spoken to her family, you replied that "the mother's statement I thought was a beautiful statement…something that I really appreciated. I thought it was terrific…I won't forget it." So, really, no need for *you* to weigh in.

Resources - Volume I – Issue 31

Greetings ! Well, the Long National Nightmare that has been The Donald's first (and hopefully last) Summer Vacation as POTUS is coming to a close. And I was worried about Slow News.

First, the recent events in Charlottesville, VA

Unite the Right rally - Wikipedia

Astor, Maggie; Caron, Christina; Victor, Daniel. "A Guide to the Charlottesville Aftermath." The New York Times. August 13, 2017.
A Guide to the Charlottesville Aftermath - The New York Times (nytimes.com)

Politico Staff. "Full text: Trump's comments on white supremacists, 'alt-left' in Charlottesville." POLITICO. August 15, 2017.*Full text: Trump's comments on white supremacists, 'alt-left' in Charlottesville - POLITICO*

My first (but thankfully not my last) "hometown"

"Bonham, Texas," Wikipedia, last edited July 13, 2023. Bonham, Texas - Wikipedia

Vanished Nazi POW camp (An astonishing story of undocumented enemy immigrants taking away American jobs ! And being rewarded with Movie Night !!)

> Davis, Tim. "Bonham's WWII Prisoner of War Camp." May 18, 2015. North Texas e-News. Bonham's WWII Prisoner of War Camp - North Texas e-News (ntxe-news.com)

Resources - Volume I – Issue 31 (continued)

"Fort Inglish," Fannin County

    Fort Inglish Vicinity of — Fannin County Historical Commission (fannincountyhistory.org)

"Sam Rayburn Obituary," The New York Times,

    Rayburn Is Dead; Served 17 Years As House Speaker (nytimes.com)

The Weekly Screed: August 27, 2017 (Volume I, Issue 32)

TO: The Donald: Rabble Rouser

FROM: Kelly: Remembering Glendale, Arizona

- Donald, watching your loathsome "campaign rally" in Phoenix the other night I couldn't help thinking back to when I attended graduate school in Arizona for one year (8/82 – 8/83). Twelve months was all I could stand.
- I crammed four semesters of work into two, plus summer school and some transferred credits, in order to escape the right-wing politics; the omnipresent and formidable insects that invaded the swamp-cooled 5th-wheeler I lived in; and the uninhabitable climate which made driving my little red moped (my only transportation) a daily life-threatening activity.
- I was there to obtain a master's degree in International Management and become a Citizen of the World and was attending a very specialized institution which (at the time) only offered that one degree. Students came from all over the globe, and we were required to also study languages and regional culture along with the usual business courses. The campus (named after its location on the WW II airbase Thunderbird Field) was a marvel of diversity, scholarship, and cosmopolitan goodwill. An oasis in the desert of local rednecks and leathery Republican snowbirds.
- At your rally, you exaggerated both the outside temps AND the time you spent "signing autographs" for your camp followers: admonished by Charlie Pierce as being so dim and ignorant that they can't recognize that they are "sliding toward something that will surprise even [themselves] with its fundamental ugliness." Even your buddy Michael the Black Man showed up from Miami for this spectacle of self-aggrandizement and mendacity.
- Along the way, you couldn't help boasting about how special you are: *"I always hear about the elite. I went to better schools than they did. I was a better student than they were. I live in a bigger, more beautiful apartment, and I live in the White House too, which is really great."*
- But really, DT, isn't this the real Phoenix you came to see? Aside from the odious "Sheriff Joe" Arpaio, Arizona has given us Barry Goldwater and Sandra Day O'Connor [the swing vote on Bush v. Gore]; an active John Birch Society in the '60s; and systemic segregation so egregious that the state was referred to as the "Mississippi of the West" and South Phoenix achieved the label of "Sunbelt Apartheid."
- It was the consummate coda to Charlottesville. It's your kind of place.

Resources - Volume I – Issue 32

To commemorate Oregon temperatures which currently rival Arizona's ......and the ridiculous campaign event in Phoenix this week......

- "Donald Trump's 57 most outrageous quotes from his Arizona speech," Gant Daily, published August 23, 2017. Donald Trump's 57 most outrageous quotes from his Arizona speech – GantNews.com

- My Arizona Alma Mater: "Thunderbird School of Global Management," Arizona State University, Thunderbird School of Global Management (asu.edu)

- Charlie Pierce, "I Have No More Patience for Trump Supporters," Esquire, August 23, 2017 Trump's Arizona Speech Shows the Danger of Supporting the President (esquire.com)

- Margaret Talbot, "Why Does Donald Trump Like Sheriff Joe?", The New Yorker, published August 25, 2017. Why Does Donald Trump Like Sheriff Joe Arpaio? | The New Yorker

- Katie Mettler, "The Story of the 'Blacks for Trump' Guy at Phoenix Rally," The Boston Globe, published August 23, 2017. The story behind the 'Blacks for Trump' guy at the Phoenix rally - The Boston Globe

- John Washington, "Phoenix Was Trump Country Long Before Trump," HuffPost, published August 23, 2017. Phoenix Was Trump Country Long Before Trump | HuffPost Latest News

The Weekly Screed: September 2, 2017 (Volume I, Issue 33)

TO: The Donald: Screed Scribe – Who Knew?

FROM: Kelly: Mistress of the Screed

- Donald, you have no idea how excited I was to tune in to MSNBC last night and hear the Breaking News from the ("FAILING") *New York Times*.
- It seems some intrepid reporters had gotten wind of the initial letter you and your gang of kids (Ivanka, Jared, and that spine-chilling Stephen Miller) had crafted to vent your wrath at James Comey back in May.
- Quoting the *Times*: "Mr. Trump ordered Mr. Miller to draft a letter and dictated his unfettered thoughts. Several people who saw Mr. Miller's multi-page draft described it as a **'screed'**."
- Wow. As you know, I myself have been sending you The Weekly Screed since January. I was so elated to learn that you too have the gift….although all I've gotten in reply from you are a couple of form letters that advise me:
"Thank you for contacting the President. We are carefully reviewing your comments." Which, frankly, doesn't sound too friendly.
- Be that as it may, when I started sending you these communications (and then re-distributing to my ever-expanding list of like-minded friends and family), I was often asked, "Kelly, just what exactly is a *screed?*"
- My American Heritage Dictionary denigrates it as "a long and monotonous piece of writing," but I prefer Merriam-Webster's portrayal of a **Screed** as "an informal piece of writing" or "a ranting piece of writing."
- Both of these capture, I think, the essence of what I try to convey to you each Sunday. I was also gratified to see the term pop up in other quarters:
- "In a *screed* that rocketed around Silicon Valley this weekend, a software engineer at Google blasted the company's efforts to increase the number of minorities and women in its ranks and leadership positions" (*Chicago Tribune*); and
- "But that speculation spiked with Trump's decision to hire as his new communications director Anthony Scaramucci, who proceeded to wage a war of words against Priebus, culminating in a profane *screed* published by the *New Yorker*" (*Milwaukee Journal Sentinel*)
- So I think this manner of communication is really catching on! The Good News is that MY Weekly Screeds won't get me fired, but yours just might get you impeached. And your little dog Pence too.

Resources - Volume I – Issue 33

Good day..........this week's offering is early because I'm going on vacation till next Sunday…. Up to Alaska to play with my friends and celebrate turning 65 !! Nothing was really gelling for me this week until I came home and watched the news. The Donald always comes through with something !

- Haberman, Maggie, and Michael S. Schmidt. "Trump Drafted Letter to Fire Comey, Times Confirms." *The New York Times*, September 1, 2017 Mueller Has Early Draft of Trump Letter Giving Reasons for Firing Comey - The New York Times (nytimes.com)

- Shear, Michael D., and Eileen Sullivan. "Trump's Morning Twitter Rant Targets Comey and Mueller." *The New York Times*, September 1, 2017. Trump Again Lashes Out at Comey's Handling of Clinton Investigation - The New York Times (nytimes.com)

- Merriam-Webster Staff. "Screed." *Merriam-Webster Dictionary*. Screed Definition & Meaning - Merriam-Webster

The Weekly Screed: September 10, 2017 (Volume I, Issue 34)

TO: The Donald: Blowhard

FROM: Kelly: No Hurricanes in Oregon!

- Donald, I just got back to Oregon after a week-long celebration of my 65th birthday in Anchorage, Alaska [ask THEM about Climate Change….]
- I haven't received Happy Returns of the Day greetings from the White House as yet, but (lucky for you) I celebrate the Birthday Month, so there's still time.
- Anyway, watching all the Harvey and Irma coverage from Texas and Florida (both places where I have friends and relatives in harm's way), I started thinking about health care in the Lone Star and Sunshine states.
- They are the two biggest Reddest States whose moronic and evil governors declined to accept the largesse that was the Affordable Care Act's expansion of Medicaid. Meaning that not only the working poor of TX and FL don't have health coverage…. their health care providers go unpaid, AND their uninsured rates and premiums for the individual and group markets are the highest in the land. Take that, Obama !!
- But what the hurricanes really brought into focus is the level of inequity in these states: Who can afford to evacuate to their second home in a drier place? Who has to sleep on the floor of a sports stadium? Who had flood insurance? Who will have health care if they are hurt during the storms?
- Both Texas and Florida land in the Top Ten States for Income Inequality [#8 and #5 respectively] No surprise, the Red States on this list did not expand Medicaid, which just adds insult to injury.
- Donald, on my flights to and from Anchorage, I read a book called: ***The Broken Ladder: How Inequality Affects the Way We Think, Live, and Die***.
It's a new book, published this year, and I thought the author might have some trenchant observations about YOU.
- Instead, the book opens with a description of air travel as a "notable microcosm…..of a status hierarchy." Who gets to board first? Who has the biggest seats? The smallest passenger-to-restroom ratio? Free drinks?
- And did you know that "the odds of an air rage incident were almost four times higher in the coach section of a plane with a first-class cabin"??
- Then (you're really gonna love this one), the author tells of the time Ivana got tossed OUT of first class for throwing a hissy fit over a crying child.

- I imagine there will lots of screaming babies in those hurricane shelters.

Resources - Volume I – Issue 34

Good evening, everyone. Hope your weather is better than Florida's tonight...........This week's offering is sort of a meandering soliloquy on Harvey, Irma, Medicaid, and Income Inequality. You'll see............

Issue Brief on "non-expansion" states. A little (okay, a lot) wonky, but informative

- Garfield, Rachel, and Anthony Damico. "The Coverage Gap: Uninsured Poor Adults in States that Do Not Expand Medicaid." *KFF*, October 19, 2016. Issue-Brief-The-Coverage-Gap-Uninsured-Poor-Adults-in-States-that-Do-Not-Expand-Medicaid (kff.org)

The impact of NOT expanding Medicaid

- Mangan, Dan. "Obamacare's Medicaid Expansion Leading to Health Insurance Boom in Some States." *CNBC*, July 20, 2016. Obamacare's Medicaid expansion leading to health insurance boom in some states (cnbc.com)
- Jost, Timothy. "ASPE: Medicaid Expansion Lowers Marketplace Premiums." *Health Affairs Blog*, August 26, 2016 ASPE: Medicaid Expansion Lowers Marketplace Premiums | Health Affairs
- Sanger-Katz, Margot. "How Expanding Medicaid May Lower Insurance Premiums." *The New York Times*, August 26, 2016. How Expanding Medicaid Can Lower Insurance Premiums for All - The New York Times (nytimes.com)

Income inequality

- Picchi, Aimee "9 U.S. States with the Highest Income Inequality." *CBS News*, June 16, 2016. 9 U.S. states with the highest income inequality (cbsnews.com)
- Kirkus Reviews Staff. "The Broken Ladder by Keith Payne." *Kirkus Reviews*, April 25, 2017. THE BROKEN LADDER | Kirkus Reviews
- Cohen, Jane. "Ivana Trump Flies into Rage at Cabin Crew over Unruly Children on Board Plane." *Daily Mail*, December 29, 2009 Ivana Trump flies into a rage at cabin crew over unruly children on board a plane say police | Daily Mail Online

The Weekly Screed: September 17, 2017 (Volume I, Issue 35)

TO:		The Donald: Exploiting Unpaid Child Labor

FROM:	Kelly: I Don't Do Lawns

- Donald, while driving around on Friday, I heard yet another story on National Public Radio that (frankly) made my skin crawl.
- I guess it was meant to be one of those feel-good dispatches about the American entrepreneurial spirit, but the notion that some deluded kid would mow the White House lawn for free to please YOU ....*And* that you would let him.....was both unsurprising and appalling.
- The event reminded me of all those accounts of you stiffing the employees and contractors who've worked at/on your properties over the years. Just last month I read an exposé of the deplorable treatment of the migrant workers building the latest luxury Trump golf resort in Dubai.
- And I know that good capitalists everywhere are applauding little Francis Xavier's "can-do" spirit and commercial genius at snagging POTUS as a client. But seriously, couldn't you have at least *tipped* him his going rate of 8 bucks? Have YOU ever mowed a lawn…or done any work for free??
- The video, of course, is priceless: little Frank manfully struggling with the power mower while you shamble along beside him. He really does ignore you until his dad intervenes and coaxes him into an awkward high-five.
- Then you condescendingly praised him as "the real future of the country." That may well come to pass, but for now the landscaping business is dominated by Hispanic laborers (43% according to the Bureau of Labor Statistics), many of whom are working here under the H2-B visa program.
- It turns out that 1 out of 3 Americans pay someone else to maintain the yard, and that (as a great article in Scientific American points out): "Lawns are the most grown crop in the U.S.—and they're not one that anyone can eat; their primary purpose is to make us look and feel good about ourselves."
- So, I guess it was a fitting photo-op for you and Frank, and he'll have a nice marketing tool for his "FX Mowing" business until he achieves his life's dream of becoming a Navy Seal and goes off to fight the North Koreans.

NPR reports that Frank clears around $20 a week from his enterprise, and that he plans to spend this summer's profits either "on a big Lego set or a smart phone."

But maybe he should heed the advice of Rep. Jason Chaffetz (R- Utah) who famously opined in March: *"rather than getting that new iPhone that [people] just love ... maybe they should invest in their own health care."* Yeah, Frank. Gosh darn it! Take some responsibility for yourself!

Resources - Volume I – Issue 35

- National Public Radio Staff. "Mowing in America: 11-Year-Old Entrepreneur Tackles White House Lawn." *NPR*, September 15, 2017. President Donald Trump Hails Young Lawn Mower Frank 'FX' Giaccio As Future Of The Country : NPR

I tried googling: Has Donald Trump ever mowed a lawn? And all I got was a link to a 2015 story about his family home in Jamaica Estates, Queens, NYC. Ironically, where I lived (but in a rent-controlled apartment) when I moved to New York after the Peace Corps and commuted via subway to my job at the World Trade Center]

- Haberman, Maggie, and Alexander Burns. "Donald Trump's Old Queens Neighborhood, Now a Melting Pot, Was Seen as a Cloister." *The New York Times*, September 22, 2015. Donald Trump's Old Queens Neighborhood Contrasts With the Diverse Area Around It - The New York Times (nytimes.com)

- Thompson, Derek. "Why the Guys Mowing Your Lawn Are Probably Foreign." *The Atlantic*, July 25, 2016. Landscaping industry become largest user of H-2b guest workers - The Atlantic

- Wray, Brittany. "The American Obsession with Lawns." *Scientific American*, July 15, 2016 The American Obsession with Lawns | Scientific American

- Morell, Sarah. "The Lunacy of the American Lawn." *The Healthy Home Economist*, June 20, 2017. The Lunacy of the American Lawn | Healthy Home Economist (thehealthyhomeeconomist.com)

- Montgomery, Mike. "No One Should Have to Choose Between Health Care and a Smartphone." *Forbes*, March 7, 2017. No One Should Have To Choose Between Health Care And A Smartphone (forbes.com)

- Goodman, Peter S. "In Dubai, the Trumps Settle for Stiffed Workers." *The New York Times*, August 26, 2017. Late Wages for Migrant Workers at a Trump Golf Course in Dubai - The New York Times (nytimes.com)

The Weekly Screed: September 24, 2017 (Volume I, Issue 36)

TO: The Donald: "Madman Across the Water"

FROM: Kelly: "I'm Still Standing" (for the 36th week in a row)

- Donald, as my mother told me, "there's only one chance to make a first impression" and you made a doozy at the United Nations this week.
- First of all, nobody hollered, pumped their fists, held up swastika signs, or wore a red hat, so I'm sure you were disappointed at the peculiar lack of enthusiasm at this particular campaign rally. Which is, after all, the only mission of the majority of your recent appearances.
- Just between you and me, I seriously think you should hire a vocal coach. Usually I try to watch The Celebrity President Show on the TV, while drinking, but this time I listened on the radio. The Good Part was I didn't have to see you make all your fatuous faces and flail about. The Bad Part was I had to concentrate on your actual locution.
- Did you realize that most of your speech pattern veers between Bellow and Sneer?? This does not make for a gracious delivery OR a gratifying listening experience. And that's just how you _sound_.
- The things you SAY are another matter. I know, you've told us that you "have the best words," but some of them seem made up.
- "NAMBIA," anyone? I know you couldn't pick it out on a map [hint, next door to South Africa], but at least you should know how to pronounce it.
Especially since you seem to so admire its health care system.
- Despite the leprosy, chronic malaria, and widespread HIV/AIDS, the country's life expectancy has skyrocketed to age 64 ! Up from age 45 in 2004!! Way to go, NAMIBIA! And that's only because they have instituted a public health care system that serves 85% of the population.
- And speaking of skyrocketing, you really just HAD to go call out the Other Crazy Guy (in #NoKo) as "Rocket Man." I know you think it's cute, but I looked up some other Elton John song titles and found one that fits you much better....even more so than "Honky Cat." See above.

But threatening North Korea again wasn't the least diplomatic part of your speech. That came during your luncheon remarks attended by African leaders: "I have so many friends [aka White Guys] going to your countries trying to get rich." This used to be called "colonialism" and didn't always go so well, especially in my old Peace Corps stomping grounds (Belgian Congo, aka Zaire, aka the Democratic Republic of the Congo). Please don't ever go to the United Nations again, Donald. SO embarrassing.

Resources - Volume I – Issue 36

Good evening. Well, it had to happen sometime. The least diplomatic person on the planet addresses the United Nations.

- Bennett, Brian. "Trump's Indecisive, Ill-Prepared Debut at the United Nations." *The Atlantic*, September 19, 2017. Trump's Indecisive, Ill-Prepared Debut at the United Nations - The Atlantic

- Robertson, Lori. "Trump's U.N. Speech." *FactCheck.org*, September 20, 2017. Trump's U.N. Speech - FactCheck.org

What a joke. And speaking of jokes, I decided to look up the complete list of Elton John song titles to see if there were some other choice parallels I could find to "Rocket Man". Lots of them! I settled on "Madman Across the Water" for The Donald, and "I'm Still Standing" for myself. Check it out:

- Songfacts Staff. "Elton John Song Titles." *Songfacts*. List of songs by Elton John (songfacts.com)

Then I decided to fact check Donald's admiration for health care in "Nambia" (rhymes with Zambia and The Gambia) but is usually known as Namibia.........

- Wikipedia Contributors. "Health in Namibia." *Wikipedia, The Free Encyclopedia*, July 10, 2024. Health in Namibia - Wikipedia

Finally, an example of going to Africa to get rich:

- Wikipedia Contributors. "Atrocities in the Congo Free State." *Wikipedia, The Free Encyclopedia*, July 10, 2024. Atrocities in the Congo Free State - Wikipedia

We are still wreaking havoc around the world.......

The Weekly Screed: October 1, 2017 (Volume I, Issue 37)

TO: The Donald: Channeling Lee Greenwood

FROM: Kelly: Choking on the Hypocrisy of it all

Verse ONE: If tomorrow all the things were gone, I'd worked for all my life

And I had to start again with just my children and my wife

I'd just declare bankruptcy (as I've often done before)

And maybe get a brand-new wife to cheat on and to bore

CHORUS: But I'm proud to be an American, where rich white guys can be free

And get five deferments from the war (bone spurs were KILLING me)

But today I'm *just fine*, playing golf, and I get to tweet all day

Yeah there ain't no doubt I love myself: God bless Trump's USA!!

Verse TWO: Now it's great to be the POTUS and to run my cons Big Time

Get to fire a lot of people and to live my life of crime.

Raising tax rates on the poor folk and declaring travel bans

Letting Russians hack elections and arresting Mexi-CANS!

[Repeat CHORUS]

Verse THREE: Now we had a little trouble when the hurricanes came through

Down in Florida and Texas, and the Virgin Islands too

And I just learned Puerto Rico is an island in the sea

Where the people are Americans, which was really news to me!

Final CHORUS: So I'm proud to be the POTUS in a country that's so swell

Where the Biggest Problem that we have is with the NFL

And to make them <u>Stand Up</u> for the song, and to love the flag like me

Cuz the country sure has gone to hell if those players take the knee.

Resources - Volume I – Issue 37

Such an eventful week, what with

- *Trumpcare III collapsing.*
- *Tom Price (Dr. Private Jetman) resigning (I hated THAT guy from Day One)*
- *The unveiling of the Top 1% Tax Giveaway Plan; and*
- *The pre-game atrocities taking place across the land.*

Oh, yeah, and I heard that Puerto Rico is still in catastrophic shambles and might need a little assistance. I'll bet that if this had happened in San Antonio instead of San Juan, help would be more forthcoming. It all put me in mind of Lee Greenwood's 1984 anthem to blind "patriotism", God Bless the USA. I actually heard him sing it LIVE during a USO tour (when I was the Director of the USO at Kadena Air Force Base in Okinawa, Japan in the late '80s). But I'm giving all y'all the link to his performance at the Trump Installation Festivities. Try to not throw up while watching.

- Lee Greenwood sings at Trump's Inaugural Concert: Lee Greenwood God Bless the USA at Donald Trump's inaugural concert (youtube.com)

- Colbert, Stephen. "Stephen Colbert on Trump and Puerto Rico." September 26, 2017. Stephen Colbert Rips Trump's Visit to Puerto Rico - Business Insider

- Mazza, Ed. "Donald Trump Explains Puerto Rico: 'An Island Surrounded by Big Water, Ocean Water'." *The Independent*, September 29, 2017. Donald Trump says Puerto Rico is 'an island surrounded by big water' | The Independent | The Independent

- Schneider, Christian. "Our President Yells at Kneelers but Does Not Have a Patriotic Bone in His Body." *USA Today*, September 29, 2017 Patriot, heal thyself: No patriotism in NFL-bashing Donald Trump (usatoday.com)

- Obama, Barack. "Obama's Take on the Issue." *YouTube*, September 27, 2017. Obama discusses Kaepernick's anthem protest (youtube.com)

- Johnson, Luke. "The Missing Verse of the Star-Spangled Banner." *YouTube*, September 15, 2017. The Missing Verse of The Star-Spangled Banner That May Change Your View Of Our Anthem. (youtube.com)

Weekly Screed: October 8, 2017 (Volume I, Issue 38)

TO: The Donald: Moron in Chief

FROM: Kelly: Trying to Stay Calm

- Donald, what the heck is REALLY wrong with you???
- Who goes to Puerto Rico, berates the territory for "throw[ing] our budget out of whack" and then launches paper towels at the assembled hurricane victims? All while disparaging the low body count compared to "a real catastrophe like Katrina" and then gushing about the F-35 fighter jet: "…we're ordering hundreds of millions of dollars' worth!"
- Say what? And *hurricane relief* is the big budget buster?
- Who, when faced with the single most horrific exercise of Second Amendment "rights" in modern American history, offers only the tiresome platitudes of "thoughts and prayers" and the right-wing bleat that NOW is certainly not the moment to talk about guns…….maybe "as time goes by."
- Who continues to poke at the North Korean tiger, hinting that "only one thing will work" and that Secretary of State Rex Tillerson's efforts in communication and diplomacy are "a waste of energy?"
- "Maybe it's the calm before the storm. Could be, the calm. The calm before the storm." Yup, I guess we'll all find out, as you've repeatedly threatened.
- Now, speaking of Rex, I had no great expectations of this guy, but he gladdened my heart with his cogent evaluation of you as a "moron." My 2000+ page American Heritage dictionary defines the term thusly: "A stupid person; a dolt. 2. *Psychology* A person of mild mental retardation having a mental age of from 7 to 12 years and generally having communication and social skills enabling some degree of academic or vocational education. The term belongs to a classification system no longer in use and is now considered offensive." In other words, it was gratuitous for Tillerson to append the adjective "f***ing" in order to get his point across.
- But is being intellectually deficient the paramount analysis of your persona? There's a new book (already sold out at my local Barnes & Noble) titled:
  The Dangerous Case of Donald Trump: 27 Psychiatrists and Mental Health Experts Assess a President by Bandy X. Lee, MD. Described as "The consensus view … that Trump is dangerously mentally ill and that he presents a clear and present danger to the nation and our own mental health", this work casts aside the old "Goldwater Rule" in favor of a "duty to warn." I can't wait to read it. And it is my fervent hope that YOU will read it too.

Resources - Volume I – Issue 38

Topic 1: Puerto Rico *So many excellent videos and coverage from the Real News, but I went with The Atlantic Monthly on this one*

Dovere, Edward-Isaac. "Trump's Puerto Rico Visit." *The Atlantic*, October 3, 2017. Trump's Puerto Rico Visit Is a Political Disaster - The Atlantic

Topic 2 Las Vegas *I'm sure I'll circle back around to this issue, and "bump stocks" in the future, but tonight I send you to a Politico article from 2014*

Bennett, Brian. "NRA Guns Second Amendment." *Politico*, May 19, 2014. How the NRA Rewrote the Second Amendment - POLITICO Magazine

Topic 3 North Korea *He's just so excited to destroy the world*

Reuters Staff. "Trump Says 'Only One Thing Will Work' with North Korea." *AOL News*, October 7, 2017. Trump says 'only one thing will work' with North Korea (aol.com)

Topic 4 Wacko in the White House

O'Donnell, Lawrence. "The Dangerous Case of Donald Trump: 27 Psychiatrists Assess." *MSNBC*, October 5, 2017. 'The Dangerous Case of Donald Trump': 27 psychiatrists assess (msnbc.com)

Goldwater rule - Wikipedia

Finally, Seth sums it all up perfectly:

Meyers, Seth. "Seth Meyers Sums It All Up." *YouTube*, October 7, 2017. Rex Tillerson Called Trump a Moron: A Closer Look (youtube.com)

The Weekly Screed: October 15, 2017 (Volume I, Issue 39)

TO: The Donald: Attitude and Platitude

FROM: Kelly: Consternation and Lamentation

- Geez, Donald, another week of awful decisions (Affordable Care Act, Iran) and scary pronouncements revealing your unmatched ego and ignorance.
- Let's start with your remarks on October 11, which found you sitting next to that dreamy Canadian Prime Minister, Justin Trudeau, who was in town to celebrate "International Day of the Girl". Eager to change both the topic and the object of the press's attention, you managed to remind us that you are still just itching to wipe out a whole bunch of international girls: "I think I have a little bit different attitude on North Korea than other people might have. And I listen to everybody, but ultimately my attitude is the one that matters, isn't it?" Too true, DT, which is why more than half the country is in an almost constant state of apprehension and despair.
- But, as the editors of the *New York Times* point out, that can be changed. The only reason that we are at the mercy of your whims and tantrums is "the Atomic Energy Act of 1946, passed when there was more concern about trigger-happy generals than elected civilian leaders." In other words, Congress could fix this system where you (and you alone) get to be The Decider of nuclear annihilation. However, given their track record….
- At a slightly less terrifying but decidedly more sanctimonious event, you became the first sitting POTUS to appear at the Values Voters Summit, on Friday the 13th, where you offered up the following howlers:
- "I met with the President of the Virgin Islands" [following Hurricane Maria]
  You knucklehead, you ARE the President of the **U.S.** Virgin Islands.
- "We see it [the "heartbeat of our great nation"] in the mothers and the fathers who get up at the crack of dawn; they work two jobs and sometimes three jobs. They sacrifice every day for the <u>furniture</u> and—future of their children. They have to go out. They go out. They work….And they make sure that the future of their children has God involved in it."
- Having a bit of trouble with the teleprompter, Donald?? Well, the entire speech is chock-full of shameless platitudes about "the power of prayer" and the magic of saying "Merry Christmas" and "stopping the attacks on Judeo-Christian values" and "We don't worship government. We worship God."

- Wrong, Donald. Most Americans worship MONEY. And POWER. Those are the "values" that govern the land. And endanger us all.

Resources - Volume I – Issue 39

A week of unparalleled hypocrisy

In a timely coincidence with the Harvey Weinstein sex scandal

CBS News Staff. "Canadian PM Justin Trudeau Celebrates International Day of the Girl in Washington." *CBS News*, October 11, 2017. Canadian PM Justin Trudeau celebrates "International Day of the Girl" in Washington - CBS News

If they were capable of doing anything, Congress could save us:

Krugman, Paul. "If They Were Capable of Doing Anything, Congress Could Save Us." *The New York Times*, October 11, 2017. Opinion | Mr. Trump Alone Can Order a Nuclear Strike. Congress Can Change That. - The New York Times (nytimes.com)

All these verbal gaffes reported verbatim at whitehouse.gov

Trump, Donald. "Remarks by President Trump at the 2017 Values Voter Summit." *The White House*, October 13, 2017. Remarks by President Trump at the 2017 Values Voter Summit – The White House (archives.gov)

Not to fear. National Character Counts Week kicks off today

Madhani, Aamer. "Trump Proclaims National Character Counts Week." *USA Today*, October 13, 2017. Trump proclaims Oct. 15-21 'National Character Counts Week' (usatoday.com)

The Weekly Screed: October 22, 2017 (Volume I, Issue 40)

TO: The Donald: Commander in Grief

FROM: Kelly: I didn't Sign Up for THIS

- Wow, DT. Both you AND your Chief of Staff, General John F. Kelly, managed to completely foul up what should have been one of the least complicated duties of your so-called presidency: offering condolences.
- I can't say I'm shocked that you would bollix this up. Having received five deferments from serving in Vietnam, you've demonstrated a pathological lack of respect and understanding for those who did….
- From dissing POW and Senator John McCain [*"He's not a war hero. He's a war hero because he was captured. I like people who weren't captured."*]…
- To actually accepting a Purple Heart from a wounded veteran at one of your campaign rallies: [*"I always wanted to get the Purple Heart. This was much easier."*]…than getting killed or dismembered?? No doubt….
- To repeatedly opining that the state of the military is *"a disaster,"* because we have fewer ships and nuclear weapons than we used to have. Yeah and there's also been a precipitous decline in the US Horse Artillery Brigade.
- But really!!….you call a grieving pregnant widow, can't remember her husband's name, and callously point out that the deceased may have been killed in action in Niger [exactly what are we doing there anyway?] but, hey, *"he must have known what he signed up for."*
- Donald, I'm willing to bet that when Sgt. LaDavid Johnson joined the Army in 2014, he never anticipated getting stuck with such a harebrained and incompetent Commander in Chief whose top priorities are:
  1) Self-aggrandizement and 2) Tax cuts for the top 1% and
  3) Tweeting night and day about all the horrible people who have wronged him (the media, Obama, Hillary, Congress, the White House staff, etc.)
- I surmise that civilians who perish while working in dangerous occupations (logging, fishing, agriculture, law enforcement, firefighting) don't deserve your sympathy either. It's their own fault they couldn't get a million-dollar start-up loan from Daddy to continue in the slum-lord business.

- Or that getting smoked at a country music concert is just the price Patriotic Americans should be willing to pay for a robust Second Amendment.
- I reckon we're really all to blame for continuing to live in a country where a nincompoop in the White House spends most of his time with one itchy finger on his remote control and another on the nuclear trigger.

Resources - Volume I – Issue 40

This week, our friend Donald demonstrates his incompetence and tone-deafness in a new arena: condolence calls.

Bever, Lindsey, and Kristine Phillips. "Fallen Sgt. La David Johnson, Caught in Trump Call Controversy, Was a Family-Oriented Soldier." *The Washington Post*, October 18, 2017. Sgt. La David T. Johnson, the soldier at the center of Trump's condolence-call controversy - The Washington Post

Lamothe, Dan. "It's Legal for Donald Trump to Accept a Purple Heart. How He Handled It Is Up for Debate." *The Washington Post*, August 3, 2016. It's legal for Donald Trump to accept a Purple Heart. How he handled it is up for debate. - The Washington Post

PBS NewsHour Staff. "How Many Americans Have Died in U.S. Wars?" *PBS NewsHour*, May 26, 2014. How many Americans have died in U.S. wars? | PBS News

CBS News Staff. "America's 10 Most Dangerous Jobs." *CBS News*, September 24, 2018. America's 10 most dangerous jobs (cbsnews.com)

The Weekly Screed: October 29, 2017 (Volume I, Issue 41)

TO: The Donald: "One of the World's Greatest Memories"

FROM: Kelly: With Apologies to Andrew Lloyd Webber

- Memory, all alone in the White House

I remember the Old Days

I could grab pussy then

I remember the time I knew what happiness was

Let the memory live again.

- All the Fake News seems to beat

A fatalistic warning

Mueller mutters and the media sputters

And soon it will be morning

- Daylight, I must wait for impeachment

To get back to my Old Life and forget CNN

When the dawn comes, that Morning Joe will say awful things

And a new day will begin

- Burnt out ends of dread-filled days

The stale cold smell of morning

I tweet blather and traduce my critics

Another day is dawning

- Touch me, please Melania, touch me,

Let's go back to Trump Tower, and our days in the sun

Can't remember the time I ever wanted this job

Look, a new day under the gun.

Resources - Volume I – Issue 41

Wikipedia Contributors. "Cats (Musical)." *Wikipedia*, Last Edited July 26, 2024. Cats (musical) - Wikipedia

Business Insider. "Old White Guy Yelling on the Lawn." *YouTube*, October 25, 2017. TRUMP: I have 'one of the great memories of all-time' (youtube.com)

Grenoble, Ryan. "Trump Brags About Having 'One of the Great Memories of All Time.'" *Huffington Post*, October 25, 2017. Trump Brags About Having 'One Of The Great Memories Of All Time' | HuffPost Latest News

Author Unknown. "Awesome Memory Except When It Isn't." *The Hill*, June 23, 2016. Trump can't recall saying he has one of the world's best memories (thehill.com)

"Mash-up from Barbra Streisand and Susan Boyle." *YouTube*, No Date. Susan Boyle & Barbra Streisand....Memory (Cats)....Mix.... (youtube.com)

The Weekly Screed: November 5, 2017 (Volume I, Issue 42)

TO: The Donald: "Don't Remember Much"

FROM: Kelly: Everybody sing along!!

- We Got a Papadopoulos for Christmas, it happened on the eve of Halloween

He was arrested way back in July,

And ever since he has been squealing to the FBI.

- We got a Papadopoulos for Christmas,

With Mueller in the role of Santa Claus

Paul Manafort and Richard Gates too,

Everyone's indicted, that's the easy thing to do.

- [Chorus] I can see me now on Christmas morning, creeping down the stairs.

Oh what joy and what surprise when I open up my eyes

To see a handcuffed Donald standing there.

- I want some more indictments please for Christmas:

Jared and Ivanka to name two.

Jeff Sessions and Mike Flynn would be a lovely win

And while you're at it, Mr. Mueller, go for Mike Pence too!

- [Chorus] Now when Papadopoulos is pleading guilty to this mess

I'm reliving history, just like poor Ms. Lewinsky, At least he wasn't wearing a blue dress.

- We got a Papadopoulos for Christmas, The Donald said he was "an excellent guy." But now he's a "liar," "low level volunteer."

I guess the campaign should have paid him hush money last year.

   Now Papadopoulos spits in its eye!

Resources - Volume I – Issue 42

Collinson, Stephen. "Donald Trump and the Mysterious George Papadopoulos Meeting." *CNN*, 3 Nov. 2017. Trump says he doesn't | CNN Politics

YouTube. "Gayla Peevey - I Want a Hippopotamus for Christmas (Original Performance)." Uploaded by AlabamaLadyRebel. November 20, 2009. I want a Hippopotamus for Christmas (youtube.com)

"I Want a Hippopotamus for Christmas." *Kididdles*. I Want a Hippopotamus for Christmas song and lyrics from KIDiddles

"I Want a Hippopotamus for Christmas." *Wikipedia*. I Want a Hippopotamus for Christmas - Wikipedia

Hayden, Michael V. "Trump, Russia, and the American Mind." *Newsweek*, 3 Nov. 2017. Mueller Vs. Trump: Papadopoulos Is the 'Big One,' Not Manafort, Ex–CIA Director Michael Hayden Says - Newsweek

Editorial Board. "The George Papadopoulos Indictment Is Very Bad for Donald Trump." *The New York Times*, 30 Oct. 2017. Opinion | Why George Papadopoulos Is More Dangerous Than Paul Manafort - The New York Times (nytimes.com)

The Weekly Screed: November 12, 2017 (Volume I, Issue 43

TO: The Donald: "A Mental Health Problem at the Highest Level"

FROM: Kelly: Indeed

- Donald, while you're on your Asian junket, making us the laughingstock of the world as usual, I'd like to remind you that just One Week ago, the latest act of American Carnage (which you promised to end, "right here and right now" on January 22) claimed 26 Texans. But at least they died in church, as the dimwits at Fox and Friends sought to put a comforting spin on things.
- Naturally, it's TOO SOON to discuss what we could *possibly* do to make the country safer by addressing the **gun problem**. Just as it was TOO SOON (41 days) to talk about banning bump stocks after Las Vegas (58 killed, 450 wounded).
- TOO SOON (518 days) following the homophobic slaughter in Orlando (49 dead); TOO SOON (878 days) after the racially motivated church killings in Charleston (9 souls); TOO SOON (1,794 days) after Sandy Hook Elementary School (26 children and teachers dispatched).
- Let's see: what do all of these tragedies have in common? Oh, yeah, the killers were all armed to the teeth, and victims of testosterone poisoning.
- You and Congress offer "thoughts and prayers" and blame the mentally ill.
- My impossibly ignorant (former) neighbor (another Texan) who of course voted for you posted on Facebook that: *It is obvious that the Anti-Gun nuts are intentionally ignoring the fact that it was another private gun owner that stopped the mass shooting. AND, the only people that will loose* [sic] *guns to more gun control are the ones that stop gun violence. Ironic twist. The Anti-Gun nuts are actually trying to increase gun violence. That guy already ignored their stupid gun control laws. What kind of morons* [sic] *think that making another law will stop gun violence?*
- Well, actually the Other Guy didn't *stop* the shooting. He continued the shooting by shooting the shooter after the main event shooting had stopped.
- Anyway, grammar aside, she does have a point. The Texas Church Shooter also ignored our stupid law against murder. Why do we still need that one, anyway? He didn't obey the Air Force's idiotic codes and wound up with a Bad Conduct Discharge. Why are we cluttering up military service with rules against assaulting your own family, fer cryin' out loud??

- Once again, I have to look to Canada on this one. Their law requires spouses (and ex-spouses and other "conjugal partners") to sign off on the "Acquisition License" for a firearm. If they don't sign, the Chief Firearms Officer of the Mounties "has a duty" to let them know. Genius.

Resources - Volume I – Issue 43

Finally, a week with some good news: Tuesday's election results !!
The rest, as usual, AWFUL, both at home and abroad.

Chappell, Bill. "Texas Shooter's History Raises Questions About Mental Health and Mass Murder." *NPR*, 7 Nov. 2017 President Trump Blames Mental Illness For Mass Shooting, Not Guns : Shots - Health News : NPR)

Mangan, Dan. "Trump Says Texas Church Shooting Caused by 'Mental Health Problem,' Not Guns." *CNBC*, 6 Nov. 2017. Trump says Texas church shooting caused by 'mental health problem' not guns (cnbc.com)

Caldwell, Leigh Ann. "Fox News Host Blames Atheists for Texas Church Shooting." *ThinkProgress*, 6 Nov. 2017. Fox News host: At least the Texas shooting victims got killed in church – ThinkProgress

"Too Soon to Debate Gun Control?" *The New York Times*, 5 Nov. 2017. Opinion | It's Not Too Soon to Debate Gun Control - The New York Times (nytimes.com)

Jacobs, Julia. "No, President Trump, It's Not Too Soon to Talk About Gun Control." *Glamour*, 6 Nov. 2017. No, President Trump, It's Not 'Too Soon' to Talk About Gun Control | Glamour

Robertson, Lori. "Trump Nixed Gun Control Rule." *FactCheck.org*, 18 Oct. 2017. Trump Nixed Gun-Control Rule - FactCheck.org

Royal Canadian Mounted Police. "Application for a Firearms License." *RCMP*, accessed 21 July 2024 Apply for a firearms licence | Royal Canadian Mounted Police (rcmp.ca)

Keller, Timothy. "Why Christians Should Support Gun Control." *The New York Times*, 11 Nov. 2017. Opinion | Why Christians Must Support Gun Control - The New York Times (nytimes.com)

The Weekly Screed: November 19, 2017 (Volume I, Issue 44)

TO: The Donald: Creep in Chief

FROM: Kelly: #Me Too

- Hey, DT, wanna hear about the first time I was sexually harassed in the workplace? I had a summer job before I went off to college (in 1970) at a horrid little franchise dessert place called The House of Pies, in Denver, Colorado. The local franchise owner/manager was a miserable scumbag named Steve who was awful to everyone. One day he was sitting at the counter with a buddy and called me over to point out to his friend what great tits I had. Guess what happened? All the employees got together and complained to the franchise HQ in California. We got Stevie FIRED.
- Sadly, the whole country now has to deal with a Pervert POTUS. Of course, almost all of us believed the accounts of the 20 women who came forward last year to tell us how you assaulted them. Just as we believe the accusers of Bill O'Reilly and Roger Ailes at Fox News, Harvey Weinstein, Kevin Spacey, Roy Moore, and (say it ain't so) Senator Al Franken.
- But here's the deal: none of those other guys are in the Oval Office.
- Really, I blame Bill Clinton for all of this. It was unbelievably *stoopid* of him to engage in any sort of intimate relationship with a young intern, no matter how "consensual" the activities. Then, he <u>lied</u> about it and got himself impeached. Dumb and dumber.
- Fast forward to Senator Kirsten Gillibrand (D-NY) opining that Clinton should have resigned over the Monica Lewinsky imbroglio.
- I agree with her but for different reasons. If Bill had done the right thing and bowed out, we would have had two years of peace and prosperity under President Gore. No Starr Report, no Little Blue Dress, no Impeachment, etc.
- Then, given <u>that</u> alternate political scenario, Dubya would have been unable to steal the 2000 election (even with the assist from Brother Jeb in Florida).
- And so it follows: no 9/11, no pointless endless conflicts in Afghanistan and Iraq, no ruination of the American economy, etc. The world would have been a much finer and safer place under a President Gore.
- In 2016, Bill's old scandal contributed a HUGE steamer trunk to the mix of Hillary's already considerable baggage, which helped lead to your triumph. The low-information voters of America threw up their hands and decided, what the hell, men are pigs, let's just go with The Donald. SAD.
- As the new hit song (from last night's SNL) goes: "Come Back Barack."

Resources - Volume I – Issue 44

Tien, James. "The Fall and Rise of the House of Pies: Send Us Your Photos of Surviving House of Pies Buildings." *LA Weekly*, 28 July 2011. The Fall and Rise of the House of Pies + Send Us Your Photos of Surviving House of Pies Buildings - LA Weekly

Borowitz, Andy. "Trump Warns That Dumping Roy Moore Could Start a Dangerous Trend of Believing Women." *The New Yorker*, 17 Nov. 2017. Trump Warns That Dumping Roy Moore Could Start Dangerous Trend of Believing Women | The New Yorker

Karni, Annie. "Gillibrand Says Bill Clinton Should Have Resigned Over Lewinsky Affair." *Politico*, 17 Nov 2017 Gillibrand remark on Clinton sends shockwaves through Democratic Party - POLITICO

Thrush, Glenn, and Maggie Haberman. "Democrats Confront a Big Question: What to Do About Bill Clinton?" *The New York Times*, 15 Nov. 2017. 'What About Bill?' Sexual Misconduct Debate Revives Questions About Clinton - The New York Times (nytimes.com)

Kantor, Jodi. "Listening to What Trump's Accusers Have Told Us." *The New Yorker*, 13 Nov. 2017. Listening to What Trump's Accusers Have Told Us | The New Yorker

Brown, Ruth Marcus. "Why Politicians Got Away with Sexual Misconduct for So Long." *The Washington Post*, 10 Nov 2017 Why politicians got away with sexual misconduct for so long - The Washington Post

"Lewinsky and Clinton Scandal: Timeline." *CNN*, 1998. A Chronology: Key Moments In The Clinton-Lewinsky Saga (cnn.com)

Baldwin, Kristen. "Chance the Rapper Sings 'Come Back Barack' on SNL." *Entertainment Weekly*, 19 Nov. 2017 SNL: Come Back Barack song with Chance the Rapper (ew.com)

The Weekly Screed: November 26, 2017 (Volume I, Issue 45)

TO: The Donald: #45

FROM: Kelly: Feeling as Thankful as I Can Under the Circumstances

- Hope you had a Happy Thanksgiving at Mar-a-Lago, DT. I know it's astonishing, but I've survived your "administration" long enough to pen as many Weekly Screeds as the country has had Presidents. Everyone who knows me can tell you that I'm usually a "glass-half-empty" sort, but I'm trying to find the silver lining this weekend. So here goes.
- Just for starters, speaking of Mar-a-Lago, I'm thankful that you have spent SO much time on the golf course, at all your freaking resorts, out of Washington, where you can do less damage. Sure, it costs a lot of taxpayer money (tens of millions, according to *Golf News Net*) but I figure it's a net WIN for the country in the long run. And you promised us that we would "get so tired of winning."
- I'm thankful that you came out in support of Roy Moore, the worse-than-usual Republican pedophile candidate for the US Senate from the Great State of Alabama. It actually does nothing to hurt the country (or even Alabama), and it got us all paying attention again to the Access Hollywood tape. I particularly enjoyed the "I'm With Perv" headlines in the *Daily News* and the *New York Post*.
- I'm thankful that you are finally shutting down that odious "charitable foundation" used to bilk donors for decades to the benefit of the Trump Crime Family. One less scam being perpetrated.
- I'm thankful that you were able to show your True Colors as "Commander in Chief" to the military on Thursday with your tone-deaf Thanksgiving address. My jaw dropped when I heard you say this:
'We're not fighting anymore to just walk around; we're fighting to win.'
I can tell you that even the *peacetime* military (with whom I worked for four years as a civilian back in the mid-1980s) wasn't just "walking around".
What an insult to the dead and wounded over the past 15 years.
- Finally, I am thankful that, for one more year at least, the country still has Obamacare, your trumped-up rants, and prevarications to the contrary. Yeah, I know that this might be a little self-serving, since helping Oregonians get coverage under the Affordable Care Act has been my job for the past four years. And I know it's not the perfect solution to the American Sickness that is our country's peculiar and inefficient system of health care. But I know for a fact that people are still living who would have died without it.

Resources - Volume I – Issue 45

Good evening, all............hope you had a lovely holiday and didn't have to argue about politics too much. I solve this problem by NOT going to Texas for turkey with the family. That said, I'm trying to put a positive spin on events in Trump World. But don't worry. I'll be fully back on the Doom and Gloom wagon next week.............Kelly

"Donald Trump's Golf Rounds Cost Taxpayers." *The Golf News Net*, 8 Oct. 2017. How much does each of Donald Trump's golf rounds cost taxpayers? (thegolfnewsnet.com)

Anything but a Democrat

Otis, Ginger Adams. "Trump Now Claims Access Hollywood Tape Might Not Be Authentic." *AOL News*, 26 Nov. 2017. Trump now claims 'Access Hollywood' tape might not be authentic (aol.com)

Crumbling Foundation

Allen, Jonathan. "Donald Trump Shutting Down His Charitable Foundation." *NBC News*, 27 Dec. 2017. Donald Trump is shutting down his charitable foundation (nbcnews.com)

Sticking it to the Troops

Lees, Isabella. "Why a Retired Lieutenant General Thinks Trump's Thanksgiving Speech to Troops Was Totally Insulting." *Bustle*, 24 Nov. 2017. Why A Retired Lieutenant General Thinks Trump's Thanksgiving Speech To Troops Was Totally "Insulting" (bustle.com)

The Weekly Screed: December 3, 2017 (Volume I, Issue 46)

TO:	The Donald: That was then

FROM:	Kelly: And this is now

THEN: "I fired him [Mike Flynn] because of what he said to Mike Pence. Very simple." -- News Conference, February 16, 2017

NOW: "I had to fire General Flynn because he lied to the Vice President *and the FBI*. [Italics mine] He has pled guilty to those lies. It is a shame because his actions during the transition were lawful. There was nothing to hide! --Tweet 11:14 AM December 2, 2017

THEN: You shared a series of Islamophobic tweets from far-right extremist group Britain First, sparking condemnation for spreading its "deplorable" ideology to a global audience. The first video, originally shared by deputy leader Jayda Fransen's account, claimed to show "Muslim migrants beating up a Dutch boy on crutches. A second re-post was captioned "Muslim destroys statue of Virgin Mary," while a third read "Islamist mob pushes teenage boy off roof and beats him to death." Then you sent a tweet to the UK Prime Minister: @ Theresa_May, "Don't focus on me, focus on the destructive Radical Islamic Terrorism that is taking place within the United Kingdom. We are doing just fine!" – 7:02 PM – November 29, 2017

NOW: Sarah Huckabee Sanders has defended the tweets, saying that *even if the content is fake,* the point is to draw attention to the underlying issue of radical Islamic extremism. Meanwhile, one member of Parliament called you a "fascist." Another described you as "stupid." A third wondered aloud whether you were "racist, incompetent or unthinking—or all three." Nov. 30, 2017

THEN: You have said the now famous Access Hollywood take which caught you boasting about sexual predation is not authentic. Last year, you acknowledged it *was* you on the tape and apologized for your actions in the hours after it surfaced in October 2016. But now, you are crying "Fake News." November 27, 2017

NOW: Unfortunately (for both you and him) you had a witness!

"He said it. 'Grab 'em by the pussy.'" – Billy Bush, December 3, 2017.

Resources - Volume I – Issue 46

Good evening. Yes, I'm in Chicago, on vacation, visiting my sisters, but The Screed cannot be delayed. This week, what used to be called "flip-flops" and now is known as Fake News. From POTUS himself. I swear, the man cannot keep a consistent or true thought in his head for more than a week.

"President Trump Changes His Story on Why He Fired Michael Flynn as National Security Adviser." *WCPO*, 2 Dec. 2017. Trump changes his story on why he fired Flynn (wcpo.com)

Fabian, Jordan. "White House: Trump Did Not Know About Britain First Leader When He Retweeted Videos." *The Hill*, 30 Nov. 2017. White House: Trump did not know about Britain First leader when he shared videos (thehill.com)

Castle, Stephen. "Trump's Tweets About Britain Stoke Outrage and Fear." *The New York Times*, 30 Nov. 2017 Trump's Tweets Manage a Rare Feat: Uniting Britain, in Outrage - The New York Times (nytimes.com)

Bush, Billy. "Yes, Donald Trump, You Said That." *The New York Times*, 3 Dec. 2017. Opinion | Billy Bush: Yes, Donald Trump, You Said That - The New York Times (nytimes.com)

Blake, Aaron. "Is Trump's Alternate Reality Full of Lies or Something Even Worse?" *The Washington Post*, Nov 29, 2017. Is Trump's 'alternate reality' built on lies … or something even worse? - The Washington Post

The Weekly Screed: December 10, 2017 (Volume I, Issue 47)

TO: The Donald: The New Face of the Republican Party

FROM: Kelly: Remembering the Last Republican I Voted For

- DT, I'm sure you remember 1980: you were 33 years old and appearing on TV to brag about erecting Trump Tower and leveling the Bonwit Teller department store in the process.
- The Metropolitan Museum of Art had asked you to preserve the Art Deco sculptures and intricate grillwork at the entrance to the building.
- At first you agreed, but then (through your fake spokesman "John Baron" who was actually YOU) declared the items to be "without artistic merit" and proceeded to jackhammer it all into oblivion. But hey, you then named your kid after your FAKE persona, so all good.
- Anyway, I'm remembering 1980 this week because John B. Anderson died on December 3, at age 95. I (along with Jacqueline Onassis and about 7% of the country) voted for him for President in 1980 and here's why:
- He was pro-gay rights; pro-choice; pro-gun control; supported The Equal Rights Amendment, environmental preservation, and the Food Stamp program; and promoted a 50-cent per gallon gasoline tax to help reduce Social Security taxes for the working stiff.
- Of course, he came in a distant third in that race. Carter refused to even debate him, and Reagan won bigly, giving rich folks a huge tax cut, union busting, and trickle-down economics.
- And, let us not forget, this was also the race when Jerry Falwell and The Moral Majority co-opted the Republican Party and became the pre-curser for Roy Moore and *his* ilk.
- John Anderson left Congress, went back to practicing law, and became one of the co-founders of FairVote, which advocated for the abolition of the Electoral College and instant-run-off voting.
- Finally, he supported Barack Obama (a fellow Illinoisan) in 2008.
- I've always seen the presidential election of 1980 as a HUGE turning point for the country: Reagan begat the Bushes….and war-mongering, and extreme income inequality, ersatz patriotism, and the mind-blowing equation of "Christian Values" with the Republican agenda.
- Because, really, I'm sure Jesus would see passing a corporate tax cut bill as much more consequential than funding CHIP (the Children's Health Care Program, which expired in September). Suffer the little children, indeed.

Resources - Volume I – Issue 47

Good evening, and Happy Holidays, everyone. Tonight, I'm remembering (fondly) the last vote I cast for a Republican. Okay, John Anderson was running as an Independent at the time, but he was one of the last R's I could find common ground with.

First, a link to what The Donald was up to in 1980: Blake, Aaron. "Donald Trump's First Media Controversy Is a Really Great Story. Just a Really Fabulous Story." *The Washington Post*, 18 Mar.2016 Donald Trump hasn't changed one bit since his first media feud in 1980 - The Washington Post

Next, some information on John B. Anderson, the National Unity Party candidate in 1980:

Simon, Scott. "Remembering John B. Anderson, National Unity Party Candidate in 1980." *NPR*. *John B. Anderson was a silver-haired, middle-of-the-road Midwest Republican Congressman of the kind you don't see today. He disliked deficits, big government and what he called moral absolutism. He supported civil rights, human rights, and the Equal Rights Amendment. He was the first candidate I ever heard endorse gay rights, or - what he called in his Illinois prairie twang - affectional preference. Toward the end of his 1980 independent campaign for president, Mr. Anderson gave his speech in San Francisco. The crowd was enormous and excited. John Anderson just said, people turn out because they see a motorcade and think it's someone important. But it's just me. John B. Anderson, a fine, funny, levelheaded man died this week at the age of 95.*

Schudel, Matt. "John B. Anderson, Fiery Third-Party Candidate in 1980 Presidential Race, Dies at 95." *The Washington Post*, 4 Dec. 2017. John B. Anderson, fiery independent candidate in 1980 presidential race, dies at 95 - The Washington Post

Sullivan, Andrew. "RIP John Anderson, the Last Liberal Republican." *New York Magazine*, 4 Dec. 2017. RIP John Anderson, the Last Liberal Republican (nymag.com)

Finally, the life and times of another figure influential in the 1980 presidential election: 3. Martin, Douglas. "Rev. Jerry Falwell, 73, Founder of the Moral Majority, Dies." *The New York Times*, 16 May Jerry Falwell, Moral Majority Founder, Dies at 73 - The New York Times (nytimes.com)

The Weekly Screed: December 17, 2017 (Volume I, Issue 48)

TO: The Donald: Idiot in Chief

FROM: Kelly: Third Generation Bureaucrat

- Season's Greetings, DT. I was all primed to cast heavy-duty aspersions on the GOP Tax Catastrophe, but something tells me it just *might* change again before you get to host your signing spectacle. So, I'm holding off. For now.
- In the meantime, I'd like to share with you an article I recently read on GovLoop, a social media blog for bureaucrats of all stripes.
- Just so you know, my paternal grandmother was a Postmistress under FDR, and my father was an HR manager for the Veterans Administration. My sister and brother-in-law both had great careers with the GAO, but I'm the only State [of Oregon] apparatchik in the bunch.
- Anyway, I get the GovLoop daily newsletter and Friday's headliner was a teaser from a book in progress titled: "365 Ways to Stop Being an Idiot". It had some good pointers on Empathy, Hope, Positive Thinking, Peace of Mind, the Problem of Attachments, and Humility, with nice quotes.
- For example, per Gandhi: "I claim to be a simple individual liable to err like any other fellow mortal. I own, however, that I have humility enough to confess my errors and to retrace my steps." You could take a lesson, DT.
- Like, just this week, you tweeted that "I was right!" following the extraordinary conclusion of the Alabama Senate race, during which you managed to back LOSERS in both the primary and general elections.
- Another tip from this article that might benefit you was #152 of the 365 Ways: Peace of Mind. As the author points out, "Lack of peace of mind breeds anger and resentment. Above all else, one's ability to make wise decisions is based on having peace of mind, uncluttered by impulsiveness."
- Sound like anyone we know? Even BEFORE you occupied the White House, a Pew Research Center survey found that "a majority of Americans believe Trump is 'too impulsive'." Wanna guess what they think NOW?
- And this from a Village Voice reporter who covered you for decades: "Donald just has no interest in information…He has no genuine interest in policy. He operates by impulse." [Wayne Barrett, shortly after the election]

- Sadly, events of the past year have validated these grim assessments. Particularly when it comes to foreign affairs, your off-the-cuff blurts and bellows are alarming a majority of the **_world_**.
- So, DT, try not to be an idiot. **_Read_** your intelligence briefings. Can't hurt.

Resources - Volume I – Issue 48

Good morning, everyone. Today, I'm trying to offer helpful tips to the POTUS as we head into this blessed season of giving and caring.

First, a little article from one of MY "daily briefings", GovLoop:

Ellis, John M. "365 Ways to Stop Being an Idiot." *GovLoop*, 23 Oct. 2017. 365 Ways to Stop Being An Idiot » Community | GovLoop

"About Us." *GovLoop*. govloop.com/about-us/

Often wrong, but never in doubt:

Parker, Ashley. "I Was Right: Being Donald Trump Means Never Saying You Were Wrong." *The Washington Post*, 13 Dec. 2017 'I was right!' Being Donald Trump means never saying you were wrong. - The Washington Post

A little problem with impulse control:

Cassidy, John. "Donald Trump: The Impulsive Demagogue in the White House." *The New Yorker*, 6 June 2017. Donald Trump, the Impulsive Demagogue in the White House | The New Yorker

Clifford, Catherine. "Trump Has Impulses, Not Beliefs." *CNBC*, 6 June 2017. Trump has impulses, not beliefs (cnbc.com)

I'm thinking that this horrible tax bill might just postpone nuclear war for a few weeks...........so Happy Holidaze, y'all..........Kelly

The Weekly Screed: December 24, 2017 (Volume I, Issue 49)

TO: The Donald: Bad Santa

FROM: Kelly: Apologies to Clement Clarke Moore

Twas the Night before Christmas and all through the land

Americans wait (with our heads in the sand)

For anything Happy or Good to befall us

Since Donald was duly installed as the POTUS.

On Day One, the Trump Show began its attacks

On the notion of Truth with "alternative facts,"

And so it began. Let's review Season One

Of the most terrifying TV show, bar none:

A cabinet stocked with folks hell-bent on killing

The missions of agencies they are now filling.

Corruption, collusion, and justice obstructed.

But Putin should be our Friend, Santa instructed.

Mass shootings at church and a concert in Vegas.

Nazis in Charlottesville; hurricanes plagued us.

Out of the climate talks! Let's build some pipelines

And drill in the Arctic and re-open coal mines.

Let's pack the courts with more zealots like Gorsuch.

Tax cuts for the rich! The middle class? Not much.

Health care for children? Much too unaffordable.

Nuclear war? It might not be too horrible.

So let's fill our stockings with bump stocks and rockets

As long as Bad Santa can still line his pockets.

Resources - Volume I – Issue 49

Good afternoon, everyone. All week long I've wrestled with which treasured holiday song I could subvert to lambast The Donald, but in the end, decided to mangle a classic poem. Hope you enjoy.

On the research front, it didn't take long to find Bad Santa bragging about how rich his Mar-a-Lago friends would be after that Big Christmas gift he inflicted on the country. [But wasn't it supposed to be all about job creation and helping out the forgotten middle class ??]

"Trump Spends Christmas at Mar-a-Lago, Brags About Tax Bill Benefits for Wealthy Friends." *CBS News*, 24 Dec. 2017. "You all just got a lot richer," Trump tells friends, referencing tax overhaul - CBS News

I was also delighted to see that the concept of "Alternative Facts" now has its own Wikipedia entry:

"Alternative Facts." *Wikipedia*, accessed 24 Dec. 2017. Alternative facts - Wikipedia

And, for your holiday entertainment,

Shouts & Murmurs. "Merry Christmas: F.A.Q." *The New Yorker*, 22 Dec. 2017. "Merry Christmas": F.A.Q. | The New Yorker

Glad Tidings to all y'all..............Kelly

The Weekly Screed: December 31, 2017 (Volume I, Issue 50)

TO: The Donald: Potentate of the United States

FROM: Kelly: Get Out!

- Donald, as you have often asked: "Hey, I'm the President! Can you believe it?" To which an anguished nation collectively replies: "Heck NO!!"
- This final issue of 2017 will hopefully be both the first and last of its kind: The Special Impeachment Issue. Yes, I'm hoping against hope that you will have your hat handed to you by Mueller well before this time next year.
- As you have lamented, this job is HARD. And, as David Letterman has noted, if you were trying to manage a Dairy Queen or work at The Gap, you'd be long gone. Your highest and best use is playing golf full-time.
- Besides being completely *unfit* to be President (you are, after all, a self-admitted sexual predator, a compulsive liar, a malignant narcissist, and an all-round ignoramus) there are actual reasons based in the law that should compel Congress to bring impeachment charges against you.
- Granted, they've only *approved* Articles of Impeachment twice in our nation's history: against Andrew Johnson (#17) in 1868 (primarily because he fired his Secretary of War) and against William Jefferson Clinton (#42) in 1998 (for perjury and obstruction of justice in the cover-up of his extramarital sexual escapades). [Tricky Dick was the only US President to ***resign*** rather than face an impeachment vote.]
- As far as most of us are concerned, you could follow either precedent. We'd delight in watching you actually hounded from office, but slinking back to Trump Tower on your own would be just dandy. Either way, we'd celebrate with nationwide bonfires of all your shoddy made-in-China MAGA gear to commemorate the stunning finale of "#45: The Celebrity President Show."
- A new 65-page White Paper titled *"The Legal Case for a Congressional Investigation on Whether to Impeach President Donald J. Trump"* has a
nifty 4-page Executive Summary that lays out 8 grounds for impeachment such as: Violating the Foreign Emoluments Clause, Abusing the Pardon Power, Undermining the Freedom of the Press, and Conspiring with Others to Commit Crimes against the United States. I highly recommend it.
- I realize that you said "No Collusion" 16 times in your recent interview with Michael Schmidt of the *New York Times*. But saying so doesn't make it so.

- Rather, it summons to mind the great quote from Ralph Waldo Emerson:
"The louder he talked of his honor, the faster we counted our spoons."

Resources - Volume I – Issue 50

Yes, it's happened. Volume I, Issue 50 is the last Screed of 2017.
Volume II, Issue 1 will be coming at you next Sunday. I'm planning on making the final issue of each year the Impeachment Issue. Unless I don't have to !! [Fingers crossed]

1) Unfit to be in charge of a Dairy Queen

France, Lisa Respers. "David Letterman Talks About His Trump Obsession." *CNN*, 12 July 2017 David Letterman: Trump's behavior 'insulting to Americans' | CNN

2) A nice history lesson for The Donald

"Impeachments of Presidents of the United States." *The History Place*. https://www.historyplace.com/unitedstates/impeachments/index.html

3) White Paper, - The Legal Case........ December 6, 2017

Bonifaz, John, Ben Clements, and Ron Fein. "The Legal Case for an Impeachment Investigation of President Donald J. Trump." *Free Speech For People*, 6 Dec. 2017.

FSFP-Legal-Case-for-Impeachment-Investigation-12-6-17-final.pdf (freespeechforpeople.org)

4) The NYT Interview - December 28, 2017

"Donald Trump's New York Times Interview: Excerpts and Analysis." *The New York Times*, 28 Dec. 2017. Excerpts From Trump's Interview With The Times - The New York Times (nytimes.com)

5) Finally, the Emerson quote is from his 1860 book *The Conduct of Life: A Philosophical Reading***, in a section called "Worship". I believe this work should be required reading before one is allowed to purchase the upcoming (and sure to be slim) volume:** *The Faith of Donald J. Trump: A Spiritual Biography* **[available on February 13, 2018]. Order yours now for your Valentine !! Happy New Year, y'all....Kelly**

THE WEEKLY SCREED

VOLUME 2 - 2018

ONE WOMAN'S
ONE WAY CORRESPONDENCE
WITH DONALD TRUMP

"I'M, LIKE, ... A VERY STABLE GENIUS"

KELLY PAIGE

Table of Contents Table - Volume Two – 2018

Issue	Topic	Date	Days Left in Office	Page
1	Button Man	Jan 7	1109	130
2	Colossal Jerk	Jan 14	1102	132
3	Come Back, Barack	Jan 21	1099	134
4	Duffer in Chief	Jan 28	1088	136
5	Pants on Fire – SOTU Edition	Feb 4	1081	138
6	Egomaniac in Chief	Feb 11	1074	140
7	Russophile	Feb 18	1067	142
8	I Hear You	Feb 25	1060	144
9	Last Responder	Mar 4	1053	146
10	Pimping Out the Press Secretary	Mar 11	1046	148
11	No Person, No Problem	Mar 18	1039	150
12	Bozo in Chief	Mar 25	1032	152
13	Congratulator in Chief	Apr 1	1025	154
14	Dumb and Dumber	Apr 8	1018	156
15	Forest Fire	Apr 15	1011	158
16	Polluter in Chief	Apr 22	1004	162
17	Talk Show Guest From Hell	Apr 29	997	164
18	Rudy ! The Musical !!	May 6	990	166
19	Art of the Un-Deal	May 13	983	168
20	Gimme That Nobel	May 20	976	170
21	Remembering Young and Beautiful Lives	May 27	969	172
22	Insulter in Chief	Jun 3	962	174
23	Minute Man	Jun 10	955	176
24	Persistently Illegal	Jun 17	948	178
25	Infesting the White House	Jun 24	941	180
26	Woe is Roe	Jul 1	934	182
27	Commander Bonespurs	Jul 8	927	186
28	Marching in the Streets	Jul 15	920	190
29	I Have the Best Words	Jul 22	913	192
30	BS in Economics	Jul 29	906	196

Table of Contents Table - Volume Two – 2018

Issue	Topic	Date	Days Left in Office	Page
31	SH*T Sayer #1	Aug 5	899	198
32	SH*T Sayer #2	Aug 12	892	200
33	SH*T Sayer #3	Aug 19	885	202
34	SH*T Sayer #4	Aug 26	878	204
35	Flag Hugger	Sep 2	871	206
36	Orange Lies Matter	Sep 9	864	208
37	Hurricane Donald	Sep 16	857	210
38	A Vast Orange Public Charge	Sep 23	850	212
39	Above the Law	Sep 30	843	214
40	Make 'Em Laugh	Oct 7	836	216
41	The Cat in the MAGA Hat	Oct 14	829	208
42	I'm Not a Baby	Oct 21	822	220
43	Ode to the MAGA Bomber	Oct 28	815	222
44	When I Can, I Tell the Truth	Nov 4	808	224
45	N.R.A.	Nov 11	801	226
46	Prison Reformer in Chief	Nov 18	794	228
47	Thankful	Nov 25	787	230
48	MAGA in Ole Miss	Dec 2	780	232
49	Putting the Fun in Funeral	Dec 9	773	234
50	Six Days of Christmas	Dec 16	766	236
51	Grinch in Chief	Dec 23	759	238
52	Special Impeachment Issue #2	Dec 30	752	240

Dear Readers, I present to You:

Trump's Second Year as Acting President of the United States (POTUS)

A Little Less **Comedy**, A Lot More **CHAOS**, Increasing **Calamity**

.....And So It Continues.....

The Weekly Screed: January 7, 2018 (Volume II, Issue 1)

TO: The Donald: Button Man

FROM: Kelly: Hanging on by a Thread

- Jiminy Christmas, DT. Couldn't we have even *one* drama-free week in 2018? I was planning on a Year-in-Review of 2017 for Issue 1 of Volume II, but now I need to change that plan pdq and toot sweet.
- Let's get this New Year's Party started with examining the Most Puerile Utterance ever made by a sitting POTUS: "Will someone from his depleted and food starved regime please inform him [Kim Jong Un] that I too have a Nuclear Button, but it is a much bigger & more powerful one than his, and my Button works!" [January 2, 4:49 pm]
- As I hope some grown-up in the White House has informed YOU by now, there Is. No. Button. Except for the red one you use to summon a kitchen minion to rustle you up another Diet Coke and cheeseburger. But there **is** a briefcase. And we're all on pins and needles hoping that you never open it.
- Then on Saturday, you let us know that you would absolutely be willing to talk with Kim (on the phone). YIKES! We don't want you to do that either! Even though you also reassured us yesterday that you are "a very stable genius….Actually, throughout my life, my two greatest assets have been mental stability and being, like, really smart…because I went to the best colleges, or college."
- I understand you felt compelled to declare yourself a brilliant mastermind in response to the release of Michael Wolff's book *Fire and Fury: Inside the Trump White House.* [Wherein you really do come off as cray-cray.]
- But the title of this new tell-all only gives me flashbacks to August 8 of last year when you took a rare break from golfing during your month-long "working vacation" in New Jersey, folded your arms across your chest and promised reporters that if North Korea continued to threaten us: "they will be met with fire and fury, and frankly power the likes of which this world has never seen before." At which point South Korea, Japan, and Guam collectively freaked out.
- At this point, Donald, I'm beginning to consider the possibility that "Rocket Man" (KJU) is actually more stable and intelligent than "Button Man" (YOU). At the very least, he seems to have a great deal more impulse control. I like that in a nuclear power head of state.
- And so the year begins. I've been responding to every "Happy 2018!" with the dire prediction that we will look back *fondly* on 2017. We'll see.

Resources - Volume II– Issue 1

Congratulations, everyone. We made it to 2018..........Such a juicy first week of the New Year ! A tell-all book, lots of nutter tweets, and a fantastically bizarre speech to reporters. Here are my 3 favorite sources for the week..........and one going back to last August.

Osnos, Evan. "Donald Trump and North Korea: Big Button, Small President." *The New Yorker*, 3 January 2018. Donald Trump and North Korea: Big Button, Small President | The New Yorker

Cillizza, Chris. "Trump Says His Nuclear Button Is 'Much Bigger' Than North Korea's." *CNN*, 3 January 2018. There's no such thing as a 'nuclear button' | CNN Politics

3. Choe, Sang-Hun. "North Korea, Sanctions, and Trump's 'Fire and Fury' Threat." *The New York Times*, 8 August 2017. Trump Threatens 'Fire and Fury' Against North Korea if It Endangers U.S. - The New York Times (nytimes.com)

Fallows, James. "How Actual Smart People Talk About Themselves." *The Atlantic*, 3 January 2018.
A Real 'Very Stable Genius' Doesn't Call Himself One - The Atlantic

On a personal note:

I'm having full knee-replacement surgery on Wednesday so hope to pre-write something for next Sunday.

On the other hand, we could experiment with what sort of Screed would emerge from an opioid haze..........Kelly

The Weekly Screed: January 14, 2018 (Volume II, Issue 2)

TO: The Donald: Colossal Jerk

FROM: Kelly: Remembering Emma Lazarus

- Donald, I can see a day, not too far in the distance, when you get tired of having New York City represented by a female (probably no more than a "3" on your scale) who offers too much misguided compassion to immigrants.
- When you come to that point, I've taken the liberty of penning a new tribute to her replacement (YOU, who else?)
- The original sonnet is inscribed on a plaque on the inside lower level of the Statue of Liberty. But it's just a National Park. These things can be rearranged. Here goes:

Quite like the brazen Sun God of Greek fame, the POTUS

Sends his tweets from land to land.

Here at our sea-washed, sunset gates shall stand

The Donald, dissing Emma Lazarus.

A Mighty Moron with a torch, whose flame

Is the imprisoned lightning, and his name

Father of Dimwits. From his beacon-hand

Glows world-wide shame; his squinty eyes command

The New York harbor that two rivers frame

"Keep, shithole lands, your tired and poor" cries he

With pursed lips. "Give me your rich, your young,

Your blond billionaires yearning to spend free,

The pale-skinned from your Scandinavian shores.

Send these, the wealthy and elite to me,

I lift my lamp beside the golden door!"

Resources - Volume II– Issue 2

Knee surgery or not: The Screed must go on !! But I had to time it around doses of oxycodone so that I could write this up somewhere between Pain Level 7 and unconsciousness.

I would encourage you to read the original sonnet before you dig into mine. Happy MLK Day to everyone...............Kelly

The History of *The New Colossus*

Lazarus, Emma. "The New Colossus." Liberty State Park, The story behind 'The New Colossus' poem on the Statue of Liberty and how it became a symbol of immigration - ABC News (go.com)

"The New Colossus." Wikipedia, accessed July 2024. The New Colossus - Wikipedia

Magness, Josh. " Norway vs USA: How the 2 countries stack up on healthcare, income and life expectancy." The Sacramento Bee, January 12, 2018. Norway, Trump's "shithole" comments & Americans moving there | Sacramento Bee (sacbee.com)

The Weekly Screed: January 21, 2018 (Volume II, Issue 3)

TO: The Donald: One Awful Year

FROM: Kelly: Soooo Missing Obama

- Donald, a recent conversation with a conservative friend of mine led me to look back on your first season of Celebrity President through a specific lens. The entire year has been a catastrophe, especially in comparison with that of the Best President in my lifetime: Barack Hussein Obama.
- *"Obama goes around signing executive orders"* said you in February of 2016. *"It's a basic disaster. You can't do it."* Actual score: YOU signed 57 EOs in your first year vs. 38 for Obama in the same time period.
- You routinely blame everyone who opposes you (Hillary, Ted Cruz, the Fake Media) as a liar. Actual score: According to the conservative methodology used by the *New York Times*, YOU uttered 103 falsehoods in your first 10 months vs. Obama's 18 in 8 years. By the *Washington Post's* tracker, you've hit 2000 lies already. Or "Lie2K" per Jimmy Kimmel.
- *"I will hire the best people"* you frequently proclaimed on the campaign trail. Ivanka backed you up on this at the Republican convention. Instead, you appointed a bunch of nitwits and ne're-do-wells and even they couldn't keep their jobs. Actual score: YOU are the only president in modern history to lose 3 Cabinet members during your first year. Total staff turnover in your administration's Year One was an astonishing 34% vs. 9% for Obama.
- *"To be honest, I inherited a mess. It's a mess. At home and abroad, a mess. ....The Middle East is a disaster. North Korea -- we'll take care of it folks. We're going to take care of it all. I just want to let you know, I inherited a mess."* So said YOU at your press conference in February. Actually, Obama handed you a vigorous economy by any measure, especially compared to the mess HE inherited from George W. Bush (two wars, and the worst economy since the Great Depression).
- *"Lock her up"* was the chant you and your (already) indicted co-conspirator General Michael Flynn used to rile up the crowds of moronic mouth-breathers at your campaign rallies. But actually, DT, Barack Obama is the **only** President since Richard Nixon who didn't face **any** investigation of his or his family's or his subordinates' activities during his two terms in office.
- Finally, Donald, you are a horrendous human being. Your complete disregard for anyone other than yourself, your assets, or your immediate family (in that order) makes you the least fit person ever to hold the office of President of the United States. You absolutely have to go.

Resources - Volume II– Issue 3

*Greetings, everyone. About the only note of humor in this week's offering is the link to the Jimmy Kimmel clip. All the rest of the links are depressing. In short, I'm feeling the pain of looking back on the last year, comparing it to 8 years of Obama, and facing 2018 with the sure knowledge that everything's gonna get worse before it gets better. Except for my left knee. I think **that's** getting better.*
Here ya go....Trump vs. Obama

Liptak, Kevin. "Trump Signs Executive Orders to Roll Back Obama Policies." *CNN*, 13 Oct. 2017. Trump has signed more executive orders than any president in the last 50 years | CNN Politics

Kimmel, Jimmy. "Jimmy Kimmel Commemorates Trump's 2,000th Lie with Documentary." *Rolling Stone*, 9 Jan. 2018. Watch Jimmy Kimmel Celebrate Trump's 2,000th Lie (rollingstone.com)

Leonhardt, David, and Stuart A. Thompson. "Trump's Lies vs. Obama's Lies: Who Is Worse?" *The New York Times*, 14 Dec. 2017. Opinion | Trump's Lies vs. Obama's - The New York Times (nytimes.com)

Aratani, Lauren. "Trump's White House Sets Record for First-Year Staff Turnover." *Fortune*, 28 Dec. 2017. Trump White House Sees Record Number of First Year Departures | Fortune

Rakich, Nathaniel. "The Incredibly (and Historically) Unstable First Year of Trump's Cabinet." *FiveThirtyEight*, 22 Dec. 2017. The Incredibly And Historically Unstable First Year Of Trump's Cabinet | FiveThirtyEight

Sherman, Amy. "Did Donald Trump Inherit a Mess?" *PolitiFact*, 17 Feb. 2017. PolitiFact | Did Donald Trump inherit 'a mess' from Barack Obama?

Haltiwanger, John. "How Trump's Russia Scandal Is Different from Nixon's Watergate." *Business Insider*, 30 Oct. 2017. Obama Only President Since Nixon Didn't Face Independent Investigation - Business Insider

The Weekly Screed: January 28, 2018 (Volume II, Issue 4)

TO: The Donald: Duffer in Chief

FROM: Kelly: Let's Talk Golf!

- Hey, Donald, I hope you enjoyed last issue's comparison between you and the hands-down best POTUS of my lifetime: Barack Hussein Obama. But here's one topic I didn't get around to last week: GOLF.
- Midway through Obama's second term, you tweeted: *"Can you believe that, with all of the problems and difficulties facing the U.S., President Obama spent the day playing golf?"*
- Then, on the campaign trail, you promised us: *"I'm going to be working for you. I'm not going to have time to play golf, believe me."*
- Hah! Not only have you already golfed 50% more than Obama, these excursions have been extremely costly to US taxpayers, who have picked up the full freight for Secret Service lodging, meals, and even golf carts at all your fancy-pants resorts.
- It must have just about killed you to be stuck in the White House during the 3-day government shutdown instead of living it up golfing and hobnobbing at Mar-a-Lago. Poor Donald. You missed your own $100,000 per couple First Anniversary Self-Congratulatory Fundraising party!! SAD.
- Anyway, one of the other reasons I've been pondering the game of golf this past week is the revelation that one of the phony-baloney "conflicts of interest" that you floated to try to persuade White House Counsel Don McGahn to fire Robert Mueller back in June was a dispute over golf fees.
- From what I've read on this scam, here's the typical scenario: You buy a golf course. People decide to quit (most likely because they don't want to be associated with anything associated with YOU), and ask for a refund of their sign-up fees, which they are contractually allowed to do. You then keep them on the hook for months or years, sometimes demanding that they keep paying annual dues, whether or not they are allowed access to the facilities. You personally pocket the sign-up fees rather than use them for maintenance and renovations. Sweet!
- In Mueller's case, he had belonged to the Lowes Island Golf Club, which you acquired in 2009 and renamed Trump National. But this isn't the only time you've been tardy on refunds. As recently as February of last year, you were court-ordered to repay refunds, with interest, to members of the former Ritz-Carlton Jupiter golf course in Florida. You have, of course, appealed.
- It's all so tawdry, DT, but (as they say) "par for the course."

Resources - Volume II– Issue 4

Good afternoon, friends. My general opinion of golf is similar to Mark Twain's: "a good walk spoiled."
But the sport and business of golf loom large in Trump World, so you are getting some pertinent factoids this week.
As for the term "duffer", Miriam-Webster lists several definitions, all of which apply to The Donald, I believe.

1.   **a** : a peddler especially of cheap flashy articles
   b : something counterfeit or worthless

2. an incompetent, ineffectual, or clumsy person; *especially* : a mediocre golfer

*I am currently reading **two** books about our Dear Leader: the first is **Fire and Fury**, by Michael Wolff, which has been in the news non-stop for the past few weeks, and another (even better, I think) by David Cay Johnston (a professor at Syracuse University of Law and frequent talking head on MSNBC, CNN, and the like). I've read other books by Johnston (**Free Lunch** and **Perfectly Legal**) and found him to be an excellent explainer, in understandable English, of tax and economic policy. His latest is titled:*
It's Even Worse Than You Think: What the Trump Administration is Doing to America *(2018) and a chapter in this book called "Refusals to Pay" outlines Trump's business model when it comes to golf.*

Sherman, Amy. "Who Plays More Golf: Donald Trump or Barack Obama?" *PolitiFact*, 10 Oct. 2017. PolitiFact | Who plays more golf: Donald Trump or Barack Obama?

Sullivan, Bob. "Trump-Mueller Dispute Over Golf Fees: It's Not Funny and It Might Lie at the Heart of the Russia Investigation." *Bob Sullivan*, 7 Aug. 2017.
Trump, Mueller dispute over golf fees? It's not funny, and it might lie at the heart of the Russia investigation — bobsullivan.net

The Weekly Screed: February 4, 2018 (Volume II, Issue 5)

TO: The Donald: Pants on Fire – SOTU Edition

FROM: Kelly: Checking the Fact Checkers

- DT, I've gotta break it to you. Whether you can bring yourself to acknowledge it or not, this was another Very Bad Week for you.
- First of all, Melania followed up her disappearance at Davos with a refusal to even ride in the same car with you to your first big State of the Union speech. She did appear in the gallery, wearing an all-white Hillary Clinton pantsuit. She did not look amused. I'm guessing Stormy Daniels fall-out.
- Your ponderous reading of the teleprompter (I thought you hated using those?) resulted in the third longest SOTU speech in history. Only two of Bill Clinton's were more time-consuming.
- And someone should really have told you that it's bad form to clap for yourself and motion people to stand up and clap some more, thus dragging out the ordeal for the rest of us. This isn't a game show.
- Now here I have a confession to make: I simply could not bring myself to watch in real time, for several reasons. <u>ONE</u>: I knew you would be reading a speech written for you by someone else, so it wasn't going to provide nearly as much entertainment value as when you speak off the cuff.
- <u>TWO</u>: I just couldn't stand to look at you and your two evil sycophants, Thing 1 and Thing 2 (aka, Pence and Ryan) sitting behind you, smirking. <u>And THREE</u>: Despite the fact that someone else wrote the speech, I foresaw that it would be jam-packed with prevarications, hyperbole, and self-aggrandizements that you would be more than happy to read out loud:
- **"We enacted the biggest tax cuts and reforms in American history"** [As long as you don't count the 3 other bigger cuts since 1940].
  "After years of wage stagnation, we are finally seeing rising wages" [As long as you ignore the wage gains under Obama, and the fourth quarter wage decline that more than wiped out your first three quarters' gains.]
  "A single immigrant can bring in virtually unlimited numbers of distant relatives" [As long as that immigrant has "unlimited" numbers of spouses and unmarried children.]
- **"We do more than any other country to help the…underprivileged all over the world "** [unless you count the United Arab Emirates, Norway, Luxembourg, Sweden, Türkiye, Denmark, the UK, Germany, the Netherlands, Belgium, Switzerland, Finland, Austria, France, and Spain.]

- And on and on, proving that our State of the Union is now totally Pathetic.

Resources - Volume II– Issue 5

Good afternoon, all………..the new "Contact the President" website has shortened the number of characters which can be submitted in the text box from 2500 to 2000. My guess is that the poor Communication Specialists who were taxed with perusing these messages from the public needed a 20% reduction in the vitriol they were required to scrutinize. So that's 500 fewer letters and spaces and punctuation marks of wisdom that I can send to The Donald every week. His loss. All y'all will, of course, continue to receive the entire Screed.

Last week I ran out of room to mention another golf-related item in the week's news. Then a friend posted this on Facebook, and it must be shared! So, I'm giving myself a mulligan on last week's Screed:

McAffee, Tierney. "Evangelical Leader Says Trump Gets 'a Mulligan' on Alleged Affair with Porn Star." People. January 24, 2018. Evangelical Leader Gives Trump Mulligan on Alleged Porn Star Affair (people.com)

Sherman, Amy, Miriam Valverde, and Louis Jacobson. "Fact-Checking Donald Trump's 2018 State of the Union Speech." *PolitiFact*, 30 Jan. 2018.
PolitiFact | Fact-checking Donald Trump's 2018 State of the Union speech

The Weekly Screed: February 11, 2018 (Volume II, Issue 6)

TO: The Donald: Egomaniac in Chief

FROM: Kelly: I have a suggestion…..

- Well, DT, another banner week. A second (albeit blessedly brief) government shutdown, this one orchestrated by Senator Rand Paul (over deficit spending) but promoted by you to blame Democrats and punish immigrants because you are just so darn ignorant and MEAN.
- Then the swift exit of another two upstanding members of your administration: your staff secretary and a speechwriter (neither of whom deserve to be named) over domestic abuse charges (made over a year ago) which somehow floated to the top of the bowl this week.
- Thankfully, you had time to work in a rally of the faithful in Ohio, where you allowed that, yeah, when opposition politicians don't leap to their feet and applaud mindlessly for you, they hate America, ergo it's TREASON.
- But the latest preposterous ego-stroking notion of yours is this military parade nonsense. I have a good parade story, DT. When I was Director of the USO at Kadena Air Force Base in Okinawa, Japan (in the late '80s), I persuaded the Base Commander to close down a few main thoroughfares so that we could put together an Easter Parade. I think we had about half a dozen floats and a couple of marching bands (of course), but the highlight of the event was the Okinawa Harley Davidson club (around 30 members strong) who proudly gunned their hogs along the route with giant stuffed Easter Bunnies riding on their handlebars. We were Proud to be Americans!
- Anyway, a good portion of this week's activities prompted Bill Maher to update his Dictator List on Friday night. Donald, you are So Close to achieving all the criteria necessary to round this out, starting with "Puts Name or Face on Buildings." The list also includes holding rallies and military parades, so you've almost got the whole thing nailed, except for….
- The Dictator Costume. The MAGA ball caps are a start, but they aren't always around when you need them, right? I'm referring to the tonsorial tragedy we all witnessed when a mighty wind caught you off-guard as you mounted the steps of Air Force One.
- So here's my suggestion, DT: Shave Your Head. Yup, just get rid of all the dyes and sprays and subterfuge. Replace them with a nice smooth pate, a big ole diamond earring, and some manly ink where the blank spot was revealed. Get a tattoo of the Army's biggest tank, stroll past the Trump International Hotel, and you can be your own damn parade every day.

Resources - Volume II– Issue 6

Collins, Sean. "How One GOP Senator, Rand Paul, Caused a Super-Short Shutdown." *USA Today*, 9 Feb. 2018. Rand Paul caused the super-short government shutdown. Here's how. (usatoday.com)

Liptak, Kevin, and Tal Kopan. "How Immigration Derailed Congress' Efforts to Avoid Another Government Shutdown." *CNN*, 6 Feb. 2018. Trump: 'I'd love to see a shutdown' over immigration | CNN Politics

"Trump Says Lives Are Being 'Destroyed' by Sexual Misconduct Allegations." *BBC*, 10 Feb. 2018. Donald Trump: Lives are being 'destroyed' by allegations (bbc.com)

Chasmar, Jessica. "Donald Trump Nearly Completes 'Dictator Checklist,' Bill Maher Says." *The Washington Times*, 10 Feb. 2018. Donald Trump nearly completes 'dictator checklist' with military parade plans: Bill Maher - Washington Times

Slattery, Denis. "Trump Slams 'Treasonous' Dems for Failing to Clap During State of the Union." *New York Daily News*, 5 Feb. 2018. President Trump slams 'treasonous' Dems for failing to clap at his first State of the Union – New York Daily News (nydailynews.com)

Walters, Joanna. "Trump Hair Mystery Solved: The Answer, My Friend, Is Blowin' in the Wind." *The Guardian*, 7 Feb. 2018. Hair-raising moment: blustery wind lifts lid on mystery of Donald Trump's mane | Donald Trump | The Guardian

The Weekly Screed: February 18, 2018 (Volume II, Issue 7)

TO: The Donald: Bleating and Tweeting

FROM: Kelly: Thoughts on Guns n Russians

- Donald, I must confess that I (like you) am a Russophile. In college, I became smitten with Russian history, literature, music, and art. My parents scraped up enough money so that I could take a class trip to Moscow and Leningrad in December of 1972. [Years before *glasnost*. Cold and grim.]
- Then I borrowed from my grandmother to fund my M.A. in Russian History [1974, Indiana University] But here's the deal, DT. I didn't borrow any money from the Russians! And I paid back my relatives.
- In *Fire and Fury*, Michael Wolff references a *Slate* article from July 4, 2016, written by Franklin Foer, which lays out six theories for your bromance with Putin. The most convincing to me, although all six are plausible, is the dirty money connection, largely due to your less than stellar credit-worthiness.
- So while the Mueller indictment this week against 13 Russians and 3 organizations focused on attempts to influence the 2016 election, I wouldn't be running around pretending this is a bigly win for you ("No collusion!")
- Of course there was collusion, DT…And obstruction…And maybe even some money laundering thrown in for good measure. But those will need to wait for future indictments, so just slow your roll a little, woncha, and try not to look like a knucklehead… as you do in your accusation that the FBI, and not easy access to an AR-15, is responsible for the Valentine's Day massacre in Florida.
- Actually, we have the Russians (well, really Soviet Senior Sgt. Mikhail T. Kalashnikov) to thank for weaponizing our citizenry (but not theirs). The *Avtomat Kalashnikova-47* used by the North Vietnamese prompted Defense Secretary Robert McNamara to order the Pentagon to develop the M-16, which was soon after available to chicken-hawk civilian gun nuts as the AR-15. The elementary school shooting in Stockton, CA, in 1989 made these weapons "popular." A ten-year ban on assault weapons was allowed to expire in 2004. And now Americans are well-equipped to maintain their 2nd Amendment rights and status as the Greatest Mass Murderers in the world.
- My book club is gathering on Tuesday to discuss an epic novel about one man's life in Russia, and then the Soviet Union. *A Gentleman in Moscow* evokes the lost elegance of the old ruling classes and the petty tyrannies of the new.

t takes me back to my old student fascinations. I know you don't usually read (anything) but take a break from "Fox and Friends" and try it.

Resources - Volume II– Issue 7

Good afternoon, comrades. Another sad week for Amerika.
- "Full Text of Mueller Indictment." *BBC News*, 16 Feb. 2018. Russia-Trump inquiry: Full text of Mueller's indictment (bbc.com)

Haberman, Maggie, and Michael S. Schmidt. "Trump Tried to Fire Mueller in December." *The New York Times*, 31 Jan. 2018. Mueller Zeros In on Story Put Together About Trump Tower Meeting - The New York Times (nytimes.com)

Kessler, Glenn, Salvador Rizzo, and Meg Kelly. "Fact-Checking Trump's Error-Filled Tweet Storm About the Russia Investigation." *The Washington Post*, 18 Feb. 2018. Fact-checking Trump's error-filled tweetstorm about the Russia investigation - The Washington Post

Nelson, Louis. "Trump Lashes Out at FBI, Obama, Democrats Over Russia Probe." *Politico*, 18 Feb. 2018. Trump attacks everyone but Russia - POLITICO

Mak, Tim. "Trump Blames Florida School Shooting on Russia Probe." *Mother Jones*, 18 Feb. 2018 Trump Blames Florida School Shooting on Russia Probe – Mother Jones

LaFrance, Adrienne. "The AR-15: America's Most Popular and Controversial Gun." *Time*, 16 Feb. 2018. Florida School Shooting: Why Civilians Started Buying AR-15s | TIME

O'Donnell, Lawrence. "Making America Great." *MSNBC*, 15 Feb. 2018. The Last Word with Lawrence O'Donnell | MSNBC The Last Word

до свидания (**do** svidaniya), *y'all......till next week.......Kelly*

The Weekly Screed: February 25, 2018 (Volume II, Issue 8)

TO: The Donald: Lying Loudly and Listening Little

FROM: Kelly: Oh yeah…..I Hear You

- Donald, of all the addle-pated, worse-than-useless, chuckle-headed, short-sighted, feather-brained, and generally cockamamie fantasies that have popped out of your mouth without benefit of rational thought, the mere notion that Arming Teachers would bring an end to school shootings might win the prize for your most ignorant idea ever.
- Summoning the grieving to the White House for an audience was BAD (You couldn't be bothered to go to Florida for something other than golf? Afraid you might be expected to attend a memorial or a funeral?).
- Forcing all these devastated kids and parents to keep thanking YOU, your lapdog Pence, and the odious Betsy DeVos for going through the motions of pretending to care about this issue was WORSE.
- Choosing to wear a shirt that had "45" stitched on the cuff to remind everyone of your pathetic presidential pomposities was truly SAD.
- Finally, needing a cue card written by someone else to keep track of "talking points" that my corgi could have come up with was beyond disturbing.
- Let's review these deeply thoughtful interrogatories…or shall we say, "Loaded questions"? [This looks like Hope Hicks handiwork, am I right?]
- At the top of the list was: *"What would you most want me to know about your experience"?* I think this was best answered by the angry father (whose daughter was killed and therefore unavailable to respond herself) who eloquently said "I'm Pissed" and pointed out that this mayhem should have been brought to an end after the *first* mass school shooting……
- Question #2 looks to read: *"What can we do to make you feel safe?"* I'd like to answer that one: Replace all Republicans in the Executive, Legislative, and Judicial branches of government with public servants in the mold of Barack Obama, Senator Jeff Merkley (D-OR), Rep. Earl Blumenauer (D-OR) and Ruth Bader Ginsburg so that we can neutralize the NRA and impose a "strict Constitutionalist" interpretation of the Second Amendment. *Now selling at Cabela's: shiny new "authentic" muskets to replace your Well-Regulated-Militia-anachronistic AR-15s and Glock 22s.!!*
- I can't seem to decipher all of talking point #3, and your little coach seemed to run out of steam with item 4: *"Resources? Ideas?"*
- Then, laughably, the most disingenuous nudge of all: *"I hear you"* which of course you weren't even able to bring yourself to utter.

Resources - Volume II– Issue 8

Good afternoon on this last Sunday of February.........can you believe it? The year is just flying by !! I'm back on the gun debate this week. Please make sure to watch a clip of The Donald's smarmy speech at the Conservative Political Action Conference of nincompoops and evil doers. Might be a new low.

"Trump Went Off-Script at CPAC. We Fact-Checked It." *NBC News*, 23 Feb. 2018. Trump went off-script at CPAC. We fact checked it. (nbcnews.com)

Bowman, Emma. "Trump Backs Arming Teachers During Emotional White House Listening Session." *NPR*, 21 Feb. 2018. Trump Backs Arming Teachers During Emotional White House Listening Session : NPR

Wang, Amy B. "This Photo of Trump's Notes Captures His Empathy Problem Better Than Anything." *The Washington Post*, 21 Feb. 2018. This photo of Trump's notes captures his empathy deficit better than anything - The Washington Post

"List of School Shootings in the United States." *Wikipedia*. [This list is continually updated. It's a very long list, but we didn't get into double digits killed until the University of Texas.] Lists of school shootings in the United States - Wikipedia

Elliott, Kennedy and Soffen, Kim "Do your Congress members support stricter gun control? *The Washington Post*. 17 Jun. 2016. Do your Congress members support stricter gun control? - Washington Post

The Weekly Screed: March 4, 2018 (Volume II, Issue 9)

TO: The Donald: Suddenly a Superhero

FROM: Kelly: Oh, the Irony!

- Donald, last week you lit on the notion that arming approximately ¾ of a million classroom instructors would be the cure for gun violence in America.
- Then, on Monday, in an inspiring speech to the nation's governors, you came up with what I believe is a more cost-effective option…a fulfillment of your boast back in July at the Republican convention: I Alone Can Fix It.
- Yes, all we need to do is get wind of another crazy white guy with a weapon of war, then whisk YOU to the scene of the action so you can vanquish him.
- But wait! On Wednesday you opined that maybe we should just preemptively relieve potential trouble-makers of their weapons. Due process might follow second in regards to the Second Amendment! Somewhere, Barack Obama is rolling on the floor laughing. And FOX Noise is exploding.
- I attempted to rework *The Charge of the Light Brigade* as a paean to these courageous statements of yours……then decided that would be disrespectful to those guys. So here's an original ode:

The Charge of The Donald.

Are heroes born or are they made? So few among us make the grade.
But here we see a champion rise: Valor flares from squinty eyes.
Red of tie instead of cape; evildoers shan't escape.
Into schools he'd bravely dash, the shooter's head completely smash.
His only weapons are his hands: tiny fists like iron bands.

While most of us might be weak-willed, The Leader is bravado-filled.
Fleet of foot, without a care, never *thinking* of his hair
'Mid the chaos of the scene, he'd emerge with mighty mien
Rescuing the innocent, he'd *step up* as president.
Trump is here to save the day, heedless of the NRA.

He used to tell us he hates gore. The sight of blood on marble floors
At Mar-a-Lago made him tremble. But now as POTUS he is nimble.
"Dating" was his Vietnam….dodging herpes, never bombs.
Bone spurs spared him from the war; now the country needs him more.
With gratitude and awe we ponder: Donald Trump, our Last Responder.

Resources - Volume II– Issue 9

Good morning, friends. I have some shockingly funny links for you today. I'll admit that sometimes I provide kind of wonky research materials, but all of these are (sadly) hilarious. And all contributed to the fashioning of today's bit of doggerel. I shamelessly borrowed a few of the best lines.

Wiedeman, Reeves. "Trump Said He Would Run into a School Shooting 'Even if I Didn't Have a Weapon.'" *GQ*, 26 Feb. 2018 Donald Trump: I Would Courageously Rush into a School Shooting Unarmed | GQ

Stein, Sam. "Unlike Obama, Trump Is Coming for Your Guns." *New York Magazine*, 1 Mar. 2018. Trump: Take the Guns First. Due Process Later (nymag.com)

Ballhaus, Rebecca. "Trump Boasted of Avoiding STDs While Dating: 'Vaginas Are Landmines. It Was My Personal Vietnam.'" *People*, 26 Feb. 2018. Donald Trump Calls Avoiding STDs His 'Personal Vietnam' (people.com)

Evans, Greg. "The Time Donald Trump Turned Away in Disgust While a Man Bled to Death in Front of Him." *The Daily Beast*, 27 Feb. 2018. The Time Donald Trump Turned Away in Disgust While a Man Was Bleeding to Death in Front of Him (thedailybeast.com)

Borowitz, Andy. "Trump Orders Parade to Celebrate His Hypothetical Act of Heroism in Florida School." *The New Yorker*, 26 Feb. 2018. Trump Orders Parade to Celebrate His Hypothetical Act of Heroism in Florida School | The New Yorker

The Weekly Screed: March 11, 2018 (Volume II, Issue 10)

TO: The Donald: Pimping Out the Press Secretary

FROM: Kelly: Channeling Sarah Huckabee Sanders

- Dear Jesus thanks for this day of rest. I get to go to church twice, AND, best of all, no press briefings on The Lord's Day. Everyone was just awful to me last week and asked hard nasty questions. Even POTUS got upset.
- On Monday, someone who goes by the name Sam Nunberg (never heard of him) started shooting his mouth off, to anyone who would listen, that he had received a subpoena from Robert Mueller that he wasn't gonna show up for.
- He then had the nerve to say that Mueller "might have something" on our Dear Leader. All I had to say was this: *"I definitely think he doesn't know that for sure, because he's incorrect. As we've said many times before, there was <u>no collusion</u> with the Trump campaign. Anything further on what his actions are? He hasn't worked at the White House, so I certainly can't speak to him or the lack of knowledge he clearly has."*
- And then HE said THIS: *"She's a joke. OK fine, yeah, she's unattractive, she's a fat slob. But that's irrelevant. The person she works for has a 30 percent approval rating."* So MEAN. Talk about casting the first stone.
- On Wednesday, that porn star payoff thing came up <u>again</u>. As an upstanding Christian wife and mother, I guess this should bother me more, but I just need to remember: Fake News. FAKE News. FAKE NEWS.
- So I sensibly responded with this: *"Look, the president has addressed these directly and made <u>very well clear</u> that none of these allegations are true. This case has already been won in arbitration. And anything beyond that, I would refer you to the president's outside counsel."*
- Which I *thought* would have shut this stupid sordid story down once and for all, but then Jim Acosta from CNN [I'll never call on <u>that</u> guy again] reported that "a source close to the White House" told him: *"POTUS is very unhappy. Sarah gave the Stormy Daniels storyline steroids yesterday."*
- Finally, on Friday, something that everyone should be So Excited about [our great stable genius Mr. Trump taking on Rocket Man] has the New York Times saying that this proposed get-together *"…has given North Korea what it has long craved: the respect and legitimacy that comes from the North Korean leader standing as an equal beside the American president."*

- This is UNFAIR because true patriotic Americans realize that North Korea only got all puffed up due to the elite media coverage of the Olympics.
- So, as I always pray every Sunday: Please, Jesus, make next week easier.

Resources - Volume II– Issue 10

Happy Spring Ahead Day to All (except Arizona and Hawaii and some countries like Iceland)........Today, I'm channeling Sarah Huckabee Sanders, who (let's face it) had an unusually difficult week. So many Breaking News topics to lie about !

On the other hand, she's really just another Trump Victim. He sullies everyone and everything he touches. And, while I don't agree with any of these people to begin with, I do have a tiny shred of sympathy for them as they come in with such high hopes for Making America Great Again (whatever that might mean to them) and then being brutally voted off the island posthaste. Let's see how long SHS lasts.

Deb, Sopan. "What President Trump's Treatment of Sarah Huckabee Sanders Tells Us." *The Denver Post*, 19 May 2017. What President Trump's treatment of Sarah Huckabee Sanders tells us (denverpost.com)

Gaffney, Adrienne. "Former Trump Aide Sam Nunberg Calls Sarah Huckabee Sanders 'Unattractive' and 'a Fat Slob'." *Newsweek*, 7 Mar. 2018. Sam Nunberg Meltdown: Former Trump Aide Calls Sarah Huckabee Sanders an 'Unattractive Fat Slob' - Newsweek

Wemple, Erik. "The Media Is Divided Over Whether Trump Was Mad. Is It Possible to Report His Moods?" *The Washington Post*, 8 Mar. 2018. Opinion | The media is divided over whether Trump was mad. Is it possible to report his moods? - The Washington Post

Wemple, Erik. "Sarah Huckabee Sanders: 'No One Elevates North Korea Like the U.S. Media.'" *The Washington Post*, 9 Mar. 2018. Opinion | Sarah Huckabee Sanders: No one elevates North Korea like the U.S. media! - The Washington Post

Rucker, Philip, and Ashley Parker. "How Sarah Huckabee Sanders Sees the World." *The Washington Post*, 10 Oct.2017 How Sarah Huckabee Sanders sees the world - The Washington Post

The Weekly Screed: March 18, 2018 (Volume II, Issue 11)

TO: The Donald: Problem-Solver in Chief

FROM: Kelly: Trying to keep up with all of the Disappeared

- Happy Saint Paddy's Day weekend, DT. Faith and begorrah, you actually managed to come out on top during your meeting with Ireland's gay-son-of-Indian-immigrants leader (Taoiseach Leo Varadkar) due to his past efforts to shut down a wind farm planned near one of your golf courses. Or, per a *Mallow News* of County Cork tweet: "Some achievement to go meet Donald Trump and be the bigger fu**ing eejit."
- But what I really want to discuss this week is the alarming parallel between your so-called "administration" and that of Stalin. I've recently read TWO books (a spy novel and a memoir) that remind us of one of Uncle Joe's favorite philosophies of personnel management: *"Yest' chelovek, yest' problema. Nyet cheloveka, nyet problemy."* ["If there is a person, there is a problem. If there is no person, there is no problem."]
- This construct has played out recently in London, with the assassination attempts and unexplained deaths of various Russian exiles. So far, extreme firings in Trump Amerika have only been accomplished via tweet and nasty bureaucratic shenanigans. [Seriously, you fire Andrew McCabe two days before his announced retirement? And think *that* will silence him???]
- Even "Red Rex" Tillerson, pre-vetted by Putin for the job, and consequently the worst Secretary of State ever, was not immune. He "disagreed" with you, so he had to go, and now we will be subject to the foreign policy expertise of Mike Pompeo, former Tea Party congressman from Kansas.
- Next on the chopping block, we are told, is either National Security Advisor [and still active-duty Army General] H.R. McMaster, mostly because he's insufficiently pro-Russian......OR maybe Deputy Attorney General Rod Rosenstein who (unforgivably) appointed Robert Mueller as FBI Special Counsel who is clearly Out To Get You. And then you could fire Mueller!
- But I've gotta say, DT, that the most entertaining News of the Week is your countersuit [citing both your real and fake names] for $20 million against Stephanie Clifford (aka Stormy Daniels), previously fired as Celebrity Mistress, whose severance package of $130,000 was inconveniently postponed until the final days of your Celebrity President campaign.
- In the spy novel I just read, one character is dispatched via a black-and-beige Montblanc Etoile pen containing golden dart frog poison.

Stephanie/Stormy should be extra cautious about signing any more documents.

Resources - Volume II– Issue 11

Naughton, John. "A Fistful of Shamrocks: Ireland's Leader Promised to Confront Trump, Then Boasts of Aiding Him." *The Intercept*, 16 Mar. 2018. Irish Leader Who Promised to Confront Trump Aided Him (theintercept.com)

"Rubio: FBI's McCabe Should Have Been Allowed to Retire." *NBC News*, 17 Mar. 2018. Rubio says FBI's Andrew McCabe should have been allowed to retire (nbcnews.com)

Ward, Alex. "Rex Tillerson's Firing Is a Sign of Bigger Problems in the Trump Administration." *Vox*, 13 Mar. 2018. Rex Tillerson has been fired. Experts say he did damage that could last "a generation." | Vox

Snell, Kelsey. "National Security Adviser H.R. McMaster Is Expected to Leave Trump Administration." *NPR*, 16 Mar. 2018. H.R. McMaster Exit Planned: National Security Adviser Is Expected To Leave Trump Administration : The Two-Way : NPR

Cillizza, Chris. "Trump's Tweetstorm Attacking Mueller and McCabe, Annotated." *CNN*, 18 Mar. 2018. Donald Trump sure looks like he is planning to fire Robert Mueller | CNN Politics

Boburg, Shawn. "New Evidence the Stormy Daniels Payment May Have Violated Election Law." *The Washington Post*, 9 Mar. 2018. How the Stormy Daniels payment may have violated election law - The Washington Post

Rubin, Jennifer. "Stormy Daniels' Parents Are Big Trump Fans." *HuffPost*, 14 Mar. 2018. Stormy Daniels' Mom Hopes Daughter's Lawsuit Doesn't Hurt Donald Trump | HuffPost Latest News

The Weekly Screed: March 25, 2018 (Volume II, Issue 12)

TO: The Donald: Bozo in Chief

FROM: Kelly: Send in the Clowns!

- DT, you probably missed this Breaking News tidbit on Thursday, so it is with a heavy heart that I must inform you: Bozo is Dead.
- That would be Frank Avruch, the first nationally-syndicated Bozo, off to the Big Top in the Sky at 89. At one point, there were 183 Bozo shows on the air in the US alone, with spin-offs in Canada, Mexico, and Brazil. The latest (out of Chicago) closed down in 2001. [By the way, Donald, the creator of Bozo, the late Larry Harman, bore a startling resemblance to you.]
- Fortunately, for kids of all ages, YOU have emerged to revive the franchise. From your downward elevator glide on June 16, 2015, to the present day POTUS Circus, you have assumed the mantle of Insane Clown President.
- This moniker, by the way, is the title of a riotous opus penned by Matt Taibbi, a columnist for *Rolling Stone*. Basically a collection of his articles for the magazine during the 2016 presidential campaign, the book is absolutely worth perusing as a recent history of how we got to this SAD place. Whoever reads your bedtime stories these days should have a go at it.
- In the meantime, the occupants of the Clown Car that passes for your "administration" have continued to enter and exit, sometimes within the same week! Case in point: Joseph diGenova, best known for his recent rantings on the Faux News Channel who, I was bitterly disappointed to learn today, will NOT be joining your crack legal team of Sekulow & Cobb.
- Turns out his wife and law firm partner is already representing other Russia probe players, so that might have created just a <u>teeny</u> conflict of interest. But it would have been entertaining to watch him go head-to-head with Mueller.
- Ah, well, as you tweeted this morning, brilliant attorneys are lining up around the block to get into the center ring spotlight: *"Fame & fortune will NEVER be turned down by a lawyer, though some are conflicted.....NO COLLUSION with Russia."*
- Donald, this just isn't true. A) Of course there was collusion. B) Maybe it's the circles I run in, but I know plenty of low-paid but dedicated public defenders and public service counselors who wouldn't even consider consorting with the likes of you.... even if you weren't infamous for stiffing every legal practitioner who crossed your path.

- It's really too bad you don't have Stormy Daniel's lawyer on your side. Now <u>that</u> guy has *cojones*. It will be The Greatest Showdown on Earth.

<u>Resources - Volume II– Issue 12</u>

Good afternoon, friends. I'm sure many of you got out and marched yesterday (like my sister). My friends in Portland marched in the cold rain. As usual, there was too much juicy material to cover in one page, so I had to go with the Bozo hook. Looking forward to tuning in to the Stormy Daniels interview tonight on 60 Minutes. Looking even more forward to the aftermath.

"RIP Bozo the Clown: Entertainer Frank Avruch Dies at 89." *CTV News*, 22 Mar. 2018. <u>TV personality known for playing Bozo the Clown dies at 89 | CTV News</u>

Zoladz, Lindsay. "Bozo the Clown Obituary: Frank Avruch." *The Ringer*, 23 Mar. 2018. <u>Bozo the Clown Has Died. Long Live Bozo the Clown. - The Ringer</u>

Taibbi, Matt. "Matt Taibbi's New Book: Insane Clown President." *Rolling Stone*, 17 Jan. 2017. <u>Matt Taibbi's New Book: 'Insane Clown President' (rollingstone.com)</u>

Kim, Seung Min. "In Another Blow to Trump's Efforts to Combat Russia Probe, DiGenova Will No Longer Join Legal Team." *The Washington Post*, 25 Mar. 2018. <u>Trump's legal team remains in disarray as new lawyer will no longer represent him in Russia probe - The Washington Post</u>

Liptak, Kevin. "Trump Bemoans Difficulty of Finding Lawyers." *CNN*, 25 Mar. 2018. <u>Trump tweets 'many lawyers and top law firms' want to join his legal team | CNN Politics</u>

Jenkins, Sally. "Stormy Daniels Lawyer Would Be Perfect for the NFL." *Sports Illustrated*, 20 Mar. 2018. <u>Stormy Daniels' Lawyer Has Faced Off in Court With Roger Goodell, Jerry Jones - Sports Illustrated</u>

The Weekly Screed: April 1, 2018 (Volume II, Issue 13)

TO: The Donald: Congratulator in Chief

FROM: Kelly: Wishing all of this was just an April Fool's joke

- DT, I see that you've been on the phone again, making inappropriate calls to two of your favorite peeps: Vladimir Putin and Roseanne Barr.
- According to a White House leak, briefing materials prepared for you ahead of the call to Putin came with the headline: "DO NOT CONGRATULATE"
- This effort presumed, or course, that a) you bother to read anything put in front of you, and b) you are ever smart enough to follow directions.
- As John McCain commented: *"an American president does not lead the free world by congratulating dictators on winning sham elections."* So, naturally, you followed your gut and not the advice of the few relatively sane adults left in the Republican Party.
- The expulsion of 60 Russian "diplomats" from the US (to show solidarity with the UK over that little poisoning episode) might lead us to assume that the bromance with Vlad could be sputtering but……..Nah. We know he still has too much on you for you to quit him.
- Meanwhile, back on the entertainment front, you phoned the eponymous star of "Rosanne" to blather on about her sitcom revival: *"Even look at Roseanne, I called her yesterday. Look at her ratings! Look at her ratings! I got a call from Mark Burnett; he did 'The Apprentice.' He's a great guy. He said, 'Donald, I called just to say hello and to tell you did you see Roseanne's ratings?' I said, 'How big where they?' They were unbelievable. Over 18 million people. And it was about us."*
- Yes, the show WAS about a little bit about you, with Rosie defending her vote by pointing out that you "talked about jobs." But it also started out with Roseanne's husband Dan [John Goodman, the best thing about this reboot] coming back from the pharmacy with "half the drugs at twice the price" due to cutbacks in the Connors' insurance plan.
- All I know is that the old "Domestic Goddess" Roseanne was a fool to vote Republican (support for Reagan was implied on the old show) just like all of the low-income and low-information voters who supported you in 2016. *"I love the poorly educated!"* you chortled after the Nevada primary.
- But the real Roseanne has some serious money now, and so she doesn't really give a rat's ass about any of the people she purports to represent. We'll see how her ratings hold up over time…and the course of the Russia investigations.

Resources - Volume II– Issue 13

Happy April Fool's Day, y'all. Our long national nightmare continues.
No Joke. Still waiting for fall-out over the Stormy Daniels interview on 60 Minutes last Sunday (62% of Americans found her "believable").
In the meantime, I tuned in to the New Roseanne..........a few good zingers, but mostly wooden delivery from all. SAD.

Wright, David, and Kevin Liptak. "Trump Calls to Congratulate Putin Despite Warnings." *CNN*, 21 Mar. 2018 Trump furious over leak of warning to not congratulate Putin | CNN Politics

Friedman, Megan. "Donald Trump Called Roseanne Barr to Congratulate Her on the Show's Revival." *Good Housekeeping*, 29 Mar. 2018. Roseanne Barr Dishes on Her Phone Call With Donald Trump (goodhousekeeping.com)

Andreeva, Nellie. "'Roseanne' Review: Revival Hits Close to Home for John Goodman & Sara Gilbert." *Deadline*, 26 Mar. 2018. 'Roseanne' Review: Revival Back Donald Trump But Misses Basics (deadline.com)

Clark, Charles. "Politics of 'Roseanne' Reboot Are More Complex Than Trump or Liberals Believe." *NBC News*, 28 Mar. 2018. The politics of the 'Roseanne' reboot are more complex than Trump or liberals believe (nbcnews.com)

The Weekly Screed: April 8, 2018 (Volume II, Issue 14)

TO: **The Donald: Dumb and Dumber**

FROM: **Kelly: Reality not as funny as the movie**

DT, even for you, this past week was chock-full of knee-slappers demonstrating your astonishing inability to grasp any concept not originating with Fox & Friends:

- Your LOL denial of any knowledge of the Stormy Daniels payoff. As Stormy's attorney Michael Avenatti put it, your one-word disavowal of the $130,000 non-disclosure agreement ("NO", when chatting with the press corps on Air Force One) was "a gift from the heavens". If you *didn't* know about the agreement, then it's invalid. If you *did* know, then you're lying, and you'll either need to reverse that lie when you get deposed in the upcoming lawsuit, or you'll need to perjure yourself.
- Your tariff tirades against China. You keep telling us what a genius you are: *"I always told people, you know I'm a very smart guy. I got good marks. I was all this, I went to the best college: the Wharton School of Finance, which to me is like the greatest business school."*
- Oh yeah? Well they sure didn't teach you much about basic economics, like the concept of Comparative Advantage, which is THE reason we have a trade deficit with China. To put it in terms you might understand: Chinese manufacturing workers are willing to work for less money and in much poorer conditions than American manufacturing workers. This gives China an advantage in producing cheap crap for Wal-Mart, as well as for the Trump Crime Family. US farmers, on the other hand, have an advantage in producing soybeans.
- Any trade war brought on by big tariffs will slow economic growth and (as you might have noticed) freak out the stock market (and your rural base). You're not gonna reverse decades of greedy business moguls exporting American jobs so that American consumers can buy stuff cheap.
- Your ignorant notion that the immigrant "caravan" of Central Americans fleeing torture and murder in their countries has resulted in a crime wave: *"Yesterday it came out where this journey coming up, women are raped at levels that nobody has ever seen before."*
- Donald, I know this Rampant Brown Rapist theory has been one of your favorites since Day One of your campaign. But it wasn't true then and it's not true now. The Wall is a paranoid fantasy that might only be cured by Mexico agreeing to pay for your psychiatric care. The only other thing they might pay for is a new Statue of Liberty lifting her torch by the Rio Grande.

Resources - Volume II– Issue 14

Good afternoon, amigos y amigas..........Kind of a slow news week, doncha think? I mean, any of this would have totally sunk another administration, but (absent more firings of corrupt officials or more Mueller indictments or more mistresses coming forward), The Donald kind of skated. Just the steady drip-drip-drip of everyday stupidity to remind us with whom we are dealing.

1) The Dumb-ass Payoff Denial

"Avenatti Reacts to Mueller-Cohen News, Trump's Stormy Comments." *MSNBC*, 10 Apr. 2018. Avenatti reacts to Mueller/Cohen news, Trump's Stormy comments (msnbc.com)

2) The Dumb-ass Tariff Idea

Karl, Jonathan. "President Trump Called Himself 'Smart' Six Times Before Announcing Tariffs." *ABC News*, 23 Mar. 2018 President Trump has called himself smart six times before - ABC News (go.com)

Amadeo, Kimberly. "U.S. Trade Deficit with China and Why It's So High." *The Balance*, 25 Mar. 2018. U.S. Trade Deficit With China and Why It's So High (thebalancemoney.com)

3) The Dumb-ass Caravan Rape Idea

Ng, Alfred. "Trump Recalls Infamous 'Rape' Comments About Mexicans." *New York Daily News*, 6 Apr. 2018. SEE IT: President Trump recalls infamous 'rape' comments about Mexicans – New York Daily News (nydailynews.com)

4) Finally, a heartbreaking story that explains why the caravan is happening

Nazario, Sonia. "When Deportation Is a Death Sentence." *The New Yorker*, 15 Jan.2018 When Deportation Is a Death Sentence | The New Yorker

The Weekly Screed: April 15, 2018 (Volume II, Issue 15)

TO: The Donald: Hair on Fire

FROM: Kelly: With Apologies to Billy Joel

Twenty-Sixteen in the fall, Lock Her Up and Build the Wall
Billy Bush and Pussy Grabbing, Comey tips his hand
January 'Seventeen, marchers fill the TV screen
Pussy hats, alternate facts, Sean and Kellyanne

Steve Bannon, Michael Flynn, Jared and Ivanka in
Tillerson is Sec of State, and Mattis for Defense,
Jeff B Sessions- DOJ, Scott Pruitt- EPA,
Goldman Sachs, party hacks, VP Mike Pence

Chorus:
We didn't start the fire, it was always burning
Since the world's been turning
"Trump is a forest fire"
Yeah we helped to light him, now we gotta fight him

Tom Price to ruin Health, Steve Mnuchin takes on Wealth
Rick Perry-Energy, and Aggies get Purdue
Ben Carson (what a dud) chosen to demolish HUD
Wilber Ross, Betsy DeVos, what can we do?

Judge Gorsuch, Muslim Ban, more troops to Afghanistan,
Liar Liar Pants on Fire, what does he care?
Out of Paris Climate Talks, Tom Price takes a walk
Tried to kill Obamacare, it's not going anywhere

Chorus
Comey out, Mueller in, Russia in the news again
Russkies in the Oval Office, Jr. screwed up
Trump Tower Russian meeting. Trump now is always tweeting
No Obstruction! No Collusion! It's a frame-up!

Fat Boy and Rocket Man; Fire and Fury is our plan
Trump is tweeting threats and taunts and Tillerson's gone
Will we meet with Kim Jong-un? Things are tense at Panmunjom,
North and South Korea, on Japan and on Guam.

Chorus

Nazis march in Charlottesville; angry white men shoot to kill
Concert-goers, folks in churches, children in schools.
Guns are good: let's arm the teachers, and the singers and the preachers,
NRA controls the Congress; we are all fools.

Stormy Daniels pay-off blues; Sarah Sanders: It's fake news
Trump can't find a lawyer who'll defend his crimes
"Where's my Roy Cohn?" Big raid on Michael Cohen
Mueller team and Rosenstein: "It's a Witch Hunt" all the time.

Chorus

Pitching towels in San Juan, Hope Hicks long gone
Drinking Diet Coke and watching Fox & Friends
Tax cuts, trade wars, trying hard to even scores
Times Up, Me Too, tell us how does this all end?

Military waiting for Trump to start a major war
Maybe in Iran over the nuclear deal?
Ambushed in Nigeria; missile strikes in Syria.
Wag the dog, smoke and fog, terror is the way we feel.

We didn't start the fire, it was always burning
Since the world's been turning
"Trump is a forest fire"
Yeah we helped to light him, now we gotta fight him
We didn't start the fire, but until he's gone

It will go on and on and on and on and on and on.....

Resources - Volume II– Issue 15

*Good Afternoon, friends..........today, a Very Special Issue of the Screed.
I've wanted to adapt this song from Day One of Trump's miserable occupation of the White House. James Comey finally gave me the perfect hook to hang it on when he bemoaned: "the forest fire that is the Trump presidency."*

Maybe I waited too long because even though it's only been about a year and a half (as opposed to 5 decades for Billy Joel), I wasn't able to cram everything in (or get it to rhyme....like "emoluments clause").

There were just way too many awful people he's appointed who've done awful things, and too many terrible things he's done (or tried to do) to give you links to each one. But I imagine there were a lot of references we didn't "get" when the original song came out in 1989.... and us without Google at the time. The Wikipedia link gives you a little tidbit on each reference in the Billy Joel song. I pondered doing the same, but then thought..........nah........because all y'all DO have Google

Kakutani, Michiko. "James Comey Has a Story to Tell. It's Very Persuasive." The New York Times, April 12, 2018. James Comey Has a Story to Tell. It's Very Persuasive. - The New York Times (nytimes.com)

Holt, Joseph. "Here's the real winner in the Trump-Comey 'war of words'." CNBC. April 16, 2018. The real winner in the Donald Trump James Comey war of words (cnbc.com)

Shear, Michael D., and Eileen Sullivan. "Trump Calls Comey an 'Untruthful Slime Ball' as Details of Book Are Released." The New York Times, April 13, 2018. Trump Calls Comey 'Untruthful Slime Ball' as Book Details Released - The New York Times (nytimes.com)

"We Didn't Start the Fire." Wikipedia. We Didn't Start the Fire - Wikipedia

"We Didn't Start the Fire." Billy Joel Official Site. We Didn't Start The Fire | Billy Joel Official Site

Resources - Volume II– Issue 15 (continued)

"The longstanding war of words between President Donald Trump and former FBI director [James Comey] escalated this weekend in advance of the highly anticipated Tuesday release of Comey's tell-all book, "A Higher Loyalty: Truth, Lies and Leadership."

Comey describes the Trump presidency as "a forest fire" in his book, and in an ABC News interview Sunday evening he compared Trump to a mob boss and said he was "morally unfit to be president."

Trump meanwhile ramped up his tweet-slams on the former prosecutor he fired last year. On Friday he called Comey an "untruthful slime ball" in a tweet, and in a Sunday tweet said that "Slippery James Comey" would "go down as the WORST FBI Director in history, by far!"

One would hope such a war of words would remain beneath the dignity of a sitting president and a former FBI director, but it has not.

Comey is winning the war chiefly because he is more credible than the president, but he has been bloodied in the process.

Comey claimed the president asked for a pledge of personal loyalty at a dinner in January. Mr. Trump tweeted Sunday that he "never asked Comey for Personal Loyalty."

If I were forced to bet my entire life's savings on the veracity of one account or the other I'd bet on Comey's account in a heartbeat. The president lies regularly and remorselessly."

>   --Joseph Holt, professor of business ethics, University of Notre Dame

The Weekly Screed: April 22, 2018 (Volume II, Issue 16)

TO: The Donald: Polluter in Chief

FROM: Kelly: In Mourning on "Trash the Earth" Day

- Well, DT, as we all predicted, absolutely positively nothing even remotely good for the planet has happened on your watch.
- Let's consider the worst of your Earth-unfriendly cabinet appointments:
    1. **Rick Perry at DOE.** Here's a man you mocked for "wearing glasses to make himself look smart," but then plucked from the obscurity of failed contestants on Dancing with the Stars to manage the nation's nuclear arsenal at an agency he once said he wanted to eliminate.
    He's largely avoided the spending scandals of the rest of your corrupt anointed [he prefers to fly Southwest Airlines], but he's still a Texas-sized tool of the fossil fuel industry and advocated for consumers to prop up failing coal and nuclear facilities.
    2. **Ryan Zinke at Interior.** Once a beard-wearing-Prius-driving-clean- energy advocate described as "the greenest Republican in the Montana Senate," Zinke has devolved into what The Wilderness Society calls: "the worst Interior Secretary ever." Eager to sell off public lands (mostly in the West) and even under the sea (in both Atlantic and Pacific), Zinke has reviewed all national monuments designated since 1996 and found that *many* of them could benefit from far less protection for wildlife, Native Americans, and paleontologists, and more commercial development like strip-mining.
    3. **Scott Pruitt at EPA.** The third (and most monstrous) of these Secretaries unflaggingly dedicated to demolishing the agencies you tapped them to "lead," Pruitt seems bent on making all of America as great as he made Oklahoma as Attorney General. Thanks to lack of regulation of water disposal related to fracking, the Sooner State is now Earthquake Central for the lower 48. Even more corrupt in DC as he was in OK, Pruitt is currently under TEN federal investigations of ethical violations. (DT, that's even more than YOU). The Environmental <u>Protection</u> Agency (established in 1970 by Richard Nixon) has never had a worse steward at the helm. According to William Ruckelshaus, its first administrator, Pruitt seems "more concerned about costs associated with regulations" designed to rein in polluters than with the actual mission of the agency.
- Fingers crossed that we all survive till your impeachment.

Resources - Volume II– Issue 16

Greetings friends...........another very SAD Earth Day. We've had 48 of them so far. Hope Mother Nature can hang in there till we get a 46th President....
As always, too much material, so I've simply focused on three very earth-unfriendly cabinet secretaries.

Rick Perry – Department of Energy

Schor, Elana. "Rick Perry's Plan to Reorganize Energy Department Faces Resistance." Politico, April 3, 2018 How Rick Perry survives in Trump's troubled Cabinet - POLITICO

"Shephard, Alex. "Rick Perry Didn't Know What the Energy Department Was a Month Ago." New Republic. January 19, 2017. (Rick Perry didn't know what the Energy Department was until about a month ago.* | The New Republic

Ryan Zinke – Department of the Interior

Friedman, Lisa. "Ryan Zinke Is Opening Up Public Lands. Just Not at Home." The New York Times, April 16, 2018 Ryan Zinke Is Opening Up Public Lands. Just Not at Home. - The New York Times (nytimes.com)

"Ryan Zinke's First Year: 14 Misdeeds That Show Why He's the Worst Interior Secretary Ever." The Wilderness Society. (Zinke, Year One: 14 misdeeds that show why he's the worst Interior secretary ever | The Wilderness Society

Scott Pruitt – Environmental Protection Agency

Bruenig, Elizabeth. "How Many Investigations Are There Against EPA Chief Scott Pruitt?" Vice News, April 5, 2018. Scott Pruitt is the target of no less than 10 federal investigations (vice.com)

Friedman, Lisa. "Scott Pruitt Before E.P.A.: Fancy Offices, a Shell Company and Friends with Money." The New York Times, April 21, 2018. Scott Pruitt Before the E.P.A.: Fancy Homes, a Shell Company and Friends With Money - The New York Times (nytimes.com)

McDermott, Jeff. "Will Scott Pruitt Bring Earthquakes to the EPA Like He Did in Oklahoma?" Newsweek, January 22, 2017. Will Pruitt Bring On Earthquakes as He Did in Oklahoma? - Newsweek

The Weekly Screed: April 29, 2018 (Volume II, Issue 17)

TO: The Donald: Talk Show Guest from Hell

FROM: Kelly: Avid Viewer

- Oh, Lordy, DT. If America ever wanted to listen to the POTUS melt down on live TV, your call-in to your preferred coffee-klatch on Thursday morning did the trick. It was a real Doocy…I mean, doozy.
- To celebrate Melania's birthday, you treated us to a rant that was exceptional even for you, while the Foxy Friendlies watched on in what I can only describe as extreme concern for your mental condition.
- While you started out by admitting that you were too busy *"to be running out looking for presents"* for your wife, you <u>did</u> have seemingly unlimited time to bellow into the phone about (in alphabetical order):
- **A+:** <u>Your</u> rating for <u>yourself</u> for your Celebrity Presidency to date.
- **CNN:** *"I don't watch them at all. I watched last night."* Wait, what?
- **Cohen, Michael:** *"[He] represents me – like with this crazy Stormy Daniels deal he represented me."* You finally admitted this! Good job!!
- **Collusion:** *"There's no collusion with me and the Russians." "So there's no collusion whatsoever." "There is no collusion with me."* Got it.
- **Comey, Jim:** *"I did a great thing for the American people by firing him."*
- **Department of Justice:** *"And our Justice Department, which I try and stay away from, but at some point I won't."* This was your <u>third</u> threat to "my Justice Department" during this harangue. Also…the DOJ includes the FBI.
  You fired the Director (Jim Comey) last year. See above.
- **Electoral College:** *"I got 306 and she got what, 223. So, remember – there was no way to break 270."* Still beating this poor dead horse race.
- **France:** *"I'll tell you what, the people of France are just – were spellbound by what happened with their great president who just left."* That might be one word for it. Or: Appalled? Disgusted? Repelled?
- **Jackson, Ronny (Dr.):** *"[He] has a perfect record. He's got this beautiful record unblemished."* Except for that alarming 2012 Inspector General's report. And now all the stuff you stirred up by trying to foist him on the VA.
- **North Korea:** *"Look, it was very, very nasty with Little Rocket Man and with the buttons – and, you know, my button's bigger than – everybody said this guy's going to get us into nuclear war." "OK, and now they're saying wow."* Yeah, wow. Our guy is as crazy as their guy.

- At the end, I hear that Rupert Murdoch called in with an emergency order for the Foxy Fiends to get you off the air before you impeached yourself.

Resources - Volume II– Issue 17

Good afternoon to MY friends……..today we review what might become (in the history books of tomorrow) a significant moment in the Decline and Fall of the 45th Presidential Regime: the train-wreck that was The Donald's F&F "interview" on Thursday.

1) 53 amazing moments

Cillizza, Chris. "Trump Says He Might Intervene in Justice Department." CNN, April 27, 2018. The 53 most stunning lines from Donald Trump's 'Fox & Friends' interview | CNN Politics

2) The Big Show

Holmes, Jack. "Trump's Fox & Friends Call Was a National Embarrassment." Esquire, April 26, 2018. Trump's Fox & Friends Call-In Was a Deranged Rant About Comey, Russia, Diamond and Silk, Ronny Jackson (esquire.com)

The Weekly Screed: May 6, 2018 (Volume II, Issue 18)

TO: The Donald: Sharing the Spotlight

FROM: Kelly: Avid FOX Viewer – Week TWO

- I get it, DT. After your already legendary melt-down on Fox and Friends on April 28, followed by your rant-filled rally in Washington, Michigan a week ago Saturday ["Kanye West….He GOTS it!"] you wanted to let someone else have a little moment on Live TV.
- And, as Jimmy Kimmel said last week about the disclosure of the raid on the office of your former physician, Dr. Harold Bornstein, "I always love it when a fun character from Season One reappears."
- But seriously, the Grand Prize for the most astonishing comeback on our national propaganda network this past week (both with Michael Cohen's *other* client, Sean Hannity, and with the Foxy Friends) goes not to you, or to the good doctor. Instead, let's applaud another recurring regular: **Rudy Giuliani**, this time playing the role of your new personal attorney.
- So when Lin Manuel Miranda gets around to writing ***"Rudy! The Musical!"*** as his political follow-up to *Hamilton,* he will surely work in the following lines concerning:
- **Cohen, Michael, on the porn star payoff:** *"Imagine if that came out on Oct. 15, 2016, in the middle of the last debate with Hillary Clinton? Cohen made it go away. He did his job."* Yes, just imagine? It might have ruined the reputation of this fine Christian candidate, so soon after the release of the Access Hollywood ("grab 'em by the pussy") tape.
- **Collusion between Trump campaign and Russia:** *"Gone. He's been cleared of that."* Ummm…Does Robert Mueller know about this?
- **Comey, Jim:** *It would have been good for God if God had kept you out of being head of the FBI…. This is a very perverted man……. who is now a pathological liar, as opposed to Donald Trump.*
Whom the *Washington Post* "Fact Checker" just announced has uttered a presidential record of 3,000 lies to the American people as of May 1.
- **Jared and Ivanka:** *I think I would get on my charger and go right into their offices with a lance if they go after Ivanka…I guess Jared is a fine man, you know that. But men are, you know, disposable. But a fine women like Ivanka?* Come on. Awww. We're so touched. Chivalry is not dead.
- **North Korea:** *I told the President, you're going to get the Nobel Peace Prize. My proudest moment is when you tell them to shove it.* Ka-boom.

Resources - Volume II– Issue 18

Good afternoon, friends, and relations........
Another hilarious week of TV viewing on FOX, The Donald's absolutely positively favorite network. This time, Rudy Giuliani (he's baaack) holds forth on matters both laughable and incriminating:

Can you imagine?

Blake, Aaron, and Eugene Scott. "Rudy Giuliani's Revealing Interview with Sean Hannity, Annotated." The Washington Post, May 3, 2018. Rudy Giuliani's revealing interview with Sean Hannity, annotated - The Washington Post

Manchester, Julia. "Giuliani: Imagine If That Came Out in the Middle of the Last Debate with Hillary Clinton." The Hill, May 3, 2018. Giuliani: Imagine if Stormy Daniels allegations came out 'in the middle of the last debate' (thehill.com)

House Intelligence Committee: No Collusion!

Hulse, Carl, and Nicholas Fandos. "House Intelligence Committee Finds No Evidence of Collusion Between Trump Campaign and Russia." The New York Times, April 27, 2018. Republicans on House Intelligence Panel Absolve Trump Campaign in Russian Meddling - The New York Times (nytimes.com)

Rudy on Comey, Jared, and Ivanka

Weigel, David. "Giuliani Tells Hannity That Comey Is 'Perverted' and He Would Totally Defend Ivanka Trump from Mueller with a 'Sword'." Slate, May 3, 2018. Giuliani tells Hannity that Comey is "perverted" and he would totally defend Ivanka Trump from Mueller. (slate.com)

Pants on Fire…….the latest

5. Kessler, Glenn, Salvador Rizzo, and Meg Kelly. "President Trump Has Made 3,001 False or Misleading Claims So Far." The Washington Post, May 1, 2018. President Trump has made 3,001 false or misleading claims so far - The Washington Post

The Weekly Screed: May 13, 2018 (Volume II, Issue 19)

TO: The Donald: Art of the Un-deal

FROM: Kelly: Dismayed..........as Usual

- Hey, DT. This morning I read that you really miss your mother. Awww. In *The Art of the Deal,* your ghostwriter mentioned that you felt you inherited <u>*"my sense of showmanship from my mother."*</u> Now that is a quality I truly value in The Leader of the Free World. I know MY mother would have voted for you, which is one of the reasons I'm *not* missing her much today. But enough about mothers. Let's talk about withdrawals.
- Your latest, from the **Iran Nuclear Agreement** *("This was a horrible, one-sided deal that should have never, ever been made,")* made me reflect on all the other catastrophes you've supposedly rescued us from:
- **TPP** You opined: *"The Trans-Pacific Partnership is another disaster done and pushed by special interests who want to rape our country."* Yep, we're out of it alright, but I'm pretty sure the only Big Winner here is China.
- **Pairs Climate Agreement** According to you, a *"terrible deal"* and a *"disaster"* for the US. *"Something could happen with respect to the Paris accords, let's see what happens."* Yeah, let's wait until Florida is submerged and then maybe we'll rethink this whole climate hoax thing.
- **The Affordable Care Act** By eliminating the penalty for non-compliance with the Individual Responsibility provision (included in the Tax Relief for Billionaires Act), *"We have essentially repealed Obamacare,"* But not to worry! *"We will come up with something much better...right after Tax Cuts!"*
- **Deferred Action for Childhood Arrivals** *"Cannot believe how BADLY DACA recipients have been treated by the Democrats...totally abandoned! Republicans are still working hard,"* you tweeted. Ummm....you *do* remember it was YOU that ended DACA, right?
- **Funding to fight Ebola** Just in time for a new outbreak in the Congo, here comes your shiny new edict: *"I herewith report 38 rescissions of budget authority, totaling $15.4 billion",* (mostly for inconsequential stuff like health care and emergency responses overseas) that you are asking Congress to withdraw from the current 2018 budget. This will probably happen because we know that Republicans are immune to infectious disease.
- Gee, what do all of these seemingly unrelated items have in common? Why, they were all Obama initiatives, and your personal animus to the Kenyan Socialist is why we can't have nice things anymore.

- Like clean air and water. And health care. Just Bread & Circuses……it's Showtime !!

Resources - Volume II– Issue 19

To all of you who are mothers……..or to all of you who had a mother ……….Happy Mother's Day ! This week's most consequential Breaking News (but far from the most entertaining, which would be more Michael Cohen/Essential Consultants revelations) is the Dear Leader's decision to unilaterally remove the US from the Joint Comprehensive Plan of Action meant to postpone Iran's development of nukes. It's just another brick in the wall of the Trump Doctrine, which I heard one NPR commentator describe this morning (very precisely) as "Belligerent Isolationism."

1) The Ultimate Withdrawal Borowitz, Andy. "Trump Considering Pulling U.S. Out of Constitution." The New Yorker, May 3, 2018. Trump Considering Pulling U.S. Out of Constitution | The New Yorker

2) Withdrawal from Trans Pacific Partnership Samuelson, Robert J. "A Year Later, Trump's Rejection of the TPP Is Still a Disaster." The Washington Post, January 30, 2018. Opinion | A year later, Trump's rejection of the TPP is still a disaster - The Washington Post

3) Withdrawal from Paris Climate Agreement Urpelainen, Johannes. "Trump's Noncooperation Threatens Climate Finance under the Paris Agreement." The Washington Post, November 21, 2017. Trump's withdrawal from the Paris agreement means other countries will spend less to fight climate change - The Washington Post

4) Withdrawal from Deferred Action for Childhood Arrivals Carlson, Lindsey. "Withdrawal from DACA Will Be Devastating." HuffPost, September 6, 2017. Withdrawal From DACA Will Be Devastating | HuffPost Religion

5) Withdrawal from the Individual Mandate Mukherjee, Sy. "The GOP Tax Bill Repeals Obamacare's Individual Mandate. Here's What That Means for You." Fortune. December 20, 2017. The GOP Tax Bill Repeals Obamacare's Individual Mandate. Here's What That Means for You (yahoo.com)

6) Withdrawal from fighting Ebola Garrett, Laurie. "Ebola Is Back, and Trump Is Trying to Kill Funding for It." Foreign Policy, May 9, 2018. Ebola Is Back. And Trump Is Trying to Kill Funding for It. – Foreign Policy

7) Withdrawal from entire Obama legacy Kwong, Jessica. "Trump Is Dismantling Obama's Legacy, and the Iran Nuclear Deal Is the Latest Casualty." Newsweek, May 9, 2018. All the Ways Trump Has Undone Obama's Legacy After Iran Nuclear Deal Withdrawal - Newsweek

The Weekly Screed: May 20, 2018 (Volume II, Issue 20)

TO: The Donald: Gimme that Nobel

FROM: Kelly: Fat Chance

- Howdy, DT. Last week we examined all the ways you want to vandalize Barack Obama's legacy. But there's One Thing he accomplished that you urgently want to duplicate: winning the Nobel Peace Prize.
- I know that *April* was National Poetry Month, but I'm going to take this opportunity in May to review some of your recent foreign policy exploits in the poetic form of *haiku*. As I'm sure you never learned, the format is three lines of 5/7/5 syllables. So, allons-y! Пойдем! ¡Vamos! 가자! Let's go!!

 1) **Threatening Europe**
    With sanctions over Iran
    There goes my Nobel…

 2) **Congo Ebola**
    Let's defund all assistance
    There goes my Nobel…

 3) **Death toll in Gaza**
    Party in Jerusalem
    There goes my Nobel…

 4) **Out of Paris talks**
    Our 400th warmest month
    There goes my Nobel

 5) **Kim Jong Un irate**
    Over joint war games down South
    There goes my Nobel….

 6) **NSA Bolton**
    Spoke of the "Libya Model"
    There goes my Nobel…

- So no matter how many gormless MAGA-hat-wearing Hoosiers chant "Nobel! Nobel!" when your handlers hold up signs, it's not gonna happen.

Resources - Volume II– Issue 20

This week focuses on The Donald's insane fantasy that he's going to be the next recipient of the Nobel Peace Prize. Hah! Only if he pries it from the cold dead hands of every living Norwegian.

Borowitz, Andy. "Trump Orders Replica Nobel Peace Prize to Display on His Desk." The New Yorker, May 3, 2018. Trump Orders Replica Nobel Peace Prize to Display on His Desk | The New Yorker

"The Nobel Peace Prize 2009." NobelPrize.org, October 9, 2009. The Nobel Peace Prize 2009 - Press release - NobelPrize.org

Borger, Julian, and Jennifer Rankin. "Let's Punish Europe Too: Trump Risks Transatlantic Trade War with Iran Sanctions." The Guardian, May 13, 2018. US threatens European companies with sanctions after Iran deal pullout | Iran nuclear deal | The Guardian

McKay, Betsy. "Ebola Funds Pledged for Recovery Are Slow to Come." The Wall Street Journal, March 20, 2018. Ebola Funds Pledged for Recovery Are Slow to Come - WSJ

Haas, Tzvi. "Colbert Rips into Ivanka and Jared as U.S. Opens Embassy in Jerusalem." Haaretz, May 17, 2018. Colbert Rips Into Ivanka and Jared as 'Peace-Treaty Barbie' Opens U.S. Embassy in Jerusalem - Israel News - Haaretz.com

Erdman, Jonathan. "Earth Had Its Third Warmest April on Record, Despite a Cool United States." The Weather Channel, May 17, 2018. April 2018 Was Earth's 400th Consecutive Warmer-Than-Average Month and the Third Warmest April on Record | Weather.com

Norton, Ben. "'Provocative Military Ruckus': North Korea Warns U.S.-South Korea War Games Could Derail Summit." Common Dreams, May 15, 2018. 'Provocative Military Ruckus': North Korea Warns US-South Korea War Games Could Derail Trump-Kim Summit | Common Dreams

Armstrong, David. "This Is Why North Korea Reacted So Strongly to Bolton's Mention of the 'Libya Model.'" The Washington Post, May 17, 2018. This is why North Korea reacted so strongly to Bolton's mention of the 'Libya model' - The Washington Post

Cochrane, Emily. The New York Times, May 9, 2018. President Trump a Nobel Laureate? It's a Possibility - The New York Times (nytimes.com)

The Weekly Screed: May 27, 2018 (Volume II, Issue 21)

TO: The Donald: Remembering "Young and Beautiful Lives"

FROM: Kelly: Me Too

- It's the second Memorial Day Weekend of your Celebrity Presidency, DT.
  So when I started reading your tweet this morning, I thought you might be wising up a bit: " *Who's going to give back the young and beautiful lives (and others) that have been devastated and destroyed by......* "
  Wait for it...*the phony Russia Collusion Witch Hunt?"*
- See, just for a New York minute, I foolishly surmised that you might be referring to ACTUAL lives destroyed.
- For example, during your first year as "Commander in Chief," the number of US troops who died in war zones around the world rose for the first time in six years. According to the Pentagon, 21 of these 33 deaths were in combat, and in places like Yemen, Niger, and Somalia, plus Iraq and Afghanistan.
- Or, in other mortality stats, the re-imposition of the Global Gag Rule has already been responsible for the fatalities of thousands of African women, as funding for contraception and all other health care has been slashed… which increases the number of unwanted pregnancies, back-alley abortions, HIV deaths, etc.
- But you and your bros Reince Priebus, Peter Navarro, Jared Kushner, Stephen Miller, and Steve Bannon looked so jolly at the signing ceremony for this death sentence that I really shouldn't have even *speculated* that you might be having second thoughts on this topic.
- In fact, you are doubling down by bringing this carnage home as you defund Planned Parenthood, the single largest provider of reproductive and other health services for low-income women.
- Last but not least, I almost flirted with the idea that you were referring to the fact that more children have been killed by firearms since the Sandy Hook Massacre than US soldiers in The War on Terror since 9/11.
- Or that being a student in 2018 was a more dangerous occupation than serving in combat. [KIA: Kids 27. Troops 13]
- Nah, the Real Victims here are the collaterally damaged wrought by the Mueller investigation (or the secondary scandals you've dragged them into): friends, family, and assorted comrades in crime. Poor Carter Page, for example, has lost a girlfriend and suffered "professional setbacks" over this!
- Indeed, for YOU, your buddies' legal fees are the real killers. SAD.

Resources - Volume II– Issue 21

The Screed was heading in a completely different direction yesterday, but when I woke up this morning and saw that tweet....well, couldn't let it go. Just never know what will "inspire" me.

"Trump: 'Beautiful Lives Have Been Destroyed by the Phony Russia Collusion Witch Hunt'." AOL News, May 27, 2018. Trump: 'Beautiful lives' have been 'destroyed by the phony Russia collusion witch hunt' (aol.com)

Tankel, Stephen. "Donald Trump's Shadow War." Politico, May 9, 2018. Donald Trump's Shadow War - POLITICO Magazine

Bergengren, Vera. "These U.S. Troops Were Killed in Combat During Trump's First Year in Office." BuzzFeed News, January 20, 2018. These US Troops Were Killed In Combat During Trump's First Year In Office (buzzfeednews.com)

Boseley, Sarah. "Trump's Global Gag Rule Is a Death Warrant for Women, Say Health Groups." The Guardian, July 21, 2017. How Trump signed a global death warrant for women | 'Global gag rule' | The Guardian

Quackenbush, Casey. "Trump's Global Gag Rule Puts 'Millions of Women's Lives at Risk,' Advocates Say." Time, January 23, 2018 Global Gag Rule: Impact of Donald Trump Abortion Funding Ban | TIME

Sit, Ryan. "Gun Violence: Children Are More Likely to Be Killed by Guns than Soldiers Are in War." Newsweek, March 23, 2018. More Children Have Been Killed by Guns Since Sandy Hook Than U.S. Soldiers in Combat Since 9/11 - Newsweek

Bump, Philip. "2018 Has Been Deadlier for Schoolchildren than Service Members." The Washington Post, May 18, 2018. 2018 has been deadlier for schoolchildren than deployed service members - The Washington Post

The Weekly Screed: June 3, 2018 (Volume II, Issue 22)

TO: The Donald: Insulter-in-Chief

FROM: Kelly: Choosing my words

- Come on, DT. You of all people are expressing outrage at a late-night comedienne just because she used an anatomical pejorative to categorize the beautiful and privileged White House princess....
- When we all know that this word is one of YOUR favorite terms of abuse for members of the female persuasion who have displeased you: Sally Yates (former Acting Attorney General, when she declined to enforce your Muslim Ban); *Philadelphia Inquirer* financial reporter Jennifer Lin (for daring to write an article about your shady casino dealings); and Jessica Leeds, one of the many women who have accused you of sexual assault.
- Meanwhile, you expressed no such opprobrium towards your favorite TV sitcom star when she took after former Obama advisor Valerie Jarrett, speculating that her progenitors might have been: "Muslim brotherhood and planet of the apes," thus reviving centuries of venomous racial stereotyping.
- Instead, you chastised Bob Iger, CEO of the Walt Disney Company, for never apologizing to YOU for *"the HORRIBLE statements made and said about me on ABC."* Because we need to remember who the Real Victim is.
- Speaking of Muslims and apes, remember when you sued Bill Maher because he asked you to produce your birth certificate to prove that your father was not an orangutan? That was really funny, DT, especially in light of your concurrent quest to prove that Barack Obama was a Muslim Socialist born in Kenya. Just think, that whole Birther Movement thing of yours kick-started your so-called political career. SAD.
- Anyway, the Samantha Bee remark correctly called out the contrast between the lovely photos of Ivanka and her offspring with your cruel decision to begin separating asylum seekers from their children (which you and current Attorney General Sessions have invidiously blamed on Democrats).
- And while most commentators focused exclusively on Samantha's use of the C word in her televised rant, I flinched at the more pointed and accurate critique offered by the F word.
- In one of life's little coincidences, a colleague of mine had (just the day before!) employed that very same adjective to describe our manager's boss, whom we had little faith would rise to support our team in putting

forth a policy protocol that would extend Medicaid coverage to more Oregonians.
- FECKLESS is indeed a spiteful and nasty put-down, Donald. Look it up.

Resources - Volume II– Issue 22

Waldman, Katy. "Ivanka Trump, Samantha Bee, and the Strange Path of an Ancient Epithet." The New Yorker, June 1, 2018. Ivanka Trump, Samantha Bee, and the Strange Path of an Ancient Epithet | The New Yorker

Ross, Martha. "Donald Trump Has Reportedly Insulted Women with the Word He Wants Samantha Bee Fired For." The Mercury News, June 1, 2018. Trump wants Samantha Bee fired for word he's used himself (mercurynews.com)

Willis, Jay. "Nothing Is the Same as Racism." GQ, June 1, 2018. Samantha Bee Calling an Administration Official a "Feckless Cunt" Is Not the Same as Racism | GQ

O'Connor, Lydia. "Trump Reacts to Roseanne's Cancellation: Who's the Real Victim Here?" HuffPost, May 30, 2018. Trump Responds To ABC's 'Roseanne' Cancellation By Making It All About Himself | HuffPost Latest News

Kruta, Virginia. "Bill Maher Defends Trump 'Orangutan' Joke." The Daily Caller, June 2, 2018. Bill Maher Defends Trump-Orangutan Joke In The Wake Of Roseanne Fallout | The Daily Caller

Naylor, Brian. "Fact Check: Are Democrats Responsible for DHS Separating Children from Their Parents?" NPR, May 29, 2018. FACT CHECK: Are Democrats Responsible For DHS Separating Children From Their Parents? : NPR

Rizzo, Salvador. "Fact-Checking Immigration Spin on Separating Families and 1,500 'Lost' Children." The Washington Post, May 30, 2018. Fact-checking immigration spin on separating families and 1,500 'lost' children - The Washington Post

The Weekly Screed: June 10, 2018 (Volume II, Issue 23)

TO: The Donald: Minute Man

FROM: Kelly: Considering Singapore

- Well, it looks like it's really gonna happen, DT. You and Rocket Man, together at last in Singapore. With Dennis Rodman jetting in just to enhance the solemnity of the occasion.
- While most real Presidents might have been boning up on a little North Korean history in preparation for this off-again on-again summit, you let us know that actually reading or learning anything was Not an Option.
- After all, you needed to spend the past week alienating all of our allies at the G-7 conference, while sucking up to Russia by announcing that they should be invited back to resuscitate the G-8.
- Fortunately, you were able to reassure everyone yesterday with your ability to rapidly size up the situation and suss out whether you'll get a Great Deal for the US: *"I think within the first minute, I'll know….Just my touch, my feel, that's what I do."*
- Yeah, we've all heard about many instances of you getting touchy-feely, and I would urge you NOT to use that approach at this meeting….
- On the other hand, your powers of perspicacity seem to have doubled over the past year. It was just last summer that White House officials dubbed you "The Two-Minute Man" due to your unique inability to sit still long enough to grasp any useful knowledge: "Even a single page of bullet points seem[s] to tax the president's attention span." [hmm…Bad news for The Screed]
- This nescience seems to extend to your appointee as State Department spokesperson, who extolled our *"very strong relationship with the government of Germany,"* by noting the upcoming D-Day anniversary.
- Sort of like Putin boasting of his strong relationship with Ukraine after seizing the Crimea….the very action that caused the G-8 to become the G-7.
- But back to Singapore. As you might imagine, I've spent the past few days mourning the passing of Anthony Bourdain, with whom I've dined vicariously for years in many far-flung "Parts Unknown." Unlike you, Bourdain was above all empathic and intellectually curious, a true citizen of the world. There was, however, one country he refused to visit: North Korea, whose leader he dismissed as "a chubby little evil f***. Most of the population is starving. Don't you think that would be in kind of bad taste?"
- He loved Singapore street food, but on one thing he was clear; when asked what dish he might serve at a Trump/Kim summit: "Hemlock."

Resources - Volume II– Issue 23

Good afternoon, friends………….I don't know about you, but I don't have a lot of high expectations for this little get-together in Singapore. I'm thinking the best we can hope for is that The Dear Leaders will postpone a nuclear exchange for a year or two. I want to live to retire!

"Germany, France Slam Trump over Group of Seven U-Turn." AOL News, June 10, 2018. Germany, France slam Trump over Group of Seven U-turn (aol.com)

Siddiqui, Sabrina; Pengelly, Martin. "Trump and Kim Jong-un: North Korea Summit Gets Underway in Singapore." The Guardian, June 9, 2018. Trump: I'll know whether Kim summit will be successful 'in first minute' | Donald Trump | The Guardian

Husband, Andrew. "Donald Trump Is Reportedly Referred to as 'Two-Minute Man' in Business Circles." Uproxx, August 4, 2017. White House Staffers Reportedly Call Trump The 'Two-Minute Man' (uproxx.com)

"Trump Appointee Heather Nauert Invokes D-Day While Praising US-Germany Relations." The Week, June 8, 2018. Trump appointee Heather Nauert invokes D-Day while praising US-Germany relations | The Week

"Anthony Bourdain's Travel Tips for Singapore." Travel Channel. Anthony Bourdain's Travel Tips for Singapore | Anthony Bourdain: No Reservations : Shows : TravelChannel.com | Travel Channel

"Anthony Bourdain Said He'd Serve Poison at Summit for Trump and Kim." Coconuts Singapore, June 9, 2018. Anthony Bourdain once joked that he'd serve poison at a summit between Trump and Kim | Coconuts

Steward, Emily. "Anthony Bourdain and Barack Obama Shared a Meal in Vietnam." Vox, June 8, 2018. Obama remembers Anthony Bourdain by tweeting photo from Vietnam meal | Vox

The Weekly Screed: June 17, 2018 (Volume II, Issue 24)

TO: The Donald: Persistently Illegal

FROM: Kelly: Enjoying your Birthday Lawsuit

- Donald, it was your 72nd birthday on Thursday, and Ivanka sent you a super profound and imaginative message on Instagram: "Happy, happy birthday Dad! I love you very much. Wishing you your best year yet!!!"
- Wow. So personal. That gal can really write. ***Three*** exclamation points!!!
- I looked you up in *The Element Encyclopedia of Birthdays,* which labels June 14 as "the Birthday of the Supervisor". It says that on the Dark Side you are "bossy, confrontational, abrupt" while At Your Best you are "authoritative and persistent." Hmmm.
- All of these stellar qualities are elucidated in the Happy Birthday lawsuit filed against you and your three eldest progeny by the Attorney General of New York. The petition "seeks to dissolve Donald J. Trump Foundation;" ban you and the kiddos from serving on the board of "any other New York charity;" and demands "restitution of $2.8 million plus penalties". Ouch.
- It turns out that the "Board of Directors" (aka your offspring) didn't meet or approve of any grants since 1999, and the Foundation "acted in a persistently illegal manner", functioning mostly as a slush fund to settle other lawsuits, fund your presidential campaign, and buy a ginormous painting of yourself.
- Of course, this flagrant misuse of charitable donations is just one slice of the vast corruption cake you've baked and served up to the American public.
- From Day One as POTUS, you've been in violation of the Constitution's emoluments clause by raking in hefty profits from the Trump Hotel, and benefitting from Chinese government loans for your new HUGE housing and resort development in Indonesia.

    Even the *lease* on the Trump Hotel (which is located in a federally owned building) violates the Government Services Administration contract which specifies that no "elected official of the Government of the United States ... shall be admitted to any share or part of this Lease, or to any benefit that may arise there from[.]"
- These financial and legal shenanigans can only presage your next Big Deal: Trump Palace Pyongyang, which South Korea will presumably pay for. I'm sure negotiations started in Singapore during your "alone time" with Kim.

- *"They have great beaches,"* you trumpeted at a recent press conference. *"You see that whenever they're exploding their cannons into the ocean. I said, 'Boy, look at that view. Wouldn't that make a great condo?'"*

Resources - Volume II– Issue 24

Winter, Tom. "Trump Used His Charitable Foundation Like a Personal Checkbook, Lawsuit Alleges." The Daily Beast, June 14, 2018. Trump Family Ran 'Persistently Illegal' Charity, New York A.G. Says in Blockbuster Lawsuit (thedailybeast.com)

Klasfeld, Adam. "NY Brings $2.8M Suit to Dissolve Trump Foundation." Courthouse News Service. June 14, 2018. NY Brings $2.8M Suit to Dissolve Trump Foundation | Courthouse News Service

Polantz, Katelyn. "Trump Emoluments Lawsuit to Move Forward After Judge's Ruling." CNN, May 1, 2018. Trump asks court to dismiss emoluments lawsuit against him | CNN Politics

Savage, Charlie. "Judge Allows Emoluments Lawsuit Against Trump to Proceed." The New York Times, June 11, 2018. Judge in Emoluments Case Questions Defense of Trump's Hotel Profits - The New York Times (nytimes.com)

Sargent, Greg. "Trump's Latest Violation of the Emoluments Clause." The Washington Post, May 15, 2018. Judge in Emoluments Case Questions Defense of Trump's Hotel Profits - The New York Times (nytimes.com)

Kennedy, Merrit. "GSA Says Trump D.C. Hotel Lease Is Valid Despite Ban on Elected Officials." NPR, March 23, 2017. GSA Says Trump D.C. Hotel Lease Is Valid, Despite Ban On Elected Officials : The Two-Way : NPR

Nguyen, Tina. "Trump's North Korea Beaches Quote Will Make You Go, 'Wait, What?.'" Bustle, June 12, 2018. Trump's North Korea "Beaches" Quote Will Make You Go, Wait, What? (bustle.com)

"Did Trump Tower Open in Pyongyang?" Snopes, June 12, 2018. Did a Trump Tower Open in Pyongyang? | Snopes.com

The Weekly Screed: June 24, 2018 (Volume II, Issue 25)

TO: The Donald: Infesting the White House

FROM: Kelly: Call the Mueller Extermination Company!!

There's a problem with Who's on the border with US

Let them in? Keep them out? It's creating a fuss.

Jefferson Sessions, that evil AG, said *Romans 13* justifies cruelty

And mandates we do as the government bids, such as taking those parents away from their kids

And locking up children and tots of all ages in detention camps made of concrete and cages

The Donald explains that all those coming here are just tools of the Democrats, and we must fear

These "animals," "rapists" infesting the nation with M-13 thugs bent on contamination of all we hold dear.

What The Donald ignores is that Grandfather Drumpf

Was a migrant from Deutschland before he was "Trump,"

And that wives One and Three were not born here as well, but Three's the "First Lady" now, so What the Hell

Was she doing in wearing that little green jacket, the back of which kicked off a media racket

Of pundits inquiring the "message" it sent when clearly the "message" was self-evident.

"I Really Don't Care, Do You?" in big white print, was perfectly plain and said just what it meant:

That FLOTUS and POTUS and all of their friends do not give a damn, and we know how this ends

People seeking asylum are sent back to die, and the "beacon of liberty" put to the lie.

Resources - Volume II– Issue 25

Good evening, all........I'm on a little vacation in Denver this week, but The Screed must go out !! There are so many vermin (Stephen Miller, Steve Bannon, Sarah Huckabee Sanders, Kellyanne Conway, Alex Azar, Kirstjen Nielsen) involved in this immigrant catastrophe but I didn't have enough room for all of them in my little poem.

Strine, Casey. "Jeff Sessions Is Using the Bible to Justify the Immoral Separation of Children from Their Parents." The Independent, June 15, 2018. This is what the Bible's Romans 13 actually says about asylum and what Jeff Sessions omitted | The Independent | The Independent

Terkel, Amanda. "Kids' Toys Are Being Seized at the Border as 'Contraband'." HuffPost, June 20, 2018. Kids Taken From Their Parents At The Border Get Their Toys Confiscated Too | HuffPost Latest News

Graham, David A. "The Language of Trump's Anti-Immigrant Rhetoric." The Atlantic, June 19, 2018. Trump Says Democrats Want Immigrants to 'Infest' the U.S. - The Atlantic

Farand, Chloe. "Trump's Grandfather Was Deported from Germany for Not Serving His Country." The Independent, August 22, 2017. Donald Trump's grandfather wrote letter begging not to be deported. Here it is | The Independent | The Independent

Wanshel, Elyse. "Melania Trump's Jacket Sparks Outrage and Memes." HuffPost, June 21, 2018. Twitter Users Came Up With Some New And Improved Jackets For Melania | HuffPost Entertainment

The Weekly Screed: July 1, 2018 (Volume II, Issue 26)

TO: The Donald: From Pro-Choice to "Lock them up"

FROM: Kelly: Woe is Roe

- DT, as you consider your next nomination to join The Supremes, you've stated that *"I'm not going to ask them that question,"* i.e., how they stand on overturning Roe versus Wade. What a crock.
- We all know that your position on this "issue" has devolved from *"I believe it is a personal decision that should be left to the women and their doctors"* (December 1999) to *"There has to be some form of punishment [for the women]"* (March 2016) to abortion rights could be left up to the states "at some point." (Today, in an interview on Fox Noise).
- Here's a little history of some of the goings-on back when women's reproductive rights were "left up to the states":
- Elizabeth Furse, former Congresswoman from Oregon, was forced to be sterilized in order to get an abortion in Los Angeles in 1961.
- A friend of mine was arrested (along with all the other women in the waiting room AND in the recovery room, plus the physician) when the clinic where she was seeking an abortion was raided in Kansas City in 1968.
- In 1970, I got pregnant at age 17, three weeks after I lost my virginity. Two words: broken condom. I couldn't get an abortion in Colorado, but (lucky for me!) the Governor of California, good old Ronald Reagan, had signed into law the second most liberal abortion law in the country in 1967. At the time, the Unitarian-Universalist church was running the Abortion Underground, connecting women with providers....I remember sitting down with a UU minister and my parents and being given the choice of Mexico, New York, or California. So, at 8 weeks, I found myself in San Francisco with my father, having a "therapeutic dilation and curettage" at a hospital.
Best decision I ever made, and the best thing Reagan ever did.
- Since the passage of Roe v. Wade in 1973, Oregon is the only state in the nation that hasn't imposed new "restrictions" on a woman's right to choose AND provides state funding for contraception and abortions for all low-income (including undocumented) women.
- Because we know that legal abortion is much safer for women than illegal abortion…which is still safer than carrying a pregnancy to term. Women (and women alone) should be able to make these decisions.

Resources - Volume II– Issue 26

I'm sorry to burden you with SO many links this week, but I just couldn't decide which to jettison. I'm not saying I'm a single-issue voter, but reproductive freedom has been my First Issue since 1970. Which is why I've pretty much voted straight Dems since 1980, when the "Moral Majority" hi-jacked the Republican party. Anyway, I'm getting the feeling we'll be backsliding even further in the near future. SAD.

Reuters. "Sen. Collins Says She Won't Support Anti-Abortion Supreme Court Nominee." AOL News, July 1, 2018. Sen. Collins says she won't support anti-abortion Supreme Court nominee (aol.com)

Langone, Alix. "President Trump Says Abortion Laws Could Be Left Up to States 'At Some Point'." Time, June 29, 2018. Donald Trump Says Abortion Rights Could Be Left Up to States | TIME

Kengor, Paul, and Patricia Clark Doerner. "Reagan's Darkest Hour." National Review, January 29, 2008. Reagan's Darkest Hour | National Review

Julie Hirschfeld Davis and Michael D. Shear. "Trump Administration Imposes New Abortion Restrictions." The New York Times, May 22, 2018. Trump Rule Would Bar Some Abortion Advice at Federally Funded Clinics - The New York Times (nytimes.com)

"Donald Trump on Abortion." On the Issues. Donald Trump on Abortion (ontheissues.org)

"Donald Trump on Abortion - From Pro-Choice to Pro-Prison." BBC News, March 30, 2016. Donald Trump on abortion - from pro-choice to pro-prison - BBC News

Resources - Volume II– Issue 26 (continued)

McMaken, Ryan. "Before *Roe v. Wade*, Abortion Had Always Been a State and Local Matter." Mises Wire. January 24, 2018. Before Roe v. Wade, Abortion Had Always Been a State and Local Matter | Mises Institute

Madera, Melissa. "6 Women Share Their Harrowing Stories of Illegal Abortion Before Roe v. Wade." Vice, January 22, 2018. 6 Women Share Their Harrowing Stories of Illegal Abortion Before Roe v. Wade – VICE

Willard Cates, Jr.; David A. Grimes; Kenneth F. Schulz. "The Public Health Impact of Legal Abortion: 30 Years Later." Guttmacher Institute, January 2003. The Public Health Impact of Legal Abortion: 30 Years Later | Guttmacher Institute

Kliff, Sarah. "Thirteen Charts That Explain How Roe v. Wade Changed Abortion Rights." The Washington Post, January 22, 2014. Thirteen charts that explain how Roe v. Wade changed abortion rights - The Washington Post

Aggeler, Madeleine. "Did Trump … Just Forget Justice Kennedy's Name?" The Cut, June 27, 2018. Did Trump Forget Justice Anthony Kennedy's Name? (thecut.com)

Farias, Cristian. "Justice Kennedy Surrendered to Donald Trump." New York Magazine, June 27, 2018. Justice Kennedy Surrendered to Donald Trump (nymag.com)

Freytas-Tamura, Kimiko. "Where Did Ireland Go? Abortion Vote Stuns Those on Both Sides." The New York Times. May 27, 2018. Where Did Ireland Go? Abortion Vote Stuns Those on Both Sides - The New York Times (nytimes.com)

Resources - Volume II– Issue 26 (continued)

Interview with Chris Matthews. "Context: Transcript of Donald Trump's Comments on Punishing Women for Abortion." PolitiFact, March 30, 2016. PolitiFact | In Context: Transcript of Donald Trump on punishing women for abortion

MATTHEWS: Do you believe in punishment for abortion, yes or no as a principle?

TRUMP: The answer is that there has to be some form of punishment.

MATTHEWS: For the woman.

TRUMP: Yeah, there has to be some form.

MATTHEWS: Ten cents? Ten years? What?

TRUMP: I don't know. That I don't know. That I don't know.

MATTHEWS: Why not?

TRUMP: I don't know.

MATTHEWS: You take positions on everything else.

TRUMP: Because I don't want to -- I frankly, I do take positions on everything else. It's a very complicated position.

The Weekly Screed: July 8, 2018 (Volume II, Issue 27)

TO: The Donald: Commander Bone Spurs

FROM: Kelly: How I spent the 4th of July

- DT, it looks like you had a pretty fine "Indepen<u>dance</u>" Day with Melania. Sure, she misspelled her holiday tweet, but she *did* hold your hand on your little White House walk-around and looked fetching in her faux-casual $2,800 ground-skimming gingham gown. Such a down-to-earth FLOTUS.
- In other family news, Don Jr. instagrammed a particularly hilarious image of you: Your pouty face and coiffed comb-over superimposed on what looks like the body of General George Washington, clutching a 50-caliber machine gun in one fist, with an eagle perched on the other upraised arm. Old Glory waves behind you and bombs are apparently bursting around your feet and the caption TRUMP. "This is Amazing" says Junior……..Indeed.
- I couldn't help but be reminded of the episode when you cowered before that real eagle when it attacked you during a TIME magazine photo-shoot in 2015, back when you thought you would be Person of the Year but it went to German Chancellor Angela Merkel instead. Those were the days.
- We also must recall that (unlike the Revolutionary War heroes you praised in your gag-worthy tweet on the 4th) YOU never wore a uniform or went into armed combat to defend "our one glorious nation under God."
- Is this why you've launched your ridiculous Trade War against Great Britain and all of our major allies? Just to pump you up until you can finagle us into a real military conflict…maybe even a nice little nuclear war with Iran or North Korea? Now <u>that</u> would be something to tweet about next Fourth!
- Meanwhile, in China, a guy named Li Jiang is revving up his factory to produce all the American flags for your 2020 campaign for *Celebrity President: Season 2*. Why don't we slap 25% tariffs on your MAGA junk?
- Here in the People's Republic of Oregon, my husband and I attended a pool party/BBQ in the neighborhood, where we wound up at a table with an eclectic group of local politicians, community activists, candidates for office, a former Senator and his wife, and the editor of the local newspaper.
- I normally try to associate only with like-minded progressives these days. But every now and then it's probably healthy for me to venture

- into somewhat civil discourse with Independents and assorted right-wingers.
- Still, I'm perturbed that some of your supporters are calling for a Civil War if you 1) get impeached; 2) lose the next election; or 3) just 'cuz. Perhaps we still ARE one nation, but maybe just for another year or two of July 4ths.

Resources - Volume II– Issue 27

I hope everyone enjoyed themselves on this mid-week holiday. My mother's birthday was the 4th of July, and one of my sisters got married on July 4, 2013, so it's always been sort of a big celebration for my family. This year I once again sat around a pool, talking to (mostly) Republicans. And I behaved myself!

1) Commander Bone Spurs

Hamblin, James. "What's a Heel Spur?" The Atlantic, August 1, 2016. Why Didn't Donald Trump Go To Vietnam? - The Atlantic

2) Looks like Melania had a good time

Clark, Andrew. " America can't spell: Melania Trump, others use #IndependanceDay — not Independence Day." IndyStar, July 4, 2018. Melania Trump, others misspell Independence Day on Twitter (indystar.com)

Carballo, Charlie. "Melania Trump's 4th of July Outfit Comes With a Stylish History Lesson." Footwear News. July 5, 2018. Melania Trump's 4th of July Dress Came With a History Lesson – Footwear News

3) The two funniest things I've seen all week:

"Donald Trump Jr. Posts Patriotic Instagram on Independence Day." Sputnik News, July 4, 2018. Warm Independence Day Regards: Trump Carrying Gun Scares Off Americans - 05.07.2018, Sputnik International (sputnikglobe.com)

"Trump and a Real Eagle." YouTube, uploaded by Inside Edition, December 10, 2015. Watch Donald Trump Dodge a Bald Eagle | Person Of The Year 2015 | TIME (youtube.com)

Resources - Volume II– Issue 27 (continued)

4) In case you missed it……..Reading from the teleprompter

Real, Evan. "Trump Delivers Independence Day Speech." The Hollywood Reporter, July 4, 2018. Trump Delivers Independence Day Speech on Twitter: Watch (hollywoodreporter.com)

5) MAGA flags from China

"US President Trump Imports Flags Made in China for 2020 Campaign." France 24, July 7, 2018. Trump to 'Make America Great Again' with Chinese-made US flags (france24.com)

6) At the Pool Party

Achen, Paris. "Before the MeToo Movement, There Was Bob Packwood." Pamplin Media, February 1, 2018. Before #MeToo movement, there was Bob Packwood | News | portlandtribune.com

Bates, Tom. "Bob Packwood: The Rise and Fall of a Senate Power Broker." Los Angeles Times, April 11, 1993. THE PACKWOOD PROBLEM : He's a Republican Senator With All the Right Friends. But Bob Packwood Also Had His Demons, and They May Forever Change the Capitol's Old Boys' Network. - Los Angeles Times (latimes.com)

7) Civil War 2.0

Armstrong, Ben. "What a Civil War?" WSAU, June 26, 2018. What? A Civil War? | WSAU News/Talk 550 AM · 99.9 FM | Wausau, Stevens Point

Manchester, Julia. "Acosta: Trump Supporter at Rally Said Media Is Going to Cause Civil War." The Hill, June 26, 2018. Acosta: Trump supporter at rally said media is going to cause 'civil war' (thehill.com)

Resources - Volume II– Issue 27 (continued)

This lady from last night's Trump rally in SC told me to tone it down. She talked about a possible civil war and people shooting each other. Just one example of some of the anger directed at the press at Trump rallies pic.twitter.com/eK2iINUcrj

— Jim Acosta (@Acosta) June 26, 2018

The Weekly Screed: July 15, 2018 (Volume II, Issue 28)

TO: The Donald: "Can't Build the Wall: Hands Too Small"

FROM: Kelly: Loving the "Carnival of Resistance"

- DT, I should have learned by now NOT to be amazed or alarmed by anything you utter, tweet, or fabricate, but your performance this past week was really a notch above all your other forays abroad.
- And we still, heaven help us, have your "summit" with your handler Vlad the Blackmailer to get through tomorrow.
- Once again, the Parade of Prevarications and Boorish Blather was in full swing, as you shot your mouth off about: NATO funding; Germany in thrall to Russia; how you miss the name "England"; Brexit strategy; the great job you're doing, in case we hadn't noticed (which we haven't); and Fake News (to describe your own recorded interview with *The Sun*). Oh, yeah, and that you retain your self-appointed status as a "very stable genius."
- The only saving grace was the astonishing number of creative, profane, witty, and almost celebratory protesters who took to the streets to commemorate your visit to Europe. So, to do my part, I've taken the liberty of re-writing a classic tune for you…..your Song of the Summer, as it were:

> Calling out around the world
> Are you ready for a brand-new beat?
> Trump is here and the time is right
> For marching in the streets
>
> They're marching up in Brussels
> Down in London town, don't forget Helsinki
> All we need is outrage! Resistance!
> There'll be protests everywhere
> There'll be banners, blimps, and paragliders,
> Marching in the street, oh!
>
> It doesn't matter what you wear, just as long as you are there
> So come on, every one, guys and girrrls, grab your signs
> around the world
> And go marching, they're marching in the street (Marching in the street!)
> It's an invitation across the nations; a chance for folks to meet
> It's a carnival of mass resistance
> Marching in the street !!

All across the UK hear them say: We're marching in the street!
Edinburgh and Glasgow (Marching in the street!)
Can't forget Belfast city (Marching in the street!)
Cardiff town down in Wales (Marching in the street!)
Grab your corgi and go; tell Trump NO
We're marching in the street……

Resources - Volume II– Issue 28

Comrades ! As we brace ourselves for the outcome of the Trump/Putin assignation, let us reflect on the highs and lows of the past week. First off, do yourself a favor and watch Bowie and Jagger's take on the Martha & the Vandellas classic anthem: David Bowie & Mick Jagger - Dancing In The Street (Official Video) (youtube.com). One factoid new to me but relevant to this Screed came from the Wikipedia entry on this song: "The song took on a different meaning when riots in inner-city America led to many young black demonstrators citing the song as a civil rights anthem to social change which also led to some radio stations taking the song off its play list because certain black advocates such as H. Rap Brown began playing the song while organizing demonstrations."

Lu, Michelle. "Trump Brought Lies to Europe." HuffPost, July 12, 2018. Trump Brought His Lies Over To Europe This Week | HuffPost Latest News

David M. Herszenhorn and Jacopo Barigazzi. "'Very stable' Trump? European leaders beg to differ." Politico, July 12, 2018. 'Very stable' Trump? European leaders beg to differ - POLITICO

"Trump's UK visit: Nine key moments."" BBC News, July 15, 2018. Trump's UK visit: Nine key moments (bbc.com)

McKirdy, Euan. "Trump's Controversial Interview with The Sun in the UK." CNN, July 13, 2018. What Donald Trump said about May, Brexit, NATO, and 'England' | CNN Politics

Frej, Willa. "Trump's UK Visit Met With Fierce Protests." HuffPost, July 12, 2018. Trump's UK Visit Met With Fierce Protests | HuffPost Latest News

Roth, Andrew. "Not Welcome: Finnish Protesters Criticize Trump-Putin Summit." The Guardian, July 15, 2018. 'Not welcome': Finnish protesters criticise Trump-Putin summit | Finland | The Guardian

The Weekly Screed: July 22, 2018 (Volume II, Issue 29

TO: The Donald: "I have the best words"

FROM: Kelly: I have located some better ones

- DT, remember back in December of 2016 when you blew your own trumpet on this topic? *"I went to an Ivy League school, I'm very highly educated. I know words, I had the best words. I have — but there's no better word than stupid."*
- I feel compelled to point out that events of the past week have proved otherwise, in particular your discombobulation over the use of "would" versus "wouldn't."
- Finally, this morning, you retreated to your old standby of "GREAT" to summarize the Humiliation in Helsinki: *"I had a GREAT meeting with Putin and the Fake News used every bit of their energy to try and disparage it. So bad for our country!"* Points for "disparage" though. Three syllables!
- Let's examine a few other terms that your voters may be googling soon:
  1) ABJECTLY, as used by Senator John McCain (R-AZ): *"No prior president has ever abased himself more abjectly before a tyrant."* Come to think of it, they might need to look up "abased" as well.
  2) APPEASEMENT, which the left has used to compare your suck-up to Vlad to Neville Chamberlin's acquiescence to Hitler (following the Nazi invasion of Czechoslovakia in 1939)....and the right has equated with JFK's wimpy encounter with Khrushchev in 1961 (which some say led to the Cuban Missile Crisis). However, in your case, perhaps we should change the spelling to AP<u>PEE</u>SEMENT, in a nod to just how injurious that rumored Moscow hooker tape might be.....which leads us to:
  3) KOMPROMAT, which Wikipedia sums up as *"short for 'compromising material' (компрометирующий материал) and* defines as *"damaging information about a politician or other public figure used to create negative publicity, for blackmail, or for ensuring loyalty."* This <u>could be</u> the "golden shower" video of the Steele Dossier, or it could be even more devastating evidence of your felonious financial shenanigans. Can't wait to find out!!
  4) VASSAL, which George Kennan employed to succinctly describe Russian international relations: *"The jealous and intolerant eye of the Kremlin can distinguish, in the end, only vassals and enemies, and the neighbors of Russia, if they do not wish to be one, must reconcile themselves to being the other."* Ukraine, which lost the Crimea to Putin in 2014, can certainly attest to the accuracy of this estimation.

5) BRAGGART, which brings us back to your "best words" self-assessment above. I leave this one to The Bard: "Who knows himself a braggart, let him fear this, for it will come to pass that every braggart shall be found an ass."

Resources - Volume II– Issue 29

As the late great Molly Ivins would have said, we were all "gobsmacked" by the summit spectacle of last Monday.

"Kansas City Star on Trump's Use of Language." The Kansas City Star, January 20, 2016. Transcript of Donald Trump's Dec. 30 speech in Hilton Head, S.C. | Kansas City Star

Milbank, Dana. "Trump Says He Has the Best Words. Merriam-Webster Disagrees." The Washington Post, April 4, 2017. Opinion | Trump says he has the 'best words.' Merriam-Webster disagrees. - The Washington Post

Loofbourow, Lili. "The Trump-Putin Summit Was Not Appeasement. It Was Worse." Slate, July 17, 2018. Trump–Putin summit was not appeasement. It was worse. (slate.com)

Wright, Robin. "Trump's Appeasement Summit with Putin." The New Yorker, July 16, 2018. Trump's Appeasement Summit with Putin | The New Yorker

Tierney, Dominic. "Trump, Putin, and the Art of Appeasement." The Atlantic, December 19, 2016. Trump, Putin, and the Art of Appeasement - The Atlantic

"Kompromat." Wikipedia. Kompromat - Wikipedia

Resources - Volume II– Issue 29 (continued)

Davidson, Adam. "A Theory of Trump Kompromat." The New Yorker, July 19, 2018. A Theory of Trump Kompromat | The New Yorker

Zakaria, Fareed. "The Kennan Diaries by George F. Kennan." The New York Times, February 23, 2014. 'The Kennan Diaries,' by George F. Kennan - The New York Times (nytimes.com)

GEOBEATS. "Trump: Media Disparaging My 'Great' Meeting with Putin Is So Bad for Our Country." AOL News, July 22, 2018. Trump: Media disparaging my 'great' meeting with Putin is 'so bad for our country' (aol.com)

Rosen, Christopher. "Donald Trump's Use of the Word 'Great' on Twitter." Entertainment Weekly, April 28, 2017. Donald Trump: Great used on Twitter 77 times in first 100 days (ew.com)

"Who knows himself a braggart, let him fear this, for it will come to pass that every braggart shall be found an ass."

— **William Shakespeare**, All's Well That Ends Well,

Act 4, Scene 3

Matthews, Jason. The Kremlin's Candidate. Simon & Schuster, 2018.

Quote from George Kennan:

The jealous and intolerant eye of the Kremlin can distinguish, in the end, only vassals and enemies, and the neighbors of Russia, if they do not wish to be one, must reconcile themselves to being the other. No matter how big and powerful, Russia always feels threatened. Even when they are feeling weak, they bluster and bully to hide their vulnerability. In this sense, Putin's policies and beliefs are largely consistent with Russian history and the legacy of the Russian Tzars.

The Weekly Screed: July 29, 2018 (Volume II, Issue 30)

TO: The Donald: BS in Economics

FROM: Kelly: MBA in International Management

- Donald, last week I poked fun at your claim that you had the "best words." Today, I'm circling back to that statement, which also included: "I went to an Ivy League school."
- Unlike the first boast, the second is undeniably true: you did in fact graduate from the Wharton School of Business at the University of Pennsylvania with a Bachelor of Science degree in Economics. Not "first in [your] class," as often reported but never denied, not on the dean's list, nor with honors…
  But hey! You were there. Except most weekends when you went back to New York to collaborate with Daddy on shady real estate deals.
- It seems to me, though, that your attendance primarily served as a handy deferment from service in a war that cost the lives of 16,899 US military in the year you graduated (1968). Only after being classified 1A following matriculation did it become necessary for you to secure your infamous "bone spur" medical deferment.
- What attending Wharton did not, apparently, accomplish was the infusion of any lasting knowledge of economics. This was made clear by Thursday's *Wall Street Journal* report on your meeting with European Commission President Jean-Claude Juncker, which occasioned the side-splitting headline:
  "European Commissioner Used Colorful, 'Very Simple' Cards to Explain Trade to Trump"
- Flash cards !! Ah, it takes me back, DT…not to MY business school studies at Harvard and the Thunderbird School of Global Management…But I do recall them from those halcyon days at Bailey Inglish Elementary School in beautiful Bonham, Texas (racially segregated, of course. It *was* the 1950s after all, when everyone in the South knew their place). But I seem to remember those pedagogical tools usually employed to drill Readin' and Ritin' and 'Rithmatic rather than the intricacies of global trade.
- Man, I'd love to get my mitts on those flashers. What exactly did you guys talk about? Did Juncker refresh your knowledge of GATT? Or its replacement, the WTO? Or why TTIP foundered? Hint: GMOs.
- I remain skeptical that this summit (like your other recent encounters with foreign leaders) will yield bigly results that benefit America. As a fan of life-long learning, however, I applaud it. Break out the nuclear war cards.

Resources - Volume II– Issue 30

As we swelter through these summer months, I look forward (as always) to September, the beginning of the School Year, and the hope that this generation is getting a better education than our current POTUS. What a nincompoop.

Today I have some lovely links to information on global trade. I know, (you are asking yourself) in a week full of headlines buzzing about Collusion with Russia, Playboy Bunny Pay-offs, and tariffs, WHY in the name of all that is holy did I feel compelled to focus on the least juicy of these topics? Because I think it got the funniest headline, and I hope you agree. Plus, I know there are many shoes to drop SOON on the other items. Also, because I learned some good stuff and want to pass it on.

Rothman, Lily. "President Trump Called Himself 'Smart' Six Times Before Breakfast." ABC News, January 6, 2018. President Trump has called himself smart six times before - ABC News (go.com)

Selk, Avi. "It's the 50th Anniversary of the Day Trump Left College and Nearly Had to Go to War." The Washington Post, May 20, 2018. Fifty years ago, Trump left Penn's Wharton School and nearly had to go to war - The Washington Post

Chait, Jonathan. "European Commission President Explains Trade to Trump with Simple Cards." New York Magazine, July 25, 2018. Trade Explained to Trump With 'Very Simple' Cards (nymag.com)

Edwards, Haley. "Crash Course Economics: International Trade." YouTube, uploaded by CrashCourse, January 15, 2015. What global trade deals are really about (hint: it's not trade) | Haley Edwards | TEDxMidAtlantic (youtube.com)

The Weekly Screed: August 5, 2018 (Volume II, Issue 31)

TO: The Donald: SH*T Sayer, #1

FROM: Kelly: Not MY President

- Howdy, Donald. I hope you are enjoying your vacation/MAGA-thon rally tour. Me, I'm working all month, plus house-sitting a friendly black cat named Chino, who loves to sit on my lap while we watch MSNBC.
- I realize it's the Dog Days of August; the last full month of reliably sweltering weather; the last gasp of estival leisure; and the calm before the storm when more (but still not most) Americans begin to focus on the mid-term elections. But I want you to know that I'm Still Paying Attention.
- As usual, I'm indulging in biblio-therapy, so my Summer Reading List includes titles such as <u>Bad Stories: What the Hell Just Happened to Our Country</u> and <u>The List: A Week-by-Week Reckoning of Trump's First Year.</u>
- The latter volume also sports this rationale for its existence on the cover: "Experts in authoritarianism advise to keep a list of things subtly changing around you, so you'll remember." Someday, we'll all look back on 2017 and…..laugh? Weep? Recall when books like this weren't banned??
- But the easiest read of them all is a little volume I checked out of the local library: <u>SH*T My President Says: The Illustrated Tweets of Donald J. Trump</u>. It was published last year, and includes pre-POTUS pronouncements, many of which are sparkly-shiny gems, including your very first tweet @RealDonaldTrump [May 4, 2009, trumpeting your appearance on Late Night with David Letterman].
- So I've decided that my four August missives to you will consider some of your twitter-patter from yesteryear, juxtaposed with contemporaneous blather from your increasingly unhinged tweets and circus performances.
- Example: "Do you think Putin will be going to The Miss Universe Pageant in November in Moscow – if so, will he become my new best friend?"
[@RealDonaldTrump June 18, 2013 11:17 PM]
- Compared to this (from your appearance before an audience of Trump-bots in Wilkes-Barre, PA on August 2): *"They [the disgusting media] wanted me to walk up and go like this,"* you said before you pretended to pummel Putin. *"They wanted me to go up and have a boxing match. Whatever happened to diplomacy?"* (Or, in this case, sycophancy.)
- Let's end today with a classic from November 10, 2012: "Many are saying I'm the best 140-character writer in the world. It's easy when it's fun."

- Still having fun, Donny? This citizen sees you as an angry ignoramus. SAD.

Resources - Volume II– Issue 31

Good afternoon, friends. I've decided to take it easy on all of us for the month of August because:
1) I hate summer (too darn hot and buggy) and 2) The Donald is "on vacation" so there <u>might</u> not be as many exciting emanations from D.C.

So for this and the next three Screeds, I plan to take my cue from a fun little book that you might enjoy: **<u>SH*T My President Says</u>** *(available from your local library if it's as progressive as the one in Lake Oswego, OR)*

Of course, this Current Occupant of the White House will never be "My President". My heart belongs to Barack. But I can't disregard an entertaining book just because I disagree with the title.

Books I'm reading NOW:

Almond, Steve. "Bad Stories: What the Hell Just Happened to Our Country." Bad Stories. (https://www.badstories.org/)

Siskind, Amy. "The List by Amy Siskind." Anchor. (https://anchor.fm/the-weekly-list)

Wheeler, Shannon. "SH*T My President Says: The Illustrated Tweets of Donald J. Trump." DoomRocket. (https://doomrocket.com/rr-shit-president-says/)

Trump Rally in Wilkes-Barre on 8/2/2018

Trump: Media wanted me to box with Putin | CNN Politics

The Weekly Screed: August 12, 2018 (Volume II, Issue 32)

TO: The Donald: SH*T Sayer, Exhibit #2

FROM: Kelly: Still Not MY President

- Greetings from the West Coast, DT. While you've been golfing on the East Coast, the rest of us have enjoyed the spectacle of your former Apprentice bestie, Omarosa, touting her new tell-all book *Unhinged*. Out next week!
- She revealed (and I'm SHOCKED) that you are "truly a racist," having come to this conclusion after listening to a tape of you using the N word.
- I'm reasonably certain that ALL of us will be treated to this recording in the near future, at which point you will deny that it is your voice, as you did in the aftermath of the Access Hollywood tape.
- But to bolster Omarosa's bold, staggering, and incendiary claim, we need look no further than your Very Own words in other settings. Herewith, a few of your Greatest Racist Hits:

  --In a 1993 radio interview, you opined that Native Americans in Connecticut were faking their ancestry. "I think I might have more Indian blood than a lot of the **so-called Indians that are trying to open up the reservations**."

  --"How is ABC Television allowed to have a show entitled 'Blackish'? Can you imagine the furor of a show, 'Whiteish'! Racism at highest level?"
  @realDonaldTrump - Oct. 1, 2014, 8:41 AM

  --You called the 1996 Miss Universe winner "Miss Housekeeping". Because she is from Venezuela, and you can't imagine any other occupation for Latinas.

  --At a June 2016 campaign rally, you pointed to one attendee and said: "Oh, look at **my African-American over here**. Look at him."
- At least, as Ivanka noted during an interview with Megyn Kelly in September of 2016: "My father can be an equal-opportunity offender." Such a comfort as we recall your soothing words from a year ago, as you noted "the very fine people, on both sides" who showed up for the murderous melee in Charlottesville, VA.
- Then yesterday, @realDonaldTrump - Aug. 11, 2018, 6:26 AM,
  "The riots in Charlottesville a year ago resulted in senseless death and division. We must come together as a nation. I condemn all types of racism and acts of violence. Peace to ALL Americans!"
- Well, maybe except Omarosa, who you now describe as a "lowlife"…or black football players, who "maybe shouldn't be in the country"…or…..

Resources - Volume II– Issue 32

Good afternoon..........I found a new little book. Looks to be self-published, from another bad poet like me, but I love the title: "Goodnight, Loon: Poems, Parodies and Jokes to Survive the Trump Presidency".
As we mark the first anniversary of our Dear Leader calling out neo-Nazis as "very fine people", here are some other notable utterances:

Alana Horowitz Satlin. "Omarosa Claims Trump Used the N-Word." HuffPost, August 10, 2018. Omarosa Claims Trump Repeatedly Used 'N-Word' During 'The Apprentice' | HuffPost Latest News

"Billy Bush Infuriated by Trump's Reported Claims on 'Access Hollywood' Tape." ABC News, December 4, 2017. Billy Bush 'infuriated' that Trump reportedly questioned authenticity of 'Access Hollywood' tape - ABC News (go.com)

Collins, Eliza. "Donald Trump's Attack on Alicia Machado." USA Today, September 27, 2016. Donald Trump: It's fine to describe ex-Miss Universe as 'Miss Piggy' (usatoday.com)

Rubin, Jennifer. "Trump Cannot Even Commemorate Charlottesville Correctly." The Washington Post, August 12, 2018. Opinion | Trump cannot even commemorate Charlottesville correctly - The Washington Post

Klein, Rick. "Trump's Both Sides on Charlottesville: Anniversary Puts Him on the Spot." ABC News, August 11, 2018. Trump said 'blame on both sides' in Charlottesville, now the anniversary puts him on the spot - ABC News (go.com)

McGraw, Meredith. "Trump Calls Omarosa a 'Low Life' as Sessions Feels 'Scared Stiff.'" ABC News, August 13, 2018. Trump calls Omarosa a 'low-life'; says Sessions is 'scared stiff' - ABC News (go.com)

Graham, David A. "Trump's Double Standard on Free Speech and the NFL." The Atlantic, May 24, 2018. Trump on Fox and Friends: NFL Protests vs. Free Speech - The Atlantic

The Weekly Screed: August 19, 2018 (Volume II, Issue 33)

TO: The Donald: SH*T Sayer, Exhibit #3

FROM: Kelly: Never will be MY President

- Salutations from the Peoples' Republic of Oregon, DT.
  You never come here to visit us. Thank you.
- I take it you are back from your "working vacation" and I'm sure you and your loving spouse are busy helping Barron get ready for "back to school."
- For your consideration, Office Depot is now offering a fine line of kiddie Kevlar products, including a bullet-proof backpack in either black or pink!
  It boasts a computer sleeve, but not a concealed carry pocket. Maybe in next year's model, depending on how many rampages the academic year brings.
- In the meantime, I see you are expending many tweets railing against Omarosa, her book *Unhinged*, and her purported audio- and video-tapes. Sinking to new depths, there was this at 7:31 AM on Tuesday:
  "When you give a crazed, crying lowlife a break, and give her a job at the White House, I guess it just didn't work out. Good work by General Kelly for quickly firing that dog!"
- Which was quickly countered by Pete Souza (the White House photographer for Obama and family) who posted a photo of Bo and Barack titled:
  "A real dog waiting for a real President."
  I have to tell you, Donald, it brought a little tear to my eye.
- Your canine castigations on Omarosa aside, this week also saw an increase in the comparisons between you and good old Nixon, as you added "enemies list" and "abuse of power" to the ongoing discussions of "obstruction of justice" and the probability that you will emerge from the Mueller investigation (at the very least) as an "unindicted co-conspirator."
- And as you compile the current Enumeration of Foes, here is a blast from the past (November 11, 2012 at 8:56 AM to be exact): "When someone attacks me, I always attack back…except 100x more. This has nothing to do with a tirade but rather, a way of life!"
- But here's the big difference between Nixon's road to resignation and the means by which **we** will end our present-day "long national nightmare": there are no Republicans with a spine who will challenge you. Gerald Ford replaced Nixon in August of 1974. I fear we be waiting till January 2021.

Resources - Volume II– Issue 33

Will summer NEVER end? Lordy I'm tired of this heat. Should break in a month or so....... Meantime, this isn't (of course) the sleepy pre-midterms-August we have experienced in the past.

Guard Dog Security ProShield II Tactical Backpack. Office Depot. Guard Dog Security ProShield II Tactical Laptop Backpack PinkBlack - Office Depot

Glasser, Susan B. "Dog Days of August, indeed." The New Yorker, August 14, 2018. Dog Days: Trump and His Toxic Twitter Insults of Omarosa | The New Yorker

A real dog waiting for a real President." Huffington Post, August 15, 2018. Pete Souza | A real dog waiting for a real President. #throwshadethenvote | Instagram

Robert Deis for Quote Investigator. "Our long national nightmare, circa 1974." This Day in Quotes, August 9, 2010. "Our long national nightmare is over." - This Day in Quotes

AlterNet Staff. "Our long national nightmare may soon be over. Here's why." AlterNet, August 10, 2018. Our Long National Nightmare May Soon Be Over -- Here's Why - Alternet.org

Doonesbury - Spineless Republican - by Garry Trudeau for August 12, 2018. Doonesbury - Spineless Republican - by Garry Trudeau for August 12, 2018 - GoComics

The Weekly Screed: August 26, 2018 (Volume II, Issue 34)

TO: The Donald: SH*T Sayer, Exhibit #4

FROM: Kelly: Shouldn't be <u>Anyone's</u> President

- Golly, Donald. Even for you, an unfortunate and awkward week. I was waiting for Mueller to declare you an "unindicted co-conspirator" but it looks like your "fixer" Michael Cohen beat him to the punch. But I think I'll focus on this 4th and final offering of the Month of Sundays of SH*T Saying on your complicated relationship with military service and Senator John McCain (R-AZ), may he rest in peace until his next incarnation.
- Your most egregious assessment of McCain (which would have pulverized the candidacy of any other presidential aspirant) came in 2015, at a town hall in Iowa: "He's not a war hero. He's a war hero because he was captured. I like people who weren't captured."
- But you'd had this McCain bee in your bonnet for a long time, hadn't you, DT? Back in 1999, in an interview with Dan Rather, you debuted your disdainful opinion of the Senator: "He was captured. Does being captured make you a hero? I don't know. I'm not sure."
- Because YOU considered <u>yourself</u> a war hero due to your avoidance of STDs, as you responded to radio shock-jock Howard Stern's *"Every vagina is a landmine, we've both said that,"* comment in 1998: "It is a dangerous world out there. It's scary, like Vietnam. Sort of like the Vietnam era," [you] said to Stern, discussing [your] sex life. "I feel like a great and very brave soldier." Mortal Combat, armed only with condoms.
- Say what you will about the Vietnam war in general, surviving 5+ years of torture as a prisoner of war might merit a few more plaudits than "being braver than any Vietnam vet because you're out there screwing a lot of women" [per Howard], which YOU then deemed deserving of "Getting the Congressional Medal of Honor, in actuality."
- I dunno, DT. You seem to exhibit all of the symptoms of tertiary neurosyphilis. Look it up......I'd get it checked out if I were you.
- By the way, free testing for syphilis is still covered under Obamacare, thanks to McCain's famous thumbs-down when the Senate tried to kill it last year.
- Fortunately for all of us, you have been pointedly disinvited to appear at McCain's funeral. Which means that (hopefully) your last word on this nemesis of yours will remain today's Instagram wishing your "deepest sympathies and respect to the family of John McCain" showing a photo of (who else?) YOU yourself gazing off into the sunset. What a feckless d*ck.

Resources - Volume II– Issue 34

Well, aren't we all "unindicted co-conspirators" at one time or another ?? What an informative week of Breaking News. The only time Trump caught a break was when McCain passed........but of course that then just served to draw comparisons and recall stupid statements from the past.

Miller, Hayley. "Fox News' Stunning About-Face on John McCain vs. Donald Trump." HuffPost, August 25, 2018. Fox News Analyst Calls Out Donald Trump Over Bland John McCain Condolences Tweet | HuffPost Latest News

BBC Staff. "Five times John McCain clashed with Donald Trump." BBC News, August 27, 2018. (https://www.bbc.com/news/world-us-canada-45313845)

Rosenberg, Alyssa. "What Donald Trump was up to while John McCain was suffering as a prisoner of war." The Washington Post, July 20, 2015. (https://www.washingtonpost.com/news/morning-mix/wp/2015/07/20/what-donald-trump-was-up-to-while-john-mccain-was-suffering-as-a-prisoner-of-war/?noredirect=on&utm_term=.587405baa51a)

Kelsey, Adam, and John Parkinson. "John McCain's Complicated Relationship with President Trump."** ABC News, August 26, 2018. (https://abcnews.go.com/Politics/john-mccains-complicated-relationship-president-trump/story?id=57398813)

Schwartz, Ian. "The Medical Theory Behind Donald Trump's Bizarre Behavior." The New Republic, February 15, 2017. (https://newrepublic.com/article/140702/medical-theory-donald-trumps-bizarre-behavior)

The Weekly Screed: September 2, 2018 (Volume II, Issue 35)

TO: The Donald: Flag Hugger

FROM: Kelly: At least I know what color it is

- Donald, Donald, Donald. I'm sure this week of listening to the endless encomiums to John McCain has been trying for you. I've pictured you sitting in front of the TV thinking: *if this LOSER gets a 10-day funeral, how grand and glorious will MINE be?* I'll bet you've started organizing it already. Maybe your old military school will put on a parade.
- But there's one aspect to the past few days that must have been beneficial for you. After all those hours staring at that flag-draped coffin, you should now have a better idea of which crayon to use, when faced with school children doing a much better job of coloring inside the lines of a flag outline.
- Hint: there are no BLUE stripes on the American standard. The BLUE part goes around the stars. The stripedy part is Red and White
- This lapse in mental acuity is troubling, DT. You've only been wearing a freaking flag lapel pin for years now. Do you close your eyes to put it on?
- And we've seen how you love to embrace Old Glory on stage, especially after delivering a really vile diatribe against immigrants. Here's what you do: you pace the stage, clapping for yourself and smirking, then you glom onto one of the hapless flags which is just standing there minding its own business and start rubbing your big old orange face and …other body parts….into it. It makes us squeamish. Get A Room !!!
- You did refrain from this unseemly display of affection for our national symbol in Evansville, Indiana the other night. Oh, how I love it when you venture into the Hoosier State. There's a certain…shall we say, quality…to the crowd that shows up for you there. They feed your darkly twisted soul.
- I can say this because I attended Indiana University in Bloomington for my Master's degree in Russian History. Back then, Republicans hated Commies. But Indiana still carried the stench of its KKK heyday in the 1920's, when (according to Wikipedia) approximately 30% of white men in Indiana, along with over half of the Indiana General Assembly, plus the Governor, were Klan members. While I was there in the early '70s, efforts to revive the glory days of the KKK were underway, and Richard Nixon felt the need to resign to avoid impeachment.
- But, as you praised the rabble last Thursday: "You love our country. You're proud of our history. And you always respect our great American flag." Yes, DT, your Very Special Brand of jingoism is…..unflagging.

Resources - Volume II– Issue 35

Greetings fellow laborers!
My theme this week is Donald Trump's appalling ignorance of, and unhealthy relationship to the American Flag. I hope you read it and laugh as hard as I did at some of this stuff. No matter what else happens, he still manages to crack me up every week.

De Maria, Meghan. "President Trump Colors American Flag Wrong During Visit to Ohio." HuffPost, August 27, 2018 This Photo Of President Trump Coloring An American Flag Has People Asking If He Knows What The Flag Looks Like | HuffPost Latest News

Aggeler, Madeleine. "Look at This Big Weirdo Fondling the Flag." The Cut, June 22, 2018 Donald Trump Hugged the American Flag Again (thecut.com)

Donald Trump Hugs American Flag.** YouTube, October 24, 2016. Donald Trump takes the stage and hugs an American flag in Tampa, Florida (youtube.com)

Cillizza, Chris. "Donald Trump Talks Economy and More in Evansville Speech." CNN, August 31, 2018. The 43 most staggering lines from Donald Trump's Indiana speech | CNN Politics

Courier Journal Staff. "KKK Cookout in Madison, Indiana Draws Hundreds Protesting."** Courier Journal, September 1, 2018.KKK cookout in Madison Indiana draws hundreds protesting (courier-journal.com)

The Weekly Screed: September 9, 2018 (Volume II, Issue 36)

TO: The Donald: Inspiring Marchers around the World!

FROM: Kelly: The Screed doesn't go on vacation…..

- DT, I'm spending several days of my Birthday Month vacation this year at the Bee-you-tee-full Oregon Coast. So I'm taking it easy on myself and forgoing my usual *hours* of research on the outrage of the week … which I'm not even aware of yet since I'm writing this early !
- Instead, I'd like to share with you the messages from some of the eloquent protest signs seen around and about. Think of it as opposition research, just so you can keep your itty-bitty fingers on the pulse of the American people.

1) From a lovely young woman in front of the White House: **TO THE WORLD: We're Sorry! Most of us voted against this idiot.**
2) Road sign with flashing lights: **Can we just admit we may have taken this "Anyone Can Grow Up To Be President" thing just a bit too far?**
3) From a gray-haired woman: **Don't Blame Trump – He did everything he could to prove he was unfit to be President.**
4) From a smiling redhead wearing sunglasses: **Does This Ass [photo of YOU] Make my Country Look Small?**
5) From a young woman in a head scarf: **2/3 of Trump's Wives Were Immigrants…proving once again we need immigrants to do the jobs most Americans wouldn't do.**
6) In bright red letters on an overpass: **Hurry Up, Mueller**
7) From Edinburgh: **Yer Maw was an Immigrant, ya Tangerine Roaster!**
8) From a woman in London: **We'll have a bigger parade when you go to jail**
9) From a smiling young girl wearing pink: **If you build a wall, MY generation will knock it down.**
10) Held up by a woman in a pink pussy cap: **We Shall Overcomb**
11) From a clean-cut young man: **I've seen better cabinets at IKEA**
12) My second personal favorite: **Sex offenders can't live in government housing (printed over a drawing of the White House)**
13) My Number One personal favorite: **Not all Trump supporters are racist, but all of them decided that racism isn't a deal breaker.**
14) And, finally, the one my sister usually carries to these events: **"Orange Lies Matter."**

Resources - Volume II– Issue 36

Good evening all y'all.........I've been off work for the past week, and on an actual weekend vacation for the last 3 days.

Yes, I've enjoyed hearing/reading about all about the various levels of White House resistance, but I'm hoping for future developments.... so I took inspiration from an email passed along from a friend which showed some very creative protest signs on the street.

No links this week, just "thanks, Duane!"............Kelly

The Weekly Screed: September 16, 2018 (Volume II, Issue 37)

TO: **Hurricane Donald**

FROM: **Kelly: They should name ALL of them after YOU**

MY hurricanes sure are magnificent things

I make myself feel really proud

Remember in San Juan I had an event where I threw paper towels at the crowd?

Obama and Sandy were really a joke.

He pretended to be presidential

I tweeted back then he just stood in the puddles and didn't do anything useful.

And don't get me started on Bush and Katrina

Now THAT was a catastrophe

Where THOUSANDS of people were killed…Oh, say what? Only one thousand, eight-ninety-three?

Now they're saying <u>three thousand</u> died due to Maria

Oh give me a break, I don't think so!

I know it's the Democrats making things up just to make me look bad. But what I know

Is I did really awesome in Houston with Harvey

I'm giving myself an A- Plus!

And Maria was really an unsung success, since those people aren't really like US.

But now a new hurricane season is coming

And I'm sure once again I'll do GREAT

And all of those people who criticize me are Big Haters who just like to HATE.

Because only My Ratings are all that's important when people are suff'ring and dying

And anyone who contradicts what I tweet out is only a LIAR who's LYING.

Resources - Volume II– Issue 37

Here in the Northwest, we don't get hurricanes. We're just waiting for the Big Earthquake !! In the meantime, Hurricane Donald strikes again.

Steward, Emily. "Trump Tweets False Claims About Puerto Rico Death Toll." Vox, September 15, 2018. Trump denies Puerto Rico death count again as Hurricane Florence hits | Vox

Wolf, Z.Byron. "George W. Bush on Donald Trump: Presidents respond differently to crises." CNN, September 12, 2018. George W. Bush vs. Donald Trump on hurricanes, 9/11 and everything else | CNN Politics

Lasker, Alix. "Trump sparks fury on Twitter with Hurricane Katrina comments." AOL, October 15, 2017 Trump sparks fury on Twitter with Hurricane Katrina comments (aol.com)

Messina, Victoria. "Donald Trump's Old Tweet About Obama and Hurricane Sandy Resurfaces." PopSugar, August 30, 2017. Donald Trump Old Tweet About Obama and Hurricane Sandy | POPSUGAR News

[The link to this tweet is broken, but here he tweeted in the third person. What a tool.]

"When Trump visited the island territory last October, OFFICIALS told him in a briefing 16 PEOPLE had died from Maria." The Washington Post. This was long AFTER the hurricane took place. Over many months it went to 64 PEOPLE. Then, like magic, "3000 PEOPLE KILLED." They hired....

...GWU Research to tell them how many people had died in Puerto Rico (how would they not know this?). This method was never done with previous hurricanes because other jurisdictions know how many people were killed. FIFTY TIMES LAST ORIGINAL NUMBER - NO WAY!"

--Trump, Donald. Twitter, @realDonaldTrump

September 14, 2018, 7:05 pm to 7:23 pm.

The Weekly Screed: September 23, 2018 (Volume II, Issue 38)

TO: The Donald: A Vast Orange Public Charge

FROM: Kelly: How low can you go?

- DT, I'd like to begin today's communiqué with a reminder of this pledge: *"I would rarely leave the White House because there's so much work to be done,"* you told <u>The Hill</u> in 2015. *"I would not be a president who took vacations. I would not be a president that takes time off."* While campaigning for the presidency in 2016, you announced: *"I'm going to be working for you. I'm not going to have time to go play golf."*
- As Saint Bernard de Clairvaux penned (c.1150), "The road to hell is paved with good intentions." And you have indeed taken us all to hell...maybe not in a handcart, but most certainly in your preferred conveyance: a golf cart.
- In fact, according to a September 6 report by <u>People</u> magazine you've spent around 20% of your first season as Celebrity President on the links, to the tune of around $77 million in American tax dollars. Over three hundred thousand of which were for golf cart fees alone.
- So I find it fitting that the Department of Homeland Security would choose this month to launch its latest attack on immigrants in the form of a "public charge" proposal. 447 pages in the Federal Register. Read all about it.
- Oh, I forgot. You don't read. So here's a summary: The concept of "public charge" surfaced in the Immigration Act of 1882, which denied entry to criminals, the insane, or "any person unable to take care of him or herself."
- Fast forward to 1996 and "welfare reform" under Bill Clinton, which substantially restricted access to public benefits for many low-income lawfully present immigrants and established the current delimitation of "public charge" benefits to Supplemental Security Income; cash assistance (e.g. Temporary Assistance for Needy Families, aka "welfare"); and long-term institutionalized care covered by Medicaid.
- Now comes the latest iteration, which considers a public charge to be a non-citizen "who is likely at any time to use or receive one or more public benefits" which have been expanded to include food, energy, or housing assistance; WIC; or health care, to which they and their families (*including their US citizen children*) are currently legally entitled.
- Approximately one in four children has at least one immigrant parent. In the Trump Crime Family, it's four out of five! And now a noxious, bigoted, misogynistic, corrupt, filthy-rich grandson, son, and husband of immigrants is, by far, the biggest burden ever charged to the American public.

Resources - Volume II– Issue 38

Hello everyone. Today's topic concerns something my work team and I have been expecting and dreading: the new, mean-spirited, "public charge" rule from the Department of Homeland Security. Ostensibly designed to save American taxpayers $2.7 billion annually by discouraging low-income legally present immigrants from accessing public benefits <u>to which they are entitled</u>, its actual aim is to reduce the number of immigrants. Period.

The new low: it would apply to benefits received or applied for during the past 36 months, AND it would also affect immigrant families, including children. Including US citizen children. In Oregon, rumors of this proposed policy have had a deleterious effect on our latest expansion of the Oregon Health Plan to all low-income children in the state, regardless of immigration status. People are understandably freaked out and worried that if they apply for health coverage, they will be deported, or prohibited from getting a green card, or be unable to reunite with other family members. Meanwhile, we're funding millions in golf vacations for the Worst Person in America. Read it and weep.

Zauzmer, Emily. "Donald Trump Has Charged U.S. Taxpayers More Than $300,000 in Golf Cart Rentals." People, September 6, 2018. Donald Trump's Golf Cart Rentals Cost Taxpayers $300K: Report (people.com)

"Hand cart? Handbasket?" The Phrase Finder. To hell in a handcart - phrase meaning and origin (phrases.org.uk)

GCIR. September 2018. DHS Proposes Vast Changes to Public Charge Definition | Grantmakers Concerned with Immigrants and Refugees (gcir.org)

Merelli, Annalisa. "Ivanka Trump Says Her Mother Came to the US Legally Thanks to Visa Scam." Quartz, August 2, 2018. Ivanka Trump says her mother Ivana came to the US legally. But only thanks to an earlier visa scam (qz.com)

Blake, Aaron. "Analysis: The Huge Questions About Melania Trump's Immigration History Nobody Will Answer." National Post, February 22, 2018. Analysis: The huge questions about Melania Trump's immigration history nobody will answer | National Post

The Weekly Screed: September 30, 2018 (Volume II, Issue 39)

TO: The Donald: Did you even watch her?

FROM: Kelly: Staying tuned in to future developments

- DT, we all know that your specialty is prevarication. But on Thursday, at 3:46 PM, you finally tweeted an unvarnished truth: "Judge Kavanaugh showed America exactly why I nominated him". Indeed.
- As we get to know him, it appears your boy Brett is proving himself to be just like YOU. Let us count the ways:
  1) He's a pervert (prone to penis waving as opposed to pussy grabbing) and sexual predator (although HIS accusers still number in the single digits).
  2) He's a stone-cold liar, like when he kicked off his "acceptance speech" lauding your unparalleled efforts to vet other possible nominees. Gimme a break. We know you picked him cuz he's the only jurist in the country who maintains that a sitting President is completely above the law.
  3) And when he isn't outright lying, he's being evasive as hell (when trying to answer Senators Harris and Feinstein about Mueller, "precedent," and "the male body"). Really, DT, you gotta watch the tape.
  4) And when he's not being evasive, he's indulging in shameless hyperbole. While unable to play the race card (like the last most odious nominee to appear before the Senate Judiciary Committee in 1991), he *was* able to throw down the Clinton card. [Yeah, this whole thing was cooked up to exact revenge for his antics during the Ken Starr investigation of Bill.]
  5) He's recklessly RUDE. Can you imagine anyone else in a job interview querying the members of the panel about their drinking habits?
  6) He has the judicial temperament of a rabid squirrel.
  7) He's a drunk. And (reportedly) a mean drunk at that. But he does enjoy a cold brewski: "I liked beer. Still like beer. I embrace drinking beer." It's his way of connecting to all the mouth-breathers in the Red States.
- Oh, wait!! I hear *you* are a teetotaler, which means that you are guilty of traits 1 through 5 without the benefit (or excuse) of any mind-altering substances. But hey…..sober or inebriated, it's gratifying to see you two share the same elitist, entitled, faux-Christian, and White Guy values.
- Donald, I know you enjoy hearing what's going on in MY life from time to time. At work, our team is in the throes of Strategic Planning; "re-branding" our unit; and crafting a new Vision Statement, Mission Statement, and "elevator speech" in order to be able to make a concise

and convincing asseveration about why we show up to the office every day.
- But nothing we come up with will be even a fraction as compelling as what was said by the two women who confronted Sen. Jeff Flake on Friday. That was an Elevator Speech for the Ages, and it may turn this whole thing around.

Resources - Volume II– Issue 39

Good evening all.........I thought I had the Screed written in my head on Thursday night, but (as so often happens) events took a dramatic turn (at least for the better this time) and the re-writing began. I didn't even have space to make fun of his second UN appearance! Or the press conference that followed......... But I'll give you a link in case you didn't catch it. Hilarious.

Pants on Fire. An update:

Kessler, Glenn, Salvador Rizzo, and Meg Kelly. "President Trump Has Made More Than 5,000 False or Misleading Claims."** The Washington Post, September 13, 2018. President Trump has made more than 5,000 false or misleading claims - The Washington Post

Brett Kavanaugh Gets a Hearing

Meyers, Seth. "A Closer Look: Trump's Latest Chaos." YouTube, September 26, 2018. Trump Holds Crazy Press Conference to Defend Brett Kavanaugh: A Closer Look (youtube.com)

Noah, Trevor. "The Daily Show: Kamala Harris Brings the Heat at Kavanaugh Hearing." YouTube. September 6, 2018. Kamala Harris Brings the Heat at Kavanaugh Hearing | The Daily Show (youtube.com)

Noah, Trevor. "The Daily Show: Trevor Noah's Summary of the Hearing." YouTube, September 27, 2018. Dr. Christine Blasey Ford Testifies Against Brett Kavanaugh | The Daily Show (youtube.com)

Kavanaugh, Brett. "Brett Kavanaugh Likes Beer." YouTube, September 27, 2018. 2023.07 Expand Background Checks 2 (youtube.com)

Malveaux, Suzanne. "Jeff Flake's Elevator Moment: A Reporter's Notebook." CNN, September 30, 2018. Jeff Flake, Ana Maria Archilla and Maria Gallagher: The elevator moment | CNN Politics

The Weekly Screed: October 7, 2018 (Volume II, Issue 40)

TO: The Donald: Make 'em laugh

FROM: Kelly: Not always the best medicine

- Happy Anniversary, DT. I'm recalling that it was merely two short years ago *today* that the nation tuned in to the 2005 "Access Hollywood "audio of your confession to sexual predation. Your intended audience was one nincompoop and sycophant, Billy Bush, who lost his job on NBC *Today* after we heard him yukking it up as you regaled him with your sexploits.
- Oh, yeah, and we also didn't appreciate the way he pimped out your next target: Arianne Zucker, his NBC colleague and a soap star on *Days of our Lives*, where you were arriving to perform a cameo. [#Tic-Tacs]
- In recent Days of our Lives, we have borne witness to other instances of unexpected or inappropriate merriment:
  1) The first was in reaction to your speechifying at the United Nations General Assembly on September 25, where you informed the astonished multitude that "in less than two years" your Amerika First scoundrels had "accomplished more than almost any administration in the history of our country." After a slight delay for translation, guffaws ensued.
  [And I would beg to differ, DT. While you and your minions *have done* your utmost to destroy the economy (tax cuts for rich guys; trade wars); the environment (radiation is good for us!); and the Affordable Care Act, you can't hold a candle to 9/11 and the Shock and Awe wars we got in the first two years of Billy's cousin Dubya Bush's Reign of Terror.]
  2) On September 27, we learned from psychology professor Dr. Christine Blasey Ford that the most painful memory of her encounter with Brett Kavanaugh and his buddy Mark Judge [come on, you know they did it] was: "…the laughter, the laugh – the uproarious laughter between the two, and their having fun at my expense."
  3) Never missing an opportunity to kick someone when they are down, you took your cue from this anguished testimony to make sport of Dr. Ford's memory lapses concerning the tangential details surrounding this traumatic event. At a rally of a repugnant racist rabble in Southaven, Mississippi, you spurred the mob to hoots and jeers with your unforgivable (and erroneous) mockery of a sexual assault survivor. Man, you KILLED it! Got 'em all energized for the "Lock her up" chant.

- Donald, I try to laugh AT you as often as possible. I know you haven't hit rock bottom. I'm braced for your next shameful (but hopefully risible) act.

Resources - Volume II– Issue 40

Good afternoon all......well, another dreadful man has been appointed to the Supremes. It's certainly the most shameful elevation since Clarence Thomas, and we await to see the new depths this court can reach. Can it get worse than Bush v. Gore?? Maybe.

Seth Meyers: A Closer Look. YouTube, October 3, 2018.
Trump Melts Down over Dr. Ford's Testimony: A Closer Look (youtube.com)

"Donald Trump Access Hollywood Tape." Wikipedia, September 15, 2018.
Donald Trump Access Hollywood tape - Wikipedia

CNN Staff. "Trump's UN General Assembly Speech Reaction." CNN, September 25, 2018.
Trump at UN: I didn't expect that reaction | CNN Politics

Vagianos, Alanna. "Christine Blasey Ford's Strongest Memory: Kavanaugh's Laughter." HuffPost, September 27, 2018.
Christine Blasey Ford Recalls 'Uproarious Laughter' During Alleged Sexual Assault | HuffPost Latest News

Guardian News. "Donald Trump Mocks Dr. Ford's Testimony in Mississippi."YouTube, October 2, 2018.
'I don't know': laughter as Trump mocks Ford's sexual assault testimony (youtube.com)

The Weekly Screed: October 14, 2018 (Volume II, Issue 41)

TO: The Donald: Hat and Hate Mongerer

FROM: Kelly: Consider me your personal book club

- Donald, from time to time I like to check into one of my new favorite books: *The List* by Amy Siskind. It's subtitled: "A week-by-week reckoning of Trump's first year" and provides me with perspective on recent antics.
- For example, this week last year, you were golfing for the fourth weekend in a row after Hurricane Maria hit Puerto Rico. And today, you spent your 210th day at the links on the first weekend after Hurricane Michael wiped out the Florida panhandle. Consistency!
- On the other hand, one short year ago, Senator Bob Corker (R-TN) who is not running for re-election, threw down major shade on you, declaring the White House "an adult day care center." Then this October he cemented his legacy as a Trumpeter by voting "Aye" on perjurer and sexual assaulter Brett Kavanaugh (officially sworn in last Sunday night). Cowardly cave-in!
- The other book I revisited this week was a Dr. Seuss favorite: *The Cat in the Hat* (1957). I was struck by its description of the chaos created by the feline sporting the iconic red-and-white-striped chapeau. He invades the home of two little kids and unleashes Thing One and Thing Two to add to the havoc.
- So let's examine a couple of events in this week's Celebrity President show:
    1) Thing One was the spectacle of Kanye West's "crazy mother-f***er" [his words, not mine] rant in the Oval Office on Wednesday. Tucker Carlson of Fox Noise described it thusly: "Sprinkled throughout his ramblings are flashes of truth, real insights into the way the world actually is rather than the way they tell us it is." And those sprinkles of sagacity informed the nation that the 13th Amendment was actually just a trapdoor to the Unabomber; Gang Lord Larry Hoover should be pardoned and set loose on the streets of Chiraq; and his Make-America-Great-Again headgear makes him feel like Superman. Which is doubly pathetic considering that the S-Man sported a cape, not a cap; and the word "Great" in MAGA is actually code for WASP, to which Kanye (let's face it) can never aspire.
    2) Thing Two was 2 more rotten rallies (this week in Iowa and Kentucky) where you railed against the Fake News media; goaded the crowd to lock up Dianne Feinstein; and gushed over KY's 2 loathsome Senators. Rand Paul is "young and spry."

3) And, Mitch McConnell is now "the greatest leader in history" and a "tough cookie." As opposed to "a smart cookie," the accolade you gave Kanye West, this week's Cat in the MAGA Hat.

Resources - Volume II– Issue 41

Good evening, all. Another ridiculous week. To top it off, I somehow accidentally deleted this Contact Group and have spent the past 4 hours (including a phone call to AOL Tech Support in Makati, Philippines) reconstructing. It's now saved in 4 formats. Ugh.

Golfing again

Darby, Luke. "Trump Golfs While Puerto Rico Faces Crisis." GQ, September 30, 2017. How Trump's Golf Weekend Made the Crisis in Puerto Rico Worse | GQ

Edwards, David. "Trump Spends 210th Day Golfing as President While Hurricane Michael Victims Pick Up the Pieces." Raw Story, October 14, 2018 Trump spends 210th day golfing as president while Hurricane Michael victims pick up the pieces - Raw Story

Kanye in the House

CNN Staff. "Kanye West's Meeting with President Trump at the White House." CNN, October 11, 2018. Trump spends 210th day golfing as president while Hurricane Michael victims pick up the pieces - Raw Story

Rosenberg, Eli. "Kanye West's White House Visit Praised by Tucker Carlson." The Independent, October 12, 2018. How Fox News covered Kanye West's White House visit compared to rappers during the Obama years | The Independent | The Independent

Lock her up

Scott, Eugene. "Trump, His Supporters and 'Lock Her Up': Due Process Gives Way." The Washington Post, October 11, 2018. For Trump and his supporters, due process gives way to 'Lock her up!' - The Washington Post

The Weekly Screed: October 21, 2018 (Volume II, Issue 42)

TO: The Donald: I'm not a baby.

FROM: Kelly: True. Most people like babies.

- DT, even from you, it was a startling denial. During your discomfiting duologue with Lesley Stahl on CBS's 60 Minutes last Sunday, you *twice* proclaimed: "I'm not a baby".
- The first instance occurred with Lesley pressed you to justify your adoration of North Korean dictator Kim Jong Un ("We fell in love"), in light of his somewhat spotty record of supporting even the most basic human rights:
  "Sure, I know all these things. I mean, I'm not a baby"
- Then came this: *"...I'm not saying I trust everybody in the White House. I'm not a baby. It's a tough business. This is a vicious place."*
- Donald, this bold declaration of non-babyhood proudly enters the pantheon of pathetic POTUS disavowals:
  1) I am not a crook
  2) I did not have sex with that woman
  3) I don't know why it *would* be Russia
  4) No collusion! No collusion!
  [Oh wait....those last 2 are yours too.]
- But I digress. Later on in the broadcast, you *did* identify who IS a baby: *"So I always used to say the toughest people are Manhattan real estate guys and blah, blah. Now I say they're babies."* [e.g., Don Junior, Eric, Jared?]
- In addition to the abjuration of infant status, you pretty much spent the remainder of the conversation denying:
  a) Russian meddling in the 2016 campaign *"I think China meddled too."*
  b) Trying to push China into an economic depression
  c) The notion that your family separation strategy is any different from Barack Obama's
  d) The very idea that you were in any way disrespectful of Dr. Ford *"It doesn't matter. We won."*
  e) And, last but not least, climate change: *"You'd have to show me the scientists because they have a very big political agenda."*
- Which might be what, DT? Maintaining life on earth for the entire world??
- But back to the baby meme (which I have to tell you is trending bigly): Here's hoping for calm weather in L.A. this week as the Diaper Donald blimp makes an appearance at Politicom. I hear it's unstable in high winds.

Resources - Volume II– Issue 42

Here in Oregon, our ballots arrived in the mail this past week. We need to make this one count. And I finally got around to seeing Michael Moore's latest movie: Fahrenheit 11/9. What a downer! But everyone in America should see it......Hope everyone found the 60 Minutes interview as entertaining as I did ! I just love it when he doesn't have a script.

I'm President and you're not.

Greene, Michael. "Trump's Recent Remarks on Various Topics." YouTube, October 15, 2018. Message from Donald J. Trump (youtube.com)

Not just a river in Egypt

Qui, Linda. "17 Things Donald Trump Said and Then Denied Saying." Politifact, July 6, 2016. PolitiFact | 17 times Donald Trump said one thing and then denied it

Graham, Ruth. "Denial: Exploring the Concept and Its Implications." The Washington Post, July 6, 2016. A history of denial (washingtonpost.com)

Helium Diaper Donald Blimp

Gumbel, Andrew. "Donald Trump Baby Blimp Comes to Los Angeles for Politicon." The Guardian, October 17, 2018. Trump baby blimp to greet commuters over Los Angeles freeways | Donald Trump | The Guardian

Lacitas, Erik. "Baby Trump Blimp Arrives on Vashon Island."The Seattle Times, August 20, 2018. 'Trump Baby' blimp arrives on Vashon Island | The Seattle Times

Long may the Baby Blimp wave !!

The Weekly Screed: October 28, 2018 (Volume II, Issue 43)

TO: The Donald: Ode to the MAGA Bomber

FROM: Kelly: [channeling The Donald's stream of consciousness]

It's too bad that my MAGA guy was captured by the FBI.
At first, I tried to make you see the fake bombs sent to Hillary
And CNN were just a hoax. Amazingly, most of you folks
Weren't buying that! So then I tried to say the *media* had lied
And *they* were who was most to blame for screwing up my great campaign.

I'd done my best to drum up fear of caravans: They're coming here
to rape our women and sell dope! Take all our jobs and shatter hope
that this great land could once again be safe for every Common Man
who likes his beer and loves his guns and wishes that the South had won.

We had a boost from Kavanaugh; those nasty Me-Too women saw
Republicans could hold the fort and send a pervert to the Court.
Just like old times! Boys will be boys. Ignore the protests and the noise
and give the FBI five days to make the trouble go away.

Yeah, everything was going fine till Cesar got it in his mind
To take out all my enemies. And now it's clear for all to see
The "False Flag" theory cannot fly. The bomber was a MAGA guy.

Resources - Volume II– Issue 43

Friends, I can only handle one attack a week............this time it's the MAGA Bomber. I'll try to deconstruct the Pittsburgh shooting next week. Unless something even worse happens. Which is always a possibility in Amerika today.

Blame the media

Miller, Haley Sweetland. "Donald Trump Blames Media for 'Anger' After Suspicious Packages Sent to Democrats." HuffPost, October 25, 2018. Donald Trump Attacks 'Hateful' Media Amid Flurry Of Suspicious Packages | HuffPost Latest News

The good ole' Hitler Days

Murdock, Sebastian. "Bomb Suspect Cesar Sayoc Wanted to 'Go Back to the Hitler Days,' Former Boss Says." AOL, October 18, 2018. Bomb suspect Cesar Sayoc 'wanted to go back to the Hitler days,' former boss says (aol.com)

The importance of spell-check

Corcoran, Kieran. "A stray fingerprint and bad spelling helped the FBI pin down the mail bombing suspect." Business Insider. October 27, 2018. Cesar Sayoc Pinned Down by FBI Thanks to Fingerprint, Bad Spelling - Business Insider

Like "father" like "son"

Cox, James. "MAGA Bomber Cesar Sayoc's Lawyer Claims His Father Was in Trump's 'Inner Circle'." The Sun, October 27, 2018. MAGA bomber suspect 'speaks like a child and found a father in Donald Trump', his lawyer says | The Sun

The Weekly Screed: November 4, 2018 (Volume II, Issue 44)

TO: The Donald: "When I can, I tell the truth"

FROM: Kelly: Maybe the truest thing you've ever said

- I have to say, Donald, you have really outdone yourself in the mendacity department these past few days. Mark Twain popularized this quote in 1906: "There are three kinds of lies: lies, damned lies, and statistics."
- And while you have often employed wildly inaccurate numbers to enhance your prevarications, I feel the need to categorize most of your recent statements into a fourth and very specific type of falsehood: Election Lies.
- One of the silliest of these came on October 22 when you announced a new 10% tax cut for the middle class and promised a resolution on this latest budget busting idea "in the next week or two." Dude, that would make it *before* the midterm election…. and when Congress has left the building.
- I get that it was just a panic attack during the week that the stock market was tanking (and wiping out all year-to-date gains), but….even from you, it was a whopper!
- In another effort to cover up the fact that your really stoopid tariff threats are doing harm to the economy in the aggregate and actual live people in particular, you tweeted on November 1 that "discussions were moving along nicely" with China.
- Sadly, this lie was almost immediately disavowed by your Fox & Friends economic advisor, Larry Kudlow: "…we are not on the cusp of a deal."
- So having decided that running on the Wall Street economy and the tax cut for Rich Old Guys might not play real great with the baser elements of your base, you opted for the sure-fire pitch: Fear & Loathing of the Other.
- "I'm a Nationalist," you've been [Jim] crowing to the vanilla red-state multitudes in the past few weeks…….forgoing the standard adjective "white" but admitting that "we're not supposed to use that word."
- Hmmm, I wonder why? Maybe one reason is because it's the first word in the National Socialist German Workers' Party (aka the Nazi Party) which turned out to be less about socialist workers and more about purifying the Fatherland by eliminating gypsies, homosexuals, and Jewish "elements".
- But it does play neatly into your demonization of George Soros: a Jew who fled Nazi-occupied Hungary only to be currently accused of funding both the Brett Kavanaugh protesters AND the invading hordes from Honduras.

- There's 50 shopping days left until Christmas but only two more lying days left until the election! I'm sure you'll make the most of them.

Resources - Volume II– Issue 44

Good evening, all. Fingers crossed for Tuesday !! Of course, I don't believe anything good until it happens.
In the immortal words of Mel Brooks: "Hope for the best....Expect the worst":
Hope for the Best, Expect the Worst - Mel Brooks (youtube.com)

Don Lemon Tonight. "Donald Trump: 'When I Can, I Tell the Truth'." CNN, November 1, 2018. Trump: I always want to tell the truth | CNN Politics)

Heath, Thomas. "Trump's Trade Dares Have Vaporized the Dow's Gains for 2018." The Washington Post, June 29, 2018. Trump's trade dares have vaporized the Dow's gains for 2018 - The Washington Post

Jones, Chuck. "Trump's Fake Midterm Economic News: 10% Tax Cut and China Deal." Forbes, November 3, 2018 Trump's 10% Middle-Class Tax Cut And China Trade Progress Is Fake News Before The Midterm Elections (forbes.com)

Sonmez, Felicia. "Trump: 'I'm a Nationalist and I'm Proud of It'." The Washington Post, October 23, 2018. Trump: I'm a nationalist and I'm proud of it - The Washington Post

Levin, Bess. "George Soros and the Caravan: How Trump Has Spread Fear of Migrants." Vanity Fair, October 31, 2018. Trump: "A Lot of People Say" George Soros Is Funding the Migrant Caravan | Vanity Fair

Streisand, Barbra. "Barbra Streisand's Lullaby to The Donald – Don't Lie to Me" YouTube, October 9, 2018. (2016) Barbra Streisand - Don't Lie to Me (Official Video) - YouTube

The Weekly Screed: November 11, 2018 (Volume II, Issue 45)

TO: The Donald: Midterms! Who Knew?

FROM: Kelly: Voting NRA in Oregon

- Donald, I know that this was a stressful week for you. You were so discombobulated by the pending menace of Nancy Pelosi taking over from that wretched lame-duck-lame-ass House Speaker Ryan that you declared Tuesday's election a "Big Victory" for you and your ilk.
- But, in a way, I agree with you. To be sure, I am exceedingly relieved that Democrats will take back the House of Representatives in January. But what continues to baffle and sadden me are two things:
- Thing One -- that ANY voter with either a functioning heart or brain would vote for ANY candidate with an "R" after his or her name, or
- Thing Two – that ANY registered voter would sit out this election. I know, most people don't pay attention. Hell, even YOU didn't pay attention most of your life. In ***FEAR,*** by Bob Woodward, he recounts an exchange between you and David Bossie (big Clinton Hater) who is trying to explain government to you in 2010, when you were considering running for Prez.
- He informs you that your voting record might be a problem…..like, you only voted in one primary election in your entire life. [1988, when you voted for Rudy Giuliani]. *"That's a fu***g lie,"* as you so eloquently retorted.
- Then, on Monday night, you rallied the dimwits assembled at the International Convention Center in Cleveland with these immortal words:

    "Whoever even heard of 'midterm'? They don't even know what it is. I've had a lot of people say: 'I don't know what "midterm" is, but now I'm watching every single minute. And I'm going out to vote.' But the key is you have to go out to vote. Because in a sense I am on the ticket."
- You even tell them they are as ignorant as you are, and they still worship you; chant "Lock Her Up" and vote the Trump ballot. SAD.
- But back to Thing One: I cannot, for the life of me, understand how there is even one lousy Republican left standing after the catastrophe we've witnessed for the past two years. This is why I'm completely committed to my new voting strategy: NRA. No Republicans Anywhere.
- Circa Ronald Regan, I abandoned the GOP in state and federal elections; only Democrats got my vote. But now I'm ferreting out closet Rs running in "non-partisan" elections. I don't want them for city council, school board, judge, sheriff, clerk of the court, sewer commissioner, or dog catcher.

- NRA! NRA! NRA! Has a familiar ring to it, doncha think?

Resources - Volume II– Issue 45

Greetings, and a happy 100th Anniversary of the end of World War I.
With the election, the on-going counts and re-counts, another rampage by a red-blooded white American male with a gun, killer wildfires, and the idiot POTUS in Paris, this week has dragged on forever. In fact, I got a jump-start on the stress by having my car's right front axle completely disintegrate Monday morning on my way to work. The 20-something tow guy arrived and while we were hooking up my sad old Subaru, we had a lively discussion on health care (he has it through his employer), his divorce and whether I thought he should try to get custody of his kids and move back to L.A., and what was going on in the election tomorrow? What was it about? I wound up explaining how the Congress works, and how impeachment works, and why for the love of all that is holy he needed to get registered, and VOTE in 2020. Not too sure we got anything sorted out. Worst news of the day: they were able to fix my car, so no new red Cadillac in my near future. All of which leads up to the subject of this week's rant. Bill Maher on HBO has given us permission to take the next year off from politics. Would that I could but The Screed must go on.

Paschal, Olivia; Carlisle, Madeleine. "The Most Notable Moments From Trump's Press Conference." The Atlantic, November 7, 2018 Trump Attacks Jim Acosta, and More, in Press Conference - The Atlantic

Ward, Alex. "Trump Calls Midterms a 'Big Victory' Despite House Loss." Vox, November 7, 2018 Trump calls midterm election results a "Big Victory." That's not true. | Vox

Waxman, Olivia B. "Why Do Midterm Elections Even Exist? Here's Why the Framers Scheduled Things This Way." TIME. November 5, 2018. What Are Midterm Elections and Why Are They Every Two Years? | TIME

The Weekly Screed: November 18, 2018 (Volume II, Issue 46)

TO: The Donald: Very Scary Times

FROM: Kelly: You Too

- Donald, I know I've been hard on you. Just because you are the most despicable person ever to occupy the Oval Office doesn't mean you can't seek redemption. So in this and (a few) future issues, I'm going to try to help you become more…palatable… to the general public.
- Let's start with Law and Order. Yesterday saw a rally in downtown Portland organized by the "Patriot Prayer" scoundrels on behalf of the "Him Too" movement. You know, the pitiful privileged white guys who are currently having a more difficult time getting away with sexual assault.
- Understandably, the Me-Too movement has rocked your world. And maybe that's one reason why you've suddenly embraced "prison reform". But I've read the highlights of the First Step bill and found it wanting.
- Why settle for a First Step? Why not be a real leader and shoot for the Whole Enchilada? I'd like to direct your admittedly brief attention span to a couple of Oregon initiatives which celebrated their 20th anniversaries this very month:
- The first is **Girl Scouts Beyond Bars**. For several years I served on the board of the Girl Scouts and was a volunteer with this program. A couple of Saturdays a month, girls visit the Coffee Creek Correctional Facility where their incarcerated female family members (mothers, grandmothers, aunts, sisters) are able to function as Troop Leaders. Songs, crafts, the GS pledge, all of it. Studies have shown that girls with a relative in prison are five times more likely to wind up in the criminal justice system themselves. And that maintaining contact with family members reduces that risk and results in less recidivism among released inmates. So fund *this* wonderful program nation-wide. Expand it to the Boy Scouts with fathers in prison. Be a hero.
- Even more relevant to prison reform would be to instantly reduce the prison population by legalizing cannabis nationwide. **The Oregon Medical Marijuana Act** passed with 56% of the vote in November of 1998. I was the first manager of the program, and the Oregon Health Division issued the first ever medical cannabis registration card in the nation in May of 1999.

- Now around 2/3 of the States enjoy some form of legal weed: either medical and/or adult use. You've already fired that Evil Elf, Attorney General Jefferson Beauregard Sessions, who once opined that "Good people don't smoke marijuana." Next step: Become the POTUS of Pot. Go for it.

Resources - Volume II– Issue 46

Good evening, all…We still have Donald Trump around to cast a pall on the holidays. This week I'm giving him some friendly advice about "prison reform".

Yan, Holly; Chavez, Nicole. "Trump says it's a 'scary time' for men. Here are the stats on false sexual assault claims." CNN, October 3, 2018. Sexual assault false reporting: What the statistics say | CNN

Dicker, Ron. " Donald Trump's Prison Reform Ideas Look Real Suspicious To Seth Meyers." HuffPost, November 17, 2018. Donald Trump's Prison Reform Ideas Look Real Suspicious To Seth Meyers | HuffPost Entertainment

Ockerman, Emma. "Here's What's in the Prison Reform Bill Trump Just Backed. "Vice News, November 15, 2018. Here's what's in the prison reform bill Trump just backed (vice.com)

Girl Scouts of Oregon and Southwest Washington. "Girl Scouts Beyond Bars." Girl Scouts of Oregon and Southwest Washington. Girl Scouts Beyond Bars | Girl Scouts (girlscoutsosw.org)

Crombie, Noelle. "Legal Marijuana in Oregon: A Look at the State's Pot History." The Oregonian, November 4, 2014 Legal marijuana in Oregon: A look at the state's pot history - oregonlive.com

McCarthy, Justin "Two in Three Americans Support Legalizing Marijuana." Gallup, October 22,2018 Two in Three Americans Now Support Legalizing Marijuana (gallup.com)

We all have more blessings than most of the people in the world. Have a Happy Thanksgiving…………Kelly

The Weekly Screed: November 25, 2018 (Volume II, Issue 47)

TO: The Donald: Thank you for letting me be myself, again

FROM: Kelly: As if we had a choice

A week of Thanksgiving Haiku from our Dear Leader:

Tuesday, November 20:

"They are tough people,"
The troops missing Thanksgiving,
Proud at the border.

Wednesday, November 21

Two ungrateful fowl:
I pardoned "Peas" and "Carrots."
Children should eat them.

Thursday, November 22

My friend MBS:
Did he murder Khashoggi?
"Maybe he didn't."

Thursday, November 22

All that I have done
Makes me grateful for myself
"Tremendous diff'rence!"

Friday, November 23

I say it's COLD now!
Science says globe is warming
Climate change a Hoax!!

Sunday, November 25

Oil prices so low
Oh "thank you President T"
"Like a big Tax Cut!"

Resources - Volume II– Issue 47

Greetings and blessings upon you all! Isn't it special that we have a POTUS who is most grateful for <u>himself</u> on Thanksgiving? That old song from Sly and the Family Stone popped into my head, so your first link is to the (truly bizarre) lyrics. Then, I took the news of the week as inspiration for some Turkey Time haiku. 17 syllables each. 3 lines of 5-7-5 syllables. It's harder than it looks.

"Sly and the Family Stone - Thank You (Falettinme Be Mice Elf Agin) Lyrics."AZLyrics.(https://www.azlyrics.com/lyrics/slythefamilystone/thankyoufalettinmebemiceelfagin.html)

Klar, Rebecca. "Trump: 'Don't Worry About Troops' Spending Thanksgiving at Border." *The Hill*, 20 Nov. 2018. (https://thehill.com/homenews/administration/417700-trump-dont-worry-about-troops-spending-thanksgiving-at-border) .

"Colbert: Trump Pardons Peas, Carrots, and Saudi Arabia." *RealClearPolitics*, 21 Nov. 2018. (https://www.realclearpolitics.com/video/2018/11/21/colbert_trump_pardons_peas_carrots_and_saudi_arabia.html)

"Donald Trump Says He's Thankful for Himself at Thanksgiving." *The Guardian*, 22 Nov. 2018. (https://www.theguardian.com/us-news/video/2018/nov/23/donald-trump-says-hes-thankful-for-himself-at-thanksgiving-video) .

Nuccitelli, Dana. "The Trump Administration Has Entered Stage 5 Climate Denial." *The Guardian*, 8 Oct. 2018. (https://www.theguardian.com/environment/climate-consensus-97-per-cent/2018/oct/08/the-trump-administration-has-entered-stage-5-climate-denial) .

Reuters. "Trump Aims Tweet at Migrant Caravans as Holiday Break Ends." *AOL*, 25 Nov. 2018.(https://www.aol.com/article/news/2018/11/25/trump-aims-tweet-at-migrant-caravans-as-holiday-break-ends/23600147/) .

The Weekly Screed: December 2, 2018 (Volume II, Issue 48)

TO: The Donald: MAGA in Mississippi

FROM: Kelly: Prefer "Becoming" in Chicago

- Oh, Donald. Another unfortunate week for you. Your former shady fixer lawyer, Michael Cohen, is making new plea deals with Mueller and singing about your FAILED business deals in Russia. Your attempts to erect a Trump Tower in Moscow and bribe Putin with a $50 million penthouse apartment apparently dragged on into the summer of 2016. When you were telling us that you had "zero" financial schemes in Russia. [But at least Cohen identified you as "Individual -1" in court. You're Number One!!]
- Then George H.W. Bush (#41) died, and people are saying nice things about him in comparison to you, using words like "decency" and "civility".
- But you did rise to the occasion on Monday night, in Biloxi, Mississippi, whipping up racial resentment and giving props to the Lynch Lady, Cindy Hyde-Smith. **_Lots_** of people in that crowd who would show up for a public hanging if we could only Make America Great Again. Your girl won, and the Senate now has 53 Republicans available to vote in more hateful judges who will support vigorous voter suppression in the Dixie states. Is it too late to let them all secede?
- Meanwhile, another campaign is in full swing: Michelle Obama's book tour. Already the Number One selling book of 2018, _Becoming_ is now also a Live Nation extravaganza, packing People Who Read Books into giant arenas all over the land. Complete with celebrity moderators, and concert T-shirts, tickets are going for thousands of dollars.
- Donald, do you remember when you had to pay actors to show up as extras for your campaign kick-off back in 2015? Those were the days.
- But I digress. Michelle's memoir describes what it was like to grow up black in Chicago and fall in love with Barack: "a toppling blast of lust, gratitude, fulfillment, wonder." [I'll bet Melania feels likewise about you.]
- However, it seems Michelle doesn't think much of you, DT. For one reason or another, she's having a hard time letting go of the whole "Birther" thing, which is really what you hung your political hat on for years.
- She also called you a "bully" and opined that you have been "challenging the dignity of our country with practically [your] every utterance." Ouch.
- Unlike you, who rushed to another MAGA rally in Pennsylvania the night Hurricane Michael was pounding Florida, Michelle is cancelling

some book tour dates to attend Poppy Bush's funeral. You can catch up with her there.

Resources - Volume II– Issue 48

Happy Holidays everyone..........with the end (finally) of the midterm elections, we can kick back a little and enjoy the eggnog. The sad outcome of the final contest in Mississippi was not unexpected, but at least no more campaign ads for a year or so.

Borowitz, Andy. "Cindy Hyde-Smith Says She Never Lost Faith in Mississippi's Racists." *The New Yorker*, 29 Nov. 2018.(https://www.newyorker.com/humor/borowitz-report/cindy-hyde-smith-says-she-never-lost-faith-in-mississippis-racists)

Liptak, Kevin. "Individual Number One! Trump Tower Moscow Planned to Give Putin a Penthouse." *CNN*, 29 Nov. 2018 (https://www.cnn.com/2018/11/29/politics/trump-tower-moscow-putin-penthouse/index.html)

Beinart, Peter. "George H.W. Bush: The Last WASP President." *The Atlantic*, 1 Dec. 2018. (https://www.theatlantic.com/ideas/archive/2018/12/george-hw-bush-last-wasp-president/577156/)

Liptak, Kevin, and Jeremy Diamond. "Selling Cindy in Biloxi: Trump Campaigns for Hyde-Smith." *CNN*, 27 Nov. 2018 (https://www.cnn.com/2018/11/27/politics/donald-trump-biloxi-cindy-hyde-smith/index.html)

Gessen, Masha. "Cindy Hyde-Smith and the True Winner in Mississippi's Senate Race." *The New Yorker*, 28 Nov. 2018.(https://www.newyorker.com/news/daily-comment/cindy-hyde-smith-and-the-true-winner-in-mississippis-senate-race)

Hohman, Maura. "Michelle Obama Shared Her Real Opinion of 'Lean In,' and a Curse Word Was Involved." *Yahoo Lifestyle*, 29 Nov. 2018. (https://www.yahoo.com/lifestyle/michelle-obama-shared-real-opinion-lean-curse-word-involved-161707335.html)

Budryk, Zack. "The Memo: Is Michelle Obama the One Critic Trump Can't Hit Back?" *The Hill*, 28 Nov. 2018. (https://thehill.com/homenews/administration/416833-the-memo-is-michelle-obama-the-one-critic-trump-cant-hit-back)

The Weekly Screed: December 9, 2018 (Volume II, Issue 49)

TO: The Donald: Putting the Fun in Funeral

FROM: Kelly: A Great Opportunity to Compare and Contrast

- Donald, I'm sure it's been many moons since you parked your own vehicle, but as we were pulling into my brother-in-law's garage this evening, I noticed he has a tennis ball hanging from the ceiling that hits the windshield when he has reached the sweet spot (aka before crashing into garbage cans).
- In MY garage, however, we still have a pinata of George Walker Bush hanging by the neck. When his wee paper feet graze the car, I have arrived.
- I'm keeping it there to remind me that, while YOU are certainly the most despicable *person* ever to occupy the White House, Dubya maintains the Top Spot in my book as the Number One Worst President EVER.
- Let us count the ways:
1) From flat-out stealing the presidency (once by voter suppression in Florida thanks to brother Jeb and The Supremes; the next time via rigged electronic paperless voter machines programmed by Diebold to flip Kerry votes); to
2) Fulfilling the evil mission of the Project for The New American Century and its manifesto by facilitating the 9/11 massacres; to
3) Starting the two longest wars in US History on completely trumped up and bogus rationales, creating millions of casualties; to
4) Standing down during the aftermath of Katrina while thousands suffered and/or perished during the "Heckuva Job Brownie" days; to
5) Destroying the economy and bringing us to the very brink of another Great Depression……well, on and on it goes, an unmeasurable sacrifice of American life and national treasure by a *feckless ignoramus chickenhawk riding Daddy's coattails to completely undeserved prominence and riches.*
- Hey, this last part sounds uncannily familiar to today's circumstances….
- Anyway, I'm not yet ready to let The Shrub skate off into simply Bad President territory. Until <u>you</u> start a nuclear war with North Korea or Iraq, and massively crash the stock market, you cannot hold a candle to #43.
- Although you ARE making a mighty effort. What a boorish display of petty arrogance at George H.W.'s funeral service on Wednesday. There you were, sitting with Robo First Lady in a line-up with three real Presidents and their (first and only) wives, manspreading to occupy as much room in the pew as possible, pouting and posturing and refusing to shake hands. Pathetic.

- Dubya is painting pictures in Dallas. That might be a good hobby to take up in prison. I'd ask him for some pointers. You are two rancid peas in a pod.

Resources - Volume II– Issue 49

Good evening, everyone........I'm sending this week's offering from bone-chilling Chicago. I know there's been exciting developments on the Mueller front, but we are in for MONTHS of that stuff. Instead I decided to focus on the Bush funeral and participants....which will quickly become last week's news but seemed significant to me.

Mark Crispin Miller, *Fooled Again: How the Right Stole the 2004 Election & Why They'll Steal the Next One Too (Unless We Stop Them)* 2005. (Fooled Again: The Real Case for Electoral Reform by Mark Crispin Miller | Goodreads)

David Ray Griffin, *The New Pearl Harbor: Disturbing Questions About the Bush Administration and 9/11*. 2005. The New Pearl Harbor: Disturbing Questions About the Bush Administration and 9/11 by David Ray Griffin (2007-04-05): David Ray Griffin: 8601410096601: Amazon.com: Books

Daniel Goleman, "Government Response to Katrina: Disaster Within a Disaster." *Newsweek*, September 5, 2005. The Government Response to Katrina: A Disaster Within a Disaster - Newsweek

Kimberly Amadeo, "Bush Administration Economic Policies." *The Balance* [Updated December 25, 2021]. President George W. Bush Economic Policies (thebalancemoney.com)

Rucker, Philip, and Dan Balz. "Bush Funeral: Trump Sits With Fellow Presidents But Still Stands Alone." *The Washington Post*, December 5, 2018. Bush funeral: Trump sits with fellow presidents but still stands alone - The Washington Post

The Weekly Screed: December 16, 2018 (Volume II, Issue 50)

TO: The Donald: Making Spirits Bright

FROM: Kelly: Enjoying the Holidays

- Donald, as I may have mentioned at some point, I watch a minimum of two hours of MSNBC per day and tune in to NPR morning and evening. The "Failing *New York Times*" arrives in our little suburban Oregon cul-de-sac every morning, and I subscribe to *The Nation*, and *The New Yorker*.
- But I've been on a little vacation for the past 10 days....with friends and relations who for unfathomable reasons are not as addicted to political news as I am; do not have a radio in every room; and would rather watch Christmas movies and sports. Go figure.
- Nevertheless, the Breaking News of the past week has been so deliriously entertaining that I feel compelled to document the events for posterity. It's the Celebrity President's "Twelve Days of Christmas"!! Try to sing along:

- ♪ **On the 10th of December, The Donald gave to Me** ♪ : an uproarious tweet proclaiming "No Smocking Gun !" Hilarity ensued, with references ranging from images of crocheted holsters to a poster of Smockey the Bear: "Only YOU can prevent Fascist Liars."

- ♪ **On the 11th of December, The Donald gave to Me** ♪ : five tweets about the Fantasy Wall ("the Military will build [it]") and a stand-off in the Oval Office with POTUS, a comatose Pence, Chuck, & a victorious Nancy.

- ♪ **On the 12th of December, on MSNBC** ♪ : I learn that Michael Cohen is heading for the hoosegow and taking you down with him.

- ♪ **On the 13th of December, I heard on NBC** ♪ : it appears you were in the room when the Mistresses Hush Money scheme was concocted. Oops!

- ♪ **On the 14th of December, The Donald gave to Me** ♪ : a new Chief of Staff (Mick Mulvaney) who has called you a "terrible human being" , replacing John Kelly, who called you "an idiot."

- ♪ **On the 15th of December, we all hear to our glee** ♪ : the resignation of Ryan Zinke!! Most malevolent Interior Secretary ever.

Resources - Volume II– Issue 50

Good evening, all. I was pretty happy with all the Breaking News this week...........except for that judge in Texas who declared the entire Affordable Care Act "unconstitutional" on Friday. That program has been in peril for so long I have to believe that the appeal of this decision will take years........or at least until MY retirement.

Gremore, Graham. "Donald Trump Smocking Gun Tweet Clowned." *Complex*, 10 Dec. 2018 (https://www.complex.com/life/2018/12/donald-trump-smocking-gun-tweet-clowned)

Gearan, Anne, and Philip Rucker. "Across Five Tweets, Trump Makes a Meandering Case for Border Wall Funding." *The Washington Post*, 11 Dec. 2018.(https://www.washingtonpost.com/politics/across-five-tweets-trump-makes-a-meandering-case-for-border-wall-funding/2018/12/11/8ea6ad64-fd35-11e8-862a-b6a6f3ce8199_story.html?noredirect=on&utm_term=.89d37cc4e513)

Kirby, Jen. "Michael Cohen Sentenced to 3 Years in Prison After Implicating Trump in Hush Money Scandal." *Vox*, 12 Dec. 2018.(https://www.vox.com/2018/12/12/18137927/michael-cohen-trump-tweet-clinton-jail)

Winter, Tom, Kristen Welker, and Hallie Jackson. "Trump Was in the Room During Hush Money Discussions, NBC News Confirms." *NBC News*, 13 Dec. 2018. (https://www.nbcnews.com/politics/justice-department/trump-was-room-during-hush-money-discussions-nbc-news-confirms-n947536)

Elkind, Peter. "Mick Mulvaney Once Called Trump a 'Terrible Human Being.'" *CBS News*, 14 Dec. 2018. (https://www.cbsnews.com/news/mick-muvlaney-called-trump-a-terrible-human-being-video-2016/)

Kirchgaessner, Stephanie, and Adam Rawnsley. "Scandal That Cost Ryan Zinke His Job Pales Compared to His Job as Interior Secretary." *The Daily Beast*, 15 Dec. 2018.(https://www.thedailybeast.com/scandal-that-cost-ryan-zinke-his-job-pales-compared-to-job-as-interior-secretary)

The Weekly Screed: December 23, 2018 (Volume II, Issue 51)

TO: The Donald: Grinch in Chief

FROM: Kelly: Rockin' the Jingle Bell News

Wow, Donald. Another week of Christmas cheer. And another fractured carol was ringing in my head all week. Everybody sing along!!

 [*CHORUS*]

Breaking News! Breaking News! What a week it was!!

So much MAGA going on: it's what The Donald does, OH!

Breaking News! Breaking News! Chaos every day.

What fun it is to watch TV and laugh our cares away.

Dashing through our lives, holiday hysteria,

Meanwhile, Donald tweets: We're out of Syria!

The ISIS threat is o'er; we've done all we can do

So Mattis says: I'm outa here…Good luck to all of you!

[*CHORUS*]

A day or two ago, on MSNBC,

I learned that (no surprise) there was no "charity."

Those Trump Foundation funds went only to the Trumps.

Now POTUS and his evil kids will have to take their lumps.

[*CHORUS*]

Now the week is done; government shut down.

No money for The Wall; the Senate has left town.

The Donald doesn't care if people don't get paid.

He's off to Mar-a-Lago to continue the charade.

Resources - Volume II– Issue 51

Good afternoon. What a mess this country is in. I have some great links for you today but could only summon the energy for a new rendition of Jingle Bells. But I did learn a few intriguing factoids about the song such as:

- *It was written by a Unitarian church organist music director in 1857*
- *It was originally intended to mark the Thanksgiving holiday*
- *It was the first song broadcast from space (in 1965).*

"Jingle Bells." Jingle Bells - Wikipedia

"Rand Paul Discusses Syria Withdrawal." *CNN* 23 Dec. 2018 Rand Paul: 'Very proud' of Trump for Syria withdrawal | CNN Politics

Gessen, Masha. "Does Donald Trump Think That the War on Terror Is Over?" *The New Yorker* 23 Dec. 2018.
Does Donald Trump Think That the War on Terror Is Over? | The New Yorker

"Editorial: Trump Foundation Scandal Exposes Definition of 'Slimy'." *San Francisco Chronicle* 23 Dec. 2018. Editorial: Trump Foundation scandal exposes grifter in chief (sfchronicle.com)

Borowitz, Andy. "Nation with Crumbling Bridges and Roads Excited to Build Giant Wall." *The New Yorker* 21 Dec. 2018. Nation With Crumbling Bridges and Roads Excited to Build Giant Wall | The New Yorker

The Weekly Screed: December 30, 2018 (Volume II, Issue 52)

TO: The Donald: Crime Boss in Chief

FROM: Kelly: Humming "Impeachable You"

- Well, it's that time again, DT. We've arrived at the end of another frantic year of your Celebrity Occupation of the White House. How the months have flown by! But one carry-over from 2017 remains: your astonishing accumulation of high crimes and misdemeanors.
- At this point last year, I expressed my wishes for a speedy impeachment. *Surely*, the law-and-order Christian soldiers of the Republican Congress would purge you from their ranks and prop up the evil (but not insane) Mike Pence to do their bidding until 2020. Sadly, this failed to occur.
- Hence, I find myself composing "The Special Impeachment Issue – Part Deux." But with a bit more hope in my heart due, of course, to the impending ascension of Nancy Pelosi to Speaker of the House. Can entertaining investigations and Articles of Impeachment be far behind?
- I know you are taking comfort from the dithering "moderates" who feel that speaking of impeachment is "going too far." To you (and them) I ask: Who in the history of the world has ever more richly deserved this particular act?
- Tom Steyer's *Need to Impeach* website details "Donald Trump's 9 Impeachable Offenses" but when I peruse this list, I find it outdated and frankly lacking. Oh sure, the low-hanging fruit of Obstruction of Justice and
  Violation of the Emoluments Clause and Undermining Freedom of the Press are still there. "Cruelly and Unconstitutionally Imprisoning Children and their Families" is a 2018 addition, thanks to your Family Separation Policy.
- But what about your treasonous suckings-up to Vladimir Putin and Mohammed bin Salman in defiance of findings by our intelligence agencies? And the de facto reveal of you as an unindicted co-conspirator in the campaign finance and collusion shenanigans leading to guilty pleas and/or criminal convictions of your assorted minions and underlings? Or your interference with the pathetic FBI probe of Brett Kavanaugh, ending with the installation of our *second* pervo Supreme Court Justice?
- BTW, "pervo" is an actual word in Scrabble, worth 12 points.
- According to the Article II, Section 4 of the *Constitution*, "The President, Vice President and all civil Officers of the United States, shall be removed from Office on Impeachment for, and Conviction of, Treason, Bribery, or other high Crimes and Misdemeanors." I say we have more than enough of these stacked up to rid ourselves of both you

and your lapdog Pence. Then Nancy Pelosi can become our first female President. Happy New Year!!

Resources - Volume II– Issue 52

Good evening, all. This being the last Sunday of the year, it's time for the Second Annual Special Impeachment Issue. Sure, it won't be easy but Gawd Almighty if not now, when ??

Graham, David A. "Tom Steyer's Plan to Impeach Trump." *The Atlantic*, 23 Oct. 2018. Tom Steyer's Plan to Impeach Trump - The Atlantic

"Trump: Impeachment Talk Swirls Around US President." *BBC News*, 17 May 2017. Trump impeachment: A very simple guide - BBC News

"Impeachable Offenses." *Justia*. Impeachable Offenses :: Article II. Executive Department :: US Constitution Annotated :: Justia

To mark the occasion, I've re-written that old Gershwin standard "Embraceable You". It's not an exceptionally long song, but its lovely sentiment and lilting melody have led many singers to cover it. Here's a link to the smooth jazzy version by Eliane Elias : Eliane Elias // Embraceable You (youtube.com)

And here's MY version, dedicated to The Donald:

Surrender, you sweet impeachable you.

Please go home, we all are beseeching you.

Just one tweet from you, and we are all in despair

You and you alone can bear to look at your hair.

We hate each and every thing that you do.

Above all, we'd love to imprison you

You've been a naughty POTUS. Come to Mueller, come to Mueller do

You sweet impeachable you.

Finally, as the year comes to a close, thus does Volume II of our hebdomadal adventures together. See you next week for Volume III, Issue 1

Table of Contents - Volume Three – 2019

Issue	Topic	Date	Days Left in Office	Page
1	Jester in Chief	Jan 6	745	248
2	National Emergency	Jan 13	738	250
3	National Embarrassment	Jan 20	731	252
4	Nancy With the Laughing Face	Jan 27	724	254
5	Withdrawer in Chief	Feb 3	717	256
6	Teleprompter Trump	Feb 10	710	258
7	Not Like the Others – Part Uno	Feb 17	703	262
8	Not Like the Others – Part Deux	Feb 24	696	264
9	Top Cover	Mar 3	689	266
10	Ode to CPAC 2019	Mar 10	682	268
11	Bikers for Trump	Mar 17	675	270
12	Concealer in Chief	Mar 24	668	272
13	March Madness	Mar 31	661	274
14	World Health Day Reckoning	Apr 7	654	276
15	I Know Nothing About WikiLeaks	Apr 14	647	278
16	I'm F**ked	Apr 21	640	280
17	Gun Nut	Apr 28	633	282
18	Only the Good Die Young	May 5	626	284
19	C Words	May 12	619	286
20	Consensual Rapist	May 19	612	288
21	I Words	May 26	605	290
22	Let Us Pray	Jun 2	598	292
23	D Words	Jun 9	591	294
24	Often Wrong, But Never in Doubt	Jun 16	584	296
25	Commander in Cockamamie	Jun 23	577	298
26	Stepping Over the Line	Jun 30	570	302
27	Potentate in Chief	Jul 7	563	304
28	The Anti-Obama	Jul 14	556	306
29	Love It or Leave It	Jul 21	549	308

Table of Contents - Volume Three – 2019

Issue	Topic	Date	Days Left in Office	Page
30	A Very Bad Thing for Our Country	Jul 28	542	310
31	A One-Man Public Health Crisis	Aug 4	535	312
32	One Sick Puppy	Aug 11	528	314
33	Watching Portland	Aug 18	521	316
34	Dissed by Denmark	Aug 25	514	318
35	MSG Liar	Sep 1	507	320
36	Homesick for Obama Blues	Sep 8	500	322
37	Strongman	Sep 15	493	324
38	Unimpeachable	Sep 22	486	326
39	Blatherskite in Chief	Sep 29	479	328
40	Emperor of the Village People	Oct 6	472	330
41	Towering Idiot	Oct 13	465	332
42	Don't Be a Fool	Oct 20	458	334
43	Crying Wolf	Oct 27	451	338
44	Bajo el Mar	Nov 3	444	340
45	Twitterpated	Nov 10	437	342
46	Bad News	Nov 17	430	344
47	Words Matter	Nov 24	423	348
48	Fowl Play	Dec 1	416	350
49	The POTUS Prayer	Dec 8	409	352
50	LOSER of the Year	Dec 15	402	354
51	#IMPOTUS	Dec 22	395	356
52	Anyone for POTUS but YOU	Dec 29	388	360

Dear Readers, I present to You:

Trump's Third Year as Acting President of the United States (POTUS)

Dwindling **Comedy**, Ballooning **CHAOS**, and Profuse **Calamity**

.....And So It Continues.....

The Weekly Screed: January 6, 2019 (Volume III, Issue 1)

TO: The Donald: Looking Like a Fool

FROM: Kelly: Let us count the ways

- Well, it's not even one full week into the New Year, but we're already in dire circumstances, and we are holding YOU completely responsible.
- Thanks to your goofy tariff and trade shenanigans, combined with the deficit created by "Tax Reform for Millionaires", and seasoned with general economic anxiety, the stock market has lost all gains from 2018.
- And now, despite total Republican control of every branch of government for the past two years, we have a government shutdown over your Stoopid Wall, which you said you were "happy to take the mantle for" but are now blaming on Nancy Pelosi. When Chuck Schumer asked why you wouldn't at least fund the parts of the spending bill you had already agreed to, you pouted that you "would look like a fool" if you compromised.
- Oh Dude…that ship has sailed!
- Sure, we've had Bad Presidents who have done more damage than you, but for sheer comic value, you are the Number One Jester-in-Chief.
- Who can forget all the times you've been played the fool by Putin: it was okay to annex Crimea "because everyone who lives there speaks Russian." Or vouching for his "extremely strong and powerful" denials of election interference? Or parroting bizarre Russian threats about Montenegro?
- **OR** this LOL evaluation of your "summit" with Kim Jong Un: "Just landed - a long trip, but everybody can now feel much safer than the day I took office. There is no longer a Nuclear Threat from North Korea." Followed by: "He's de-nuking, I mean he's de-nuking the whole place." Then when subsequent satellite images proved the contrary: "I don't believe it."
- **OR** your assertion that you could run for any office in Europe and win.
- **OR** your (two) meetings with Bill Gates when you flat-out asked him "if there was a difference between HIV and HPV." [Hint: you probably don't have the first one but it would be a miracle if you don't have the second.]
This sort of query belies your self-proclaimed "natural instinct for science."
- **OR** your solution for the "Pleasure" wildfire: Finnish forest floor raking.
- So, Happy New Year, DT. I'm hoping 2019 will be the Worst Year of Your Life, as predicted by the *LA Times*. It certainly won't "Be Best," and probably not for Melania or the Trump Crime Family either.

- But I am feeling hopeful that it will be a much better year for the rest of the world.

Resources - Volume III, Issue 1

As the year begins, our blunderbuss of a POTUS is afraid to negotiate the government shutdown because it might make him "look like a fool." Normally the fear of looking foolish [FOLF?] is primarily experienced by insecure adolescents but now The Leader of the Free World is in thrall to it. SAD. As we all know by now, however, The Donald has raised tomfoolery to an art form and manages to look breath-takingly ridiculous almost every day. And I continue to hold to the theory that the best way to get through it all is to relax, laugh out loud, and enjoy it.

Egan, Timothy. "Trump Is Finally Making Political Satire Great Again." *The New York Times*, 4 Jan. 2019. Opinion | We Need to Keep Laughing - The New York Times (nytimes.com)

Lithwick, Dahlia. "Trump Says He'd Look 'Foolish' If He Agreed to Reopen the Government Without Wall Funding." *Slate*, 3 Jan. 2019. Trump says he'd "look foolish" if he agreed to reopen the government without wall funding. (slate.com)

Johnson, Eliana. "Trump Is Lonely and Fed Up With Governing." *Politico*, 2 Jan. 2019. Trump says he was lonely over the holidays - POLITICO

"Looking Like a Fool Over Montenegro." *YouTube*, Trump goes after Montenegro, warns they could start World War III (youtube.com)

Sargent, Greg. "North Korea Played Trump for a Fool, Just as We Knew They Would." *The Washington Post*, 12 Nov. 2018. Opinion | North Korea played Trump for a fool, just as we knew it would - The Washington Post

James, Geoffrey. "Bill Gates Just Politely Called Trump a Lecherous Fool." *Inc.*, Publication Date. Bill Gates Just (Politely) Called Trump a Lecherous Fool | Inc.com

Wiener, Jon. "Coming Up: The Worst Year of Trump's Life." *Los Angeles Times*, 3 Jan. 2019. 2019 will be the worst year of Donald Trump's life - Los Angeles Times (latimes.com)

The Weekly Screed: January 13, 2019 (Volume III, Issue 2)

TO: The Donald: We have a National Emergency!

FROM: Kelly: Indeed. It's YOU

- Congratulations, DT! You have now caused and presided over the longest government shutdown in US history. You're Number One! And *of course* we have a National Emergency......but it ain't at the southern border.
- Far too often, your hi-jinks conjure up songs in my head that I feel compelled to re-write in honor of the reality/musical-comedy show we are all enduring until you are impeached, indicted, or compelled to quit.
- I doubt that you are familiar with the operetta **Pirates of Penzance** by Gilbert and Sullivan, but it was the only one of their productions to premiere in these United States: New York City, in fact, on New Year's Eve, 1879.
- The showstopper of this little opera was the "Major-General's Song," sung by a pompous and preposterous prevaricator at the end of Act I. I urge you to find it on the YouTubes and sing along to these lyrics I wrote *just for you*:

I know that I'd have been a brave and awesome Major General

Much better than McMaster, Kelly, Flynn, and Mattis: Losers All!

I went to military school and know all things historical

Oh yes, I'm sure I would have been at least a six-star General!

   Cuz being "Commander-in-Chief" just isn't quite enough for me.

The title doesn't live up to my ego and my vanity.

It isn't powerful enough to let me rule with tyranny

I think "Dictator Emperor Supreme" would be the best for me.

   I am the very model of a National Emergency

Imperiling alliances and threat'ning the economy

Despoiling the environment and tweeting foreign policy

Oh yes, I'm proud to be the Potentate of Idiocracy.

Resources - Volume III, Issue 2

Good evening, all. Couldn't resist adapting the Major General's Song from the Pirates of Penzance for The Donald to sing.

Author Unknown. "Major-General's Song from The Pirates of Penzance - Live and with Lyrics!" *YouTube*, No Date. Major-General's Song from The Pirates of Penzance - live and with lyrics! (youtube.com)

Wikipedia Contributors. "The Pirates of Penzance." *Wikipedia*, Last Edited July 26, 2024. The Pirates of Penzance - Wikipedia

Gorton, Ben. "Why George Washington Is History's Only Six-Star General." *Mental Floss*, No Date. Why George Washington Is History's Only Six-Star General (mentalfloss.com)

Benen, Steve. "Trump: 'I Think I Would Have Been a Good General'." *MSNBC*, January 3, 2019. Trump: 'I think I would have been a good general' (msnbc.com)

Timm, Trevor. "Trump Surrounds Himself with Generals Who Are Masculine but Also Obedient." *NBC News*, December 10, 2017. Trump surrounds himself with generals who are masculine — but also obedient (nbcnews.com)

And, in the meantime, the shutdown continues. This article graphically depicts the damage:

Zhou, Li. "The Shutdown Drags On." *Vox*, January 11, 2019. Government shutdown 2019: The astonishing effects of the shutdown, in 8 charts - Vox

It was 60 degrees and sunny in Portland today. Hope everyone is having a safe and warm New Year!............Kelly

The Weekly Screed: January 20, 2019 (Volume III, Issue 3)

TO: The Donald: A National Embarrassment

FROM: Kelly: MANEAC

- Donald, can it be just two short years since you began your misbegotten occupation of the White House? There's the actual damage you have done to the judiciary, the environment, our international standing, etc., etc.
- And then there's the sheer chagrin, discomfiture, and mortification that all rational and knowledgeable Americans (aka <u>not</u> the MAGA voters) have had to endure during the years of your campaign and reign.
- You might say we only have ourselves to blame. Legend has it that you decided to throw your hat in the ring following the 2011 White House Correspondents' Dinner, when President Obama and Seth Meyers made sport of your political aspirations and your qualifications thereto.
- I can tell you were deeply traumatized and embarrassed by this event. You're the first President not to appear at the dinner since Ronald Reagan skipped it in 1981. His excuse was: recovering from an attempted assassination. Yours was: recovering from personal humiliation.
- You showed us though, didn't you? Thanks to the Russians and the Electoral College, you overcame the popular vote to star in the Celebrity President Show and inflict your particular brand of pratfalls and faux pas on the land.
- As a tonic, for the past year, Andy Borowitz (a satirical columnist for *The New Yorker*) has been appearing throughout the country (okay, mostly the Blue States) on his "Make America Not Embarrassing Again" tour.
- On Friday night he finally made it to Portland, in the ornately uncomfortable Arlene Schnitzer Concert Hall, to which the faithful flocked in the pouring rain, seeking comfort in the company of other like-minded folk. Or, as Borowitz put it: "It's so great to be in a room where everyone reads!"
- There's MANEA merchandise (all proceeds of which go to the International Refugee Committee). I bought the hat for my husband and the bumper sticker for my ancient Subaru, where it now lives next to "Bernie 2016".
- Of course, MANEA (the state we will all be in once you've been deposed) rhymes with MANIA, a condition (along with malignant narcissism) with which I believe you are currently afflicted. According to one definition:

- The symptoms of mania include: elevated mood, inflated self-esteem, decreased need for sleep, racing thoughts, difficulty maintaining attention, increase in goal-directed activity, and excessive involvement in pleasurable activities. These manic symptoms significantly impact a person's daily living. [And all of ours as well, Donald….sadly, all of ours….]

Resources - Volume III, Issue 3

Good evening, friends……….On this somber second anniversary of the Installation of the Dear Leader, I give you my 101st Screed. If there is a God, there won't be a third anniversary. Anyway, I had a delightful time on Friday night. Andy Borowitz (of The Borowitz Report), to whom I bow down in awe, was in town, on his "Make America Not Embarrassing Again" tour.

In the meantime, I'm happy to offer you Trump's most embarrassing moments from the past two years:

Jenny Starrs. "Trump's Strangest Moments of 2017." *The Washington Post*, December 28, 2017. Trump's strangest moments of 2017 (washingtonpost.com)

Jenny Starrs. "Trump's Most Awkward Moments of 2018." *The Washington Post*, December 19, 2018. Trump's most awkward moments of 2018 (washingtonpost.com)

And, from happier times, one of the events that contributed to our current woes:

Merica, Dan. "2011 White House Correspondents' Dinner: Trump, Meyers, Obama Jokes." *CNN*, April 28, 2016. TBT: Obama and Seth Meyers lampoon Trump at the 2011 WHCD | CNN Politics

Finally, more on Andy Borowitz:

Baer. April and Meza, Claudia. "Andy Borowitz Interview." *OPB*, January 11, 2019. Andy Borowitz On Surviving The Death Of Satire - OPB

6. South, Phil. "Andy Borowitz: Make America Not Embarrassing Again." *NJ.com*, March 2018. Andy Borowitz wants to 'Make America Not Embarrassing Again' - nj.com

7. Scott, A.O. "Reviewing 2016 with New Yorker Satirist-in-Chief Andy Borowitz." *NPR*, December 27, 2016. Reviewing 2016 With 'New Yorker' Satirist-In-Chief Andy Borowitz : NPR

The Weekly Screed: January 27, 2019 (Volume III, Issue 4)

TO: The Donald: Nancy with the laughing face

FROM: Kelly: Or "Nancy" as you call her

It wasn't your finest week, DT. You failed valiantly, on several fronts:

- Capitulating on the longest and most expensive ($6 billion) government shutdown in the nation's history without getting a single penny or peso for your barrier/steel-slat-fence/dog-run/duck-blind.
- Postponing delivering a "great" State of the Union speech from an undisclosed location after the Speaker of the House pointedly disinvited you from her venue. "Her prerogative" as you allowed.
- Watching another of your cronies, Roger Stone, slide under the Mueller Bus, with indictments on seven felony counts. [Not on the list, but clearly a criminal act: the tattoo of Richard Nixon that Roger sports on his back. As Stephen Colbert said: "I pity his cellmate."]
- Floundering for but not finding a suitable nickname for your nemesis: "Nancy Pelosi or, as I call her, 'Nancy.'" "Oh, SNAP! Even Alec Baldwin came up with "Nancy Peloser" on Saturday Night Live.

Not helping the situation were your assorted minions/spokespersons:

- Lara (Mrs. Eric) Trump opining that while the government shutdown might be causing federal workers and contractors "a little bit of pain," the ultimate goal of solving "our immigration problem" [aka keeping brown people out of the country] is "so much bigger than any one person." Get this woman an anchor job on Fox Noise, stat!
- Wilbur Ross, Commerce Secretary, Mr. Magoo look-alike, and arguably the Most Corrupt Member of your cabinet had his own "let them eat cake" moment by suggesting that furloughed workers simply take on low-interest loans to bridge the shutdown gap.
- Sarah Sanders [or "The Huckabeast" per Rick Wilson….now THAT's a nickname!] blaming the shutdown on the Democrats, while you fulfill your "No. 1 priority as commander in chief, which is to protect the American people" ostensibly from the aforementioned brown folk.

- Most entertaining, as usual, was your No. 1 Legal Eagle Rudy Giuliani, aka "With a defense lawyer like this, who needs a prosecutor?"
- With every outing, Rudy digs a deeper hole, informing us that you were indeed negotiating the Moscow Trump Tower up to Election Day 2016; and wistfully noting "I am afraid it will be on my gravestone: Rudy Giuliani: He lied for Trump." RIP, Rudy.

Resources - Volume III, Issue 4

Good afternoon, friends. This week's Screed title name checks a Frank Sinatra song from the 1960's AND most of the recent photos of the Speaker of the House. As heard on Real Time with Bill Maher on Friday, custody of Trump's manhood has passed from Ann Coulter to Nancy Pelosi.

Mazza, Ed. "Stephen Colbert Gives Nancy Pelosi a New Nickname." HuffPost, January 25, 2019. Colbert Bestows Pelosi With A Fearsome New Nickname For Winning Trump Showdown | HuffPost Entertainment

Burnett, Erin. "Trump crashes into nickname wall: 'Nancy, as I call her'." CNN, January 25, 2019. Trump crashes into nickname wall: 'Nancy, as I call her' | CNN Politics

ABC News. "Government Shutdown Cost the US Economy at Least $6 Billion." ABC13, January 27, 2019. Government shutdown cost the US economy at least $6 billion, Simple & Poor says - ABC13 Houston

Papenfuss, Mary. "Steve Martin's Roger Stone Asks Trump for Pardon on SNL." HuffPost, January 27, 2019. Steve Martin's Wild And Crazy Roger Stone Pleads With Trump On 'SNL': Pardon Me! | HuffPost Entertainment

Leonhardt, David. "Wilbur Ross and the Shutdown." The New York Times, January 25, 2019. Opinion | The Wilbur Ross Debacle - The New York Times (nytimes.com)

Smith, Allen. "What's Wrong with Rudy? Longtime Giuliani Watchers Stunned by Gaffes." NBC News, January 25, 2019. What's wrong with Rudy? Longtime Giuliani watchers stunned by gaffes (nbcnews.com)

And speaking of deals gone awry:

Weber, Peter. "Trump apparently tried to renegotiate a deal with Frank Sinatra. It backfired." The Week. October 9, 2017**.** Trump apparently tried to renegotiate a deal with Frank Sinatra. It backfired. | The Week

The Weekly Screed: February 3, 2019 (Volume III, Issue 5)

TO: The Donald: Withdrawer-in-Chief

FROM: Kelly: Not Reassured

- Donald, in my…shall we say…interpersonal relationships, I've never trusted "The Withdrawal Method," believing it to be a sure-fired precursor to an unwanted event. And having also learned (thanks to Stormy Daniels) that you are disinclined to partake in precautionary safeguards, I have cast a jaundiced eye on all your withdrawals during the past two years.
- It wasn't supposed to be this way. Time and time again, you regaled us with attestations of your deal-*making* virtuosity, vowing that only a negotiator of your amazing experience and proficiency could fashion the extraordinary agreements that would keep the country safe.
- But, golly Donald. All I've seen is deal-*breaking;* repealing (but seldom replacing) partnerships, deals, treaties, and arrangements that have led to peace, prosperity, and strong relationships with our allies. [Note: an "ally" is a civilized country which used to have some measure of respect for us.]
- This week's announcement of our blast-off from the 1987 Reagan-Gorbachev Intermediate-Range Nuclear Forces (INF) Treaty is just the latest in a long string of "worst-deals ever" that you have yanked us out of:
    1. The Trans-Pacific Partnership (winner: China)
    2. The Iran Nuclear Deal (winner: European Union, maybe)
    3. The United Nations Educational, Scientific and Cultural Organization, aka UNESCO (losers: education, science, and culture)
    4. The United Nations Human Rights Council (winner: tyrants)
    5. The United Nations Relief and Works Agency for Palestinian Refugees (loser: Middle East Peace)
    6. The Special Measures Agreement with South Korea (winner: NoKo)
    7. The Paris Climate Agreement (winner: Big Oil; loser: Earth)
    8. NATO….oh wait, you've just *threatened* to withdraw from that.
- If you want a good laugh, DT, you should go back and read *The Art of the Deal*, upon which (rumor has it) you wanted to place your stubby wee hand to take the Oath of Office two years ago. It contains these words of wisdom: "You can't con people, at least not for long. You can create excitement, you can do wonderful promotion and get all kinds of press, and you can throw in a little hyperbole. But if you don't deliver the goods, people will eventually catch on."

- Too true, DT. And until you pull out of the White House, the country is definitely feeling SCREWED.

Resources - Volume III, Issue 5

Good afternoon all. This month we celebrate Valentines Day, Black History Month, and The Year of the Pig. All good things. On the other hand, have you noticed the frequency with which this country is being pulled out of deals and treaties which were to our benefit in the past?

Here's an entertaining link to the many times The Donald explained to us what a great Deal Maker he was......and please note, this compilation only goes up to the defeat of his Repeal/Replace effort on Obamacare....in 2017:

Burris, Sarah. "All the times Trump said he was the best dealmaker and everyone else sucked at dealmaking." *YouTube*, CNN. March 24, 2017. All the times Trump said he was the best dealmaker and everyone else sucked at dealmaking (youtube.com)

Ward, Alex. "INF Treaty: USA and Russia Withdraw." *Vox*, February 1, 2019.
Shesgreen, Deirdre. State of the Union: US leaving INF Treaty nuclear deal with Russia - Vox

"Donald Trump's Foreign Policy: Iran, NAFTA, Russia, Mexico, Canada Trade." *USA Today*, November 21, 2018. Trump has dropped out of a number of deals, groups internationally (usatoday.com)

Chappell, Bill. "U.S.-South Korea Forces Agreement Set to Expire with No New Deal in Place." *NPR*, December 31, 2018. U.S.-South Korea Forces Agreement Set To Expire With No New Deal In Place : NPR

Suebsaeng, Asawin. "Trump Doesn't Want Alliances Like NATO; He Wants US Soldiers to Be Guns for Hire." *The Daily Beast*, January 15, 2019. Trump Wants to Turn America's Alliances Into Protection Rackets (thedailybeast.com)

The Weekly Screed: February 10, 2019 (Volume III, Issue 6)

TO: The Donald: Teleprompter Trump

FROM: Kelly: Listening between the lines

- Donald, we all know that you don't like to read. A lot of us think you *can't* read very well. Maybe that's why when you are <u>forced</u> to read the teleprompter rather than just rant at rallies, the results sound so phony.
- Even more telling, you make some pretty entertaining mistakes (Freudian slips?) when you have to muddle through words someone else has written in order to make you appear "presidential."
- One of those came on Thursday, at the National Prayer Breakfast: "*Since the founding of our nation, many of our greatest strides – from gaining our independence to abolition of civil rights to extending the vote for women – have been led by people of faith,*" you struggled to read out loud.
- Oopsidoodle. I'm sure the teleprompter actually said something on the lines of "abolition of <u>slavery</u>" and some platitude about the civil rights movement, but (forgive my impertinence here), I would contend that "people of faith" have often used their religious scriptures to <u>justify</u> slavery and diminish women. So maybe, accidentally, you didn't misspeak at all.
- The Apostle Paul was particularly stern on these topics:
  Let your women keep silence in the churches: for it is not permitted unto them to speak; but they are commanded to be under obedience as also saith the law. And if they will learn anything, let them ask their husbands at home: for it is a shame for women to speak in the church. [1 Corinthians 14: 34-35] Hint: that's pronounced "First" (not "One") Corinthians.... Remember your gaffe at Liberty University, January 2016?
- Paul also advised slaves to obey their masters, and instructed masters how to manage their slaves in the service of the Almighty. [Ephesians 6:5-11]
- And let us not forget the Apostle Peter's admonitions: "Slaves, submit yourselves to your masters with all respect, not only to the good and gentle but also to the cruel." [1 Peter 2:18]
- Followed up by: "Likewise you wives, be submissive to your husbands." [1 Peter 3:1]. Oh yeah, the Bible is replete with civil rights heroes and feisty suffragettes.
- By the way, DT, General Dwight D. Eisenhower (who was elected President the year I was born) was the first POTUS to use a teleprompter AND to attend a National Prayer breakfast. Also (fun fact) the top

marginal tax rate during his administration was 91 %. But that's a topic for another Screed.

Resources - Volume III, Issue 6

- *The past few days have seen "Teleprompter Trump" (as opposed to "Twitter Trump" or my personal favorite "Tarmac Trump") lying, threatening, and being his usual bombastic ignorant self. They have also reminded us that The Man Cannot Read.*

David Pakman. "Uh-Oh: Does Donald Trump Know How to Read?" *YouTube*, February 2, 2017. Uh-Oh: Does Donald Trump Know How to Read? (youtube.com)

- *This was made crystal clear as he bumbled through our premier annual exercise in hypocrisy and unctuousness known as The National Prayer Breakfast:*

Gonzales, Richard. "At National Prayer Breakfast, Trump Pledges 'I Will Never Let You Down'." *NPR*, February 7, 2019. At National Prayer Breakfast, Trump opposes abortion, supports religious liberty : NPR

- *You can all dig out the family Bible and check out my next few references, after watching The Donald's display of scriptural ignorance while trying to pander to the good Christian students at Liberty University in 2016:*

Cohen, Jason. "Donald Trump's Scriptural Ignorance at Liberty University." *Mashable*, January 18, 2016. Donald Trump flubs Bible verse during speech at Christian university | Mashable

- *If you are interested, Wikipedia has a fact-filled entry for "teleprompter":*

Wikipedia Contributors. "Teleprompter." *Wikipedia*, Last Edited July 26, 2024. Teleprompter - Wikipedia

- *Finally, a bit of a swerve into President Eisenhower's tax policy*

Bell, Jonathan. "Eisenhower's Tax Policies Invested in the Future, Not Just the Present." *Zócalo Public Square*, December 19, 2017. Eisenhower's Tax Policies Invested in the Future, Not the Few | Essay | Zócalo Public Square (zocalopublicsquare.org)

Resources - Volume III, Issue 6 (continued)

As a bonus, I'm also attaching a copy of the response I received today from the White House when I sent The Donald this week's Screed. A longer form letter than usual. This also puts to rest any notion that he ever reads these valentines from his subjects.

From: The White House <noreply@whitehouse.gov>
Date: February 10, 2019 at 3:00:49 PM PST
To: "kellypaige2012@gmail.com" <kellypaige2012@gmail.com>
Subject: Thank You For Your Message

The White House

February 10, 2019

Thank you for taking the time to write. **My staff will review your correspondence shortly.**

More women participate in America's workforce today than ever before. Their contributions benefit every sector of our economy and bring wealth to communities across our Nation. But promoting the empowerment of women is not just a domestic priority, it is also critical to achieving greater peace and prosperity around the world. Yesterday, I was honored to sign a National Security Presidential Memorandum establishing the Women's Global Development and Prosperity Initiative, or W-GDP. The initiative will invest in women entrepreneurs by expanding their economic participation, with the aim of boosting global economic output by an additional $12 trillion by 2025.

By advancing workforce development and vocational training, while eliminating legal, regulatory, and cultural barriers that hinder women from becoming active in their local economies, W-GDP will strive to help 50 million women in developing countries realize their economic potential.

To watch yesterday's signing event, and to learn more about my Administration's effort to empower women and increase American and global prosperity, please click here.

Sincerely,

[His big ugly scrawl here but it can't be copied]

Resources - Volume III, Issue 6 (continued)

If you're going to quote scripture in a room of fervent Christians, you better know your stuff.

GOP presidential front-runner Donald Trump learned that lesson the hard way Monday, when he spoke to students at Liberty University, a Christian school in the heart of Virginia.

After vowing to protect Christians across the globe, Trump read a verse from Second Corinthians — one of the books in the New Testament. But Trump flubbed the name, pronouncing it "Two Corinthians," as it's often written in text.

Reporters and political pundits got in on the fun.

Getting the general impression that by saying 2 Corinthians rather Second Corinthians, Trump schlonged his Biblical reference— Ben Jacobs (@Bencjacobs) January 18, 2016

Cahn, Emily. "Donald Trump flubs Bible verse during speech at Christian university." Mashable. January 25, 2016. Donald Trump flubs Bible verse during speech at Christian university | Mashable

The Weekly Screed: February 17, 2019 (Volume III, Issue 7)

TO: The Donald: Not Like the Others – Part Uno

FROM: Kelly: Pondering Presidents' Day

- Donald, one of the things I most appreciate about our little correspondence is the discovery of fun-filled facts I happen upon as I conduct my "research" into your behavior from the past week. For example (and I bet you didn't know this either), the concept of celebrating "President's Day" on the third Monday of February was first broached by NATO (as in the National Association of Travel Organizations) in the 1950's.
- In other words, what began as a way to honor George Washington and Abraham Lincoln, and has since evolved into a shameless retail blow-out, had its origins as a promotion of American tourism.
- But as I am not buying anything or going anywhere tomorrow, I have the leisure to consider YOU, the Donald, in comparison to past POTUSes. As usual, I find you wanting in almost every respect. Here's how a couple of events from the past week have distinguished you from your predecessors:
    1) <u>You hate dogs.</u> Except maybe "a good old-fashioned German shepherd," as you mused at your Monday night rally in El Paso. Perhaps like "Blondi," Hitler's German Shepherd, who came in handy when der Führer needed to test the cyanide capsules provided to him during his last days in the bunker. (Spoiler: the capsules worked). Besides, it might make you resemble, in one small way, Barack Obama, as one of your MAGAts in the audience pointed out. Can't have that.
    2) <u>You are, far and away, the King of the Non-Sequitur.</u> To wit: "Yeah, Obama had a dog. You're right. Both parties should come together to finally create a safe and lawful system of immigration." Huh? These two sentences should *not* have come together. Not only are you incapable of reading (see last week's Screed) but you can barely speak without a script. In this you do resemble Reagan and Dubya.
    3) <u>You love dictators and tyrants.</u> As you were declaring your phony National Emergency on the White House lawn on Friday, you veered into Adulation of Murderous Strongman territory with this shout-out to Chinese President Xi: "And when I asked President Xi, I said do you have a drug problem? No, no, no, I said you have 1.4 billion people what do you mean you have no drug problem...I said why? Death penalty. We give death penalty to people that sell drugs, end of problem."

- So much un-Presidentialness. So little space. To be continued next week.

Resources - Volume III, Issue 7

Good evening, all. Presidents' Day is tomorrow ! Yippee ! And I'm starting a 2-part series on how The Donald differs from his predecessors.

The inspiration for the title comes from the Sesame Street song: "One of these Things is Not Like the Others"

One of these things is not like the others,
One of these things just doesn't belong,
Can you tell which thing is not like the others
By the time I finish my song?

And the inspiration for the content derives from two disturbing non-TelePrompTer appearances by No. 45:

His rally in El Paso on Monday, February 11 Speech: Donald Trump Holds a Political Rally in El Paso, Texas - February 11, 2019 (youtube.com)

His National Emergency speech on Friday the 15th. Full Video: Trump Declares National Emergency - The New York Times (nytimes.com)

Snopes Staff. "Presidents' Day." *Snopes*, February 16, 2003. What Is Presidents Day? | Snopes.com

Delkic, Melina. "Does Donald Trump Hate Dogs? Why Would He?" *Newsweek*, October 25, 2017. Why Does President Donald Trump Hate Dogs? - Newsweek

Shapira, Avner. "Why Did the Nazis Like Dogs?" *Haaretz*, April 9, 2013. Why Did the Nazis Like Dogs? - Jewish World - Haaretz.com

Suebsaeng, Asawin. "Daily Show's Trevor Noah Mocks Trump's Bizarre Anti-Dog Rant." *The Daily Beast*, February 12, 2019. 'Daily Show's Trevor Noah Mocks Trump's Bizarre Anti-Dog Rant (thedailybeast.com)

Blake, Aaron. "Trump's Bewildering National Emergency Press Conference, Annotated." *The Washington Post*, February 15, 2019. Transcript of Trump national emergency press conference, annotated - The Washington Post

The Weekly Screed: February 24, 2019 (Volume III, Issue 8)

TO: The Donald: Not Like the Others – Part Deux

FROM: Kelly: Still Pondering Presidents' Day

- Donald, I'm continuing to celebrate Presidents' Day Month this week. Because as I considered your unique qualifications to the post, and your exceptional job performance to date, I just didn't have enough space to do you justice in comparison to POTUS Numbers 1 through 44.
- BTW, what led me down this path was that little song from Sesame Street that many of the characters have sung to help small children develop their cognitive abilities: "One of These Things is Not Like the Others." I return to your February 15 declaration of National Emergency to make my point:

4) <u>For starters, no urgency about declaring this big emergency</u>. Most presidents have made this a rather brief but solemn announcement (usually via Executive Order) befitting the occasion. You, on the other hand, rambled on about trade deals and all the great relationships you had with China, Russia, both Koreas, Japan, and the UK. The last I found perplexing, as I had recently been alerted to this response to the question, "Why do some British people not like Donald Trump?" *Trump lacks certain qualities which the British traditionally esteem. For instance, he has no class, no charm, no coolness, no credibility, no compassion, no wit, no warmth, no wisdom, no subtlety, no sensitivity, no self-awareness, no humility, no honour and no grace – all qualities, funnily enough, with which his predecessor Mr. Obama was generously blessed.*

5) <u>A National Emergency Unlike all Others</u> At first, you tried to make it the same: "It's been signed by other presidents…There's rarely been a problem. They sign it; nobody cares. I guess they weren't very exciting. But nobody cares. They sign it for far less important things in some cases – in many cases." But then you start whining about how you're gonna get sued and get "a bad ruling" in the lower courts but hopefully get a "fair shake and win in the Supreme Court." Finally, you confess: "I could do the wall over a longer period of time, I didn't need to do this, but I'd rather do it much faster." So, actually, NOT an emergency at all. But you have already been sued! So spot-on prediction.

6) <u>Fun fact:</u> As of January 2019, the United States is under 31 continuing declared states of national emergency, most concerning sanctions. None of the others call out the military to build a concrete wall. Just saying.

Resources - Volume III, Issue 8

Good afternoon from snowy sunny Anchorage. I'm here to play with my friends AND for the annual winter festival: Fur Rendezvous. Aka "Fur Rondy" which culminates in the start of the Iditarod on Saturday. I usually come up here to visit in late summer, but I needed a snow fix.

Continuing the Presidents' Day theme, I'm still dogging the Donald over his ridiculous National Emergency. And waiting for the Mueller report to drop.

- *Several of you have forwarded Nate White's explanation of why the Brits hate Trump so I thought I should make sure I communicated it to him. If you haven't read it yet:*

White, Nate. "Quora: Nate White Hilariously Answers the Query 'Why Do British People Not Like Trump?' February 15, 2019 Why Do British People Not Like Donald Trump? | Obliviots

- *I was also surprised to learn that we are currently [as of Feb. 24, 2019] under 31 states of emergency!*

Wikipedia Contributors. "List of National Emergencies in the United States." *Wikipedia*, Last Edited July 26, 2024. List of national emergencies in the United States - Wikipedia [This site is continuously updated.]

- *And in case you missed Trump's aggrieved comments about the judicial system:*

Shear, Michael D., and Julie Hirschfeld Davis. "Trump's Highly Annoying Sing-Songy Complaint About How Unfair the Courts Are." *The New York Times*, February 15, 2019. Trump Declares a National Emergency, and Provokes a Constitutional Clash - The New York Times (nytimes.com)

The Weekly Screed: March 3, 2019 (Volume III, Issue 9)

To: The Donald – "And we'll take care of it for Alaska. Right?"

From: Kelly – That's exactly what I'm afraid of

- DT, I really enjoy the very rare times when you and I have something in common. So, this week I'd like to celebrate both of us being in Anchorage, Alaska at the same time! Imagine my delight.
- I'm here for a week and a bit, visiting my friends and enjoying the gorgeous weather and scenery: blue skies and sunshine every day; perfect for the annual Fur Rendezvous Festival and the kick-start of the Iditarod.
- YOU, on the other hand, were only briefly in Alaska on your way home from Vietnam and your pathetic "summit" with the murderous dictator, Kim Jong Un, your new bestie…. stopping at Elmendorf Air Force Base to refuel Air Force One. But by golly, you made the most of it:
- "So, we're coming in and we're landing, and I say, "You know, I have a choice: I can stay on the plane and relax as we fuel up, right?"
  But since you are <u>pretending</u> to be the freaking "Commander in Chief," you move your lazy ass and summon the moxie to speak to the troops: "I said, "All right, so let's go. Put on the tie. Put on the shirt. But I wanted to be with you. And it's an honor to be with you."
  Man, that's real leadership. No One has ever seen anything like it.
- Two comments, DT. 1) Most males of my acquaintance put on the shirt *before* the tie, but maybe you're special that way. 2) Here's a bunch of service members freezing their tuckases off in the Last Frontier, and you are *deigning* to appear before them. You aren't fit to lick their frosty feet.
- Then you pander: "Since the Second World War, our intrepid service members in Alaska have proudly stood at the "top cover for North America." You are a powerful warning to the world to never strike American soil."
- When what you really mean is: My dictator buddy Kim Jong Un can *easily* strike Anchorage from Pyongyang, so get ready for martyrdom in WW III.
  We'll use Alaska as an excuse to pulverize the entire Korean peninsula.
- Finally, you suck up to Alaska's latest governor, the odious, towering (6'7") Mike Dunleavy: "I just want to say he has been an incredible warrior. He's not only one of the best governors in the United States; he's definitely the largest.
- "Where is Mike? Look at that man. He's all man. He ran an incredible campaign. He won easily. Look at him. " Gross. Get a room.

Resources - Volume III, Issue 9

Good evening all.........I'm actually just arrived back in Oregon from Alaska but wanted you to share in another thrilling episode in the Celebrity President Show.

This one didn't get much coverage last week, what with all the other goings-on. But since I was in the vicinity for it, it floated to the surface as Screed-Worthy.

So only one link tonight...............the remarks of our Dear Leader to the troops at "J-Ber" (Joint Base Elmendorf -Richardson)

"Donald Trump Remarks to Troops at Elmendorf AFB, Alaska." February 28, 2019. President Trump Speaks To Troops Stationed At Joint Base Elmendorf In Anchorage, Alaska (youtube.com)

Back when I lived in Anchorage there were TWO bases: Elmendorf Air Force Base and Army Garrison Fort Richardson, but they got themselves consolidated (right-sized?) on the recommendation of the 2005 Defense Base Closure and Realignment Commission. At the time, I was married to an Air Force retiree, so spent many happy hours availing myself of the Elmendorf AFB services like a low-priced commissary and free socialized medicine. Those were the days.

But I digress ! Rick Wilson (one of the frequent talking heads on MSNBC) described this past week of Trump-related shenanigans as "a dumpster fire on top of Burning Tire Mountain" and I think that sums it up well.

The Weekly Screed: March 10, 2019 (Volume III, Issue 10)

To: The Donald – Losing it

From: Kelly – Losing Sleep

Ode to CPAC 2019 (With Quotes)

1) Now I lay me down to sleep; "My Pillow," though, I cannot keep.

No longer can I rest my head on something made by he who said:

"I see the greatest president in history. Of course he is, he was chosen by God"

2) Sebastian Gorka told the crowd that hamburgers are not allowed

by Democrats like AOC. The Green New Deal's a fantasy:

"It's a watermelon," Gorka told the audience members, imploring them to use his metaphor themselves. "Green on the outside, deep, deep communist red on the inside....This is what Stalin dreamt about but never achieved."

3) A "work of art" was on display that showcased every cheap cliché:

An eagle! And the Flag! In Space! Next to The Donald's stalwart Face!

Three hundred pounds of gilded frame, called: "Unafraid and Unashamed"

Thus spake Julian Raven, the creator of this 8 x 16-foot, 300 pound monstrosity, "When we depart from our Judeo-Christian values, the boundaries of right and wrong are lost. People have lost respect for our country."

4) And then God's Chosen did appear to tell the folk who hold him dear:
- *"What we've done together has never been done in the history—maybe of beyond our country, maybe in the history of the world."*
- *"From that day we came down the escalator, I really don't believe we've had an empty seat at any arena, at any stadium."*
- *"See, I don't have white hair."*
- *"I'm in love, and you're in love. We're all in love together."*
- *"I spent my New Year's all by myself....I figured it would look good if I stayed in the White House so that you people all love and vote for me, okay?"*
- *"This is how I got elected, by being off script....And if we don't go off script, our country is in big trouble, folks.... I'm going to regret this speech."*

Resources - Volume III, Issue 10

Well, it happened again last weekend: the annual display of nincompoopery known as the Conservative Political Action Conference. At the inaugural CPAC in 1974, Ronald Reagan was the keynote speaker and won the straw poll for the preferred possible presidential candidate. George Wallace came in second.

- Wikipedia Contributors. "Conservative Political Action Conference." *Wikipedia*, Last Edited July 26, 2024. Conservative Political Action Conference - Wikipedia

By now the whole shebang has now devolved into a MAGA circus, or as Bill Maher called it on Friday night: "a virtual Woodstock of the mentally impaired." Trump did his flag-hugging schtick, of course, and a parade of speakers made fools of themselves.

Heisenberg, J. "Chosen by God? Kirk, Owens, My Pillow Guy Make for Surreal CPAC Circus." *Heisenberg Report*, March 2, 2019. 'Chosen By God': Kirk, Owens, My Pillow Guy Make For Surreal CPAC Circus – Heisenberg Report

Ward, Alex. "Trump Goes on and On for Over 2 Hours at CPAC." *Vox*, March 2, 2019. CPAC 2019: "General Raisin Cain" and Trump's other odd speech points - Vox

Parker, Ashley, and Philip Rucker. "The 10 Personas of Donald Trump in a Single Speech." *The Washington Post*, March 9, 2019. The 10 personas of Donald Trump in a single speech - The Washington Post

Borowitz, Andy. "God Offers People of Alabama New Bibles to Replace Ones Trump Signed." *The New Yorker*, March 9, 2019. God Offers People of Alabama New Bibles to Replace Ones Trump Signed | The New Yorker

The Making Of Trump Painting 'Unafraid And Unashamed' By Artist Julian Raven (youtube.com) December 27, 2015.

I hope you are keeping up on the Cohen testimony, the Manafort sentencing, the Jared security clearance flap, and the 81 entities being investigated by Congress. All Screed-Worthy indeed, but there's only so much room in any given week.

I will leave you however, on this first Sabbath of Lent, with the image of Trump signing a Bible in while offering comfort to tornado victims in Alabama.

The Weekly Screed: March 17, 2019 (Volume III, Issue 11)

To: **The Donald – Enjoying "the support of Bikers for Trump"**

From: **Kelly – Remembering the Bunny Bikers of Okinawa**

- DT, on the eve of one of the most horrific massacres in recent history (committed, as usual, by a White Guy with a Gun, but this time in New Zealand), you put the American people on notice: *"I have the support of the police, the support of the military, the support of the Bikers for Trump – I have the tough people, but they don't play it tough – until they go to a certain point, and then it would be very bad, very bad."*
- As so often happens, your moronic utterances make me hearken back to happier times: the late '80s, specifically, when I was convinced that Ronald Reagan would be the Worst President in my lifetime….and your televised racial invective was focused on the (later exonerated) Central Park Five.
- This particular comment also revived a memory of when the Air Force and the military police and bikers had MY back….when I was the Director of the largest USO operation in the world, at Kadena Air Force Base in Okinawa, Japan, a mere 30 years ago.
- We were always coming up with morale-boosting events to keep the Airmen and Marines and their families entertained (in the era of Airmail, not email; before the World Wide Web, and Twitter) so in 1989 I persuaded the base commander to shut down the main drag on a Sunday in March so that the USO could put together an Easter Parade.
- And what a time we had! Floats, marching bands, and (bringing up the rear) just about every American in Okinawa who owned a motorcycle, sporting huge stuffed Easter rabbits strapped to their handlebars. Many combat-hardened Vietnam Vets riding those bunny-adorned bikes.
- I bring this up because I don't think you've ever "gotten" the military, Donald. I know you went to a military academy in the early '60s and played soldier there. Heck, you were even front and center in a Columbus Day parade down Fifth Avenue. But when it came time to answer your country's call to service you played the phony "bone spurs" card and chickened out.
- It was this same mindset that led you to dismiss John McCain as a war hero because he was shot down, imprisoned, and tortured for years [*"I like people who weren't captured."*] and still propels you into Twitter wars with McCain's daughter over his legacy. Happening today, even as I write this.
- So, I for one am not concerned that the armed forces will stage a coup to keep you in office. They know a coward and a racist when they see one.

Resources - Volume III, Issue 11

Happy St. Paddy's Day to most of you.........with the rise of genetic testing I believe almost everyone in the world has discovered at least a smidgen of Irish heritage. But this week's Screed focuses on another holiday memory from my past that ties into the latest threats from the Dear Leader.

Author Unknown. "New Zealand Mosques Attack Suspect Praised Trump in Manifesto." *Al Jazeera*, March 15, 2019. New Zealand mosque attacks suspect praised Trump in manifesto | New Zealand Attack News | Al Jazeera

Papenfuss, Mary. "Be Afraid: Donald Trump and Breitbart Violence Supporters." *HuffPost*, March 14, 2019. Trump Raises Specter Of Supporters Turning Violent If They Don't Get Their Way | HuffPost Latest News

Interview with Larry King. "Trump 1989 Central Park Five Interview." *CNN*, October 7, 2016. Trump 1989 interview on the 'Central Park Five' | CNN Business

Fahrenthold, David A., and Michael Kranish. "Decades Later, Disagreement Over Young Trump's Military Academy Post." *The Washington Post*, January 9, 2016. 50 years later, disagreements over young Trump's military academy record - The Washington Post

Author Unknown. "Trump Attacks McCain Over Dossier, Meghan McCain Swipes Back." *KDVR*, March 17, 2019. Trump attacks McCain over dossier; Meghan McCain swipes back (kdvr.com)

Lapham, Lewis H. "1989 Was the Year That Brought Us Trump." *The Nation*, No Date. 1989 Was the Year That Brought Us Trump | The Nation

The Weekly Screed: March 24, 2019 (Volume III, Issue 12)

To: The Donald – Concealer in Chief

From: Kelly – Let us accessorize

- Let's face it, DT....We all have something to hide. For you, it's your balding pate, your sexcapades, your business shenanigans, foreign emoluments, collusion with Russians, and obstruction of justice.
- For many women AND men, head coverings of many sorts are either required or recommended as faith-appropriate garments. Consider the Jewish kippah; the Sikh turban; the Hasidic schtreimel; or (as sported by your good buddy, fellow tyrant, and Guy Who <u>DID</u> Get Away with Murder, Saudi Arabian Prince Muhammad Bin Salman) a nice shemagh, with igal.
- This made Judge Jeanine Pirro's recent diatribe describing Congresswoman Ilhan Omar's hijab as "antithetical to the Constitution" both ignorant AND sexist. And prompted Faux News to pull her from their rotation of bombastic and bigoted chowder-heads. That action naturally inspired multiple twitter pleas from you and the MAGA Hatters to restore the good judge to her rightful place in the pantheon of Foxy FOTs (Friends of Trump).
- But if we're gonna ban headscarves in the House as an example of separation of Church and State, we'd also better go after crosses and crucifixes, as they most definitely identify the religious beliefs of the wearer.
- An online shopping excursion for this particular accessory took me to a purveyor called Bling Jewelry, which offered a Sterling Silver Multi-Skull Cross Pendant (perfect for Halloween); and a fake turquoise and rhinestone cross bracelet billed as "Easter Party Bling." Cuz nothing says "Good Friday" like tarting up an execution with imitation diamonds!
- And to a site called Hollywood Life which inquires: "What better way to show off your faith than by wearing a gorgeous cross necklace?" [They should check out Paul's first letter to Timothy, Chapter 2, Verses 9-10.]
- Big showy bejeweled crosses also appear on many concealed-carry handbags ("Will comfortably hold a revolver or a semi-automatic"), often appearing along with Bible verses about God-given strength stitched into the leather. Sold by brands like "Cowgirl Bling" and "Gun Tote'n Mamas," they truly beg the question: What Would Jesus Pack?
- This circles back to another woman excoriated for wearing a headscarf in solidarity with her Muslim citizens:

- New Zealand PM Jacinda Ardern, who skipped straight over thoughts-and-prayers to declaring an assault weapons ban. Now this, Donald, is moral leadership. Call the Nobel Committee!

Resources - Volume III, Issue 12

Good afternoon, friends. A moment of silence for the lily-livered report from the Special Counsel. But as the Boston Globe proclaims: Mueller Time is Over. Now It's Impeachment Time.

Clements, Ben and Fein, Ron. "Mueller Time is Over. Now it's Impeachment Time. March 24, 2019. The Boston Globe. Mueller time is over. Now it's impeachment time - The Boston Globe

Meanwhile, what captured my attention this week were the headscarves and guns debates both here and in New Zealand. The hypocrisy of the "Christian" gun nuts never ceases to amaze. Here we go:

Patten, Dominic. "Fox News, Donald Trump, Jeanine Pirro Pulled for Second Week Over Racist Remark." *Deadline*, March 18, 2019. Fox News Risks Donald Trump Wrath, Keeping Jeanine Pirro Off Another Week (deadline.com)

Wikipedia Contributors. "Christian Head covering." *Wikipedia*, Last Edited July 26, 2024. Head covering for Christian women - Wikipedia

La Croix, Jane. "Celebs Wearing Cross Necklaces." *Hollywood Life*, March 30, 2018. Celebs Wearing Cross Necklaces: See Pics Of Stars With The Jewelry – Hollywood Life

"Justin West Concealed Carry Western Croc Cross Duo Color Shoulder Handbag Purse." *Amazon*, No Date. Justin West Concealed Carry Western Croc Cross Duo Color Shoulder Handbag Purse (Purple Flat Wallet): Handbags: Amazon.com

McKirdy, Euan. "New Zealand's Assault Weapons Ban." *CNN*, March 20, 2019. Assault rifles to be banned in New Zealand in aftermath of massacre | CNN

The Weekly Screed: March 31, 2019 (Volume III, Issue 13)

To: The Donald – March Mischaracterization

From: Kelly – March Madness

- DT, we've been watching a lot of basketball at our house during MSNBC commercials. [Go Ducks!] The back-and-forth and ups-and-downs on the court have seemed to parallel the various narratives attempting to explain the fall-out from the end of the investigation by the Special Counsel.
- Firstly, the William Barr Summary of the Principal Conclusions of the Robert Mueller Report….NOT a Summary of the Report itself, as Barr hastened to clarify….assured an anxious public that there was No Evidence Beyond A Reasonable Doubt that either you or anyone in your circle of Misfit Toys was clever or committed enough to *criminally conspire* with the Russians in their attempts to destroy American democracy. Whew!
- The best description I heard of this tortured determination was that perhaps you and Don Jr. and all the other indicted (and soon-to-be-indicted) felons in your administration were "collusion-curious" but not quite In It to Win It.
- Nextly, that same letter to Congress (four pages of flim-flam, if you ask me) saved the House of Representatives the burden of deciding whether Mueller's dithering over Obstruction of Justice was any big deal either.
- In a move-along-folks-nothing-to-see-here conclusion, Barr announced that he and Deputy AG Rod Rosenstein had reached a gentlemen's agreement that nothing in the Mueller Report was "sufficient to establish that the President committed an obstruction-of-justice offense." A grateful nation is now free to consign this whole messy exercise to the dustbin of history.
- YOU, as per usual, were not content to graciously accept this generous whitewash and move on. Instead, you just <u>had</u> to start bellowing about "total and complete exoneration" and threatening to investigate the FBI, Congress, the media, and anyone else who had hurt your widdle feelings over the past two years. "We can never let this happen to another President again" you whined in the Oval Office. WAH!
- On Thursday, in a typical going-overboard move, the Republican members of the House Intelligence Committee decided to suck up to you by sending a nastygram to current Chairman Adam Schiff, demanding his resignation because he had the temerity to talk about what all of us have seen *with our very own eyeballs*: massive evidence of collusion with the Russians.

- I hope you watched it, Donald, cuz the guy you demeaned as a "pencil-neck" handed all their heads to them in a blistering rebuttal. Best TV of the week.

Resources - Volume III, Issue 13

Good afternoon, all..............what a maddening week of obfuscation. But there were two stellar moments on TV that confirmed my take on the whole messy conclusion of the Mueller investigation:

"Robert Mueller Hits The Dusty Trail." YouTube. Robert Mueller Hits The Dusty Trail (youtube.com)

Hear Schiff's heated response after calls for resignation CNN, March 28, 2019. Hear Schiff's heated response after calls for resignation | CNN Politics

In case you haven't read it yet, here's the Barr Summary of the Conclusions, but not the Report, of the Mueller Report. I won't believe anything in these letters until I see the actual report,

Heffernan, Virginia. "Schiff vs. Barr." Los Angeles Times, March 29, 2019. Column: Forget what William Barr wrote about collusion. Listen to Adam Schiff instead - Los Angeles Times (latimes.com)

"Barr on March 24 [Here's the Summary]." The New York Times, March 24, 2019. Read Attorney General William Barr's Summary of the Mueller Report - The New York Times (nytimes.com)

"Barr on March 29 [Why the Summary wasn't really a summary]." Axios, March 29, 2019. New Barr letter: Mueller report will be sent to Congress by mid-April (axios.com)

"What Barr's Letter About Mueller Report Says and Doesn't Say." The Washington Post, March 24, 2019. Opinion | What Barr's letter about the Mueller report says and doesn't say - The Washington Post

Next week (BARR-ing any more alarming developments): the latest attempt to make me retire earlier by cancelling the Affordable Care Act.

Feels like every Day is April Fool's Day but enjoy it tomorrow...........Kelly

The Weekly Screed: April 7, 2019 (Volume III, Issue 14)

To: The Donald – *"healthiest individual ever elected to the presidency"*

From: Kelly – Contemplating health care for all

- Donald, today is World Health Day, and not a moment too soon. A headline on the cover of the April issue of <u>The New Republic</u> caught my eye: "Why Global Autocracy is bad for Your Health." That would be you and your ilk.
- Inside, the accompanying article is titled: "The Plague Years" and goes on to describe how *"Distrust of expertise, suspicion of immigrants, [and] shunning of international cooperation"* are leading to measles outbreaks, the persistence of polio, and renewed threat from Ebola.
- Ironically, the article then notes: *"immigrants typically pose less of a health risk to the American public than other U.S. residents do"* and cites citizens of Nicaragua, Costa Rica, and Mexico as having higher average vaccination rates than good ole red-blooded Americans.
- I know this to be true of Oregon, which has the highest percentage of "anti-vaxxers" in the country, due to the shameful ease with which the misinformed can "opt out" of vaccination for "philosophical" reasons.
- And while you are urging the Department of Justice to support the district court ruling in Texas (in December of last year) which declares the entire Affordable Care Act "unconstitutional", not a single Republican has ever (in 70 attempts at repeal) come up with a replacement that is, as you promise: *"something that is going to be much less expensive than Obamacare for the people ... and we're going to have (protections for) pre-existing conditions and will have a much lower deductible. So, and I've been saying that, the Republicans are going to end up being the party of health care."*
- To which I can only reply: Not Bloody Likely.
- Meanwhile, the goal of the 50-year-old World Health Organization for 2019 is stated as "Universal health coverage: everyone, everywhere" because pathogens don't give a flying fig for border walls or tariffs and *will* find a way to make their presence known around the globe.
- Here in Oregon, Senate Bill 770 ("Relating to statewide health care coverage; declaring an emergency") is being advanced to provide a
- Plan, to be administered by the Oregon Health Authority, where I work!! If it passes, I might have to delay my retirement again.

- And by the way, DT, contrary to the letter you dictated for your wacko doctor to sign, you rank as the 26th healthiest POTUS. Obama was #2.

Resources - Volume III, Issue 14

Good afternoon, all...........it IS World Health Day. We sure aren't the healthiest country on the planet (that would be Spain), but by God, we've got the most prisoners and the most firearms. I'm sure these rankings are not related in any way.

"Spain Tops Italy as World's Healthiest Nation While U.S. Slips." Bloomberg, February 24, 2019. Healthy Nation Rankings: These Are the Healthiest Countries - Bloomberg

"Right Wing Dictators are Bad for Your Health." The New Republic. The Rise of Right-Wing Nationalism Is Jeopardizing the World's Health | The New Republic

"Oregon is NOT Progressive on the Vaccine Issue." Kaiser Health News. For Many Countries, Poverty Lays At The Heart Of Why Measles, Once Nearly Vanquished, Has Returned - KFF Health News

"But Oregon is on the Right Track Here." Oregon Legislative Information System.

SB770 2019 Regular Session - Oregon Legislative Information System (oregonlegislature.gov) Introduced (oregonlegislature.gov)

"What Universal Health Care Looks Like to the World Health Organization." World Health Organization. World Health Day 2019: About the campaign (who.int)

"Amazingly, Trump Not the Healthiest Person Ever to Occupy the Oval Office." Voice of America News. Healthiest Presidents Ever? New Compilation Doesn't Place Trump Among Fittest (voanews.com)

Alonso-Zaldivar, Ricardo. "Trump's Battle with 'Obamacare' Moves to the Courts." Associated Press, March 31, 2019. Trump's battle with 'Obamacare' moves to the courts | AP News

The Weekly Screed: April 14, 2019 (Volume III, Issue 15)

To: The Donald – ""I know nothing about WikiLeaks."[4/11/19]

From: Kelly – It's Your Thing

- Oh, Donald…just because *you* suffer from CRS (Can't Remember Sh**) Syndrome, it doesn't mean the rest of us do. Take Thursday's arrest of Julian Assange, the founder of WikiLeaks, hauled kicking and screaming from his hidey hole in the Ecuadorian embassy in London.
- You're like a 4-year-old trying to deny ever eating the chocolate cake while we can clearly recall you covered head-to-toe in gooey brown frosting.
- I guess the multiple times you praised WikiLeaks during the 2016 campaign didn't count as actually being cognizant of it:
  "WikiLeaks, I love WikiLeaks." [10/10/16]; *"This WikiLeaks is like a treasure trove."* [10/31/16]; *"This WikiLeaks stuff is unbelievable. It tells you the inner heart, you gotta read it."* [10/12/16]; *"Boy, I love reading those WikiLeaks."* [11/4/16]; --*"Very little pick-up by the dishonest media of incredible information provided by WikiLeaks. So dishonest! Rigged system!"* [10/12/16]
- And it wasn't just you touting their services. As your odious lackey Roger Stone bragged to the Southwest Broward Republican Organization in August of 2016, "I actually have communicated with Assange. I believe the next tranche of his documents pertain to the Clinton Foundation, but there's no telling what the October surprise may be."
- Umm, that turned out to be the WikiLeaks release of hacked email from Clinton's campaign manager John Podesta within an hour of the <u>Washington Post</u> release of the Access Hollywood ("Grab 'em by the pussy") video.
- Even Don Jr. was in direct cahoots, with WikiLeaks emailing him on October 12, 2016: "Hey Donald, great to see you and your dad talking about our publications."
- And why is any of this important anyway? Well, it's because it was a crucial part of the Russian cyber-war on American democracy, during which WikiLeaks was one of many third parties used by Putin to help elect YOU over your rivals and install his "useful idiot" in the White House.

- I just finished reading a fascinating book called House of Trump; House of Putin (The Untold Story of Donald Trump and the Russian Mafia), written last year. I would highly recommend it to you, as a memory refresher, so you don't keep saying things like: "Russia has never tried to use leverage over me. I HAVE NOTHING TO DO WITH RUSSIA." [1/11/17]

Resources - Volume III, Issue 15

"This Photo Got Julian Assange Kicked Out of Ecuadorian Embassy." New York Post, April 14, 2019. This photo got Julian Assange kicked out of Ecuadorian embassy (nypost.com)

"Ecuador Explains Why It Gave Up Julian Assange." The New York Times, April 12, 2019. As Ecuador Harbored Assange, It Was Subjected to Threats and Leaks - The New York Times (nytimes.com)

As always, I can't make this stuff up....But Republicans can

"Trump Was Joking About Loving WikiLeaks, Sarah Sanders Says." NBC News. Trump was joking about loving WikiLeaks, Sarah Sanders says (nbcnews.com)

"Mike Pence and Trump Try to Rewrite History on WikiLeaks." Vox, April 12, 2019. Pence's defense of Trump's WikiLeaks comments makes no sense - Vox

"Republican Reaction to Trump and WikiLeaks." CNN, April 11, 2019. Donald Trump's past praise for WikiLeaks leaves Republicans at a loss | CNN Politics

"What Really Happened." Politico, April 11, 2019. Trump today: 'I know nothing about WikiLeaks.' Trump in 2016: 'Oh, we love WikiLeaks' - POLITICO

"Trump's Campaign Speeches on WikiLeaks and Julian Assange." Business Insider, November 2017. 5 Times Trump Praised WikiLeaks During His 2016 Election Campaign - Business Insider

"Trump Russia: The saga in 350 words. 24 July 2019. BBC News. Trump Russia: The saga in 350 words (bbc.com)

"House of Trump/House of Putin." The Washington Post, August 16, 2018. Book review of House of Trump, House of Putin: The Untold Story of Donald Trump and the Russian Mafia by Craig Unger - The Washington Post

The Weekly Screed: April 21, 2019 (Volume III, Issue 16)

To: ▮▮▮ The Donald – "This is the end of my presidency. I'm ▮▮▮."

From: Kelly – I concur, with redactions

Donald, I know you haven't yet (and never will) READ the Mueller Report. Which is a shame because whatever your shyster lawyer (excuse me, the Attorney General of the United States) Bill Barr is feeding you seems to have you confused as to the meaning of actual words. And then you look like a ▮▮▮ idiot. In my work with the Oregon Health Authority, I have compiled a Glossary of Terms related to the Affordable Care Act, which I give to the people I train. Likewise, I offer you a small sample of terms used in the Report:

1. **Collusion.** Described on Volume I Page 2 of the Report as "…not a specific offense or theory of liability found in the United States Code". But here's a definition I found: "secret or illegal cooperation or conspiracy, especially in order to cheat or deceive others." The Report then goes on to describe this type of activity for hundreds of pages. So, while it might not be *criminal*, it sure as ▮▮▮ happened.
2. **Coordination.** Also described on Page 2 as a term that "does not have a settled definition in federal criminal law" but which the investigators understood "to require an agreement …between the Trump Campaign and the Russian government on election interference…..which requires more than the two parties taking actions that were informed by or responsive to the other's actions or interests." So I guess since they couldn't find a signed-in-blood contract, there wasn't any coordinating going on in getting you installed in the Oval Office.
3. **Canoodling.** Not actually in the report, but maybe could be used to describe Don Junior's amorous response to the offer of dirt on Hillary "as part of Russia and its government's support for Mr. Trump" [V I, P.14]. DJTJ replies: "If it's what you say I love it" [This must be an example of being "responsive."]
4. **Exoneration.** Donald, you don't even have to know what this means. Just know that on Volume II Page 8, it says that "this report does *not* exonerate" you. So when you keep saying it does, you appear to be mentally ▮▮▮.
5. **Indictment.** Two "opinions" issued by the Department of Justice (in 1993 and 2000) say that it is "impermissible" to indict a sitting President. To which I say: "▮▮▮." Because whenever this comes up, I think back to when you said you could shoot someone on Fifth Avenue and get away with it. And then I wonder, if you actually did this, would the DOJ *still* think that you were too busy being a stone-cold murderer to be taken away from your important executive duties as POTUS? Somehow, I think that circumstance might change their "opinion."

Resources - Volume III, Issue 16

Good day, everyone. Happy Easter or Passover if you so celebrate. Happy Earth Day tomorrow. I had been planning a global-warming Screed, but the release of the Mueller report intervened. Apart from the Report itself, I have some located some lovely holiday reading for you!

"Mueller Report: Bad Guys Play Dirty, Trump Democrats' Duty." The Guardian, April 19, 2019. The Mueller report shows that bad guys who play dirty, like Trump, always win | Jonathan Freedland | The Guardian

Let's just call it "Canoodling" with the Russians. Canoodle Definition & Meaning - Merriam-Webster

"Trump Jr. and Russians: An In-Depth Look." The New York Times, July 11, 2017. Russian Dirt on Clinton? 'I Love It,' Donald Trump Jr. Said - The New York Times (nytimes.com)

Why NO ONE should not be above the law

"Why a Sitting POTUS Should Not Be Above the Law." Time. Robert Mueller Was Wrong. President Trump Can Be Indicted | TIME

"Trump, Midterms, and the Fifth Avenue Comment." The New York Times, August 28, 2018. Opinion | What if Trump Did Actually Shoot Someone on Fifth Avenue? - The New York Times (nytimes.com)

*Have **you** read The Mueller Report yet? I sure haven't (the book version is on order) but I did get through the Executive Summaries for Volume I and Volume II. And the April 18 print edition of the New York Times (delivered right to my driveway all the way across the country to Oregon).* Read the Mueller Report: Searchable Document and Index - The New York Times (nytimes.com)

It looks like 400+ pages worth of impeachable offenses to ME, and that doesn't include all the other on-going investigations. Much will be revealed in days to come, I'm sure.

The Weekly Screed: April 28, 2019 (Volume III, Issue 17)

To: The Donald – Gun Nut

From: Kelly – Purse-aholic

- Donald, you might remember me ranting about Christian bling conceal-carry handbags a few weeks ago. These accessories first came to my attention when I attended a Christmas Bazaar in Imbler, Oregon in December 2017.
- Imbler is in Union County, in Eastern Oregon, which is the NRA-friendly part of the state. A majority of the population out there voted for you, and routinely sends Greg Walden (R-OR) back to Congress, so that he can vote against their best interests. Example: Walden was front and center in the House bill to kill Obamacare in 2017, despite his territory being the Number One Republican district in the entire country whose citizens gained health coverage via the Affordable Care Act. But I digress.
- I have come to consider this past week as Bill of Rights week in these here United States. Two big events compete for our attention: the annual National Rifle Association convention (this year in Indianapolis, pumping up the Second Amendment) and the National Correspondents Dinner (always in Washington, D.C., celebrating the First Amendment). And for the third year in a row, you have boycotted the latter event to hold a rally in some other benighted city where you tell lies and threaten the rest of us.
- This year saw more drama than usual at the NRA meeting: reports of financial shenanigans; a power struggle between President Oliver North and VP Wayne LaPierre; and the concurrent sentencing of Russian spy Maria Butina in part due to her efforts to infiltrate the organization. It was a doozy.
- Then YOU showed up and proceeded to sign away any future US influence over illegal international arms deals by "un-signing" (with great flourish) our commitment to the 2014 U.N. Arms Trade Treaty. Never mind that this treaty was never ratified by the Senate and didn't do what you said it did (**"We will never allow foreign bureaucrats to trample on your Second Amendment freedom."**) Donald, you are such a doofus.
- Anyway, back to Imbler and that Christmas bazaar, where I did actually purchase (for myself) a tasteful (but adorable) red leather concealed-carry purse, complete with an illustrated guide that answers the

question: "How do you carry your pistol?" I believe it would nicely hold either of the weapons you purport to own, but I use the compartment for my copy of the *Constitution* and the book *On Tyranny*. Highly recommended reading, DT.

Resources - Volume III, Issue 17

Greetings y'all. This past week we witnessed another disturbing convention of the addled acolytes attending the annual NRA meeting. In the little book On Tyranny, Timothy Snyder warns: "When the men with guns who have always claimed to be against the system start wearing uniforms and marching with torches and pictures of a leader, the end is nigh." There are hundreds of paramilitary organizations in this great land of ours. Just saying. In the meantime, we are still free to go shopping and read books.

Bannow, Tara. "Bend Rally Urges Walden to Save Obamacare." February 2, 2017. Bend Bulletin. Bend rally urges Walden to save Obamacare | Health | bendbulletin.com

Qui, Linda. "Trump's NRA Speech Fact-Checked." The New York Times, April 26, 2019. Fact-Checking Trump's Speech to the N.R.A. - The New York Times (nytimes.com)

Mak, Tim. "Oliver North Says He Will Not Seek a 2nd Term as NRA President." NPR, April 27, 2019. Oliver North Says He Will Not Seek A 2nd Term As NRA President : NPR

Chappell, Bill. "Trump Moves to Withdraw U.S. from U.N. Arms Trade Treaty." NPR, April 26, 2019. Trump Moves To Withdraw U.S. From U.N. Arms Trade Treaty : NPR

"Maria Butina: Putin 'outraged' at sentencing of Russian spy." 27 April 2019. BBC News. Maria Butina: Putin 'outraged' at sentencing of Russian spy. bbc.com

Males, Jesse. "Here Are Donald Trump's Chosen Concealed Carry Weapons." November 1, 2019. Wide Open Spaces. Here Are Donald Trump's Chosen Concealed Carry Guns (wideopenspaces.com) ["Whether he is carrying his Smith & Wesson .38 special, or his H&K 45, you won't want to be on the receiving end of either of the two."]

Miller, Emily. "Donald Trump's Guns." The Washington Times. November 14, 2012. MILLER: Donald Trump's guns - Washington Times

The Weekly Screed: May 5, 2019 (Volume III, Issue 18)

To: The Donald – Only the Good Die Young

From: Kelly – I'm Glad I'm Not Young Anymore

Oh, Donald……I just love it when you mouth off to reporters before getting on a helicopter. It's stand-up comedy at its finest.

Last week, on your way to address the NRA in Indianapolis, we were treated to your special brand of self-adulation. Declining to declare Joe Biden too old to run for President, you reassured an anxious public: "I'm a young and vibrant man!" then gave a little crotch-thrust to emphasize your "energy." Puh-leeze.

Then on to Green Bay, Wisconsin to rally the low-information voters, feed them a bunch of hooey, and diss the rest of the democratic candidates.

To help you along next time, I've written you a campaign song, with apologies to Rodgers and Hammerstein, and titled **Younger:**

> (Intro) Can you believe I'm the President? Some people say I've been Heaven-sent! I'm here to lead the Caucasian race, and to wrap the flag in my embrace….

Younger than Biden am I.

Hotter than Beto am I.

Whiter than Swalwell, Inslee, and even Hickenlooper….

Richer than Bernie am I

Gayer than Mayor Pete am I

Tougher than all those dames who believe they stand a chance

And when I see the likes of Cory B,

And Kamala and Julián, then

I know the Nazis like ME.

Mouth-breathing Bigots love ME.

They'll vote for me and I'll be the President for Life!

Resources - Volume III, Issue 18

Good day everyone…….It's Cinco de Mayo, but I spent Quatro de Mayo at a memorial service for my beautiful, brilliant, generous, and accomplished niece, who left us all too early at age 41. Stephanie had been fighting a very aggressive form of breast cancer for four years…you can read all about it at the website for the Triple Negative Breast Cancer Foundation: https://www.tnbcfoundation.org/

This proves that, as the Billy Joel song goes, Only the Good Die Young, and the wretched Donald Trump remains.

Fabian, Jordan. "Trump: 'I Am a Young, Vibrant Man.'" April 26, 2019. The Hill. Trump: 'I am a young, vibrant man' (thehill.com)

Cillizza, Chris. "The 48 Most Wait-What? Moments from Trump's Recent MAGA Rally in Wisconsin." CNN, April 29, 2019. The 43 most mind-boggling lines from Donald Trump's Wisconsin campaign rally | CNN Politics

*This week, I've written a song for him. You can watch the video of the lovely original, from the 1958 movie **South Pacific**, which was controversial at the time for its depiction of inter-racial romance. It was also a time when the word "gayer" meant "happier."*

"South Pacific (1958) - Original Song Performance." YouTube. South Pacific - Younger Than Springtime (youtube.com)

Finally, as Maurice Chevalier sang in the (also 1958) musical Gigi, "I'm glad I'm not young anymore" but I hope I live long enough to see The Donald in an orange jump suit.

The Weekly Screed: May 12, 2019 (Volume III, Issue 19)

To: The Donald – A Walking Talking C Word

From: Kelly – Channeling the Cookie Monster

- Donald, thanks to you, I watch a lot more television than I used to. Primarily MSNBC. But there's another long-running favorite that both you and I are too old to have experienced when it would have done us the most good. I'm speaking, of course, of Sesame Street, currently celebrating its 50th Anniversary. While I adore the Muppets [Miss Piggy is a personal role model], the show also helped millions of kids learn the alphabet and the English language. Something you could use a little help with.
- For example, there are a lot of "C" words in the news right now. Let's look at a few of these, their definitions, and how to properly use them in a sentence! Here we go:
- **Corrupt:** having or showing a willingness to act dishonestly in return for money or personal gain.
  How to use in a sentence: Donald Trump is the most corrupt POTUS ever.
- **Colluded, Coordinated, Conspired:** These terms have been bandied about for months. *How to use in a sentence*: While The Mueller Report failed to provide sufficient evidence that you knowingly conspired or criminally coordinated with the Russians during the 2016 election, there are multiple ways that you've colluded with them since 1984.
- **Cover-up:** An attempt to prevent people from discovering the truth about a serious mistake or crime. *How to use in a sentence:* When you slept with women other than the First Lady, you tried to cover-up by paying them hush money, in violation of campaign laws.
- **Contempt of Congress:** The act of obstructing the work of the United States Congress or one of its committees. Also, what I often feel when I listen to most of its members. *How to use in a sentence*: When your minion Steve Mnuchin is found in contempt of Congress, he will be subject to a maximum fine of $1,000 and 12 months in the Capitol Hill jail.
- **Constitutional Crisis**: "In political science, a constitutional crisis is a problem or conflict in the function of a government that the political constitution or other fundamental governing law is perceived to be unable to resolve." [Wikipedia] *How to use in a sentence*: Following your impeachment or the elections of 2020, you will probably lock

yourself in the Oval Office and refuse to come out, which will be a constitutional crisis.
- **Cookies**: When I watch you on TV, I want to cry and eat a lot of cookies.

Resources - Volume III, Issue 19

A Happy Mother's Day to all of you who consider themselves mothers (of children, corgis, kitties, dragons) and the valiant he-men who co-parent.

As I was researching the most outrageous notion of the week set forth by Jerry Fallwell, Jr., who believes The Donald is owed an extra two years on his current term in office......."reparations" from the trials and tribulations of the Mueller investigation..., I kept bumping up against an inordinate number of words beginning with the letter C.

This inspired me to check out Sesame Street's (and especially Cookie Monster's) take on words starting with C from September 1, 2012. Sesame Street Letter C (youtube.com)

Now let's consider Colluded, Coordinated, and Conspired

Paul, Deanna. "Colluded, Coordinated, and Conspired." The Washington Post, March 25, 2019. Mueller's proof of conspiracy and collusion: What Barr's letter says - The Washington Post

Next, Contempt of Congress

Shapira, Ian. "Contempt of Congress." The Washington Post, May 9, 2019. Nancy Pelosi's Capitol jail joke: Can Congress imprison Trump officials who are in contempt? - The Washington Post

Are we already in a Constitutional Crisis? Nancy Pelosi says yes.........I say she should use the constitutional remedies available to her and impeach his ass !

Goldberg, Michelle. "Are We Already in a Constitutional Crisis?" The New York Times, May 9, 2019. Opinion | If This Is a Constitutional Crisis, Act Like It - The New York Times (nytimes.com)

Stanley-Becker, Isaac. "Claiming Two Years of His Presidency Were Stolen, Trump Suggests He's Owed Overtime." The Washington Post, May 6, 2019. President Trump echoes Jerry Falwell Jr.'s 'reparations' for two years 'stolen' by Mueller - The Washington Post

The Weekly Screed: May 19, 2019 (Volume III, Issue 20)

To: The Donald – Consensual Rapist

From: Kelly – We asked for it

- We need to give you props for this one, DT. You *promised* that you would pack all of the courts with "pro-life" justices. And, by golly, you have.
- I mean, compared to the other ways you vowed to screw over the country [Repeal and Replace Obamacare on Day One! Build a Big Beautiful Wall and Have Mexico Pay for it! Lock her up!], you really came through on this judge thing, especially with White Walker Gorsuch and I-Like-Beer Brett.
- Of course, I refer to these judicial specimens and their political counterparts as "pro-birth/pro-death." Because let us review the "pro-life" agenda :
    1. The zygote is a "person" which absolutely must be carried to term.
    2. After birth, this infant should pull itself up by its own diaper pins: Medicaid, food stamps, welfare payments, and public housing all enable sloth and dependence and must be slashed. No freebies.
    3. The Second Amendment is the only one that counts. Let's have plenty of weapons everywhere, so those babies have access to them as soon as their pudgy little fingers can pull a trigger. [Remember the toddler who killed his mother at the Wal-Mart?]
    4. This *might* result in gun violence. But then we can lock *them* up and make sure the death penalty is alive and well. Pro-life indeed.
- Naturally, the reason I feel the need to rant about this today is the moronic statements of (male) legislators in various red states that have coincided with the rash of pro-birth bills in the pipeline to the Supreme Court.
- I'm looking at you, John Becker (Ohio) who believes that ectopic pregnancies can be "replanted" from the fallopian tube into the uterus. Hah!
- And Barry Hovis (Missouri) who shared his vast law enforcement experience with us: "Most [rapes] were date rapes or consensual rapes…"

- And the 25 guys in Alabama who voted for the strictest pro-birth legislation ever: 99 years in prison for doctors who perform abortions at any stage of the pregnancy, even in cases of rape (consensual or otherwise) or incest.
- Which, when you think about it, Donald, is much more logically consistent than *your* (latest) stand on the topic. I mean, **if** abortion is MURDER, it is **still** MURDER no matter *how* the female [i.e., vessel] got knocked up: Assaulters and incestuous male family members should have just as much right to fatherhood as boyfriends, fiancés, and husbands!!!!
- Can I get an A*men*?

Resources - Volume III, Issue 20

"Trump on Abortion: I Am Pro-Life with Three Exceptions." AOL, May 19, 2019. Trump on abortion: I am 'pro-life' with 'three exceptions' (aol.com)

[Can I please note for the record that Ronald Reagan and Donald Trump were both pro-choice....before they weren't?]

Bump, Philip. "How Trump Became an Abortion Hard-Liner." The Washington Post, May 15, 2019. How Trump became an abortion hard-liner - The Washington Post

Tackett, Michael. "Trump, Abortion, and Evangelicals: A 2020 Strategy." The New York Times, May 16, 2019. Trump Fulfills His Promises on Abortion, and to Evangelicals - The New York Times (nytimes.com)

Iati, Marisa and Paul, Deanna. "Recent Sorties in the War on Roe." The Washington Post, May 17, 2019. Abortion laws in Alabama, Georgia, Missouri mount challenge to Roe v. Wade - The Washington Post

Epstein, Kayla. "Sponsor of Ohio Abortion Bill Thinks You Can Reimplant Ectopic Pregnancies. You Can't." The Washington Post, May 10, 2019. Ohio abortion bill includes false claim about ectopic pregnancy - The Washington Post

Russo, Amy. "Missouri's Barry Hovis and His 'Consensual Rapes' Comment." HuffPost. Missouri Lawmaker Backpedals On Suggestion That 'Consensual Rapes' Exist | HuffPost Latest News

Finally, a look-back to the pro-life consequences of the Second Amendment:

"Idaho Toddler Shoots, Kills Mother in Walmart." The Guardian, December 30, 2014. Idaho toddler shoots and kills his mother inside Walmart | Idaho | The Guardian

The Weekly Screed: May 26, 2019 (Volume III, Issue 21)

To: The Donald – Can't imagine the "I Word"

From: Kelly – I can

- Poor Donald …your tender feelings were hurt very badly this week: *"I hear last night, they're going to have a meeting right before this meeting to talk about the I-word. The I-word. Can you imagine?"*
- First of all, heck yeah! But then you went on to ponder a situation in which a future Democratic president could be I-worded over practically nothing! Which is just crazy talk because something like ***that*** could *never ever* happen. [#1998blowjob] We didn't have Twitter then; I'm just imagining.
- I know it's only been a couple of weeks since we considered the many C words surrounding the current catastrophe of your continual combat against constitutional government, but I found myself ruminating over several I- words this week, and not just the Big One:
- **Investigation:** Way back at this year's State of the Union address (delayed until February 5 due to YOUR government shutdown), you threatened the country thusly: *"If there is going to be peace and legislation, there cannot be war and investigation."* I keep hoping you don't mean this literally.
- **Infrastructure [week]:** What has now become an annual exercise in futility, when supposedly bi-partisan efforts to shore up collapsing bridges devolve into you doing something outrageous… like going on strike…as you did on Thursday…as you hearkened back to your SOTU pledge to do absolutely nothing unless everyone is nice to you.
- **Impromptu:** The above-mentioned hissy fit was billed as an unscheduled event which only resulted from your **ire** at being accused of a cover-up. Really, the nerve. But the Rose Garden stage set-up and the bigly printed signs gave the lie to anything resembling spontaneity.
- **Impeachment** This is such a no-brainer, DT. No one has ever deserved it more than you. And if Congress can't come up with some new ones soon, the last "impeachable offense" in the history of the US will be "lying about oral sex". And I really don't think that was what the Founders had in mind as a "high crime and misdemeanor."
- **"Ill-tempered," "immoral," "ignorant," "illegal," "illicit," "infantile," "incompetent," "inappropriate," "insufferable," and "imminently impeachy."**

- All used in a song written for the *Late Night with Stephen Colbert* show which aired Wednesday evening. Watch the video, Donald!

Resources - Volume III, Issue 21

Good evening to all of you from The Land of the Midnight Sun, Fairbanks, Alaska. My corgi is snoozing at my feet after winning a fistful of ribbons at this sweet little all-breeds dog show up here. One more session tomorrow, then back to Anchorage for a week.

Meanwhile, The Screed never rests. The Donald cannot bring himself to say the "I" word" but I have no such qualms. He has fled to Japan for a few days and (if we are lucky) he won't get the North Koreans too riled up while he's there. I was considering a poem or a song, but the Late Show with Stephen Colbert beat me to it, so I provide that link here: Colbert Cooks Up a Children's Song Response After Trump Calls Impeachment 'the I-Word' (Video) - TheWrap

Shephard, Alex. "Trump and the Impeachment Trap." The New Republic, May 23, 2019. Trump v. The "I" Word | The New Republic

Prokop, Andrew. "Trump's State of the Union: Investigations and Legislation." Vox, February 5, 2019. State of the Union 2019: Trump demands Democrats not investigate him - Vox

Haberman, Maggie, and Peter Baker. "Trump Abandons Infrastructure Week After Pelosi Clash." The New York Times, May 22, 2019. How 'Infrastructure Week' Became a Long-Running Joke - The New York Times (nytimes.com)

Brotherton-Bunch, Elizabeth. American Manufacturing Staff. "Insert Your Infrastructure Week Joke Here." American Manufacturing, May 22, 2019. [Insert Your Infrastructure Week Joke Here] - Alliance for American Manufacturing

Shephard, Alex. "Trump's Do-Nothing Presidency." The New Republic, May 24, 2019. The Do-Nothing President | The New Republic

Wikipedia Contributors. "Impeachment in the United States." Wikipedia, 2019. Impeachment in the United States - Wikipedia

The Weekly Screed: June 2, 2019 (Volume III, Issue 22

To: The Donald – Let Us Pray

From: Kelly – But for ourselves, not *your* sorry ass

- Donald, is this a new hair style? I'm looking at a photo of you taken this morning where it's kind of slicked straight back instead of that weird curly que dippity-do it's usually shellacked into. Makes you look less dorky.
- But I digress. According to the White House, you put in a celebrity appearance at McLean Bible Church in Vienna, Virginia, "to visit with the Pastor and pray for the victims and community of Virginia Beach."
- And there you are, head bowed, eyes closed, clutching a golf cap, while a crazed-looking pastor lays hands on you and waves the Bible around.
- Preacher Man must not have gotten the White House message though, cuz HIS prayer was for YOU, not all the people who got shot up on Friday.
- See, what happened was that the right reverend Franklin Graham had called on Men and Women of God across this great land of ours to lift their voices to the heavens on a Special Day of Prayer on behalf of YOU today:
I [also] hope thousands of pastors across the nation will take a moment in their service this Sunday to pray for the President with their congregations. The Bible tells us, "The prayer of a righteous person has great power ..." (James 5:16). I believe there is power in prayer!
@Franklin_Graham 2:02 PM - May 30, 2019
- Twitter-verse replies to this plea included the following:
    1. "I pray every day that he gets impeached or eats one cheeseburger too many. No preference there."
    2. "I pray trump gets what he deserves. 40 to life."
    3. "As the sound guy at my church, I will turn off his mic if he tries that bull."
- Then, inconveniently, Another Disgruntled American Man with a Gun (the world's deadliest species) killed a bunch of government employees at his former workplace and suddenly the nation needed to divert some of its thoughts and prayers to the victims and their loved ones.
- It sorta messed up the whole day. Because the article I read stated that "the president did not make remarks from the stage before departing." Your Big Day communing with a whole lot of hypocrites and the Guy Upstairs spoiled by yet another national exercise of someone else's Second Amendment rights. But at least you got in a lot of golf this weekend! So not a total loss.

Resources - Volume III, Issue 22

Good evening, all...........this week I'm writing to you from one of my favorite places, Anchorage, Alaska. It's 57 degrees and sunny. In other words, PERFECT summer weather. And I'm in a celebratory mood because my corgi Triston (aka The Triscuit) is now an AKC Registered Champion !! My only previous exposure to the world of dog shows was watching the movie "Best in Show" (hilarious) and also tuning in to the annual Westminster Dog Show (televised live from Madison Square Garden, NYC) But for the last two weekends I've attended 7 of these events, watching my friend Betty trot Triston's furry little butt around in circles. And am here to reassure you that I will not be adopting this lifestyle. My doggy and I will fly back to Portland tomorrow and retire from the ring.

And now to my usual Sunday topic: The Donald. As we know, golf is his church, but he did step in to a real church this morning to celebrate a Special Day of Prayer........for himself.......which he relentlessly promoted over the weekend.

Brigham, Bob. "Donald Trump Went on Post-Golf Twitter Rampage Begging Americans to Pray for His Failed Administration." Raw Story, June 1, 2019. Donald Trump went on post-golf Twitter rampage -- begging Americans to 'pray' for his failed administration - Raw Story

Samuels, Brett. "Trump Makes Unannounced Stop at Virginia Church." The Hill. June 2, 2019. Trump makes unannounced stop at Virginia church (thehill.com)

The Weekly Screed: June 9, 2019 (Volume III, Issue 23)

To:	The Donald – D Day Dolt

From:	Kelly – The D doesn't stand for "Donald"

- Oh, Donald……I guess it's time for another vocabulary lesson. We've recently explored "I" words and "C" words. Let's tackle the letter "D."
- **D-Day**: It's celebrated on June 6, every year. And is meant to commemorate the day the Allied forces stormed the beaches of Normandy in order to defeat the Nazis in World War II. *Not*, as proclaimed by Republican National Committee Chairwoman Ronna McDaniel, *"...the time where we should be celebrating our president."* It's not always about YOU.
- **Disgraceful**: With the graves of the fallen in the background, you granted a televised interview to Fox News, filled with your usual petty sniping at your personal and political enemies. [Pelosi. Mueller.] Very bad optics, DT.
- **Deluded**: Donald, you really need to learn to read the room. While the Trump Baby Blimp (from last summer); and Trump Toddler Tweeting on the Toilet Blimp (new this year) floated around London, you remained convinced of your popularity. These were your assessments of the trip:
    1. *"There are those that say they have never seen the Queen have a better time, a more animated time."* [Have you looked at the photos????]; and
    2. *"I am really loved in the U.K."* [Dude, check out all the protestors and the embarrassing stuff projected onto buildings around town.]
- **Dismissive**: In a June 5 interview with Piers Morgan, you declared yourself *"never a fan"* of the Vietnam war, plus it was in a country *"nobody had ever heard of"* before the US entered the fray. Fortunately, Daddy was able to secure 5 draft deferments for you, and some other poor bastard got to go in your place. I sure hope HE was a fan.
- **Disgusting**: This word describes the tab (millions of dollars) that US taxpayers are picking up for the Trump Crime Family Summer Vacation. Sure, we'd all like our kids to meet the Queen, but exactly what service to the nation is Tiffany providing by touring the Churchill War Room? Or how do we benefit from Junior and Eric's pub crawl in Ireland? Just asking.

- **Dummkopf:** Granted, this is a German term, but it perfectly describes your staggering ignorance of all matters, both foreign and domestic:
    1. Like your total cluelessness about the possible effect of Brexit on relations between Ireland and Northern Ireland (part of the UK); and
    2. Declaring that NASA should be focusing on *"Mars (of which the Moon is a part)"* for our next space adventure. [Words fail me.]

Resources - Volume III, Issue 23

History Editors. "Why Was It Called D-Day?" History, 2019. Why Is It Called D-Day? | HISTORY

Milbank, Dana. "For D-Day, Trump Recalls the Heroism of… Donald Trump." The Washington Post, June 5, 2019. Opinion | For D-Day, Trump recalls the heroism of … Donald Trump - The Washington Post

Bennhold, Katrin. "Trump in France for D-Day." The New York Times, June 6, 2019. D-Day Remembrance: Trump Mixes Solemnity With Swipes at Mueller and Pelosi - The New York Times (nytimes.com)

Carrell, Severin. "Trump UK State Visit: People Had Never Seen the Queen Have a Better Time." The Guardian, June 7, 2019. Trump on UK visit: 'People had never seen the Queen have a better time' | Donald Trump | The Guardian

Mackey, Robert. "Donald Trump Welcomed to the U.K. with Video of Boris Johnson Calling Him Unfit for Office." The Intercept, June 3, 2019. Video of Boris Johnson Mocking Trump Projected on Big Ben (theintercept.com)

Business Insider Staff. "Trump UK Visit: Londoners' Reaction." Business Insider, 2019. Donald Trump in Britain: How 12 People in London Feel About Trip - Business Insider

Poniewozik, James. "Stephen Colbert on Trump and Piers Morgan." The New York Times, June 6, 2019. Stephen Colbert Skewers Trump's Interview With Piers Morgan - The New York Times (nytimes.com)

Quartz Staff. "Trump's Kids Meeting the Queen During UK Visit Will Cost Millions." Quartz, 2019. Trump's kids meeting the Queen during UK visit will cost millions (qz.com)

Staff and Agencies. "Ireland Visit: Donald Trump Arrives for Discussions with Leo Varadkar." The Guardian, June 5, 2019. Trump likens Irish border to wall between US and Mexico | Donald Trump | The Guardian

Staff and Agencies. "Trump: Moon Is Part of Mars, Tweet NASA." The Guardian, June 7, 2019. Trump attacks Nasa and claims the moon is 'a part' of Mars | The moon | The Guardian

The Weekly Screed: June 16, 2019 (Volume III, Issue 24)

To: The Donald – Often wrong, but never in doubt

From: Kelly – NOW can we impeach you???

Oh, Donald, you made several astonishing statements this past week.

- The first came on Wednesday, when you reassured your Bromance Buddy, Little Rocketman, that you would NEVER (under your *"auspices"*) utilize CIA intel against him, like when Kim's half-brother was a CIA informant (which got him killed). That would be a shocking betrayal of trust!
- The next day, you promised (on TV!) that you <u>would</u> willingly take info on your Democratic opponents from any foreign government. *"Oppo research,"* you informed your interviewer (George Stephanopoulos, ABC).
- When George helpfully reminded you that the FBI Director (Christopher Wray, your pick) had declared this to be a crime, you doubled down with, *"The FBI Director is WRONG!"* [No, actually that would be you.]
- And what is this obsession with Norway? Back in January of 2018, you expressed a desire for more immigrants from there (instead of from all of those "shithole countries" sending us their tired, poor, huddled masses).
- And now you speculate that <u>Norway</u> might just come through with valuable information to help you in your next campaign. I hate to break it to you, DT, but Norway just isn't that into you, if you catch my drift.
- But never mind, I've composed a little song for you to sing to yourself as you recall these past few days of verbal *faux pas*. I'm sure you remember the tune to *Norwegian Wood,* by The Beatles (from *Rubber Soul,* 1965):

In twenty-sixteen, I got some aid from Russia then.
Now I need more help. It would be good if Norway would.
I said on TV that I'd take any "oppo research,"
From anyone willing and able my foes to besmirch.

I've seen lots of things in my stupendous life of crime.
But I've never thought to notify the FBI.
I wouldn't take intel against my good friend Kim Jong Un.
But dirt against all of those Democrats can't come too soon.

So I'm asking *all* my foreign friends, help me again.
If I had my pick, it would be good if Norway would.

Resources - Volume III, Issue 24

Happy Father's Day to all those who qualify ! This week was chock-full of alarming statements from the Dear Leader. And as sometimes happens, I felt a song coming on as I listened to his criminal rantings. Just to refresh your memories of the tune, hearken back to 1965 (if you were born during or before the '50s) and have a stroll down memory lane: Norwegian Wood (This Bird Has Flown) (Remastered 2009) (youtube.com) *And here's some "background" on the song itself*: Norwegian Wood (This Bird Has Flown) – song facts, recording info and more! | The Beatles Bible

First, let's hear what he had to offer up to the Dictator in the North:

Graham, David A. "Trump Sides With North Korea Against the CIA." The Atlantic. June 11, 2019. Trump to Kim: No North Korea Spying Under My Auspices - The Atlantic

Next, let's move on to the kind of intel he would accept:

Smith, Rebecca. "FEC Chairwoman Tweets It's Illegal to Accept Anything of Value from Foreign National in U.S. Election." CBS News, June 13, 2019. FEC chairwoman Ellen Weintraub tweets "it is illegal" to accept anything of value from a foreign national in U.S. election - CBS News

Rizzo, Salvador. "Why Trump's Comment About Accepting Foreign Help Is So Astounding." The Washington Post, June 13, 2019. Trump just mused openly about committing what might well be a crime - The Washington Post

Ewing, Philip. "Fact Check: Foreign Interference and Opposition Research Are Not the Same." NPR, June 13, 2019. Fact Check: Trump Compares Foreign Election Interference To Oppo Research : NPR

Finally, his inappropriate crush on Norway. Sure, they are very white and blond, but hasn't anyone told him they are socialists???

Gramer, Robbie. "Norway Rejects Trump's Backhanded Praise on Immigration." NBC News, 2019. In Norway, Trump's comments on immigration rejected as backhanded praise (nbcnews.com)

Lowe, Josh. "Trump May Love Norway, but Norwegians Can't Stand the U.S. President." Newsweek, 2019. Trump May Love Norway, But Norwegians Can't Stand the U.S. President, Say He's a 'Threat to World Peace' - Newsweek

The Weekly Screed: June 23, 2019 (Volume III, Issue 25)

To: The Donald – Commander- in- Cockamamie

From: Kelly – Not exactly a cock-eyed optimist

- Donald, your latest **cock-up** of the English language afforded a grateful nation at least *some* levity in the face of your most alarming and dangerous Game of Chicken yet: the decisions to 1) dispatch missiles to Iran and then 2) call them off.
- The comedians and the Twitter-verse made great sport of your "**cocked and loaded**" reference to this bit of military brinksmanship. Bill Maher (*Real Time* on HBO) helpfully discovered a gay porn movie with the same title.
- Many commentators (including Maher) opined that what you probably meant to say was "**locked and loaded**", which is the turn of phrase you used about two years ago (before the beautiful pen pal relationship) to threaten North Korea and Kim Jong Un.
- But (as I learned) *that* phrase is itself a malapropism for "**loaded and locked**," which is what Marion Morrison (aka John Wayne) was *supposed* to say in the 1949 (non-porn) movie "*Sands of Iwo Jima*". But he got it backwards and they filmed it that way and now we're stuck with it.
- In other news of the week, we saw you officially kick off your 2020 campaign to continue your Reign of Error as Celebrity President.
- And, as usual at these rallies, you went off **half-cocked** on matters small and great; reliving your Top Hits of the 2016 road show and acting like Hillary Clinton was still your opponent…."**Lock her up!**" cried the faithful, as neo-fascists and white supremacists marched outside the arena in Orlando.
- Meanwhile, here in Oregon, Republican state senators (whose party lost bigly in the last election) fled to Idaho in order to deny Democrats the quorum needed to vote on (and pass) a climate change bill.
- "We will not stand by and be bullied by the majority party any longer," Senate Republican Leader Herman Baertschiger Jr. (Grants Pass) whined.
- Governor Kate Brown responded by authorizing the Oregon State Police to round up the miscreants and bring them back to do their jobs, which led to this from Senator Brian Boquist (Dallas): "Send bachelors and come heavily armed. I'm not going to be a political prisoner in the state of Oregon."

- Then militia groups threatened violence against Democratic lawmakers and state staff, leading to a Capitol shutdown. **Cocka-doodle-doom.**

Resources - Volume III, Issue 25

Well, it almost happened this week: the kick-off to World War III. Fortunately, our Drama Queen in the White House pulled out at the last minute, despite being "Cocked and Loaded"

1. "George Conway on Trump's Handling of Iran: 'To Say This Is Amateur Hour Would Defame Amateurs.'" AOL, June 22, 2019. George Conway on Trump's handling of Iran: 'To say this is amateur hour would defame amateurs' (aol.com)

2. "Trump's Abrupt Decision to Call Off Iran Strike." The New York Times, June 21, 2019. Trump Says He Was 'Cocked and Loaded' to Strike Iran, but Pulled Back - The New York Times (nytimes.com)

3. "Cocked & Loaded: Twitter Takes Aim." Yahoo News. Cocked & Loaded: Twitter Takes Aim At Trump Phrase; Andrew Dice Clay Might Hold Clue (yahoo.com)

4. "Trump's 'Half-Cocked and Loaded' Tweet Draws Barrage of Reaction." The Jerusalem Post. Trump's half-cocked and loaded tweet draws barrage of reaction - The Jerusalem Post (jpost.com)

5. Maher, Bill. "Real Time with Bill Maher." YouTube, June 21, 2019. Monologue: Cocked and Loaded | Real Time with Bill Maher (HBO) (youtube.com)

6. "Trump 2020 Campaign Kickoff in Orlando." CNN, June 19, 2019. Donald Trump's 2020 kickoff rally: The 34 most memorable lines | CNN Politics

7. "Donald Trump's Orlando Rally Attracts Extremists." HuffPost. Trump's 2020 Campaign Kickoff Attracted Extremists To A City That Hates Trump | HuffPost Latest News

8. "Oregon GOP Tweets Out the Wrong Photo Claiming Heavily Armed Militia Lays Siege to the Capitol." ThinkProgress. Oregon GOP tweets logger protest photo, says 'heavily armed militia' is laying siege to the Capitol – ThinkProgress

9. Cohen, Roger. "Opinion: Trump and Iran." The New York Times, June 21, 2019. Opinion | Trump's Slouching Toward War With Iran Is a Disgrace - The New York Times (nytimes.com)

What will next week bring? Will we go to war? Will my office be occupied by armed militia?? Stay tuned !............Kelly

Resources - Volume III, Issue 25 (continued)

Glossary of Terms (in order of appearance):

- **Cockamamie** describes something that is ridiculous or implausible. Like a Trump Presidency.

    https://grammarist.com/usage/cockamamie/

- **Cock-eyed** can be traced to the Gaelic word "*caog*", meaning squint-eyed.

    http://www.word-detective.com/2011/07/cockeyed/

- **Cock-up** is basically a synonym for screw-up

    https://www.phrases.org.uk/meanings/cock-up.html

- **Cocked and loaded** : Some have suggested that this is the Secret Service code for Don Jr. and Eric

- **Locked and loaded (or, correctly, loaded, and locked)**

    https://www.phrases.org.uk/bulletin_board/61/messages/230.html

    https://www.lawfareblog.com/what-exactly-does-locked-and-loaded-mean

- **Half-cocked:** not quite fully prepared

    https://www.urbandictionary.com/define.php?term=half-cocked

- **Lock her up:** What MAGA folk say when they hear the words Hillary Clinton.
  Former national security advisor, Michael Flynn led a "Lock Her Up!" chant at the 2016 Republican National Convention. He awaits sentencing on his conviction of lying to the FBI.

    https://www.dailykos.com/stories/2017/10/30/1711184/-The-Ukrainian-Origins-of-LOCK-HER-UP

- **Cockadoodledoom** : This great word shows up as the answer to the crossword puzzle clue "Dire early morning warning"

Resources - Volume III, Issue 25 (continued)

- **Cocked and locked:** Okay, not actually in The Screed, but I found a website saying this was the safest way to carry your pistol. Consider this your bonus definition.

    https://www.usacarry.com/cocked-locked-carry-unsafe/

President Trump has been all over the place on Iran, which is what happens when you take a serious subject, treat it with farcical superficiality, believe braggadocio will sway a proud and ancient civilization, approach foreign policy like a real estate deal, defer to advisers with Iran Derangement Syndrome, refuse to read any briefing papers and confuse the American national interest with the Saudi or Israeli.

--Roger Cohen,
for *The New York Times*
June 21, 2019

The Weekly Screed: June 30, 2019 (Volume III, Issue 26)

To: The Donald – Stepping Over the Line on the World Stage

From: Kelly – Appreciating the Line-up on the Debate Stage

- Donald, I know that some people will criticize your publicity stunt at the Korean Demilitarized Zone this morning. They will bemoan your photo-op with Little Rocket Man and your gushy bromance statement: *"Stepping across that line is a great honour. Great progress has been made, great friendships have been made and this has been, in particular, a great friendship."* [Oh, puh-leeze. Get a room.]
- Likewise, many took offense at your jocular encounter with Putin a few days ago at the G20 Summit. Wearing one of the ugliest ties I've ever seen, you adopted your usual Meeting-with-Strongmen posture (sitting on the edge of the chair, legs akimbo, forming a wee heart-sign with your pudgy little fingers just in front of your crotch). Here's how the NY Times described it: *Turning to Mr. Putin, he said, with a half-grin on his face and mock seriousness in his voice, "Don't meddle in the election, President."*
- Going on to disparage a free press, you considered a solution: *"Get rid of them,"* Mr. Trump said. *"Fake news is a great term, isn't it? You don't have this problem in Russia, but we do." "We also have,"* Mr. Putin insisted in English. *"It's the same."* It's just easier to actually murder journalists in Russia when Putin wants to shut them up.
- And speaking of murder, you also heaped praise on Crown Prince Mohammed Bin Salman, who recently dispatched *his* most pesky critic (*Washington Post* reporter Jamal Khashoggi) by carving him up in the Saudi Embassy in Istanbul, Turkey: *"It's an honor to be with the Crown Prince of Saudi Arabia, a friend of mine, a man who has really done things in the last five years in terms of opening up Saudi Arabia. And I think especially what you've done for women. I'm seeing what's happening; it's like a revolution in a very positive way."* Yeah, a real freakin' beacon of liberty.
- Your other notable statement of the week was your cursory assessment of the Democratic debates: *"BORING,"* you tweeted.
- But I beg to differ, Donald. I was thrilled to watch 20 men and women who were all, to a person, intelligent, compassionate, thoughtful, and Not Crazy.
- Last month I was stopped behind a slightly beat up white Econoline van sporting this bumper sticker: **Any Functioning Adult - 2020**.

- Now that's a campaign slogan <u>all</u> Americans should be able to promote!

Resources - Volume III, Issue 26

Greetings, one and all...........As I mentioned in this week's issue, I came away happy after watching the Democrats debate for four hours. Sure, I have my preferences, but learned a lot about each person, and believe we will wind up with a worthy opponent to the Orange One. As usual, Andy Borowitz nailed it: Terrified Trump Writes Check to Biden Campaign | The New Yorker

I'm currently leaning toward either Warren, Booker, or Harris for the top of the ticket, and Julian Castro as the perfect VEEP for any of them.

Koerth, Maggie, et al. "The First Democratic Debate in Five Charts." FiveThirtyEight, 2019. The First Democratic Debate In Five Charts | FiveThirtyEight

Maddow, Rachel. "Democratic Debate: Presidential Hopefuls Put Substance First." MSNBC, 2019. In Democratic debate, presidential hopefuls put substance first (msnbc.com)

Borger, Julian. "Trump and Kim's DMZ Meeting Proves More Than Just a Photo Op." The Guardian, 2019.. Trump and Kim's DMZ meeting proves more than just a photo op | Donald Trump | The Guardian

ABC News. "Trump Meets Vladimir Putin." YouTube, 2019. Trump tells Putin at G20 summit: Don't meddle in U.S. elections (youtube.com)

Shear, Michael D., and David E. Sanger. "Trump and Putin Discuss Election Interference." The New York Times, June 28, 2019. Trump and Putin Share Joke About Election Meddling, Sparking New Furor - The New York Times (nytimes.com)

Politico Staff. "Trump's Meeting with MBS at G20 Amid Khashoggi Controversy." Politico, June 29, 2019. Trump praises Saudi crown prince, ignores questions on Khashoggi killing - POLITICO

Eloquent as always, Trump interrupted his trip to Japan to offer some commentary on the Democratic debate. "BORING!" he declared in a single-word missive on Twitter.

Shabad, Rebecca. "'Boring' Trump Yawns at Democratic Debate. NBC News. June 26, 2019. "BORING!' Trump yawns at Democratic debate (nbcnews.com)

P.S. In other news, I slipped and fell Friday night (visiting a friend, in her bathroom) and Broke My Elbow !! But I can still waggle my fingers on my left hand enough to type, so The Screed will survive.

The Weekly Screed: July 7, 2019 (Volume III, Issue 27)

To: The Donald – Potentate in Chief

From: Kelly – An Ode to the "Salute to America"

"Our Army manned the air, it rammed the ramparts, it took over airports, it did everything it had to do. And at Fort McHenry, under the rockets' red glare, had nothing but victory. When dawn came, the star-spangled banner waved defiant."

        -----The Donald, addressing the nation, July 4, 2019

'Twas the birthday of freedom from crazy King George
When patriots gathered in backyards to gorge
On hamberders*, hot dogs, and way too much beer
Singing anthems of liberty we hold so dear.

While out on the Mall there arose such a clatter
The Fake News swarmed in to see what was the matter.
King Donald was trying to put on a show,
But the rain made the dang teleprompter go slow

So the message was garbled, but he let us know:
That our brave US army, they got the job done!
They rammed all the ramparts and that's how we won.
They took over the airports in just such a manner
That dawn came and with it the Star-Spangled Banner!!

Those "new Sherman tanks" were an awesome surprise
The fly-overs lifted our eyes to the skies
We searched overhead and we looked all around
But Baby Blimp Trump never came off the ground.

Melania stunned in her rainbow-striped frock.
The spectacle <u>did</u> have a great deal to mock,
But better the POTUS play tough here at home
Than start a real war with an outcome unknown.

So cheers to the Red, White, and Blue on this day
Valor! Purity! Vigilance! All on display,

For Red States and Blue States alike to proclaim
As we watch our democracy go down in flames.

Resources - Volume III, Issue 27

Good day all............Hope everyone had a relaxing holiday weekend. Of course, I have to poke fun at The Donald's "Salute to America" antics on the 4th. Maybe this tweet from a history professor (Seth Cotlar, Willamette University, Salem, OR) put it best:

"Trump's speech at the Lincoln Memorial is like a low energy Super Bowl halftime show, swapping out Bruno Mars for your angry grandpa reading a 5th grader's book report on American Military History." @SethCotlar 4:16 pm - 4 July 2019

Brockell, Gillian. "Turns Out There Weren't Airports Back Then." The Washington Post, July 5, 2019. Trump blames teleprompter for his Fourth of July #RevolutionaryWarAirports screw up - The Washington Post

Task and Purpose. "Trump Claims Brand-New World War II Sherman Tanks Will Be Part of July 4th Salute to U.S. Military." The National Interest, July 2, 2019. Trump Claims 'Brand New' World War II Sherman Tanks Will Be Part of July 4th Salute to U.S. Military (nationalinterest.org)

Zak, Dan. "Evening in America: What It Felt Like on Trump's 4th of July." The Washington Post, July 5, 2019. Trump's 4th of July: What it felt like in Washington - The Washington Post

Wade, Peter. "Russian State TV Laughs at Trump's July Fourth." Rolling Stone, July 6, 2019. Russian State TV Laughs at Trump's Fourth of July Parade (rollingstone.com)

Colonial Flag Staff. "Symbolism of the Red, White, and Blue." Colonial Flag, 2019. Symbolism of the American Flag – Colonial Flag

Remnick, David. "Little Rocket Man." The New Yorker, July 3, 2019. Donald Trump: Little Rocket Man | The New Yorker

*"Trump Eats "Hamberders" While Government Remains Shut Down." Jimmy Kimmel . YouTube. January 15, 2019. (2079) Trump Eats "Hamberders" While Government Remains Shut Down - YouTube

P.S. Broken Elbow surgery scheduled for Thursday. Hope I can type again by Sunday.

The Weekly Screed: July 14, 2019 (Volume III, Issue 28)

To: The Donald – The Anti-Obama

From: Kelly – Missing Barack

- Good afternoon, Donald….can we get REAL today? Usually, I attempt to gather whatever shreds of humor I can find in the events of the past week so that *whoever* reads these submissions to www.whitehouse.gov can view the news through the lens of satire rather than despair.
- But I'm just not up to that on this fine Sunday in Oregon. Because as I contemplate recent headlines, I'm struck by the immense damage you are wreaking on the nation just to get back at your predecessor.
- Let us count the ways:
    1. **Cancelling the Affordable Care Act:** Largely ignored by the media (fake, liberal, or otherwise), oral arguments began on Tuesday in the 5th Circuit Court of Appeals, in New Orleans. Having repeatedly failed to Repeal-and-Replace Obamacare in Congress, the latest gambit is to declare the entire law unconstitutional through the court system. In December, in **Texas v. United States**, a District court judge did just that. You then tweeted: *"As I predicted all along, Obamacare has been struck down as an UNCONSTITUTIONAL disaster! Now Congress must pass a STRONG law that provides GREAT healthcare and protects pre-existing conditions. Mitch and Nancy, get it done!"*
    2. **Cancelling the Iran nuclear deal:** Who cares if we have World War III in the Middle East? In a new batch of leaked diplomatic cables from the former British ambassador to the US (my new hero Kim Darroch), we learned *"The administration is set upon an act of diplomatic vandalism, seemingly for ideological and personality reasons - it was Obama's deal."* You called it *the "worst deal ever."*
    3. **Cancelling environmental regulations:** Of course you also hated the Paris Climate Agreement …*"The Paris accord will undermine [the U.S.] economy," and "puts [the U.S.] at a permanent disadvantage."*) And have undone 83 other attempts by Obama to save the planet. You even reinstated sales of plastic water bottles in National Parks because banning them had cut down on too much litter.

- No, you still aren't the Worst President Ever (yet). In terms of body count and economic calamity, Good Old Dubya (#43) still ranks higher. But you are, without a doubt, the Most Despicable Person ever to occupy the White House. I believe your place in history is secure on that count.

Resources - Volume III, Issue 28

Good afternoon, all. I had surgery on my elbow on Thursday, and the new cast restricts me more than the pre-op version. So I'm typing with one finger, which really slows my roll. I'm also in a fair amount of pain, so if I weren't naturally cranky over the latest attempts to undo the Affordable Care Act, this is the icing on the cake. Sorry The Screed is such a downer this week........but sometimes I just miss my Real President a lot. Here's some info on the Great Undoing by the Insane Clown President:

Rovner, Julie. "The Affordable Care Act Is Back in Court: 5 Facts You Need to Know." NPR, July 9, 2019. Affordable Care Act Is Under Attack In Court Again: 5 Things To Know : Shots - Health News : NPR

Bachmann, Elizabeth. "Appeals Court to Uphold ACA: Health Care a Basic Human Right, Says CHA." Angelus News, 2019. Appeals court to uphold ACA; health care a basic human right, says CHA (angelusnews.com)

Keith, Katie. "The Affordable Care Act and Its Ongoing Legal Challenges." Health Affairs, July 9, 2019. Texas v. United States: Where We Are Now And What Could Happen Next | Health Affairs

Al Jazeera Staff. "UK Envoy: Trump Left Iran Nuclear Deal to Spite Obama." Al Jazeera, July 14, 2019. UK envoy said Trump left Iran nuclear deal to spite Obama: Report | Donald Trump News | Al Jazeera

Dale, Daniel; Gaouette, Nicole; Cohen, Zachary. "Fact Check: Trump Wrong on Iran Enrichment." CNN, July 11, 2019. Fact check: Trump wrong on all 3 claims in tweet on Iran deal | CNN Politics

BBC Staff. "Trump on the Iran Deal: 'Worst, Horrible, Laughable'." BBC, 2019. Trump on the Iran deal: 'Worst, horrible, laughable' (bbc.com)

Popovich, Nadja, et al. "Trump's Environment Rollbacks." The New York Times, 2019. The Trump Administration Is Reversing Nearly 100 Environmental Rules. Here's the Full List. - The New York Times (nytimes.com) [This site was updated October 15, 2020]

Nix, Joanna. "The National Park Service Ends Bottled Water Ban." Mother Jones, September 2017. The National Park Service Just Ended Its Bottled Water Ban—After Finding It Worked – Mother Jones

The Weekly Screed: July 21, 2019 (Volume III, Issue 29)

To: The Donald – Love it or Leave it

From: Kelly – Looking for the Exits

- Donald, you have outdone even *your* bigoted and misogynistic self this week. Last Sunday, you inquired of the four Congresswomen of "The Squad": *"Why don't they go back and help fix the totally broken and crime infested places from which they came…"*
[Umm… New York City? Boston? Detroit? Minneapolis?]
- On Tuesday, you reassured us that [just like Joe Biden recently announced]:
"I don't have a racist bone in my body!"
- Which comes as a huge relief, because on Wednesday, you held a rally of the White Faithful in North Carolina and posed at the podium until the [amazingly spontaneous and unified] chant of "Send Her Back" waxed and waned through the assembled multitude. Which you later repudiated. But then commended. [It's this election season's "Lock Her Up!"]
- At any rate, it set me to wondering where I could flee given, as you later put it: *"if you hate our Country, or if you are not happy here, you can leave!"*
- Or as one of my cousins plaintively tweeted: "Ancestry DNA….where should I go back to?"
- Since the seventies, I've harbored fantasies of becoming a Canadian. After George W. Bush stole his second term in 2004, I sent away for the paperwork. And, at the time, I could have squeaked in…young enough, educated enough, with passable French. But my spouse was reluctant, so we stayed put, outlasted Dubya, and basked in the glow of Obama for 8 years.
- But now we have YOU. And now, I'm too old and don't have enough money to retire in Canada. [Wait? Did you think only the glorious United States of America has immigration restrictions??]
- Lately, I've been subscribing to <u>International Living</u> magazine. "Since 1979" proclaims the masthead, which is when I was internationally living (and trying not to die young) in Zaire as a Peace Corps volunteer.
- The July 2019 issue touts Croatia as "Perfect for Part-time European Living" and promotes "Taking Things Easy in Small-Town Vietnam."

- There's also an article profiling "A Full Life Living on Social Security in Cotacachi." (In Ecuador……don't feel bad; I didn't know where it was either.)
- But now I'm seriously considering Scotland. From which the Buchanan clan side of my family emigrated. I look like them. They might take me in.

Resources - Volume III, Issue 29

Q: Can somebody explain how a huge crowd of people can spontaneously erupt in the same chant at the exact time a remark is made about the 'squad' without a cheerleader or a Jumbotron leading them on? I think the Borg only existed in Star Trek: Next Generation. **A:** it can happen if they all share one little brain

Guardian Staff. "Donald Trump Said He Tried to Stop the 'Send Her Back' Chants, But Did He?" The Guardian, July 19, 2019. Donald Trump said he tried to stop the 'send her back' chants ... but did he? - video | Donald Trump | The Guardian

Gessen, Masha. "The Weaponization of National Belonging: From Nazi Germany to Trump." The New Yorker, July 21, 2019. The Weaponization of National Belonging, from Nazi Germany to Trump | The New Yorker

Boot, Max. "Why 'Send Her Back' Is Even Worse Than 'Lock Her Up'." The Washington Post, July 21, 2019. Opinion | Why 'send her back' is even worse than 'lock her up' - The Washington Post

Wang, Esther. "A Brief, Recent History of 'I Don't Have a Racist Bone in My Body'." Jezebel, June 20, 2019. A Brief Recent History of 'I Don't Have a Racist Bone in My Body' (jezebel.com)

LaPonsie, Maryalene. "7 Tips for Retiring to Canada." U.S. News & World Report, March 10, 2017. 7 Tips for Retiring to Canada (usnews.com)

Top Retirements Staff. "Top Places to Retire in Scotland." Top Retirements, 2019. State Guides | SCOTLAND Retirement Guide (topretirements.com) [Note: this site was last updated in November 2023. I still want to move there.]

Trattner, Esther. "Best Countries to Retire on $1 Million." MoneyWise, January 25, 2019. 15 Places You Can Comfortably Retire With $1 Million | Moneywise

Cobb, Jelani. "Donald Trump's Idea of Selective Citizenship." The New Yorker, July 21, 2019. Donald Trump's Idea of Selective Citizenship | The New Yorker

P.S. My cast is off; the stitches are out; I have a metal plate and 6 pins in my arm. I can type and drive again and touch the top of my head. Back to work tomorrow !!

The Weekly Screed: July 28, 2019 (Volume III, Issue 30)

To: The Donald – "Our President, ME"

From: Kelly – The Lovers, the Dreamers, and ME

Why are there so many books about Donald that I have felt compelled to read?

Tomes about Russians; obstruction of justice; delusions of grandeur; and greed.

I have good friends who think he is terrific; I know they're wrong, wait and see:

> Someday we'll get us a much better POTUS
>
> For lovers, and Dreamers, and me.

He said that Mueller was just on a Witch Hunt, a sentiment echoed by Barr

Some people heard that, and others believed it; Look what it's done so far.

We should impeach him for all of his misdeeds, his ignorance, and cruelty.

> Someday we'll get us a much better POTUS
>
> For lovers, and Dreamers, and me.
>
>> Half of the country is under his spell
>>
>> I think everyone has gone crazy!

Have you been paying attention to all this? The damage he does with his lies?

What does he have to do to make us all wake up before our democracy dies?

Writing this Screed is my small contribution; it's something that I'm supposed to be….

> Someday we'll get us a much better POTUS
>
> For lovers, and Dreamers, and me.

La lala la lala la dee da do ! La lala la la, dee da do !!

Resources - Volume III, Issue 30

Good morning, all. I took inspiration from this week's message from:

1) The Mueller Report and hearing

2) The Muppet Movie 40th Anniversary

3) The unhinged jibber-jabber between Tarmac Trump and reporters just before he left for West Virginia:

The White House put out a transcript of this event, where the Dear Leader said (and this is an exact quote): "This has been a very bad thing for our country. And despite everything we've been through, it's been an incredible two and a half years for our country. **The administration, our President -- me --we've done a great job."**

The Muppet Movie hook came from an NPR story about the fortieth anniversary of the film, wherein they played a little bit of one of my favorite songs of all time: The Rainbow Connection. I hope my re-write doesn't spoil it (for any of us) for all time.

Holmes, Linda. "Rainbows, Frogs, Dogs And 'The Muppet Movie' Soundtrack At 40" NPR. July 25, 2019. 'The Muppet Movie' At 40: Kermit, Fozzie And A Lot Of Good Songs : NPR

Please do yourself a favor and watch Kermit (and a bunch of New Yorkers) sing his signature song at Lincoln Center:

(1931) "Rainbow Connection" with Kermit the Frog, Choir! Choir! Choir!, and New Yorkers at Lincoln Center - YouTube

I'm finally finishing up the Mueller Report.........all 476 pages and 1002 footnotes. It's a doozy !

The Weekly Screed: August 4, 2019 (Volume III, Issue 31)

To: The Donald – A One-Man Public Health Crisis

From: Kelly – Health Care Bureaucrat….and Alarmist

- Gosh, Donald. This has been quite the week in Health Care News. And I must say you have played your standard part in all of it.
- Let's begin with just one of your 20 egregious lies from this week's rally in Cincinnati: *"...We will always protect patients with pre-existing conditions, always."* Hah! Mandatory coverage of pre-existing conditions was THE signature insurance market reform of the Affordable Care Act. Which you are now trying to kill via the courts in your support of *Texas v. United States*. [Still in the Fifth District Court in New Orleans. Next stop, the Supreme Court.]
- Of course, you have a plan for terrific health care waiting in the wings, right? The one you have been promising since 2015, and which "White House Officials" say you *might* be unveiling in September. Or again, maybe not.
Because the article I read about this "stressed that the plans have not been completed" and "the ideas have yet to get [your] sign off."Okey dokey.
- Much has been made of the Democratic presidential candidates competing visions for universal health care coverage, from tweaking the ACA to full-fledged Medicare for All, but at least one thing is clear: they are all trying to expand affordable coverage while you are still obsessed with Repealing Obamacare, with or without the Replacement part.
- Next, we turn to climate change, specifically in the Arctic. While it was super nice of you to offer Vladimir Putin aid in putting out fires in Siberia, what might be more helpful is abandoning your "Chinese hoax" explanation of global warming AND to stop overturning Obama-era environmental regulations AND to rejoin the Paris Climate Agreement. These modest moves might ameliorate all the ways We The People (and I include Republicans) might soon die of the hunger, heat, drowning, wildfire, air pollution, and disease caused by climate catastrophe and continued reliance on fossil fuels.
- Finally, the biggest elephant in the room threw back its head and trumpeted that mass shootings in this country constitute an extraordinary threat to public health. As regular folk attempted to go about their business (at the Gilroy, CA Garlic Festival; at a Wal-Mart in El Paso, TX; and at Ned Pepper's western themed bar in Dayton, OH),

White Male American Citizens with guns decided once again that their Second Amendment rights trumped everyone else's Rights to Life, Liberty, and the Pursuit of Happiness. YOU came back early from golfing to offer condolences.

Resources - Volume III, Issue 31

Dale, Daniel, Subramaniam, Tara, and Lybrand, Holmes. CNN "Trump Cincinnati Rally Fact-Check." CNN, August 2, 2019. Trump made numerous false claims at his Ohio rally | CNN Politics

"White House Weighs September Rollout of Health Plan to Contrast with Democrats' Ideas." MarketWatch, August 3, 2019. White House weighs Sept rollout of health plan to contrast with Democrats' ideas - MarketWatch

Uhrmacher, Kevin; Schaul, Kevin; Firozi, Paulina; Stein, Jeff. "Where 2020 Democrats stand on Health Care" The Washington Post. [Updated April 8, 2020] Medicare-for-all: Where Democrats stand on health-care issues - Washington Post

Jayapal, Pramila. "It's Time Democrats Get Their Facts Right on Medicare for All." The Washington Post, August 1, 2019. Opinion | Pramila Jayapal: It's time for Democrats to get their facts right on Medicare-for-all - The Washington Post

Abram, Nerilie. "Time will tell if this is a record summer for Greenland ice melt, but the pattern over the past 20 years is clear". The Conversation. July 2, 2019. Time will tell if this is a record summer for Greenland ice melt, but the pattern over the past 20 years is clear (theconversation.com)

Achakulwisut, Ploy. "Climate Change is a Public Health Emergency." Scientific American. January 23, 2019. Climate Change Is a Public Health Emergency | Scientific American

Lutz. Eric. "Trump Offers to Help Putin with Siberian Wildfires." Vanity Fair, August 1, 2019. Forestry Expert Donald Trump Offers to Help Putin with Siberian Wildfires | Vanity Fair

Silverstein, Jason. "2019 Mass Shootings: More Than Days in the Year." CBS News. [Updated January 2, 2020] Mass shootings in U.S. 2019: There were more mass shootings than days in 2019, according to Gun Violence Archive - CBS News

Villa, Lissandra; Elliott, Philip; Berenson Rogers, Tessa. "Trump's Reaction to El Paso and Dayton Shootings." Time, August 7, 2019. 2020 Democrats Contrast With Trump Response to Shootings | TIME

Rubin, Jennifer. "There Is No Excuse for Supporting This President." The Washington Post, August 4, 2019. Opinion | The two recent mass shootings show there is no excuse for supporting Trump - The Washington Post

The Weekly Screed: August 11, 2019 (Volume III, Issue 32)

To: The Donald – One Sick Puppy

From: Kelly – Not a Veterinarian, but I know of some good ones

- So, Donald, it's the Dog Days of August, and once again the sound of gunfire echoes across the land. Per usual, due to your ignorance and stunning lack of empathy, you are beyond useless in these situations.
- For starters, you decided *not* to read the teleprompter when delivering your first remarks to the nation following the massacres in "Texas and Ohio" and went with your gut, calling out the cities of El Paso (Correct!) and Toledo (WRONG). But you did ask God to bless us, so there's that.
- Then you visited Dayton and El Paso, ostensibly as Comforter-in-Chief, which (of course) just made things worse by:
- 1) Attacking both Senator Sherrod Brown (D-OH) and Mayor Nan Whaley of Dayton as being insufficiently enthusiastic about your PR photo-ops with hospital staff; and
- 2) Posing for the cameras and grinning, with your tiny thumb up, while our robo-First Lady stood next to you holding a 2-month old infant orphaned by the white nationalist shooter inspired by your hateful rhetoric.
- Because, really, wasn't all of this about YOU? As your social media director informed a grateful nation: *"The president was treated like a Rock Star inside the hospital, which was all caught on video. They all loved seeing their great President!"* Gag me.
- Of course, you are blaming both shootings on mental illness and video games, neither of which has been shown to have any meaningful correlation with gun violence. What really matters is how *dangerous* people are.
- As part of my Summer Reading program, I finally got around to yet another alarming tome about YOU: The Dangerous Case of Donald Trump, published in 2017, and subtitled "27 Psychiatrists and Mental Health Experts Assess a President." I highly recommend this book to you, DT.
- One of my favorite chapters was "The Issue is Dangerousness, Not Mental Illness" which concludes that you are "unprecedentedly and abnormally dangerous" to the nation: "He has his finger on the triggers of a thousand or more of the most powerful thermonuclear weapons in the world."

- You have previously characterized both the Marine who gunned down 12 people in Thousand Oaks, California (last year) AND Kim Jong Un (in 2017) as "Sick Puppies". This year, I believe that diagnosis belongs to you.

Resources - Volume III, Issue 32

Good afternoon, all. As we ponder the possible remedies to the ever-escalating gun violence in this great land of ours, I'm convinced the only thing that will work is an outside-the-box idea from Chris Rock: Chris Rock Netflix Special Takes on Gun Debate - Business Insider

Owen, Helaine. "Trump's Speech Was Like a Hostage Video." The Washington Post, August 5, 2019. Opinion | Trump's speech was like a hostage video - The Washington Post

Goldiner, Dave. "Joe Biden and Trump both stumble over weekend gun rampages in 'Houston,' 'Michigan' and 'Toledo.'" New York Daily News, August 5, 2019. Joe Biden and Trump both stumble over weekend gun rampages in 'Houston,' 'Michigan' and 'Toledo' – New York Daily News (nydailynews.com)

Bseiso, Faris. "In Dayton and El Paso." CNN, August 8, 2019. Dayton mayor 'at a loss' for why Trump aired grievances following hospital visit | CNN Politics

Wood, Graeme. "Trump's El Paso Photo Is Obscene." The Atlantic, August 2019. Trump's El Paso Photo Is Obscene - The Atlantic

Herman, Ken. "Trump Was Rock Star When We Needed President." Austin American-Statesman, August 7, 2019. Trump was a 'rock star' when we needed a president (statesman.com)

Allen, Jonathan. "In Visit to Dayton, Trump Finds a Victim: Himself." NBC News, August 7, 2019. In visit to Dayton, Trump finds a victim — himself (nbcnews.com)

Finnegan, Joanne. "President Trump Links Mass Shootings to Mental Health; Experts Say He Has It Wrong." Fierce Healthcare, August 8, 2019 President Trump links mass shootings to mental health. Experts say he has it wrong | Fierce Healthcare

Perry, Douglas. "Psychiatrists use Mueller Report to track Donald Trump's mental health, warn: 'There is very little time now'". OregonLive, July 12, 2019. Psychiatrists use Mueller Report to track Donald Trump's mental health, warn: 'There is very little time now' - oregonlive.com

The Weekly Screed: August 18, 2019 (Volume III, Issue 33)

To: The Donald – Watching Portland

From: Kelly – Ho Hum

- Was this supposed to scare us, Donald? Your little girly-man tweet from yesterday? *"Major consideration is being given to naming ANTIFA an "ORGANIZATION OF TERROR." Portland is being watched very closely. Hopefully the Mayor will be able to properly do his job! "*
- You really are off your rocker. Along with the most despised man in the Senate, Ted Cruz (R-TX), who couldn't find time to visit his constituents in El Paso after a *real* domestic terror attack but has devoted his evil energies to Senate Resolution 279, "calling for the designation of Antifa as a domestic terrorist organization."
- Puh-leeze. You obviously have no clue what sorts of serious hate groups we've had to put up with in Oregon ever since, well, the very beginning. Sure, the People's Republic of Portland has evolved into a proud bastion of latte-swilling kale-eating socialist cyclists, but it wasn't always thus.
- Oregon's first constitution actually banned black people from residing in the state and didn't ratify the 15th Amendment to the Constitution until 1959, when I was 7 years old. [I know you've only heard about the Second Amendment, but the post-Civil War 15th gave black *men* the right to vote.]
- Meanwhile we've either harbored or home-grown a slew of despicable and violent right-wing confederacies: the Northwest Hammerskins (a white nationalist group founded in Dallas, OR, 30 years ago); ACT for America, an anti-Muslim group in Silverton; a Salem branch of the National Socialist Movement (the Nazi guys, not the Bernie guys); the Pacific Coast Knights of the Ku Klux Klan; the Wolves of Vinland (neo-pagan Norse white supremacists); and Oregonians for Immigration Reform (anti-foreigners and Holocaust deniers) based in the lovely wine-country town of McMinnville.
- To name just a few. Of course, the Proud Boys and the Oath Keepers and the Three Percenters and the Patriot Prayer nuts all made the pilgrimage to Portland yesterday, hoping to get a rise out of Rose City Antifa (which doesn't show up unless the Fascists show up first) and create major mayhem.
- But mostly everyone just walked back and forth over bridges, and a few scuffles resulted in 13 arrests and 6 injuries. Fortunately, the Portland Hot Sauce Expo, the PDX Adult Soap Box Derby, the third annual

Oregon Bigfoot Festival, and the Corgi Walk in the Pearl came off without a hitch.

Resources - Volume III, Issue 33

Good afternoon, all.........the nation watched breathlessly as just about every right-wing-nut outfit descended on the Rose City yesterday. Would it be another Charlottesville? Or Hong Kong? My main concern was the safety of Portland's corgis, as the organizers of the annual Corgi Walk in the Pearl decided to Keep Calm and Corgi On in the face of the fascist invasion. Corgi Walk in the Pearl .

Fortunately, as coverage from Montana (!) showed, no corgis were harmed in this event: The 12th annual Corgi Walk held in Portland despite protests | Billings News | kulr8.com

Meanwhile, other media covered the actual demonstration of testosterone overload, which was organized to protest Rose City Antifa, although Rose City Antifa doesn't protest anyone unless actual fascists deliberately come to town to cause trouble.

Papenfuss, Mary. "Proud Boys Deem Portland a Success Because Trump Sided With Right-Wing Extremists." HuffPost Latest News, August 8, 2019. Proud Boys Deem Portland A Success Because Trump Sided With Right-Wing Extremists | HuffPost Latest News

Wilson, Jason. "Portland rally: Proud Boys vow to march each month after biggest protest of Trump era." The Guardian, August 17, 2019. Portland rally: Proud Boys vow to march each month after biggest protest of Trump era | Portland | The Guardian

Baker, Mike; Bogel-Burroughs, Nicholas. "Antifa and Far-Right Groups Face Off in Portland as Trump Weighs In. " The New York Times, August 17, 2019. Antifa and Far-Right Groups Face Off in Portland as Trump Weighs In - The New York Times (nytimes.com)

Perry, Douglas. "Oregon has prominent place on Southern Poverty Law Center's new list of U.S. hate groups" OregonLive, February 21, 2018. Oregon has prominent place on Southern Poverty Law Center's new list of U.S. hate groups - oregonlive.com

Semuels, Alana. "The Racist History of Portland." The Atlantic, July 22, 2016. The Racist History of Portland, the Whitest City in America - The Atlantic

Gupta, Arun. "Riotlandia: Why Portland Has Become the Epicenter of Far-Right Violence" The Intercept, August 16, 2019. Why Portland Has Become the Epicenter of Far-Right Violence (theintercept.com)

The Weekly Screed: August 25, 2019 (Volume III, Issue 34)

To: The Donald – Dissed by Denmark

From: Kelly – Let's Go Greenland !

- Poor Donald. Your latest real estate venture was rejected out-of-hand by the current owner. How dare Denmark refuse to even haggle with you over your proposed purchase of Greenland ? Who does that "nasty" Prime Minister think she is anyway?? Boy, you showed her who was boss.
- I'm sure that if Denmark floated the idea of acquiring, say, Alaska, you would give it your usual thoughtful and informed consideration, and promptly schedule a red-carpet welcome for the bargaining delegation. I mean, we only spent $7.2 million to buy the place from the Russkies way back in 1867. I'm sure you could get our money back and more, even though half the state is presently engulfed in flames.
- But back to Greenland. Honestly, I'm surprised you even offered to buy the place. We already maintain an honest-to-god Air Force Base there: Thule AFB, profiled in a *Life* magazine article, "Birth of a Base," dated September 22, 1952. I mean, Denmark should be paying **us** take the whole chunk of ice off its hands. There certainly isn't much to write home about: the climate is lousy; the mosquitoes are ferocious; and there are only 2 *golfklubs*.
- The capital city, Nuuk, sports a Country Club with a 9-hole course played on "arctic grass". And the delicious Scottish whiskey liqueur Drambuie sponsors the annual (weather permitting) World Ice Golf Championship in Uummannaq. But I'm convinced that the Trump Organization could work its usual magic and create a world-class resort on the shores of Diskobay.
- Okay, maybe Denmark wants to hold on the world's biggest island for bragging rights? Strategic location? All those valuable minerals hiding out beneath the permafrost? But there's only about 56,000 Inuit living there full time. We have a proud history of decimating the homelands of indigenous peoples, so one more wouldn't matter much in the grand scheme of things.
- Denmark's military is certainly no match for ours, and I doubt that NATO would weigh in to help. While Amerika, on the other hand, could probably rely on our good friend and ally Vladimir Putin to support our invasion.

- About 16 years ago, we determined that a bunch of OUR oil was located under the sands of Iraq and just went in to claim what was rightfully ours. I'm willing to bet that if we took over Greenland, we would be greeted as liberators in Kangerlussuaq, just like in Kirkuk.

Resources - Volume III, Issue 34

Good afternoon, friends. I've been thinking that our next military adventure would be Iran.........or maybe North Korea if the bromance fizzles. But now I'm considering that The Donald just might go after Greenland. If you can't buy it, take it !

Real Estate

Bildt, Carl. "Trump's Denmark Saga of the Absurd." The Washington Post, August 21, 2019. Opinion | Carl Bildt: Trump's Denmark saga goes beyond the absurd - The Washington Post

Bender, Jeremy. "We're Already There - Life on Thule AFB." Business Insider, November 24, 2014. What It's Like to Serve at Thule Air Base - Business Insider

Hitting the Links

Zuk, Sean. "Golfing on Greenland." Golf.com, August 17, 2019.** If President Trump buys Greenland, the U.S. would gain these golf courses

World Ice Golf: World Ice Golf Championship, Ummannanaq, Greenland (youtube.com)

It's Not Like It's the First Time We've Done Something Like This.

Longley, Robert. "Did Oil Drive the US Invasion of Iraq?" Thought.Co. [Updated on October 04, 2021] Did Oil Drive the US Invasion of Iraq? (thoughtco.com)

Bonus videos - Greenland ice

Iceberg crashing in Diskobay: iceberg crashing in Diskobay, Greenland (youtube.com)

Ever see an iceberg tip over? (1925) Ilulissat Icefjord - Large iceberg breaking over - YouTube

Greenland: GREENLAND - LAND OF ICE 4K (youtube.com)

Finally, as it just so happens, I'm reading an excellent book about past explorations and current climate change investigations of Greenland.

The Ice At The End Of The World by Jon Gertner (2019)

The Weekly Screed: September 1, 2019 (Volume III, Issue 35)

To: The Donald – MSG Liar

From: Kelly – I can help you out

- Not your finest week, Donald. There were so many milestones of malfeasance, I was forced to borrow the acronym for that nasty additive to Chinese food (mono sodium glutamate). But in your case, MSG stands for:
- <u>MEAN</u> -- The headline in the *New York Times* says it all: "*Sick Migrants Undergoing Lifesaving Care Can Now Be Deported*" …in 33 days. This has the sticky malevolent fingerprints of your Senior Evil Policy Advisor Stephen Miller all over it, and constitutes a new low, even for you.
- <u>STUPID</u> – The Associated Press thoughtfully gathered your top six idiotic statements of the week on the topics of:
  1) Puerto Rico hurricane aid ("*Will it ever end?*"); When hurricanes end.
  2) General Motors *("…once the Giant of Detroit, is now one of the smallest auto manufacturers there.")*; Umm, still the largest.
  3) North Korea *("the first lady has gotten to know Kim Jong-Un*); NOT
  4) Iran *("We gave them $150 billion and & 1.8 billion and we got nothing)*
  Well, actually these were previously frozen Iranian assets, & an unpaid debt.
  5) The environment *("We're right now having the cleanest air and cleanest water on the planet.");* Hello! Switzerland is #1; we are #27.
  6) Wind energy *("… windmills, which frankly aren't working too well.")*. That would be wind <u>turbines</u>, Donald Quixote, which are working just fine.
- <u>GREEDY</u> -- In your latest attempt to violate the emoluments clause of the Constitution, you have put forward the truly lousy idea of hosting next year's G-7 summit at your bedbug ridden FAILING Doral Resort in Florida, within 5 a five-mile radius of odiferous attractions such as the Medley landfill and Covanta Waste Energy facility. Spectacular, I'm sure.
- <u>LIAR</u> –The *Washington Post* has reported a new record of presidential prevarication: 12,019 "false or misleading claims" since taking office.
- But here's where I can be of assistance, Donald: To save you from committing one more impeachable offense, I suggest holding the next G-7 fête in Eastern Oregon. May I offer the Retreat, Links, and Spa at

Silvies Valley Ranch? It has its own airstrip (daylight landings only) and provides "once-in-a-lifetime Western experiences." Both at the ranch itself, and the nearby metropolis of Burns. Plus, instead of worrying about hurricanes, world leaders can enjoy the annual Harney County Fair & Rodeo. Giddy-up.

Resources - Volume III, Issue 35

Good afternoon, one and all. I'm feeling happy today because it's September which means autumn begins this month! The approach of fall has not improved The Donald's mood, however. In fact, it's been a true s***storm of a week, full of mean, stupid, and greedy blatherings, actions, lies, and missteps.

Mean

Jordan, Miriam, Dickerson, Caitlin. "Sick Migrants Undergoing Lifesaving Care Can Now Be Deported." The New York Times, August 29, 2019. Sick Migrants Undergoing Lifesaving Care Can Now Be Deported - The New York Times (nytimes.com)

Stupid

Associated Press. "AP Fact Check: Trump's Swipe at Puerto Rico and G-7 Comments." PBS NewsHour, August 2019. AP fact check: Trump's swipe at Puerto Rico, G-7 comments | PBS News Weekend

Greedy

Leena, Kim. " Everything We Know About the Trump Resort in Doral, Florida." Town & Country, August 2019. [Updated October 19, 2019] All About the Trump Doral Resort in Florida - Donald Trump G7 Summit at Golf Club (townandcountrymag.com)

Liar

Kessler, Glenn, et.al. "President Trump Has Made 12,000 False or Misleading Claims." The Washington Post, August 12, 2019. Trump has made more than 12,000 false or misleading claims - The Washington Post

Now, here's MY suggested venue for the G-7 summit next year, even though they spelled "accommodations" wrong at their website....I used to drive through this place all the time when I commuted between Burns and John Day in eastern Oregon, and it's beautiful. The Retreat at Silvies Valley Ranch - Oregon Golf Spa Resort | The Retreat at Silvies Valley Ranch.

Attendees could also visit the lovely metropolis of Burns [Burns, Oregon | Things to do in Burns, OR (traveloregon.com)] and environs Malheur National Wildlife Refuge - Travel Oregon (site of the famous 2014 Occupation!)

The Weekly Screed: September 8, 2019 (Volume III, Issue 36)

To: The Donald – Wannabe Weatherman

From: Kelly – I know which way the wind blows

Donny's in the White House thinking 'bout tweets sent
I'm watching TV thinking 'bout the government
Mike Pence, suspense, will he get laid off?
Might know too much, might need a payoff

Look out, kid, it's somethin' you did. God knows when, but you're doin' it again. You better stay at Trump resorts; play at his golf course
Air Force diverts to stay at Turnberry
Too bad per diem is the only cash you carry

Alabama governor said she wore black face
Long time ago but it's still sure a disgrace
She won't resign, don't care what they say
God must approve cuz the hurricane stayed away

Look out, kid, don't matter what you did. Walk on your tiptoes, get woke with No Doz. Protesters in the streets watch out for the fire hose
Keep a clean nose, wear the right color clothes
You don't need a weatherman to know which way the wind blows

Ah, get sick, get well, migrants going through hell
Obamacare in the courts; might be the death knell
Try hard, get barred, get back beyond the pale
Get jailed, jump bail, get deported if you fail

Look out, kid, you're gonna get hit. By users, MAGA men, loud-mouth losers
Hangin' 'round with cheaters. Guy in the White House playing with his sharpie
Don't follow leaders, they're all bottom feeders.
Oh, get born, keep warm, climate change coming fast
Learn to dance, get blessed, try to be a success
Please her, please him, buy gifts, don't grift
Go to college, get out, paying rent's a heavy lift

Look out, kid, they keep it all hid. persevere, resist, light yourself a candle
Pay attention, read the news, stay up on the scandals
Outrage in the air, listen up, you gotta care.

Can't let the country succumb to the vandals.

Resources - Volume III, Issue 36

Well, it happened again..........a line from a long-ago song just popped into my head, and I was compelled to mangle the lyrics. This week's offering is: **Homesick for Obama Blues -(apologies to Robert Zimmerman, Nobel Prize for Literature, 2016)** *Here's the video of the original. First rap ever made. First official lyric video ever.* (1925) Bob Dylan - Subterranean Homesick Blues (Official HD Video) - YouTube

Harvey, Josephine. "Trump's Sharpie Memes Over Hurricane Alabama." HuffPost, September 4, 2019. Trump Sharpie Memes Show How He Could Solve All His Problems With Pen | HuffPost Latest News

Borenstein, Seth. "NOAA Assailed for Defending Trump's Hurricane Dorian Claim." AOL News, September 7, 2019. NOAA assailed for defending Trump's Hurricane Dorian claim (aol.com)

Connor, Jay. "Alabama Gov. Kay Ivey Refuses to Step Down Over Blackface Controversy." The Root, September 5, 2019. Alabama Gov. Kay Ivey Refuses to Step Down Over Blackface Scandal (theroot.com)

Bertrand, Natasha and Bender, Bryan. "Air Force Crew Stayed at Trump's Scottish Retreat." Politico, September 6, 2019. Air Force crew made an odd stop on a routine trip: Trump's Scottish resort - POLITICO

Thiessen, Mark. "Air Force Disputes Alaska Crew Favored Trump Scottish Hotel." AOL News, September 8, 2019. Air Force disputes Alaska crew favored Trump Scottish hotel (aol.com)

Young, Neil J. "Mike Pence: Lackey in Chief." The Week, September 2019. Lackey in chief | The Week

Helmore, Edward. "Mike Pence accused of humiliating hosts in Ireland." The Guardian, September 5, 2019. Mike Pence accused of humiliating hosts in Ireland | Mike Pence | The Guardian

Goodnough, Abby. Appeals Court Seems Skeptical About Constitutionality of Obamacare Mandate." The New York Times, July 9, 2019. Appeals Court Seems Skeptical About Constitutionality of Obamacare Mandate - The New York Times (nytimes.com)

The Weekly Screed: September 15, 2019 (Volume III, Issue 37)

To: **The Donald – Strongman**

From: **Kelly – I could knock you over with a feather**

- Donald, you have a lot of communication quirks: you frequently refer to yourself as "a stable genius;" you often claim ignorance ("I don't know...I don't know") when the true answer to the question is "yes"....as in "Yes, I drew the bubble on the weather map with my trusty Sharpie."
- But the word you keep coming back to again and again is: Strong, or strongly. Especially when you are lying about something... or have no intention of doing what you say you are going to do...or when you are fixing to do something dastardly.
- Or sometimes it's just plain old hilarious. Like this past week when you were holding your little press conference about the horrors of vaping. And you pointed at Melania (who, as per usual, was in typical Stepford Wife mode, expressionless and silent) and said the following:

"That's how the first lady got involved. She's got a son," (awkward pause) "together." After recalling that this so-called "son" [aka Barron] might also be yours, you added: [he] "is a beautiful young man, and she feels very, very strongly about it." Nice save, doofus.

- Or take delaying the 2020 census because the courts wouldn't let you add the "Are you a citizen?" question (which would have resulted in a huge undercount.)"We're looking at that...So we are trying to do that. We're looking at that very strongly." Bozo. Not gonna happen.
- Or your *current* stand on reproductive choice: "As most people know, and for those who would like to know, I am strongly Pro-Life, with the three exceptions - Rape, Incest and protecting the Life of the mother - the same position taken by Ronald Reagan." [After RR was pro-choice in the '70s.]
- Or your extremely temporary consideration of stronger gun control legislation following the summer blood baths: "I'm saying Congress is going to be reporting back to me with ideas. And I'll look at it very strongly." Fat chance.

- But, ultimately, you wanna BE a strongman, just like your dictator buddies Putin, Duterte, Xi, Kim, and Erdogan. Here's how you start: by declaring martial law and canceling the 2020 general election. I'm sure you are already considering it strongly.

Resources - Volume III, Issue 37

Good morning, everyone........I'm at rainy (but still beautiful) Gleneden Beach this weekend. Sitting in a coffee shop that has the only (on-again, off-again) wi-fi for miles around. But no obstacles can stop The Screed !! Today's puzzlement: How anyone, even his most idiotic supporters, can think that this guy is a Strong He-Man Leader is beyond me....but he's definitely trying to convince us of that at all times.

Moye, David. "Twitter Users Mock Trump's Parenting Skills After He Says Melania 'Has A Son' HuffPost, September 11, 2019. Twitter Users Mock Trump's Parenting Skills After He Says Melania 'Has A Son' | HuffPost Latest News

Fabian, Jordan. "Trump looking 'very strongly' at delaying census" The Hill, July 2019. Trump looking 'very strongly' at delaying census (thehill.com)

Ertelt, Steven. "President Trump Tweets 'I'm Strongly Pro-Life'." LifeNews, May 20, 2019. President Trump Tweets "I'm Strongly Pro-Life." Says "We Must Stick Together for Life and Win in 2020" - LifeNews.com

Rubin, Jennifer. "Trump's Inevitable Cave on Gun Safety Has Arrived." The Washington Post, August 19, 2019. Opinion | Trump's predictable cave on gun safety has arrived - The Washington Post

Balluck, Kyle. "Trump: 'I Strongly Pressed Putin on Election Interference'." The Hill, July 9, 2017. Trump: I 'strongly pressed' Putin on election meddling (thehill.com)

Milligan, Susan. "Postpone the 2020 Election? Many GOP Voters Say Yes." U.S. News & World Report, August 10, 2017. Postpone the 2020 Election? Many GOP Voters Say Yes (usnews.com)

The Weekly Screed: September 22, 2019 (Volume III, Issue 38)

To: The Donald – ♫ Unimpeachable ♫

From: Kelly – ♫ That's what you are ♫

- Donald, I usually reserve my rant about your ever-mounting list of impeachable offenses for the last Screed of the year, but I find myself unable to delay commenting on the events of the past week.
- It appears that the *very day* following Robert Mueller's testimony before Congress……..when it became clear that you would never be held accountable for the many high crimes and misdemeanors outlined in his report….you doubled down and decided that the 2020 election could also be swayed with assistance from a foreign power:
- In this case, the President of Ukraine, Volodymyr Zelensky, who (it appears) you tried to bully into providing dirt on Joe Biden's son Hunter and his business dealings in that country. I reckon you figured if it worked with Vladimir and Hillary, why not use the same tactics to smear Uncle Joe?
- All this comes to us by way of a whistle-blower complaint about said phone conversation which was found to be "credible and of urgent concern" by the Intelligence Community Inspector General, Michael Atkinson, who is <u>required by law</u> to turn such a complaint over to Congress.
- True to form for your administration, the acting Director of National Intelligence, Joseph McGuire, who has been in this position for about 6 weeks, [after the hasty exit of former DNI Dan Coats and his Deputy Sue Gordon, and the aborted appointment of Congressman (R-TX) and toady John Ratcliffe] has blocked this move. Unprecedented and illegal, but hey.
- Well, I'm sure the whole thing will be cleared up quickly, since you said today that you are just fine with releasing the transcript of the call since it *"was largely the fact that we don't want our people, like Vice President Biden and his son creating to the [sic] corruption already in the Ukraine."*
- *Contributing* to the eloquence of political discourse, as always.
- Donald, I get a lot of mail from Nancy Pelosi and the DNC, begging me for money, and urging me to please check off what I feel are the top Democratic priorities for 2020. These lists never include "Impeach the Sumbitch" [as they would say in my native Texas] as a choice, so I

- always write it in, and inform the sender that they will get my dollars only when that happens.
- I have no worries that I will ever write that check, DT. You remain untouchable, much to the disgrace of our Congress and our country.

Resources - Volume III, Issue 38

Good afternoon, everyone.... Way back on Valentine's Day, 2017, The Screed contained a re-write ("Reprehensible") of that Nat King Cole standard ("Unforgettable") from 1951. Today, another version that it pained me to pen:

Unimpeachable, that's what you are, just like Kavanaugh, or William Barr

Doesn't matter how nefarious,/ Democrats don't want to make a fuss

Never before has someone been more...

Unimpeachable, in every way and I do despair that's how you'll stay.

That's why, Donald, it's a mystery that a POTUS with your history

Stands invincible, unaccountable too.

Tenbarge, Kat. "Trump Talked About Both Joe and Hunter Biden with Ukraine Leader." Business Insider, September 22, 2019. Trump Says He Hopes 'They Release' Ukraine Call on Joe, Hunter Biden - Business Insider

Nichols, Tom. "Trump's Ukraine Call Is a Clear Impeachable Offense." The Atlantic, September 21, 2019. Trump's Ukraine Call: A Clear Impeachable Offense - The Atlantic

Rozsa, Matthew. "AOC: Democratic Refusal to Impeach Trump Is a Bigger National Scandal Than Trump's Lawbreaking." Salon, September 22, 2019. AOC: Democratic refusal to impeach Trump is a "bigger national scandal" than Trump's lawbreaking | Salon.com

As so often happens lately, I agree with Elizabeth Warren on this one: "A president is sitting in the Oval Office, right now, who continues to commit crimes," Warren tweeted. "Today's news confirmed he thinks he's above the law. If we do nothing, he'll be right."

Rizvi, Nayyirah. "Reiterating Call for Impeachment, Warren Accuses Congress of Complicity in Trump's Continued Crimes." Common Dreams, September 21, 2019. Reiterating Call for Impeachment, Warren Accuses Congress of Complicity in Trump's Continued Abuses | Common Dreams

The Weekly Screed: September 29, 2019 (Volume III, Issue 39)

To: The Donald – Blatherskite in Chief

From: Kelly – Bombarded by Blather

- My goodness, Donald….what a difference a week makes! In my dispatch last Sunday, I was bemoaning the fecklessness of Nancy Pelosi and the hand-wringers in Congress urging "caution" in calling you to account.
- Then we all were provided with two documents so sweetly short and succinct that even *you* might be able to read them (and I hope you have):
  1) A 5-page "Memorandum of Telephone Conversation", which was "Declassified by order of the President September 24, 2019"; and
  2) An Unclassified 7-page memo (with a 2-page Classified and redacted Appendix) from an as-yet Unknown Whistleblower. This communication was addressed to the Chairmen of the Senate and House Committees on Intelligence and dated August 12 (but was held up by the DNI and DOJ and not provided to Congress until September 25).
- The release of these bombshells was followed by a public hearing on September 26 wherein Acting Director of National Intelligence Joseph McGuire had his hat handed to him by the House Intelligence Committee.
- These three events resulted in a majority of House Dems *finally* on-board for an official Impeachment Inquiry, even my own reluctant Representative, Kurt Schrader, a notorious DINO (that's "Democrat In Name Only", if you aren't up on political lingo)….And even, at long last, Speaker Pelosi herself, who needed to get out ahead of the "moderate" freshman Democrats she was "protecting" from political backlash in the hinterlands.
- Now I realize that you, The Stable Genius, have purported to "have the Best Words"……….as in the words you used in the "absolutely perfect" July 25th shakedown phone call with Ukrainian President Volodymyr Zelensky.
- So perfect, in fact, that the transcript and all other notes of the call were sent to a hidey-hole secret server normally reserved for the most clandestine of national security materials…..So perfect that your communications clean-up detail felt it necessary to blast a "Talking Points" email to all House Republicans (and, oopsie, Democrats as well)….So perfect that I (as one of your frequent correspondents)

received a "Resolute Reads" email from the White House [Real News President Trump Doesn't Want You to Miss] with links to articles such as *"After Failing on Russia, Democrats Try a New Hoax"* from The Washington Times. Blather, blather, and blather indeed.

Resources - Volume III, Issue 39

Greetings to all. I think we can safely say that The Donald really put his foot in it this week. And then attempted major damage control, which did not turn out so well. Which called to mind a Word-of-the-Day I received on September 10, and am quite fond of:

Blatherskite [bla-thər-skīt] Origin: *Scottish English, 17th century* Nonsense/ A person who is prone to speaking nonsense

While this term seems to have reached maximum popularity around 1930, I predict a come-back. To begin, just in case you haven't gone there on your own yet, here are links to what might be the two most important documents of the year (so far). They are much more bite-size and digestible than The Mueller Report:

Full Document: Trump's Call With the Ukrainian President
By THE NEW YORK TIMES UPDATED Oct. 30, 2019
Full Document: Trump's Call With the Ukrainian President - The New York Times (nytimes.com)

"The Whistleblower Complaint." House Intelligence Committee, August 12, 2019. Read the full text of the Trump-Ukraine whistleblower complaint (nbcnews.com)

Brooks, Brad. "Pelosi: Public Shifting to Support of Impeachment Inquiry." AOL News, September 29, 2019. Pelosi: Public shifting to support of impeachment inquiry (aol.com)

Nilson, Ella. "Moderate House Democrats Call for Impeachment Investigation." Vox, September 24, 2019 Impeachment: Moderate House Democrats are suddenly eager for an impeachment investigation - Vox

Rubin, Jennifer. "A 'Perfect Call' for Those Dense Enough to Say So." The Washington Post, September 26, 2019. Opinion | The 'perfect' call — and those dense enough to say so - The Washington Post

Morrow, Brendan. "White House Accidentally Emailed Ukraine Talking Points to Nancy Pelosi." The Week, September 2019. The White House accidentally emailed its Ukraine talking points to Nancy Pelosi | The Week

The Weekly Screed: October 6, 2019 (Volume III, Issue 40)

To: The Donald – Emperor of the Village People

From: Kelly – Once Again, the Emperor Has No Clothes

- Uh-Oh, DT. Another not-so-good week for you.
    1) You doubled down on the impeachable offense of soliciting election interference from a foreign power, this time from China :
    "China should start an investigation into the Bidens, because what happened in China is just about as bad as what happened with Ukraine,"
    2) We were treated to a delicious stream of tweets showing (per <u>The New York Times</u> headline) "Envoys Saw Quid Pro Quo in Ukraine."
    3) Just this morning, another whistle-blower on the Ukraine mess has emerged. Let's call this one WB 2.0, in the interest of keeping track. I think we might wind up with a long list of WBs.
- But you did have *some* fun last week, when you appeared before hundreds of deluded supporters in The Villages, Florida. As usual, you were able to damn with faint praise AND get away with a bunch of outright lies:
- *"I'm thrilled to be here in one of the most famous and thriving communities anywhere in Florida, and really anywhere in the world, as far as I'm concerned — The Villages. (Applause.) In fact, I was thinking about moving to The Villages, but I just couldn't leave Mar-a-Lago. I couldn't leave it. (Laughter.) I got stuck at Mar-a-Lago. I don't know."*
Translation: You poor losers may think you have it great here, but it can't hold a candle to my truly spectacular Mar-a-Lago. Neener, neener, neener.
- *"And we met the folks that built The Villages and that run The Villages, and they're out here someplace. And they've done a fantastic job. You know, in my old days, I would have been jealous. Now I couldn't care less about them. (Laughter.) It's amazing. It's amazing how being President can do that to you. (Laughter.)"*
Translation: I'm the President, and you're not.
- *"But they may go by different names, whether it's "single payer" or the so-called "public option*
- *,"* but they're all based on the totally same, terrible idea. They want to raid Medicare to fund a thing called socialism. Any socialists in the room? I don't think so. Not too many. Anybody? AUDIENCE: Booo —

Translation: Medicare-for-Seniors is just dandy, but Medicare-for-All is for deep-state socialists and communists and illegals and freedom-haters.
- As long as I'm President, no one will lay a hand on your Medicare benefits. And that's what we're here to do today. (Applause.)
Translation: I'm SO here to lay a hand on your Medicare by taking the first step to privatize the hell out of it. Suckers!

Resources - Volume III, Issue 40

Buckley, Chris. "Trump Urges China to Investigate Bidens." The New York Times, October 5, 2019. China Loves News About Trump's Controversies. Not This Time. - The New York Times (nytimes.com)

Emmons, Alex. "Trump's Ukraine Call." The Intercept, October 4, 2019. Trump-Ukraine Call Was Anything but "Routine," Texts Show (theintercept.com)

McCarthy, Tom. "Second Whistleblower Comes Forward in Trump-Ukraine Scandal." The Guardian, October 6, 2019. Second whistleblower comes forward in Trump-Ukraine scandal | Trump impeachment inquiry (2019) | The Guardian

But, as usual, our Dear Leader took the time to rally the faithful in what looks to me like one of the Worst Places on Earth: The Villages, in central Florida. Along with the unbearable heat, enough alligators to stock a border moat, and Stand Your Ground laws, this deep-red Republican haven boasts (according to its official website): [A] Fun and affordable active adult community where everything you could possibly want, need, or dream of doing in your retirement years is just a golf car ride away... The Villages® Florida: Active Retirement Living at Its Best

Yeah, that's my Dream Retirement all right: no need to leave the compound, just drive my $25,000 golf cart around in circles with a bunch of old codgers who proudly call themselves the M-T Heads (that's pronounced "Empty Heads", get it?)

Johnson, Akilah. "The Villages Trump Visit: Medicare Advantage for Retirees, the Government Pays for It." ProPublica, October 3, 2019. They're Retired. They're Insured. The Government Pays for It. And Trump Loves It. — ProPublica

Simmons-Duffin, Selena. "Targeting Medicare for All Proposals, Trump Lays Out His Vision for Medicare." NPR, October 3, 2019. Trump Signs Executive Order On Medicare, Critiques 'Medicare For All' : Shots - Health News : NPR

Luthra, Shefali. "Fact-Checking Trump's Claims About Medicare in The Villages." Politifact, October 3, 2019. PolitiFact | Fact-checking Trump's claims about Medicare at The Villages in Florida

Remarks by President Trump at Signing of an Executive Order Protecting and Improving Medicare for our Nation's Seniors | Ocala, FL – The White House (archives.gov)

The Weekly Screed: October 13, 2019 (Volume III, Issue 41)

To: **The Donald – Towering Idiot**

From: **Kelly – Just trying to keep up with the headlines**

- Uh-Oh, DT. Another not-so-good week for you:
- Marie Yovanovitch, the former ambassador to Ukraine, testified before three House committees leading the impeachment inquiry against you. As you predicted in The Gift That Keeps on Giving (the transcript of your July 25 phone call with Ukraine President Zelensky) she did indeed turn out to be "bad news" [for you]. You should read her prepared remarks. Ouch!
- I know you claim not to know these guys, but it turns out that one of Rudy Giuliani's "business associates" who were arrested on Wednesday (just before leaving the country) attended your "invitation-only" election night party. This upstanding gentleman (Lev Parnas) founded a company called "Fraud Guarantee." His comrade-in-crime Igor Fruman owns a Black Sea beach club called "Mafia Rave." I cannot make this stuff up.
- And more adverse events in a slew of court rulings, which declared that you have to turn over your financial records to Congress; placed a nation-wide injunction on your nasty "public charge" rule; and declared that you can't reallocate money for your Stupid Border Wall.
- But it was an even worse week for our heretofore allies, the Kurds. After they've spent years fighting ISIS, you apparently agreed with the President of Turkey (Recep Tayyip Erdoğan) that those same Kurdish fighters might be the real terrorists and gave the green light for Turkey to go after them.
- In what was maybe the most craven rationale for abandoning an ally in US history, you explained that this was just fine because *"they didn't help us in the Second World War. They didn't help us with Normandy, as an example."* True. But neither did Turkey, which was still licking its wounds after siding with Germany in World War I and remained neutral in World War II.
- But here's most likely the real deal behind this sordid betrayal: *"I have a little conflict of interest 'cause I have a major, major building in Istanbul,"* you said in a 2015 interview. *"It's a tremendously <u>successful job. It's called Trump Towers</u> — two towers, instead of one, not the usual one: it's two. And I've gotten to know Turkey very well. They're amazing people...They have a strong leader."* [Another one of your favorite odious autocrats.]

- I guess this is our new foreign policy (to paraphrase the former chairman of GM): What's good for the Trump Organization is good for America.

Resources - Volume III, Issue 41

Desiderio, Andrew; Cheney, Kyle; Toos, Nahal. Yovanovitch, Marie. "Deposition to Congress." *Politico*, October 11, 2019. Marie Yovanovitch says Trump ousted her over 'unfounded and false claims' - POLITICO

Yovanovitch, Marie. "Prepared Remarks to Congress." *DocumentCloud*.Marie Yovanovitch prepared remarks to Congress - DocumentCloud

Samuelsohn, Darren; Schreckinger, Ben. Indicted Giuliani associate attended private '16 election night party for 'friend' Trump. POLITICO. October 11, 2019. Indicted Giuliani associate attended private '16 election night party for 'friend' Trump - POLITICO

Cassidy, John. "Rudy Giuliani's Two Indicted Associates Could Have a Lot to Say." *The New Yorker*, October 11, 2019. Rudy Giuliani's Two Indicted Associates Could Have a Lot to Say | The New Yorker

Samuelsohn, Darren; Gerstein, Josh. "Trump Loses Appeal to Withhold Financial Records from Democrats." *Politico*, October 11, 2019. Trump loses appeal to withhold financial records from Democrats - POLITICO

Hesson, Ted. "Judge Blocks Trump Green Card Public Benefits Regulation." *Politico*, October 11, 2019. Judge blocks Trump move to deny green cards to recipients of government benefits - POLITICO

Gerstein, Josh. "Judge Rules Against Trump Border Wall." *Politico*, October 11, 2019.** Another judge rules against Trump on border wall - POLITICO

Specia, Megan. "A Little History." *The New York Times*, October 9, 2019. Why Is Turkey Fighting the Kurds in Syria? - The New York Times (nytimes.com)

Patterson, Robert W. "What's Good for America." *National Review*, July 1, 2013. 'What's Good for America . . .' | National Review

Papenfuss, Mary. "Conflict of Interest: Donald Trump, Syria, Kurds, Turkey." *HuffPost*, October 11, 2019. Trump On Turkey: 'I Have A Little Conflict Of Interest ... It's Called Trump Towers' | HuffPost Latest News

Date, S.V. "Turkey Versus Kurds Dispute, Trump Chooses The Side Where He Has A Condo Complex." *HuffPost Latest News*. October 12, 2019. In Turkey Versus Kurds Dispute, Trump Chooses The Side Where He Has A Condo Complex | HuffPost Latest News

Finally, all the stuff we might need to defend in the future: List of things named after Donald Trump - Wikipedia

The Weekly Screed: October 20, 2019 (Volume III, Issue 42)

To: The Donald to Erdoğan: Don't be a fool!

From: Kelly: I don't think he got the message.

- Uh-Oh, DT. Another not-so-good week for you. [I think this is a pattern.]
- Your acting Chief of Staff, Mick Mulvaney, confessed on live TV that there was, indeed, a quid-pro-quo in Ukraine; that you guys do this "all the time"; that the Trump Doral would be the perfect site for the G-7 meeting (despite the fact that holding it there would be your most blatant violation of the Emoluments Clause ever); and that "At the end of the day he (the President) still considers himself to be in the hospitality business." Yikes!
- I predict that (if he's lucky) Mulvaney will soon need to spend more time with his family......or sleep with the fishes (if he isn't).
- There have been so many interesting quotes around the Turkey/Syria/Kurds catastrophe that I've written a song for you. I'm sure you remember this old tune from late-greats Frank Sinatra (in 1940) and Rick Nelson (in 1963):

Fools rush in where angels fear to tread.

The Turks invaded Syria; now many Kurds are dead.

I can't see the danger there.

There's lots of sand for all, so I don't care.

Fools rush in where wise men never go.

My great and unmatched wisdom says

Let Putin run this show.

PKK is even worse than ISIS was.

Pence made the Turks so happy that they called a pause.

Fools rush in where wise men never go

Sometimes you have to let them fight.......Get in a couple blows.

We can always go back in and BLAST

Our soldiers will go to Iraq; the die is cast.

Resources - Volume III, Issue 42

Good afternoon, everyone. So much outrage, so little space. Once again, the perfect song sprang to mind. But before you read my version in The Screed, please enjoy watching impossibly young and handsome Ricky Nelson sing it (on the Ozzie and Harriet Show): Ricky Nelson Sings Fools Rush In (youtube.com)

Fools Rush In (Where Angels Fear to Tread) - Wikipedia

And now for the sad facts behind my version:

Trump: "History will look upon you favourably if you get this done the right and humane way. It will look upon you forever as the devil if good things don't happen. Don't be a tough guy. Don't be a fool!"

Walker, James. "Erdogan Threw Trump's Syria Letter in Trash." *Newsweek*, October 17, 2019. Turkey's Erdogan Threw Trump's Letter in the Trash, President's Plea Against Syria Offensive Was 'Thoroughly Rejected': Report - Newsweek

Pelosi: "all roads with you lead to Putin,"

Rogers, Katie. "Inside the Derailed White House Meeting." *The New York Times*, October 16, 2019. Inside the Derailed White House Meeting - The New York Times (nytimes.com)

Trump: claims Kurds 'no angels' as he boasts of his own 'brilliant' strategy

Borger, Julian; Safi, Michael. "Trump: Claims Kurds 'No Angels' as He Boasts of His Own 'Brilliant' Strategy." *The Guardian*, October 16, 2019. Trump claims Kurds 'no angels' as he boasts of his own 'brilliant' strategy | Donald Trump | The Guardian

Shinkman, Paul D. "Trump Touts 'Strategically Brilliant' Decision to Abandon Kurds in Syria." *U.S. News*, October 16, 2019. Trump Touts 'Strategically Brilliant' Decision to Abandon Kurds in Syria (usnews.com)

Resources - Volume III, Issue 42 (continued)

Trump: Syria has "got a lot of sand over there," Trump said. "So there's a lot of sand that they can play with."

Berger, Miriam. "Trump: Syria Has 'Got a Lot of Sand Over There'." *The Washington Post*, October 17, 2019. Trump's statements on Syria and sand -- and what's wrong with them -- explained - The Washington Post

Trump: I view the situation on the Turkish border with Syria to be, for the U.S., strategically brilliant. Our soldiers are out of there, our soldiers are totally safe. They have to work it out. Maybe they can do it without fighting. Syria is protecting the Kurds," Trump said in wide-ranging remarks to reporters in the Oval Office alongside Italian President Sergio Mattarella.

Brennan, David. "Trump's Remarks on Syria with Italian President Mattarella." *Newsweek*, October 17, 2019. Trump's Translator Looks Perplexed by His Comments on Syria: 'They've Got...A Lot of Sand That They Can Play With' - Newsweek

Trump: "my great and unmatched wisdom"

Noor, Poppy. "Trump's 'Great and Unmatched Wisdom'." *The Guardian*, October 7, 2019. 'In my great and unmatched wisdom': Trump makes modest claim about his intellect | Donald Trump | The Guardian

Trump: Trump said the Kurdistan Workers' Party (PKK), which has waged a decades-long armed campaign against Ankara, were "probably" a bigger "terrorist threat" than the Islamic State in Iraq and the Levant (ISIL, or ISIS) armed group.

"Trump on PKK and ISIL." *Al Jazeera*, October 17, 2019. Trump says Kurds 'not angels', dubs PKK 'worse than ISIL' | Donald Trump News | Al Jazeera

Resources - Volume III, Issue 42 (continued)

Pence: [The agreement with Turkey] "ends the violence — which is what President Trump sent us here to do." Turkey's foreign minister, Mevlut Cavusoglu, immediately contradicted the description of the agreement, saying it was not a cease-fire at all, but merely a "pause for our operation." He added that "as a result of our president's skillful leadership, we got what we wanted." **Trump:** Later, at a rally in Dallas, the president defended his approach to the conflict as "tough love." "Sometimes you have let them fight," he said, "like two kids in a lot."

Karni, Annie; Jakes, Lara; Kingsley, Patrick.. "Pence and Turkey Agreement." *The New York Times*, October 17, 2019. Turkey Agrees to Pause Fighting, but Not to Withdraw Forces From Northern Syria - The New York Times (nytimes.com)

Trump: I was elected on getting out of these ridiculous endless wars, where our great Military functions as a policing operation to the benefit of people who don't even like the USA. The two most unhappy countries at this move are Russia & China, because they love seeing us bogged down, watching over a quagmire, & spending big dollars to do so. When I took over, our Military was totally depleted. Now it is stronger than ever before. The endless and ridiculous wars are ENDING! We will be focused on the big picture, knowing we can always go back & BLAST!

Hall, Colby. "Trump on Ending Endless Wars." *Mediaite*, October 7, 2019. Trump on Syria Troop Withdrawal: 'Can Always Go Back & BLAST!' (mediaite.com)

Trump: "It's time to bring our soldiers back home," Trump said Wednesday. They are not coming home, although Trump tweeted Sunday: "USA soldiers are not in combat or ceasefire zones" and "Bringing soldiers home!"

Baldor, Lolita C. "Trump on Bringing Soldiers Back Home." *Military Times*, October 20, 2019. Pentagon chief says American troops leaving Syria will conduct anti-ISIS operations from Iraq (militarytimes.com)

The Weekly Screed: October 27, 2019 (Volume III, Issue 43)

To: **The Donald: Crying Wolf**

From: **Kelly: I feel really bad about the dog**

- <u>This just in</u>: "Last night the United States brought the world's No. 1 terrorist leader to justice. Abu Bakr al-Baghdadi is dead. He was the founder and leader of ISIS….I got to watch much of it." [I know you love to watch.]
- However, here's what you said on <u>August 11, 2016</u>: "Isis is honoring President Obama. He is the founder of Isis. He founded Isis. And, I would say the co-founder would be crooked Hillary Clinton."
- But back to today, as you vividly described Baghdadi's final moments: "He died like a dog; he died like a coward." Reassuringly, the only US casualty was a military canine, "a beautiful dog" in your words. SAD.
- So I'm guessing that with yesterday's grisly victory we have irrevocably definitively 100% defeated ISIS? As you have been trumpeting repeatedly for the past year or so? Like last <u>December</u> when you declared: "We have won against ISIS….Our boys, our young women, our men — they're all coming back, and they're coming back now." Frankly, I believe there's more to come on this front. As they say on the TV, I will stay tuned.
- In other news, you continue to be utterly baffled by some of the personally peskier parts of the Constitution, like "you people with this phony emoluments clause" (psst, it's right here: Article I, Section 9, Paragraph 8); and the impeachment inquiry, which really has you flummoxed.
- "So someday, if a Democrat becomes President and the Republicans win the House, even by a tiny margin, they can impeach the President, without due process or fairness or any legal rights." Yuppers. That's pretty much exactly how it works, and you can read all about it in Article II, section 4.
- Then you just *had* to go lower, so you added: "All Republicans must remember what they are witnessing here – a lynching." Shame on you.
- But the best retread of the week was your lie about The Wall, this time with a special spin: "…we're building a wall in Colorado, we're building a beautiful wall, a big one that really works that you can't get over…" Hmm.
-

- Maybe this section of the border barrier will keep out the New Mexicans, who remain our last best defense against the Old Mexicans, unless they all find out about the annual Albuquerque Balloon Fiesta….Up, Up & Away!

Resources - Volume III, Issue 43

Karam, Zeina; Abdul-Zahra, Qassim, Bilginsoy, Zeynep. "ISIS Leader Baghdadi Killed in US Military Raid." *NBC Washington*, October 27, 2019. President Trump Says Islamic State Leader Is Dead Following US Raid in Syria – NBC4 Washington (nbcwashington.com)

Siddiqui, Sabrina. "Donald Trump Calls Barack Obama the Founder of ISIS." *The Guardian*, August 11, 2016. Donald Trump calls Obama the 'founder of Isis' | Donald Trump | The Guardian

Smith, Allan. "Fifteen Stunning Moments from Trump's Press Conference on al-Baghdadi's Death." *NBC News*, October 27, 2019. Fifteen stunning moments from Trump's announcement of al-Baghdadi's death (nbcnews.com)

Durkee, Alison. "Trump, G7 at Doral, and the Emoluments Clause." *Vanity Fair*, October 21, 2019. Trump Blasts "Phony Emoluments Clause" In Post-Doral Meltdown | Vanity Fair

Slater, Georgia. "Donald Trump Calls Impeachment 'Lynching'." *People*, October 22, 2019. Donald Trump Calls Impeachment Inquiry 'Lynching' (people.com)

The Dear Leader got a standing ovation when he announced the Colorado border wall at a speech in Pittsburgh. He should really stick to the teleprompter, but I love it when he doesn't. But the guy who won the Internet last week was Vermont Senator Patrick Leahy, when he tweeted out a new map of the USA:

Hernandez, Salvador. "Trump Border Wall in Colorado." *BuzzFeed News*, October 23, 2019. President Trump Said He's Building A Wall In Colorado (buzzfeednews.com)

Meanwhile, with New Mexico now located beyond our southern border, I predict this will be the preferred way to surmount the barricades: Albuquerque International Balloon Fiesta

The Weekly Screed: November 3, 2019 (Volume III, Issue 44)

To: The Donald - Future Denizen of the Deep

From: Kelly - Just another reason to boycott Florida

- Donald, Halloween Week seemed to be a mixed bag for you. You got booed at a World Series baseball game; the House formalized impeachment proceedings against you; and that candy distribution thing at the White House party didn't seem to go too well….it was kind of a dirty trick for you AND Melania to put treats on that Minion kid just to watch them slide off.
- On the other hand, the "Build the Wall" activity where the little tykes got to print their names on paper "bricks" was a special holiday touch. In fact, it could be the inspiration for a new wall design, since it seems that the metal bollards in the recently completed sections are easily overcome by inexpensive power tools and ladders. We still need that alligator moat!
- Meanwhile, on the other side of the country, wildfires in California came close to engulfing the Reagan Presidential Library. What a stunning loss *that* would have been! Especially since Don Jr. is scheduled to read from his latest book, "Triggered" at a SOLD-OUT event at the library on Nov.10.
- According to the library website: *"From his childhood summers in Communist Czechoslovakia that began his political thought process…to the major achievements of President Trump's administration, Donald Trump, Jr. spares no details and delivers a book that focuses on success and perseverance, and proves offense is the best defense."* We're also told that this tome is about "standing up for what you believe in." Deep.
- But the heroic effort of firefighters that saved the library wasn't quite what Reagan believed in, was it? *"The nine most terrifying words in the English language are 'I'm from the government and I'm here to help."* So, I doubt he would be truly appreciative of either the emergency assistance, or the annual event in May when the Ventura County Fire Department deploys hundreds of goats to munch down the brush around the complex to create a fire break.
- This led me to ponder where YOUR presidential library will be. Most likely at Mar-A-Lago, your new "official" residence. I'm thinking the best location for your important "papers" (framed tweets?) might be the tower on the property.

- Since all the rest of it will soon be underwater (or Bajo-El-Mar) due to climate change. On the bright side, you will finally get your alligator moat, free of charge OR pesky government assistance.

Resources - Volume III, Issue 44

Today's topic is Presidential Libraries. Plus climate change. You wouldn't think these two are linked, but as it turns out they are! But first, it was Halloween Week:

VanHoose, Benjamin. "Donald and Melania Trump Pass Out Halloween Candy — Including a Viral Moment with a Kid in Minion Costume" *People*, October 31, 2019. Donald, Melania Trump Pass Out Halloween Candy (people.com)

Linge, Mary Kay. "Build the Wall Game at Kids' White House Halloween Party." *New York Post*, November 2, 2019. Kids told to 'Build a Wall' for Halloween at White House (nypost.com)

Cranley, Ellen. "Smugglers Reportedly Cutting Holes in Trump's Newly Constructed Border Wall." *AOL News*, November 2, 2019. Smugglers are reportedly cutting holes in Trump's newly constructed border wall with saws and power tools (aol.com)

Times Editorial Board. "Trump Suggests Moat with Alligators at the Border." *Los Angeles Times*, October 2, 2019. Opinion: Trump's gator-filled 'moat' may be the silliest of his harebrained ideas - Los Angeles Times (latimes.com)

Waldman, Paul. "Wildfires Threatening Reagan Library." *The Washington Post*, October 31, 2019. Opinion | Wildfires are threatening the Reagan Library. Call in the government! - The Washington Post

Miller, Ryan W; Woodyard, Chris; Harris, Mike. [USA TODAY] " Easy Fire: Goats help save Ronald Reagan Presidential Library in Simi (vcstar.com)" *Ventura County Star*, October 30, 2019.

Fottrell, Quentin. "Trump's Move from New York to Florida for Tax Purposes." *MarketWatch*, November 4, 2019. All the reasons Trump's move from New York to Florida for tax purposes could be 'doomed' - MarketWatch

Garfield, Leanna. "Trump on Climate Change and Sea Level Rise at Mar-A-Lago." *Business Insider*, July 14, 2017. Sea-Level Rise Is Overtaking Trump's Favorite Vacation Spot - Business Insider

Author's Last Name, First Name. "How Mar-A-Lago's Denizens Nurtured Donald Trump's Ego." *The Washington Post*, February 6, 2019. Book review of Mar-a-Lago: Inside the Gates of Power at Donald Trump's Presidential Palace by Laurence Leamer - The Washington Post

The Weekly Screed: November 10, 2019 (Volume III, Issue 45)

To: The Donald – Twitterpated

From: Kelly – Educated

Trump Praises Trump 2,026 times (analysis of his tweets by The New York Times)

We now have a POTUS named Trump

Who loves to be out on the stump.

He went to Kentucky but didn't get lucky.

The voters gave Bevin the dump.

Trump can't read or write, so he tweets.

His language is not always sweet

He hates the Fake News and Democrat views

But praises himself and his feats.

He targets Pelosi and Schiff

"*A Witch Hunt*" is his favorite riff.

Sometimes it's a reach to achieve "*lasting peach*,"

And he often winds up in a tiff.

But Donald's the POTUS we've got.

He tweets if we like it or not.

His phone calls are worse: read the transcripts and curse

At the tragedy voters have wrought.

Resources - Volume III, Issue 45

Good evening, everyone.............another humdrum week of scandal and turmoil. The most interesting article I read all week was the *New York Times* "Special Section" last Sunday that analyzed 11,390 White House tweets. So, I made life easy for myself and sent The Donald a little poem about his Twitter habit. And isn't "Twitterpated" a delightful word? It made its first appearance in the 1942 Disney movie "Bambi." I felt it was so appropriate here since we know the only person Trump is romantically attached to is himself (this is borne out by his Tweets of Praise).

Van Syckle, Katie. "Trump's Twitter Data and Insights." *The New York Times*, November 2, 2019. The Journalists Who Read All of President Trump's Tweets. Twice. - The New York Times (nytimes.com)

Shear, Michael; Haberman, Maggie; Confessore, Nicholas; Yourish, Karen; Buchanan, Larry; Collins, Keith. "Trump's Twitter Presidency." *The New York Times*, November 2, 2019. How Trump Reshaped the Presidency in Over 11,000 Tweets - The New York Times (nytimes.com)

Knutsen, Jacob. "Trump Sets Personal Best for Tweets in September and Breaks Record in October." *Axios*, October 2, 2019. Trump set personal record by tweeting over 800 times last month (axios.com)

Knutsen, Jacob. "Trump's 82-Tweet Plane Trip to Alabama Football Game." *Axios*, November 10, 2019. Donald Trump sets Twitter record amid impeachment inquiry over Ukraine (usatoday.com)

Abadi, Mark. "Trump's Typos and Spelling Errors in Tweets." *Business Insider*, July 19, 2017. Here Are Trump's Worst Typos and Spelling Mistakes - Business Insider

Finally, in a rare instance of Good News, we did have an "off-year" election that took down the Republican Governor of Kentucky and flipped both the House and the Senate of Virginia legislature from red to blue. Trump said last night that if Gov. Matt Bevin lost in Kentucky, 'they're going to say Trump suffered the greatest defeat in the history of the world... You can't let that happen to me!' OOOPS.

The Weekly Screed: November 17, 2019 (Volume III, Issue 46)

To: The Donald – YOU are the "bad news"

From: Kelly – Another woman who has been through "some things"

- Donald, I have to tell you that watching the three exemplary Foreign Service Officers testify (eloquently) at your impeachment inquiry this week brought up a lot of traumatic memories for me. Let's say I was "triggered."
- As yesterday's *New York Times* front-page headline summed it up: "Ex-Envoy 'Devastated' as Trump Vilified Her." I know exactly how she felt.
- Thirty-six years ago, I was denied a career as an FSO…not because of my (stellar) scores on the Foreign Service exams or any lack of professional or educational qualifications…but because I was likewise vilified by my former Peace Corps Zaire supervisor, who had moved on to the State Department.
- I was black balled by this person (JL) because, while I was teaching English courses at the National University of Zaire, I fell in love with, and lived with, a handsome and highly educated man who was doing business in the city we lived in (Kisangani). Unfortunately, this guy was also a Muslim of Pakistani descent (born in Kenya, university in England) and was therefore deemed an unsuitable suitor by Peace Corps HQ in Kinshasa, Zaire.
- My one other female Peace Corps colleague in Kisangani was also dating a foreign businessman, but he was a white Frenchman, so that was just fine. My male Peace Corps colleagues in Kisangani tended to keep company with local (Zairian) prostitutes, but that was considered typical, so also okay.
- But during the background check for my security clearance, JL declared that I would be a "genuine security risk" because of my "demonstrated lack of discretion." And, just to put the icing on the cake, opined that were I to work for the Foreign Service, "within a year, she would be giving secrets away to her Russian boyfriend." Case closed. No appointment. No appeal.
- I went on to work overseas for most of the next decade, with Intercontinental Hotels, and as Director of two non-profit agencies affiliated with the military. But I always lamented my lost career with the Foreign Service….

- ….Until Friday, when I realized that I would have probably had the same professional trajectory as Marie Yovanovitch (first posting in Africa due to my Peace Corps experience; then on to former Soviet republics, due to my Master's degree in Russian history and language) and might have wound up on the chopping block anyway, due to the double standard still applied to female FSOs. The main difference: I would have retired under Obama.

Resources - Volume III, Issue 46

Good afternoon, everyone. Today's Screed does not lambaste The Donald for his despicable behavior toward the Foreign Service Officers we heard testify this past week, especially Marie Yovanovitch….or the contradictions between White House statements about the phone calls to Ukraine compared to the actual transcripts. You can read all about that in the links I'm providing.

Instead, this is a rather personal autobiographical memo. After all, I know everything about Donald Trump, so (as a loyal pen pal) I feel he should know more about me. To my old friends, this is old news. Certainly not something I dwell on frequently but watching the impeachment inquiry turned over some decades-long rocks in my memory and recalled a truly pivotal event in my life: the time when I spent two years (1981-1983) applying to be a Foreign Service Officer (yes, it takes that long), only to be denied a security clearance thanks to a relationship I had while I was in the Peace Corps in Zaire (1978-79). While I suppose there is some cachet to having one's romantic life declared a threat to national security, it really doesn't make up for losing a career. But it happened and you can read the sad story here ! In the meantime, some links to my research for the week:

First Phone Call (April 21, 2019)– No mention of "corruption", just a lot of fawning. Zelensky effusively expresses his gratitude to Trump 10 times and otherwise praises him as a "great example" another half-dozen times. Trump bragged about "owning" the Miss Universe competition and favorably commented on the Ukrainian contestants. Classy.

Keith, Tamara. "The White House Just Released a Log of Trump's First Call with Zelenskiy." *NPR*, November 15, 2019. Trump Releases Rough Transcript Of First April Call With Zelenskiy : NPR

Resources - Volume III, Issue 46 (continued)

Transcript of Trump's First Call With Ukraine's President." *The New York Times*, November 15, 2019. Read Trump's First Call With the New Ukrainian President - The New York Times (nytimes.com)

**Kiely, Eugene and Farley, Robert. "Discrepancy in White House Versions of First Trump-Zelensky Phone Call." *FactCheck.org*, November 15, 2019. Discrepancy in White House Versions of First Trump-Zelensky Phone Call - FactCheck.org

Second Phone Call (July 25, 2019) – Where he calls Ambassador Yovanovitch "bad news" (prompting Zelensky to agree with him) and then ominously promises that "she's going to go through some things", which Yovanovitch testified that she took as a "threat."

Trump-Zelensky Transcript | PDF | Government (scribd.com)

First Meeting (September 25, 2019)

Remarks by President Trump and President Zelensky of Ukraine Before Bilateral Meeting | New York, NY – The White House (archives.gov)

Best-timed tweet ever – So, to double-down, Trump twittered another denigrating tweet *as Yovanovitch was testifying.* Which allowed Adam Schiff (Chairman of the House Intelligence Committee) to read this communication into the record as yet another impeachable offense (witness intimidation) committed live, by the Dear Leader, during his own impeachment inquiry. Perfection.

Donald J. Trump on X: "Everywhere Marie Yovanovitch went turned bad. She started off in Somalia, how did that go? Then fast forward to Ukraine, where the new Ukrainian President spoke unfavorably about her in my second phone call with him. It is a U.S. President's absolute right to appoint ambassadors." / X   (November 15, 2019)

Resources - Volume III, Issue 46 (continued)

Politi, Daniel. "Trump Is a Big, Dumb Baby." *Slate*, November 15, 2019. Fox Business host Lisa Kennedy calls Trump a big dumb baby for Yovanovitch attack. (slate.com)

Many expressed outrage when President Donald Trump took to Twitter to attack former U.S. ambassador to Ukraine, Marie Yovanovitch, while she testified in the impeachment investigation. And it wasn't just his opponents. Even traditional allies said the president had gone too far. "Should the president be tweeting at her mid-hearing? No," Fox Business Network host Lisa Kennedy said. "It makes him look like a big dumb baby."

While Yovanovitch was testifying, Trump slammed her on Twitter, claiming that "everywhere Marie Yovanovitch went turned bad." The House Intelligence Committee Chairman Adam Schiff interrupted the questioning to read the tweet aloud and ask for Yovanovitch's reaction. Trump defended himself later in the day. "It's a political process, it's not a legal process," Trump said. "I'm allowed to speak up." He added that "I have the right to speak, I have freedom of speech."

The Weekly Screed: November 24, 2019 (Volume III, Issue 47)

To: **The Donald – Use your "inside" voice**

From: **Kelly – Words matter**

- Donald, I know we were both very busy at work last week. I led a couple of Very Important Meetings, worked on a policy project for my boss, and delivered an all-day training on the Affordable Care Act (Medicaid and Marketplace) because, hey! We still have Obamacare! And my job is to help get Oregonians enrolled!
- You, on the other hand, were occupied with verbally trashing, lying about, and downright endangering the men and women who testified at your Impeachment Inquiry (oh, it gladdens my heart to write those two "I" words). Keep that up and we might get "Witness Intimidation" added to the eventual Articles of Impeachment.
- And you also carved out a whole *hour* of your Friday schedule for a frenzied call-in rant to Fox & Fiends….er, "Friends." At one point, even Brian Kilmeade had the temerity to question one of your more improbable and downright wack-a-doodle assertions: *"Are you sure they did that?"*
- *"Well, that's what the word is,"* you replied. Because, really, sadly, you don't know anything for sure and you comprehend even less.
- Let's see…….what else did you accomplish in the past week? No rallies. Still licking your wounds from your 2 visits to Louisiana earlier this month, when your guy lost the governor's race to the Democrat? No awkward visits from World Leaders sitting stoically by while you make a fool of yourself.
- But you did travel to Austin with Ivanka to tour a factory. Afterwards, you tweeted: *"Today I opened a major Apple Manufacturing plant in Texas that will bring high paying jobs back to America."* OOPS! That plant actually started up in 2013, back when we had a real President.
- Another risible moment came right before that trip to Austin when you claimed **(a)** to barely know Gordon Sondland [hint: he was the guy whose call you took on an unsecured cell phone from a restaurant in Kiev, where you were bellowing so loudly that half the diners heard the conversation] and **(b)** then went on to claim that "he seems like a nice guy, though" and that his testimony had exonerated you [just like the Mueller report did…not]

- I recently saw a t-shirt that proclaimed: "English is weird. It can be understood through tough, thorough, thought though." Donald, I know you are trying to tough it out right now. Think through your words, though.

Resources - Volume III, Issue 47

Good afternoon, y'all. Today's musings consider some of The Donald's words: specifically his inability to understand certain terms (like exonerate) and how he uses his pathetic vocabulary to bully others, more often to his detriment than theirs. After I'd written this week's offering, I read Maureen Dowd's column on this very topic in The New York Times: Opinion | Trump's White Whale - The New York Times (nytimes.com) November 23, 2019.

Frazin, Rachel. "Impeachment Witnesses Come Under Threats, Harassment." *The Hill*, November 23, 2019. Impeachment witnesses come under threats, harassment (thehill.com)

Perez, Hilton. "Donald Trump's Call with Fox & Friends Lasted Nearly an Hour!" *Perez Hilton*, November 22, 2019. Donald Trump Goes Too Far For 'Fox And Friends' In Hour-Long Crazypants Rant - Perez Hilton

Mekelburg, Madlin. "Did Trump open a 'major Apple Manufacturing plant' in Austin? No.." November 21, 2019. PolitiFact | Did Trump open a 'major Apple Manufacturing plant' in Austin? No.

Gage, John. "Trump Denies Knowing Sondland 'Very Well'." *Washington Examiner*, November 20, 2019. Trump denies knowing Sondland 'very well' - Washington Examiner

Lofgren, Kristine. "Donald Trump Claims Gordon Sondland Exonerated Him Despite Impeachment Testimony To The Contrary." Inquisitr. November 20, 2019. Donald Trump Claims Gordon Sondland Exonerated Him Despite Impeachment Testimony To The Contrary - Inquisitr

Hayes, Christal; Wu, Nicholas. "Trump Impeachment Inquiry: Officials Who Testified Before Congress." *USA Today*, November 22, 2019. Trump impeachment inquiry: The officials who testified before Congress (usatoday.com)

Wishing everyone a lovely Thanksgiving with food and people you like.............Kelly

The Weekly Screed: December 1, 2019 (Volume III, Issue 48)

To: The Donald – Fowl Play

From: Kelly – Go Fish

- Donald, for the past couple of weeks, I've played an ice-breaker game at my work meetings: Best or Worst Thanksgiving Ever. Participants trotted out the usual tales of woe (burnt turkeys; cancelled flights; blizzard road trips) and joy (surprise homecomings, new babies, awesome bi-cultural feasts).
- <u>My</u> favorite Thanksgiving celebrations have happened far away from home. Top of the list are the years in Okinawa, Japan, when I was the Director of Kadena Air Force Base USO, and we kept the facility open for 72 hours so that the troops could stop by for a turkey dinner, watch a movie, and use the overseas phones. [This was the late '80s: no email or cell phones.]
- I was remembering those happier holidays as I watched you ruin Thanksgiving for all Americans-with-functioning-brains this year:
    1) Cracking wise about impeachment as you "pardoned" Bread and Butter, the White House turkeys: *"...they've already received subpoenas to appear in Adam Schiff's basement on Thursday..."*
    2) Sneering at the *"radical left"* at a rally in Florida: *"People have different ideas why it shouldn't be called Thanksgiving, but everybody in this room, I know, loves the name Thanksgiving. And we're not changing."* Wow. That's the bold leadership we need in these times.
    3) Pooh-poohing rumors that your recent unscheduled visit to Walter Reed Hospital was to forestall a heart attack: *"I have a gorgeous chest."*
    4) Surprising *"the toughest, strongest, best and bravest warriors on the face of the earth,"* with a visit to Afghanistan and a fake news announcement about a ceasefire with the Taliban, after complaining about not having enough time to eat a proper meal: *"I never got the turkey. A gorgeous piece of turkey."* Haven't the troops suffered enough without their Chicken-Hawk-in-Chief spoiling a well-earned day of R & R?
- Me, I'm trying to maintain a spirit of gratitude this year and counting my blessings: I live in Oregon (which has the best climate and fewer natural disasters than anywhere else in the country right now);

- I have great health care (with my employer) and will receive an actual pension when I retire at the end of the year; I enjoy loving friends and family and a cute little dog; and I had sufficient household income to partake of Thanksgiving dinner at a fine restaurant this year. In solidarity with Bread & Butter, I ordered the fish.

Resources - Volume III, Issue 48

Happy Thanksgiving Weekend, y'all.........today I reflect on Trump's holiday shenanigans. Hopefully only one more Thanksgiving with this moron in the White House.

Trump in D.C. - The War on Turkeys

Jarvis, James. "Trump Cracks Impeachment Jokes During Turkey Pardon, Says Bread and Butter Had Been Subpoenaed." *The Hill*, November 26, 2019. Trump cracks impeachment jokes during turkey pardon, says Bread and Butter were subpoenaed (thehill.com)

Levine, Jon. "Turkeys Pardoned by Presidents Still Live Short, Sad Lives: PETA." *New York Post*, November 30, 2019. Pardoned turkeys still live short, sad lives: PETA (nypost.com)

Trump in Florida – The War on Thanksgiving

Steward, Emily. "Trump Rally: The War on Thanksgiving." *Vox*, November 27, 2019. War on Thanksgiving: Trump falsely says liberals want to rename holiday - Vox

Cathey, Libby. "Trump Denies Heart Attack, Praises 'Gorgeous Chest' in Florida." *ABC News*, November 27, 2019. Trump denies heart attack, praises his 'gorgeous chest' at Florida rally - ABC News

Trump in Afghanistan – The War

Colvin, Jill. " Trump thanks troops in Afghanistan, says Taliban want a deal." *Associated Press*, November 28, 2019. Trump thanks troops in Afghanistan, says Taliban want a deal | AP News

Hope you had a safe and lovely holiday. One month from today, I will be officially RETIRED.........Kelly

The Weekly Screed: December 8, 2019 (Volume III, Issue 49)

To: The Donald – The POTUS Prayer

From: Kelly – Let us pray

- **Nancy Pelosi:** *"At night and in church on Sunday, I pray for [Trump]. The prayer is that God will open his heart to meet the needs of the American people. I said to my pastor, 'These prayers are not working.' He replied, 'Maybe you're not praying hard enough.'"* (Harper's Bazaar, October 2019)
- **James Rosen** (reporter, Sinclair Broadcast Group) *"Do you hate the president, Ms. Speaker?"* (Pelosi's weekly press briefing at the Capitol, December 5, 2019).
- **Nancy Pelosi:** *"As a Catholic, I resent your using the word 'hate' in a sentence that addresses me. I don't hate anyone. I was raised in a way that is a heart full of love, and always pray for the president. And I still pray for the president. I pray for the president all the time. So don't mess with me when it comes to words like that."*
- Within the hour, <u>you</u> responded on Twitter, *"Nancy Pelosi just had a nervous fit. She hates that we will soon have 182 great new judges and sooo much more. Stock Market and employment records. She says she 'prays for the President.' I don't believe her, not even close."*
- All of which led me to ponder how I, Kelly Paige, might pray for you, DT.

I would wager my left arm that you could never recite the actual Lord's Prayer [see Matthew 6: 9-13], but here's my version, just for you:

Our POTUS, which art in D.C., Donald be thy name
Thy kingdom comes to Mar-A-Lago, not all 50 states….yet.
Thy will is toxic, on earth AND in heaven,
Thanks to your denial of climate change.
Instead of giving us our daily bread, you cut food stamps for the poor.
And forgive the debts of corporations with massive tax cuts.
You have always succumbed to the temptations of the flesh and filthy lucre,
And delivered us unto the evildoings of your vile cabinet and vicious judges.
For thine is corruption, and ignorance, and vainglory….forever,
Or until you get impeached, voted off the island, resign, defect to Russia, whatever-the-hell it takes. Can I get an AMEN?????

Resources - Volume III, Issue 49

We got schooled on the history of impeachment by four law professors:

Pierce, Charles P. "Trump's High Crime Was to Assault Every American's Right to Free and Fair Elections." *Esquire*, December 4, 2019. Pamela Karlan Testifies Trump's Ukraine Crime Assaulted Free and Fair Elections (esquire.com)

We got another completely unqualified conservative judicial appointment

Pierce, Charles P. "The Senate Just Confirmed a Trump Judge With No Real Trial or Litigation Experience." *Esquire*, December 5, 2019. Senate Confirms Trump Judge Sarah Pitlyk Despite Zero Trial Experience (esquire.com)

In this season of giving, Trump takes food out of the mouths of babes

Spross, Jeff. "Trump's Food Stamp Cuts Are Cruel Politics, Bad Economics." *The Week*, December 6, 2019. Trump's food stamp cuts are cruel politics and bad economics | The Week

Nancy Pelosi takes down a conservative reporter

Chiu, Allyson. "'#DontMessWithNancy': Pelosi's viral clash with reporter inspires trending hashtag, backlash — and merchandise." *The Washington Post*, December 6, 2019. #DontMessWithNancy trends after Nancy Pelosi's clash with Sinclair Broadcasting's James Rosen - The Washington Post

Naturally, my thoughts turned to the Bible after listening to the latest Pelosi/Trump kerfuffle, so I'm attaching several Sunday School lessons for those so inclined.

Pastor Ikechukwu Chinedum. "The Meaning Of The Lord's Prayer Verse By Verse - Everyday Prayer Guide." Everyday Prayer Guide TV. February 12, 2019.

Blank, Wayne. "What Is "Filthy Lucre"? One year bible plan - Bible Study (keyway.ca) The Greek word pronounced *af-il-ar-goo-ros* means *without covetousness* i.e. "filthy lucre" is a violation of the Tenth Commandment ("[20:17] Thou shalt not covet thy neighbour's house, thou shalt not covet thy neighbour's wife, nor his manservant, nor his maidservant, nor his ox, nor his ass, nor any thing that is thy neighbour's" Exodus 20:17 KJV).

Filthy Lucre | The King's English (kingsenglish.info)

The Weekly Screed: December 15, 2019 (Volume III, Issue 50)

To: The Donald – Loser of the Year

From: Kelly – I love when it all comes full circle

- Oh, Donald, you just HAD to go there didn't you? You were only a runner-up for TIME magazine's Person of the Year award this year (along with also-rans the Hong Kong protesters; Nancy Pelosi; and the Whistleblower).
- But you LOST to a 16-year-old autistic Swede who speaks English better than you do. That's gotta be a blow.
- Still, did you really need to cyber-bully this kid? *"So ridiculous. Greta must work on her Anger Management problem, then go to a good old-fashioned movie with a friend! Chill Greta, Chill!* (Says the most temper-tantrum- prone POTUS in American history.) And then let your campaign photo-shop your giant orange head on top of Greta's body to create an alternate cover? It SO clashes with her pink hoodie.
- What's truly extraordinary is that the First Family had to pile on as well. Don Jr. (who recently made headlines for killing an endangered sheep) opined that the choice of Greta Thunberg as Person of the Year was merely a "marketing gimmick." Yes, just a craven ad campaign to save the planet.
- And Melania (whose stated mission is to <u>stop</u> bullying on social media) declined to stick up for Greta: *"'Be Best' is the first lady's initiative, and she will continue to use it to do all she can to help children,"* Stephanie Grisham, the White House press secretary, said in a statement first reported by CNN. *"It is no secret that the president and first lady often communicate differently — as most married couples do."* Well, isn't that special…. Apparently remaining silent is the best that FLOTUS can be in this instance.
- Who's next? We've yet to hear from the other Trump spawn, two of whom (Ivanka and Eric, along with Don Jr.) have been sentenced to "compulsory charity training" for their part in the Trump Foundation fraud.
- And while we're on this topic: Just this week, you paid a court-ordered $2 million to eight charities to settle the judgment against you and your phony foundation. Even better, you are required to be under "special supervision" if you ever dare to practice philanthropy in New York state again.

- Meanwhile, the American Institute of Philanthropy's Charity Watch gives the Clinton Foundation an "A" rating....Which reminds me of another female you lost bigly to (by 2.8 million popular votes) in 2016...which was, coincidentally, the only time you *were* declared TIME Person of the Year.

Resources - Volume III, Issue 50

Good morning, all. I did not address impeachment (again) this week. Instead, I simply had to comment on Trump's hissy fit over losing TIME Person of the Year, as well as what should be (and would be for any other POTUS) another impeachable offense: the illegal activities of Trump's Phony Fake Foundation (not the orange face make-up), the thing that was supposed to dispense charitable donations. What a scam.

Trump First Family reacts

Heinbrod, Camille." "Donald Trump Lambasted For Putting His Face Over Greta Thunberg's On Time Cover." *International Business Times*, December 12, 2019. Donald Trump Lambasted For Putting His Face Over Greta Thunberg's On Time Cover | IBTimes

Levin, Bess. " Donald Trump, Malignant Tumor, Attacks Greta Thunberg Over *Time* Magazine Cover." *Vanity Fair*, December 12, 2019. Donald Trump, Malignant Tumor, Attacks Greta Thunberg Over Time Magazine Cover | Vanity Fair

Rogers, Katie. " Despite 'Be Best' Campaign, Melania Trump Stays Mum as Husband Mocks Greta Thunberg" *The New York Times*, December 13, 2019. Despite 'Be Best' Campaign, Melania Trump Stays Mum as Husband Mocks Greta Thunberg - The New York Times (nytimes.com)

The Trump Foundation Scandal

Raymond, Adam K. "Trump Pays $2 Millin Fine for Abusing His Own Charity." *New York Magazine*, December 10, 2019. Trump Pays $2 Million Fine for Abusing His Own Charity (nymag.com)

Kessler, Glenn. "Foundation Face-Off: The Trump Foundation Versus the Clinton Foundation." *The Washington Post*, June 27, 2018. Foundation faceoff: The Trump Foundation vs. the Clinton Foundation - The Washington Post

Calabresi, Massimo. "Hillary Clinton Wins Popular Vote by Nearly 2.9 Million." *TIME*, December 20, 2016.

The Weekly Screed: December 22, 2019 (Volume III, Issue 51)

To: **The Donald – #IMPOTUS (IMpeached President Of The United States)**

From: **Kelly – Thank you, George, for this new moniker**

- Well, Donald….it finally happened: Impeached! And during the Happy Holidays!! Two lovely articles of coal for your Christmas stocking. [Do you hang up a stocking? I'll bet it is Perfect, spun from 18K gold thread.]
- At any rate, among many other of My Favorite Things this month, George Conway (Kellyanne's husband…how does THAT still work?) was inspired to gift us with the above abundantly marvelous and everlasting hashtag.
- And while *The New York Times* boldly proclaimed: **TRUMP IMPEACHED** on December 19, the honor for "Headline of the Day" absolutely must go to Victoria Merlino of *The Queens Daily Eagle*:
Queens man impeached [Page 16, below the fold] Former Jamaica Estates resident Donald Trump was impeached Wednesday by the U.S. House of Representatives. He is the third president to be impeached in United States history — and the first from Queens.
- DT, did I ever tell you that I *also* lived in Jamaica Estates once upon a time? When I moved to New York after my stint in the Peace Corps in the Congo and found a big, beautiful rent-controlled apartment right on the E-train line, upon which I commuted to my job in the World Trade Center? [Or, as my father opined: "From one jungle to another."] Those were the days….
- But I digress. You, of course, are pooh-poohing this event, referring to it as "Impeachment Lite." And, for once, I whole-heartedly agree with you. Me? I would have thrown the book at you:
    1) Thousands of violations (foreign and domestic) of the Emoluments Clause of the Constitution from Day One of your ill-gotten tenure in the White House. And I say "ill-gotten" due to Russian interference, *plus*:
    2) The campaign finance violations (hundreds of thousands of dollars of pay-offs to former inamoratas on the eve of the 2016 election) for which your former attorney Michael Cohen is currently serving prison time.
    3) Also, *all* of the obstructions of justice outlined in the Mueller Report which (were you not a "sitting President" and protected by that

bogus Department of Justice "policy" against indictments) would have resulted in multiple criminal convictions……..And finally, on daily display:
4) "Conduct grossly incompatible with the presidency." [Indeed. See the 1974 House Judiciary Committee report justifying the Nixon articles.]

Resources - Volume III, Issue 51

Best Christmas Miracle Ever, huh ?? What a week.........of course, lost in the impeachment news was the tidbit that the Fifth Court of Appeals in New Orleans declared the "individual mandate" part of the Affordable Care Act to be "unconstitutional" (the part that says everyone has to have health coverage so that the insurance companies will keep covering "pre-existing conditions"). Turns out that reducing the tax penalty to $0.00 dollars for NOT having coverage rendered the mandate moot. But I see this as a win......first of all, the Appeals Court didn't declare the entire ACA unconstitutional (which would have meant an immediate appeal to the Supreme Court).....instead the whole mess is remanded back to the District Court in Texas that got this whole party started last year and ordered that judge to go at his ruling "with a finer-toothed comb." So this comb-over should take at least another few months. Meanwhile, we still have Obamacare.

But history was made in Washington DC with the third impeachment ever of a president. Here is my favorite coverage of the aftermath:

Best Nickname Ever (brought to us by George Conway)

Weber, Peter. "George Conway Gives Trump a Savage New Nickname Post-Impeachment." *The Week*, December 20, 2019. George Conway has a savage new nickname for post-impeachment Trump | The Week

IMPOTUS (IMpeached President Of The United States) @realDonaldTrump is accusing @SpeakerPelosi of political malpractice. I don't think so. #IMPOTUS https://t.co/a4WoLJgaqr — George Conway (@gtconway3d) December 20, 2019

Best Headline Ever (brought to us by Rachel Maddow)

Merlino, Victoria. "Queens Man Impeached." The Queens Daily Eagle. December 220, 2019 Best New Thing: In Other News, Local Man Impeached | Rachel Maddow | MSNBC (youtube.com)

Resources - Volume III, Issue 51 (continued)

Worst Person Ever

Holmes, Jack. "The President Attacked a Widow at a Rally Because His Offenses Are Not Just Against the Constitution." *Esquire*, December 19, 2019. Trump Suggests John Dingell Is in Hell After Widow Debbie Dingell Voted for Impeachment (esquire.com)

What should have been included

Leonhardt, David. "The Eight Counts of Impeachment That Trump Deserves." *The New York Times*, December 8, 2019. Opinion | The Eight Counts of Impeachment That Trump Deserves - The New York Times (nytimes.com)

Emoluments explained

Milhiser, Ian. "The Emoluments Clause, Explained for Donald Trump." *Vox*, October 22, 2019. The emoluments clause, explained for Donald Trump - Vox

Finally, thanks to my dear friend Sharon in Anchorage for sending me this last link! See an excerpt on the next page.

Hanukkah starts tonight ! Merry Christmas in 3 days !! Kwanzaa kicks off on December 26 !!! Happy Holidays to all !!!!...........Kelly

Resources - Volume III, Issue 51 (continued)

Someone on Quora asked "Why do some British people not like Donald Trump?" Nate White, an articulate and witty writer from England wrote the following response:

A few things spring to mind. Trump lacks certain qualities which the British traditionally esteem.

For instance, he has no class, no charm, no coolness, no credibility, no compassion, no wit, no warmth, no wisdom, no subtlety, no sensitivity, no self-awareness, no humility, no honour and no grace – all qualities, funnily enough, with which his predecessor Mr. Obama was generously blessed.

So for us, the stark contrast does rather throw Trump's limitations into embarrassingly sharp relief.

Plus, we like a laugh. And while Trump may be laughable, he has never once said anything wry, witty, or even faintly amusing – not once, ever.

I don't say that rhetorically, I mean it quite literally: not once, not ever. And that fact is particularly disturbing to the British sensibility – for us, to lack humour is almost inhuman.

But with Trump, it's a fact. He doesn't even seem to understand what a joke is – his idea of a joke is a crass comment, an illiterate insult, a casual act of cruelty.

Trump is a troll. And like all trolls, he is never funny and he never laughs; he only crows or jeers.

And scarily, he doesn't just talk in crude, witless insults – he actually thinks in them. His mind is a simple bot-like algorithm of petty prejudices and knee-jerk nastiness.

There is never any under-layer of irony, complexity, nuance or depth. It's all surface.

Some Americans might see this as refreshingly upfront.

Well, we don't. We see it as having no inner world, no soul.

Patten, John. "British Writer Pens the Best Description of Trump I've Read." *Red Lake Nation News*, October 21, 2019. British Writer Pens The Best Description Of Trump I've Read - Red Lake Nation News

The Weekly Screed: December 29, 2019 (Volume III, Issue 52)

To: The Donald – Still the IMPOTUS

From: Kelly – All I want NEXT Christmas is a Happy 2021

- So, Donald….it seems you've had a nice relaxing vacay at Mar-A-Lago, golfing and tweeting happy holiday hate-filled messages to the faithful, including the purported name of this year's hero, the Whistleblower.
- Barack Obama, on the other hand, posted his list of Favorite Books of 2019. I could just weep.
- As you know, for the past two years, I've reserved this last issue of the current volume of our correspondence to focus on your impeachment.
- But since we've already achieved that glorious event (hooray!), I'd like to close out 2019 with a catchy little song.
- Okay, I didn't write the original (that debuted in 1994, during the tenure of our *last* impeached President), but I've penned [mostly] new lyrics just for YOU. Here we go:

All I Want for Christmas Is [Anyone But] You

- I don't want a lot next Christmas. There is just one thing I need:

Someone else to be the POTUS so I get to stop The Screed.

I don't really need to love them. They just need to take your place.

Santa Claus can make me happy with a different POTUS face.

I just want for you to GO, more than you could ever know.

Make my wish come true! Anyone for POTUS but YOU, YOU, Donald!

- I won't ask for much next Christmas. I won't even wish for snow.

I just can't wait for the ending of this SAD reality show.

I have made a list and sent it to the North Pole for Saint Nick.

Any one of the contenders wouldn't be as big a dick.

'Cuz the country can't survive four more years of toxic vibe.

What more can I do? Donald, anyone for POTUS but YOU, YOU, YOU!

- Oh you so deserved impeachment; I can't count the ways.

Even Pence would be a better POTUS for these days.

Liz or Cory would be FINE; Bernie, Amy, I don't mind.

Santa won't you bring me the ONE we really need?

Won't you send a real POTUS to me???

- Oh, I don't want a lot next Christmas. This is all I'm asking for:

I just want a brand new POTUS standing in the White House door.

I just want for you to GO, more than you could ever know.

Even Yang would do! Donald, any other POTUS but YOU, YOU, Donald!

Anyone for POTUS but YOU, Donny

Anyone for POTUS but YOU, Donny

Anyone for POTUS but YOU, Donny

Anyone for POTUS but YOU, Donny

Anyone for POTUS but YOU, Donny

Resources - Volume III, Issue 52

Dear Ones......Another year of Weekly Screeds has come to an end. Time to say goodbye to Volume III and ring in Volume IV next year! A couple of significant changes are planned:

- *Since I will be RETIRED next year, I'm taking my weekends back, and will be sending out the Screed on **Mondays**, starting on January 6.*
- *I am planning a 3.5-month road trip next summer (taking Highway 20 from Newport, OR to Boston, MA) so look forward to the Screed Show on the road.*

This week, two wildly different communications from the former and current Occupants of the White House:

Trump's Latest Twitter-Storm." *BBC News*, December 28, 2019.** Trump faces criticism after sharing tweet naming alleged whistleblower (bbc.com)

Next, I'm also sending along Barack Obama's list of favorite books of 2019, just to remind you of a happier time when we had an actual grown-up in charge.

Wallace, Kelly. "Barack Obama's 2019 Favorite Books List." *CNN*, December 28, 2019. Barack Obama lists his favorite books of 2019 | CNN Politics

Finally, probably more than anything you wanted to know about one of America's Best Selling Christmas Songs Ever. Number 1 is White Christmas and Number 2 is Silent Night, both performed by Bing Crosby. But we're here to celebrate the 25th Anniversary of Number 3.

"All I Want for Christmas Is You." *Wikipedia*. All I Want for Christmas Is You - Wikipedia

In a CBS interview, Mariah Carey reveals "All I Want for Christmas Is You" hit in 1994: **From the archives: Mariah Carey reveals "All I Want for Christmas Is You" hit in 1994 (youtube.com)**

Carey, Mariah. "Mariah Carey Releases New 'All I Want for Christmas Is You' Music Video Featuring Kids." *Entertainment Weekly*, December 20, 2019. Mariah Carey drops new All I Want for Christmas Is You music video

Bonus Video, Celebrity Edition (December 23, 2019)
Mariah Carey - All I Want For Christmas Is You (Celebrity Edition) (youtube.com)

Table of Contents Table - Volume Four – 2020+

Issue	Topic	Date	Days Left in Office	Page
1	Still the IMPOTUS	Jan 6	380	368
2	I Like to Obey the Law	Jan 13	373	370
3	Under the Bus	Jan 20	366	372
4	Still a Very Stable Genius	Jan 27	359	374
5	Know-Nothing in Chief	Feb 3	352	376
6	SOTU Voce	Feb 10	345	378
7	Daytona Don	Feb 17	338	380
8	Five-Alarm Pre-Existing CON-dition	Feb 24	331	382
9	Commander in Chaos	Mar 2	324	384
10	CDC Clown	Mar 9	317	386
11	Con Man in Chief	Mar 16	310	388
12	Flipper in Chief	Mar 23	303	390
13	Waffler in Chief	Mar 30	296	392
14	Playing Favorites	Apr 6	289	396
15	The Bad Decider – Version 2	Apr 13	282	398
16	POTUS Horribilius	Apr 20	275	402
17	POTUS Hilarious	Apr 27	268	404
18	POTUS Fabulist	May 4	261	406
19	Onward MAGA Warriors	May 11	254	408
20	The Comeback Kid	May 18	247	410
21	Open Up the Churches	May 25	240	412
22	Please Fence Me In	Jun 1	233	416
23	Boogie Woogie Bunker Bully Boy	Jun 8	226	420
24	Pandering to the Basest of the Base	Jun 15	219	422
25	True Colors – Part 1	Jun 22	212	426
26	True Colors – Part 2	Jun 29	205	428
27	Open Mouth, Insert Foot	Jul 6	198	430
28	Who Was That Masked Man?	Jul 13	191	434
29	Uncle Donald	Jul 20	184	436
30	Five Words	Jul 27	177	438

Table of Contents Table - Volume Four – 2020+

Issue	Topic	Date	Days Left in Office	Page
31	Nobody Likes Me	Aug 3	170	440
32	It Is What It Is	Aug 10	163	442
33	Kamala For The People	Aug 17	156	444
34	Who Cares ?	Aug 24	149	446
35	Nobody Outside the Beltway Really Cares	Aug 31	142	448
36	Suckers and Losers	Sep 7	135	450
37	We Got To Open Up Our Schools	Sep 14	128	452
38	Leader of the Herd	Sep 21	121	454
39	Deflector in Chief	Sep 28	114	458
40	COVID Karma	Oct 5	107	460
41	Regenerated	Oct 12	100	462
42	Underlevered	Oct 19	93	464
43	Rounding the Corner	Oct 26	86	466
44	Going In With Our Lawyers	Nov 2	79	468
45	First Runner-Up	Nov 9	72	470
46	Sore Loser	Nov 16	65	472
47	Cuckoo in Chief	Nov 23	58	474
48	Pardoner of Three Turkeys	Nov 30	51	476
49	The Donald Went Down to Georgia	Dec 7	44	478
50	Chiseler in Chief	Dec 14	37	480
51	Bad Santa (Encore)	Dec 21	30	482
52	Scrooge in Chief	Dec 28	23	484
53	Loser in Chief	Jan 4	16	486
54	Mob Boss	Jan 11	9	488
55	Impeachable You	Jan 18	2	490
56	Lest We Forget	Jan 21	-1	492

Dear Readers, I present to You:

Trump's Fourth Year as Acting President of the United States (POTUS)

Scarcely Any **Comedy**, Off-the-Charts **CHAOS**, and Almost Constant Calamity

.....And So It ends.....

The Weekly Screed: January 6, 2020 (Volume IV, Issue 1)

To: The Donald –Still the IMPOTUS

From: Kelly – What's the Rush?

- Happy New Year, Donald! To start the decade off with a bang, you "directed" a nice assassination (and threatened 52 other attacks) that just might kick off another Middle East conflagration. What a Great Leader!
- In other combustion news, the entire continent of Australia is becoming a smoldering funeral pyre for half a billion humans, koalas, wombats, and wallabies, but I don't see you paying any mind to that. After all, just another major ally….somewhere out there in one of the big wet oceans.
- Meanwhile, Congress is reassembling in Washington D.C. after the holiday revels, and the question of the hour becomes: When will Nancy Pelosi send those darn articles of impeachment over to the Senate so that Mitch McConnell can have his way with them?
- I have three words for this impending process: Not So Fast.
- Because when I hear McConnell declare his intention for a quick acquittal (with no evidence considered or witnesses called) in a Senate impeachment kangaroo court "trial," it reminds me of another McConnell decree that played fast and loose with traditional Senate proceedings.
- Remember way back to February 13, 2016, when Supreme Court Justice Antonin Scalia was found stone-cold dead at a hunting ranch [offering "many exciting on-site opportunities for adventure,"] in Marfa, Texas?
- President Obama (a real President) quickly nominated Merrick Garland (Chief Judge of the DC Circuit Court of Appeals, who had bi-partisan support) to replace Scalia. But citing "the Biden rule" (from a 1992 speech by then-Senator Joe), Moscow Mitch declined to hold any hearings on Garland and wait for the *next president* to name Scalia's replacement.
- Speaking in Kentucky in August of 2016, McConnell said: "One of my proudest moments was when I looked Barack Obama in the eye and I said, 'Mr. President, you will not fill the Supreme Court vacancy.' "
- I'm now on board with this logic. I'm calling on Speaker Pelosi to let the *next Senate* consider your articles of impeachment. Send them over on January 4, 2021. With any luck, Chuck Schumer (D-NY) will then be the Senate Majority Leader and YOU will have just a few days left in office.

- But time enough for a speedy little trial, and you can become the only impeached President ever convicted by the Senate and rendered "Unpresidented."

Resources - Volume IV, Issue 1

Happy New Year, one and all ! Plus, we get a new decade. And hopefully the last new Volume (IV) of The Weekly Screed. I'm officially retired, so (as I promised last week), the Screed is moving to Mondays for the duration. Hang in there with me for one more year!........Kelly

Romero, Dennis; Talmazan, Yuliya. "Trump Threatens Iran with Attacks on 52 Sites." *NBC News*, January 4, 2020. Trump threatens attacks on 52 sites if Iran retaliates for Soleimani killing (nbcnews.com)

Sykes, Tom. "Australia's New South Wales Declares Week-Long Emergency Over Extreme Fire Danger." *The Daily Beast*, January 2, 2020. 'Go On, Piss Off!': Australia's Prime Minister Heckled by Angry Wildfire Victims (thedailybeast.com)

Drucker, David. "Mitch McConnell's Biggest Impeachment Problem: Donald Trump." *Vanity Fair*, January 3, 2020. Mitch McConnell's Biggest Impeachment Problem Isn't Democrats—It's Donald Trump | Vanity Fair

Rhodan, Maya. "Antonin Scalia Dies at Cibolo Creek Ranch." *TIME*, February 14, 2016. Antonin Scalia Dead: See the Ranch Where He Died | TIME

Davis, Julie Hirschfeld. "Joe Biden Argued for Delaying Supreme Court Picks in 1992." The New York Times. February 22, 2016. Joe Biden Argued for Delaying Supreme Court Picks in 1992 - The New York Times (nytimes.com)

Elving, Ron. "What Happened with Merrick Garland in 2016 and Why It Matters Now." *NPR*, June 29, 2018. What Happened With Merrick Garland In 2016 And Why It Matters Now : NPR

Kilgore, Ed. "Pelosi Hints at Delaying Senate Trial; McConnell in No Hurry." *New York Magazine*, December 19, 2019. Pelosi Hints at Delaying Senate Trial; McConnell in No Hurry (nymag.com)

The Weekly Screed: January 13, 2020 (Volume IV, Issue 2)

To: The Donald –"I like to obey the law"

From: Kelly – On what planet?

- Hey, Donald, we're not even two weeks into the New Year and you've given us at least one good laugh. On Tuesday, while hosting the Prime Minister of Greece, you had a little press conference in the Oval Office and (while manspreading from your favorite yellow chair) sort of walked back your tweet-threat to target 52 sites in Iran in retaliation of its retaliation for you dropping a drone strike on its top general, Qasem Soleimani.
- When asked about your pledge to include cultural sites among those targets (aka, a War Crime), you whined about how Iran was "allowed" to kill, maim, blow up, etc., etc., all our stuff and folks, and then offered up this knee-slapper: *"And we are, according to various laws, we're supposed to be very careful with their cultural heritage. And you know what? If that's what the law is…I like to obey the law."*
- As you can imagine, the twitter-verse immediately responded with comments like this one: *"Unless it's embezzlement, defrauding a charity, tax evasion, bribery, blackmail, or rape. Laws against those, not so much."*

- The rest of the meeting followed the usual pattern of :
  1) Reporters asking impertinent questions having absolutely nothing to do with [insert name of country here].
  2) The leader of [whatever country du jour] forced to listen as you equivocate and prevaricate your meandering way though the topics you choose to respond to….which on Tuesday included impeachment , which you described as *"… a totally partisan hoax, witch hunt. And, frankly, it's been going on from before I came down the escalator with our great First Lady. I mean, it — this has gone on for three years, and probably longer than that.* "[Oy vey with the escalator again.]
  3) The afore-mentioned Robo-First Lady and her foreign counterpart sitting stiffly as you drone on, expressionless and silent on the side couches.

- I'd like to note, however, that there is one law that you **do** have to follow, and that is the Law of Unintended Consequences.... which so far includes the Iraqi Parliament voting unanimously to expel all or our troops from the country; and the accidental Iranian missile strike against a civilian air flight which killed all 176 souls aboard. More tragedies to come, I predict.

Resources - Volume IV, Issue 2

Good afternoon, all. Another catastrophic week in world news. I can't blame The Donald for the Australian wildfires, but I can lay the Ukrainian flight shoot down at his feet. But the most hilarious thing he said this week came during one of those awkward and awful press conferences with random foreign leaders. This week's victim was the Prime Minister of Greece:

"Full Transcript: President Trump and PM Mitsotakis." *Greek City Times*, January 8, 2020. Full Transcript Of Opening Remarks Between President Trump And Greek PM Before Bilateral Meeting (greekcitytimes.com)

Moye, David. "Twitter Users Greatly Amused After Trump Says, 'I Like To Obey The Law'." *HuffPost*, January 7, 2020. Twitter Users Greatly Amused After Trump Says, 'I Like To Obey The Law' | HuffPost Latest News

The Law of Unintended Consequences in action

Arraf, Jane. "Iraqi Parliament Votes to Expel U.S. Troops; Trump Threatens Sanctions." *NPR*, January 6, 2020. Iraqi Parliament Votes To Expel U.S. Troops, Trump Threatens Sanctions : NPR

"Protests in Iran as Government Admits to Downing Plane: Latest Updates." *Al Jazeera*, January 12, 2020. Anger after Iran admits downing plane: All the latest updates | Soleimani assassination News | Al Jazeera

Then he told us that the Impeachment Hoax predates his campaign announcement in June of 2015. I went back and watched it, and you can too!

Donald Trump Presidential Campaign Announcement Full Speech (C-SPAN) Bing Videos

The Weekly Screed: January 20, 2020 (Volume IV, Issue 3)

To: **The Donald – Under the Bus**

From: **Kelly – Enjoying the Ride**

- Oh, Donald, we have reached so many milestones today:
1) It's the Third Anniversary of your installation, and our correspondence.
2) In only one year, the <u>Next</u> President of the United States will be inaugurated, and our long national nightmare will come to an end.
3) <u>The Washington Post</u> "Fact Checker" announced its latest tally of your prevarications: "President Trump made 16,241 false or misleading claims in his first three years". Now that's an impressive total. Especially when you consider that your 2019 canards outnumbered the lies you told in 2017 and 2018 *combined*. As Mark Twain observed, "If you tell the truth, you don't have to remember anything. " So, I say, great recall effort on your part, DT!
4) You chose to observe *this* MLK Day (which celebrates the birthday of the Reverend Martin Luther King, Jr., who was assassinated by a gunman in 1968) by tweeting support for a pro-gun rally in Richmond, Virginia, where security has been increased due to "credible threats of violence."
- And tomorrow is another Very Big Day for you as well. It's the start of your Impeachment Trial in the US Senate! This will indeed be Must See TV.
- But the big show to watch this past week was the Rachel Maddow interview with Lev Parnas on MSNBC. Over two nights (and with a re-broadcast on Sunday….I'm sure you could catch it On Demand if you missed it), good ole' Lev implicated pretty much everyone except Ivanka in your Ukraine "corruption" scheme. Here's a list of the folks who became human speed bumps as The Wheels on the Bus [Went] Round and Round:
1) You; and Your Vice-President (Mike Pence); and
2) Your Attorney General (William Barr); and your Secretary of State (Mike Pompeo); and your Secretary of Energy (Rick Perry); and
3) Almost all of your attorneys: Rudy Giuliani, and John Dowd, and Jay Sekulow, and Joe diGenova, and Victoria Toensing; and, finally
4) Your Number One lapdogs in the House (Devin Nunes); and in the Senate (Lindsey Graham).

- I realize Lev has been indicted on campaign finance charges, but that alone doesn't make him (and his trove of documents and photos) impeachable (unlike you). As Winston Churchill once said: *The truth is incontrovertible; malice may attack it, ignorance may deride it, but in the end, there it is.*

Resources - Volume IV, Issue 3

Good afternoon, everyone. The Donald just tweeted: *It was exactly three years ago today, January 20, 2017, that I was sworn into office. So appropriate that today is also MLK Jr. DAY. African-American Unemployment is the LOWEST in the history of our Country, by far. Also, best Poverty, Youth, and Employment numbers, ever. Great!* 11:59 AM - Jan 20, 2020

Yes, SO appropriate. Here's another take on Trump observation of this holiday: Edwards, David. "'Embarrassingly incompetent': NAACP official scolds Kellyanne Conway who can't explain Trump's diss of MLK Day." *Raw Story*, January 20, 2020. 'Embarrassingly incompetent': NAACP official scolds Kellyanne Conway who can't explain Trump's diss of MLK Day - Raw Story

Today also marks the third anniversary of the Most Lies Told by ANY American President: Kessler, Glenn, et.al. "President Trump Made 16,241 False or Misleading Claims in His First Three Years." *The Washington Post*, January 20, 2020. President Trump made 16,241 false or misleading claims in his first three years - The Washington Post

But the most delicious event of last week was the Rachel Maddow/Lev Parnas interview on MSNBC. Here's some coverage: Cassidy, John. "Rudy Giuliani's Bagman, Lev Parnas, Blows Up Trump's Ukraine Defense." *The New Yorker*, January 16, 2020. Rudy Giuliani's Bagman Lev Parnas Blows Up Trump's Ukraine Defense | The New Yorker

Borowitz, Andy. "Trump Stays Up All Night with Sharpie Crossing Out Lev Parnas in Photos with Him." *The New Yorker*, January 16, 2020. Trump Stays Up All Night with Sharpie Crossing Out Lev Parnas in Photos with Him | The New Yorker

Rubin, Jennifer. "New Evidence of Impeachable Conduct: Could It Get Worse for Trump?" *The Washington Post*, January 15, 2020. Opinion | New evidence of impeachable conduct: Could it get worse for Trump? - The Washington Post
As you can imagine, I'm very happy that I'm retired and don't have to call in "sick" to watch the Senate impeachment proceedings......starting tomorrow !

The Weekly Screed: January 27, 2020 (Volume IV, Issue 4)

To: The Donald – "A Very Stable Genius"

From: Kelly – Very Seriously Concerned

- Yee-gads, Donald, I have certainly enjoyed watching the hours (and hours) of Impeachment Reality TV (on multiple networks!) this week.
- And now we have a leaked tome from your former National Security Advisor, which you've dismissed out of hand ["If John Bolton said this, it was only to sell a book"] and your threatening tweet directed at Adam Schiff ["He has not paid the price, yet, for what he has done to our Country!"] and your reported messages to wavering Republican Senators: [Someone you know told CBS news that GOP Senators have been warned: "Vote against the president, and your head will be on a pike."] Yikes!
- What next? The suspense is killing me. Fortunately, when the hearings aren't on, I'm able to dig into <u>A Very Stable Genius</u>, the latest tell-all book authored by two Pulitzer Prize winning journalists from *The Washington Post* (Carol Leonnig and Philip Rucker), which came out on Tuesday.
- You've invoked that title phrase in reference to yourself on at least five occasions, but it never fails to remind me of another quote commonly attributed to Albert Einstein: *"Everybody is a genius. But if you judge a fish by its ability to climb a tree, it will live its whole life believing that it is stupid."* Of course, the fish is aware of its limitations, while you are not. You believe your temperament and talents make you a genius…the rest of us know you are manifestly unfit for any occupation or human relationship.
- But did Einstein really write that thing about the fish? Maybe not….but what he did say is this: *"There are only a few enlightened people with a lucid mind and style and with good taste within a century. What has been preserved of their work belongs among the most precious possessions of mankind."*
- Ironically, though, it's akin what you had to say about Elon Musk on Wednesday: *"He's one of our great geniuses, and we have to protect our genius,"* you said. *"You know, we have to protect Thomas Edison, and we have to protect all of these people that came up with originally the light bulb, and the wheel and all of these things. And he's one of our very smart people, and we want to cherish those people."*

- I hate to break it to you like this, DT, but Edison died in 1931. And I've read that the wheel might have been invented in what is now Ukraine!! Around 4000 BC. Probably that person doesn't need our protection either.

Resources - Volume IV, Issue 4

Good evening, all......what an action-packed week! Impeachment hearings non-stop AND the coronavirus. But not to fear. Our Dear Leader says he has the outbreak "totally under control."

Chalfant, Morgan. "Trump Says U.S. Has Coronavirus 'Totally Under Control'." *The Hill*, January 22, 2020. Trump says US has coronavirus 'totally under control' (thehill.com)

Phew. That's a relief. Meanwhile,

Haberman, Maggie and Schmidt, Michael S. "In Book, Bolton Says Trump Tied Ukraine Aid to Inquiries He Sought." *The New York Times*, January 26, 2020. Trump Tied Ukraine Aid to Inquiries He Sought, Bolton Book Says - The New York Times (nytimes.com)

Sonmez, Felicia; Viebeck. "Trump Says Schiff Has Not 'Paid the Price' for Leading Impeachment Inquiry." *The Washington Post*, January 26, 2020. Schiff 'has not paid the price' for impeachment, Trump says in what appears to be veiled threat - The Washington Post

Pettigrew, Todd. "Why We Should Forget Einstein's Tree-Climbing Fish." *Maclean's*, January 23, 2020. Why we should forget Einstein's tree-climbing fish | Maclean's Education (macleans.ca) [Updated to January 14, 2022]

Derysh, Igor. "Trump's Fitness to Stand Trial Questioned by Professionals." *Salon*, January 24, 2020. Trump's fitness to stand trial questioned by professionals: "Serious signs of deterioration" | Salon.com

Happy Year of the Rat, everyone !!.........Kelly

The Weekly Screed: February 3, 2020 (Volume IV, Issue 5)

To: The Donald – Ignoramus in Chief

From: Kelly – Pay no attention to that man behind the curtain

- Once again, Donald, I've been glued to the TV much of the week, what with the Senate Impeachment show; Breaking News of the Coronavirus; and Super Bowl LIV (that's #54 to you).
- The only common denominator linking these 3 events is your mind-bending nescience of constitutional law [according to you, Article II allows you "to do whatever I want"]; communicable disease [you've got that Coronavirus thing "totally under control"]; and US geography [you congratulated the Kansas City Chiefs on representing "the Great State of Kansas ...so very well!"]. OOPS: they play in Kansas City, *Missouri,* which is why former *Missouri* Senator (and current MSNBC commentator) Claire McCaskill has been wearing a Chiefs lapel pin all week. There's no place like home.
- As you know, I'm one of those people who has advocated for your impeachment from Day One, when you began violating both the foreign and domestic emoluments clauses of the Constitution. This was the low-hanging fruit and should have been the first Article of Impeachment drawn up by the Congress. It certainly would have buttressed the eventual charges in Article One (for Abuse of Power) as you solicited a very large Thing of Value from the President of Ukraine (investigation of your political opponents) at the same time you withheld US support from our ally who is at war with Russia.
- Your defense against the articles of impeachment that *did* make their way to the Senate has ranged from "a perfect call"… to the charge of overturning the last election [duh, that's what impeachment ALWAYS does]… to the circular reasoning of Alan Dershowitz: Your every action might be detrimental to the country, but if YOU only <u>believe</u> that your shenanigans are beneficial….then they are! And how can that be impeachable??
- It fell to Sen. Lamar Alexander, retiring Republican from Tennessee, to put the final nail in the coffin of anything resembling an actual Senate trial. He conceded that the House Managers had "proved" their case and that your actions undermined "the principle of equal justice under the law." However, "… if you've got eight witnesses saying that you left the scene of an accident, you don't need nine." Truer words were never spoken.

- Donald, you are, indeed, the one-man scene of the greatest head-on crash in the history of American democracy, hands-down guilty of manslaughter.

Resources - Volume IV, Issue 5

Greetings to all....I'm not compulsively watching the Senate impeachment catastrophe full-time. But I'm probably paying attention more than the average bear. And I'll probably watch the State of the Union address just to say I caught Trump's last performance at that event. Meanwhile, other things are going on.

The Coming Plague

Al-Arshani, Sarah. "Trump's Tweet on U.S. Coronavirus Cases Contains Wrong Information." *Business Insider*, January 30, 2020. Trump Got Number US Coronavirus Cases Wrong in Tweet - Business Insider

The Superbowl

Reyes, Lorenzo. "Donald Trump deletes tweet after congratulating Kansas, not Missouri, for Chiefs' Super Bowl win." *USA Today*, February 2, 2020. Trump congratulates Kansas, not Missouri, in tweet for Super Bowl win (usatoday.com)

The Emoluments Clause.......and everything else he should have been impeached for......I just can't let this one go.

"What Is the Emoluments Clause?" *Britannica*. What Is the Emoluments Clause? | Britannica

Le Miere, Jason. " Trump Impeachment Articles: Here Are All the Ways the President Has Been Accused of Violating the Constitution." *Newsweek*, January 8, 2019. Trump Impeachment Articles: Here Are All the Ways the President Has Been Accused of Violating the Constitution - Newsweek

Feldman, Noah. "Yes, Abuse of Power Is Impeachable." *Yahoo News*, January 30, 2020. Yes, Abuse of Power Is Impeachable (yahoo.com)

Lily livered cowards, all those Senate Republicans

Naylor, Brian. "Sen. Alexander Explains Decision Not to Call Witnesses in Trump Impeachment Trial." *NPR*, January 31, 2020. Lamar Alexander Explains Decision Against Trial Witnesses : NPR

The Weekly Screed: February 10, 2020 (Volume IV, Issue 6)

To: **The Donald – SOTU Voce**

From: **Kelly – At least there was a happy ending**

- Gosh, Donald. Your most recent (and hopefully last) State of the Union address was certainly one for the record books. I agree with Nancy Pelosi, who opined that you looked "sedated." You hardly yelled at all, but when you did open your mouth, you managed to work in the usual complement of half-truths, misstatements, fibs, and prevarications we've come to expect.
- Let's set aside the Celebrity POTUS Game Show stagecraft ("First Class Sergeant Townsend Williams, come on down!!")
- And Best Black Friends moments (That Tuskegee Airman who I promoted to Brigadier General! That cute little girl in the pink sweater who got the "opportunity scholarship"! See, they all love ME!!)
- And demeaning forever the Presidential Medal of Freedom by having Vanna….excuse me, Melania, fasten the thing around the neck of cancer-ridden racist Rush Limbaugh, who (at your request) delayed treatment for his malady to participate in this unfortunate spectacle.
- When you arrived at the Policy Portion of the program, you had the chutzpah to read from the teleprompter lines like:
    1. *The years of economic decay are over* [thanks to eight years of Obama dragging us back from the Bush Depression of 2008]
    2. *Under my administration, 7 million Americans have come off food stamps* [cuz you changed the income rules and threw them off]
    3. *Socialism destroys nations,* [Huh? Like Norway??] *but, always remember, freedom unifies the soul*. [What the hell does that mean?]
    4. *We will always protect patients with preexisting conditions*. [Oh, Donald, you're such a kidder!]
    5. *Our spirit is still young. The sun is still rising. God's grace is still shining. My fellow Americans, the best is yet to come.*
- This fatuous declaration appeared to be the last straw for the Speaker of the House, who neatly jogged the pages of your speech and then tore 'em up!
- Alas, whatever restraint you demonstrated on Tuesday night, you reverted to form for the rest of the week, rampaging through the National Prayer Breakfast on Thursday, then working yourself into a

lather of self-pity and rage, swearing vengeance on your enemies, both foreign and domestic.
- Oh yeah....the "best"...or the Beast...is yet to come, I truly fear.

Resources - Volume IV, Issue 6

Good afternoon, all. What an amazing week! The circular firing squad of the Iowa caucus; the State of the Union circus; the 52-48 vote in the Senate to let Trump skate; the Middle East "peace" plan designed solely to help keep Netanyahu out of prison; the profane National Prayer Breakfast (aka, the Sermon of the Mouth); the Friday Night Massacre of national security and diplomatic personnel who had testified in the House Impeachment hearings.........well, as you will see, I only had room to express my thoughts on the SOTU.

The State of the Union address

"Trump State of the Union 2020 Live Fact-Check Transcript." *Politico*, February 4, 2020. Trump State of the Union 2020: Live fact-check & transcript (politico.com)

Astor, Maggie. "Trump's State of the Union Appeals to Black Voters." *The New York Times*, February 4, 2020. Trump's State of the Union Speech Continues a Theme: Courting Black Voters - The New York Times (nytimes.com)

**Johnson, Kevin. "Trump Suggests Pelosi's Speech-Tearing Could Be Illegal, But Experts Disagree." *USA Today*, February 7, 2020. Trump: 'illegal' for Pelosi to tear up speech, but experts disagree (usatoday.com)

The rest of the week that was

Dionne, E.J. "Trump's Friday Night Massacre Is Just Beginning; I Fear What's to Come." *The Washington Post*, February 8, 2020. Opinion | Vindman and Sondland are just the beginning for Trump. I fear what's to come. - The Washington Post

Sargent, Greg. "This Vulgar Man Has Squandered Our Decency." *The Washington Post*, February 7, 2020. Opinion | This vulgar man has squandered our decency - The Washington Post

The Weekly Screed: February 17, 2020 (Volume IV, Issue 7)

To: **The Donald – Daytona Don**

From: **Kelly – Probably your highest and best use as POTUS**

- Happy President's Day, Donald. I see you found a fitting way to celebrate re-tweeting *@NASCAR: The President of the United States gives the command for the 2020#DAYTONA500.*
- Wow. What a leader. So a real pilot buzzed the speedway while you lounged on Air Force One, then a real driver chauffeured you and Melania around in a circle (sticking to the safe "apron" of the track) in your "presidential" limo (aka "The Beast") following your halting little speech ending with you bellowing: *"Gentlemen, start your engines!"*
- Note: You were supposed to say "DRIVERS, start your engines," which has been the standard since Danica Patrick became a top racer in 2012. Plus, there's an all-female team at Daytona this year. Just saying.
- Also, I hate to sound elitist here, but is there any more useless human enterprise than auto racing? Excuse me, "motorsports?" We will spend billions of dollars a year to watch people go vroom-vroom around and around and around on a journey to nowhere in vehicles unfit for actual roads, until (hopefully) someone dies in a fiery crash. Isn't that what the fans are there for?
- I saw all of the Oscar-nominated Best Pictures this year, the most tedious being "Ford vs. Ferrari". Lots of footage of grimacing and downshifting interspersed with evil corporate overlords being either bungling bureaucrats or rapacious money-grubbers. Until the inevitable tragic ending when Christian Bale (as British driver Ken Miles) manages to die on a test drive.
- I suppose it's less unseemly than Wrestle Mania, and at least no non-human animals are harmed (unlike the poor abused and doomed creatures in dog and horse racing). But, more than most athletic endeavors, it seems that the majority of drivers need to be RICH in order to compete, with the amount of money they bring into a team mattering more than skill behind the wheel.
- So, I guess it's exactly your type of sport, DT! I mean, that's how you picked most of your cabinet and ambassadors, right? From your big donors? Rather than from among people actually qualified to run an agency or be a diplomat with any knowledge of a foreign land?

- I suppose I'm especially cranky today cuz it's "President's Day" and you are such a ludicrous excuse for Leader of the Free World, especially compared with your predecessor. I hope I'm in a better mood this time next year.

Resources - Volume IV, Issue 7

Happy Last President's Day for Donald Trump! I believe that sincerely. Vote Blue No Matter Who !! As the Department of Justice unravels, I decided to hold off on unpacking that drama, and focus on the biggest inanity of the week: The Donald trying to look "presidential" at the Daytona 500. Which was, sadly, rained out on Saturday, but did resolve today in the massive crash that all the fans were hoping for! I'm sure a good time was had by all. Except maybe the poor guy who wound up in the hospital. As always, I learned something new by digging into this topic, which does not interest me at all.

McGraw, Meredith. "Trump's Reelection Campaign Goes 'Pedal to the Metal' at Daytona 500." *Politico*, February 17, 2020. Trump's reelection campaign goes pedal to the metal at Daytona 500 - POLITICO

Fryer, Jenna. "Trump Arrives at Daytona 500, Sets Off Raucous Celebration." *PBS News*, February 16, 2020. Trump arrives at Daytona 500, sets off raucous celebration | PBS News Weekend

Cole, Frederick. "Will NASCAR Bring Back 'Gentlemen, Start Your Engines'?" *FanBuzz*. February 19, 2020. NASCAR fans are wondering if one tradition will return with Danica Patrick retiring - FanBuzz

Perkins, Chris. "Katherine Legge on Racing and the Future of Motorsports." *Road & Track*, January 24, 2020. Katherine Legge on Racing Daytona With All-Female Driver Lineup (roadandtrack.com)

Perez, Jerry. "Behind the Shadowy Billion-Dollar Payouts of F1, NASCAR, and IndyCar." *The Drive*, July 15, 2019. Show Me the Money: The Finances Behind IndyCar, NASCAR, and Formula 1 (thedrive.com)

Bromberg, Nick. "Denny Hamlin Wins Daytona 500 as Ryan Newman Flips at Finish." *AOL News*, February 17, 2020. NASCAR: Denny Hamlin wins second straight Daytona 500 (aol.com)

P.S. I'm having double knee surgery on Wednesday, so if next week's Screed sounds like it's written by someone on drugs, you'll know why !

The Weekly Screed: February 24, 2020 (Volume IV, Issue 8)

To: The Donald – Five Alarm Preexisting CON-dition

From: Kelly – In the Beginning, there were PECs

- Donald, remember back just a few short years ago, almost 3 years to the day, when you were dipping your little (supposedly) bone-spur-plagued feet into the icy waters of health care policy?
- *"Nobody knew that health care could be so complicated,"* you whined at the time (2/27/17). Well, just about everyone trying to function as an adult in the current economy knew that health care was *perilously, life-and-death, existentially* complicated. Except YOU. Because you are, as your departed Secretary of State Rex Tillerson told us: A F #$%ing Moron.
- One of the more nuanced points of the health care debate is the topic of "preexisting conditions." You are obviously baffled by this concept, but you acknowledge you are supposed to understand and support "it"... Them??
- *"We will always protect patients with preexisting conditions, very importantly,"* you announced with one side of your noggin (on May 9, 2019), while the other side was furiously and concurrently supporting its polar opposite (*Texas v. Azar*), before the federal appellate court, which would demolish whatever remains of the afore-mentioned Patient Protection & Affordable Care Act (aka Obamacare), whose 10-year anniversary as the law of the land will be celebrated next month.
- Knowing that actually deciding this case would be bad for "optics" during an election year, your handlers have wisely postponed winning *Texas v Azar* for the insurance companies. And then sending it along to the Supremes, where your Gang of Five could sound the final death knell. Better to let the Russians….excuse me, the voters….weigh in first.
- I'm thinking a lot about preexisting conditions these days, DT, because
  a) I just switched my health coverage over to Medicare.
  b) I just retired from a job where I helped to enroll people into expanded Medicaid and marketplace plans (aka the ACA).
  c) And I have many preexisting conditions, primarily Two Bad Knees.
- And so do YOU, Donald: hair replacement surgery; those Vietnam-era bone spurs; unspecified mental health maladies [like your delusional declarations from today about the stock market]. But you take it one step further, DT. You **ARE** a Preexisting Condition. On the body politic. A

preexisting Con Job we all could see coming. Not even Medicare can save us from you.

Resources - Volume IV, Issue 8

Good Evening one and all ! As you can see, I have survived the double knee surgery, with one weird complication: some sort of allergic reaction to the mesh dressing over the incision, resulting in a Biblical plague of boils and blisters on the right knee. [See Exodus 9: 8-35] I will spare you the photo.

I'm seeing the surgeon tomorrow and start PT on Friday. Meanwhile the coronavirus continues to be TOTALLY under control (not) and the stock market has now registered a negative result for the year. The Donald is not perturbed.

Chalfant, Morgan. "Trump Asserts Coronavirus Under Control as Stocks Plunge." *The Hill*, February 24, 2020. Trump asserts coronavirus 'under control' as stocks plunge (thehill.com)

Fortunately, we all still have the Affordable Care Act, Medicaid, and Medicare

Luthra, Shefali. "Trump's Talk on Preexisting Conditions Doesn't Match His Administration's Actions." *Kaiser Health News*, May 16, 2019. Trump's Talk On Preexisting Conditions Doesn't Match His Administration's Actions - KFF Health News

Kunkle Roberts, Danielle. "Does Medicare Cover My Pre-Existing Conditions?" *Boomer Benefits* January 19, 2020. Medicare and Pre-existing Conditions: What's Covered | Boomer Benefits

And The Donald's ailments are considered PEC as well.

"Hair Loss Treatments and Preexisting Conditions." *Mayo Clinic*. Hair loss - Diagnosis and treatment - Mayo Clinic

"Is a Bone Spur Considered a Pre-Existing Condition?" *Answers*. Is a bone spur considered a pre-existing condition? - Answers

The Weekly Screed: March 2, 2020 (Volume IV, Issue 9)

To: The Donald – Commander in Chaos

From: Kelly – Haikus for a Hoax

1) Prophesier in Chief

The Dear Leader says:

"Like a miracle someday

It will go away."

2) Delegator in Chief

Mike Pence is in charge.

He can pray the plague away.

Just like HIV.

3) Comforter in Chief

The first soul we lost:

"Such a wonderful woman."

Oh wait.... What a guy!

4) Emergency Preparedness

Defund CDC.

Eliminate NSC,

Global health office.

5) Blamer in Chief

First the Russian Hoax.

Impeachment was a Hoax too.

Democrats did this.

6) Doing the Hard Work

"We order a lot.

Elements of medical--

A lot of supplies."

7) Consequences

All Purel sold out.

"Cancel trip" trends on Google.

There goes my pension.

8) Accessorizing for the Apocalypse

Pandemic couture:

Fascist fashionistas sport

Red MAGA face masks. *

*Okay, I made this one up, but maybe a good project for Ivanka?

Resources - Volume IV, Issue 9

I'm back in the hospital, 10 days after surgery on February 19, with an infected right knee. In the meantime, you might have heard a few things about the coronavirus:

Levin, Bess. "Trump Claims Coronavirus Will "Miraculously" Go Away by April." *Vanity Fair*, February 11, 2020. Trump Claims Coronavirus Will "Miraculously" Go Away by April | Vanity Fair

Martin, Jeffrey. "Mike Pence's 'Pray On It' Plan To Combat Indiana HIV Outbreak Resurfaces After Trump Taps VP to Lead Coronavirus Response ." *Newsweek*, February 28, 2020. Mike Pence's 'Pray On It' Plan To Combat Indiana HIV Outbreak Resurfaces After Trump Taps VP to Lead Coronavirus Response - Newsweek

Heimbrod, Camille. "Trump's Mental Deterioration Rumors: POTUS Makes Huge Mistake About Coronavirus Patient." *International Business Times*, March 2, 2020. Trump Mental Deterioration Rumors: POTUS Makes Huge Mistake About Coronavirus Patient, CDC Takes Responsibility | IBTimes

Krugman, Paul. "When a Pandemic Meets a Personality Cult." *The New York Times*, February 27, 2020.** Opinion | When a Pandemic Meets a Personality Cult - The New York Times (nytimes.com)

Egan, Laura. "Trump Calls Coronavirus Democrats' 'New Hoax'." *NBC News*, February 28, 2020. Trump calls coronavirus Democrats' 'new hoax' (nbcnews.com)

Porter, Tom. "Pence Refuses to Condemn Trump Jr. for Saying Dems Want Coronavirus to Spread." *Business Insider*, March 2, 2020. Pence Refuses to Condemn Trump Jr for Saying Dems Want Coronavirus Deaths - Business Insider

Sheth, Sonam. "Trump Orders Medical Supplies Amid Coronavirus Concerns." *Business Insider*, February 28, 2020. Trump Says He's Ordering Many 'Elements of Medical' for Coronavirus - Business Insider

Biron, Bethany. "Purell Hand Sanitizer Sells Out on Amazon Amid Coronavirus Fears." *Business Insider*, February 28, 2020. Purell Hand Sanitizer Sells Out on Amazon Amid Coronavirus Fears - Business Insider

The Weekly Screed: March 9, 2020 (Volume IV, Issue 10)

To: The Donald – Centers for Disease Control Clown

From: Kelly – Gobsmacked

- Donald, every now and again you really out-do yourself. I've become accustomed to the moronic and misspelled tweets; the bellowing of BS at your rallies; the daily lies and insults. But you were somehow able to bring all of it together in a singularly unhinged visit to the CDC on March 6.
- My reaction to that spectacle [knowing full well that I'm not supposed to touch my face] comes from the Scottish word "gob", meaning "mouth", meaning I literally clapped my hand over my mouth while watching it.
Fortunately, we have the transcript:
- [16 minutes and 34 seconds in] *"So we have 240 cases, 11 deaths, everything is too much and it's true. ...I would have said does anybody die from the flu? I didn't know people died from the flu."*
- Your own grandfather died from the Spanish flu in 1918, you cretin.
- [27:15] *"But I think importantly, anybody right now and yesterday, anybody that needs a test, gets a test... and the tests are all perfect, like the letter was perfect. The transcription was perfect, right?"*
- Yes, DT, our entire testing protocol (in terms of availability and reliability) for this Coronavirus catastrophe has been pretty much on par with the phone call to Ukraine that got you impeached. Good comparison there.
- [29:37, re the cruise ship anchored off California] *"I like the numbers being where they are, I don't need to have the numbers double because of one ship that wasn't our fault..., they're mostly Americans, so I can live either way with it. I'd rather have them stay on, personally."*
- How soon can we book the entire Trump Crime Family on a 3-hour tour to Gilligan's Island??
- [37: 58] *"My uncle is a great person who was at MIT. He taught at MIT for I think a record number of years. He was a great, super genius. Dr. John Trump. I like this stuff. I really get it. People are surprised that I understand that I understand it. Every one of these doctors said, 'How do you know so much about this?' Maybe I have a natural ability. Maybe I should have done that instead of running for President. I understand that whole world. I love that world. I really do. I love that world."*

- Yes, you *might* have been able to pass the Certified Nursing Assistant course at a community college and we all could have been spared this nightmare.

Resources - Volume IV, Issue 10

On his way to play golf in Florida, Trump dropped in to the Centers for Disease Control in Atlanta. Reporters were on the scene. 45 minutes of what-the-hell ensued.

Here's the transcript:

"Transcript: Donald Trump Visits CDC, Calls Jay Inslee a 'Snake'." *Rev*, March 6, 2020. Transcript: Donald Trump Visits CDC, Calls Jay Inslee a "Snake" | Rev

Trump learns something new that everyone else has known forever:

Zorllner, Danielle. "Trump Says He Didn't Know People Died from the Flu." *Business Insider*, March 8, 2020. Trump Said He 'Didn't Know People Died From the Flu' - Business Insider

I survived a cholera quarantine on a steamboat trip down the Congo River in 1979. This no laughing matter!

Chappell, Bill; Romo, Vanessa. "Coronavirus: Grand Princess Cruise Ship Docks Off California Coast." NPR. March, 2020. Coronavirus: Grand Princess Cruise Ship Docks Off California Coast : Shots - Health News : NPR

The current head of the CDC does not inspire confidence:

Choma, Russ. "Trump's CDC Director Has a History of Controversial Opinions on Controlling Viruses." *Mother Jones*, March 7, 2020. Trump's CDC Director Has a History of Controversial Opinions on Controlling Viruses – Mother Jones

Knee surgery update: back home from the hospital, but still taking oxycodone and antibiotics. This recovery will take a while.

The Weekly Screed: March 16, 2020 (Volume IV, Issue 11)

To: The Donald – Con-Man in Chief

From: Kelly – Calling you out

- Holy Cow, DT. I just watched your performance at the daily Pandemic Press Briefing, with the stock market LIVE in the lower right corner, plunging with every word. I'm pretty sure it hit 3,000 points down (an all-time record!) right around the point when you gave yourself a 10 out of 10 for your handling of this catastrophe.
- It's been quite a week for bungled outings for you, though. First there was your Oval Office address to the nation on Wednesday night, where you came off as a stoned orangutan squinting at the teleprompter and trying to make sense of the script (which alternated between inane and alarming) hastily penned for you by Jared Kushner and Stephen Miller.
- Usually you excel at mendacity when you are unconstrained by the printed word, but in this speech you managed to lie about "contacts with our allies", the "foreign virus", the "speed and professionalism" of your response to the crisis, details of the European response [Italy cut off travel from China three days before we did], the notion that the European travel ban was inclusive of "trade and cargo" [it wasn't] but did not include the countries in Europe where you have golf courses, and (finally) the lie that health insurance companies had agreed to provide no-cost treatment for the coronavirus.
- Please. Pigs will fly on the day we get anything free from insurance companies or Big Pharma that hasn't been mandated under Obamacare.
- Next came your Rose Garden press conference on Friday. When asked by a reporter about why you closed the National Security Agency pandemic response office in 2018, you responded first with: "[that's] a nasty question" and then: "I don't know anything about it" when you are actually on tape in February explaining why you closed it: "I'm a businessperson; I don't like having thousands of people around when you don't need them."
- If we follow that logic, we should disband the entire military now and send everyone home until we're actively involved in a declared conflict. That would save a LOT of money!
- Finally, on March 10, you tweeted that "We need the Wall more than ever!", ostensibly to keep out the hordes of infected scum from the southern border. Just one problem: on that day, the US had 1,000

confirmed cases of the coronavirus; Canada had 100; and Mexico had 8. You are a doofus.

Resources - Volume IV, Issue 11

So, what a difference a week makes, eh? I think we'd better get used to cataclysmic changes coming quickly for quite some time. As usual, The Donald has been out there LYING about his administration's response to the coronavirus crisis. It's getting real, folks:

The Wednesday night in the Oval Office lies

Kessler, Glenn; Rizzo, Salvador. "Fact-Checking Trump's Address to the Nation on Coronavirus." *The Washington Post*, March 12, 2020. Fact-checking Trump's address to the nation on the coronavirus - The Washington Post

The Friday in the Rose Garden lies

Capehart, Jonathan. "The Buck Never, Ever Stops with Trump." *The Washington Post*, March 16, 2020. Opinion | The buck never, ever stops with Trump - The Washington Post

Badash, David. "How We Know Trump Was Lying About the Pandemic Office." *Raw Story*, March 13, 2020. How we know Trump was lying when he said, 'I didn't do it' and 'I don't know anything about' closing the pandemic office - Raw Story

The Wall will save us

Rizzo, Salvador. "Trump's Wobbly Claim That His Wall Could Stop Coronavirus." *The Washington Post*, March 12, 2020. Trump's wobbly claim that his wall could stop the coronavirus - The Washington Post

I beg my Republican friends and relatives to read this one:

Wehner, Peter. "The Trump Presidency Is Over." *The Atlantic*, March 13, 2020. Peter Wehner: The Trump Presidency Is Over - The Atlantic

Even though both of my county libraries are closed, I have enough reading material stockpiled in the house to last me through ten quarantines. It's not a bad time to be laid up with bad knees and forced to stay inside! Wishing you all health and peace as we get through this........Kelly

The Weekly Screed: March 23, 2020 (Volume IV, Issue 12)

To: The Donald – Wartime Whiny Little Bitch

From: Kelly – March Sadness

- Donald, one of the things I'm missing most from Life as I Knew It is the reliably risible reality checks from late night comics. I could record all my favorites (Colbert, Seth, Trevor, Jimmy K, John Oliver, and Bill Maher) and watch at least the opening monologues. I know they would have had a field day with your appearances at the daily Coronavirus Task Force Briefings, which I've had to make do with as the New Normal Comedy Hour.
- While it's not my favorite epithet for you, the appellation that most often comes to mind as I'm taking in your performances is the one offered up by Bill Maher way back on May 6, 2016: Whiny Little Bitch.
- "Irrational, pouty, vain, thin-skinned, hysterical and just not that bright, does that sound like anyone we know today?" Maher queried the audience.
- While you've often played the Victim Card over the past few years, your querulous self-pity is particularly stark in juxtaposition to your recent self-proclaimed ascension to "Wartime President."
- Setting aside the fact that any single one of your acts of negligence and corruption would have resulted in the summary court-martial of any other commander in actual wartime, your blubbering during this crisis is particularly offensive.
- Take your grouching (while millions of Americans are newly unemployed and impoverished due to stay-at-home orders) about your selfless donation of your presidential paycheck ("Nobody cared, no one said thank you very much…. I get excoriated all the time….") WAH.
- Or how much you've sacrificed in order to ruin the country with your tenure as POTUS ("It's cost me billions of dollars to be president of the United States.") Cue the tiny violins.
- But the carping that really got to me was your unbelievably wussy reaction to the coronavirus test that you had to endure while millions of Americans have been begging to get one: "Not something I want to do every day, I can tell you that," you whimpered. "Nothing pleasant about it."
- I recently had double knee surgery that resulted in a nasty infection requiring the same type of test for MRSA (long swab up the nostril into

the sinuses). Trust me, DT, it was certainly the *least* invasive and painful procedure that I've undergone in the past 6 weeks. Man up, snowflake.

Resources - Volume IV, Issue 12

Greetings from Oregon, where the Governor finally issued Executive Order No. 20-12: Stay Home, Save Lives. This week I'm focusing on what an absolute wimp The Dear Leader is:

Bill Maher called it early on

Boucher, Geoff. "Bill Maher Calls Trump 'Whiny Little Bitch' on Real Time." *Deadline*, August 3, 2019. Bill Maher Roots For Recession, Calls Trump "A Whiny Little Bitch" (deadline.com)

No one appreciates him

Jefferson, Andrea. "Trump Complains No One Thanks Him for Giving Up Presidential Salary During Virus Press Conference." *Political Flare*, March 22, 2020. Trump Uses Virus Presser to Whine that No One Thanks Him for Giving Up Presidential Salary (politicalflare.com)

He could be even more corrupt

Burris, Sarah K. "Trump Claims Being President Is Costing Him Billions." *Raw Story*, March 22, 2020. Trump goes down in flames after whining 'it costs me billions to be president' - Raw Story

Mommy, it hurt :(

Trump explains getting tested for Coronavirus (youtube.com) March 16, 2020

As our Governor said, Stay Home ! and Stay Healthy ....Kelly

The Weekly Screed: March 30, 2020 (Volume IV, Issue 13)

To: The Donald – Waffler in Chief

From: Kelly – March Madness

- It has gone by many names: yo-yoing, flip-flopping, backtracking, waffling. And it's taken down many politicians a thousand times more honorable, decent, intelligent, and fit for office than you.
- Let's look at <u>just three</u> of your most head-snapping declarations and reversals regarding COVID 19:
  1) Heckuva Job (Not)
- "…We have it totally under control. It's one person coming in from China. It's going to be just fine." -- *January 22*
- "And again, when you have 15 people [infected], and the 15 within a couple of days is going to be down to close to zero, that's a pretty good job we've done."---*February 26*
- "And so, if we can hold that down, as we're saying, to 100,000 — that's a horrible number — maybe even less, but to 100,000, so we have between 100- and 200,000, we all together have done a very good job." - *March 29*
- *[Wow. Zero to Two Hundred Thousand in a month. No matter WHAT happens, you will go down in history as being the Worst President Ever in a time of national crisis.]*

  2) Shipping Supplies (Not)
- "The federal government is not supposed to be out there buying vast amounts of items and then shipping. <u>We're not a shipping clerk</u>." ---- *March 20*
- [And yet, somehow, you shipped close to 18 tons of medical equipment to China way back on February 7. No such concern for American governors, mayors, or hospitals.]

  3) In your Easter bonnet (Not)
- "I would love to have it [the country] open by Easter. I will tell you that right now. I would love to have that. It's such an important day for other reasons. But I'll make it an important day for this, too. I would love to have the country opened up and just raring to go by Easter."---*March 24*

- "Wouldn't it be great to have all the churches full? You'll have packed churches all over our country. I think it'll be a beautiful time." --- *March 24*
- "The better you do, the faster this whole nightmare will end. We can expect that by June 1, we will be well on our way to recovery. We think, by June 1 . . . a lot of great things will be happening." --- March 29
- *[Oh Gawd…I was SO looking forward to seeing you, Melania, and your evil (but sanctimonious) spawn all lined up in the pew on Easter Sunday…with the exception of the Kushners, of course. But here's what we could do by Easter: change the name of the White House to the "Waffle House."]*

Resources - Volume IV, Issue 13

*Good afternoon all…………I hope you are all having a reasonably good time with your loved ones…..all together…..all the time…..This week, I have to step back from a long held conviction and throw in the towel: These past few years, I've tried to draw the distinction between recognizing Donald Trump as the Worst **Person** Ever to be installed in the White House, but clinging to my opinion that George W Bush was the Worst **President** Ever, due to wrecking the economy and the sheer body count (between 9/11, the Iraq and Afghanistan wars, and Katrina). But now that we've already surpassed every country in the world in damage done to our economy (projected unemployment rate of 32%, tanking the stock market, etc.) AND in the number of cases of COVID-19, and the boorish behavior, and the LIES, I've gotta hand it to The Donald. Hope it's enough to do him in come November. This week, let's look at his flip-flopping, some of it at such breakneck speed I have had to reappraise The Screed on an almost hourly basis:*

Heckuva Job

Saunders, Josh. MacMillan, Arthur. "Trump's Reality Struggle During Coronavirus Crisis." *Express*, March 28, 2020. Coronavirus crisis: How Donald Trump may be worsening the pandemic by 'fighting reality' | World | News | Express.co.uk

Resources - Volume IV, Issue 13 (continued)

Fenwick, Cody. "13 Times Trump's Coronavirus Claims Have Gone Down in Flames." *Salon*, March 10, 2020. 13 times Trump's coronavirus claims have gone down in flames | Salon.com

Leonhardt, David. "A Complete List of Every Time Trump Tried to Play Down the Coronavirus." *The Durango Herald*, March 17, 2020. David Leonhardt: A complete list of every time Trump tried to play down the coronavirus – The Durango Herald

Shipping Clerk in Chief

U.S. Shipped Tons Of COVID-19 Supplies To China As Trump Dismissed Threat Here | HuffPost Latest News

In Your Easter Bonnet

Lucas, Fred. "Open by Easter? Trump Wants Nation Shut by Coronavirus 'Raring to Go'." *The Daily Signal*, March 24, 2020. 'Open by Easter'? Trump Wants Nation Shut by Coronavirus 'Raring to Go' (dailysignal.com)

André Gagné. "Coronavirus: Trump and religious right rely on faith, not science." *The Conversation*, March 29, 2020. Coronavirus: Trump and religious right rely on faith, not science (theconversation.com)

Rowan, Nicholas. "Churches Won't Be Packed for Easter Despite Trump's Call." *Washington Examiner*, March 25, 2020. Churches won't be 'packed' for Easter despite Trump call - Washington Examiner

Statistics

The Centers for Disease Control: Coronavirus Disease 2019 (COVID-19) | COVID-19 | CDC

Johns Hopkins University COVID-19 Map - Johns Hopkins Coronavirus Resource Center (jhu.edu)

Resources - Volume IV, Issue 13 (continued)

Prosperity gospel preacher Kenneth Copeland told a Christian magazine that the fear of the coronavirus was a sin. He said when people fear they give the devil a pathway to their bodies.

On Twitter he told his 432,000 followers: "No weapon meant to hurt you will succeed ... No disease. NO VIRUS. ... Believe it. Receive it. Speak it in Jesus' Name!"

Copeland, who is wealthy, also told people to continue tithing to the church even if they lose their jobs due to the coronavirus.

--André Gagné for The Conversation, 3/29/20

The Weekly Screed: April 6, 2020 (Volume IV, Issue 14)

To: The Donald – Playing Favorites

From: Kelly – I Love New York

- Donald, about a month ago, in the good old pre-plague days, when I was in the hospital, recovering from a post-surgery infection, I remember having a conversation with one of my nurses that went something like this: "Just wait……he's <u>not</u> going to send medical supplies to Blue States like Washington and New York. He's waiting for Florida and Texas to blow up, and then he'll come to the rescue."
- Gawd, sometimes I hate it when I'm right. Just recently, with New York leading the nation in cases and deaths, and screaming from the rooftops for PPE and ventilators, Florida (just coincidentally, I'm sure) received 100% of its request for supplies, even before its dim-bulb Governor issued a stay-at-home order for the state.
- But, hey, your idiot son-in-law has declared that New York is just being a big whiney-pants state that doesn't duly appreciate the Dear Leader: "I have all this data about ICU capacity. I'm doing my own projections, and I've gotten a lot smarter about this. New York doesn't need all the ventilators." …so, who are we going to believe? Jared Kushner, Boy Wonder and One-Man Multi-Portfolio Moron or the Governor of New York, Andrew Cuomo [who, if there is a god, will be our next President]??
- Meanwhile, both you and Jared have declared the federal stockpile to be "for us, not the states," and even changed the official wording of the Strategic National Stockpile's website to reflect this new philosophy. It SO reminds me of when FDR told the states to make their own tanks and airplanes during WWII [just kidding]. And who the hell is "us"? The Trump Crime Family? Republicans Only?
- Donald, we are all getting whiplash from your all-over-the-map pronouncements. One day, you are the "Wartime President." The next day, you are just a "backup." One day you are warning us about all the "terrible death" about to descend on us. The next, you are back to happy talk about filling the stadiums for the upcoming NFL season ["Sports weren't designed for this" ….as if anything in our world was].
- I even remember one glorious day back in July of 2016 (at the Republican National Convention) when you proclaimed: "I alone can fix it". Which has since devolved to "I take no responsibility." Of course, you won't. It's all Obama's fault.

- What all this blame-shifting and kicking-the-can-down-the-road has brought into focus is our need to get rid of the Electoral College as the determiner of US presidential elections. Long an anachronism, this pitting of red states against blue states allows politicians like you to play favorites instead of considering the popular vote in all 50 states.
- How do you think the people of Staten Island (57 % of whom voted for you in 2016) feel when you deny life-saving medical supplies to NYC? More than a third of the people of New York, 38% of the population of Washington state, and 47% of Michiganders voted for your sorry ass. But their governors are Democrats, so they are SOL for now.

Resources - Volume IV, Issue 14

Treviso, Perla for ProPublica. "In Case You're Wondering Why Florida Got All the Good Stuff..." *Crooks and Liars*, March 30, 2020. In Case You're Wondering Why Florida Got All The Supplies They Requested... | Crooks and Liars

Dye, Liz. "Kushner Dismisses New York's Ventilator Needs." *Wonkette*, April 2, 2020. Jared Kushner's Magical MBA Knows New York Whiners Don't Need Thousands Of Vents (wonkette.com)

Brodkin, Jon. "US Edits National Stockpile Website After Kushner Claims It's Not for States." *Ars Technica*, April 3, 2020. US edits National Stockpile website after Kushner claims it's not for states | Ars Technica

Rupar, Aaron. "Trump Tells Governors to Be 'Nice' for Coronavirus Help." *Vox*, March 25, 2020. Trump to governors: "They have to treat us well" if they want coronavirus help - Vox

Armour, Nancy. "Donald Trump Can't Bully NFL into Starting Season Before Safe." *USA Today*, April 4, 2020. Donald Trump can't bully the NFL into starting season before it's safe (usatoday.com)

Woodward, Calvin; Yen, Hope. "AP Fact Check: Trump, Wartime Pandemic Leader or Backup?" *PBS NewsHour*, April 4, 2020. AP FACT CHECK: Trump, 'wartime' pandemic leader or 'backup'? | PBS News Weekend

Every now and then, I'm reminded of how great it is to live in Oregon: this past week our governor, Kate Brown, sent 140 ventilators to New York, just because they need them more than we do right now. Would that we had leadership at the top like this. There's a lot of pandemic parody songs going around the Internet. Here's one of my favorites from this week: "Stayin' Inside" - Coronavirus Bee Gees Parody (youtube.com)

The Weekly Screed: April 13, 2020 (Volume IV, Issue 15)

To: The Donald – The (Bad) Decider, Version 2

From: Kelly – I Love the USPS

- Golly, Donald, you really triggered my PBSD [Post Bush Stress Disorder] with your tweet today: *"For the purpose of creating conflict and confusion, some in the Fake News Media are saying that it is the Governors decision to open up the states, not that of the President of the United States & the Federal Government. Let it be fully understood that this is incorrect. It is the decision of the President, and for many good reasons."*
- Which took me straight back to April of 2006 (the height of the Iraq War) when another dim-bulb Republican POTUS announced: *"I'm the decider, and I decide what's best."*
- Of course, Dubya never made a good decision in his life, and you have by far exceeded even his dismal record in both business and politics. So let me just note for the record that (before you exponentially multiply the COVID death toll by prematurely packing the sports stadiums and houses of worship) you have just recently made another terrible decision NOT to give aid to the United States Post Office during this Time of Troubles.
- The American people couldn't expect you to realize this, but (fun fact) the Constitution of the United States actually empowered Congress to establish a postal service. And with the Post Office Act of 1791, they made it happen, and thereby greatly expanded access to information throughout the land.
- I recently read a nice little book (published last year by Harvard University Press) titled "The Public Option: How to Expand Freedom, Increase Opportunity, and Promote Equality." I know you probably don't hold these concepts in high regard, cuz they do sound vaguely socialist, but the book quotes historian Richard R. John as crediting the postal service thusly: *"The citizen-farmer had no trouble securing access to a steady flow of information on public affairs, making it possible for him to participate in national politics without leaving the farm."* Of course, the "citizen-farmer" in the early days of our republic was exclusively white, male, and owned property (including other people!) but, hey, that's the majority of your base today, right?

- And you might not be aware of this, either, but there's a whole bunch of Republican voters in rural America who don't have reliable access to the Internet, and REALLY appreciate 6 day a week mail delivery.
- Which brings me to the other thing you've disparaged this past week that depends on a vital postal service: Vote by Mail…. declaring live on Fox & Friends that efforts to fund this system would be "crazy." *"They had things, levels of voting that if you'd ever agreed to it, you'd never have a Republican elected in this country again!"*
- Would that it were so, DT, but (trust me on this one) Oregon has had 100% Vote by Mail for 20+ years and we've still managed to elect plenty of evil and moronic GOP candidates who routinely attempt to subvert democracy in our state. More on this soon!

Resources - Volume IV, Issue 15

Good afternoon……..I hope none of you attended any sort of religious service in person this past week. I live-streamed the Unitarians on Sunday, and ordered groceries on Instacart, all from the comfort of my recliner. I could get used to this. Meanwhile, the Orange One (who had previously urged us to "pack the pews" for Easter Services) continued his "Do as I say, not as I do" style of leadership, voting absentee in the Florida primary while forcing Wisconsinites to line up in person, during a pandemic, for hours to cast their votes. Thanks, 5-4 Supreme Court emergency ruling !! Anyway, I love the United States Post Office, especially when I get to vote by mail, so I'm particularly perturbed by the Dear Leader's attacks on this institution.

I'm the Decider

Wilson, Christopher. "Trump Claims He Can Overrule States on Ending COVID-19 Shutdowns." *AOL*, April 13, 2020. Trump claims he can overrule states on ending COVID-19 shutdowns [Video] (aol.com)

Stolberg, Sheryl Gay. "The State of Our Union Is … Complex." *The New York Times*, December 24, 2006.** The Decider - The New York Times (nytimes.com)

Deciding to Kill the Post Office

Steinberg, Neil. "Cruise Ships Safe, Post Office Dies." *Chicago Sun-Times*, April 12, 2020. Airlines safe, but Trump would let post office die - Chicago Sun-Times (suntimes.com)

Resources - Volume IV, Issue 15 (continued)

Johnson, Jake. "Sanders Says Congress Must Stop Trump from Exploiting COVID-19 Crisis." *Common Dreams*, April 12, 2020. Sanders Says Congress Must Stop Trump From Exploiting Covid-19 Crisis to 'Bankrupt and Privatize the Postal Service' | Common Dreams

Deciding on Voter Suppression

Levine, Sam. " Trump says Republicans would 'never' be elected again if it was easier to vote." *The Guardian*, March 30, 2020. Trump says Republicans would 'never' be elected again if it was easier to vote | Donald Trump | The Guardian

Allen, Greg. "Trump Denounces Vote-by-Mail, GOP in Florida Relies on It." *NPR*, April 11, 2020. Despite Trump Criticism, Republicans Also Rely On Vote By Mail : NPR

Gardner, Amy and Viebeck, Elise. "GOP Pushes Voting by Mail—with Restrictions." *The Washington Post*, April 12, 2020. GOP pushes voting by mail — with restrictions — while Trump attacks it as 'corrupt' - The Washington Post

How Oregon did it

"Vote-by-Mail in Oregon." *Wikipedia*. Vote-by-mail in Oregon - Wikipedia

Oregon GOP Walkout." *The Washington Post*, February 24, 2020. Oregon Republicans walk out again to avoid cap-and-trade vote - The Washington Post

I have much more to say on this topic, so consider this Vote By Mail - Part One.

Resources - Volume IV, Issue 15 (continued)

During the White House coronavirus briefing Tuesday [April 7], Trump said, "I think that mail-in voting is a terrible thing" and followed up the next day with several tweets calling on Republicans to oppose statewide mail-voting, claiming without evidence that the practice hurt GOP candidates and was susceptible to widespread fraud.

---Greg Allen. NPR. 4/11/20

The Weekly Screed: April 20, 2020 (Volume IV, Issue 16)

To: The Donald – POTUS Horribilis

From: Kelly – I Love the USPS

- Donald, let this past week be remembered for the 5-day interval when you pivoted from
  --<u>Autocracy</u>: "When somebody's the president of the United States, the authority is total." [Monday, April 13] to
  --<u>Acquiescence</u>: "I will be speaking to all 50 governors very shortly. And I will then be authorizing each individual governor of each individual state to implement a reopening, very powerful reopening plan of their estate in a time in a manner which is most appropriate." [Tuesday, April 14] to
  --<u>Anarchy</u>: "LIBERATE MINNESOTA" .... "LIBERATE MICHIGAN" .... "LIBERATE VIRGINIA and save your great 2nd Amendment. It is under siege!" [Friday, April 17]
- I gotta tell you, DT, this encouragement of armed insurrection against the coronavirus is not playing too well, even in the heartland. That's because most Americans (even Republicans) are smarter than you are and realize that re-opening Cracker Barrel for fine sit-down dining and gift-shopping won't cure COVID-19. And that ventilators are more potent weapons than firearms in this particular situation.
- But hey, according to you, these Virus Deniers are "good people" (just like the Good Nazis of Charlottesville in 2017) who are entitled to issue death threats to state governors and public health officials as a justifiable response to "cabin fever."
- I hate to employ another firearm reference here, but I'm thinking this sort of protest might backfire. Most intelligent people are already reluctant to get out and enjoy themselves without access to COVID-19 testing, a vaccine, or anything approaching a reliable treatment. Do you really think that we'll be more likely to "get the economy going again" if the streets are clogged with the soon-to-be infected disaffected MAGA Morons waving confederate flags and brandishing armaments? Not an enticing scenario.
- But what IS trending favorably is Vote by Mail. Which is now being championed by Michelle Obama and believe me you don't want to get in front of that train. As I mentioned last week, Oregon was the national pioneer in this endeavor, and I've long maintained that we have the freest and fairest elections in the country.

- If you check out the website of the Oregon Secretary of State (a female Republican, if you can believe it) you will see how we actually encourage all Oregonians (even Republicans!) to exercise their franchise. It's a radical notion, but somehow it works.
- As I mentioned last week, Oregon has been conducting vote-by-mail exclusively for twenty years. In 2015, we led the country again by implementing Motor Voter (by which new voters are automatically registered at the Department of Motor Vehicles). In 2017, we expanded voter registration to 16-year-olds. And just last year, the State legislature voted to provide pre-paid postage on ballot return envelopes. All good enough, but I have an idea to make Vote by Mail even more popular. I'll share this with you next week.

Resources - Volume IV, Issue 16

Wise, Alana. "Trump Falsely Claimed 'Total Authority' Over States; Now He's Backpedaling." *NPR*, April 14, 2020. Trump Backpedals 'Total' Authority Comments : NPR

Peters, Jeremy W. "Trump's 'Liberate' Call Fits Right Into Anti-Government Playbook." *The Washington Post*, April 17, 2020. Trump's 'LIBERATE' tweets might be both unconstitutional — and criminal - The Washington Post

Relman, Eliza. "Trump Defends Protesters Making Death Threats Against Governors, Calling Them 'Very Good People'." *Business Insider*, April 20, 2020. Trump Calls People Resisting Lockdowns 'Good People' - Business Insider

"Yahoo News/YouGov Coronavirus Poll: Most Americans Reject Anti-Lockdown Protests." *AOL*, April 20, 2020. Yahoo News/YouGov coronavirus poll: Most Americans reject anti-lockdown protests (aol.com)

Pilkington, Ed. "Michelle Obama Backs Vote-by-Mail Push Amid Coronavirus Pandemic." *The Guardian*, April 13, 2020. Michelle Obama announces new vote-by-mail push | Michelle Obama | The Guardian

"Vote-by-Mail in Oregon." *Wikipedia*. Vote-by-mail in Oregon - Wikipedia

**Ruben, Joey. "Oregon's Motor Voter Law Increases Turnout, Diversity." *Oregon Public Broadcasting*, April 17, 2020. Study: Oregon 'Motor Voter' Program Boosted Turnout And Diversity Of Voters - OPB

The Weekly Screed: April 27, 2020 (Volume IV, Issue 17)

To: The Donald – POTUS Hilarious

From: Kelly – I Love the USPS

- I gotta hand it to you, Donald. This past week, you provided me (and the rest of the world, I'm sure) with more guffaws and LOL moments than at any other time in at least the past 3 months. I know, it was inadvertent, but still…. I wanna say "thanks" on behalf of a grateful planet.
- I'm referring of course to your performance at the April 23 Coronavirus Taskforce Briefing, during which you queried the doctors sitting on the sidelines as to the possibility of using disinfectants and UV lighting "internally" to clean up COVID-19.
- These musings spawned a bounty of snarky responses on Twitter and You-Tube: a photo of a bottle of "Clorox Chews"; a yard sign for Biden with the slogan: "He Won't Make You Drink Bleach!"; a song parody from Randy Rainbow tweaking the lyrics to that timeless Mary Poppins tune, "A Spoonful of Sugar."
- Almost as laughable: your lame attempt at a press conference in the Oval Office the next day to spin your comments as "sarcasm" designed to punk the press. Pathetic.
- But you also used that press conference to attack the United States Postal Service again: *"The Postal Service is a joke because they're handing out packages for Amazon and other Internet companies. And every time they bring a package, they lose money on it."* Then you threatened not to sign off on any relief funds unless the USPS raises its prices on Amazon deliveries. Because you hate Jeff Bezos. Because he also owns *The Washington Post*. Because it publishes "nasty" and "Fake News" stories about you. Because all of this worldwide health and economic emergency is really All About You.
- YOU got to vote by mail in the Florida primary election last month *["I'm allowed to"]*
  But everyone ELSE who sends in a ballot is "cheating" and "corrupt." Once again, Donald, you are missing a golden opportunity on this issue. I've got to tell you, mail-in ballots were already popular, but now (after watching the Wisconsin Pandemic Primary debacle) they are the wave of the future. So, grab your surfboard, DT.

- First, embrace "National Vote by Mail." Next, establish the Great National Election Door Prize. You could fund it in a piece of CARES legislation. Here's how it could work:
    1) Every registered voter gets a ballot sent to them, which they return in a postage-paid envelope showing their name and address. The voter must sign the envelope.
    2) The envelope is received at the local County Clerk's office. The Clerk registers the envelope as being returned and verifies the voter's signature on the envelope.
    3) The envelope is opened. The (secret) ballot goes off for the votes to be recorded.
    4) The envelope is used as the Door Prize ticket (unless the voter marks "Decline to Participate.") Each state conducts a million-dollar drawing for each national election.
- Just think of it, Donald! People would love it! Voter registration and participation would sky-rocket. Morale would soar. What a legacy. I just hope it doesn't get you re-elected.

Resources - Volume IV, Issue 17

I'm still beating the drum for National Vote by Mail, and today I'm sending The Donald a Bright Idea that might make him get behind it. I'm not the only person to come up with it....Google searches reveal similar attempts in Florida and Arizona. But I've long thought that Oregon could really make it work...Let me know what you think......

Funke, Daniel. "In Context: What Donald Trump said about disinfectant, sun and coronavirus." PolitiFact. April 24, 2020. PolitiFact | In Context: What Donald Trump said about disinfectant, sun, and coronavirus

Nichols, John. "Vote-by-Mail in the U.S.: A Growing Debate Amid COVID-19." *The Nation*, April 24, 2020. What's Super Popular? Voting by Mail. | The Nation

Epstein, Reid J. "Why Republicans Are So Afraid of Vote-by-Mail." *The New York Times*, April 8, 2020. Why Republicans Are So Afraid of Vote-by-Mail - The New York Times (nytimes.com)

Levine, Carrie. "Coronavirus Sparks Battle Over Vote-by-Mail." *NBC News*, April 14, 2020. Coronavirus has ignited a battle over voting by mail. Here's why it's so controversial. (nbcnews.com)

The Weekly Screed: May 4, 2020 (Volume IV, Issue 18)

To: The Donald – POTUS Fabulist

From: Kelly – Still Reality Based

"Nobody's seen this I would say since 1917, which was the greatest of them all..." 4/4/2020

"Who would think you could have a stock market at 24,000 after we've gone through the worst pandemic since 1917? That's over 100 years." 4/29/20

In the grand scheme of things, it's a small nit to pick from the mountain of lies and distortions.

You inflict on us daily your wacko ideas and denials in infinite portions.

But there's one little fact that you always get WRONG and I can't understand why you say it.

It's incontrovertible! Can't be dismissed as "sarcasm" however you play it.

A lot of stuff happened the year that you mention: particularly World War One.

The Czar of all Russia stepped down from his throne; the Romanov dynasty done.

Mata Hari was killed by a French firing squad; New York women were granted the vote.

Brazil entered the war when one of its ships was sunk by a German U-boat.

The White Sox became the World Series champs; the Green Corn Rebellion took place.

The Great Thessaloniki Fire in Greece left tens of thousands displaced.

In Illinois, two hundred fifty were killed in the race riots of East St. Louis.

The first of the Pulitzer Prizes were granted; tornadoes killed hundreds of us.

Yet meanwhile, in Kansas, the fatal pandemic had not yet begun to emerge.

So, when you say otherwise, I grit my teeth, and try to extinguish my urge

To scream at the TV: "You ignorant moron!" and fling projectiles at the screen

No matter how often you try to deny it, the "Spanish Flu" happened in **Nineteen Eighteen**.

Resources - Volume IV, Issue 18

Glasser, Susan B. "Trump and the 1917 Pandemic That Wasn't." *The New Yorker*, April 30, 2020. History According to Trump: The President and the 1917 Pandemic That Wasn't | The New Yorker

Norman, Tony. "Trump, Truth, and the 1917 Pandemic." *Pittsburgh Post-Gazette*, April 7, 2020. Tony Norman: Who are you going to believe — POTUS or an actual expert? | Pittsburgh Post-Gazette

Rupar, Aaron. "Trump's Mistaken Reference to the 1918 Flu Pandemic." *Vox*, May 1, 2020. Trump won't stop saying the 1918 flu pandemic happened in 1917 - Vox

Melvin, Tessa "1917: When Women Won the Right to Vote." *The New York Times*, November 1, 1987. 1917: WHEN WOMEN WON RIGHT TO VOTE - The New York Times (nytimes.com)

Andrews, Evan. "Why Was It Called the Spanish Flu?" *History*. January 12, 2016. Why Was It Called the 'Spanish Flu?' | HISTORY [Updated July 12, 2023]

"First Cases Reported in Deadly Influenza Epidemic." *History*. First cases reported in deadly 1918 flu pandemic | March 4, 1918 | HISTORY

Finally, the last organized insurrection against the US government (which I had never heard of until I read about it on Wikipedia this morning):

Grant, Richard. "The Socialist Revolution in Oklahoma Crushed: The Green Corn Rebellion." *Smithsonian Magazine*, May 2020. When the Socialist Revolution Came to Oklahoma—and Was Crushed | Smithsonian (smithsonianmag.com)

The Weekly Screed: May 11, 2020 (Volume IV, Issue 19)

To: The Donald – "Leading" from way, way behind

From: Kelly – AWOL

Asked Wednesday [May 6] if the nation needs to accept greater loss of life, Trump said "Hopefully it won't be the case, but it may very well be the case."

Onward MAGA warriors, marching with our guns, swastikas, and nooses: Time to have some fun!
We've been home for far too long; learning how to Zoom; ordering on Instacart and cowering in our rooms.
Onward MAGA soldiers, marching as to war, with Confederate banners going on before!

COVID's in the White House. Fauci's quarantined; testing yields alarming outcomes unforeseen.
We can pray this plague away if we only choose. Let's go storm the beaches and get us some new tattoos.
Onward MAGA soldiers! We'll pretend it's war, and get back to normal, like we were before.

Only cowards wear the mask. Trump and Pence are brave! Lives come cheap where there is money to be saved.
Let's muzzle the CDC; guidelines override; "civil rights" trump public health when God is on our side.
Onward MAGA soldiers, mount your monster trucks. Safety is for whiners; all we need is luck.

Testing's overrated; vaccines take too long. Suck it up and go forth! Sing the victor's song.
We can all be warriors! Pack the parks and pews. Eat more bacon, get a haircut, what have we to lose?
Onward MAGA soldiers; we can't question why. Trump's is to command us; ours to do and die.

Resources - Volume IV, Issue 19

Greetings, fellow combatants. As a young Presbyterian in small town Texas, I belted out "Onward Christian Soldiers" with the best of them. Here's a link to the original, so you can refresh your memories (if you have them) or learn a new tune! Onward Christian Soldiers w lyrics piano worship video - video Dailymotion

But now I'm a Unitarian-Universalist, and we're having a bit of a national crisis, so I've re-written this old hymn to make it a little more "relevant."

Megerian, Chris. "Trump Calls Americans 'Warriors' in Push to Reopen Economy." *Los Angeles Times*, May 6, 2020. Trump calls Americans 'warriors' in fight to open economy - Los Angeles Times (latimes.com)

Stableford, Dylan. "Trump: People in Pennsylvania Want Their Freedom Now, But Democrats Delay Reopening to Hurt Him." *AOL*, May 11, 2020. Trump: Pennsylvanians want to reopen and are 'fully aware of what that entails' (aol.com)

Graham, Bryan Armen. "Michigan's Governor Faces Racism and Protests Amid Lockdown Orders." *The Guardian*, May 3, 2020. 'Swastikas and nooses': governor slams 'racism' of Michigan lockdown protest | Michigan | The Guardian

**"CDC Guidelines for Reopening Businesses." *DocumentCloud*.CDC-Business-Plans.pdf (documentcloud.org)

Walch, Tad. "Trump Hosts Multifaith Prayer Service at White House." *Deseret News*, May 7, 2020. National Day of Prayer features Latter-day Saints, evangelicals, Catholics, Muslims, Jews, and Hindus – Deseret News

**"Where Is Trump's Battle Plan Against Coronavirus?" *Cleveland.com*, May 10, 2020. If Americans are 'warriors' against the coronavirus,' where is President Trump's battle plan? - cleveland.com

Letter to the Editor, from Steve Jones, South Euclid, Ohio Posted May 08, 2020

This week, President Donald Trump argued that Americans are warriors willing to risk death to immediately re-pump the economy. Americans may well be warriors, but the commander-in-chief should not send his soldiers into battle without armor, without weapons, without ammunition and without a battle plan -- especially when all credible reconnaissance screams that engagement is nothing short of a death sentence.

The Weekly Screed: May 18, 2020 (Volume IV, Issue 20)

To: The Donald – The Comeback Kid

From: Kelly – No so fast

We're Coming Back (Apologies to The Angels from The Donald)

(Intro) I'm in the White House and COVID's around. It bothers me all day and night. And when I get mad and fire everyone, you say things that aren't very nice.

We're coming back and there's gonna be trouble (Hey-la-day-la we're coming back) With no vaccine the death rate's gonna double (Hey-la-day-la we're coming back!)

Whistleblower lies are mean and untrue (Hey-la-day-la we're coming back!) So, look out, Bright, cuz I'm coming after you! (Hey-la-day-la we're coming back!)

We've been locked down for such a long time (Hey-la-day-la we're coming back!) We'll open up and things will be fine! (Hey-la-day-la we're coming back!)

Obama will be sorry he was ever born (Hey-la-day-la we're coming back!) 'Cause my brain is big and I'm awful strong (Hey-la-day-la we're coming back!)

Hey, Obama's always cheatin'. And now he's gonna get a beatin'

How does he think you'll believe all his lies? (Ah ooo. Ah ooo)

He thinks he's smart, but I'll cut him down to size (Ah oo) Wait and see !!!!!

The stock market's gonna save my reputation (Hey-la-day-la we're coming back!) Or else I'll have to take a permanent vacation (Hey-la-day-la we're coming back!)

Don't need no testing! We're coming back…No contact tracing! We're coming back…Masks are for sissies! We're coming back… Vaccines don't matter! We're coming back…

Resources - Volume IV, Issue 20

Good afternoon to all my fellow self-imposed shut-ins. I don't know about your state or situation, but I'm in one of the few Oregon counties that has NOT been cleared to re-open. Which is just fine with me. I have the HUGE privilege of not being in any rush. The quote that inspired this week's song came on Friday, when The Donald proclaimed: "Vaccine or No Vaccine, We're Back!" This rallying cry does not inspire confidence, and just makes me want to stay in lockdown even longer. But it did trigger a memory from the '60s, so (as an antidote to last week's old moldy hymn) I give you fresh lyrics to a peppy little pop song. Enjoy the old black and white video (the Ed Sullivan Show October 6, 1963): The Angels - My Boyfriend's Back 1963 (youtube.com)

And then read all about it. Apparently, mine is not the first parody. My Boyfriend's Back (song) - Wikipedia

Perez, Matt. "Unveiling Effort to Speed COVID-19 Vaccine, Trump Says 'Vaccine or No Vaccine, We're Back'." *Forbes*, May 15, 2020. Unveiling Effort To Speed COVID-19 Vaccine, Trump Says, 'Vaccine Or No Vaccine, We're Back' (forbes.com)

Bella, Timothy. "Trump Criticizes Whistleblower Rick Bright's Testimony." *The Washington Post*, May 18, 2020. Trump says coronavirus whistleblower Rick Bright is 'causing great injustice and harm' - The Washington Post

Goldberg, Michelle. "Obamagate Is a Fake Scandal. Rick Bright Described a Real One."*The New York Times*, May 15, 2020. Opinion | Obamagate Is a Fake Scandal. Rick Bright Described a Real One. - The New York Times (nytimes.com)

Rubin, Jennifer. "Why Trump Is Back to Attacking Obama." *The Washington Post*, May 18, 2020. Opinion | This is why Trump is back to attacking Obama - The Washington Post

Zeeshan, Aleem. "Obama Criticizes Trump's Response in Commencement Speech." *Vox*, May 16, 2020. Barack Obama's commencement speech criticizes Trump's coronavirus response - Vox

**Friedman, Vanessa. "The Politics of Wearing Masks During the Pandemic." *GQ*, May 15, 2020. Your Mask Is Now Your Political Identity | GQ

The Weekly Screed: May 25, 2020 (Volume IV, Issue 21)

To: The Donald – Open up the Churches

From: Kelly – You go first

Open Up the Church on Time (apologies to Lerner & Loewe)

It's time to open up the churches; ding-dong the bells are gonna chime!

Let's all start singing, praises we're bringing! And get us to the church on time.

Let's kill some people in the morning: old folk, and young folk in their prime.

Jesus will save us, we are the bravest, let's all go to the church on time.

> It is essential to do this now
>
> I'll sue the Governors, that's my solemn vow!

Oh, I will be golfing in the morning. Church is for suckers like Mike Pence.

Build our alliance! Ignore the science, it really doesn't make much sense.

> People are breaking the church doors down
>
> It's time to worship all around the town!

I'm gonna wait and see what happens, count up the bodies as they fall.

Time for the faithful to show what they're made of and sacrifice themselves for all!

> Me? I'll be golfing and have more fun
>
> With God on my side, shoot a hole-in-one!

So, fill up the pews on Sunday morning. Ding-dong the bells are gonna chime.

Don't mind the virus, the saints will admire us, so get yourselves to church,

Get yourselves to church, for MY sake get yourselves to church on time!

Resources - Volume IV, Issue 21

Well, it's another especially sad Memorial Day, hopefully the last Trumpian one we'll see. Thanks to him, we have tens of thousands more Americans to mourn, due to 6 weeks of inaction in February and March. And we'll also be seeing another surge in the death toll this summer, thanks to premature re-openings of businesses, beaches, and churches.

I really don't have a good feeling about this....my church (First Unitarian-Universalist of Portland) has already announced that we'll continue to stream services until June of 2021. And the final nail in the coffin to my travel plans for this year was the announcement that, for the first time since World War Two, there will be no Alaska State Fair. That does it for me !! I'm staying at home for the duration !

Meanwhile, the Dear Leader "ordered" churches, synagogues, and (with some hesitation) mosques, to open across the land, deeming houses of worship "essential." At least to everyone except the Trump Crime Family.........I didn't see any of their pointy little heads in the pews yesterday. Just His Orangeness glad-handing the caddies and speeding around in his golf cart on Saturday and Sunday.
So, I'm closing out the May Screed Poetry Slam with a Broadway tune today: "Get Me To The Church on Time", from My Fair Lady.

You can take your pick of two versions....one is a lively theatrical production, and one is by Frank Sinatra, Old Blue Eyes at his smarmiest.

Get Me to the Church on Time MY FAIR LADY | Get Me to the Church On Time (youtube.com)

Sinatra (1952) Frank Sinatra (Live) - Get Me To The Church On Time - YouTube

Meanwhile, despite the documented dangers of congregating and singing in enclosed spaces, The Donald is urging us to comply with his pronouncements:

Woodward, Aylin. "Trump declared houses of worship essential. Mounting evidence shows they're super-spreader hotspots." *Business Insider*, May 28, 2020. Houses of Worship, Which Trump Says Are Essential, Are Coronavirus Hotspots - Business Insider

Resources - Volume IV, Issue 21 (continued)

Breuninger, Kevin; Higgins-Dunn, Noah. "Trump Demands Governors Reopen Houses of Worship 'Right Now'." *CNBC*, May 22, 2020. Trump slams governors, demands they open houses of worship 'right now' (cnbc.com)

Baker, Peter. "Trump Pushes to Reopen Churches, Creating Clash with Governors." *The New York Times*, May 22, 2020. Firing a Salvo in Culture Wars, Trump Pushes for Churches to Reopen - The New York Times (nytimes.com)

Finally, after touring a Ford mask production facility (while declining to wear a mask), Trump addressed African American leaders in Ypsilanti, Michigan:

"And we're going to open our churches again. I think CDC is going to put something out very soon. I spoke to them today; I think they're going to put something out very soon. We've got to open our churches. People want to go in. I saw a scene today where people are trying to break into a church to go into the church — not to break in and steal something, to break in — they want to be in their church. I said, "You better put it out." And they're doing it and they're going to be issuing something today or tomorrow on churches. We got to get our churches open."

"Remarks by President Trump at Listening Session with African-American Leaders in Ypsilanti, MI." *The White House*, May 21, 2020. Remarks by President Trump in Listening Session with African American Leaders | Ypsilanti, MI – The White House (archives.gov)

Dizikes, Peter. "Who gets ventilator priority?" *MIT News* May 13, 2020. Who gets ventilator priority? | MIT News | Massachusetts Institute of Technology

Lord have mercy ! Stay safe and sane.........Kelly

Resources - Volume IV, Issue 21 (continued)

In some cases — as an example, Florida and — I guess I've heard from about six governors where they have far more testing than they have people that need the test, so that's something. Nobody has done the job on testing like we have. Nobody has done the job on ventilators like we have. You're going to see that in a little while at the Ford plant where they're making thousands and thousands of ventilators. And nobody that's needed a ventilator in this entire country has not gotten one. And very importantly, all over the world now they're calling us for help on ventilators. They're very hard to make and they're calling for help on ventilators.

--Donald Trump. Remarks to African American Leaders in Ypsilanti, MI on 5/21/20

In May 2020, the demand for ventilators surged dramatically due to the COVID-19 pandemic. The U.S. government invoked the Defense Production Act to increase the production of ventilators, partnering with manufacturers to boost supply[1]. Despite these efforts, the demand was still challenging to meet, with some areas like New York City forecasting a need for tens of thousands of additional ventilators.

National Estimates of Increase in US Mechanical Ventilator Supply

The Weekly Screed: June 1, 2020 (Volume IV, Issue 22)

To: The Donald – Please Fence Me In

From: Kelly – Mourning George Floyd

Hey, Donald. I was watching the country go to hell the other night and a visual from our nation's capital caught my eye: "The White House Fence Replacement Project" printed in tasteful script on a white wall in front of the fence surrounding your current government housing, framing a tableau of the Secret Service vs We the People. Unlike nuclear arms treaties, environmental regulations, and affordable health care, this seems to be the one initiative from the Obama era that you've gotten behind. Literally.

As you tweeted on Saturday, *"Great job last night at the White House by the U.S.@SecretService. They were not only totally professional, but very cool. I was inside, watched every move, and couldn't have felt more safe."* You went on: *"...nobody came close to breaching the fence. If they had they would have been greeted with the most vicious dogs, and most ominous weapons, I have ever seen. That's when people would have been really badly hurt, at least."* Finally, attempting to incite the faithful, you beseeched: *"Tonight, I understand, is MAGA NIGHT AT THE WHITE HOUSE???"* And later, in comments to reporters, you clarified: *"By the way, they love African American people, they love black people.... MAGA loves the black people."* I'm sure this declaration came as Breaking News to all concerned.

Meanwhile, you and your loved ones had been hustled into a bunker, presumably deep in the bowels of the residence, secure from the mayhem you had incited. But by this morning, you were upbraiding the nation's governors in a phone call. *"Most of you are weak! You have to dominate.... you have to arrest people, you have to track people, you have to put them in jail for 10 years, and you'll never see this stuff again."* Um-hmm. This is legacy-building stuff, DT. Decades from now, school children will be reading these words and thinking "Golly gee. Now that's the kind of empathic, inspirational leadership our country got when we really needed it." But back to that fence. We learn from The White House Historical Association's Timeline Overview that the original post-and-rail version was installed by a real President (Thomas Jefferson) in 1801. A stone wall erected in 1808 enclosed the White House Grounds and also included a barrier that kept livestock away from the gardens. 1818 saw the first iron fence, but the grounds remained open to the public until

President Ulysses S. Grant (an actual war hero) began closing them at sunset, in 1873.

And now you are having a go at it. Maybe someday, visitors to the White House will be able to cross the bridge over the alligator-filled Pennsylvania Avenue Moat and be herded through the gates of the "restored" fence (50-feet tall, reinforced concrete topped with electrified razor wire), wearing our haz-mat suits and gas masks, under the scrutiny of black-loving MAGA Secret Service warriors brandishing "ominous" firearms and holding back snarling German shepherds. And then Amerika will be Great Again.

Resources - Volume IV, Issue 22

Please Fence Me In

(Apologies to Cole Porter)

Oh, I am here in the White House under siege from Antifa!
Please fence me in.
Let me tweet and repeat all the nasty threats I love.
Please fence me in.
Don't leave me by myself as the evening breeze
Scatters all the tear gas through the cheery trees
Send me to the bunker with my family!
Please fence me in.
Don't turn me loose to the mercy of the looters
Underneath the smoky skies
Unleash the dogs and the pepper spray and guns
Till the anarchy subsides.
I want to be safe inside as the riot commences
Summon the MAGA folk to my defenses.
I'll hide in the White House.
I don't care where Pence is.
Please fence me in.

Resources - Volume IV, Issue 22 (continued)

Well, it happened again. I was inspired to write another song, but it is attached here as a bonus. I listened to several versions of this tune and settled on Willie Nelson and Leon Russell as my favorite: [Don't Fence Me In (youtube.com)](youtube.com) *- 1979*

Of course, the Coward in the White House wants nothing more than to be protected from the citizenry by the biggest bad-ass barrier possible. After the events of the past week, the plans drawn up by the Obama administration might not suffice.
It was just last week that COVID-19 was our only nationwide crisis. What a difference 9 minutes in Minneapolis made. These are strange and mournful days indeed.

Haberman, Maggie. "Trump Threatens Protesters with 'Dogs' and 'Weapons'." *The New York Times*, June 1, 2020. [Trump Threatens White House Protesters With 'Vicious Dogs' and 'Ominous Weapons' - The New York Times (nytimes.com)](nytimes.com)

Blake, Aaron. "Trump's 'Bunker' Retreat Crystallizes His AWOL Response to George Floyd Unrest." *The Washington Post*, June 1, 2020. [Trump's bunker retreat crystallizes his AWOL response to George Floyd unrest - The Washington Post](#)

Bierman, Noah; Stokols, Eli; Megerian, Chris. "Trump Tells Governors to 'Dominate' as He Shrinks from Crisis." *Los Angeles Times*, June 1, 2020. [Trump calls for 'law and order,' threatens to deploy troops to major cities - Los Angeles Times (latimes.com)](latimes.com)

"History of the White House Fence." *The White House Historical Association*. [History of the White House Fence - White House Historical Association (whitehousehistory.org)](whitehousehistory.org)

Resources - Volume IV, Issue 22 (continued)

About the White House Historical Association

First Lady Jacqueline Kennedy envisioned a restored White House that conveyed a sense of history through its decorative and fine arts. She sought to inspire Americans, especially children, to explore and engage with American history and its presidents. In 1961, the nonprofit, nonpartisan White House Historical Association was established to support her vision to preserve and share the Executive Mansion's legacy for generations to come. Supported entirely by private resources, the Association's mission is to assist in the preservation of the state and public rooms, fund acquisitions for the White House permanent collection, and educate the public on the history of the White House. Since its founding, the Association has given more than $115 million to the White House in fulfillment of its mission.

To learn more about the White House Historical Association, please visit WhiteHouseHistory.org.

The Weekly Screed: June 8, 2020 (Volume IV, Issue 23)

To: The Donald – Boogie Woogie Bunker Boy

From: Kelly – Persevering in Portland

He was the famous Donald Trump from Mar a Lago way.
He liked to build casinos and to golf all day
His only genius was for graft; he was a privileged brat
And good at dodging the draft
But he's the POTUS now, and scared as he can be
He's the Boogie Woogie Bunker Boy of White House, D.C.
He's s'posed to serve The People & his Uncle Sam
But he's just in it for himself, don't give a damn
His minions seem to understand that with this
Clown in the House they get to grab all they can
He's Mitch's bitch for sure, & dumb as he can be
He's the Boogie Woogie Bunker Boy of White House, D.C.
And then, in MN, an awful thing was done
And thousands took to the streets to raise their voices
And folks they woke up from the lockdown and they saw they have some choices
And they don't really like the POTUS that they see
He's the Boogie Woogie Bunker Boy of White House, D.C.
He went *down, down, down* to the Bunker just to check it all out (make an "inspection")
And thought he'd revive the Eighteen Oh Seven Act of Insurrection
Then took a photo op, with a Bible prop,
He's the Boogie Woogie Bunker Boy of White House, D.C.
He gasses the protesters every day and night
To dominate the streets and make sure all is right
For all the wealthy in this land
But Black Lives Matter too much for us to not take a stand
Whoa, whoa, we'll vote him out on November 3
He's the Boogie Woogie Bunker Boy of White House, D.C.

Resources - Volume IV, Issue 23

Okay, I guess you know what's coming........here are two versions of the real song. I couldn't make up my mind which I liked better:

The Andrews Sisters (1941) – recording a "V-Disc" .....like MTV for WWII (I'm not old enough to remember this one, but it makes me nostalgic for my USO days) (1957) The Andrews Sisters - Boogie Woogie Bugle Boy (V-Disc 1945) - YouTube

The Divine Miss M (1973) – on Johnny Carson....with Barry Manilow on piano (I AM young enough to remember Bette Midler sing this one! It's the year I graduated from college.) Lullaby Of Broadway Boogie Woogie Bugle Boy - Bette Midler - Johnny Carson 1973 (youtube.com)

Borowitz, Andy. "Trump Says Inspection Revealed Bunker Was Dusty Because Obama Never Used It." *The New Yorker*, June 3, 2020. Trump Says Inspection Revealed Bunker Was Dusty Because Obama Never Used It | The New Yorker

Colarossi, Natalie. "History of the Insurrection Act and How Trump Could Use It Against Protests." *Business Insider*, June 4, 2020. How Trump Could Use the Insurrection Act to Stop George Floyd Protests - Business Insider

Curuvilla, Carol. "Trump Defends Bible and Church Photo Op After Tear Gassing Protesters." *HuffPost*, June 4, 2020. Trump Defends Church Photo Op: 'I Think It Was Very Symbolic' | HuffPost Latest News

But the Absolute Worst Thing the Idiot-in-Chief said last week:

Superville, Darlene. "Trump Declares Friday a 'Great Day for George Floyd'." *Portland Press Herald*, June 5, 2020. Trump declares Friday 'a great day' for George Floyd (pressherald.com)

Finally, a Public Service Announcement: *I have* **SHINGLES**. *YOU do not want to have shingles !! Get vaccinated !!!!!*

The Weekly Screed: June 15, 2020 (Volume IV, Issue 24)

To: The Donald – Pandering to the Basest of the Base

From: Kelly – Persevering in Portland

- Donald, as you know, my first early childhood memories are of segregated small-town life in northeast Texas. My mother was a homemaker. My father was the Personnel Director for the local VA Hospital. One of the best things that ever happened to me was when he was transferred to the VA Hospital in Denver, Colorado, in 1960, and my family escaped full-time immersion in Southern "culture".

- I must emphasize "full-time," however, because my parents' idea of summer vacation was to load up the Pontiac with 3 little girls and drive to southeast Texas every year to visit the kinfolk, who lived primarily in Woodville (big timber) and Port Arthur (big oil). Both of my grandfathers worked in those extraction industries. Some of my relatives employed The Help. Some voted for George Wallace in 1968. There were rumors of an uncle in the KKK. [On the plus side, I learned to fish and ride horses, and the food was scrumptious.]

- I was always cautioned ahead of these visits that a few of these relatives might speak differently about black people than we were accustomed to in Colorado….they might use words that we were never supposed to use, but we were not to say anything about it. My sisters and I were still supposed to be Polite and Ladylike. That's just the way things were in Texas.

- Last week, one of my cousins (a lifelong Texan) posted this on Facebook:

Dear Congressman Gohmert,

I am asking that you do everything you can to oppose this outrageous proposal to rename the army bases. These Confederate generals were all American heroes (well not Gen. Bragg so much) and it is an insult to our heritage and the great men and women who were ever stationed at these forts. BTW, I also read the invitation from the Secretaries of Defense and the Army to have a "bipartisan discussion". I wish that you would convey to them that I will proudly accept their offer and represent the American people who love freedom and cherish our Southern Heritage. Those two can represent the other side. Your obedient servant, _____

- <u>No longer having my mother around to shush me, I replied:</u>

I have to disagree with you on this one, Cousin...Confederate generals were traitors to the nation who put dedication to the institution of slavery above fealty to the United States of America. There's much that I love about Texas, including my family, but the racism I grew up with and still witness is the part of "Southern heritage" that this country needs to put behind us.

Rename the bases for real war heroes and heroines. Put the Confederate statues in a museum somewhere. The men who lost the Civil War should no longer be held up as an inspiration to white people or stand as a silent intimidation to people of color. Black lives mattered so little in our past that the South was willing to secede to maintain its right to exploit them. Events of the past few weeks have demonstrated that (finally) a vast majority of this country believes they matter now.

- <u>Good ole' Cousin _____ responded:</u> None of what you said is true though I certainly don't doubt your sincerity. Have a nice day. 😊

Well, I tried, because I no longer ascribe to "being polite," but to saying something when I see something. I know you think your strongman bigot persona is playing well in the heartland, but when the GOP-led Senate Armed Services Committee thinks we need to change those base names, you might want to pay attention. You and my Cousin are relics and chickenhawks. Time's Up, Corporal Bonespurs!!

Resources - Volume IV, Issue 24

Kheel, Rebecca. "Senate Panel Votes to Require Pentagon to Rename Bases Named After Confederates." *The Hill*, June 11, 2020. <u>Senate panel votes to require Pentagon to rename bases named after Confederates (thehill.com)</u>

Robinson, Eugene. "Trump Might Go Down in History as the Last President of the Confederacy." *The Washington Post*, June 11, 2020. <u>Opinion | Trump might go down in history as the last president of the Confederacy - The Washington Post</u>

Resources - Volume IV, Issue 24 (continued)

Haberman, Maggie. "Trump's Walk Down Ramp at West Point Raises Health Questions." *New York Daily News*, June 13, 2020. Trump's Walk Down Ramp at West Point Raises Health Questions - The New York Times (nytimes.com)

Proposed names for Army bases honoring Confederates

1. Fort Moore, Georgia. (Fort Benning, 1917): Renamed for Army Lt. Gen. Hal Moore, awarded the Distinguished Service Cross during the Vietnam War and his wife Julia, a military advocate.
2. Fort Eisenhower, Georgia. (Fort Gordon, 1917) Renamed after President Dwight D. Eisenhower, Supreme Allied Commander in Europe during WWII and a five-star General in the Army.
3. Fort Liberty, North Carolina (Fort Bragg, 1918)
4. Fort Cavazos, Texas. (Fort Hood, 1942): Renamed for Army General Richard E. Cavazos, who earned the Distinguished Service Cross during the Vietnam conflict.
5. Fort Novosel, Alabama (Fort Rucker, 1942): Renamed for Army Chief Warrant Officer 4, Michael J. Novosel, who earned the Medal of Honor after rescuing 29 soldiers in a medevac mission.
6. Fort Johnson, Louisiana. (Fort Polk, 1941): Renamed for Army Sergeant William Henry Johnson who was posthumously awarded the Medal of Honor for actions in France in WWI.
7. Fort Walker, Virginia (Fort A.P. Hill, 1941): Established in 1941. Renamed for Dr. Mary Edwards Walker, the only female surgeon during the Civil War, and the only woman ever awarded the Medal of Honor.
8. Fort Barfoot, Virginia. (Fort Pickett, 1941): Renamed for Army Tech Sgt. Van T. Barfoot who received the Medal of Honor for his actions in Italy during WWII.
9. Fort Gregg-Adams, Virginia. (Fort Lee, 1917): Renamed for Lt. General Arthur Gregg who played a key role in integrating the Army and for Lt. Colonel Charity Adams, one of the highest-ranking female soldiers in WWII.

List of U.S. Army installations named for Confederate soldiers - Wikipedia

"John Oliver Explains the Confederate Monuments Controversy." *YouTube*, October 8, 2017. Confederacy: Last Week Tonight with John Oliver (HBO) (youtube.com)

Resources - Volume IV, Issue 24 (continued)

"The American Civil War ... was an act of treason at the time against the Union, against the Stars and Stripes, against the U.S. Constitution – and those officers turned their backs on their oath," Army Gen. Mark Milley told the House Armed Services Committee.

June 9, 2020

"The United States of America trained and deployed our HEROES on these Hallowed Grounds, and won two World Wars," Trump tweeted on June 10. "Therefore, my Administration will not even consider the renaming of these Magnificent and Fabled Military Installations."

June 10, 2020

Like the Civil War itself, "Lost Cause" symbology is simply and entirely about white supremacy. It has nothing to do with "heritage" or "tradition" or any such gauzy nonsense. The heavily armed "liberate Michigan" mob that invaded the statehouse in Lansing, egged on by President Trump, had no historical reason to be waving the Confederate flag. That banner represents the knee that has been kept on the necks of African Americans not just for eight minutes and 46 seconds, the time Derek Chauvin spent crushing the life out of George Floyd, but for 401 years.

--Eugene Robinson, for the *Washington Post*,

June 11, 2020

The Weekly Screed: June 22, 2020 (Volume IV, Issue 25)

To: The Donald – Showing your True Colors (Part One)

From: Kelly – Color Me Outrageously Entertained

- Poor Donald, such a terrible, horrible, very bad week for you: two Supreme Court decisions that displeased you; the Bolton book and interview; the kerfuffle over the firing of the US Attorney for the SDNY; that pitiful rally in Tulsa and your Walk of Shame off the helicopter; and non-stop derision over your West Point appearance....
- Here's my question: How soon will Mike Pence (and then the rest of the Cabinet) start drinking water with both hands to a) protect their clothing and b) make you look stronger than a toddler? Or how about a new line of Make America Great Again Sippy-Cups?
- But I digress. What I really want to talk about today is a Super Special Item that I received in the mail (yes, from the United States Postal Service!) for the low, low price of $25: my very own OFFICIAL TRUMP COLORING BOOK which contains:
"16 artistic depictions of our great leader and is perfect for both adults and youth." [Illustrations by Keith Tomczyk, who according to Twitter is the "Official Artist for @realdonaldtrump, 2020 Presidential Campaign, USAF Vet, Catholic, UNLV, CSN, Rancho HS, God Bless Las Vegas & USA! VAN HALEN STILL RULZ!"]
- The back cover advises: "Enjoy this relaxing pastime as you spark your creativity and let your imagination run free. Each image of our Nation's 45th President is single-sided, allowing you to remove and proudly display your art piece around your home or workplace." Perfect activity for lockdown! Soon to adorn countless refrigerators!
- I was able to obtain this treasure (to which I'm sure YOU gave your blessing) because I donate one dollar (that's $1.00) a month to your campaign, making me (as I'm constantly assured in relentless emails) among your most loyal and indispensable supporters. Today, you invited me to join the Trump 100 Club. I need only contribute $25 by 11:59 PM.
- Offers pour in almost daily for MAGA merchandise [Trump/Pence playing cards ($20); a one-of-a-kind beer cozy ($15) for Father's Day; a Paige Family Trump/Pence 2020 doormat ($75)] but I was immune to all blandishments until the coloring book appeared. This, I am convinced, will become a true collector's item, so I intend to maintain it in pristine condition until I can make a killing on eBay someday.

- One thing that Keith's (often unintentionally hilarious) illustrations are missing though, Donald, are thought bubbles coming out of your face, containing your greatest pronouncements. I'd like to offer up a couple of suggestions for the second edition:
- YOU, in front of a brick wall, sleeves rolled up, wearing a tie and a hard hat, and gripping a trowel: "I will build a great wall-and nobody builds walls better than me—and I'll build them very inexpensively. I will build a great, great wall on our southern border, and I will make Mexico pay for that wall. Mark my words."
- YOU, in prayer, head bowed, eyes closed, hands clasped, American flag in the background: "I am the Chosen One. And you know what? We're winning!"
- More to come next week………...in the meantime, go golfing and lick your wounds.

Resources - Volume IV, Issue 25

The Supremes Disappoint Trump:
Newser Editors. "Obama and Trump Have Very Different Reactions to DACA Ruling." *Newser*, June 18, 2020. 'Do You Get the Impression the Supreme Court Doesn't Like Me?' (newser.com)

John Bolton Disappoints Trump:
Wade, Peter. "Trump Threatens Bolton as Judge Rejects Block on Book." *Rolling Stone*, June 20, 2020. Trump Threatens Bolton With 'Bombs Dropped on Him!' (rollingstone.com)

Geoffrey Berman Disappoints Trump:
Rosenzweig, Paul. "Why Bill Barr Got Rid of Geoffrey Berman." *The Atlantic*, June 21, 2020. Why Bill Barr Got Rid of Geoffrey Berman - The Atlantic

Tulsa Disappoints Trump
Lach, Eric. "Donald Trump's Empty Campaign Rally in Tulsa." *The New Yorker*, June 21, 2020. Donald Trump's Empty Campaign Rally in Tulsa | The New Yorker

Mark, Michelle. "Trump's Tulsa Rally and West Point Ramp Reenactment." *Business Insider*, June 20, 2020. Trump Gives Lengthy Explanation at Tulsa Rally About Ramp Incident - Business Insider

O'Neil, Luke. "Trump's 'Sad Walk of Shame' After Tulsa Rally Inspires Memes." *The Guardian*, June 22, 2020. 'Everybody hurts': Trump's sad 'walk of shame' after Tulsa rally delights critics | Donald Trump | The Guardian

The Weekly Screed: June 29, 2020 (Volume IV, Issue 26)

To: The Donald – Showing your True Colors (Part Two)

From: Kelly – Color Me Outraged

- Donald, it's hard to imagine this week being worse than the one before, but I feel we've gotten there. So, I'd like to continue my progress through the OFFICIAL TRUMP COLORING BOOK that I began last week and provide more appropriate thought bubbles to accompany the illustrations therein.
- Did I mention that the coloring book also arrived with some colored pencils? Alas, no orange! I'm still refraining from doing any actual coloring in the book (although I'm told it would have a relaxing effect) so I'll just have to keep imagining your mandarin hue.
- Let's begin with the inaner events and work up to the unbelievably awful. I'm choosing for our first illustration (and quote), your attempted spin on the Tulsa Rally: Picture, please, your giant head, mouth agape, bellowing, and (coming over your left shoulder, which I don't believe is anatomically possible) an enormous fist (supposedly yours, but clearly not drawn to scale) poised to punch out the viewer: *"WOW! The Trump Rally gives @FoxNews the "LARGEST SATURDAY NIGHT AUDIENCE IN ITS HUSTORY." Isn't it amazing that virtually nobody in the Lamestream Media is reporting this rather major feat!"* Yes, it IS amazing that so many people (including me) tuned in to watch you fail miserably at this hus-torical event full of empty seats.
- Next up, there's a drawing of you in front of the flag, arms folded, attempting a friendly smile, bringing to mind your recent complaint to Sean Hannity about John Bolton:
"He's the only man I think I ever met – I knew him for a year – I don't think I ever saw him smile once. I said to him, 'John, do you ever smile?' And it tells you something about somebody." Indeed. I'm trying to think of when I've ever seen a genuine smile on <u>your</u> face, DT. As opposed to your customary grimaces, smirks, pouts, and sneers.
- Perhaps the most gag-worthy rendering of you in this coloring book shows you in profile, standing in front of some sort of institutional-type building cradling a sweet baby girl. We know the gender of this child as she is sporting a huge bow around her little bald head, an earring in her left ear, and what look to be false eyelashes. Did you personally rescue her from one of the immigrant children holding pens which ICE was

directed to empty by next month by a US District Judge, citing "horrific conditions." Hmm?
- Finally, I'm choosing an image of you ripping your jacket and shirt open to reveal an American flag t-shirt (?) tattoo (?), as you tug off your tie and pose in a profile-in-courage, neck bulging, as fighter jets swarm overhead. *"Nobody briefed or told me, @VP Pence, or Chief of Staff @MarkMeadows about the so-called attacks on our troops in Afghanistan by Russians, as reported through an "anonymous source" by the Fake News @nytimes. Everybody is denying it & there have not been many attacks on us...."*
You lily-livered coward traitor chicken-hearted Putin-loving "Commander in Chief."
- Oh, one last thing. You did show your True Colors this week as you re-tweeted a video of one of your supporters, in a golf cart, shaking his fist and hollering "White Power!"

Resources - Volume IV, Issue 26

Feldman, Josh. "Trump Touts Record Fox News Saturday Ratings for Tulsa Rally." *Mediaite*, June 22, 2020. Trump Touts Records Fox News Ratings for Tulsa Rally (mediaite.com)

Chan, J. Clara. "Comedian Sarah Cooper Mocks Trump for Low Tulsa Rally Crowd Size in Latest Video." *The Wrap*, June 22, 2020. Comedian Sarah Cooper Mocks Trump for Low Tulsa Rally Crowd Size in Latest Video - TheWrap

O'Reilly, Andrew. "Trump Discusses Bolton, Seattle, and Democrats in Hannity Interview." *Fox News*, June 25, 2020. Trump blasts Bolton, Seattle, Democrats in 'Hannity' interview | Fox News

"Judge Orders ICE to Free Detained Immigrant Children Due to COVID-19." *NPR*, June 26, 2020. Judge Orders ICE To Free Detained Immigrant Children Because Of COVID-19 : Coronavirus Updates : NPR

Boggioni, Tom. "Trump Knew About Russian Bounties on US Military Earlier Than Admitted, Says Ex-RNC Head." *Raw Story*, June 28, 2020. Trump knew about Russian bounties on US military much earlier than he's letting on: Ex-RNC head - Raw Story

Samuels, Brett. "McEnany: Trump Shared Video of Man Shouting 'White Power' to Stand With Supporters." *The Hill*, June 29, 2020.

The Weekly Screed: July 6, 2020 (Volume IV, Issue 27)

To: The Donald – Open Mouth, Insert Foot

From: Kelly – Can we survive until next July 4 ???

Donald, this past week was notable as the halfway point of the Year 2020, your last Independence Day as Celebrity POTUS, and certainly the greatest collection of ignorant statements uttered by an Occupant of the White House in four short days.

"Do people still not understand that this is all a made-up Fake News Media Hoax started to slander me & the Republican Party? I was never briefed because any info that they may have had did not rise to that level." July 1, on Twitter, speaking of the Russia/Taliban/Bounty national security scandal. [Um, A) NOT made up; and B) you *were* briefed but you are too addled to remember what people tell you (especially if it's bad news about Putin) and too busy watching Fox & Friends to read your Presidential Daily Brief. Which if you COULD read, you should.]

"Actually, I had a mask on. I sort of liked the way I looked, OK? I thought it was OK. It was a dark, black mask, and I thought it looked OK. Looked like the Lone Ranger. But, no, I have no problem with that. I think — and if people feel good about it, they should do it." July 1, interview with Fox Business. [Note: cover the Pie Hole, not the eyes, DT]

"I think we're going to be very good with the coronavirus. I think that, at some point, that's going to sort of just disappear, I hope." [Same stupid interview, see above.]

"If you look, we were talking this morning, something to think about. China was way early, and they're getting under control just now. And Europe was way early, and they're getting under control. We followed them with this terrible China virus. And we are likewise getting under control. ... But other places were long before us, and they're now... It's a life. It's got a life. And we're putting out that life because that's a bad life that we're talking about....So I want to thank everybody for being here today. These are historic numbers in a time that a lot of people would have wilted. They would have wilted, but we didn't wilt, and our country didn't wilt, and I'm very honored to be your president."

[At which point you dash for the exit, already wilted by threat of questions from the press.] July 2 – White House Press Briefing

"Likewise, testing — there were no tests for a new virus, but now we have tested over 40 million people. But by so doing, we show cases, 99 percent of which are totally harmless. Results that no other country will show, because no other country has testing that we have — not in terms of the numbers or in terms of the quality." [July 4, from an actual speech on the White House Lawn. Imbecilic and dangerous, on every level imaginable.]

"I am here as your President to proclaim, before the country and before the world, this monument will never be desecrated." July 3 at Mount Rushmore. [Which is good news because the Sioux already consider the monument to be a desecration of their land, and you've already threatened to blast your big ugly face up there, when the only other person who should ever be added to Mount Rushmore is Barack Obama. Just saying.]

Resources - Volume IV, Issue 27

Greetings Fellow Americans. Hope you all had a safe and delicious Fourth of July. Donald Trump had many ignorant things to say last week.

Let's get to them !

On the Russia/Taliban/Bounty scandal

Moore, Mark. "Trump Calls Russia-Taliban Bounty Report a 'Fake News Media Hoax'." *New York Post*, July 1, 2020. Trump: Russia-Taliban bounty report is a 'Fake News Media Hoax' (nypost.com)

On wearing a mask, and the virus disappearing

TooFab Staff. "Trump Says Mask Makes Him Look Like the 'Lone Ranger'; Bette Midler Responds." *TooFab*, July 2, 2020. Celebs Mock Donald Trump's Lone Ranger Mask Boast (toofab.com)

Resources - Volume IV, Issue 27 (continued)

Murphy, Mike. "Trump Says a Face Mask Makes Him Look Like the Lone Ranger. One Problem With That..."MarketWatch. July 1, 2020. Trump says a face mask makes him look like the Lone Ranger. One problem with that ... - MarketWatch

Krawczyk Kathryn. "Trump Still Saying Coronavirus Will 'Just Disappear'." *The Week*, July 1, 2020. Trump is still saying coronavirus will 'just disappear' | The Week

On not wilting

**"Donald Trump July 2 Press Conference Transcript on Coronavirus and New Job Numbers." *Rev*, July 2, 2020. Donald Trump July 2 Press Conference Transcript on Coronavirus, New Job Numbers | Rev

On testing for COVID-19

Smith, David. "Trump Claims 99% of US COVID-19 Cases Are 'Totally Harmless'." *The Guardian*, July 4, 2020. Trump claims 99% of US Covid-19 cases are 'totally harmless' as infections surge | Coronavirus | The Guardian

At Mount Rushmore

"Mount Rushmore National Memorial." *History*. Mount Rushmore - Presidents, Facts & Controversy (history.com)

Fearnow, Benjamin. "Trump 'Totally Serious' About His Face On Mount Rushmore,' South Dakota Republican Says." *Newsweek*, April 26, 2018. Trump 'Totally Serious' About His Face On Mount Rushmore, South Dakota Republican Says - Newsweek

Fredericks, Bob. "Trump Staffer Tweets Photo of 'Improved' Mt. Rushmore." *New York Post*, July 3, 2020. Trump staffer tweets photo of 'improved' Mount Rushmore (nypost.com)

What's next? Ivanka as the face of Lady Liberty?? At least he doesn't have enough time left in office to deface any national monuments.........

Resources - Volume IV, Issue 27 (continued)

"We got hit by the virus that came from China," the president said, prompting a strange whoop and applause from someone in the audience. "We've made a lot of progress. Our strategy is moving along well. It goes out in one area; it rears back its ugly face in another area. But we've learned a lot. We've learned how to put out the flame."

The number of infections now regularly tops 50,000 per day, higher than in April when the US was in the first grip of infections. Dr Anthony Fauci, the nation's top infectious diseases expert, warned this week: "I think it's pretty obvious that we are not going in the right direction."

Trump returned to his now familiar and baseless complaint that America has a high caseload because it performs more tests. "Now we have tested almost 40m people. By so doing, we show cases, 99% of which are totally harmless. Results that no other country can show because no other country has the testing that we have, not in terms of the numbers or in terms of quality."

--David Smith for *The Guardian*, 7/4/2020

The Weekly Screed: July 13, 2020 (Volume IV, Issue 28)

To: The Donald – Who WAS that Masked Man??

From: Kelly – Finally, a good look for you

- Gosh, I'm proud of you, DT. You masked up for a visit to Walter Reed Hospital in a tasteful navy-blue mask with the Presidential seal. And I must say that when we only have to look at your little squinty eyes instead of your entire face, it's an improvement!
- It sure has been a long time coming…remember back in April when the CDC first issued "voluntary" mask-wearing recommendations at a White House Coronavirus Task Force Briefing? [Ah, those were the days…] At which time you reassured an anxious nation: *"I'm feeling good. I just don't want to be doing, somehow sitting in the Oval Office behind that beautiful resolute desk, I think wearing a face mask as I greet presidents, prime ministers, dictators, king, queens, I don't know somehow, I don't see it for myself. I just don't. Maybe I'll change my mind."* Absolutely, you wouldn't wanna look like a wimp in front of your favorite dictators.
- And then last month, you expressed displeasure with <u>other</u> people wearing masks: *"They put their finger on the mask, and they take them off, and then they start touching their eyes and touching their nose and their mouth. And then they don't know how they caught it."* Yeah, they do the hokey-pokey and they turn themselves around….
- Of course, all this talk of masks sent me to my bookshelves, from which I plucked <u>"Complete Stories of Edgar Allen Poe"</u> and refreshed my memory of (I know you know where I'm going here) <u>"The Masque of the Red Death."</u> It's pretty creepy, and does not end well, but there are several surprising parallels to our current situation, given that it was written in 1842. [Note: Poe was paid $12 for this story.]
- The tale begins: *"The Red Death had long devastated the country. No pestilence had ever been so fatal, or so hideous…But the Prince Prospero was happy and dauntless and sagacious. When his dominions were half depopulated, he summoned to his presence a thousand hale and light-hearted friends from among the knights and dames of his court, and with these retired to the deep seclusion of one of his castellated abbeys."*
- C'mon, Donald, don't tell me you haven't thought of something like this. Gathering your nearest and dearest and retreating to a lockdown at your golf resort in Scotland?

- Anyway, there's a big party... *"a gay and magnificent revel. The tastes of the duke were peculiar...his conceptions glowed with barbaric lustre. There are some who would have thought him mad. His followers felt that he was not."* Which pretty much explains your mind-boggling yet consistent approval rating of 40%, huh?
- So, on the story goes until (you guessed it) and in spite of all precautions, a masked stranger appears, *"tall and gaunt, and shrouded from head to foot in the habiliments of the grave."* He embodies the Red Death, and he infects everyone, and they all die. SAD.
- But let no one accuse YOU of not doing enough to depopulate your dominions. I believe your decree to open the schools next month might just about do it. That should produce the Big Spike in all 50 states, and the rise in the Red Death rates we've been waiting for!

Resources - Volume IV, Issue 28

Good Afternoon, fellow masked ones. I know you're as excited as I am that the Dear Leader finally covered his face covering. The less we see of him, the better!

Mark, Michelle. "Trump Wears Face Mask in Public for First Time." *Business Insider*, July 11, 2020. Trump Wears Face Mask in Public for First Time Since COVID-19 Began - Business Insider

Woodall, Hunter. "CDC Recommends Masks, White House Response Varied." *The Daily Beast*, April 3, 2020. Trump Says CDC Recommends Masks, but He Won't Wear One (thedailybeast.com)

Sheth, Sonam. "Trump: Americans Wearing Masks to Show Disapproval, Not for Safety." *Business Insider*, June 18, 2020. Trump: Americans Wear Masks to Show Disapproval, Not As Preventive Measure - Business Insider

"The Masque of the Red Death." *Wikipedia*. The Masque of the Red Death - Wikipedia

Smith-Schoenwalder, Cecelia. "Trump: 'We Will Pressure Schools to Reopen in Fall'." *U.S. News & World Report*, July 7, 2020. Trump: We Will Pressure Schools to Reopen in Fall (usnews.com)

The Weekly Screed: July 20, 2020 (Volume IV, Issue 29)

To: The Donald – AKA "Uncle Donald"

From: Kelly – Oh, yeah…. I read the book

- It really is such a shame that you can't read, DT. Because the book your niece Mary wrote [Too Much and Never Enough] is SO enlightening. You would think that all the other books published about you in the past three years (most of which I've also read) would have covered just about all the angles. And they have, except for one significant arena: Family of Origin. Which in your case was dysfunctional beyond belief.
- And while Mary undeniably takes you to task, she also demonstrates toward you what other authors have been unable to summon, which is a sense of empathy. And then she goes on to explain why YOU can never, ever feel empathy towards anyone else in your family, your work, or the citizens of these United States, whom you are sworn to protect.
- Here's an example from this week: three summer schoolteachers in Arizona contracted COVID-19 and one perished. When asked about this event in the context of your demand that schools open nationwide, you had this to say: *"I think there's a lot of politics going along. I think they think they'll do better if they can keep the schools closed in the election."* In other words, this lovely woman died so that Democrats could prove a point, and garner a few more electoral votes. Gosh, that makes sense to me!
- As Mary sums it up: "The simple fact is that Donald is fundamentally incapable of acknowledging the suffering of others. Telling the stories of those we've lost would *bore* him. Acknowledging the victims of COVID-19 would be to associate himself with their weakness, a trait his father taught him to despise." [page 210]
- But it's not just Mary who considers you manifestly unfit for your current position as Celebrity President. "He's a clown," was the opinion offered by your oldest sister, US Appeals Court Judge Maryanne Barry [page 8]. While there have been many instances in your tenure that bear out this assessment, this week offered one shining moment for our enjoyment. You, in the Rose Garden, in front of True Believers only:
- *"We're bringing back consumer choice in home appliances so that you can buy washers and dryers, showerheads and faucets. So, showerheads,"* [you] continued. *"You take a shower, the water doesn't come out. You want to wash your hands, the water doesn't come out. So, what do you do? You just stand there longer or you take a shower*

longer? Because my hair — I don't know about you — but it has to be perfect. Perfect."
- And then, in a nod to "the people who do the dishes"….(no one in the current audience, to be sure) *"Dishwashers," you said, "You didn't have any water, so you — the people that do the dishes — you press it, and it goes again, and you do it again and again. So, you might as well give them the water because you'll end up using less water. And in many places — in most places of the country — water is not a problem."*
- Because when you, Donald Trump, have somehow managed to combine the pandemic of 1918, the economic freefall of 1929, and the civil unrest of 1968, into the fourth year of your reign, what is **really** on the minds of Americans in 2020? Low flow appliances!

Resources - Volume IV, Issue 29

Good afternoon, comrades. The New Gestapo is patrolling the streets of the People's Republic of Portland, but I didn't have time to get to that this week, because I had to talk about Mary Trump's book. Hopefully by next week some judge will have issued an injunction against the feds and the jack-booted thugs will have retreated. Of course, all is calm in the privileged enclaves of Lake Oswego. And if any Scary Federales show up at the front door, I will unleash The Attack Corgis !!

Roberts, Laurie. "Trump Pushes to Reopen Schools Despite COVID-19 Concerns in Arizona." *AZCentral*, July 13, 2020. Donald Trump dismissed the COVID-19 death of an Arizona teacher. Why? (azcentral.com)

Arizona Teacher Dies As Trump Pushes For School Re-Openings | The Beat With Ari Melber | MSNBC, July 14, 2020. Arizona Teacher Dies As Trump Pushes For School Re-Openings | The Beat With Ari Melber | MSNBC (youtube.com)

Cillizza, Chris. "The 45 most incoherent lines from Donald Trump's rambling Rose Garden speech." CNN. July 15, 2020. The 45 most incoherent lines from Donald Trump's rambling Rose Garden speech - CNNPolitics

Hutchinson, Bill. "Trump's Comments on Shower Heads and Dishwashers." *People*, July 13, 2020. Donald Trump Complains About Dishwashers Again (people.com)

Flood, Alison. "Review of 'Too Much and Never Enough' by Mary Trump." *The Guardian*, July 12, 2020. Too Much and Never Enough review: Mary Trump thumps Donald | Donald Trump | The Guardian

The Weekly Screed: July 27, 2020 (Volume IV, Issue 30)

To: The Donald – Five More Words to Remember

From: Kelly – Test Taker Extraordinaire

- Oh, Donald, I'm so excited to let you know that we have something in common! We both passed (almost) the same test. It turns out that once you turn 65, Medicare insists that you take either the Montreal Cognitive Assessment Test (MoCA), OR the Mini-Cog as part of your standard "wellness check." Have you had one of these recently???
- "The Mini-Cog© can be used to screen for cognitive impairment quickly during both routine visits and other clinical settings. It serves to identify patients who need more thorough evaluation." Like YOU, since you were given the full MoCA.
- Since my doctor knows that I'm not completely addled, she gave me the Mini-Cog, which I absolutely crushed. I only had to remember three words, but I did have to draw the face of a clock, like you did. I'll bet mine was prettier than yours!
- Anyway, we've all had these five words drilled into our skulls all week: **Person. Man. Woman. Camera. TV.** I'd like to play a little game with you and see if you can tell where I'm going with these other sets of five words.
- **Testing. Makes. Us. Look. Bad.** Yes, you actually said those very words. During the same interview with a Fox News TV doctor (trying to keep a straight face) when you were bragging about your "acuity" test. Can I explain to you how coronavirus testing actually works? What really matters is the positivity rate and……. oh, never mind.
- **I. Wish. Her. Well. Frankly.** These were the astonishing words you uttered when asked about Ghislaine Maxwell at one of your Coronavirus Task Force Meetings. Having a memory lapse? Here's the whole exchange: *"I don't know," [you] shrugged Tuesday, when asked if [you] thought Ghislaine Maxwell would reveal which powerful men [like you] were involved in her late ex-boyfriend Jeffrey Epstein's sex-trafficking ring. "I haven't really been following it too much. I just wish her well, frankly. I've met her numerous times over the years, especially since I lived in Palm Beach, and I guess they lived in Palm Beach. But" [you] said again, "I wish her well, whatever it is."* Got it!
- **"Innocent." Mothers. Are. A. Scam.**
Donald, I'm very perplexed over this one. With your strong record on Family Values, I was just sure that when the Wall of Moms and the Dads

with Leaf Blowers showed up to protest the jack-booted thugs occupying Portland city streets, you would throw up your hands and call them off. Instead, you are now threatening to send the storm troopers to other cities. *"We're looking at Chicago, too. We're looking at New York,"* [you] said. *"All run by very liberal Democrats. All run, really, by the radical left."* Um. Hmm.

- **Putin. Russia. Bounties. Troops. Silent.** This was a tweet sent by VoteVets.org, which was preceded by: "Someone ask Trump if he can recall this in order." OUCH. This is arguably the worst scandal of your administration, and we have heard NOTHING from you on how you plan to respond to your buddy Vladimir on this one. I think you must simply wish him well, frankly.

Resources - Volume IV, Issue 30

Syal, Akshay. "Trump's Cognitive Test: What Is the Montreal Cognitive Assessment Exam?" *NBC News*, July 23, 2020. Trump cognitive test: What is the Montreal Cognitive Assessment exam? (nbcnews.com)

Rogers, Katie. "Trump's Cognitive Test Results and Comments." *The New York Times*, July 22, 2020. Trump Defends His Cognitive Testing Results on Fox News. Again. - The New York Times (nytimes.com)

**Janison, Dan. "Trump Comments on Ghislaine Maxwell, Epstein, and Portland Protests." *Newsday*, July 22, 2020. Donald Trump says 'Wish her well' of alleged pimp Maxwell, not 'Lock her up' - Newsday

Miroff, Nick, Berman, Mark. "Trump Defends Portland Crackdown, Plans to Deploy Feds to Other Cities." *The Washington Post*, July 20, 2020. Trump threatens to deploy federal agents to Chicago and other U.S. cities led by Democrats - The Washington Post

Savage, Charlie; Crowley, Michael; Schmitt, Eric. "Trump Says He Did Not Ask Putin About Suspected Bounties to Kill U.S. Troops." The New York Times. July 29, 2020. Trump Did Not Ask Putin About Russia's Bounties on U.S. Troops - The New York Times (nytimes.com)

Crump, James. "'Benedict Donald': New ad from veterans' group compares Trump to America's greatest traitor over Russia bounties." The Independent. July 4, 2020. 'Benedict Donald': New ad from veterans' group compares Trump to America's greatest traitor over Russia bounties | The Independent | The Independent.

The Weekly Screed: August 3, 2020 (Volume IV, Issue 31)

To: The Donald – "Nobody Likes Me"

From: Kelly – You can fix this

- OMG, Donald. You actually said it. The sad little boy id broke through the big bad bully super-ego while you were complaining about the "high approval ratings" of Dr. Anthony Fauci. It happened at your COVID Press Conference on Tuesday, July 28. You also threw Dr. Deborah Birx into the mix: *"They are highly thought of, but nobody likes me. It can only be my personality, that's all."*
- At this point, I'm sure you expected the assembled audience to rise as one, rip off their masks, and proclaim their fealty and love to YOU, their Dear Leader. When that didn't happen, you went on to tout (once again) hydroxychloroquine as a cure for the coronavirus.
- Now see, this is the problem, DT. Sure, we don't like your personality. It's awful and scary. But the real reason nobody likes you is because you've spent the past 3.5 years demonstrating that YOU don't like US. This has become crystal clear in 2020 with YOU playing Victim-in-Chief during the pandemic/economic collapse/protests in the streets.
- Yes, the worldwide pandemic evolved from a "Democratic hoax" to a Chinese plot, to an actual problem but only insofar as it destroyed the economy, not that it's killed (as of today) 157,179 Americans. Plus, it's also put a stop to your ridiculous rallies and your glorious GOP nominating convention in North Carolina, and then Florida *"The pageantry, the signs, the excitement were really, really top of the line."* Oh, well.
- And the destruction of the economy is an actual problem only because it makes you "look bad" and hurts your re-election chances, not because it's destroyed thousands of small businesses, and millions of jobs, and damaged tens of millions of your fellow citizens.
- And just when you thought things couldn't get any worse, here come the Black Lives Matter protesters, (whose slogan you deemed "a symbol of hate") painting said slogan on Fifth Avenue, right in front of Trump Tower AND in Lafayette Square, across from the White House.
- So, here's how you turn this around, Donald: institute a nationwide mask mandate (it would really help); become the head cheerleader for nationwide "Vote from Home" so that no one dies from standing in line to cast a ballot in November; get the Senate to ratify the HEROES Act

passed by the House in May. Just for a little while, pretend YOU really care about, and *like*, us.

Resources - Volume IV, Issue 31

Dear Ones, Are you still (mostly) at home? Good, because Dr. Birx says things are going to get worse, fast. As usual, the events of the week have overwhelmed the one-page boundary of The Screed. I can only rely on the certainty that things will "get worse before they get better" and I will have an opportunity to revisit the multiple catastrophes that confront us in the future. With that in mind, today's offering focuses on my favorite Quote of the Week from our beleaguered POTUS.

Associated Press. "'Nobody Likes Me,' Trump Says as He Defends Disproved Coronavirus Treatment." *Syracuse.com*, July 29, 2020. 'Nobody likes me,' Trump says as he defends disproved coronavirus treatment - syracuse.com

Parker, Ashley, Rucker, Philip, Dawsey, Josh. "Trump as the Victim-in-Chief: Complaints About Pandemic Impact." *The Washington Post*, July 9, 2020. Trump the victim: President complains in private about the pandemic hurting himself - The Washington Post

Kim, Juliana. "Trump Calls BLM 'Symbol of Hate' as Mural Painted Near Trump Tower." *The New York Times*, July 28, 2020.** 'Black Lives Matter' Mural Outside Trump Tower Is Vandalized Multiple Times - The New York Times (nytimes.com)

Lutz, Eric. "Contagion Nation: GOP Reluctance to Attend Trump Convention in Florida." *Vanity Fair*, July 14, 2020. Sad: No One Wants to Go to Trump's COVID Convention | Vanity Fair

Downie, James. "GOP's Stimulus Disaster Starts with the President." *The Washington Post*, August 2, 2020. Opinion | The GOP's stimulus disaster starts with the president - The Washington Post

Bort, Ryan. "Trump Suggests Delaying Election as Economy Tanks." *Rolling Stone*, July 30, 2020. Trump Suggest Delaying Election as Economy Tanks (rollingstone.com)

The Weekly Screed: August 10, 2020 (Volume IV, Issue 32)

To: The Donald – "It is what it is"

From: Kelly – Except when it isn't

- Another BIG week for you, DT. Another batch of COVID briefings filled with lies (including your alarmist characterization of the Beirut explosion as an "attack"); signing four fake Executive Orders at your Bedminster Golf Club; tweeting your smirking self, superimposed on Mount Rushmore, index finger pointing heavenward, as though God had already made it so.
- But what dominated both the news and the late-night comedy routines was your bonkers interview with <u>Axios</u> reporter Jonathan Swan. Lordy, Donald, it was EPIC. So many jaw-dropping moments, including your verbal shrug regarding the American COVID-19 death rate. Here's the exact exchange:

President Donald J. Trump:
Yeah. Under the circumstances right now, I think it's under control. I'll tell you what-

Jonathan Swan:
How? 1,000 Americans are dying a day.

President Donald J. Trump: *They are dying. That's true. And it is what it is. But that doesn't mean we aren't doing everything we can.*

- Even earlier in the interview, you had already lied about the travel ban on China ("*it was very early in January*" – except that it was on January 31); the Spanish flu of "1917" – except that it started in 1918; the trade war with China ("*With the tariffs and everything else I did, we were taking in billions of dollars*" – except that's not how tariffs work, you moron), your Tulsa Death Rally (you blamed Black Lives Matter protesters for the low turn-out, saying they turned the venue into "an armed camp," but then doubled the actual attendees from 6,000 to 12,000, so they must have snuck through);
"*We wiped out ISIS*" – except you didn't. Seeing a pattern here?
- In fact, the entire interview is an exercise in blame-shifting (China, governors, the Obama administration); disparagement (Hilary, mail-in

voting; Lyndon Johnson and the Civil Rights Act; John Lewis) ; more well-wishing for Ghislaine Maxwell (accused of sex trafficking); plus, an extremely entertaining fumbling with charts during which you tried to prove that *"We're lower than the world."* And on that one, you may have a point.
- I gotta tell you though, this was my favorite knee-slapper: *"I comprehend extraordinarily well, probably better than anybody that you've interviewed in a long time."* And bless him, Mr. Swan did <u>not</u> say: "That just *isn't* true."

Resources - Volume IV, Issue 32

Good afternoon, all....still waiting on Biden's pick for Veep.........in the meantime:

Summary of the Axios interview (Nine Wackiest Moments)

**Chait, Jonathan. "The 9 Wildest Answers in Trump's Interview With Jonathan Swan." *New York Magazine*, August 4, 2020. Trump's Axios Interview: His 9 Wildest Answers, Ranked (nymag.com)

Entire transcript of the Axios interview

"Donald Trump Interview Transcript with Axios on HBO." *Rev*, August 4, 2020. Donald Trump Interview Transcript With Jonathan Swan of Axios on HBO | Rev

A little reality checking

Dale, Daniel; Subramaniam, Tara. "Fact Check: Trump Litters Briefing with False Claims on Voter Fraud, COVID Response, and Beirut Explosion." *CNN*, August 4, 2020. Fact check: Trump litters briefing with false, unsubstantiated claims on voter fraud, Covid response and Beirut explosion | CNN Politics

Giglio, Mike; Gilsinan, Kathy. "The Inconvenient Truth About ISIS." *The Atlantic*, February 5, 2020. Is ISIS Gone? No, Kurdish Leader Says. - The Atlantic

The Weekly Screed: August 17, 2020 (Volume IV, Issue 33)

To: The Donald – POTUS Insultas

From: Kelly – For "Kamala for The People"

- Donald, I realize last week was a tough one for you. Your younger brother (and "best friend") Robert died on Saturday. I mean you did show up at the hospital on Friday but the next day you went golfing. Thoughts and prayers.
- But what seemed to give you the most angst was the announcement of Kamala Harris as Joe Biden's running mate. It sucked up almost all of the news coverage! Thank heaven you came up with a really punchy nickname for her: Phony Kamala. That'll win a lot of hearts and minds.
- Fortunately, since I give you a dollar a month, I'm on all of your email lists, so I'm on the inside track and get the real scoop on how I'm supposed to think/feel/react to this development. Here's a sample:
- <u>Wednesday, August 12</u>: "Kelly, While President Trump and Vice President Pence are working to **RESTORE LAW AND ORDER,** Slow Joe and Phony Kamala are trying to *DESTROY* our Nation. **They will RAISE your taxes. They will cut critical police funding. They will KILL vital American energy jobs. They will open our borders to illegal immigrants. And they will appease SOCIALIST dictators.**"

[One quick question on this last point…. are there any SOCIALIST dictators left in the world? I mean besides Bernie Sanders? Just checking, cuz you seem to have cornered the market in ACTUAL Dictator appeasement: Vladimir Putin, Kim Jong Un, Rodrigo Duterte, Jair Bolsonaro, Recep Tayyip Erdogan, etc.]

- <u>And then on Thursday, August 13</u>: **Kamala Harris is the meanest, most horrible, most disrespectful, MOST LIBERAL of anyone in the U.S. Senate, and I cannot believe that Joe Biden would pick her as his running mate.** [I'm proud to say Oregon's Jeff Merkley is more liberal.]
- It didn't take you long though to revert to true form and slip into slimy innuendo designed to fire up the base: a sparkling new birther conspiracy! This time it's not about *where* she was born (Oakland, CA) but whether she is a *citizen* due to her shady parentage (immigrants from India and Jamaica).
- "I heard it today that she doesn't meet the requirements," you told us at your COVID Reality Show on Thursday. Adding coyly: "I have no idea if that's right."
- Given another opportunity to discredit this new theory, you decided to double down the next day: "I read something about it. It's not something

that bothers me. … It's not something that we will be pursuing." Well, that's a big relief, you Son-of-a-Scottish-Immigrant.

Resources - Volume IV, Issue 33

Will you be watching the first Zoom convention for the next three nights ?? I know I will. Looking forward to hearing from smart, kind people for a change. And speaking of, I'm pretty, pretty pleased with Kamala for VEEP. An excellent choice for these times we find ourselves in. Can't wait to watch her demolish Mike Pence in October.

Borowitz, Andy. "Trump Questions Whether Oakland Is Located in United States." *The New Yorker*, August 15, 2020. Trump Questions Whether Oakland Is Located in United States | The New Yorker

Borowitz, Andy. "Obama Hurt by Trump's Reuse of Birther Strategy: 'I Thought It Was a Special Thing Between Him and Me'." *The New Yorker*, August 14, 2020. Obama Hurt By Trump's Reuse of Birther Strategy: "I Thought It Was a Special Thing Between Him and Me" | The New Yorker

Borowitz, Andy. "Kamala Harris's Approval Rating Soars After Trump Reminds Nation How 'Nasty' She Was to Kavanaugh." *The New Yorker*, August 12, 2020. Kamala Harris's Approval Rating Soars After Trump Reminds Nation How "Nasty" She Was to Kavanaugh | The New Yorker

Romano, Nick. "Late-night hosts react to Kamala Harris VP pick: Joe Biden 'went Black and he's not going back.'" ." *Entertainment Weekly*, August 12, 2020. Late-night hosts react to Kamala Harris VP pick (ew.com)

Norris, Michele L. "Phony Kamala Is Just Another Predictable Trump Slur." *The Washington Post*, August 13, 2020. Opinion | Trump wants to define what it means to be truly American. His Kamala Harris nickname exemplifies that. - The Washington Post

Solender, Andrew. "Trump Calls Harris 'Mad Woman' and Questions Her VP Eligibility." *Forbes*, August 13, 2020. Trump Calls Harris 'Mad Woman' As Top Campaign Advisor Questions Her VP Eligibility (forbes.com)

Frost, Natasha. Donald Trump: A Look at His Family's Ancestry." *History* July 13, 2018. The Trump Family's Immigrant Story | HISTORY

The Weekly Screed: August 24, 2020 (Volume IV, Issue 34)

To: The Donald – "Who Cares?"

From: Kelly - I do! I do!!

- Donald, I realize last week was another tough one for you.
- A judge said you had to pay Stormy Daniels' legal fees of $44,100. Added to the $130,000 you paid for her "non-disclosure agreement" and that's gotta be the most expensive one-night stand you ever had.
- Your former campaign CEO and White House Chief Strategist Steve Bannon was indicted for fraud on a "build the wall" scam and arrested by agents from the United States Postal Investigative Service. Sweet.
- Your niece Mary released hours of conversations she had with your big sister Maryanne which were definitely not flattering. "Donald is cruel."
- And I'm sure you were positively seething throughout the incredibly well-produced Democratic National Convention. We know because you did a lot of tweeting in ALL CAPS all week. Here are MY favorite quotes:
- **Bernie Sanders**: *"Nero fiddled while Rome burned. Trump golfs."* [I know you need an historical note here, DT. So, Nero was a Roman emperor, described by Suetonius (his first biographer) as the kind of fellow who "practiced every sort of obscenity," …kind of a Q-Anon fellow.]
- **Kristin Urquiza** [you've never heard of her], whose father, Mark died on June 30 from COVID-19 after going to a karaoke bar following the precipitous re-opening of Arizona. *"My dad was a healthy 65-year-old. His only preexisting condition was trusting Donald Trump, and for that, he paid with his life."* Ouch. One less MAGA voter in Phoenix.
- **Michelle Obama**: *"Donald Trump ... cannot meet this moment. He simply cannot be who we need him to be for us. It is what it is."* Nailed it!
- **John Kerry**: *"When this president goes overseas, it isn't a goodwill mission, it's a blooper reel."* That one really cracked me up, Donald.
- **Barack Obama** (speaking of YOU): *"He's shown... no interest in treating the presidency as anything but one more reality show that he can use to get the attention he craves."* ♪ Zing! Went the strings of my heart!! ♪
- **Julia Louis-Dreyfus**: *"When Donald Trump spoke at his inauguration about 'American Carnage' I assumed that was something he was against – not a campaign promise."* Maybe the only one you have truly met.
- So many smart kind compassionate people. So hard to go back to reality. But I'll be watching the RNC horror show all this week. I'm psyched.

Resources - Volume IV, Issue 34

Yes, I watched every minute of every day of the Democratic National Convention so you wouldn't have to ! But if you didn't watch it, you missed out. Sure, some of the speakers and musical numbers fell flat (to my ears) but I'll bet someone else loved them. Let's just hope that enough people (like me) came around to be fans of Uncle Joe. I do think he and Kamala are the perfect ticket for these plague-ridden and catastrophic times. And so much else juicy stuff going on! None of it good for the Donald !! Here we go:

Stormy Weather

Associated Press. "Trump Ordered to Pay Stormy Daniels' Legal Fees." *USA Today*, August 22, 2020. Stormy Daniels: Donald Trump ordered to pay $44,100 in legal fees (usatoday.com)

Bannon Bamboozle

Sheth, Sonam. "Trump Contradicts Himself on Steve Bannon and Border Wall Scheme." *Business Insider*, August 21, 2020. Trump Appears to Contradict Himself on Steve Bannon Border Wall Operation - Business Insider

Sibling Rivalry

Rahman, Khaleda. "Trump Responds to Sister's Secret Audio Recording." *Newsweek*, August 24, 2020. Trump Says 'Every Day It's Something Else, Who Cares' to Sister's Secret Audio Recording - Newsweek

The Speech of Joe Biden's Life

Bruni, Frank. "The Speech of Joe Biden's Life." *The New York Times*, August 21, 2020. Opinion | With the Speech of His Life, Joe Biden Becomes the Man for This Moment - The New York Times (nytimes.com)

The Weekly Screed: August 31, 2020 (Volume IV, Issue 35)

To: The Donald – "Nobody outside the beltway really cares."

From: Kelly - I do! I do!!

- Donald, the quote above actually came from your Chief of Staff, Mark Meadows, and not you. And it was referring to the Hatch Act, a quaint little law that prohibits all federal employees (except for you and Mike Pence) from using any federal property for political purposes. Which means that it was violated countless times over the course of the Republican National Convention. Especially Night 4. But I know you don't care either.
- I watched a lot of this horrible spectacle. And I tried to take notes but gave up. Because I knew that I could rely on the New York Times Fact Checker to do the job for me. I had gone to them after the DNC and had found a few "misleading" or "exaggerated," but no "false" statements. But guess what? Pages and pages of all three were uttered night after night at the RNC. Here's a few of the outright "False" statements.
- Nikki Haley (former Governor of South Carolina) lied that Joe Biden was going to ban fracking. When it's just new leases on public lands.
- Steve Scalise (US Representative from Louisiana) lied about the loss of manufacturing jobs under Obama/Biden and about Biden supporting defunding the police.
- Matt Gaetz (US Representative from Florida) lied that the Democrats would disarm the citizenry, empty the prisons, fill the burbs with MS-13, and disband the police! YIKES.
- YOU lied about The China Virus (it's NOT going away), the China Tariffs (they didn't pay them, we did), and Democrats getting rid of postal workers. Right.
- Patty McCloskey (currently indicted with her husband for brandishing weapons at peaceful protesters) lied that Joe Biden wanted to abolish the suburbs altogether! Mercy!
- Kimberly Guilfoyle (Don Jr.'s girlfriend…and why was she speaking anyway?) decried the Democrat's "socialist agenda" then lied that she was a first-generation American because her mother was an immigrant (wrong, she was a Puerto Rican American citizen). Screaming the whole time to an empty room. [Note: back when she had better taste in men and was married to California Governor Gavin Newsom, she was quite lovely. Now she looks like Elvira, Mistress of the Dark].
- Another note: all of the above falsehoods were spewed on Night One!!

- And I know this may be catty, but Melania's appearance in a Nazi prison matron uniform to deliver her hostage-video comments about your honesty and compassion was really weird, DT. Someone should have vetted the speech AND the outfit. SAD.
- Of course, the most jarring tone of all four nights was the impression that not only would Democrats destroy the country if elected in November, but that all of the terrible things happening now *were already taking place* in Joe Biden's America. Particularly the absence of LAW AND ORDER, as you are so fond of tweeting.
- Let's turn to Ted Wheeler, Mayor of Portland, for his take on this: *"Do you seriously wonder, Mr. President, why this is the first time in decades that America has seen this level of violence? It's you who have created the hate and the division."* Amen.

Resources - Volume IV, Issue 35

Howdy, y'all. So glad to have the Republican National Convention in the rear-view mirror as we continue our Mad Max Road Warrior journey to Election Day. As usual, one page could not do justice to the past week's shenanigans and tragedies. All I could fit in was the blatant lies from Night One of the convention. But there was one funny moment I must bring your attention to. Tim Scott (the lone Black Republican Senator) did his level best to prop up his party line, but at one point he warned us that Democrats would bring us a "socialist utopia". I cheered HOORAY!! No poverty ! Everyone would have health care! I'm sure he meant "dystopia", but that is what we have NOW.

"The RNC Was An Avalanche Of Corrupt Hatch Act Violations." *Rantt Media*, August 29, 2020. The RNC Was An Avalanche Of Corrupt Hatch Act Violations - Rantt Media

"KIMBERLY GUILFOYLE Delivers Bizarre Speech ...YOU GOTTA SEE THIS!!!" *TMZ*, August 24, 2020. Kimberly Guilfoyle Delivers Bizarre Speech at RNC in Support of Trump (tmz.com)

Mesh, Aaron. "Portland Mayor Blames President Trump for Fatal Shooting Amid Protests." *Willamette Week*, August 30, 2020. Portland Mayor Blames President Trump for Fatal Shooting Amid Protests (wweek.com)

[Note: at press time for this Screed, it appears that an Antifa guy killed a Patriot Prayer guy on Saturday night in Portland. More to come.]

The Weekly Screed: September 7, 2020 (Volume IV, Issue 36)

To: The Donald – My Musings on the Military Suckers and Losers

From: Kelly - Channeling your thoughts

Raindrops were falling on my head, so I was disinclined to visit LOSERS who were dead……in some old cemetery for Marines who died in the First World War. I never really got what they were fighting for. *"Who were the good guys in this war?"*

I mean, those guys were SUCKERS for getting killed at Belleau Wood. And since I didn't go to that creepy cemetery, I got to spend more time at the French Ambassador's house. Brought back some awesome artwork for the White House. Why should SHE have all that nice stuff?

And while we're at it, everyone was SO upset when I told that widow (can't ever remember the dead guy's name) that *"He knew what he signed up for"* in Niger. Why should I care?

And speaking of people I don't care for, *"I never was a fan of John McCain."* They said that my campaign was over when I said *"He was a 'hero' because he was captured. I prefer people who weren't captured."* Guess I showed them, AND him. Another *"f**king loser."* He didn't even invite me to his lousy funeral. And just because I stood next to General John Kelly at his son's grave on Memorial Day and said to him *"I don't get it. What was in it for them?"*

What's the big deal? That guy was a useless Chief of Staff. *"He got eaten alive. He was unable to handle the pressure of this job."* Sure, he was a four-star general in the Marine Corps but that doesn't make him so tough.

And can you believe they wanted me to include "wounded warriors" in my 2018 military parade? The last thing I wanted was to see a bunch of amputees rolling down the street. Gross. And I'll bet the American people are with me on this one. *"Nobody wants to see that."*

Finally, it's one thing for The Atlantic, which is a *dying* magazine, to report all this crap. But then this so-called reporter from FOX (!!!) confirms it. She *"should be fired"* …or maybe poisoned!! But I guess I oughta save *that* for my next term.

Resources - Volume IV, Issue 36

Today I'll join the crowd raking The Donald over the coals for his military comments. None of this is surprising from such a sniveling bullying coward. I was in the Peace Corps, not the War Corps, but I did spend 4 years working as a civilian with the armed forces in the Pacific in the '80s. In fact, I also opened and operated a Stars and Stripes bookstore on Naval Station Guam right before I moved to Okinawa. I would have been really annoyed if the Pentagon had shut down the Stars and Stripes operation! Here's the article that set off the firestorm this week.

Goldberg, Jeffrey. "Trump: Americans Who Died at War Are 'Losers' and 'Suckers'." *The Atlantic*, September 3, 2020. Trump: Americans Who Died in War Are 'Losers' and 'Suckers' - The Atlantic

Here's a couple of confirming reports. Another tidbit: Chuck Hagel was my boss at USO, before he became a Senator from Nebraska, and Secretary of Defense.

Choi, Inyoung. "Chuck Hagel: Atlantic Report In Line with Trump's Words and Actions." *Business Insider*, September 6, 2020. Chuck Hagel: Atlantic Report Is in Line With Trump's Words and Actions - Business Insider

Kranish, Michael. "Trump's History of Disparaging Military Service." *The Washington Post*, September 6, 2020. Trump, under fire for alleged comments about veterans, has a long history of disparaging military service - The Washington Post

Baker, Sinead. "Trump Took Art from US Ambassador's Home in France." *Business Insider*, September 7, 2020. Trump Took Art From Diplomat in Paris After Canceled WWI Event: Report - Business Insider

Bendix, Aria. "Trump Allegedly Disparaged General John Kelly at Arlington Cemetery." *Business Insider*, September 5, 2020. Trump Blasts John Kelly After Reports of Rude Remark at Arlington - Business Insider

Barr, Jeremy. "Jennifer Griffin Defended by Fox News Colleagues After Trump Twitter Attack." *The Washington Post*, September 5, 2020. Jennifer Griffin defended by Fox News colleagues after Trump Twitter attack over confirmation of Atlantic reporting - The Washington Post

The Weekly Screed: September 14, 2020 (Volume IV, Issue 37)

To: The Donald – "We got to open up our schools"

From: Kelly – You go back first, Donald

- First of all, DT, the above quote from last month is grammatically incorrect. It should be "We <u>have</u> got to open up" or even "<u>We've</u> got to open up." Contractions are almost always permissible.
- Secondly, the schools that *have* opened up are seeing some decidedly bad outcomes. Thousands and thousands of students have tested positive, and teachers have died in five states. Universities have sent COVID-positive students back home to infect their respective communities and suspended or expelled others for attending super-spreader parties.
- But why should students refrain from partying like it's 2019? It's not like they're seeing a particularly good example set by the Leader of the Free World. From the last night of the Republican National Convention to your airplane-hanger assemblies during the past two weeks, you have gathered the faithfully ignorant base, shoulder to shoulder and mask-less, to listen to nonsense, threats, and mendacities.
- You have even taken to subverting various state health laws at these death rallies by labeling them as "peaceful protests" instead of campaign events. That's extremely clever, Donald. Unless you care about your voters living until Election Day.
- Of course, I am staying home as much as possible reading the many intriguing books written about YOU that have been released this month. Not to mention <u>Melania and Me</u> by Stephanie Winston Wolkoff (Sept. 1).
- First out of the gate was <u>Donald Trump v. The United States</u> by Michael Schmidt (Sept. 1) which let us know that you thought you could somehow negotiate with Robert Mueller, like, you know, a real estate deal.
- Then came the one I ordered right away: <u>Disloyal</u> by Michael Cohen. This is sure to be the most entertaining of the litter (out Sept. 8).
- "In our country, the lie has become not just a moral category, but a pillar of the State." Peter Strzok, author of <u>Compromised</u> (also Sept. 8) , quoted Alexandr Solzhenitsyn to get started on Rachel Maddow's pick of the bunch.

- Last, but not least, you gave eighteen hours of TAPED interviews to Bob Woodward for his book Rage (out on Sept. 15). What were you thinking???
  This is even more damaging than the transcript of your "perfect" phone call with the President of Ukraine, and *that* got you impeached. Please let this be the final nail in the coffin of your odious "presidency."

Resources - Volume IV, Issue 37

Hello all. We're still having Hazardous air quality. The backyard smells like an ashtray, and that's as far as I've gone since last week, but we were far enough from the major conflagrations to avoid fleeing for our lives. So many parts of our beautiful state were just destroyed. And they are saying this is only the beginning of peak fire season. But the Screed must go on. The Donald is back risking the lives of his base, but not just theirs. Because they will leave his rallies and infect others. All this is shameful. Meanwhile, a bunch of books dropped in September. There are many reviews online so I will let you google to your heart's content. I won't be buying the Woodward book for the same reason I didn't buy the Bolton book: they both knew dreadful things were happening and saved them for publication. All the same, there's lots of juicy tidbits in Woodward's and at least we are finally learning about them.

Miller, Tim. "Trump's Reckless, Atrocious, Deceitful Rally." *The Bulwark*, September 14, 2020. Trump's Reckless, Atrocious, Deceitful Rally (thebulwark.com)

Papenfuss, Mary. "Trump Instigates 'Lock Him Up' Chant for Obama at Rally." *AOL News*, September 14, 2020. Trump instigates 'lock him up' chant for Obama at rally (aol.com)

Blum, Jeremy. "Trump Calls North Carolina Rally 'Peaceful Protest'." *HuffPost*, September 10, 2020. Trump Brags About Rally Crowds, Mockingly Calls Supporters 'Peaceful Protesters' | HuffPost Latest News

Pierce, Charles P. "Bob Woodward's Revelations on Trump and COVID-19." *Esquire*, September 10, 2020. Bob Woodward Knew Trump Was Downplaying Covid-19 for Months (esquire.com)

The Weekly Screed: September 21, 2020 (Volume IV, Issue 38)

To: The Donald – Leader of the Herd

From: Kelly – Channeling The Notorious RBG

"And you'll develop – you'll develop herd -- like a herd mentality. It's going to be – it's going to be herd-developed, and that's going to happen. That will all happen." - DTrump

Herd Immunity would require 200 million infections and result in 6 million dead Americans

A DC State of Mind (a COVID Rap)

By Notorious RBG

Ayo, Donald Trump, it's high time to GO.
It's time, DT, straight back to the bigly dungeon of your soul.

Herd immunity rises as does my mentality.
I won't disappear, 'cause that's the essence of finality.
Beyond 6 million cases, life is defined.
I think of COVID when I'm in a DC state of mind.

My vitality don't like no herd mentality.
Run up the mortality and get the plurality.

What more you want? The herd immunity?
Killin' brothers and sisters with impunity?
Somebody gotta speak up for the community.

Two hundred million infections is quite the collection.

Six million lost be our own Holocaust.

I can't take that body count, it ain't no hoax.
I guess you don't fear it if you don't love folks.

That's why you gotta go, DT; give us Biden and bring back Fauci.

Thinking of the COVID. Yaz, thinking of the COVID.

Resources - Volume IV, Issue 38

*Well, we have no one to blame but ourselves. To the half of registered voters who sat out the last presidential election, to the mere quarter of registered voters who pulled the lever for Trump, to the tiny but significant number who voted Green Party, to the morons who sent a majority of Republicans back to the Senate in 2018, the chickens have come home to roost. This minority of the population will make the Supreme Court of the United States the most regressive body of government for the next generation. But we are **all** totally screwed.*

Now that I have that rant out of the way, let's get to the most hilarious, yet terrifying, malapropism of the year. At his recent Town Hall (in Philadelphia, on September 15), Trump confused "herd mentality" (which is evident at his MAGA Death Rallies) with "herd immunity", which he has decided is the best way out of this COVID mess. Here's the full exchange with the ABC Moderator:

'It would go away without the vaccine?' [George] Stephanopoulos asked him.

'Sure, over a period of time. Sure, with time it goes away,' Trump responded.

'And many deaths,' Stephanopoulos told him, as the nation approached 200,000 of them due to the coronavirus.

'And you'll develop – you'll develop herd -- like a herd mentality,' Trump said. 'It's going to be – it's going to be herd-developed, and that's going to happen. That will all happen,' he said.

But here's the catch. As communicable disease experts have pointed out, achieving herd immunity through infection alone would require approximately 70% of the population to become infected. That would mean that over 230 million Americans would need to contract COVID. As opposed to the close to 7 million so far. The current death rate is over 3%. So if you do the math, herd immunity would result in almost 7 million deaths. And that's what the Dear Leader deems acceptable. Because he really doesn't give a flying fork about We the People.

Hope you enjoy my first rap song............Kelly

Resources - Volume IV, Issue 38 (continued)

Kessler, Glen. "Trump's ABC News Town Hall: 'Four Pinocchios,' Over and Over Again." *The Washington Post*, September 15, 2020. Trump's ABC News town hall: Four Pinocchios, over and over again - The Washington Post

"Herd Immunity and COVID-19: What You Need to Know." *Mayo Clinic*. Herd immunity and COVID-19: What you need to know - Mayo Clinic

Haltiwanger, John. "Trump Suggests RBG's Dying Words to Keep Seat Vacant Are a Democratic Hoax." *Business Insider*, September 21, 2020. Trump: RBG's Dying Wish to Keep Seat Vacant May Be a Democratic Hoax - Business Insider

Brockell, Gillian. "Ruth Bader Ginsburg's Legacy and Jewish Identity." *The Washington Post*, September 19, 2020. The Holocaust and Jewish history fueled Ruth Bader Ginsburg's quest for justice - The Washington Post

"Amy Dorris' Trump Sexual Assault Allegation Deserves America's Full Attention." *NBC News*, September 17, 2020. Amy Dorris' Trump sexual assault allegation deserves America's full attention (nbcnews.com)

Filipovic, Jill. "Trump Faces New Sexual Assault Accusations from Amy Dorris." *The Guardian*, September 17, 2020. How many Trump accusers does it take for his supporters to care? | Jill Filipovic | The Guardian

Resources - Volume IV, Issue 38 (continued)

President Donald Trump on Monday suggested that Ruth Bader Ginsburg's dying wish, reportedly dictated to her granddaughter, that her Supreme Court seat not be filled until a new president is elected "came out of the wind" and was made up by Democrats in Congress.

"I don't know that she said that, or was that written out by Adam Schiff and Schumer and Pelosi? I would be more inclined to the second," Trump said during a phone interview with "Fox & Friends."

"That came out of the wind, it sounds so beautiful. But that sounds like a Schumer deal or maybe a Pelosi or Shifty Schiff," he said, adding, "Maybe she did and maybe she didn't."

--John Haltiwanger for Business Insider, 9/21/20

The Weekly Screed: September 28, 2020 (Volume IV, Issue 39)

To: The Donald – Deflector in Chief

From: Kelly – I'm here for some answers, dammit!

- Donald, when researching today's pen-pal letter, I accessed the Way-Back Machine of the interwebs and came up with this gem from 2017: "White House officials are quick to use the term 'fake news' for any reporting that casts the president or his administration in a negative light—yet they routinely refuse to answer reporters' very real questions." Sound familiar?
- The article went on to cite six examples of Sean Spicer and then Sarah Sanders (remember them?) dismissing any uncomfortable inquiry as "highly inappropriate," "100 percent false", "cherry picking facts", "yellow journalism" or (my personal favorite) "elitist clickbait."
- But Sean, Sarah, Stephanie Grisham (who never held a single press conference !) and now Kayleigh McEnany are pikers when compared to you, DT. I mean, you *really* know how to insult, evade, and disparage reporters. All of these comebacks are from a November 2018 press conference:

  ---To Jim Acosta (when he had the temerity to ask about the Russia investigation) *"CNN should be ashamed of itself having you working for them....You are a rude, terrible person."*

  ---When NBC reporter Pete Alexander came to Acosta's defense: *"Well, I'm not a big fan of yours either, to be honest with you."*

  ---When Yamiche Alcindor (PBS Newshour) questioned you about the Republican Party's support of white nationalists, *" That's such a racist question…What you just said is so insulting to me."*

- But lately, Donald, I fear you are slipping. Instead of lame ripostes, or schoolboy taunts, you simply flee the stage or call on someone else (often from a "friendlier" news outlet) in hopes of rescue.

  ---On August 13, S.V. Dáte, from HuffPost, asked: "Do you regret all of the lying you have done to the American people?" After fumbling about for a bit, you simply pointed to another reporter and said, *"Go ahead please."*

  ---But the most egregious example of this type of evasion came last Tuesday on the White House lawn, when a reporter queried: "Why haven't you said anything about the 200,000 deaths from COVID?" A normal president (or human being) would have replied, "Yes, it's a tragic milestone and we're doing everything we can to avoid future losses to this abominable scourge." However, you are The Donald, the Worst President Ever, and a stone-cold sociopath, so you just turned away and asked: *"Anyone else?"*

Resources - Volume IV, Issue 39

No, today's Screed does not address Trump's unseemly tweet that he would nominate Amy Comey Barrett while RBG was still lying in state at the Capitol, OR the pathetic tax returns "bombshell". Can it be shocking if we knew it all along? These stories have time to percolate. What made my head snap around this past week was a Trump interview with reporters on the White House lawn last Tuesday. I've been spitting mad about it all week, but you'll have to read all the way through The Screed to find out why. Maybe you'll be as outraged as I was. Of course, this has been a long time coming.

Solis, Marie. "5 Times Trump White House Has Refused to Answer Reporters' Questions." *Newsweek*. October 23, 2017. Six Times Donald Trump's White House Has Refused to Answer Reporters' Questions - Newsweek

Samuels, Brett. "7 Times Trump Clashed with Reporters in Hostile Post-Midterms Press Conference." *The Hill*. November 7, 2018. 7 times Trump clashed with reporters in hostile post-midterms press conference (thehill.com)

Rogers, Katie; Haberman, Maggie. "Trump Has a New Press Secretary Who Knows How to Defend Him." *The New York Times*. April 7, 2020. Who Is Kayleigh McEnany? President Trump's New Press Secretary - The New York Times (nytimes.com)

Mackey, Robert. "Two Female Reporters Refuse to Let Trump Bully Them." *The Intercept*. May 12, 2020. Reporters Refused to Let Trump Bully Them, So He Ran Away (theintercept.com)

Wilkinson, Joseph. "Trump Refuses to Answer 'Lying' Question from Reporter." *New York Daily News*. August 14, 2020. SEE IT: Trump refuses to answer question on 'all the lying you've done to the American people' – New York Daily News (nydailynews.com)

Schwab, Nikki; Earle, Geoff. "Donald Trump ignores question about the U.S. hitting 200,000 coronavirus deaths and then calls it 'a shame' - after rival Joe Biden tweeted about the milestone for hours. Daily Mail. September 22, 2020. Trump ignores question about the U.S. hitting 200,000 COVID deaths and then calls it 'a shame' | Daily Mail Online

The Weekly Screed: October 5, 2020 (Volume IV, Issue 40)

To: **The Donald – COVID Karma Strikes**

From: **Kelly – No one more deserving than you**

- Seriously, DT, did you believe the MAGA Gods could outwit biology? Heaven knows you certainly tempted fate, in both word and deed, for the past nine months. *"Democratic Hoax!" "Kung-flu!"*
- What's most repulsive (but true to form) is your deliberate exposure of others to your vile infected self: the fundraiser at your golf course in Bedminster on Thursday, after you knew for a fact that you had been in close proximity with Hope Hicks who had tested positive; the drive-around to wave at your deluded supporters with two poor Secret Service guys in the same car. Boy, did *they* pick the short straws on that detail.
- What's next? A rally in the ER at Walter Reed? Heck, I can't get even two steps into my doctor's lobby without filling out a contact tracing form and having my temperature taken. But everyone around you is fair game.
- I'll be very annoyed if you somehow managed to contaminate Joe Biden with this virus at the "debate" on Tuesday. He should have kept his mask on, what with you bellowing and spitting all over the stage.
- And speaking of that "debate," the polling is not good for you, Donald. I read that only 21% of voters in Pennsylvania and Florida who watched thought you "won." Which is about 20% too many, but only half of your usual approval rating. And in crucial swing states, oh dear!
- Me? I found the entire show quite entertaining (Biden crushed it) and will be exceedingly disappointed if there isn't an encore.
- I know your doctors have pulled out all the stops to keep your sorry ass alive and kicking, but I've been looking at the risk factors that indicate you just might not survive this thing:

Gender: Not very manly, but technically Male   ☑

Age: Over 65 (You behave like a toddler, but are 74)   ☑

Obesity: BMI >30 (Yup if you weigh what you say)   ☑

Underlying Conditions: Besides Ramp Shuffling, Two-handed Water-Sipping, Word Slurring, and Near-Constant Rage, who knows??? But I'm gonna give you a ☑

Person of Color: Orange, so yeah, ☑

- Meanwhile, enjoy the Presidential Suite at the hospital. Thoughts & Prayers.

Resources - Volume IV, Issue 40

So, I started the week thinking this week's Screed might be about the Supreme Court, or Trump's taxes. Then I watched the debate on Tuesday and thought it would most definitely be about THAT. Now we have COVID infecting half the administration and the Dear Leader. It's just too much for one small page! Looking forward to the VP debate on Wednesday !! Unless Pence isn't also at Walter Reed by then.

Cohn, Nate. "Polls and Election Analysis for Florida and Pennsylvania." *The New York Times*, October 3, 2020. Poll Finds Voters in Two Crucial States Repelled by Trump's Debate Behavior - The New York Times (nytimes.com)

Houston, Jordan. "WATCH: Trump Mocks Biden During Debate, 'I Don't Wear Masks Like Him'." *Heavy*, October 2, 2020. WATCH: Trump Mocks Biden, 'I Don't Wear Masks Like Him' (heavy.com)

Dawsey, Josh; Leonnig, Carol D.; Knowles, Hannah. " Secret Service agents, doctors aghast at Trump's drive outside hospital." The Washington Post. October 4, 2020. Trump's drive outside Walter Reed hospital criticized by Secret Service members, doctors - The Washington Post"

Connelly, Aileen AJ. "Inside Walter Reed's Presidential Suite Where Trump Is Staying." *New York Post*, October 3, 2020. Inside Walter Reed's 'Presidential Suite' where Trump is staying (nypost.com)

The Weekly Screed: October 12, 2020 (Volume IV, Issue 41)

To: The Donald – Regenerated

From: Kelly – I'm Speaking

Donald, what I've come to appreciate about our weekly correspondence is the fact that I'm in charge. Having watched the last two "debates" of this election season, most memorable for both you and your sidekick, Silent Mike, butting in and yelling over your opponents AND the moderators, it's satisfying that I don't have to worry about those discourtesies. You just get ME, unvarnished and uninterrupted.

So quit squirming and "Just shut up, man" (in the immortal words of Joe Biden) while I provide my musings on The Week That Was. Let's start with your dramatic arrival at the White House via Marine One and your (literally) hair-raising appearance on the balcony of the People's House as the helicopter lifted into the skies and you ripped off your mask. This allowed you to infect even more staffers of the West Wing as you strode inside.

Over the next few days, we were treated to videos of you on the White House lawn, assuring a Grateful Nation that you were feeling hale, hearty, and yay, even twenty years younger following the miracle cure of "Regeneron." That puts you at 54. If you take another dose, will you regress to 34? That would make you too young to be President. But let's not go down that rabbit hole.

And is it just me, or doesn't the brand name for this so-called remedy for COVID-19 bring to mind late-night commercials for Male Sexual Enhancement, or the label ascribed to some sci-fi dystopian novel nostrum meant to revive corpses? Or, perhaps in your case, all three?? Oh, the horror!

Just let it be said that the origins of Regeneron sprang from aborted fetal tissue, normally *verboten* in your Administration, but in this case permitted due to the life-saving benefits of said tissue to serve The Dear Leader.

Not to forget the most important part of this story: stocks are soaring for Regeneron, which is notable given that its CEO is a member of your golf club (Trump National) in Briarcliff Manor, New York. In fact, you, and "Lenny" (Leonard Schleifer) just happened to meet in May to discuss his firm's new line of pharmaceuticals. What a blessed coincidence.

But let's circle back to the VP debate and the two most delightful minutes of the past week. I'm speaking, of course, of the time that The Fly perched on Pence's snow-white noggin, which detracted bigly from his attempt to look dignified and Pen-sive. Kamala Harris could barely keep a straight face. As the Good Book warned in another time of plague: "Behold, I will send swarms of flies on you…"[Exodus 8:21-22]

Resources - Volume IV, Issue 41

It is exactly, and only, 100 days until January 20, 2021. At which time, God willing, and the creek don't rise, Joe Biden will be inaugurated and the Orange Ogre banished to Mar-a-Lago. Until then we can expect more weeks like the past one:

Yashari, Leora. "Kamala Harris: 'I'm Speaking Now' at VP Debate." *Refinery29*, October 7, 2020.* How Kamala Harris Won The Debate With "I'm Speaking" (refinery29.com)

Papenfuss, Mary. "Trump's Use of Regeneron and Fetal Tissue Hypocrisy." *HuffPost*, October 9, 2020.* Trump's COVID-19 'Miracle' Treatment Relied On Cells Linked To Aborted Fetus | HuffPost Latest News

Hart, Robert. "While Trump Touts Cure Made by Regeneron, Its CEO Is a Member of Trump Golf Club." *Forbes*, October 8, 2020.* While Trump Touts 'Cure' Made By Regeneron, Its CEO Is A Member Of Trump Golf Club (forbes.com)

"Fly in Mike Pence's Hair Steals VP Debate Spotlight." *The West Australian*, October 2020.* US Vice Presidential debate: Fly in Mike Pence's hair steals debate as he faced off against Kamala Harris | The West Australian

The Weekly Screed: October 19, 2020 (Volume IV, Issue 42)

To: The Donald – Underlevered

From: Kelly – You Think You're So Clever

- Donald, when you condescend to a woman, it helps to have your facts (and "best words") straight. Case in point…During your Town Hall on Tuesday, Savannah Guthrie (moderator extraordinaire) asked the following: "The question is, on behalf of voters, who do you owe $421 million to?"
- You replied with a rambling and defensive vomitus of un-answers like: *"When I decided to run, I'm very underlevered, fortunately, but I'm very underlevered. I have a very, very small percentage of debt compared. In fact, some of it, I did as favors to institutions that wanted to loan me money."*
- Savannah: "Any foreign bank? Any foreign entity?"
- YOU: *"Not that I know of, but I will probably, because it's so easy to solve, and if you'd like to do, I will let you know who I owe, whatever small amount of money. I want to say two things. Number one, it's a very small amount of money. Number two, it's very straight. It's very, very straight, but it's a tiny percentage of the worth. Did you ever hear the expression underlevered?"*
- Savannah: "Yeah." [Underlever defined: a lever behind the trigger guard of a rifle.]
- YOU: *"I am extremely underlevered."*
- ME: (screaming at the TV) "It's under<u>leverage</u>d, you dolt."
- Or, as used properly in a sentence: "2019 was a fantastic year for our country and one of the best years in the history of Trump Organization, as shown in the President's Financial Disclosure Form released today, our businesses thrived with strong revenues while remaining <u>underleveraged</u> and maintaining very low levels of debt." ---Eric Trump, July 31, 2020
- The Town Hall was otherwise notable for your dodge-and-weave to questions asked by other women like Moriah Geene: "…if Roe v. Wade is ultimately overturned in the future, what protections would be put in place or kept for where the mother's life is in jeopardy in relation to high-risk pregnancies?"
- To which you non-responded by yammering on about how you would *never* have a discussion with *any* of your Supreme Court nominees about *anything* like this. Right.

- Or, when Cristy Montesinos Alonso inquired: "What is your plan now in 2020 to make healthcare costs affordable for Americans like myself?"
- YOU: *"Good. So, we got rid of the individual mandate on Obamacare, which was the worst part of Obamacare, and now you could actually say it's not Obamacare because that's how big it was, where you had to pay a fortune for the privilege of not having to pay for bad health insurance, so we got rid of that. That was a big, big thing. And by doing that, and we will always have…"* Blah, blah, blah.
- And all of the above is why you are having to BEG suburban women to like you.

Resources - Volume IV, Issue 42

Savannah Guthrie, Host. "Donald Trump NBC Town Hall Transcript." *Rev*, October 15, 2020. Donald Trump NBC Town Hall 10/15 | Transcripts (rev.com)

Glasser, Susan B. "Mister Rogers Versus Nasty Uncle Trump." *The New Yorker*. October 16, 2020. The Presidential Town Halls Were Mister Rogers Versus Nasty Uncle Trump | The New Yorker

Alexander, Dan. "Donald Trump Has at Least $1 Billion in Debt." *Forbes*, October 16, 2020. Donald Trump Has At Least $1 Billion In Debt, More Than Twice The Amount He Suggested (forbes.com)

Kassidy, Vavra. "Trump's Financial Documents and Ivanka's Income." *The Sun*. August 1, 2020. Trump financial docs reveal Mar-a-Lago suffered $1.3m slump while Ivanka and Jared earned $36m in outside income in 2019 | The Sun

Chapman, Matthew. "Trump Begs Suburban Women to Stop Loathing Him." *Raw Story*, October 13, 2020. Trump begs suburban women to stop loathing him: 'Will you please like me?' - Raw Story

Worthington, Aliza. "Trump Tries to Scare Suburban Women with Threat of Cory Booker." *Crooks and Liars*, September 1, 2020. Twitter Scoffs After Trump Tries To Scare Suburban Women With Threat Of Cory Booker | Crooks and Liars

The Weekly Screed: October 26, 2020 (Volume IV, Issue 43)

To: **The Donald – Rounding the Corner**

From: **Kelly – Keeping Count Till I'm Dizzy**

1) We'll be coming round the corner very soon (34 of the last 56 days)

COVID "goes away in April" with the heat (February 2020)

We have cases cuz we test; otherwise, we'd be the best. (October 2020)

We'll be rounding COVID Corner any day.

2) Health care will be "taken care of" very soon (January 2017)

It's "fantastic" and "terrific," just you wait (February 2017)

But we're "not voting on it till the end of the election;" (April 2019)

Still, I promise you it really will be "great." (August 2019)

3) I will sign a health bill "in the next 4 weeks." (May 2019)

Oh, I really meant "2 months" before I sign, (June 2019)

Now I think it's "within two weeks," or it's "sometime very soon," (July 2020)

"Prior to the end of the month" will be fine. (August 2020)

4) If you vote by mail " it doesn't work out well

For Republicans," it isn't very nice. (April 2020)

If you live in North Carolina, you should vote by mail and then

Show up in person too, it's better to vote twice. (September 2020)

5) Oh, Election Day is just around the bend, and I promise you it's going to be BIG.

If I lose, "I'll count on [SCOTUS]" They will count the votes right for us.

"The only way I lose" is if [it's] "rigged." (September and August 2020)

Resources - Volume IV, Issue 43

Howdy y'all..........Every time someone talks about "rounding the corner," my addled brain summons up that old folk song "She'll be Coming Round the Mountain". This was one of the songs my mother made us sing in the (un-air-conditioned) car driving down to Texas every summer in the early '60s. Ugh.

There are many versions online, many of them kiddie cartoons, but I'm giving you a link to my favorite old timey version: (1976) Day 17 - "She'll Be Comin' Round the Mountain" performed at Roan Mountain State Park - YouTube

In addition to rounding the corner on COVID, another thing The Donald keeps saying is that the only reason we have so many COVID cases is because we do so many tests. This makes me absolutely crazy, but he said it again on "60 Minutes" last night. What an idiot. You may have heard that he was so cheesed off about the interview, he released his own version a couple of days earlier. Again, what an idiot. Because HIS version showed him once again needing two hands to drink a glass of water, whereas "60 Minutes" was kind enough to edit that out. And you really need to see the Lincoln Project ad that's a mash-up of Trump promising a health care plan over the past 4 years. Hilarious. This article from Forbes provides that ad, plus a Daily Show "rounding the corner" compilation.

Lee, Bruce Y. "Lincoln Project Ad Shows Trump Promising a Health Care Plan Since January 2017." *Forbes*, October 24, 2020. Lincoln Project Ad Shows Trump Promising A Healthcare Plan Since January 2017 (forbes.com)

Finally, some of the disturbing things he's said about the election. Just a week from tomorrow! Fingers crossed !!!

Dzhanova, Yelena. "Trump Slams Mail-in Voting, Says It 'Doesn't Work Out Well for Republicans'." *CNBC*. April 8, 2020. Trump slams mail-in voting, says it 'doesn't work out well for Republicans' (cnbc.com)

Chalfant, Morgan. "Trump: 'The Only Way We Are Going to Lose This Election Is If It's Rigged'." *The Hill*. August 17, 2020. Trump: 'The only way we're going to lose this election is if the election is rigged' (thehill.com)

The Weekly Screed: November 2, 2020 (Volume IV, Issue 44)

To: **The Donald –** *"Going in with our lawyers"*

From: **Kelly –** "Once more unto the breach"

- Donald, let me tell you where I was on Election Day, 2016. Instead of being safe among My People in True-Blue Oregon, I was dining on catfish and hush puppies (delicious) with Trumpeter kinfolk in Jasper, Texas.
- When you google Jasper, you'll find the city website touting Jasper's "southern charm" and "rich heritage," but you'll also quickly find out about the June 7, 1998, murder of James Byrd, Jr.
- Byrd was dragged behind a truck by three white supremacists until his head and right arm were disengaged from the rest of his body when he hit a culvert. This heinous lynching resulted in the first conviction of white men for the death of a black man in the freaking ENTIRE HISTORY of TEXAS.
- It also resulted in the bi-partisan passage of the "Matthew Shepard and James Byrd Jr. Hate Crimes Prevention Act," in 2007, which George W. Bush threatened to veto. It was signed into law by Barack Obama in 2009.
- I give you this background to remind you that we (progressive Dems) have gone through all of this before. Baby Bush was an illegitimate president who was handed his first election in 2000 via voter purging by Big Brother Jeb (Governor of Florida at the time) and then by the Supreme Court.
- He went on to steal the 2004 election fair and square thanks to no-paper-trail electronic voting machine shenanigans in Ohio. Conveniently, both the CEO of Diebold voting machines, <u>AND</u> the Ohio Secretary of State had both pledged to "deliver" the state to Bush.
- Now Supreme Court Associate Justice/Sexual Predator Brett Kavanaugh is toying with the idea of using 2000's <u>Bush v Gore</u> decision as "precedent" in a lawsuit you haven't even filed yet….even though that decision itself specifically stated it was "limited to the present circumstances."
- Kavanaugh also opined in a recent SCOTUS ruling that "States want to avoid the chaos and suspicions of impropriety that can ensue if thousands of absentee ballots flow in after election day and potentially flip the results of an election," to which Justice Elena Kagan (in her

dissent) replied: "There are no results to 'flip' until all valid votes are counted." Oh, SNAP!
- We can't say we haven't been warned though. Just last night, in a quote sure to be remembered for the ages, you told a crowd of reporters: *"I think it's a terrible thing when ballots can be collected after an election."*
- Indeed. Terrible and dangerous to collect and count all those pesky ballots.

Resources - Volume IV, Issue 44

In 2016, I was in Jasper, Texas for Election Day....and the Morning After. Kind of a long story, but fortunately my sister was with me. Someone needed to drive us to the Houston airport while I sobbed hysterically for hours in the passenger seat. Anyway, I'm more hopeful for tomorrow's results. I mean, you and I knew this guy was going to be a train wreck from the jump, but now we've had four years of his hijinks to convince more Americans. Although the fact that this monster still has ANY support is beyond me.

Robinson, Campbell. "Texas Executes White Supremacist for 1998 Dragging Death of James Byrd Jr." The New York Times. April 24, 2019. Texas Executes White Supremacist for 1998 Dragging Death of James Byrd Jr. - The New York Times (archive.ph)

Marley, Patrick. "Supreme Court: Wisconsin Mail Ballots Must Be Received by Nov. 3." *Milwaukee Journal Sentinel/USA Today*, October 27, 2020.**

"Trump: Counting of Late-Arriving Ballots a 'Terrible Thing'." *Bloomberg*, November 1, 2020. Watch Trump: Counting of Late-Arriving Ballots a 'Terrible Thing' - Bloomberg

Pierce, Charles. " Trump's Plan Isn't Merely Cheating. It's a Hijacking." *Esquire*, November 1, 2020. Trump Campaign Will Pretend He Won the 2020 Election (esquire.com)

Finally, over the past four years, I've become more and more concerned about the security of our border…with Idaho. Check out this photo.

Speare-Cole, Rebecca. "Idaho Protest Against Coronavirus Measures Features Lt. Gov. with Gun and Bible." *Newsweek*, October 30, 2020. GOP Lt. Gov. Drives Around With Gun and Bible To Protest COVID Restrictions in Idaho as Cases Soar - Newsweek

The Weekly Screed: November 9, 2020 (Volume IV, Issue 45)

To: The Donald – First Runner-Up

From: Kelly – Not feeling like Miss America yet

- Donald, I hate to be the one to tell you this, but you LOST the election.
- I know, it's almost impossible to imagine. After four unprecedented years of mayhem, misery, malapropisms, and mendacity, it's simply *shocking* that the majority of voters chose "Sleepy Joe" and that "monster," Kamala Harris over YOU and Mayonnaise Mike.
- Let's consider all you have done for us:
    - Removed the US from the Paris Climate Accords and the nuclear arms deal with Iran, making us immeasurably less safe.
    - Overturned every Obama environmental and financial regulation you could get your tiny little mitts on.
    - Separated kids from their parents and put them in cages, while making asylum seekers wait it out in dangerous Mexican slums.
    - Tried mightily (but failed, thus far) to eliminate the Affordable Care Act and (along with it) protection for people with pre-existing medical conditions…But I'm sure the Supreme Court will finish off the ACA.
    - And speaking of which, appointed fully one-third of the Supremes, each one more repellant than the last.
    - Destroyed the Obama-Biden economy, ushering in the worst recession since the Great Depression, and guaranteeing that you will leave office as the *only* President with a net loss of American jobs.
    - And, last but not least, made America First in coronavirus cases and deaths. We're Number One !!!
    - Oh, and you even got IMPEACHED. Only the third Prez in history!
- What's astonishing to me is not that you LOST on this horrendous record, but that you persuaded *more* people to vote for you in this election than in 2016. It's lovely that the Biden-Harris ticket secured the most votes in American history, but it's pathetic that the Trump-Pence ticket came in second with the second-most votes in American history!! What the hell???
- Maybe this little speech from the November 1 episode of *Fargo* explains it best. "Loy," played by Chris Rock, says to "Odis" (Jack Huston):

"Every country has its own type of criminal. In America, we got the confidence man, snake oil salesman, grifter. They don't rob you as much as trick you into robbing yourself. See, 'cause in America, people want to *believe*. They got that *dream*. And a dreamer, you can fleece."

Resources - Volume IV, Issue 45

Are you pinching yourself? Breathing a sigh of relief? I'm certainly happier with this outcome than what could have happened, but I'm still on the edge of my seat, and will be until January 20, 2021. I expect more shenanigans over the next two months than in the past 46. Hope I'm wrong. But we must get our laughs in where we can. This week, the winner was Guiliani's press conference at Four Seasons Total Landscaping....as opposed to the assumed venue of the Philadelphia Four Seasons Hotel. The gardening company is already selling stickers proclaiming: "Make America Rake Again" and "Lawn and Order."

Bekiempis, Victoria. "'Make America rake again': Four Seasons Total Landscaping cashes in on Trump fiasco." *The Guardian*, November 9, 2020. 'Make America rake again': Four Seasons Total Landscaping cashes in on Trump fiasco | Donald Trump | The Guardian

CAP Action. "President Trump Has the Worst Economic Record in Recorded History." *Medium*, November 2020. President Trump has the worst economic record in history | by CAP Action | Medium

And a good explanation of what could befall us if the Supreme Court strikes down the Affordable Care Act:

Alonso-Zaldivar, Ricardo. "Much at Stake as Supreme Court Weighs Future of Obamacare." *Associated Press*, November 9, 2020. Much at stake as Supreme Court weighs future of 'Obamacare' | AP News

Fargo season 4 - Wikipedia

Finally, some of my faithful readers have inquired when I will cease and desist with The Weekly Screed. Never fear. I will keep going until Trump is dragged from the White House feet first or until Biden is inaugurated. Whichever comes last. In the meantime, let's all rejoice and celebrate, but with reservations........Kelly

The Weekly Screed: November 16, 2020 (Volume IV, Issue 46)

To: The Donald – Sore Loser

From: Kelly – Almost Believing You'll Be Gone Soon

- Donald, I hate to be the one to tell you this again, but you are <u>still</u> the LOSER of the 2020 presidential election. And by a wider margin than when I first broke this news to you last week.
- In fact, and I'm almost reluctant to point this out, Joe Biden is now the apparent winner of 306 electoral votes. That's exactly the number that you won in 2016! At which time, both you and that harridan Kellyanne Conway characterized your win over Hillary Clinton as a "landslide."
- Let's look at Kellyanne's exact quote (from a tweet on November 28, 2016, 12:35 PM): "306. Landslide. Blowout. Historic." It still gives me chills.
- Face it, DT. This is also the second time you have LOST the popular vote, aka "the will of the people." Which means 5.6 million more American voters preferred Joe Biden to YOU as Leader of the Free World. SAD.
- Nevertheless, here you are, stomping your feet and banging your little fists, calling this election a "fraud," and chalking up the popular vote to all those "illegal" mail-in votes. In 2016, you blamed it on busloads of "illegal<u>s</u>" voting in various states, so this year's excuse is a tad less xenophobic.
- You are also proclaiming that you *really* won….but that the election was "rigged" which fulfills your pre-election prognostications that "the only way they're going to win is by a rigged election." [August 20 Super-Spreader rally in Old Forge, Pennsylvania]
- It's actually pretty nifty the way you teed this up: You would only lose if the election were rigged; the election was rigged, so you lost. The circular logic is flawless, except for the part where you now won't admit that you lost, even though the election was rigged. I'm getting dizzy.
- For just a moment yesterday, you stumbled over the Cliff of Concession, tweeting: "he [Biden] won because the Election was Rigged." Then you caught yourself on a jutting branch and hauled your old orange ass back onto the ledge, this time blaming the "FAKE NEWS MEDIA" for pushing the false narrative that somehow Joe Biden was the President-Elect.

- "I WON THE ELECTION!" you frantically tweeted last night, as Toto pulled back the curtain and Twitter alerted us in red print that "Official sources called this election differently."
- This is getting humiliating, Donald. Even your hair has gone gray. I suggest an extended golf holiday at Mar-a-Lago, perhaps until January 20, 2021?

Resources - Volume IV, Issue 46

Dear Friends, Are you all breathing a little easier? I know I (finally) am. The Trump legal challenges all seem to be going nowhere fast, and there's too many states that need to be flipped for the Supremes to pull off another Bush v Gore. The only nagging fear I have is if Trump minions still get it together to thwart the will of the people in their states and steal the electoral college.

Phillips, Amber. "Could the Electoral College Be Stolen from Biden?" *The Washington Post*, November 12, 2020. Could the electoral college be stolen from Biden? - The Washington Post

Court, Andrew. "Trump Debuts Gray Hair at White House Press Conference." *Daily Mail*, November 14, 2020. Trump sends social media into meltdown as he debuts GRAY HAIR at White House press conference | Daily Mail Online

Alexander, Harriet. "Trump reveals his 'truly great' legal team: A conspiracy theorist accused of antisemitism and his wife, a lawyer who retweets Q-Anon and a campaign legal adviser who says gays are 'sinners'... all led by Rudy Giuliani."*Daily Mail*, November 2020. Trump's fab five! The president names his legal team to fight the election through the courts | Daily Mail Online

Lynch, Sarah N.; Heavey, Susan. "Trump Backtracks on Acknowledging Biden's Win." *AOL News*, November 15, 2020. Trump backtracks on acknowledging Biden won election, concedes 'nothing' (aol.com)

Finally, a nice article from The New Yorker on the importance of Good Losers.

Gopnik, Adam. "Democracy Depends on Good Losers." *The New Yorker*. November 14, 2020. Democracy Depends on Good Losers | The New Yorker

More mischief in the days ahead, I'm sure. Also, I don't know about where you live, but Oregon is having an all-time record surge of COVID cases, and we are going into a partial shutdown again next week. Stay home if you can ! ...Kelly

The Weekly Screed: November 23, 2020 (Volume IV, Issue 47)

To: The Donald – Still the LOSER

From: Kelly – Offering Haikus for the Attempted Coup.

1) Giuliani says

    "I know crimes. I can smell them."

    We can smell flop sweat.

2) Sidney Powell says

    Hugo Chavez is involved

    Even though he's dead

3) The My Pillow guy

    Bails out Kenosha shooter

    Smile for the camera!

4) *"I won, by the way."*

    "Big Pharma [was] against us."

    "Waited and waited."

5) Jenna Ellis said

    That you were an "idiot."

    In 2016.

    Now she says that you

    Are the best president in

    Modern history.

6) They count and recount

    All the votes from the swing states

    Results still the same.

7) While G-20 meets,

    You golf while the nation dies……Play while we perish.

Resources - Volume IV, Issue 47

Holmes, Jack. " Trump's Stupid Coup—Which Hasn't Failed Yet—Is Distracting Us From What Needs to Be Done." *Esquire*.November 20, 2020. Trump's Stupid Coup Ropes in Michigan Republican Legislators (esquire.com)

Reed, Brad. "Exiled Trump Lawyer Sidney Powell Vows Epic Lawsuit to Stop America from Being Stolen by Communists." *Raw Story*. November 23, 2020. Exiled Trump lawyer Sidney Powell vows 'epic' lawsuit to stop America from being 'stolen by communists' - Raw Story

Farberov, Snejana; Associated Press. "Kenosha Shooter Kyle Rittenhouse Released from Custody After Posting $2M Bail." *Daily Mail*. November 20, 2020.Kenosha shooter Kyle Rittenhouse, 17, is released from custody after posting $2M bail | Daily Mail Online

Bhardwaj, Naina. "Donald Trump Says, 'I Won, by the Way' and Lashes Out at Pfizer Claiming It Delayed News of the COVID-19 Vaccine Until After the Election." Business Insider. November 21, 2020. Trump Says 'I Won, by the Way,' Lashes Pfizer Over COVID-19 Vaccine - Business Insider

Kaczynski, Andrew; Steck, Em; McDermott, Nathan. "Trump's Legal Adviser Jenna Ellis in 2016 Called Him an 'Idiot' and Said His Supporters Didn't Care About 'Facts or Logic'." *CNN Politics*. November 18, 2020. Trump's legal adviser Jenna Ellis in 2016 called him an 'idiot' and said his supporters didn't care about 'facts or logic' | CNN Politics

Cathey, Libby. "Could Recounts and Lawsuits Help Trump Flip the Election? Reality Check." *ABC News*. November 12, 2020. Could recounts and lawsuits help Trump flip the election?: Reality check - ABC News (go.com)

Fidel, Manny. "Trump, Rudy Giuliani Voter Fraud Lawsuits Are a Sad, Incompetent Coup." *Business Insider*. November 22, 2020. Trump, Rudy Giuliani Voter Fraud Lawsuits Are a Sad, Incompetent Coup - Business Insider

Karni, Annie; Rappeport, Alan. "G20 Summit Closes With Little Progress and Big Gaps Between Trump and Allies." *The New York Times*. November 22, 2020. G20 Summit Closes With Little Progress and Big Gaps Between Trump and Allies - The New York Times (nytimes.com)

The Weekly Screed: November 30, 2020 (Volume IV, Issue 48)

To: The Donald – Pardoner of Three Turkeys

From: Kelly – Grateful: Only 10 more Weekly Screeds to go !!!!

- Donald, you remain forever the LOSER of the 2020 presidential election. And I am forever grateful for that outcome, along with the majority of not just the nation, but the entire civilized world.
- More about what I'm grateful for in a bit, but first I would like to acknowledge the fact that you pardoned more turkeys this Thanksgiving than any other POTUS in history, with not just one (Corn) or two (Cob) but three (Michael Flynn, who got into trouble by, among other things, serving as an undeclared foreign agent for Turkey, the country.)
- As for the rest of us, you encouraged *"...all Americans to gather, in homes and places of worship, to offer a prayer of thanks to God for our many blessings."* Let the Holiday COVID Contagion begin!
- So, here's some of the other things I was grateful for on November 26:
1. The fact that someday soon we will have public health officials who are intelligent, admired, and consulted, as opposed to the current spokesman for the Coronavirus Task Force, erstwhile radiologist and former FOX fulminator Dr. Scott Atlas. The only person who listens to this "herd immunity" quack is YOU, so this month Dr. Atlas advised us all to pack in tight around the table with our loved ones…particularly those of the elderly persuasion…since "for many people this is their last Thanksgiving."
2. I was also grateful, as I took in all the horrific news at home and abroad, that neither I nor any of my loved ones had succumbed to the coronavirus; or were "food insecure"; or had lost livelihoods; or had our homes foreclosed on, swept away by hurricanes, or consumed by wildfires.
3. Fingers crossed; I was grateful that you haven't yet plunged us into a nuclear conflagration just to stave off Joe Biden's inauguration. I know, there's still time, but it might not look good on your list of achievements as you gin up for your presidential run in 2024. Which, I hate to tell you, might be difficult from behind bars. You will most likely go up the river for state charges, from which no one can pardon you. Sing-Sing perhaps?
4. Lastly, I was grateful to turn to my 11/26/20 Page-A-Day Trump Out of Office calendar and find this 2018 quote from you: *"Time, time, turkey*

for Thanksgiving. My mother would say, oh, eight hours. I said, eight hours? She made the greatest turkey I've ever had. It takes time."
- And you, Donald, will soon have nothing BUT time.

<u>Resources - Volume IV, Issue 48</u>

<u>Dear All,</u> This season of gratitude finds me thankful for YOU, my faithful readers. Not even one of you has asked to "unsubscribe", with the exception of one of my sisters. It's a long story. Family. Anyway, I'm sure you are as happy as I am that this is my final Thanksgiving Screed.

Crowley, James. "Lincoln Project Releases Thanksgiving Ad Thanking Poll Workers, Activists, Patriots." *Newsweek*. November 26, 2020. <u>Lincoln Project Releases Thanksgiving Ad Thanking Poll Workers, Activists, Patriots - Newsweek</u>

Monkman, Betty C. "Pardoning the Thanksgiving Turkey." *White House Historical Association*. <u>Pardoning the Thanksgiving Turkey - White House Historical Association (whitehousehistory.org)</u>

Rosario, Isabella for Ames Tribune. "Presidential Turkey Pardon: Names of Iowa Birds Vying for Trump's Approval." *Des Moines Register*. November 24, 2020. <u>Presidential turkey pardon: Names of Iowa birds vying for Trump's revealed (desmoinesregister.com)</u>

Frum, David. "Trump Pardoned Flynn to Protect Himself." *The Atlantic*. November 25, 2020. <u>Trump Pardoned Flynn to Protect Himself - The Atlantic</u>

Sumner, Mark. "Trump's Coronavirus Chief Urges Americans to Gather for 'Their Last Thanksgiving'." *Daily Kos*. November 17, 2020.<u>Trump's coronavirus chief urges Americans to gather for 'their last Thanksgiving' (dailykos.com)</u>

Singman, Brooke. "Dr. Scott Atlas Resigns as Special Adviser to Trump on Coronavirus." *Fox News*. November 30, 2020. <u>Dr. Scott Atlas resigns as special adviser to Trump on coronavirus | Fox News</u>

Cillizza, Chris. "The 40 Most Utterly Unhinged Lines from Donald Trump's First Post-Election Interview." *CNN. November 30, 2020. <u>The 40 most utterly unhinged lines from Donald Trump's first post-election interview | CNN Politics</u>

The Weekly Screed: December 7, 2020 (Volume IV, Issue 49)

To: The Donald – Went Down to Georgia

From: Kelly – Peachy Keen: Only 9 more Weekly Screeds to go !!!!

- *"I don't like doing them [rallies] for other people,"* Trump said in an odd moment of candor. *"They are a lot of work…. I shouldn't do this for them, it costs too much money."*-----Rally in Valdosta, Georgia, to get out the vote for the Senate run-off election in January ---Saturday, Dec. 5, 2020

- The [Donald] Went Down to Georgia; he was lookin' to Stop the Steal. He was in a bind 'cause he was way behind. He was willing to make a deal.
  He said he'd talk about Perdue and Loeffler, but only if along the way He could rant about how **he'd** really won in Georgia on Election Day.

- So the maskless MAGA masses went
  Marching Through Georgia that night.
  They got all the way to Valdosta and then they put up a fight
  For the freedom to catch the COVID just like Giuliani did
  While they were Marching Through Georgia.

- It wasn't a Rainy Night in Georgia
  It was a nice warm place to spend the night but
  The anguished cries of "Four More Years"
  Seemed to send a sad refrain through the night.
  How many times they counted; the votes still come out the same
  No matter how you look at it or think of it
  Biden won and you just got to play the game.

- And so Trump's leaving on that Midnight Plane from Georgia
  Yeah, he's going back to find a place where he won, in his mind.
  And Melania will be with him (you know she will), on that Midnight Plane from Georgia.
  But how long will she and Barron stay? NYC is looking pretty fine.

- Trump said "Georgia, oh Georgia, the whole day through
  Just a lot of work for Kelly Loeffler and David Perdue.
  Other candidates may reach out to me; other eyes cry desperately.

But I won't be doing this for anyone else too soon."
On this trip to Georgia, Georgia, no peace did Trump find.
Just another loss keeps Georgia on [His] Mind.

Resources - Volume IV, Issue 49

It's December, Dear Ones. Which means that we will rid ourselves of this Orange Ogre next month! Something to make the season bright. But before we can all relax, there's a Senate run-off election in Georgia on January 5 which will determine the Fate of the Earth (or at least control of the Senate).

Cohen, Arienne. "How to Donate to the Georgia Senate Runoff Election: 8 Ways to Help the Races Before January." *Fast Company* November 8, 2020. How to donate to the Georgia Senate runoff election: 8 ways to help the races before January - Fast Company

In case you missed it, Trump held a rally in Valdosta, GA on Saturday evening, ostensibly in support of the Republican candidates, both of whom should be Locked Up for insider trading, but that's another story. Anyway, he seemed quite peeved to be there, and spent most of the time talking about HIMSELF, naturally.

Fowler, Stephen. "Trump Continues Attacks on Election Results at Georgia Senate Runoff Rally." *NPR*. December 5, 2020. Trump Continues Attacks On Election Results At Georgia Senate Runoff Rally : NPR

Associated Press. "Trump Urges Backers to 'Take Revenge' by Voting." *AP News* December 5, 2020. The Latest: Trump urges backers to 'take revenge' by voting | AP News

I started out thinking about that good ole country song, The Devil Went Down to Georgia, but then other Georgia songs kept popping into my head, so I felt the need to mash up four more. If I didn't get to your favorite, here's a list of 64 Georgia tunes.

Baker, Elaina. "77 Songs About the Great State of Georgia." *Spinditty*. [Updated April 2, 2023] 77 Songs About the Great State of Georgia - Spinditty

"Joe Biden won in Georgia, flipping a state Donald Trump won in 2016.*Politico*. [Last updated January 6, 2021] Georgia Election Results 2020 | Live Map Updates | Voting by County & District (politico.com)

The Weekly Screed: December 14, 2020 (Volume IV, Issue 50)

To: The Donald – Chiseler-in-Chief

From: Kelly – In the Christmas Spirit: Only 7 Weekly Screeds to go !!!!

- I hear people asking, Why won't Trump concede the election? To which I reply, "Because there is SO much money to be made by not conceding!"
- As you know, Donald, and as you reassure me relentlessly, I **am** among your TOP supporters with my HUGE donation to "WinRed" of one dollar (that's $1.00) <u>per month</u>. And for my generous contribution to your cause, I am pelted daily with overtures, pleas, and exhortations, to give MORE, or "enter to win," or (in the spirit of the season) acquire unique merchandise.
- Here's a sample of recent texts I've received from YOU:

Pres. Trump has a special CHRISTMAS GIFT for his TOP supporters, like YOU! You have 1 HR to claim your Trump Christmas Stickers! Act NOW!" [Naturally, I was excited.] A click on the link reveals my "gift" to be two stickers proclaiming, "We're Saying MERRY CHRISTMAS Again" and a warning that if I don't "contribute $15 IMMEDIATELY to claim your FREE set of Trump Christmas Stickers," they will be "released to the next Patriot in line." [Since when does a FREE GIFT cost 15 smackaroos?]

CONGRATULATIONS! President Trump has selected YOU to receive one of our ICONIC 2020 Trump Christmas Ornaments FOR FREE. This one-time offer for a FREE ornament is available to you for ONE HOUR, so don't wait. <u>Please contribute $45 IMMEDIATELY to claim your FREE 2020 Trump Christmas Ornament! (This donation qualifies for the gift offer!)</u> And I *really* wanted this Free Gift, your face on a red ball, pointing a finger at me, wearing a MAGA hat….but for $45, I can get 45 red ornaments at the Dollar Store and paint "MAGA 2020" on them.

Pres. Trump: We will not bend. We will not break. We will never give in.

    We will never give up. We will NEVER surrender!

    FIGHT BACK! Reply YES to donate $45.[When I didn't fall for this one, the next text was a "1000% Impact Offer for One Hour"….which was "Extended" for another hour in the next text, and "Reactivated" in the next.] Then you gave up on me.

Resources - Volume IV, Issue 50

Good morning, all. There's hope on a few fronts:

1. Vaccines are arriving for health care workers and long-term care residents.
2. Those two guys in Georgia just might win their Senate races on January 5 (send $$ if you can to Home | Fair Fight); and
3. Rumor has it that moving vans are scheduled to arrive at the White House next week.

AND Melania looks for a nice school in Florida for Barron.......A Christmas Miracle !!

Marx, Linda. "Mar-a-Lago and Trump Residences Being Renovated While Melania Looks at Schools." *People*. December 3, 2020. Mar-a-Lago Trump Apartments Being Renovated While Melania Looks at Schools for Barron | PEOPLE.com

- Meanwhile, The Donald and his deluded supporters (18 State Attorneys General, who should all be disbarred) and 106 Republican members of Congress (who should all be censured by the rest of the House of Representatives) were unable to persuade the Supreme Court to debase itself enough to overturn the election.

Parks, Miles. "Supreme Court Dismisses Texas Lawsuit Aiming to Overturn Election Results." *NPR*, December 12, 2020. Supreme Court Dismisses Texas Lawsuit Aiming To Overturn Election Results : NPR

- But that hasn't stopped him from continuing to "fundraise" from the gullible. I probably receive 6-8 texts a day and another 4-5 emails, mostly from The Donald himself, but also from Don Jr., Eric, and Eric's lovely wife Lara. But never from Ivanka and Jared, who must be above such groveling. The ones from the kids usually start out with "My father asked me to reach out to you" or "Can I tell my Dad you'll step up?" or "I spoke with my father, and he chose YOU." The sad thing is, this stuff must work on someone, since the "campaign" has pulled in over $200 million *since* the election.

Associated Press. "Trump Has Raised More Than $200 Million Since Election Day." *MarketWatch*. December 3. Trump has raised more than $200 million since Election Day - MarketWatch

And yes, the texts in The Screed are actual texts that came to my very own phone !

Text 1. December 9, 9:11 am PST

Text 2. December 6, 4:19 pm PST

Text 3. December 11, 8:06 am PST. I think this one was right after the Supreme Court issued its ruling.

The more frantic they get, the more hilarious I find them.

The Weekly Screed: December 21, 2020 (Volume IV, Issue 51)

To: The Donald – Bad Santa (Encore)

From: Kelly – Fa-la-la-la-la !!! : Only 6 Weekly Screeds to go !!!!

'Twas the week before Christmas, the year: Twenty-Twenty.
The nation was plagued with problems a-plenty.
For starters, the plague itself (COVID Nineteen)
Had killed and infected in numbers unseen. Hospitals are full.
ICU beds at zero. The country's in need of a Holiday Hero.
When back at the White House there rose such a clatter,
I turned on the news to see what was the matter?!?
It seemed that Mike Flynn (who you pardoned this year)
Had an idea so CRAZY, it's perfectly clear that you LOVED it!
Let's do it! Declare Martial Law! Overturn the election!!
Forget that we saw the Electoral College give Biden the win…It's a HOAX!
But reality finds us back in the heartland where food lines are terribly long.
Unemployment is rising. It just seems so wrong that a nation as rich as the
U S of A should let people go hungry on this Christmas Day,
When we've suffered so much for the entire year.
But wait! There's another big crisis, we hear:
The Russians have hacked half the country's email using ORION "updates"
So they could assail the systems of governments, businesses too!
We look to Our Leader to see what to do!
But as usual, Donald, you're brainless and LAME,
You sent out a tweet pinning all of the blame on China!
Yes, *China's* the villain again! Like they were for the virus
And Hunter Biden! Maybe he's in cahoots with them!
You never know. What a great episode for the Donald Trump Show!
The "Celebrity POTUS," oh when will it end?
Even with 2021 just round the bend, it still seems so endless.
We fear the Last Days. We know all the havoc that you can still raise.
Martial law, fighting in the streets, even a war
With Iran or Korea, no matter what for.
Donald Trump, you're a creepy and nasty old elf
Who is only concerned with your dastardly self.
But there's only One Month till you're gone from our sight!
Merry Christmas to All! And to all, a good night.

Resources - Volume IV, Issue 51

Dear Ones, it's beginning to look a lot like Christmas (although it's 55 degrees here today) !

Hanukkah ended Friday and Kwanzaa starts on Saturday, so I hope all of these holidays find you happy and warm.

I waxed poetic again this week, and will only burden you with two research links:

Liptak, Kevin; Brown, Pamela. "Heated Oval Office meeting included talk of special counsel, martial law as Trump advisers clash." CNN. December 20, 2020. Heated Oval Office meeting included talk of special counsel, martial law as Trump advisers clash | CNN Politics

Reston, Maeve. "Donald Trump Is Still Only Out for Himself." CNN Politics. December 20, 2020. Donald Trump is still only out for himself | CNN Politics

Sink, Justin. "Trump Downplays Huge Hack Tied to Russia, Suggests China." Bloomberg. December 21, 2020. Trump Downplays Huge Hack Tied to Russia, Suggests China - Bloomberg

As at Christmases Past, I've drawn inspiration from:

A Visit From Saint Nicholas, by Clement Clarke Moore.
A Visit from St. Nicholas - Wikipedia

The Weekly Screed: December 28, 2020 (Volume IV, Issue 52)

To: The Donald – The Ebenezer Scrooge-in-Chief

From: Kelly – Sincere Apologies to Dickens: Only 5 Weekly Screeds to go

Stave One: A visit from The Ghost of Roy Cohn, chains rattling, oozing a nasty stench. "Bah! Humbug!" proclaims The Donald. But then, "Speak comfort to me, Roy!" The Ghost replies, "I have none to give. You will be haunted by Three Spirits." The apparition walks backward from him and disappears into the bleak, dark night.

Stave Two: A visit from the Ghost of Christmas Past who tells The Donald: "I have seen your nobler aspirations fall off one by one, until the master-passion, Gain, engrosses you." *"Oh, yeah?"* replied Donald Trump. *"Engross this!"*

Happy New Year to all, including to my many enemies and those who have fought me and lost so badly they just don't know what to do. Love! [Tweet from Dec. 31, 2016]
People are proud to be saying Merry Christmas again. I am proud to have led the charge against the assault of our cherished and beautiful phrase. MERRY CHRISTMAS!!!!! [Tweet from Dec 24, 2017]
I am all alone (poor me) in the White House waiting for the Democrats to come back and make a deal on desperately needed Border Security. At some point the Democrats not wanting to make a deal will cost our Country more money than the Border Wall we are all talking about. Crazy!"
[Dec 24, 2018, after YOU, Donald Trump, shut down the government]

2019 HOLIDAY RETAIL SALES WERE UP 3.4% FROM LAST YEAR, THE BIGGEST NUMBER IN U.S. HISTORY. CONGRATULATIONS AMERICA!
[Dec 25, 2019, because isn't this what Christmas is all about ??]

Stave Three: A visit from the Ghost of Christmas Present who tells The Donald: "There are some upon this earth of yours who lay claim to know Us, and who do their deeds of passion, pride, ill-will, hatred, envy, bigotry, and selfishness in Our name, who are as strange to Us as if they had never lived." You countered:
"So, you're the President of the United States, and you just went through an election where you got more votes than any sitting President in history, by far – and purportedly lost. You can't get 'standing' before the Supreme Court, so you 'intervene' with wonderful states……...that, after careful study and consideration, think you got 'screwed,' something which will hurt them also. Many others likewise join the suit but, within a flash, it is thrown out and gone, without even looking at the many reasons it was brought. A Rigged Election, fight on!" [Tweet from Dec 25, 2020]

Stave Four: A visit from the Ghost of Christmas Yet to Come, who leads Scrooge, excuse me, YOU, to listen to a group of Florida businessmen conversing: "1) I don't know much about it. I only know he's dead. 2) Why? What was the matter with him?

I thought he'd never die! 3) It's likely to be a cheap funeral, for upon my life I don't know of anybody to go to it. 4) I don't mind going if a lunch is provided. [General laughter.]"

From @realMelaniaTrump: *Well, I don't have time to go to his stupid funeral. I'm still working like my ass off at Christmas stuff. You know, who gives a fuck about Christmas stuff and decoration, but I need to do it, right?"* [Dec 24, 2021]

Resources - Volume IV, Issue 52

Dear Friends, it's the last Weekly Screed of 2020 ! Having just watched A Christmas Carol, it put me in a Dickensian frame of mind for this week's message to The Donald. A Christmas Carol - Wikipedia. In the novella, which uses the term "Stave" for "Chapter", Scrooge is visited first by the specter of his late business partner, Marley. For whom I substituted Trump's former attorney, the execrable Roy Cohn. All his other business "associates" are in prison or recently pardoned.

Kruse, Michael. "Roy Cohn and Donald Trump: A Documentary." *Politico Magazine*, September 19, 2019. The Final Lesson Donald Trump Never Learned From Roy Cohn - POLITICO Magazine

Scrooge is also visited by The Ghosts of Christmases Past, Present, and Yet to Come, which gave me the opportunity to revisit some of Trump's greatest holiday tweets, and this year's beauty in which, of course, he is still in denial about the election. Next year's fictional tweet comes from Melania, but most of the wording is from her recorded phone conversation with her (former) friend Stephanie Winston Wolkoff, and which we just learned about this year in the book Melania and Me.

Mazza, Ed. "Twitter Users Mock Melania Trump's 'Who Gives A F**k About Christmas' Tree." HuffPost. November 24, 2020. Twitter Users Mock Melania Trump's 'Who Gives A F**k About Christmas' Tree | HuffPost Latest News

And, really, won't we miss the Barbie Robot First Lady almost as much as Our Dear Leader? He also took time out on Christmas Day to whinge about her zero magazine covers as FLOTUS (especially compared to Michelle Obama's twelve). I think what he fails to understand is that a cover image is usually accompanied inside the publication by a story and/or interview with the subject, and since Melania is a bot there wouldn't be much there, would there??

O'Connell, Oliver. "Trump Finds Time to Complain That Melania Has Not Been Featured on Enough Magazine Covers, Despite Mounting Crises." The Independent. December 26, 2020. Trump finds time to complain that Melania has not been featured on enough magazine covers, despite mounting crises | The Independent

The Weekly Screed: January 4, 2021 (Volume IV, Issue 53)

To: The Donald – Loser in Chief – Give it up already!

From: Kelly – Auld Lang Syne! Only 4 Weekly Screeds to go !!!!

- Donald, the presidential election was 2 months ago, but there you were, on the phone to the Georgia Secretary of State, trying to talk him into (criminally) subverting the election results and "find 11,780 votes" for you. Meanwhile you've already labelled the Georgia Senate run-off election (tomorrow) "illegal and invalid." This has not stopped every Republican in Christendom from badgering me for money to save the soul of America from the forces of darkness and Communist pedophiles (aka Democrats).
- Here are the swamp creatures I've heard from in just the last 48 HOURS !!!!!

    Kelly Loeffler and David Perdue
    I cannot wait to bid adieu
    Mitch McConnell as well as "Team Mitch"
    Can't be too soon for me to ditch
    Martha McSally and Rafael (Ted) Cruz
    To see your names gives me the blues.
    Kevin McCarthy and Gingrich, Newt
    I long to give you both the boot.
    Louie Gohmert and Tom Cotton
    I'd like to see you both forgotten.
    Karl Rove and Michelle Steel
    The nausea you make me feel
    Is just as strong as when I see
    An email from Nikki Haley
    Mike R. Pence and Rick L. Scott
    Will I miss you? I will not.
    Marco Rubio, George P. Bush
    I wish to kick you in the tush.
    And please, I beg you, no more pleas
    From the NRCC or the State GOPs
    As well as each and every Trump
    My shoe print on your every rump.
    I'd like to plant A.S.A.P. and banish you from my TV.
    Hooray for 2021! The fundraising will soon be done.
    With so much joy, I can't describe when I can click on "Unsubscribe."

Resources - Volume IV, Issue 53

Happy New Year to All ! Here's to a safe passage to January 20, after which things just have to get better. As you know, I give $1 a month to Donald Trump, which has put me on the mailing lists of every past and present Republican in the land. And since I've given a lot of money to Dems over the past 4 years, I'm on all of their mailing lists too. I'm looking forward to getting off all those lists, but not until after the Biden inauguration.

I was familiar with all the names I've listed in this week's Screed, except for Michelle Steel....who turns out to be a brand-new Republican representative from California. So, she hasn't had time to perform any dastardly deeds yet. Give her time. Fingers crossed for the Georgia Senate run-off tomorrow !! ....Kelly

Shear, Michael D.; Saul, Stephanie. "Trump, in Taped Call, Pressured Georgia Official to 'Find' Votes to Overturn Election." *The New York Times*. January 3, 2021. Trump, in Taped Call, Pressured Georgia Official to 'Find' Votes to Overturn Election - The New York Times (nytimes.com)

Papenfuss, Mary for HuffPost . "Trump Declares Georgia Senate Races 'Illegal and Invalid' Days Ahead of Vote." *AOL News*. January 2, 2021. Trump Declares Georgia Senate Races 'Illegal And Invalid' Days Ahead Of Vote (aol.com)

The Weekly Screed: January 11, 2021 (Volume IV, Issue 54)

To: The Donald – Mob Boss

From: Kelly – Anxious - Still 3 Weekly Screeds to go…Anything Can Happen

- Donald, for the past four years I've attempted to put a light-hearted spin on these weekly communications. Like the late-night comedians, I adopted the theory that ridicule was my most effective medium. But I feel hard-pressed to find anything entertaining about the past week.
- Oh, there WAS reason for celebration in the outcome of the Georgia Senate run-off. In four short years you have managed to flip the presidency and both houses of Congress from Republican to Democrat for the first time since 2008. Now that's what *I* call Making America Great Again.
- But the horror show that unfolded on live television on January 6 was unfathomable, even though I have imagined far worse from you (martial law, nuclear strike). You have often come across as a wanna-be Mafia Don, most recently in your attempt to shake down the Georgia Secretary of State.
- However, this time you had an actual deluded violent mob at your disposal, ginned up and primed to follow marching orders from you and your henchmen. Rudy Giuliani (who never served a day in his life) called for "trial by combat." Rep. Mo Brooks from Alabama (another chicken-hawk) urged the crowd to start "kicking ass." Don Jr. threatened lawmakers that they should "choose wisely" between being "a hero or a zero."
- Then it was your turn. And as you surveyed the rabble before you, you decided that this was precisely the right time to incite an insurrection, not only against Congress, but against your own Vice-President.
- And who were these fine Patriots, who overcame the inexplicably weak security forces at the Capitol, chanted "Hang Pence!," defecated in the halls, and screamed threats against Nancy Pelosi that I can't repeat here?
- They were Your People, carrying flags and wearing shirts, caps, and pins to identify their specific brands of twisted psychoses: white supremacists sporting Virginia Confederate battle flags and Thin Blue Line flags; Neo-Nazis (didn't you love the guy in the Camp Auschwitz t-shirt?); evangelical Christians (Appeal to Heaven, and "Jesus is my Savior, Trump is my President" flags); worshippers of Kek, the Egyptian God of Darkness waving the Republic of Kekistan flag.

- Q-Anon flags and apparel abounded; and several sycophants waved the Trump/Rambo banner (I'm sure this was your favorite).
- Yes, it was so glorious until it wasn't, and five people lay dead. And at the end? Vice President Mike Pence still declared Joe Biden President-Elect.

Resources - Volume IV, Issue 54

Dear Ones, It's been another tumultuous week in American history. Don't know about you, but I watched TV for 14 hours straight on January 6. I finally gave up around 11:30 PM Pacific Time after getting the estimate from Ali Velshi on MSNBC that the Congressional festivities would last another 3 hours or so.

Phillips, Jack for Epoch Times." 'Massive Amounts of Evidence Will Be Presented' on Jan. 6: Trump." January 1, 2021. Posted by Front Sight. So, this is what President Trump plans to do on January 6… (ignatius-piazza-front-sight.com)

Washingtonian Staff. "PHOTOS: DC on the Eve of the January 6 Pro-Trump March." *Washingtonian* January 5, 2021. PHOTOS: DC on the Eve of the January 6 Pro-Trump March - Washingtonian

Multiple Photographers. "Scenes of Terror in Washington as Trump Rioters Swarm the Capitol." *Vanity Fair* January 7, 2021. Scenes of Terror in Washington as Trump Rioters Swarm the Capitol | Vanity Fair

Campanile, Carl; Steinbuch, Yaron. "Rioters Left Feces, Urine in Hallways and Offices During Mobbing of US Capitol." *New York Post* January 8, 2021. Rioters left feces, urine in hallways and offices during mobbing of US Capitol (nypost.com)

Briggs, Jimmie. "The Unbearable Whiteness of Storming the Capitol." *Vanity Fair*. January 7, 2021. The Unbearable Whiteness of Storming the Capitol | Vanity Fair

Quito, Anne; Shendruk, Amanda. "Decoding the Pro-Trump Insurrectionist Flags and Banners." *Quartz*.**Decoding the pro-Trump insurrectionist flags and banners (qz.com)

Sweeney, Dan. "Where Did the Mobsters Live in South Florida?" *South Florida Sun-Sentinel* March 9, 2020. Where did the mobsters live in South Florida? - South Florida Sun-Sentinel (sun-sentinel.com)

I have two more Screeds after this one: Next Monday and next Thursday, the day after the Inauguration. We'll get through this. Till then, stay alert.

The Weekly Screed: January 18, 2021 (Volume IV, Issue 55)

To: The Donald – Impeachable You

From: Kelly – Next to Last Screed…Anything Can Happen in 2 days

- Congratulations, Donald. Thanks to the events of January 6, you have become the only President of the United States to have been impeached TWICE. Which makes *you* Number One amongst impeached POTUSes.
- I must confess…I'm one of those radical socialist Democrats who believed you committed numerous impeachable offenses both before and during your term in office. Were it up to me, we could have maintained a rolling impeachment process for the past four years: bring up articles of impeachment in the House, vote, send to the Senate, vote, rinse, and repeat.
- <u>Examples</u>: violation of the Fair Housing Act; employment of undocumented persons; convictions arising from your fraudulent "charitable foundation" and "university"; violation of the appropriations and emoluments clauses and the Presidential Records Act; abuse of power; soliciting foreign interference; campaign finance crimes; obstruction of justice; contempt of Congress; obstruction of Congress; violation of human rights; abuse of Presidential pardons; felony witness tampering and retaliation; etc., etc.
- But I must hand it to you, you saved the best for last: "willfully inciting violence against the Government of the United States." No other President has even *considered* that one! And this time, there's a body count.
- In honor of which, I've written a farewell song for you, to be sung to that old Gershwin standard, "Embraceable You."

Last year we were sure that ONE time would do.
But now we can see it has to be TWO.
This time your high crime was broadcast live on TV,
Urging insurrection for the whole world to see.
For four years, we watched you cheat, steal, and lie.
Above all, we want to bid you goodbye.
You've been a horrid POTUS.
Please depart for Mar-a-Lago, do!
You Vile Impeachable You.

Resources - Volume IV, Issue 55

You will be receiving one final Screed on the first full day of the Biden-Harris administration, but (fingers crossed) we will have been able to pry The Donald out of the White House by then, so I won't be able to send it to him there. Ah, well, maybe someday he will buy the book on Amazon.

The Daily Show (January 12, 2021) covers the January 6 rally: Jordan Klepper Sees It All at The Capitol Insurrection | The Daily Social Distancing Show - YouTube

Naylor, Brian. "Full Text: Trump Impeachment Article for 'Incitement of Insurrection'." *NPR*. [Updated February 9, 2021.] Full Text: Trump Impeachment Article For 'Incitement Of Insurrection' : House Impeachment Vote: Live Updates : NPR

President Donald Trump and Impeachable Offenses | Constitution Annotated | Congress.gov | Library of Congress

"Embraceable You." *Wikipedia*. Embraceable You - Wikipedia

Wishing a peaceful MLK Day for all of us..........Kelly

Dear Friends,

I have something a little different for The Final Screed: 3+ pages of The Donald's All-Time Hits in the "Best Words" department. With links to my research, of course!

These may or may not be your choices but (in my humble opinion) they convey the essence of the man, and a summary of what we have endured for the past four and a half years. And since for many of us, The New Year did not begin until twelve noon yesterday, here's an observance of renewal from another poet:

**"For last year's words belong to last year's language,
And next year's words await another voice.
And to make an end is to make a beginning."**

T. S. Eliot, from "Little Gidding"

The Weekly Screed: January 21, 2021 (Volume IV, Issue 56)

To: My Readers – The Donald's Best Words (June 2015 to January 2021)

From: Kelly – Lest We Forget

December 30, 2015

I'm telling you, I used to use the word incompetent. Now I just call them stupid. I went to an Ivy League school. I'm very highly educated. I know words, I have the best words...but there is no better word than stupid. Right?

June 15, 2015: When Mexico sends its people, they're not sending their best…They're bringing drugs. They're bringing crime. They're rapists. And some, I assume, are good people….I will build a great, great wall on our southern border. And I will have Mexico pay for that wall.

July 20, 2015: [John McCain] was not a war hero…he's a war hero because he was captured. I like people that weren't captured.

January 23, 2016: I could stand in the middle Fifth Avenue and shoot somebody, and I wouldn't lose any voters.

February 23, 2016: We won the evangelicals. We won with young. We won with old. We won with highly educated. We won with poorly educated. I love the poorly educated.

May 26, 2016: We're going to win so much, you're going to be so sick and tired of winning, you're going to come to me and go 'Please, please, we can't win anymore.'

July 27, 2016: Russia, if you're listening — I hope you are able to find the 30,000 emails that are missing. I think you will probably be rewarded mightily by our press. Let's see if that happens.

January 20, 2017: [Today] will be remembered as the day the people became the rulers of this nation again. The forgotten men and women of our country will be forgotten no longer. Everyone is listening to you now…This American carnage stops right here and stops right now. (Inaugural address)

February 2, 2017: Frederick Douglass is an example of somebody who's done an amazing job and is getting recognized more and more, I notice.

May 4, 2017: How am I doing? Am I doing OK? Hey, I'm president! I'm president! Can you believe it?

August 15, 2017: …you had some very bad people in that group [neo-Nazis], but you also had people that were very fine people, on both sides. (Charlottesville rally)

September 30, 2017: [Puerto Rico] is an island surrounded by water, big water, ocean water.

October 7, 2017: The media is—really, the word, I think one of the greatest of all terms I've come up with—is fake. I guess other people have used it perhaps over the years, but I've never noticed it.

January 6, 2018: Actually, throughout my life, my two greatest assets have been mental stability and being, like, really smart… I went from VERY successful businessman, to top T.V. Star … to President of the United States (on my first try). I think that would qualify as not smart, but genius … and a very stable genius at that!"

January 11, 2018: Why are we having all these people from shithole countries come here?

June 28, 2018: I said, 'Oh, I am so smart. I am the smartest person.' My uncle was a great professor at MIT for 40 years. Can you believe? Forty years. I said, 'But I'm smarter than him. I'm smarter than anybody.'

September 19, 2018: This [Florence] is a tough hurricane, one of the wettest we've ever seen from the standpoint of water.

September 27, 2018: China has total respect for Donald Trump's very, very large brain. [Speaking of himself]

November 27, 2018: They're making a mistake because I have a gut, and my gut tells me more sometimes than anybody else's brain can ever tell me. [Can we ever forget the inspiring "I Have a Gut" speech?]

January 10, 2019: When during the campaign I would say, 'Mexico's going to pay for it,' obviously I never said this and I never meant they're going to write out a check.

February 21, 2019: How about the word 'caravan?' Caravan? I think that was one of mine.

March 24, 2019: No Collusion, No Obstruction, Complete and Total EXONERATION. KEEP AMERICA GREAT! [Release of Mueller Report]

April 26, 2019: I think that — I just feel like a young man. I'm so young. I can't believe it. I'm the youngest person. I am a young, vibrant man.

July 4, 2019: Our army manned the air, it rammed the ramparts, it took over the airports, it did everything it had to do, and at Fort McHenry, under the rockets' red glare, it had nothing but victory.
[Speaking of the Revolutionary War, before airplanes were invented, then inadvertently switching to the War of 1812, when the "Star-Spangled Banner" was written.]

September 9, 2019: Under the normal rules, I'll be out in 2024 so we may have to go for an extra term.

October 2, 2019: The call was perfect, the real call, the call I made.

[To the Ukrainian President Vladimir Zelensky, which kicked off Impeachment #1]

January 20, 2020: It's one person coming in from China. We have it under control. It's going to be just fine.

February 26, 2020: When you have 15 people…within a couple of days it's going to be down to close to zero. That's a pretty good job we've done.

February 27, 2020: "It's going to disappear. One day, it's like a miracle -- it will disappear."

March 6, 2020: "I like this stuff. I really get it. People are surprised that I understand it... Every one of these doctors said, 'How do you know so much about this?' Maybe I have a natural ability. Maybe I should have done that instead of running for president." (on scientific research for treatments)

March 11, 2020: "The virus will not have a chance against us. No nation is more prepared or more resilient than the United States."

April 3, 2020: "I'm feeling good. I just don't want to be doing -- somehow sitting in the Oval Office behind that beautiful Resolute Desk, the great Resolute Desk, I think wearing a face mask as I greet presidents, prime ministers, dictators, kings, queens, I don't know, somehow I don't see it for myself. I just don't.

April 23, 2020: [To William Bryan, undersecretary of science and technology at the Department of Homeland Security, White House press conference, with Dr. Deborah Birx cringing in her chair] So, supposedly we hit the body with a tremendous, whether it's ultraviolet or just very powerful light, and I think you said that hasn't been checked, but you're going to test it. And then I said supposing you brought the light inside the body, which you can do either through the skin or in some other way. And I think you said you're going to test that, too. Sounds interesting, right? And then I see the disinfectant, where it knocks it out in one minute. And is there a way we can do something like that, by injection inside or almost a cleaning, because you see it [COVID] gets in the lungs and it does a tremendous number on the lungs, so it'd be interesting to check that, so that you're going to have to use medical doctors with, but it sounds interesting to me. So, we'll see, but the whole concept of the light, the way it kills it in one minute. That's pretty powerful.

June 5, 2020: Hopefully, George [Floyd] is looking down right now and saying, 'This [May jobless rate] is a great thing that's happening for our country.'… this is a great day for him, this is a great day for everybody.

July 9, 2020: I actually took one [a mental impairment test] when I -- very recently, when I --when I was -- the radical left was saying, is he all there? Is he all there? And I proved I was all there because I got -- I aced it. I aced the test. I took it at Walter Reed Medical Center in front of doctors. And they were very surprised. They said, that's an unbelievable thing. Rarely does anybody do what you just did.

August 3, 2020: They are dying, that's true. And it is what it is. But that doesn't mean we aren't doing everything we can. It's under control, as much as you can control it.

August 17, 2020: We have to win the election. We can't play games. Go out and vote. Make sure because the only way we're going to lose this election is if the election is rigged.

November 4, 2020: This is a fraud on the American public. This is an embarrassment for our country. As far as I'm concerned, we already have won it.

December 10, 2020: How can you give an election to someone who lost the election by hundreds of thousands of legal votes in each of the swing states? How can a country be run by an illegitimate president?

December 19, 2020: Big protest in D.C. on January 6th. Be there, will be wild!

January 6, 2021: Our country has had enough. We will not take it anymore and that's what this is all about. To use a favorite term that all of you people really came up with, we will stop the steal. Today I will lay out just some of the evidence proving that we won this election, and we won it by a landslide.... if Mike Pence does the right thing, we win the election. All he has to do... States want to revote. The states got defrauded. They were given false information. They voted on it. Now they want to recertify. They want it back. All Vice President Pence has to do is send it back to the states to recertify, and we become president, and you are the happiest people.... Now it is up to Congress to confront this egregious assault on our democracy. After this, we're going to walk down and I'll be there with you. ...We're going walk down to the Capitol, and we're going to cheer on our brave senators, and congressmen and women. We're probably not going to be cheering so much for some of them because you'll never take back our country with weakness. You have to show strength, and you have to be strong. [Cue Impeachment #2]

January 6, 2021: I know your pain, I know you're hurt. We had an election that was stolen from us. It was a landslide election and everyone knows it, especially the other side….There's never been a time like this, where such a thing happened, where they could take it away from all of us. From me, from you, from our country. This was a fraudulent election, but we can't play into the hands of these people. We have to have peace. So go home. We love you, you're very special.

January 20, 2021: Have a good life; we'll see you soon.

Resources - Volume IV, Issue 56

User Clip: TRUMP I KNOW WORDS | C-SPAN.org

Full text: Donald Trump announces a presidential bid - The Washington Post

Donald Trump Says "I Like People Who Weren't Captured", Calls John McCain "Loser" - Transcript - Rev

Donald Trump quote: I could stand in the middle Fifth Avenue and shoot... (azquotes.com)

Donald Trump: 'I love the poorly educated' (yahoo.com)

Trump: 'We're going to win so much, you're going to be so sick and tired of winning' | 406 Politics | billingsgazette.com

Trump broke US law by asking Russians to find Hillary Clinton emails (usatoday.com)

The Inaugural Address – The White House (archives.gov)

Trump implied Frederick Douglass was alive. The abolitionist's family offered a 'history lesson.' - The Washington Post

President Trump: 'Hey, I'm president! Can you believe it?' (theweek.com)

PolitiFact | In Context: Donald Trump's 'very fine people on both sides' remarks (transcript)

Donald Trump says Puerto Rico is 'an island surrounded by big water' | The Independent | The Independent

Donald Trump just claimed he invented 'fake news' (cnn.com)

Resources - Volume IV, Issue 56 (continued)

Trump: I'm a 'very stable genius' (cnn.com)

Trump Called El Salvador, Haiti 'Shithole Countries': Report | Time

Donald Trump's 54 most outrageously over-the-top lines from his North Dakota speech (cnn.com)

Donald Trump Makes A Stunning Observation About The Wetness Of Water | HuffPost Latest News

Trump's "Very, Very Large Brain" Comment Underscores Myth About Intelligence (inverse.com)

'My Gut Tells Me More Than Anybody Else's Brain': Trump's Bizarre Washington Post Interview Was Totally Bonkers (thenewcivilrightsmovement.com)

Trump Revises History on Mexico's Wall Payment - FactCheck.org

BBC cameraman assaulted during Trump rally in El Paso - Vox

Trump on Mueller report: 'Complete and total exoneration' | TheHill

Trump, 72, declares he's a 'young, vibrant man' compared with Joe Biden, 76 - The Washington Post

Trump Says Revolutionary War Troops 'Took Over the Airports' | Time

Trump jokes about running for third term in 2024 | The Times of Israel

Trump's Inaccurate Claims About His 'Perfect' Call - FactCheck.org

Six months of Trump's COVID denials: 'It'll go away … It's fading' | World news | The Guardian

'Like a miracle, it will disappear': Trump's most notable quotes on COVID-19- The New Indian Express

Trump suggesting injecting disinfectant: video, transcript - Business Insider

Trump says he hopes George Floyd 'is looking down' and celebrating jobs report: 'This is a great day for him' (yahoo.com)

Trump claims he 'aced' cognitive test but offers no proof - CNNPolitics

Trump tells Axios rising COVID-19 death toll 'is what it is' (usatoday.com)

Resources - Volume IV, Issue 56 (continued)

Trump: 'The only way we're going to lose this election is if the election is rigged' | TheHill

What Donald Trump Said in Premature Election 'Victory' Statement—Full Transcript of President's Extraordinary White House Speech (newsweek.com)

Trump Calls Biden an 'Illegitimate President' in Tweet-Storm About Election Results (ijr.com)

'Be There. Will Be Wild!': Trump All but Circled the Date - The New York Times (nytimes.com)

Trump's speech that 'incited' Capitol violence: Full transcript | US Elections 2020 News | Al Jazeera

Trump's Message to Capitol Protesters: 'Go Home, We Love You' - Variety

Trump departs White House after self-congratulatory farewell speech (nydailynews.com)

Don't see your favorite quote here? Try these sites:

Donald Trump Quotes From the 2016 Election (thoughtco.com)

15 Most Memorable Trump Quotes of 2017 - Craziest Things Donald Said in 2017 (townandcountrymag.com)

The 41 most unreal Donald Trump quotes of 2018 (cnn.com)

Trump's 10 Most Hilariously Stupid Things He Said in 2019 (thenewcivilrightsmovement.com)

Donald Trump's 199 wildest lines of 2019 (cnn.com)

Trump's Weirdest Quotes of 2020 | NowThis (youtube.com)

TO: The Donald: Having a BAD summer vacation

FROM: Kelly: Fast Forward Three-and-a-Half Years

DATE: August 25, 2024

- Gosh, Donald….long-time, no hear. Following the counting of the votes, you kept quite busy trying to keep the votes from being certified. That little insurrection on January 6 was Must-See TV. It even got you impeached again! Then, once you (finally) left the White House (with your hundreds of boxes of purloined documents), I had nowhere to send my weekly missives.
- I also figured you'd be too busy enjoying your retirement to keep up with the likes of ME: golfing at your eponymous resorts; cavorting with the grand-kids at the Mar-a-Lago swimming pool; finally getting to spend some quality time with Melania and Barron after four hectic years of destroying the country. Plus the relief you must have felt at not being convicted by the Senate for a second time would make you want to slow your roll.
- Boy was I wrong! You immediately started campaigning again for the 2024 presidential election (because, hey, you could), all the while bleating that you had absolutely won the 2020 contest. Rally after rally, griping about how the presidency had been stolen from you by evil and corrupt forces and how your low-information supporters could help you Stop the Steal if they would just reach deep into their Social Security pay-outs and help you find the evidence of all this malfeasance.
- And donate they did, but it soon became clear that those funds were required to pay your skyrocketing legal bills. Oh, those indictments! It's so hard to keep track, so I'm sending you a helpful link to a very useful summary (as of last month) from The New York Times: Trump Criminal Cases, Explained: Charges and Status of Each Inquiry - The New York Times (nytimes.com)
- Anyway, you wound up spending a LOT of time trying to stay out of court; being in court; sleeping in court; losing in court; and complaining about all of the above instead of counting the blessings the Good Lord gave you. And speaking of THAT, angels came down to wrap themselves in the American flag on July 13 and save your sorry ass…I mean, ear…from a would-be assassin. Talk about literally dodging a bullet. Almost makes a person believe in miracles.
- Lastly, you got to run in and win a bunch of primaries against Nikki Haley and choose a sympatico running mate from a shallow pool of scoundrels. J.D. Vance used to call you "America's Hitler" and call himself a "Never-Trumper" but you brought him around and into the cult of Project 2025.

- Yeah, you were riding pretty high in the saddle, Donald. You absolutely crushed Joe Biden in your televised debate on June 27 in Atlanta and cruised to your cringe-worthy convention in "horrible" Milwaukee, Wisconsin last month. Everyone left that icky event thinking that you had the election sewn up. You wouldn't even have to try to overturn the results this time!
- But then events took a turn, so to speak. Another miracle! On the other side of the debate, Joe took a few weeks to mull over what the next six months of his life would be like if he had to run against YOU and still be the sitting President. And then what the rest of his life would be like if he lost that race and became responsible for the Ruination of the Free World. I know I'd do just what he did if I'd been in his shoes: let Kamala take that hit!
- Funny thing, though. It appears many Americans seem to like Kamala and her salt-of-the-earth choice for VEEP, Coach Walz. They are nicer, smarter people than you and JD. They're now the IT Couple, packing the stadiums and fairgrounds and raising many hundreds of millions of campaign dollars. And she doesn't even have to siphon off any of that cash to pay her personal attorneys.
- Meanwhile I'm starting to worry about your mental health, DT. Kamala Harris has SO gotten under your skin. You've gone from mocking her laugh, to pretending not to know how to pronounce her name, to professing not even to know who she is. But I guess you've finally been able to identify her well enough to let us know you now you think you are "better looking than Kamala." Ouch! That's really gonna make her lose sleep.
- Donald, we're all in for a few exciting months between now and November 5. I don't know about you, but I can't wait to see how badly Kamala beats you at the polls. And how many people show up to vote for her and then vote "D" all the way down the ballot. And how big the Democratic majorities will be in the House and the Senate. Which will allow us to load up the Supreme Court with justices who don't want to run the country like a Catholic boarding school. Ultimately, the measure of her victory will make it difficult for you to claim that this election was RIGGED! Best of all, when Kamala becomes President, I won't have to worry about reviving our correspondence. As much as I enjoyed our little chats, it was exhausting trying to keep up with your shenanigans week in and week out. I was so happy when Biden won, but I'll be even more JOYFUL when we inaugurate our first female POTUS. I know you'll be up to no good no matter what the outcome, but at least I won't be responsible for pointing out your shortcomings. As I saw on a t-shirt recently: "I can explain it to you, but I can't make you understand it." I'm quitting you, DT. Kelly OUT.

ACKNOWLEDGEMENTS

This publication would not be in your hands without the inspiration and support of the following:

1) My clueless pen-pal, Donald J. Trump. His toxic and narcissistic personality, disdain for any knowledge of domestic or foreign policy, and contempt for the American public provided ample fodder for my weekly commentary. I'm also thankful that he never personally read any of my little memos, so I remain safe in Oregon, and not (yet) in danger of being sent to a cell at the Naval Station Guantanamo Bay Detention Camp in Cuba.

2) My long-suffering husband, Tom, who was compelled to be my first reader and editor every week for four years. He also was solely in charge of the corgis every Screed day and recruited many new victims to my ever-expanding email list.

3) My team at SelfPublishing.com, especially Allison.

4) My talented friends Wayne for taking my photo; and Sonja for drawing a cartoon of Trump for my cover.

5) My faithful and enthusiastic readers, who endured my TMI wonkiness and cheesy doggerel for the duration of the Trump occupation of the White House.

6) Some of my cherished readers died during those years:
Ann M, Ron H, Farid B, Jeremy T, Jill S, Glady B. Peggy M.

   Some have since passed away:
   Jan S, Janet B, Norma G, Harold B, Tom O, Clyde N.

One of those is the first person to whom I sent Volume I, Issue 1: my best friend from the fourth grade, Laura Beth Walker Brown. This was her final feedback for Volume IV, Issue 56:

The Screed for four years is an absolutely extraordinary accomplishment!!! And Congratulations on your PERFECT final Screed!!! PERFECT!!! 👏🖤👏🖤👏🖤👏

I miss you so much, Laura, and hope that, in some incarnation, you will be able to read this book you so tirelessly urged me to produce.

With gratitude to all, Kelly.

Lake Oswego, Oregon

September, 2024

BIBLIOGRAPHY

Section 1: (Mostly) Books About Donald Trump, and More Worthy Topics

[**A Note:** Some of these books are cited in the Weekly Screeds. But many others I read before, during, and after The Donald's Reign of Error. All of them informed my thinking and writing, so I recommend them to you here.]

Section 2: Bible Verses Cited

[**A Note:** Usually from the King James Version, because the Trump Bible was not yet available.]

Section 3: Songs and Poems that Inspired Me

[**A Note:** As I was composing my thoughts, the works listed sprang unbidden into my brain, and stayed there until I mangled them into parodies with which I could mock The Donald and his minions. They were created for entertainment purposes only, and not intended to defame or infringe upon the rights of the original creators. The results are not endorsed or authorized by, nor do they represent the views or opinions of the original artists, creators, or any affiliated parties.]

Section 1: (Mostly) Books

Author	Title	Year	Topic
Alexander, Michelle	The New Jim Crow: Mass Incarceration in the Age of Colorblindness	2010	Race
Almond, Steve	Bad Stories: What the Hell Just Happened to Our Country	2018	Trump
Applebaum, Anne	Red Famine: Stalin's War on Ukraine	2017	Ukraine
Bender, Michael C.	"Frankly, We Did Win This Election": The Inside Story of How Trump Lost	2021	Trump
Bliss, Eula	Having and Being Had	2020	Economics
Blumenthal, Max	Goliath: Life and Loathing in Greater Israel	2013	Middle East
Bolton, John	The Room Where It Happened: A White House Memoir	2020	Trump
Borowitz, Andy	Profiles in Ignorance: How America's Politicians Got Dumb and Dumber	2022	American History
Brody, David & Lamb, Scott	The Faith of Donald Trump: A Spiritual Biography	2018	Trump
Browder, Bill	Red Notice: A True Story of High Finance, Murder, and One Man's Fight for Justice	2015	Russia
Buettner, Russ and Craig, Susanne	Lucky Loser: How Donald Trump Squandered His Father's Fortune and Created the Illusion of Success	2024	Trump
Busse, Ryan	Gunfight: My Battle Against the Industry that Radicalized America	2021	Guns
Campbell, Josh	Crossfire Hurricane: Inside Donald Trump's War on the FBI	2019	Trump
Cheney, Liz	Oath and Honor: A Memoir and a Warning	2023	Trump

Cohen, Brian Tyler	Shameless: Republicans' Deliberate Dysfunction and the Battle to Preserve Democracy	2024	American History
Cohen, Michael	Disloyal, A Memoir: The True Story of the Former Personal Attorney to President Donald J. Trump	2020	Trump
Corn, David	American Psychosis: A Historical Investigation of How the Republican Party Went Crazy	2022	Political Science
Cox, John Woodrow	Children Under Fire: An American Crisis	2021	Guns
Dawes, Daniel E.	150 Years of ObamaCare	2016	Health Care
Department of Justice	The Mueller Report: The Final Report of the Special Counsel into Donald Trump, Russia, and Collusion	2019	Trump
Dershowitz, Alan	Supreme Injustice: How the High Court Hijacked Election 2000	2001	Bush
Desmond, Matthew	Poverty, by America	2023	Political Science
Dias, Elizabeth & Lerer, Lisa	The Fall of Roe: The Rise of a New America	2024	Health Care
Dickens, Charles	A Christmas Carol: In Prose. Being a Ghost Story of Christmas	1843	Novella
Dimmack, Gordon J.	Trumpisms: The Trump-to-English Dictionary	2017	Trump
Dowd, Maureen	The Year of Voting Dangerously: The Derangement of American Politics	2016	Trump
Dr. Seuss	The Cat in the Hat	1957	Poem
Dr. Seuss	How the Grinch Stole Christmas	1957	Poem
Egan, Timothy	A Fever in the Heartland: The Ku Klux Klan's Plot to Take Over America, and the Woman Who Stopped Them	2023	American History
Emerson, Ralph Waldo	The Conduct of Life: A Philosophical Reading	1876	Philosophy
Erdozain, Dominic	One Nation Under Guns: How Gun Culture Distorts Our History and Threatens Our Democracy	2024	Guns

Fauci, Anthony	On Call: A Doctor's Journey in Public Service	2024	Health Care
Foer, Franklin	The Last Politician: Inside Joe Biden's White House and the Struggle for America's Future	2023	Biden
Franken, Al	Giant of the Senate	2017	American History
Franken, Al	Lies and the Lying Liars Who Tell Them: A Fair and Balanced Look at the Right	2003	Political Science
Garrett, Laurie	The Coming Plague: Newly Emerging Diseases in a World Out of Balance	1994	Health Care
Garrett, Laurie	Betrayal of Trust: The Collapse of Global Health Care	2000	Health Care
Gertner, Jon	The Ice at the End of the World: An Epic Journey Into Greenland's Buried Past and Our Perilous Future	2019	Environment
Goodell, Jeff	The Heat Will Kill You First: Life and Death on a Scorched Planet	2023	Environment
Gore, Al	Earth in the Balance	1992	Environment
Gore, Al	An Inconvenient Truth: The Planetary Emergency of Global Warming and What We Can Do About It	2006	Environment
Gorski, Philip S. & Perry, Samuel L.	The Flag + The Cross: White Christian Nationalism and the Threat to American Democracy	2022	Public Policy
Haberman, Maggie	Confidence Man: The Making of Donald Trump and the Breaking of America	2022	Trump
Hannah-Jones, Nikole	The 1619 Project: A New Origin Story	2021	Race
Hill, Marc Lamont & Plitnick, Mitchell	Except for Palestine: The Limits of Progressive Politics	2021	Middle East
Hutchinson, Cassidy	Enough	2023	Trump

Author	Title	Year	Category
Immerwahr, Daniel	How to Hide an Empire: A History of the Greater United States	2019	American History
Isenberg, Nancy	White Trash: The 400-Year Untold History of Class in America	2016	American History
Isikoff, Michael & Corn, David	Russian Roulette: The Inside Story of Putin's War on America and the Election of Donald Trump	2018	Trump
Ivins, Molly & Dubose, Lou	Shrub: The Short but Happy Political Life of George W. Bush	2000	Bush
Ivins, Molly & Dubose, Lou	Bushwacked: Life in George W. Bush's America	2003	Bush
Jacobs, A.J.	The Year of Living Constitutionally: One Man's Humble Quest to Follow The Constitution's Original Meaning	2024	American History
Johnston, David Cay	Free Lunch: How the Wealthiest Americans Enrich Themselves at Government Expense (and Stick You with the Bill)	2007	Economics
Johnston, David Cay	Perfectly Legal: The Covert Campaign to Rig Our Tax System to Benefit the Super Rich – -and Cheat Everybody Else	2005	Economics
Johnston, David Cay	It's Even Worse Than You Think: What the Trump Administration is Doing to America	2018	Trump
Jones, Robert P.	The Hidden Roots of White Supremacy and the Path to a Shared American Future	2023	Race
Katyal, Neal with Koppelman, Sam	Impeach: The Case Against Donald Trump	2019	Trump
Kendi, Ibram X.	How to be an Anti-Racist	2019	Race

Kessler, Glenn & Rizzo, Salvador & Kelly, Meg	Donald Trump and His Assault on Truth: The President's Falsehoods, Misleading Claims and Flat-Out Lies	2020	Trump
Klay, Phil	Redeployment	2014	Military - Fiction
Kozol, Jonathan	An End to Inequality: Breaking Down the Walls of Apartheid Education in America	2024	Political Science
Kristof, Nicholas D. & WuDunn, Sheryl	Tightrope: Americans Reaching for Hope	2020	Public Policy
Landrieu, Mitch	In the Shadows of Statues: A White Southerner Confronts History	2018	Race
Leamer, Laurence	Mar-A-Lago: Inside the Gates of Power at Donald Trump's Presidential Palace	2019	Trump
Lee, Bandy X.	The Dangerous Case of Donald Trump: 27 Psychiatrists and Mental Health Experts Assess a President	2017	Trump
Leibovich, Mark	Thank You for Your Servitude: Donald Trump's Washington and the Price of Submission	2022	Trump
Leonnig, Carol & Rucker, Philip	I Alone Can Fix it: Donald Trump's Catastrophic Final Year	2021	Trump
Lichtman, Allan J	The Case for Impeachment	2017	Trump
Lynas, Mark	Our Final Warning: Six Degrees of Climate Emergency	2020	Environment
Maddow, Rachel	Prelude: An American Fight Against Fascism	2023	American History
Manigault Newman, Omarosa	Unhinged: An Insider's Account of the Trump White House	2018	Trump

Marlantes, Karl	Matterhorn: A Novel of the Vietnam War	2010	Military - Fiction
Matthews, Jason	Red Sparrow	2013	Russia - Fiction
Matthews, Jason	Palace of Treason	2015	Russia - Fiction
Matthews, Jason	The Kremlin's Candidate	2018	Russia - Fiction
McCann, Anthony	Shadowlands: Fear and Freedom at the Oregon Standoff	2019	American History
Moore, Michael	Dude, Where's My Country?	2003	Bush
Moore, Michael	Fahrenheit 9/11	2004	Bush
Murray, Melissa & Weissmann, Andrew	The Trump Indictments: The Historic Charging Documents with Commentary	2024	Trump
Mystal, Elie	Allow Me to Retort: A Black Guy's Guide to the Constitution	2022	Public Policy
Obama, Barack	A Promised Land	2020	Obama
Payne, Keith	The Broken Ladder: How Inequality Affects the Way We Think, Live, and Die	2018	Public Policy
Poe, Edgar Allen	The Masque of the Red Death	1842	Short Story
Pomerantz, Mark	People vs. Donald Trump: An Inside Account	2023	Trump
Reilly, Rick	Commander in Cheat: How Golf Explains Trump	2019	Trump
Rich, Nathaniel	Losing Earth: A Recent History	2019	Environment
Richardson, Heather Cox	Democracy Awakening: Notes on the State of America	2023	Public Policy
Rucker, Philip and Leonnig, Carol	A Very Stable Genius: Donald J. Trump's Testing of America	2020	Trump
Schiff, Adam	Midnight in Washington: How We Almost Lost Our Democracy and Still Could	2021	Trump

Schmidt, Michael	Donald Trump v. The United States: Inside the Struggle to Stop a President	2020	Trump
Seidel, Andrew L.	The Founding Myth: Why Christian Nationalism is Un-American	2019	Public Policy
Select Committee; Remnick, David; Raskin, Jamie	The January 6th Report	2022	Trump
Serwer, Adam	The Cruelty is the Point: The Past, Present, and Future of Trump's America	2021	Trump
Shuster, Simon	The Showman: Inside the Invasion That Shook the World and Made a Leader of Volodymyr Zelensky	2024	Ukraine
Simpson, Glenn & Fritsch, Peter	Crime in Progress: Inside the Steele Dossier and the Fusion GPS Investigation of Donald Trump	2019	Trump
Siskind, Amy	The List: A Week-By-Week Reckoning of Trump's First Year	2018	Trump
Sitaraman, Ganesh & Alstott, Anne L.	The Public Option: How to Expand Freedom, Increase Opportunity, and Promote Equality	2019	Public Policy
Snyder, Timothy	On Tyranny: Twenty Lessons from the Twentieth Century	2017	Political Science
Strzok, Peter	Compromised: Counterintelligence and the Threat of Donald J. Trump	2020	Trump
Swofford, Anthony	Jarhead: A Marine's Chronicle of the Gulf War and Other Battles	2003	Military
Taibbi, Matt	Insane Clown President: Dispatches from the 2016 Circus	2017	Trump
Theroux, Paul	Deep South: Four Seasons on Back Roads	2015	Race
Tirado, Linda	Hand to Mouth: Living in Bootstrap America	2014	Public Policy
Toobin, Jeffrey	Too Close to Call: The thirty-Six-Day Battle to Decide the 2000 Election	2001	Bush

Toobin, Jeffrey	The Nine: Inside the Secret World of the Supreme Court	2007	Public Policy
Towles, Amor	A Gentleman in Moscow	2016	Russia - Fiction
Trudeau, G.B.	YUGE ! 30 Years of Doonesbury on Trump	2016	Trump
Trudeau, G.B.	#SAD ! Doonesbury in the Time of Trump	2018	Trump
Trudeau, G.B.	Former Guy: Doonesbury in the Time of Trumpism	2022	Trump
Trudeau, G.B.	Day One Dictator: More Doonesbury in the Time of Trumpism	2024	Trump
Trump, Donald & Schwartz, Tony	The Art of the Deal	2987	Trump
Trump, Mary L	Too Much and Never Enough: How My Family Created the World's Most Dangerous Man	2020	Trump
Unger, Craig	House of Bush, House of Saud	2004	Bush
Unger, Craig	House of Trump, House of Putin: The Untold Story of Donald Trump and the Russian Mafia	2018	Trump
Vance, J.D.	Hillbilly Elegy: A Memoir of a Family and Culture in Crisis	2016	Economics
Wallace-Wells, David	The Uninhabitable Earth: Life After Warming	2019	Environment
Walter, Barbara F.	How Civil Wars Start and How to Stop Them	2022	Political Science
Watson, Brian T.	Headed Into the Abyss: The Story of Our Time, and the Future We'll Face Paperback	2019	Public Policy
Webb, James	Fields of Fire	1978	Military - Fiction
Wheeler, Shannon	SH*T My President Says: The Illustrated Tweets of Donald J. Trump	2017	Trump
Whitlock, Craig	The Afghanistan Papers	2021	Military

Whitman, James	Hitler's American Model: The United States and the Making of Nazi Race Law	2017	Race
Wilkerson, Isabel	Caste: The Origins of Our Discontents	2020	Race
Wilson, Rick	Everything Trump Touches Dies: A Republican Strategist Gets Real About the Worst President Ever	2018	Trump
Wilson, Rick	Running Against the Devil: A Plot to Save America From Trump - And Democrats From Themselves	2020	Trump
Wolff, Michael	Fire and Fury: Inside the Trump White House	2018	Trump
Wolff, Michael	Siege: Trump Under Fire	2019	Trump
Wolff, Michael	Landslide: The Final Days of the Trump Presidency	2021	Trump
Wolkoff, Stephanie Winston	Melania and Me	2020	Trump
Woodward, Bob	The Last of the President's Men	2015	Nixon
Woodward, Bob	Fear: Trump in the White House	2018	Trump
Woodward, Bob	Rage	2020	Trump
Young, Damon	What Doesn't Kill You Makes You Blacker: A Memoir in Essays	2019	Race
Ziegler, Mary	Roe: The History of a National Obsession	2023	Health Care

Section 2: From the Good Book

Volume/Issue/Page	Topic	Chapter and Verse
I-9 p. 38	Budget Anti-Christ	2 Corinthians 3:17
		Exodus 21:24
		Matthew 5: 38-39
		Matthew 5:9
		Acts 9:25
		Matthew 25: 41-43
II-25 p. 180	Infesting the White House	Romans 13:1
III-6 p. 258	Teleprompter Trump	1 Corinthians 14:34-35
		Ephesians 6: 5-11
		1 Peter 2: 18
		1 Peter 3: 1
III-12 p. 372	Concealer in Chief	Timothy 2:9-10
III-22 p. 292	Let Us Pray	James 5:16
III-49 p. 352	The POTUS Prayer	Matthew 6:9-13
IV-41 p. 462	Regenerated	Exodus 8:21-22

Section 3: Songs and Poems

First Performed by	Title	Year	Composed by	Volume & Issue & Page
Andrews Sisters	*Boogie Woogie Bugle Boy*	1941	Don Raye and Hughie Prince wrote the song for the movie *Buck Privates*	IV-23
Angels	*My Boyfriend's Back*	1963	Bob Feldman, Jerry Goldstein, and Richard Gottehrer wrote the song	IV-20
Baring-Gould, Sabine	*Onward Christian Soldiers*	1865	The Anglican priest wrote the lyrics and Arthur Sullivan wrote new music in 1871	IV-19
Beatles	*Norwegian Wood*	1965	John Lennon & Paul McCartney for the album *Rubber Soul*	III-24
Blondie	*Call Me*	1980	Giorgio Moroder (Music) & Debbie Harry (Lyrics)	I-29
Carey, Mariah	*All I Want for Christmas is You*	1994	Mariah Carey and Walter Afanasieff co-wrote the song for the *Merry Christmas* album	III-52 360

Carmichael, Hoagy	*Georgia on My Mind*	1930	Hoagy Carmichael and Stuart Gorrell wrote the song	IV-49 478
Cast of *The Pirates of Penzance*	*Major General's Song*	1879	W.S. Gilbert (lyrics) & Arthur Sullivan (music) for the comic opera	III-2 250
Charlie Daniels Band	*The Devil Went Down to Georgia*	1979	Written and recorded by the Band for the *Million Mile Reflections* album	IV-49 478
Cole, Nat King	*Unforgettable*	2016	Irving Gordon	I-4 28
Crosby, Bing & the Andrews Sisters	*Don't Fence Me In*	1944	Cole Porter & Robert Fletcher wrote the music and lyrics	IV-22 416
Dr. Suess	*The Grinch Who Stole Christmas*	1957	Theodore Suess Geisel wrote the children's book of the same name	I-23 66
Dylan, Bob	*Subterranean Homesick Blues*	1965	Bob Dylan wrote the music and lyrics	III-36 322
Eberle, Ray (with the Glenn Miller Orchestra)	*Fools Rush In*	1940	Johnny Mercer (lyrics) & Rube Bloom (music)	III-42 334
Gladys Night & the Pips	*Midnight Train to Georgia*	1973	Written by Jim Weatherly and originally titled "Midnight Plane to Houston"	IV-49 478

Greenwood, Lee	*God Bless the USA*	1984	Lee Greenwood	I-37 96
Henson, Jim (as Kermit the Frog)	*The Rainbow Connection*	1979	Paul Williams & Kenneth Ascher wrote the song for *The Muppet Movie*	III-30 310
Holloway, Stanley & Cast	*Get Me to the Church On Time*	1956	Alan Jay Lerner (lyrics) & Frederick Loewe (music) for *My Fair Lady*	IV-21 412
Joel, Billy	*We Didn't Start the Fire*	1989	Billy Joel wrote the song for his album *Storm Front*	II-15 158
Lazarus, Emma	*The New Colossus*	1883	Emma Lazarus authored the poem of the same name	II-2 132
Martha & the Vandellas	*Dancing in the Street*	1964	William Stevenson, Marvin Gaye, and Ivy Jo Hunter wrote the song	II-28 190
Matt Monro	*From Russia With Love*	1963	Lionel Bart (for the James Bond film of the same name)	I-25 70
Moore, Clement Clarke	*A Visit From Saint Nicholas*	1822	Clement Clark Moore authored the poem of the same name	I-49 120
Paige, Elaine	*Memory (from Cats)*	1981	Andrew Lloyd Webber (Music) & Trevor Nunn (Lyrics based on poems by T.S. Eliot)	I-41 104
Peevey, Gayla	*I Want a Hippopotamus for Christmas*	1953	John Rox	I-42 106
Pell, Johnny	*Jingle Bells*	1857	James Lord Pierpont wrote the song for a Thanksgiving church service	II-51 238

Rogers, Ginger	*Embraceable You*	1930	George Gershwin (music) & Ira Gershwin (lyrics)	II-52 240 & IV-55 490
Tabbert, William	*Younger Than Springtime*	1949	Richard Rodgers (music) & Oscar Hammerstein II (lyrics) for *South Pacific*	III-18 284
Unknown, at a banquet for the Saint-Jean Baptiste Society in Quebec	*O Canada* Officially adopted as Canada's national anthem on July 1, 1980	1880	Calixa Lavallee (music) & Sir Adolphe-Basile Routhier (French lyrics). Robert Stanley Weir (English Lyrics - 1908)	I-24 68
Unknown, but most likely by children as a game	*The Twelve Days of Christmas*	1909	Music by Frederic Austin from a folk tune; lyrics from various sources (1780 on)	II-50 236
Unknown, but most likely by Union Army soldiers as a marching song	*Marching Through Georgia*	1865	Henry Clay Work composed the song to commemorate Gen. Sherman's "march to the sea" from Atlanta to Savannah during the Civil War	IV-49 478
White, Tony Joe	*Rainy Night in Georgia*	1969	Tony Joe White wrote the song for his album *Continued*	IV-49 478
Whitter, Henry	*She'll be Coming 'Round the Mountain*	1924	Origins are unknown but this song might have been written by slaves	IV-43 466

INDEX

Section 1: All Things Trump

Section 2: People

Section 3: Places

Section 4: Everything Else

Note: These Indexes are in table form, and list Volume-Issue as well as page numbers (which refer to the first page of the Weekly Screed, but the entry might also be found in the accompanying Resources).

Also, I = Introduction; FF = the Fast Forward memo dated August 25, 2024; and Bib = Bibliography

Section 1: All Things Trump

Topic	Subtopic	Volume	Issue	Page
Access Hollywood Tape		1	45	**112**
		1	46	**114**
		2	18	**166**
		2	32	**200**
		2	40	**216**
		3	15	**278**
Air Force One		2	6	**140**
		2	14	**156**
		3	9	**266**
		4	7	**380**
Alias (John Baron)		1	47	**116**
Apprentice (The)		1	1	**22**
		1	3	**26**
		2	13	**154**
		3	32	**314**
Art of the Deal (The)		2	19	**168**
		3	5	**252**
Baby Blimp		2	28	**190**
		2	42	**220**
		3	23	**252**
Calls to World Leaders		1	4	**28**

Topic	Subtopic	Volume	Issue	Page
		1	30	**80**
		2	13	**154**
		3	39	**328**
		3	41	**332**
		3	46	**344**
		4	10	**386**
		4	22	**416**
		4	37	**452**
Christmas (on)		1	39	**100**
		4	50	**480**
		4	52	**484**
Coloring book		4	25	**426**
		4	26	**428**
Debates		2	18	**166**
		4	40	**460**
		4	41	**462**
		FF		**500**
Executive orders		1	1	**22**
		1	2	**24**
		1	3	**26**
		1	20	**60**
		2	3	**134**
		3	40	**330**
		3	41	**332**
		4	32	**442**
Family				
	Brother (Robert Stewart)	4	33	**444**
	Daughter #1 (Ivana Marie Trump, aka Ivanka)	1	11	**42**
		1	16	**52**
		1	33	**88**
		2	3	**134**
		2	15	**158**
		2	18	**166**
		2	20	**170**
		2	22	**174**
		2	24	**178**
		2	32	**200**
		2	38	**212**

Topic	Subtopic	Volume	Issue	Page
		3	47	**348**
		3	50	**354**
		4	3	**372**
		4	9	**384**
		4	27	**430**
		4	42	**464**
		4	50	**480**
	Daughter #2 (Tiffany Ariana Trump)	3	23	**294**
	Daughter-in-Law (Lara Trump, married to Eric)	3	4	**254**
		4	50	**480**
	Father (Frederick Christ Trump Sr.)	2	22	**174**
		4	29	**436**
	Grandfather (Friedrich Trump); immigrant from Germany	2	25	**180**
		4	10	**386**
	Mother (Mary Anne MacLeod Trump); immigrant from Scotland	2	19	**168**
		4	48	**476**
	Niece (Mary Lea Trump, daughter of Donald's oldest brother, Fred Trump, Jr.)	4	29	**436**
		4	34	**446**
		Bib		
	Sister (Maryanne Trump Barry)	4	29	**436**
		4	24	**422**
	Son #1 (Donald John Trump, Jr., aka DJTJ)	1	26	**72**
		2	15	**158**
		2	27	**186**

Topic	Subtopic	Volume	Issue	Page
		2	44	**224**
		2	50	**236**
		3	15	**278**
		3	16	**280**
		3	23	**294**
		3	25	**298**
		2	44	**224**
		2	50	**236**
		4	9	**384**
		4	35	**448**
		4	42	**464**
		4	50	**480**
	DJTJ Girlfriend Kimberly Guilfoyle	4	35	**448**
	Son #2 (Eric Frederick Trump)	2	42	**220**
		3	23	**294**
		3	25	**298**
		3	50	**354**
		4	42	**464**
		4	50	**480**
	Son #3 (Barron William Trump)	2	33	**202**
		3	37	**324**
		4	49	**478**
		4	50	**480**
		FF		**500**
	Son-in-Law (Jared Kushner, husband of Daughter #1 Ivanka)	1	26	**72**
		1	33	**88**
		1	42	**106**
		2	15	**158**
		2	18	**166**
		2	20	**170**
		2	21	**172**
		2	42	**220**
		4	11	**388**
		4	13	**392**
		4	14	**396**
		4	42	**464**

Topic	Subtopic	Volume	Issue	Page
		4	50	**480**
	Wife #1 (Ivana Marie Zelnickova Trump); mother of Don Jr., Eric, & Ivanka; immigrant from Czechoslovakia	1	30	**80**
		1	34	**90**
		1	38	**98**
	Wife #2 (Marla Ann Maples); mother of Tiffany	1	30	**80**
	Wife #3 (Melania Knauss Trump, born Melanija Knavs); mother of Barron; immigrant from Slovenia, Yugoslavia)	1	7	**34**
		1	19	**58**
		1	22	**64**
		2	5	**138**
		2	17	**164**
		2	25	**180**
		2	27	**186**
		2	38	**212**
		2	48	**232**
		3	1	**248**
		3	27	**304**
		3	37	**324**
		3	44	**340**
		3	50	**354**
		4	6	**378**
		4	7	**380**
		4	35	**448**
		4	37	**454**
		4	50	**480**
		4	52	**484**
		FF		**500**
Firearms		3	17	**282**
Foundation		2	24	**178**
		2	51	**238**
		3	50	**354**

Topic	Subtopic	Volume	Issue	Page
Golf (playing)		1	45	112
		2	4	136
		2	38	212
Golf Clubs & Resorts				
	Trump National Golf Club, Bedminster, NJ	1	29	78
		1	32	86
		1	40	102
	Trump National Doral Golf Club, Miami, FL	3	35	320
		3	42	334
		3	43	338
	Trump National Golf Club Jupiter, FL (formerly the Ritz-Carlton Jupiter)	2	4	136
	Trump National Golf Club, Washington DC, Loudoun County, VA (formerly Lowes Island Golf Club)	2	4	136
	Trump National Golf Club Westchester, Briarcliff Manor, NY	4	41	452
	Trump Turnberry, Scotland	3	36	322
Hair		1	7	34
		2	6	140
		3	10	268
		3	22	292
		4	8	382
		4	29	436
		4	46	472
Hotels	Trump International (Washington DC)	2	6	140
		2	24	178
	Trump Turnberry (Scotland)	3	36	322

Topic	Subtopic	Volume	Issue	Page
Household appliances		3	29	**309**
Hush money payments (Stormy Daniels)		2	5	**138**
		2	10	**148**
		2	11	**150**
		2	12	**152**
		2	14	**156**
		2	17	**164**
		2	18	**166**
		2	50	**236**
		3	5	**256**
		3	19	**286**
		4	34	**448**
Impeachment		1	50	**122**
		2	52	**240**
		3	12	**272**
		3	21	**290**
		3	38	**326**
		3	39	**326**
		3	40	**330**
		3	41	**332**
		3	43	**338**
		3	44	**340**
		3	45	**342**
		3	46	**344**
		3	47	**348**
		3	48	**350**
		3	49	**325**
		3	51	**356**
		3	52	**360**
		4	1	**368**
		4	2	**370**
		4	3	**372**
		4	4	**374**
		4	5	**376**
		4	10	**386**
		4	55	**490**
		4	56	**492**
		Bib		

Topic	Subtopic	Volume	Issue	Page
Lone Ranger		4	27	**430**
Lies (aka lying, mendacity, prevarication) [Note: not an inclusive list of every falsehood. Please see pretty much every page in the book containing a Trump quote.]				
		1	1	**22**
		1	5	**30**
		1	21	**62**
		1	32	**86**
		2	8	**144**
		2	14	**156**
		2	44	**224**
		3	47	**348**
		4	2	**370**
		4	11	**388**
		4	39	**458**
		4	45	**470**
Mar-a-Lago (Palm Beach, Florida)		1	14	**48**
		1	45	**112**
		1	49	**120**
		2	4	**136**
		2	9	**146**
		2	51	**238**
		3	40	**330**
		3	44	**340**
		3	49	**352**
		3	52	**360**
		4	42	**464**
		4	50	**480**
		4	55	**490**
		FF		**500**
		Bib		
Memory		1	41	**104**
Mental acuity		4	30	**438**

Topic	Subtopic	Volume	Issue	Page
Mental health		1	38	**98**
		2	1	**130**
		2	35	**206**
		3	32	**314**
		4	9	**384**
		4	56	**492**
		Bib		
Merchandise		1	27	**74**
		1	50	**122**
		2	6	**140**
		2	27	**186**
		4	25	**426**
		4	50	**480**
Military deferments		2	30	**196**
Military "service"		2	34	**204**
		3	2	**250**
		3	11	**270**
Miss Universe pageant		2	31	**198**
		2	32	**200**
		3	46	**344**
"My African-American" (Gregory Cheadle)		2	32	**200**
Promises (made, kept, broken)		1	1	**22**
		1	15	**50**
		1	23	**66**
		1	28	**76**
		1	43	**108**
		1	45	**112**
		2	4	**136**
		2	44	**224**
		3	14	**246**
		3	20	**288**
		3	24	**296**
		3	46	**344**

Topic	Subtopic	Volume	Issue	Page
		4	43	466
Protests against		1	13	46
		1	14	48
		1	21	62
		1	31	82
		1	37	96
		2	28	190
		2	32	200
		2	35	206
		2	36	208
		3	23	294
		3	33	316
		4	16	402
		4	22	416
		4	23	420
		4	30	438
		4	31	440
		4	34	446
		4	37	452
		4	56	492
Purple Heart		1	40	102
Rallies (Mostly in chronological order)		1	10	40
		1	20	60
	Phoenix, AZ	1	32	86
	Ashburn, VA	1	40	102
	Cincinnati, OH	2	6	140
	Washington, MI	2	18	166
	West Columbia, SC	2	27	186
	Wilkes-Barre, PA	2	31	198
	Redding, CA	2	32	200
	Southaven, MS	2	40	216
	Council Bluffs, IA and Richmond, KY	2	41	218
	Johnstown, PA	2	48	232
	El Paso, TX	3	7	262
	Green Bay, WI	3	18	284
	Orlando, FL (2020 Campaign "Kick-off")	3	25	298

Topic	Subtopic	Volume	Issue	Page
	Greenville, NC	3	29	309
	Cincinnati, OH	3	31	312
	The Villages, FL	3	40	330
	Dallas, TX	3	42	334
	Sunrise, FL	3	48	350
	Battle Creek, MI	3	51	356
	Tulsa, OK	4	25	426
		4	26	428
		4	32	442
	Henderson, NV	4	37	452
	Old Forge, PA	4	46	472
	Valdosta, GA	4	49	478
	Washington DC (Jan 6)	4	55	490
		4	56	492
		FF		500
Tax returns		1	13	46
Terrorism (on)		1	18	56
		1	46	114
		2	51	238
		3	33	316
		3	41	332
		3	42	334
		3	43	338
Trump Tower				
	Istanbul, Turkey	3	41	332
	Meeting (2016 – NYC)	2	7	142
	Moscow	2	48	232
	New York City	1	1	22
		1	7	34
		1	47	116
		2	7	142
		4	31	440
Turkey (the bird)		3	48	350
		4	48	476
Twitter		1	2	24
		1	7	34
		1	10	40

Topic	Subtopic	Volume	Issue	Page
		1	12	**44**
		1	33	**88**
		1	46	**114**
		2	7	**142**
		2	15	**158**
		2	21	**172**
		2	25	**180**
		2	27	**186**
		2	29	**192**
		2	31	**198**
		2	33	**202**
		2	34	**204**
		2	37	**210**
		2	50	**236**
		3	22	**292**
		3	25	**298**
		3	26	**302**
		3	27	**304**
		3	28	**306**
		3	33	**316**
		3	37	**324**
		3	45	**342**
		3	46	**344**
		3	49	**352**
		3	52	**360**
		4	2	**370**
		4	4	**374**
		4	5	**376**
		4	13	**392**
		4	15	**398**
		4	17	**404**
		4	25	**426**
		4	27	**430**
		4	30	**438**
		4	36	**450**
		4	39	**458**
		4	42	**464**
		4	46	**472**
		4	52	**484**
Voting		2	45	**226**

Section 2: People

Name	Volume	Issue	Page
Abu Bakr Al-Baghdadi	3	43	338
Acosta, Jim	2	10	148
	2	27	186
	2	45	226
	4	39	458
Ailes, Roger	1	44	110
Alcindor, Yamiche	4	39	458
Alexander, Lamar	4	5	376
Alexander, Pete	4	39	458
Anderson, John	1	47	474
Ardern, Jacinda	3	12	272
Arpaio, Joseph	1	32	86
Assange, Julian	3	15	278
Atkinson, Michael	3	38	326
Atlas, Scott	4	48	476
Avenatti, Michael	2	14	156
Avruch, Frank	2	12	272
Baertschiger Jr., Herman	3	25	298
Baldwin, Alec	3	4	254
Bale, Christian	4	7	380
Bannon, Steve	1	6	32
	2	15	158
	2	21	172
	4	34	446
Baron, John	1	47	116
Barr, Roseanne	2	13	154
	2	22	174
Barr, William	3	13	274
	3	38	326
	4	3	372
Barrett, Amy Coney	4	39	258

Name	Volume	Issue	Page
Barrett, Wayne	1	48	118
Barry, Maryanne Trump	4	29	436
	4	34	446
Bashar al-Assad	1	12	44
Becker, John	3	20	288
Bee, Samantha	2	22	174
Berman, Geoffrey	4	25	426
Best, Ricky John	1	20	60
Bevin, Matt	3	45	342
Bezos, Jeff	4	17	404
Biden, Hunter	3	38	326
	4	51	482
Biden, Joseph	Intro		11
	FF		500
	3	18	284
	3	29	309
	3	32	314
	3	38	326
	3	40	330
	4	1	368
	4	17	404
	4	33	442
	4	34	446
	4	35	448
	4	38	454
	4	39	458
	4	40	460
	4	41	462
	4	45	470
	4	46	472
	4	48	476
	4	49	478
	4	51	482
	4	54	486
	4	56	492
Birx, Deborah	4	31	440
	4	55	490
Blackwell, Ken	2	49	234
Blumenauer, Earl	2	8	144
Bolsonaro, Jair	4	33	444
Bolton, John	2	20	170

Name	Volume	Issue	Page
	4	4	374
	4	25	426
	4	26	428
	4	37	452
	Bib		
Bonham, James Butler	1	31	82
Booker, Cory	3	18	284
	3	26	302
	3	42	334
	3	52	360
Boquist, Brian	3	25	298
Bornstein, Harold	2	18	166
Borowitz, Andy	1	44	110
	2	9	146
	2	19	168
	2	20	170
	2	48	232
	2	51	238
	3	3	252
	3	10	268
	Bib		
Bossie, David	2	45	226
Bourdain, Anthony	2	23	176
Bright, Rick	4	20	410
Brooks, Mo	4	54	488
Brown, Kate	3	25	298
	4	14	396
Brown, Sherrod	3	32	314
Burnett, Mark	2	13	154
Bush, Billy	1	46	114
	2	15	158
	2	32	200
	2	40	216
Bush, George H.W.	2	48	232
	2	49	234
Bush, George W. (aka Dubya)	1	12	44
	1	32	86
	1	44	110
	2	3	134
	2	37	210

Name	Volume	Issue	Page
	2	40	216
	2	49	234
	3	7	262
	3	28	306
	3	29	308
	4	6	378
	4	13	392
	4	15	398
	4	44	468
	4	46	472
Bush, Jeb	1	44	110
	2	49	234
	4	44	468
Butina, Maria	3	17	282
Buttigieg, Pete	3	18	406
Byrd Jr., James	4	44	468
Calvo, Eddie Baza	1	30	438
Carey, Mariah	3	52	360
Carter, Jimmy	1	47	115
Castro, Julian	3	18	284
	3	26	302
Cavasoglu, Mevlut	3	42	334
Chaffetz, Jason	1	35	320
Chamberlin, Neville	2	29	192
Chance the Rapper	1	44	110
Chauvin, Derek	4	24	422
Chavez, Hugo	4	47	474
Cheadle, Gregory	2	32	200
Chevalier, Maurice	3	18	284
Christian, Jeremiah Joseph	1	20	60
Chun Doo-hwan	1	30	80
Churchill, Winston	4	3	372
Clarno, Bev	4	16	402
Clifford, Stephanie (also see Daniels, Stormy)	2	11	150
Clinton, Hillary	Intro		11
	1	2	24
	1	7	34
	1	12	44
	1	17	54
	1	18	56
	1	25	70

Name	Volume	Issue	Page
	1	33	**88**
	1	40	**102**
	2	3	**134**
	2	5	**138**
	2	18	**166**
	2	43	**222**
	2	45	**226**
	3	15	**278**
	3	16	**280**
	3	20	**288**
	3	25	**298**
	3	38	**326**
	3	43	**338**
	3	50	**354**
	4	46	**472**
	4	56	**492**
Clinton, William Jefferson (Bill)	1	18	**56**
	1	44	**110**
	1	50	**122**
	2	5	**138**
	2	38	**212**
	2	39	**214**
Coats, Dan	3	38	**326**
Cohen, Michael	Bib		
	2	14	**156**
	2	15	**158**
	2	17	**164**
	2	18	**166**
	2	19	**168**
	2	34	**204**
	2	48	**232**
	2	50	**236**
	2	51	**238**
	4	37	**452**
Cohen, Roger	3	25	**298**
Cohn, Roy	2	15	**158**
	4	52	**484**
Colbert, Stephen	1	22	**64**
	1	30	**80**
	1	37	**96**

Name	Volume	Issue	Page
	2	20	170
	2	47	116
	3	4	254
	3	21	290
	3	23	294
	4	12	390
Cole, Nat King	1	4	28
	3	38	326
Cole, Natalie	1	4	28
Comey, James	1	17	54
	1	18	56
	1	21	62
	1	33	88
	2	15	158
	2	17	164
	2	18	166
Conway, George	3	25	298
	3	51	356
Conway, Kellyanne	1	2	24
	2	25	180
	4	3	372
	4	46	472
Copeland, Kenneth	4	13	392
Corker Bob	2	41	218
Cotlar, Seth	3	27	304
Cotton, Tom	4	53	486
Crosby, Bing	3	52	360
Crowley, Monica	1	5	30
Cruz, Ted	2	3	134
	3	33	316
	4	53	486
Cuomo, Andrew	4	14	396
Daniels, Stormy	2	5	138
	2	10	148
	2	11	150
	2	12	152
	2	13	154
	2	14	156
	2	17	164

Name	Volume	Issue	Page
	2	18	**166**
	3	5	**256**
	4	34	**446**
Darroch, Kim	3	28	**306**
Date, S.V.	4	39	**458**
DeClairvaux, Bernard	2	38	**212**
Dershowitz, Alan	4	5	**376**
	Bib		
DeVos, Betsy	1	14	**48**
	1	22	**64**
	2	8	**144**
	2	15	**158**
Dickens, Charles	4	52	**484**
	Bib		
DiGenova, Joseph	2	15	**158**
	4	3	**372**
Dorris, Amy	4	38	**454**
Dowd, John	4	3	**372**
Dr. Seuss (Theodor Seuss Geisel)	1	23	**66**
	2	41	**218**
	Bib		
Dunleavy, Mike	3	9	**266**
Duterte, Rodrigo	3	37	**324**
	4	33	**444**
Dylan, Bob	3	36	**322**
Edison, Thomas	4	4	**374**
Einstein, Albert	4	4	**374**
Eisenhower, Dwight D.	3	6	**258**
	4	24	**422**
Eliot, T.S.	4	56	**492**
Ellis, Jenna	4	47	**474**
Emerson, Ralph Waldo	1	50	**122**
	Bib		
Erdogan, Recep Tayyip	3	37	**324**
	3	42	**334**
	4	33	**444**
Eyre, Eric	1	13	**46**
Falwell, Jerry	1	47	**116**
Fauci, Anthony	Bib		

Name	Volume	Issue	Page
	4	19	**408**
	4	27	**430**
	4	31	**440**
	4	38	**454**
Feinstein, Diane	2	39	**214**
	2	41	**218**
Fletcher, Micah	1	20	**60**
Floyd, George	4	22	**416**
	4	24	**422**
	4	56	**492**
Flynn, Michael (Mike)	1	18	**56**
	1	25	**70**
	1	42	**106**
	1	46	**114**
	2	3	**134**
	2	15	**158**
	3	2	**250**
	3	25	**298**
	4	48	**476**
	4	51	**482**
Foer, Franklin	2	7	**142**
	Bib		
Ford, Christine Blasey	2	39	**214**
	2	40	**216**
Foreman, George	1	26	**72**
Franken, Al	1	21	**62**
	1	44	**110**
	Bib		
Fransen, Jayda	1	46	**114**
Fruman, Igor	3	41	**332**
Furse, Elizabeth	2	26	**182**
Gaetz, Matt	4	35	**448**
Gandhi	1	48	**118**
Garland, Merrick	4	1	**368**
Gates, Bill	3	1	**248**
Gates, Richard	1	42	**106**
Geene, Mariah	4	42	**464**
Giaccio, Francis (Frank)	1	35	**92**

Name	Volume	Issue	Page
Gilbert & Sullivan	3	2	250
Gillibrand, Kirsten	1	44	110
Gingrich, Newt	4	53	486
Ginsburg, Ruth Bader	2	8	144
	4	38	454
Giuliani, Rudy	2	18	166
	2	45	226
	3	4	254
	3	41	332
	4	3	372
	4	46	472
	4	47	474
	4	54	488
Glaspie, April	1	12	44
Gohmert, Louie	4	24	422
	4	53	486
Goldstone, Rob	1	26	72
Goldwater, Barry	1	32	86
	1	38	98
Goodman, John	2	13	154
Gordon, Sue	3	38	326
Gore, Albert (Al)	Bib		
	1	32	86
	1	44	110
	4	44	468
	4	46	472
Gorka, Sebastian	3	10	268
Gorsuch, Neil	1	3	26
	1	49	120
	2	15	156
	3	20	288
Graff, Rhona	1	26	72
Graham, Franklin	3	22	292
Graham, Lindsay	4	3	372
Grant, Ulysses S.	4	22	416
Greenwood, Lee	1	37	96
Grisham, Stephanie	3	50	354
	4	39	458
Guilfoyle, Kimberly	4	35	448
Guthrie, Savannah	4	42	464

Name	Volume	Issue	Page
Hagel, Chuck	4	36	450
Haley, Nikki	1	12	44
	4	35	448
	4	53	486
	FF		500
Hannity, Sean	2	18	166
	4	26	428
Harman, Larry	2	12	152
Harris, Kamala	Intro		
	1	22	64
	2	39	210
	3	18	284
	3	26	302
	4	33	444
	4	34	446
	4	41	462
	4	45	470
	4	55	490
	FF		500
Hickenlooper, John	3	18	284
Hicks, Hope	2	8	144
	2	14	156
	4	40	460
Hitler, Adolph	2	29	192
	2	43	222
	3	7	262
	FF		500
Hoover, Larry	2	41	218
Hovis, Barry	3	20	288
Hussein, Saddam	1	12	44
Huston, Jack	4	45	472
Hyde-Smith, Cindy	2	48	232
Iger, Bob	2	22	292
Inslee, Jan	3	18	284
	4	10	386
Ivey, Kay	3	36	322
Ivins, Molly	2	29	192
	Bib		
Jackson, Ronny	2	17	164
Jarrett, Valerie	2	22	174

Name	Volume	Issue	Page
Jefferson, Thomas	4	22	416
Jesus	1	9	38
	1	19	58
	1	47	116
	2	10	148
	3	12	272
	4	13	392
	4	21	412
	4	54	488
Joel, Billy	2	15	158
	3	18	284
John, Richard R.	4	15	398
Johnson, Boris	3	23	294
Johnson, LaDavid	1	40	102
Johnson, Lyndon B.	4	32	442
Johnston, David Cay	2	4	136
	Bib		
Jones, Steve	4	19	408
Judge, Mark	2	40	216
Juncker, Jean-Claude	2	30	196
Kaepernick, Colin	1	37	96
Kagan, Elena	4	44	468
Kalashnikov, Mikhail	2	7	142
Karman, Tawakkol	1	12	44
Kavanaugh, Brett	2	39	214
	2	40	216
	2	41	218
	2	43	222
	2	44	224
	2	52	240
	3	38	326
	4	33	444
	4	44	468
Kelly, John Francis	1	29	78
	4	36	450
Kelly, Megyn	2	32	200
Kennan, George	2	29	192
Kennedy, Anthony	2	26	302
Kennedy, John F. (JFK)	2	29	192

Name	Volume	Issue	Page
Kennedy Onassis, Jacqueline	1	47	**116**
	4	22	**416**
Kennedy, Lisa	3	46	**344**
Kerry, John	2	49	**234**
	4	34	**446**
Khashoggi, Jamal Ahmad	2	47	**230**
	3	26	**302**
Khruschev, Nikita	2	29	**192**
Kilmeade, Brian	3	47	**348**
Kim Jong Un	1	30	**80**
	2	1	**130**
	2	15	**158**
	2	20	**170**
	2	23	**176**
	2	43	**222**
	3	1	**248**
	3	9	**266**
	3	25	**298**
	3	32	**314**
	3	35	**320**
	4	33	**444**
Klobuchar, Amy	3	52	**360**
Kristof, Nicholas	1	20	**60**
	Bib		
Kunstler, James Howard	1	28	**76**
Kushner, Jared	1	26	**72**
	1	33	**88**
	1	42	**106**
	2	15	**158**
	2	18	**166**
	2	20	**170**
	2	21	**172**
	2	42	**220**
	4	11	**388**
	4	13	**392**
	4	14	**396**
	4	42	**464**
	4	50	**480**
LaPierre, Wayne	3	17	**317**
Lazarus, Emma	2	2	**132**

Name	Volume	Issue	Page
Leahy, Patrick	3	43	338
Lee, Bandy X.	1	38	98
	Bib		
Leeds, Jessica	2	22	174
Leonnig, Carol D.	4	4	374
	Bib		
Letterman, David	1	50	122
	2	31	198
Lewinsky, Monica	1	42	106
	1	44	110
Lewis, John	4	32	442
Li Jiang	2	27	186
Limbaugh, Rush	4	6	378
Lin, Jennifer	2	22	174
Lindell, Mike	3	10	268
	4	47	474
Loeffler, Kelly	4	49	478
	4	53	486
Louis-Dreyfus, Julia	4	34	446
Machado, Alicia	2	32	200
MacLeod, Mary Anne Trump	2	19	168
Macron, Emmanuel	1	19	58
Maddow, Rachel	1	1	22
	3	26	302
	3	51	356
	4	3	372
	4	37	452
	Bib		
Manafort, Paul	1	42	106
Manigault-Newman, Omarosa	2	32	200
	2	33	202
	Bib		
Maples, Marla	1	30	80
Markovic, Dusko	1	19	58
Mattarella, Sergio	3	42	334
Matthews, Chris	2	26	182
Matthews, Jason	2	29	192
	Bib		
Mattis, James N.	1	22	64
	2	15	158

Name	Volume	Issue	Page
	2	51	238
	3	2	250
Maxwell, Ghislaine	4	30	438
	4	32	442
May, Theresa	1	46	114
McCabe, Andrew	2	11	150
McCain, John	1	40	102
	2	13	154
	2	29	192
	2	34	204
	2	35	206
	3	11	270
	4	36	450
	4	56	492
McCarthy, Kevin	4	53	486
McCaskill, Claire	4	5	376
McCloskey, Patty	4	35	448
McConnell, Mitch	2	41	218
	4	1	368
	4	53	486
McDaniel, Ronna	3	23	294
McEnany, Kayleigh	4	39	458
McGahn, Don	2	4	136
McGuire, Joseph	3	38	326
	3	39	328
McMaster, H.R.	2	11	150
	3	2	250
McNamara, Robert	2	7	140
McSally, Martha	4	53	486
Meadows, Mark	4	26	428
	4	35	448
Merkel, Angela	2	27	186
Merkley, Jeff	1	11	42
	1	23	66
	2	8	144
	4	33	444
Merlino, Victoria	3	51	356
Meyers, Seth	1	38	98
	2	39	214
	2	40	216

Name	Volume	Issue	Page
	2	46	**228**
	3	3	**252**
Michael the Black Man (Maurice Woodside; aka Michael Symonette and Mikel Israel)	1	32	**86**
Miles, Ken	4	7	**380**
Miller, Stephen	1	33	**66**
	2	21	**172**
	3	35	**320**
	4	11	**388**
Miranda, Lin Manuel	2	18	**166**
Mitsotakis, Kyriakos	4	2	**370**
Mnuchin, Steve	2	15	**158**
	3	19	**286**
Mohammed bin Salman	2	52	**240**
	3	26	**302**
Moore, Michael	Intro		**11**
	Bib		
	2	42	**220**
Mueller, Robert	1	18	**56**
	1	33	**88**
	1	41	**104**
	1	42	**106**
	1	50	**122**
	2	4	**136**
	2	7	**142**
	2	10	**148**
	2	11	**150**
	2	12	**152**
	2	14	**156**
	2	15	**158**
	2	18	**166**
	2	21	**172**
	2	23	**176**
	2	25	**180**
	2	34	**204**
	2	36	**208**
	2	39	**214**
	2	48	**232**

Name	Volume	Issue	Page
	2	52	**240**
	3	4	**254**
	3	12	**272**
	3	13	**274**
	3	16	**280**
	3	19	**286**
	3	23	**294**
	3	30	**310**
	3	32	**314**
	3	38	**326**
	3	51	**356**
	4	37	**452**
	4	56	**492**
	Bib		
Mulvaney, Mick	2	50	**236**
	3	42	**334**
Murdoch, Rupert	2	17	**164**
Musk, Elon	4	4	**374**
Namkai-Meche, Taliesin Myrddin	1	20	**60**
Nauert, Heather	2	23	**176**
Navarro, Peter	2	21	**172**
Nero	4	34	**446**
Newsom, Gavin	4	35	**448**
Nixon, Richard	1	8	**36**
	1	18	**56**
	2	3	**134**
	2	16	**162**
	2	33	**200**
	2	35	**206**
	3	4	**254**
	3	51	**356**
Noah, Trevor	2	39	**214**
	3	7	**262**
	4	12	**390**
North, Oliver	3	17	**282**
Nunberg, Sam	2	10	**148**
Nunes. Devin	4	3	**372**
Obama, Barack	Intro		**11**

Name	Volume	Issue	Page
	Bib		
	1	2	**24**
	1	4	**28**
	1	7	**34**
	1	9	**38**
	1	10	**40**
	1	11	**42**
	1	12	**44**
	1	15	**50**
	1	18	**56**
	1	19	**58**
	1	21	**62**
	1	34	**90**
	1	37	**96**
	1	40	**102**
	1	47	**116**
	2	3	**134**
	2	4	**136**
	2	5	**138**
	2	7	**142**
	2	8	**144**
	2	9	**146**
	2	10	**148**
	2	11	**150**
	2	12	**152**
	2	15	**158**
	2	18	**166**
	2	19	**168**
	2	21	**172**
	2	34	**204**
	2	37	**210**
	2	40	**216**
	2	47	**230**
	3	3	**252**
	3	7	**262**
	3	8	**264**
	3	14	**276**
	3	28	**306**
	3	31	**312**
	3	36	**322**

Name	Volume	Issue	Page
	3	43	**338**
	3	46	**344**
	3	51	**354**
	3	52	**360**
	4	1	**368**
	4	6	**378**
	4	14	**396**
	4	20	**410**
	4	22	**416**
	4	23	**420**
	4	25	**426**
	4	26	**428**
	4	32	**442**
	4	34	**446**
	4	37	**452**
	4	44	**468**
	4	45	**470**
Obama, Michelle	2	48	**232**
	4	16	**402**
	4	34	**446**
	4	35	**448**
	4	52	**484**
Ocasio Cortez, Alexandria	3	29	**308**
O'Connor, Sandra Day	1	32	**86**
O'Donnell, Lawrence	1	38	**98**
	2	7	**142**
Oliver, John	4	12	**390**
	4	26	**428**
Omar, Ilhan	3	12	**272**
	3	29	**308**
O'Reilly, Bill	1	44	**110**
O'Rourke, Beto	3	18	**284**
Packwood, Bob	2	27	**186**
Page, Carter	2	21	**172**
Papadopoulos, George	1	42	**106**
Parnas, Lev	3	41	**332**
Patrick, Danica	4	7	**380**
Pena, Enrique	1	29	**78**
Pence, Michael (Mike)	1	22	**64**
	1	33	**88**

Name	Volume	Issue	Page
	1	42	106
	1	46	114
	2	5	138
	2	8	144
	2	15	158
	2	50	236
	2	52	240
	3	15	278
	3	36	322
	3	42	334
	3	51	356
	4	3	372
	4	9	384
	4	19	408
	4	21	412
	4	22	416
	4	25	426
	4	26	428
	4	33	444
	4	35	448
	4	41	462
	4	45	470
	4	53	486
	4	54	488
	4	56	492
Perdue, David	4	49	478
	4	53	486
Perry, Rick	1	22	64
	2	15	158
	2	16	162
	4	3	372
Pierce, Charlie	1	26	72
	1	32	86
	3	49	352
	4	37	452
	4	44	468
Pirro, Jeanine	3	12	272
Pitlyk, Sarah	3	49	352
Podesta, John	3	15	278
Poe, Edgar Allen	4	28	434

Name	Volume	Issue	Page
	Bib		
Pompeo, Mike	2	11	**150**
	4	3	**372**
Pope Francis	1	19	**58**
Powell, Sidney	4	47	**474**
Pressley, Ayanna	3	29	**308**
Price, Thomas (Tom)	1	22	**64**
	1	28	**76**
	1	37	**96**
	2	15	**158**
Priebus, Reince	1	6	**32**
	1	28	**76**
	1	33	**88**
	2	21	**172**
Pruitt, Scott	1	14	**48**
	1	22	**64**
	2	15	**158**
	2	16	**162**
Putin, Vladimir	1	18	**56**
	1	25	**70**
	1	29	**78**
	1	49	**120**
	2	7	**142**
	2	11	**150**
	2	13	**154**
	2	23	**174**
	2	28	**190**
	2	29	**192**
	2	31	**198**
	2	48	**232**
	2	52	**240**
	3	1	**248**
	3	15	**278**
	3	17	**282**
	3	26	**302**
	3	31	**312**
	3	34	**318**
	3	37	**324**
	3	42	**334**

Name	Volume	Issue	Page
	4	26	**428**
	4	27	**430**
	4	30	**438**
	4	33	**444**
Puzder, Andrew	1	5	**30**
Raffensperger, Brad	4	53	**486**
	4	54	**488**
Rand, Paul	2	6	**140**
	2	41	**218**
	2	51	**238**
Ratcliffe, John	3	38	**326**
Rather, Dan	2	34	**204**
Raven, Julian	3	10	**268**
Rayburn, Sam	1	31	**82**
Reagan, Ronald	1	47	**116**
	2	13	**154**
	2	26	**182**
	3	3	**252**
	3	5	**256**
	3	7	**262**
	3	10	**268**
	3	11	**270**
	3	20	**288**
	3	37	**324**
	3	44	**340**
Rittenhouse, Kyle	4	47	**474**
Robinson, Eugene	4	24	**422**
Rock, Chris	3	32	**314**
	4	45	**470**
Rodgers & Hammerstein	3	18	**284**
Rodman, Dennis	3	49	**352**
Rosen, James	3	49	**352**
Rosenstein, Rod	1	18	**56**
	2	11	**150**
	2	15	**158**
	3	13	**274**
Ross, Wilbur	3	4	**254**
Rove, Karl	4	53	**486**
Rubio, Marco	4	53	**486**
Ruckelshaus, William	2	16	**280**

Name	Volume	Issue	Page
Rucker, Philip	4	4	374
	Bib		
Ryan, Paul	1	15	50
Sanders, Bernie	1	11	42
	1	22	64
	3	52	360
Sanders, Sarah Huckabee	1	46	114
	2	10	148
	2	15	158
	3	4	254
	3	15	278
	4	15	398
	4	39	458
Sayoc, Cesar	2	43	222
Scalia, Antonin	4	1	368
Scalise, Steve	4	35	448
Scaramucci, Anthony	1	28	76
	1	33	88
Schiff, Adam	Bib		
	3	45	342
	3	46	344
	3	48	350
	4	4	374
Schleifer, Leonard	4	41	462
Schmidt, Michael	Bib		
	4	37	452
Schrader, Kurt	3	39	328
Schumer, Chuck	3	1	248
	4	1	368
	4	38	454
Schwarzenegger, Arnold	1	3	26
Scott, Rick	4	53	486
Scott, Tim	4	35	448
Sekulow, Jay	2	12	152
	4	3	372
Sessions, Jefferson Beauregard (Jeff)	1	14	48
	1	22	64
	1	28	76
	1	42	106
	2	15	158

Name	Volume	Issue	Page
	2	22	**174**
	2	25	**180**
	2	46	**228**
Shakespeare	2	29	**192**
Shepard, Matthew	4	44	**468**
Sinatra, Frank	3	4	**254**
	3	42	**334**
	4	21	**412**
Siskind, Amy	2	31	**198**
	2	41	**218**
	Bib		
Slonso, Cristy Montesinos	4	42	**464**
Smith, David	4	27	**430**
Soleimani, Qasem	4	2	**370**
Solzhenitsyn, Alexandr	4	37	**452**
Sondland, Gordon	3	47	**348**
Soros, George	2	44	**224**
Souza, Pete	2	33	**202**
Spacey, Kevin	1	44	**110**
Spicer, Sean	1	1	**22**
	1	2	**24**
	1	28	**76**
	4	39	**458**
Stahl, Lesley	1	8	**36**
	2	42	**220**
Stalin, Joseph	3	10	**268**
Starr, Ken	1	44	**110**
	2	39	**214**
Steel, Michelle	4	53	**486**
Stephanopoulos, George	3	24	**296**
	4	38	**454**
Stern, Howard	2	34	**204**
Steyer, Tom	2	52	**240**
Stone, Roger	3	4	**254**
	3	15	**278**
Strzok, Peter	4	37	**452**
	Bib		
Suetonius	4	34	**446**
Swalwell, Timothy	3	18	**284**
Swan, Jonathan	4	32	**442**

Name	Volume	Issue	Page
Taibbi, Matt	2	12	**152**
	Bib		
Thunberg, Greta	3	50	**354**
Tillerson, Rex	1	12	**44**
	1	25	**70**
	1	38	**98**
	2	11	**150**
	2	15	**158**
	4	8	**382**
Tlaib, Rashida	3	29	**308**
Toensing, Victoria	4	3	**372**
Tomczyk, Keith	4	25	**426**
Trudeau, Justin	1	24	**68**
	1	39	**100**
Trump, Barron	2	33	**202**
	3	37	**324**
	4	49	**478**
	4	50	**480**
	FF		**500**
Trump, Donald J. (see Trump Index)			*Every*
Trump, Jr., Donald J.	1	26	**72**
	2	15	**158**
	2	27	**190**
	3	13	**274**
	3	15	**278**
	3	16	**280**
	3	23	**294**
	3	25	**298**
	3	44	**340**
	3	50	**354**
	4	9	**384**
	4	35	**448**
	4	42	**464**
	4	50	**480**
Trump, Eric Frederick	2	42	**220**
	3	23	**294**
	3	25	**298**
	3	50	**354**
	4	42	**464**

Name	Volume	Issue	Page
	4	50	480
Trump Frederick Christ	2	22	174
Trump, Friedrich	2	25	180
Trump, Ivana Marie Zelnickova	1	30	80
	1	34	90
	1	38	98
Trump, Ivana Marie (aka Ivanka)	1	16	52
	1	33	88
	2	3	134
	2	15	158
	2	18	166
	2	20	170
	2	22	174
	2	24	178
	2	32	200
	2	38	212
	3	47	348
	3	50	354
	4	3	372
	4	9	384
	4	27	430
	4	42	464
	4	50	480
Trump, Lara Lea	3	4	254
	4	50	480
Trump, Mary Anne MacLeod	2	19	168
Trump, Maryanne (see Barry, Maryanne Trump)			
Trump, Mary Lea	4	29	436
	4	34	446
	Bib		
Trump, Melania Knauss	1	7	34
	1	19	58
	1	22	64
	2	5	138
	2	17	164
	2	25	180
	2	27	186
	2	38	212
	2	48	232

Name	Volume	Issue	Page
	3	1	248
	3	27	304
	3	37	324
	3	44	340
	3	50	354
	4	6	378
	4	7	380
	4	35	448
	4	37	454
	4	50	480
	4	52	484
	FF		500
Trump, Robert Stewart	4	33	444
Trump, Tiffany Ariana	3	23	294
Turnbull, Malcolm	1	16	52
	1	29	78
Twain, Mark	2	4	136
	2	44	224
	4	3	372
Urquiza, Kristen	4	34	446
Urquiza, Mark	4	34	446
Varadkar, Leo	2	11	150
	3	23	294
Veselnitskaya, Natalia	1	26	72
	2	7	142
Viola, Vincent	1	5	30
Walden, Greg	3	17	282
Warren, Elizabeth	3	26	302
	3	38	326
	3	52	360
Wayne, John	3	25	298
Webber, Andrew Lloyd	1	41	104
Weinstein, Harvey	1	39	100
	1	44	110
West, Kanye	2	18	166
	2	41	218
Whaley, Nan	3	32	314
Wheeler, Ted	4	35	448
Williams, Townsend	4	6	378
Wilson, Rick	3	4	252

Name	Volume	Issue	Page
	3	9	266
	Bib		
Wolff, Michael	2	1	130
	2	4	136
	2	7	142
	Bib		
Wolkoff, Stephanie Winston	4	37	452
	4	52	484
	Bib		
Woodward, Bob	2	45	226
	4	37	252
	Bib		
Wray, Christopher	3	24	296
Xi Jinping	3	7	262
Yang, Andrew	3	51	256
Yates, Sally	1	3	26
	2	22	174
Yovanovitch, Marie	3	41	332
	3	46	344
Zelensky, Volodymyr	3	38	326
	3	39	328
	3	41	332
	3	46	344
	4	56	492
Zinke, Ryan	2	16	162
	2	50	236
Zucker, Arianne	2	40	216

Section 3: Places

Country	State/Region	City	Vol.	Iss.	Page
Afghanistan			1	44	**110**
			2	15	**158**
			2	21	**172**
Belgium			2	5	**138**
		Brussels	2	28	**190**
Canada			1	10	**40**
			1	24	**68**
			1	43	**108**
			2	12	**152**
			3	5	**256**
			3	29	**308**
			4	11	**388**
Democratic Republic of the Congo (DRC)			I		**11**
			4	46	**472**
		Kisangani	I		**11**
			4	46	**472**
Denmark			2	5	**138**
			3	34	**318**
France			2	5	**138**
			2	17	**164**
			2	23	**176**
			3	23	**294**
			4	25	**426**
			4	36	**450**
		Paris	1	6	**32**
Finland			2	5	**138**
			2	28	**190**
			2	45	**226**
		Helsinki	2	28	**190**
			2	29	**192**
Gaza			2	20	**170**
Germany			2	5	**138**
			2	23	**176**
			2	25	**180**
			2	28	**190**

Country	State/Region	City	Vol.	Iss.	Page
			3	29	**308**
			3	41	**332**
		Hamburg	1	25	**70**
Greenland			3	23	**294**
			3	34	**318**
		Nuuk	3	34	**318**
Guam (USA)			1		**11**
			1	30	**80**
			2	1	**130**
			2	14	**156**
			4	46	**472**
Honduras			2	44	**224**
Iran			1	39	**100**
			2	14	**156**
			2	19	**168**
			2	20	**170**
			3	5	**256**
			3	25	**298**
			3	28	**306**
			3	35	**320**
			4	2	**370**
Iraq			2	21	**172**
			3	34	**318**
			3	42	**334**
			4	2	**370**
			4	13	**392**
			4	15	**398**
Israel			1	19	**58**
			2	20	**170**
			3	25	**298**
		Jerusalem	2	20	**170**
Japan			1		**11**
			1	10	**40**
			1	37	**96**
			2	1	**130**
			2	6	**140**
			2	14	**156**
			3	8	**264**
			3	11	**270**
			3	21	**288**

Country	State/Region	City	Vol.	Iss.	Page
			3	26	**302**
			3	45	**342**
		Okinawa	I		**11**
			3	11	**270**
			3	48	**350**
			4	36	**450**
Korea			1	14	**48**
			3	8	**264**
		Demilitarized Zone (DMZ)	3	26	**302**
	North Korea (NoKo)		1	36	**94**
			1	38	**98**
			1	39	**100**
			2	14	**156**
			2	17	**164**
			2	18	**166**
			2	20	**170**
			2	23	**176**
			2	24	**178**
			2	42	**220**
			3	1	**248**
			3	5	**256**
			3	21	**290**
			3	24	**422**
			3	25	**426**
			3	35	**320**
		Pyongyang	1	30	**80**
			2	24	**178**
			3	9	**266**
	South Korea		I		**11**
			1	30	**80**
			2	1	**130**
			2	3	**134**
			2	10	**148**
			2	14	**156**
			2	20	**170**
			3	5	**256**
		Incheon	1	30	**80**
		Seoul	1	30	**80**

Country	State/Region	City	Vol.	Iss.	Page
Mexico			1	2	24
			1	29	78
			2	14	156
			2	26	182
			3	5	256
			3	14	276
			3	20	288
			3	22	292
			4	11	388
			4	25	426
			4	26	428
Montenegro			1	19	58
			3	1	248
Namibia			1	36	94
New Zealand			3	11	270
			3	12	272
Niger			1	40	102
			2	21	172
			4	36	450
Nigeria			2	14	156
Norway			2	2	132
			2	5	138
			3	24	296
			4	6	378
Puerto Rico (USA)			1	37	96
			1	38	98
			2	37	210
			2	41	218
			3	35	320
			4	56	492
Russia			1	2	24
			1	7	34
			1	13	46
			1	17	54
			1	18	56
			1	24	68
			2	3	134
			2	4	136

Country	State/Region	City	Vol.	Iss.	Page
			2	7	142
			2	11	150
			2	12	152
			2	13	154
			2	15	**158**
			2	17	**164**
			2	18	**166**
			2	21	**172**
			2	23	**176**
			2	25	**180**
			2	26	**182**
			2	28	**190**
			2	29	**192**
			2	35	**206**
			2	37	**210**
			2	42	**220**
			2	48	**232**
			3	1	**248**
			3	3	**252**
			3	5	**256**
			3	8	**264**
			3	12	**272**
			3	13	**274**
			3	15	**178**
			3	16	**280**
			3	17	**282**
			3	19	**286**
			3	24	**296**
			3	26	**302**
			3	27	**304**
			3	30	**310**
			3	39	**328**
			3	42	**334**
			3	46	**344**
			3	51	**356**
			4	5	**376**
			4	8	**382**
			4	9	**384**
			4	18	**406**

Country	State/Region	City	Vol.	Iss.	Page
			4	26	**428**
			4	27	**430**
			4	30	**438**
			4	39	**458**
			4	51	**482**
			4	56	**492**
Saudi Arabia			1	19	**58**
			2	47	**230**
			3	12	**272**
			3	25	**298**
			3	26	**302**
Singapore			2	23	**176**
			2	24	**178**
Somalia			2	21	**172**
			3	36	**322**
Sweden			1	6	**32**
			2	5	**138**
Switzerland			2	5	**138**
			3	35	**320**
		Davos	2	5	**138**
Syria			1	2	**24**
			1	6	**32**
			1	12	**44**
			2	14	**156**
			2	51	**238**
			3	41	**332**
			3	42	**334**
			3	43	**338**
Turkey			3	20	**288**
			3	26	**302**
			3	41	**332**
			3	42	**334**
			4	48	**476**
		Istanbul	3	26	**302**
			3	41	**332**
Ukraine			2	23	**174**
			2	29	**192**
			2	40	**216**
			3	38	**326**
			3	39	**328**

Country	State/Region	City	Vol.	Iss.	Page
			3	40	**330**
			3	41	**332**
			3	42	**334**
			3	45	**342**
			3	46	**344**
			3	49	**352**
			4	3	**372**
			4	4	**374**
			4	5	**376**
			4	10	**386**
			4	37	**452**
			4	51	**482**
			4	56	**492**
	Crimea		2	29	**192**
United Arab Emirates (UAE)			2	5	**138**
		Dubai	1	35	**92**
United Kingdom (UK)			1	46	**114**
			2	5	**138**
			2	13	**154**
			2	28	**190**
			3	8	**264**
			3	23	**294**
			3	28	**306**
		London	2	11	**150**
			2	28	**190**
			2	36	**208**
			3	15	**278**
			3	23	**294**
United States of America (USA)					
	Alabama		1	45	**112**
			1	48	**118**
			3	10	**268**
			3	25	**298**
			3	36	**322**
			3	45	**342**
			4	21	**412**
	Alaska		I		**11**

Country	State/Region	City	Vol.	Iss.	Page
			1	34	90
			3	9	266
			3	34	318
			3	36	322
			4	21	412
		Anchorage	1	34	90
		Fairbanks	3	21	290
	Arizona		I		11
			1	32	86
			2	10	148
			4	17	404
			4	29	436
			4	31	440
		Glendale	1	32	86
		Phoenix	1	32	86
			4	34	446
	California		1	44	110
			2	26	182
			3	44	340
			4	10	386
			4	35	448
			4	53	486
		Gilroy	3	31	312
		Los Angeles	2	26	182
		Redding	2	32	200
		San Francisco	1	47	116
			2	26	182
		Stockton	2	7	142
		Thousand Oaks	3	32	314
	Colorado		I		11
			2	26	182
			3	43	338
			4	24	422
		Denver	1	31	82
			1	44	110
			4	24	422
	District of Columbia	Washington	4	55	490
			4	56	492
			FF		500

Country	State/Region	City	Vol.	Iss.	Page
	Florida		1	34	**90**
			1	34	**90**
			1	44	**110**
			2	4	**136**
			2	7	**142**
			2	8	**144**
			2	35	**206**
			2	41	**218**
			2	48	**232**
			2	49	**234**
			3	35	**320**
			3	40	**330**
			3	44	**340**
			3	48	**350**
			4	10	**386**
			4	14	**396**
			4	15	**398**
			4	17	**404**
			4	21	**412**
			4	31	**440**
			4	35	**448**
			4	40	**450**
			4	44	**468**
			4	50	**480**
			4	54	**488**
		Mar-a-Lago (see Trump Index)			
		Orlando	3	25	**298**
		Sunrise	3	48	**350**
		The Villages	3	40	**330**
	Georgia		3	20	**288**
			4	24	**422**
			4	50	**480**
			4	53	**486**
			4	54	**488**
		Valdosta	4	49	**478**
	Hawaii		2	10	**148**
	Idaho		3	20	**288**
			3	25	**298**

Country	State/Region	City	Vol.	Iss.	Page
			4	44	**468**
	Illinois		1	47	**116**
			4	18	**406**
		Chicago	1	21	**62**
			2	12	**152**
			2	48	**232**
			4	30	**438**
		East St. Louis	4	18	**406**
	Indiana		I		**11**
			2	7	**142**
			2	35	**206**
			4	9	**384**
		Bloomington	2	35	**206**
		Evansville	2	35	**206**
		Indianapolis	3	17	**282**
			3	18	**284**
		Madison	2	35	**206**
	Iowa	Council Bluffs	2	41	**218**
	Kansas		4	5	**376**
			4	18	**406**
		Kansas City	4	5	**376**
	Kentucky	Richmond	2	41	**218**
	Louisiana		3	47	**348**
			4	24	**422**
			4	35	**448**
		New Orleans	3	28	**306**
			3	31	**312**
			3	51	**356**
	Massachusetts	Boston	I		**11**
			3	12	**272**
			3	29	**308**
			3	52	**360**
	Michigan				
		Battle Creek	2	18	**166**
		Detroit	3	29	**308**
		Washington	2	18	**166**
	Mississippi		1	32	**86**
		Biloxi	2	48	**232**
		Southaven	2	40	**216**
	Missouri		3	20	**288**

Country	State/Region	City	Vol.	Iss.	Page
			4	5	376
		Kansas City	4	5	376
			2	26	182
	Nevada		2	13	154
		Henderson	4	37	452
		Las Vegas	1	43	108
			2	38	212
			4	25	426
	New York		I		11
			2	24	178
			2	26	182
			2	30	196
			3	50	354
			4	14	396
			4	18	406
		Jamaica Estates	3	51	356
		New York City	2	2	132
			3	2	250
			3	29	308
			4	14	396
			4	21	412
			4	30	438
		Queens	1	35	92
			3	51	354
	North Carolina	Greenville	3	29	318
	Oklahoma	Tulsa	4	25	426
			4	26	428
			4	32	442
	Ohio		2	6	140
			2	35	206
			3	20	288
			3	32	314
			4	44	468
		Cincinnati	2	6	140
		Cleveland	2	45	226
		Dayton	3	31	312
			3	32	314
	Oregon		I		11
			1	1	22
			1	5	30

Country	State/Region	City	Vol.	Iss.	Page
			1	21	62
			1	24	68
			2	26	182
			2	36	206
			2	38	212
			2	42	218
			2	46	228
			3	14	276
			3	33	316
			3	48	350
			4	14	396
			4	15	398
			4	16	402
			4	20	410
			4	44	468
		Burns	3	35	320
		Dallas	3	25	298
		Enterprise	1	10	40
		Grants Pass	3	25	298
		Harney County	3	35	320
		Imbler	3	17	282
		John Day	3	35	320
		McMinnville	3	33	316
		Ontario	1	31	82
		Oregon Outback	1	5	30
		Pendleton	1	5	30
		Portland	1	20	60
			1	24	68
			2	12	152
			2	46	228
			3	3	252
			3	33	316
			4	29	436
			4	30	438
			4	35	448
		Salem	3	27	430
			3	33	316
		Silverton	3	33	316

Country	State/Region	City	Vol.	Iss.	Page
		Silvies Valley Ranch	3	35	**320**
	Pennsylvania				
		Johnstown	2	48	**232**
		Old Forge	4	48	**476**
		Wilkes-Barre	2	31	**198**
	Texas		1		**11**
			1	31	**82**
			1	34	**90**
			1	37	**96**
			1	43	**108**
			3	14	**276**
			3	28	**306**
			3	31	**312**
			3	32	**314**
			3	38	**326**
			3	47	**348**
			3	51	**356**
			4	8	**382**
			4	14	**396**
			4	19	**408**
			4	25	**426**
			4	43	**466**
			4	44	**468**
			4	50	**480**
		Austin	3	47	**348**
			2	8	**144**
		Bonham	1	31	**82**
			2	30	**196**
		El Paso	3	7	**262**
		Jasper	4	44	**468**
		Marfa	4	1	**368**
		Sutherland Springs	1	43	**108**
	Virginia		3	6	**378**
			3	45	**342**
			4	16	**402**
			4	24	**422**
			4	54	**488**
		Ashburn	1	40	**104**

Country	State/Region	City	Vol.	Iss.	Page
		Charlottesville	1	31	82
		Richmond	4	3	372
		Vienna	3	22	292
		Virginia Beach	3	22	292
	West Virginia		1	13	46
			3	30	310
	Wisconsin	Green Bay	3	18	284
Virgin Islands (USA)			1	37	96
			1	39	100
Yemen			1	12	44
			2	21	172
Zaire (now DRC)			1		11
			1	36	94
			3	29	308
			4	46	472

Section 4: Everything Else

Topic	Sub-topic	Vol	Issue	Page
Abortion		1	2	24
		2	21	172
		2	26	182
		3	20	288
Affordable Care Act (ACA) (aka Obamacare) (see Bibliography)		Intro		11
		1	1	22
		1	5	30
		1	6	32
		1	8	36
		1	10	40
		1	12	44
		1	15	50
		1	23	66
		1	28	76
		1	34	90
		1	39	100
		1	45	112
		2	15	158
		2	19	168
		2	40	216
		2	50	236
		3	13	274
		3	14	276
		3	16	280
		3	17	282
		3	20	288
		3	28	306
		3	31	312
		3	36	322
		3	38	326
		4	8	374
		4	42	464
		4	45	470
		4	47	474
		4	51	482
	Texas v Azar	4	8	374
	Texas v United States	3	31	312
		3	28	306
Alternative facts		1	2	24
		1	49	120

Topic	Sub-topic	Vol	Issue	Page
Atomic Energy Act of 1946		1	39	**100**
Beatles, The		3	24	**296**
Bible	Bib	1	9	**38**
		1	15	**50**
		1	25	**70**
		3	6	**258**
		3	10	**268**
		3	12	**272**
		3	22	**292**
	Bib			
Biden rule		4	1	**368**
Black Lives Matter		1	31	**82**
		4	23	**420**
		4	32	**442**
Border Wall		1	2	**24**
		1	6	**32**
		1	9	**38**
		1	23	**66**
		1	29	**78**
		2	14	**156**
		2	15	**158**
		2	36	**208**
		2	50	**236**
		2	51	**238**
		3	1	**248**
		3	8	**264**
		3	20	**288**
		3	41	**332**
		3	43	**338**
		3	44	**340**
		4	11	**388**
		4	25	**426**
		4	34	**446**
		4	52	**484**
		4	56	**492**
Bump stocks (see Guns – Bump stocks)				
Bush v. Gore		1	32	**82**
		2	40	**216**
		4	44	**468**
		4	46	**472**

Topic	Sub-topic	Vol	Issue	Page
Cabinet		Intro		**11**
		1	1	**22**
		1	5	**30**
		1	6	**32**
		1	14	**48**
		1	22	**64**
		1	49	**120**
		2	3	**134**
		2	16	**162**
		2	36	**208**
		3	4	**254**
		3	49	**352**
		4	7	**380**
		4	25	**426**
Census (2020)		3	37	**324**
Centers for Disease Control and Prevention (CDC)		4	9	**384**
		4	10	**386**
		4	13	**392**
		4	19	**408**
		4	21	**412**
		4	28	**434**
Congressional Medal of Honor		2	34	**204**
Central Intelligence Agency (CIA)		1	1	**22**
		1	21	**62**
		3	24	**296**
Central Park Five		3	11	**270**
Checks and Balances - see Constitution		1	15	**50**
Children's Health Insurance Program (CHIP)		1	47	**116**
Civil War		1	31	**82**
		2	27	**186**
		3	33	**316**
		4	24	**422**
Classified information		1	18	**56**
		3	39	**328**
Climate change		1	14	**48**

Topic	Sub-topic	Vol	Issue	Page
		1	34	**90**
		1	49	**120**
		2	15	**158**
		2	19	**168**
		2	42	**220**
		2	47	**230**
		3	5	**256**
		3	25	**298**
		3	31	**312**
		3	34	**318**
		3	36	**322**
		3	44	**340**
		3	45	**342**
		3	49	**352**
Clinton Foundation		3	15	**278**
		3	50	**354**
Coffee Creek Correctional Facility (Oregon)		2	46	**228**
Confederate flag, monuments, statues		1	31	**82**
		4	16	**402**
		4	19	**408**
		4	24	**422**
		4	54	**488**
Congress (US)		1	7	**34**
		1	9	**38**
		1	10	**40**
		1	12	**44**
		1	15	**50**
		1	23	**66**
		1	39	**100**
		1	40	**102**
		1	43	**108**
		1	47	**116**
		1	50	**122**
		2	8	**144**
		2	11	**150**
		2	14	**156**
		2	19	**168**
		2	26	**182**
		2	44	**224**
		2	45	**226**

Topic	Sub-topic	Vol	Issue	Page
		2	52	**240**
		3	10	**268**
		3	12	**272**
		3	13	**274**
		3	17	**282**
		3	19	**286**
		3	21	**290**
		3	28	**306**
		3	29	**308**
		3	37	**324**
		3	38	**326**
		3	39	**328**
		3	41	**332**
		4	1	**368**
		4	5	**376**
		4	15	**398**
		4	24	**422**
		4	38	**454**
		4	50	**480**
		4	54	**488**
		4	55	**490**
		4	56	**492**
	House Intelligence Committee	2	18	**166**
		3	13	**274**
		3	39	**328**
		3	46	**344**
	Senate Intelligence Committee	1	18	**56**
		1	22	**64**
Conservative Political Action Conference (CPAC)		1	6	**32**
Constitution (US)		Intro		**11**
		1	2	**24**
		1	3	**26**
		1	5	**30**
		1	10	**40**
		1	15	**50**
		2	8	**144**
		2	19	**168**
		2	24	**178**
		2	50	**236**

Topic	Sub-topic	Vol	Issue	Page
		2	52	**240**
		3	8	**264**
		3	12	**272**
		3	14	**276**
		3	17	**282**
		3	19	**286**
		3	21	**290**
		3	28	**306**
		3	35	**320**
		3	36	**322**
		3	43	**338**
		3	52	**360**
		4	5	**376**
		4	15	**398**
		4	16	**402**
		4	24	**422**
		4	55	**490**
	Amendments			
	First	1	6	**32**
		3	17	**282**
	Second	1	38	**98**
		1	40	**102**
		2	8	**144**
		2	9	**146**
		3	17	**282**
		3	20	**288**
		3	22	**292**
		3	31	**312**
		3	43	**338**
	Thirteenth	2	41	**218**
	Fifteenth	3	33	**316**
	Articles			
	Article I, Section 9	3	43	**338**
	Article II, Section 1	Intro		**11**
	Article II, Section 4	2	52	**240**
		3	43	**338**
	Checks and Balances	1	15	**50**
	Electoral College (see Elections – Electoral Vote)			

Topic	Sub-topic	Vol	Issue	Page
	Emoluments clause	1	50	**122**
		2	24	**178**
		2	52	**240**
		3	35	**320**
		3	42	**334**
		3	43	**338**
		3	51	**356**
		4	5	**376**
		4	55	**490**
	Voting	4	15	**398**
		4	17	**404**
		4	43	**466**
		4	49	**478**
Corgis		1	8	**36**
		2	28	**190**
		3	33	**316**
COVID -19		4	13	**392**
(aka Severe Acute Respiratory Syndrome Coronavirus 2)		4	15	**398**
		4	16	**402**
		4	17	**404**
		4	19	**408**
		4	20	**410**
		4	21	**412**
		4	22	**416**
		4	26	**428**
		4	27	**430**
		4	29	**436**
		4	31	**440**
		4	32	**442**
		4	34	**446**
		4	37	**452**
		4	38	**454**
		4	39	**458**
		4	40	**460**
		4	41	**462**
		4	43	**466**
		4	46	**472**
		4	47	**474**
		4	48	**476**
		4	49	**478**

Topic	Sub-topic	Vol	Iss	Page
		4	51	**482**
		4	56	**492**
Dads with Leafblowers (Portland, Oregon)		4	30	**438**
Deferred Action for Childhood Arrivals (DACA)		2	19	**168**
		4	25	**426**
Democratic candidates debate		3	19	**286**
Democratic National Convention (DNC) - 2020		4	35	**448**
Department of Energy (DOE)		1	22	**64**
		2	15	**158**
		2	16	**162**
		4	3	**372**
Department of Health and Human Services (HHS)		1	1	**22**
		1	6	**32**
		1	28	**76**
Department of Homeland Security (DHS)		2	22	**174**
		2	38	**212**
		4	56	**492**
Department of (the) Interior (DOI)		2	16	**162**
		2	50	**236**
Department of Justice (DOJ)		1	14	**48**
		1	15	**50**
		1	17	**54**
		3	16	**280**
		3	39	**328**
Department of Labor (DOL)		1	30	**80**
Dogs		2	33	**202**
		3	7	**262**
		3	43	**338**
		4	22	**416**
Ebola		2	19	**168**

Topic	Sub-topic	Vol	Iss	Page
		2	20	**170**
		3	14	**276**
Economy (US)		2	35	**206**
		2	43	**222**
		2	44	**224**
		2	49	**234**
		3	2	**250**
		3	4	**254**
		3	6	**258**
		3	28	**306**
		4	8	**382**
		4	13	**392**
		4	16	**402**
		4	19	**408**
		4	31	**440**
		4	45	**470**
	Comparative Advantage	2	14	**156**
	Economic nationalism	1	6	**32**
	Foreign trade	2	14	**156**
		2	20	**170**
		2	27	**186**
		2	30	**196**
		2	40	**216**
		2	44	**224**
		3	1	**248**
		3	5	**256**
		3	8	**264**
		3	17	**282**
		4	11	**388**
		4	32	**442**
	Stock market	2	14	**156**
		2	44	**224**
		2	49	**234**
		3	1	**248**
		3	49	**352**
		4	8	**382**
		4	11	**388**
		4	13	**392**
		4	18	**406**
		4	20	**410**

Topic	Sub-topic	Vol	Issue	Page
	Tariffs	2	14	**156**
	Tax cuts	1	22	**64**
		1	37	**96**
		1	49	**120**
		2	19	**168**
		2	44	**224**
Elections				
	1980	1	47	**116**
	2000	1	44	**110**
	2004	4	44	**468**
	2016	1	2	**24**
		1	13	**46**
		4	44	**468**
	2019	3	45	**342**
	2020	4	43	**466**
		4	44	**468**
		4	45	**470**
		4	52	**484**
		4	53	**486**
		4	56	**492**
		FF		**500**
	2024	FF		**500**
	Electoral vote	Intro		**11**
		1	2	**24**
		1	3	**26**
		1	13	**46**
		1	47	**116**
		2	17	**164**
		3	3	**252**
		4	14	**396**
		4	46	**472**
		4	51	**482**
	Midterms	2	45	**226**
	Opposition research	3	24	**296**
	Popular vote	1	2	**24**
		3	3	**252**
		3	50	**354**
		4	46	**472**
	Russian interference in	3	1	**248**
		3	16	**280**
		3	24	**296**

Topic	Sub-topic	Vol	Issue	Page
		3	26	**302**
		3	37	**324**
		3	40	**330**
		3	51	**356**
		4	55	**490**
	Voting machines - Diebold	2	49	**234**
		4	44	**468**
Environment				
See Climate Change				
See Global Warming				
See Hurricanes				
See Paris Climate Agreement				
See Wildfires				
See Wind Energy				
Environmental Protection Agency (EPA)		1	6	**32**
		1	14	**48**
		1	16	**52**
Facebook		1	43	**108**
		4	24	**422**
"Fargo" (Hulu)		4	45	**470**
Federal Bureau of Investigation (FBI)		1	10	**40**
		1	15	**50**
		1	17	**54**
		1	18	**56**
		1	42	**220**
		2	7	**142**
		2	11	**150**
		2	18	**166**
		2	43	**222**
		2	52	**240**
		3	13	**274**
		3	24	**296**
Foreign Policy		2	20	**170**
		3	2	**250**
		3	25	**298**
		3	41	**332**

Topic	Sub-topic	Vol	Issue	Page
	G-7 (Group of Seven)	2	23	**176**
		3	35	**320**
		3	42	**334**
	G-8 (Group of Eight)	2	23	**176**
	G-20 (Group of Twenty)	1	25	**70**
		4	47	**474**
Foreign Service		3	46	**344**
General Motors		3	35	**320**
Girl Scouts Beyond Bars (Oregon)		2	46	**228**
Global gag rule		1	2	**24**
		2	21	**172**
Global warming		1	14	**48**
		3	31	**312**
Goldwater rule		1	38	**98**
GOP health care bill		1	10	**40**
Government Services Administration (GSA)		2	24	**178**
Gulf War I		1	12	**44**
Guns				
	Arming teachers	2	8	**144**
	Assault weapons ban			
	New Zealand	3	12	**372**
	United States	2	7	**142**
	Bump stocks	1	38	**98**
		1	43	**108**
		1	49	**120**
	Mass Shootings			
	Charleston, SC	1	43	**108**
	Dayton, OH	3	31	**312**
	El Paso, TX	3	31	**312**
	Gilroy, TX	3	31	**312**
	Las Vegas, NV	1	38	**98**
		1	43	**108**
	New Zealand (Christchurch)	3	11	**270**
		3	12	**272**
	Orlando, FL	1	43	**108**
	Parkland, FL	2	7	**142**
		2	8	**144**

Topic	Sub-topic	Vol	Issue	Page
	Sandy Hook, (Newtown, CT)	1	43	**108**
	Stockton, CA	2	7	**142**
	Sutherland Springs, TX	1	43	**108**
	Thousand Oaks, CA	3	32	**314**
	Mental health and	1	43	**108**
		3	32	**314**
	NRA (see National Rifle Association)			
	Second Amendment (see Constitution)			
Halliburton		1	12	**44**
Harney County Fair and Rodeo (Oregon)		3	35	**320**
Hatch Act		4	35	**448**
Hate crime (Portland, Oregon)		1	20	**60**
Hate groups				
	Ku Klux Klan	1	31	**82**
		2	35	**206**
		4	24	**422**
	National Socialists (Nazi)	1	31	**82**
		2	44	**224**
		3	29	**308**
		3	33	**316**
		4	44	**468**
		4	56	**492**
		Bib		
	Oath Keepers	3	33	**316**
	Oregonians for Immigration Reform	3	33	**316**
	Pacific Coast Knights of the KKK	3	33	**316**
	Patriot Prayer	2	46	**228**
		3	33	**316**
		3	35	**320**
	Q-Anon	4	46	**472**
		4	54	**488**
	Republic of Kekistan	4	54	**488**
	Thin Blue Liners	4	54	**488**

Topic	Sub-topic	Vol	Issue	Page
	Three Percenters	3	33	**316**
	Wolves of Vinland	3	33	**316**
Health Care		Intro		**11**
(see also Medicaid and Medicare)		1	1	**22**
		1	8	**36**
		1	10	**40**
		1	14	**48**
		1	16	**52**
		1	22	**64**
		1	23	**66**
		1	34	**90**
		1	35	**92**
		1	36	**94**
		1	45	**112**
		2	19	**168**
		2	21	**172**
		2	38	**212**
		2	45	**226**
		3	14	**276**
		3	28	**306**
		3	31	**312**
		4	8	**382**
		4	35	**448**
		4	43	**464**
	Pre-existing conditions	3	14	**276**
		3	28	**306**
		3	31	**312**
		3	51	**356**
		4	5	**376**
		4	6	**378**
		4	8	**384**
		4	34	**446**
	Public Option	3	40	**330**
		4	15	**398**
	Vaccination	3	14	**276**
		4	16	**402**
		4	20	**410**
		4	38	**454**
		4	47	**474**
		4	50	**480**

Topic	Sub-topic	Vol	Issue	Page
Hurricanes				
	Dorian	3	36	**322**
	Florence	4	56	**492**
	Harvey	1	34	**90**
	Irma	1	34	**90**
	Katrina	2	37	**210**
	Maria	1	38	**98**
		1	39	**100**
		2	37	**210**
		2	41	**218**
	Sandy	2	37	**210**
Immigration		1	3	**26**
		1	35	**92**
		2	2	**132**
		2	5	**138**
		2	6	**140**
		2	14	**156**
		2	22	**174**
		2	25	**180**
		2	36	**208**
		2	38	**212**
		2	44	**224**
		2	47	**230**
		3	4	**254**
		3	7	**262**
		3	24	**296**
		3	29	**308**
	US Immigration and Customs Enforcement (ICE)	4	26	**428**
Impeachment				
	Clause (also see Constitution, Article II, Section 4)	2	52	**240**
	Clinton, William Jefferson	1	44	**110**
		1	50	**122**
		3	21	**290**
	Johnson, Andrew	1	50	**122**
	Trump, Donald (see Trump Index, Impeachment)			
Indiana University			Intro	**11**

Topic	Sub-topic	Vol	Issue	Page
		2	7	**142**
		3	35	**320**
Indictments		1	42	**106**
		2	3	**250**
		2	7	**142**
		3	4	**256**
		3	16	**280**
		3	41	**332**
		4	3	**374**
		4	34	**446**
		4	35	**448**
		FF		**500**
Inequality		1	34	**90**
		1	47	**116**
Iran nuclear arms deal		2	19	**168**
		2	20	**170**
		3	5	**256**
		3	28	**306**
Islamic State of Iraq and Syria (ISIS)		1	2	**24**
		2	51	**238**
		3	41	**332**
		3	42	**334**
		3	43	**338**
		4	32	**442**
January 6 Insurrection		4	54	**488**
		4	55	**490**
		4	56	**492**
		FF		**500**
Kompromat		2	29	**192**
Kurdistan Workers Party (PKK)		3	42	**334**
Liberty University (Lynchburg, VA)		1	9	**38**
		3	6	**258**
Libya model		2	20	**170**
MAGA Bomber		2	43	**222**
MAGA Night		4	22	**416**
Malheur National Wildlife Refuge		3	35	**322**
Mara Salvatrucha (M-13)_		2	25	**180**
Martial law		4	51	**482**

Topic	Sub-topic	Vol	Issue	Page
Me Too Movement		1	44	110
Medicaid		Intro		11
		1	8	36
		1	23	66
		1	34	90
		2	38	212
		3	20	288
		3	47	348
		4	8	382
Medicare		1	8	36
		1	16	52
		3	31	312
		3	40	330
		4	8	382
		4	30	438
Military (US)		Intro		11
		1	30	80
		1	40	102
		1	45	112
		2	6	140
		3	8	264
		3	11	270
		3	27	304
		3	34	318
		3	42	334
		3	43	338
		4	24	422
		4	36	450
	Air Force	1	37	96
		1	43	108
		2	6	140
		3	9	266
		3	11	270
		3	34	318
		3	36	322
		3	48	350
	Army	1	40	102
		2	11	150
		3	9	266
		3	27	304
		4	24	422
		4	56	492

Topic	Sub-topic	Vol	Issue	Page
	Congressional Medal of Honor	2	34	**204**
	Navy	1	7	**34**
		1	30	**80**
	Trump deferments from service	2	30	**196**
	United Seamen's Service (USS)	1	30	**80**
	United Service Organizations	1	37	**96**
		2	6	**140**
		3	11	**270**
		3	48	**350**
		4	36	**450**
Mount Rushmore		4	27	**430**
		4	32	**442**
Mueller Report		3	13	**274**
(also see Bibliography)		3	16	**280**
		3	19	**286**
		3	32	**314**
		3	51	**356**
		4	56	**492**
Muslim ban		1	2	**24**
		1	15	**50**
		1	21	**62**
		1	24	**68**
National Aeronautics and Space Administration (NASA)		1	14	**48**
		3	23	**294**
National Association for Stock Car Auto Racing (NASCAR)		4	7	**380**
National Association of Travel Organizations (NATO)		3	7	**262**
National Commission on Forensic Science (NCFS)		1	14	**48**
National Day of Prayer		4	19	**408**
National Institutes of Health (NIH)		1	14	**48**

Topic	Sub-topic	Vol	Issue	Page
National Oceanic and Atmospheric Administration (NOAA)		1	14	48
		3	36	322
National Park Service		3	28	306
National Prayer Breakfast		1	3	26
		3	6	258
		4	6	378
National Republican Congressional Committee		4	53	486
National Rifle Association (NRA)		1	38	98
		2	8	144
		2	15	158
		2	45	226
		3	17	282
		3	18	284
National Security Council		4	9	384
National Socialist Movement (aka Nazis) – see Right Wing Organizations				
Native Americans		1	31	82
		2	16	162
		2	32	200
Nobel Peace Prize		1	12	44
		2	18	166
		2	20	170
		3	36	322
North Atlantic Treaty Organization (NATO)		1	19	58
		2	28	190
		3	5	256
Obamacare (see Affordable Care Act – ACA)				
Opposition research		3	24	296
Oregon Board of Investigators		1	21	62
Oregon Health Authority		Intro		11
		3	14	276

Topic	Sub-topic	Vol	Issue	Page
		3	16	**280**
Oregon Medical Marijuana Act		2	46	**228**
Paris Climate Agreement		2	15	**158**
		2	19	**168**
		3	5	**256**
		3	28	**306**
		3	31	**312**
		4	45	**470**
Patient Protection and Affordable Care Act (see ACA)				
Peace Corps		Intro		**11**
		1	35	**92**
		1	36	**94**
		3	29	**308**
		3	45	**342**
		3	51	**356**
Physicians for a National Health Program		1	8	**36**
Presidential Records Act		Intro		**11**
		4	55	**490**
Presidents Day		3	7	**262**
		3	8	**264**
		4	7	**380**
Prison Reform		2	46	**228**
Public Charge		3	38	**326**
		3	41	**332**
Racism		Intro		**11**
		2	22	**174**
		2	32	**200**
		2	36	**208**
		4	19	**408**
		4	24	**422**
		Bib		
Republican National Committee		4	35	**448**
Roe v Wade		2	26	**182**
(see Abortion)		4	42	**220**
		Bib		
Rose City Antifa		3	33	**316**

595

Topic	Sub-topic	Vol	Issue	Page
Russian Interference (see Elections,) (see Putin, Vladimir in People Index)				
SCOTUS (see Supreme Court of the United States)				
Sesame Street		3	7	**262**
		3	19	**286**
		3	30	**310**
Social safety net				
	Food Stamps	3	20	**288**
		3	49	**352**
		4	6	**378**
	Special Supplemental Nutrition Program for Women, Infants, and Children (WIC)	1	9	**146**
		2	38	**212**
	Supplemental Security Income (SSI)	2	38	**212**
	Temporary Assistance to Needy Families (TANF) (aka Welfare)	2	38	**212**
Social Security		1	47	**116**
		3	29	**308**
Spanish flu		4	10	**386**
		4	18	**406**
		4	32	**442**
State of the Union (SOTU)		1	7	**34**
		2	5	**138**
		2	6	**140**
		3	4	**254**
		3	5	**256**
		3	21	**290**
Supreme Court of the United States (SCOTUS)				
		1	3	**26**
		2	26	**182**
		2	52	**240**
		3	8	**264**
		3	20	**288**

Topic	Sub-topic	Vol	Issue	Page
		3	30	**310**
		4	1	**368**
		4	15	**398**
		4	25	**426**
		4	38	**454**
		4	42	**464**
		4	43	**466**
		4	44	**468**
		4	50	**480**
		4	51	**482**
		FF		**500**
		Bib		
Taliban		3	48	**350**
		4	27	**430**
Texas v Azar and Texas v US (see Affordable Care Act)				
Thunderbird School of Global Management (at Arizona State University)		Intro		**11**
		1	32	**86**
Trans-Pacific Partnership (TPP)		2	19	**168**
Triple Negative Breast Cancer Foundation		3	18	**284**
Unitarian Universalist Church		2	26	**182**
		2	51	**238**
United Nations		1	36	**94**
		2	40	**216**
		3	5	**256**
United Seamen's Service (USS) (see Military)				
United Service Organizations (USO) (see Military)				
United States Postal Service (USPS)		4	15	**398**
		4	17	**404**
US Air Force, Army, Navy (see Military)				
Values Voter Summit		1	39	**100**

Topic	Sub-topic	Vol	Issue	Page
Vietnam War		1	40	**102**
		2	7	**142**
		2	9	**146**
		2	27	**186**
		2	34	**204**
		3	23	**294**
		4	24	**422**
		Bib		
Voting (see Elections)				
Wall of Moms (Portland, Oregon)		4	30	**438**
Walter Reed Hospital		3	48	**350**
		4	28	**434**
		4	40	**460**
		4	55	**490**
Welfare Reform		2	38	**212**
Wharton School		2	14	**156**
	(at University of Pennsylvania)	3	30	**310**
White House		Intro		**11**
		1	1	**22**
		1	17	**54**
		1	28	**78**
		1	32	**86**
		1	35	**92**
		1	40	**102**
		2	3	**134**
		2	4	**136**
		2	8	**144**
		2	23	**176**
		2	27	**186**
		2	33	**202**
		2	36	**208**
		2	38	**212**
		2	41	**218**
		2	42	**220**
		3	6	**258**
		3	7	**262**
		3	10	**268**
		3	30	**310**
		3	42	**334**
		3	44	**340**
		3	48	**350**

Topic	Sub-topic	Vol	Issue	Page
		4	22	**416**
		4	23	**420**
		4	31	**440**
		4	39	**458**
		4	48	**476**
		4	52	**484**
White House (National) Correspondents' Dinner		3	3	**252**
		3	17	**282**
WikiLeaks		1	12	**44**
		3	15	**278**
Wildfires		3	1	**248**
		3	31	**312**
		3	44	**340**
		4	1	**368**
Wind energy		2	11	**150**
		3	35	320
World Ice Golf Championship		3	34	318
World Trade Center		1	30	80
		3	51	356
World Trade Organization (WTO)		2	30	196

Kelly Paige was born in Georgia; grew up in Texas and Colorado; and has lived in eight other states and eleven countries in Europe, Africa, and Asia. She holds graduate degrees in Russian History and International Management, and survived teaching English at the National University of Zaire, in the Peace Corps.

Kelly worked in the insurance, banking, and hospitality industries; was an Executive Director for three non-profit agencies and two regulatory boards; and spent twenty-five years working for the State of Oregon, primarily in public health. She is a licensed substitute teacher and lives in Oregon with her husband and two rambunctious corgis.

AND NOW, FOR SOMETHING COMPLETELY DIFFERENT.......

In 1959, when Kelly Paige was a second-grade student in a small-town Texas public school, she was assigned a Christmas project that resulted in this little book.

A unique rendition of a timeless tale, the original version was produced on Big Chief tablet paper and construction paper with a #2 pencil and crayons. Read the story to the children in your life, then let them create their own artwork from the coloring book section included in this publication. Available on Amazon.

Made in the USA
Monee, IL
09 October 2024

67508845R00332